INSIGHT GUIDE

W9-BZV-441

COnTInEnTaL
EUROPE

T 19991

APA PUBLICATIONS
Part of the Langenscheidt Publishing Group

INSIGHT GUIDE
Continental Europe

ABOUT THIS BOOK

Editorial

Project Editor
Roger Williams
Editorial Director
Brian Bell

Distribution

UK & Ireland
GeoCenter International Ltd
The Viables Centre, Harrow Way
Basingstoke, Hants RG22 4BJ
Fax: (44) 1256-817988

United States
Langenscheidt Publishers, Inc.
46–35 54th Road, Maspeth, NY 11378
Fax: (1) 718 784-0640

Canada
Thomas Allen & Son Ltd
390 Steelcase Road East
Markham, Ontario L3R 1G2
Fax: (1) 905 475 6747

Australia
Universal Press
1 Waterloo Road
Macquarie Park, NSW 2113
Fax: (61) 2 9888 9074

New Zealand
Hema Maps New Zealand Ltd (HNZ)
Unit D, 24 Ra ORA Drive
East Tamaki, Auckland
Fax: (64) 9 273 6479

Worldwide
Apa Publications GmbH & Co.
Verlag KG (Singapore branch)
38 Joo Koon Road, Singapore 628990
Tel: (65) 865-1600. Fax: (65) 861-6438

Printing

Insight Print Services (Pte) Ltd
38 Joo Koon Road, Singapore 628990
Tel: (65) 865-1600. Fax: (65) 861-6438

©2002 Apa Publications GmbH & Co.
Verlag KG (Singapore branch)
All Rights Reserved
First Edition 1984
Fifth Edition 2000; updated 2002

CONTACTING THE EDITORS

We would appreciate it if readers
would alert us to errors or outdated information by writing to:
**Insight Guides, P.O. Box 7910,
London SE1 1WE, England.**
Fax: (44) 20 7403-0290.
insight@apaguide.demon.co.uk

This guidebook combines the interests and enthusiasms of two of the world's best known information providers: Insight Guides, whose titles have set the standard for visual travel guides since 1970, and Discovery Channel, the world's premier source of nonfiction television programming.

The editors of Insight Guides provide both practical advice and general understanding about a destination's history, people, culture and institutions. Discovery Channel and its website, www.discovery.com, help millions of viewers explore their world from the comfort of their own homes and encourage them to explore it first hand.

This updated edition of *Insight Guide: Continental Europe* is carefully structured to convey an understanding of the Continent and its culture as well as to guide readers through its sights and activities:

◆ The **Features** section, indicated by a yellow bar at the top of each page, covers Europe's history and its culture, which is summed up in 26 short essays, from Architecture to Zeitgeist.

◆ The main **Places** section, indicated by a blue bar, is a complete guide to all the sights and areas worth visiting. After an introduction, each country begins with its capital city, followed by a tour of of the country's main regions and places of interest. Places of special interest are co-ordinated by number with the maps.

EXPLORE YOUR WORLD
Discovery CHANNEL

Above: rowing into Santorini, Greece.

◆ The **Travel Tips** listings section at the end of the book, with an orange bar, provides a point of reference for information on travel, hotels, shops and restaurants. This section is indexed on the back flap.

The contributors

Though substantially revised, the fifth edition of *Insight Guide: Continental Europe* is built on the previous editions of this popular title. Changes have been made to reflect the changes in holiday travel, in particular to the Continent's principal cities, which have become popular for weekend visits. The sections on Spain and Greece have both been enlarged, and a new chapter by travel writer **Shaun Sheehan** has been added on Slovakia and the Croatian Coast, the most attractive, accessible and peaceful part of the former Yugoslavia.

The new edition still owes much to the original editor, **Rolf Steinberg**, a graduate of Columbia University School of Journalism, who brought his many years' experience as a foreign correspondent to produce a modern-day "Grand Tour" of Europe. Writers whose work is still reflected in this edition include **Rowlinson Carter, Uli Schmetzer, Petra Dubulski, Oliver Henderson, Tan Chung Lee, West J. Perry, Sarah Béhar, Lee Foster, Thomas C. Lucey, Linda White, Wilhelm Klein, F. Lisa Beebe** and **Paul Sullivan**.

This edition was overseen by **Roger Williams**, project editor of the previous edition. **Helen Partington**, who edited the latest edition of *Insight Guide: Spain*, took on the substantial editing work required to bring the book right up to date in its busy new format, using Insight Guides' European specialists.

The chapters on Europe's history were written by **Pam Barrett**, a historian who has since become a regular Insight Guide project editor, and *Europe A–Z* was compiled by editorial director **Brian Bell** and Williams, who also wrote the introductory chapter, *Heart of the Old World*.

The Travel Tips section was compiled by **Siân Lezard**. The book was proofread by **Bryony Coleman** and indexed by **Elizabeth Cook**.

The photographs, which always make Insight Guides stand out from the crowd, were provided by Insight Guides' extensive library and by such favourite regulars as **Bodo Bonzio, Guglielmo Galvin, Michael Jenner, Catherine Karnow, Lyle Lawson** and **Bill Wassman**.

Map Legend

—— ·· —	International Boundary
———	Regional Boundary
– – – –	Province/State Boundary
⊖	Border Crossing
—·▲·—	National Park/Reserve
– – – –	Ferry Route
Ⓜ	Metro
Ⓢ	S–Bahn
Ⓤ	U–Bahn
✈ ✈	Airport: International/ Regional
⛌	Bus Station
Ⓟ	Parking
❶	Tourist Information
✉	Post Office
✝ † ✟	Church/Ruins
†	Monastery
☪	Mosque
✡	Synagogue
■ ▣	Castle/Ruins
∴	Archaeological Site
∩	Cave
𝚰	Statue/Monument
★	Place of Interest

The main places of interest in the Places section are coordinated by number with a full-colour map (e.g. ❶), and a symbol at the top of every right-hand page tells you where to find the map.

CONTENTS

Maps

Europe **76**
FRANCE **84**
Paris **86**
Loire Valley **106**
Riviera **114**
BELGIUM **128**
Brussels **132**
NETHERLANDS **144**
Amsterdam **148**
GERMANY **164**
Berlin **168**
Romantic Road **178**
SWITZERLAND **196**
AUSTRIA **216**
Vienna **218**
Prague **242**
Warsaw **246**
Kraków **247**
Budapest **250**
ITALY **258**
Rome **260**
Florence **276**
Venice **280**
The Lakes **286**
GREECE **314**
Athens **318**
SPAIN **340**
Madrid **342**
Barcelona **350**
Southern Spain **366**
PORTUGAL **378**
Lisbon **382**

Inside front cover:
Europe: Political
Inside back cover:
Europe: Physical

Introduction

The Heart of the World 15

History

Decisive Dates 22
Beginnings 25
Conquerors of the World 33
Modern Times 43

Europe from A to Z

Architecture 52
Beaches 52
Corruption 53
Driving 54
European Union 55
Food 55
Gestures 56
Humour 57

Immigrants 57
Jet Set 58
Kissing 58
Lavatories 59
Monarchies 59
Nature 60
Oath-making 60
Punctuality 61
Queues 61
Robbery 61
Status 62
Television 62
Umbrellas 63
Vendetta 64
Wine-making 64
Xenophobia 65
Yacht Watching 66
Zeitgeist 67

The Louvre,
Paris.

Insight on ...

Treasures of the Louvre 89
Germany's Festivals 188
Rome's Colosseum 272
Greek Islands Flora 332
Castles in Spain 370

Travel Tips

General Tips 394
France 402
Belgium 408
The Netherlands 412
Germany 417
Switzerland 422
Austria 425
Budapest 428
Warsaw and Kraków .. 431
Prague 433
Italy 436
Croatia 440
Greece 441
Spain 446
Portugal 450

◆ **Full Travel Tips index
   is on page 393**

Places

Introduction 75
FRANCE 83
Paris 89
Around France 101
BELGIUM 127
Brussels 131
Around Belgium 135
THE NETHERLANDS 143
Amsterdam 147
Around the Netherlands 153
GERMANY 163
Berlin 167
Around Germany 173
SWITZERLAND 195
Around Switzerland ... 199
AUSTRIA 215
Vienna 221
Around Austria 227
EXCURSIONS TO THE EAST 239
Prague 241
Warsaw and Kraków 245
Budapest 249

ITALY 257
Rome 263
The Vatican 271
Florence 275
Venice 279
Around Italy 285
THE BALKAN COAST 301
Slovenia & Croatian Coast .. 303
Albania 307
GREECE 313
Athens 317
Around Greece 323
SPAIN 339
Madrid 345
Barcelona 351
Around Spain 357
PORTUGAL 377
Lisbon 381
Around Portugal 385

THE HEART OF THE OLD WORLD

Seen from space, it's quite a small continent. But over the centuries Europe has produced the richest mix of cultures anywhere on earth

This is the world of châteaux and champagne, La Scala and Monte Carlo, gondolas and gypsy violins. It is the home of democracy, Christianity, the Renaissance, royalty, Michelangelo, Mercedes-Benz, Beethoven, Brigitte Bardot, pasta and goulash. Its art is admired, its wines are drunk, its clothes are copied and its languages are spoken in every corner of the world.

Europeans have always been hazy about the boundaries of their continent. To French politicians, it is a collection of well-off countries who need to get together for their own self-interest. To former Soviet republics, it is a fold that they can return to now that communism has gone. Romantics see Paris as its centre, bureaucrats see Brussels, style-setters see Milan; classicists look to Athens, Catholics to the Vatican, bankers to Bonn, while Mittel Europeans have their eyes on somewhere much mistier, further east.

The continent has its actual centre in an unmarked field north of Vilnius in Lithuania. Only Lithuanians know this. However, like its Baltic neighbours, including all of Scandinavia, Lithuania could not be squeezed into this book. But it is fully covered in *Insight Guide: Baltic States*, and also in *Insight Guide: Eastern Europe*, along with Bulgaria, Romania, Moldova, Belarus, Ukraine, Georgia, Armenia, Azerbaijan and much of Russia, all of which lay claim to a place on the world's second smallest continent.

Nor can islands be added to a guide about a mainland. Malta, Cyprus, Ireland and Great Britain are thus excluded – although Britain might have been banned through arrogance: "Fog in Channel: Continent isolated" was a memorable headline in the London *Times*. The Channel Tunnel, of course, has consigned that attitude to history's scrapheap.

Wide divisions

Its countries may be physically attached, but Continental Europe is not homogeneous, and all efforts to unite its unruly tribes have come to nothing. Charlemagne and Napoleon failed, and so have the European Community bureaucrats. The fact is that Europeans, in spite of all the

handshaking and treaty signing, do not see themselves as a single unity.

Indeed, they often don't see themselves as part of the country to which they belong. Basques, Bretons, Catalans, Flemings, Lombards, Prussians and inhabitants of sundry former empires and city states still dream of resurrecting independent nationhood. Minorities must be hard: they vote and may lob the occasional bomb. Taking the wrong line over the question of Macedonia, a nation that has not existed for over 2,000 years, can still bring down the government of Greece.

Mistrust runs deep, and stereotypes are still used in the nations' popular newspapers to stir

---

PRECEDING PAGES: fence-peeping in the Paris Tuileries; carnival pageant in Basel, Switzerland; in Austria's mountains; Breton fishermen.
LEFT: celebrating Cologne's carnival.
RIGHT: a Burgundy wine confraternity meeting.

up feeling. In moments of sudden angst, they also publish reports about what other Europeans think about them. There are epigrams to sum up every nation, every region, every city, sayings to reinforce ideas about their stubbornness or *joie de vivre*, their cleverness or stupidity. Such cartoon characters are easy to sketch, from the hard working Teutonic races of the north to the excitable Latins of the south, from boisterous Bavarians and emotional Poles to arrogant French, devious Greeks and boring Belgians.

ROMAN RULE

Pax Romana was administered by many people, often from sundry tribes outside Italy. The great Emperor Diocletian (284–305) was born in Dalmatia, SW Croatia.

poorer, more rural "midday" lands of the south – the Midi in France, the Mezzogiorno in Italy. In Spain the industrious northerner has no time for "lazy" flamenco-playing Andalusians. Such prejudices are put aside at holiday time as northerners head for the sun. The whoops from otherwise sober Germans are said to be audible as their cars cross the Alps and slip down into Italy. Only a love of football seems to unite Europeans, though the games themselves are often replays of earlier hostilities.

"A typical Spaniard," the Viennese psychoanalyst Sigmund Freud said of the painter Salvador Dalí. "Quite mad." His statement does not bear analysis.

The north-south divide is the most noticeable: the industrious peoples of the colder climates scorn the backward and lazy siesta-seeking peasants of sunnier parts. Visually, the strapping, healthy, fair-skinned northerner gets darker, lazier, louder and smaller towards the south. Even within countries there can be divisive stereotypes: Germany's northern Prussians tend to look down on the beer-swilling Bavarians. The richer inhabitants of northern France and Italy look down on the

Roman occupation

The nearest Europe came to being united was not under one country, but under one city, ancient Rome. Pax Romana stretched all around the Mediterranean and north to the River Danube, and ruled in every country in Continental Europe.

Perhaps Rome's most significant bequest was a written language from which European "Romance" languages subsequently evolved, and as a result a Frenchman, an Italian, a

ABOVE: money-minded Swiss tram sweeping through the centre of Zürich.
RIGHT: haycart in Poland's rural heartland.

Spaniard and a Portuguese can all roughly understand what the other is trying to say – although their hand gestures are probably equally intelligible to each other.

Teutonic tribes shaped the languages in the north, Slavs to the east. To the west, all but pushed into the sea, are the last of the Celtic-speakers, the Bretons. Trapped in pockets in between are little-used languages such as Romansch in part of Switzerland, and Basque, spoken on the western border of France and Spain and related to Hungarian.

Language is no respecter of the borders – which have anyway failed to remain firm. At the beginning of the 20th century few countries looked the shape they do today. Italy and Germany had not long been invented. Albania, Bulgaria and Yugoslavia had not been thought of. Prussia had disappeared, Austria and Hungary dramatically deflated.

Since then, Germany has divided and united, Czechoslovakia united and divided, Poland re-emerged, and Yugoslavia has been pieced together and then blown apart again.

It can be reassuring sometimes to be reminded that Prince Hans Adam II or Prince Rainier are still quietly getting on with life in Liechtenstein and Monaco, microscopic princi-

EUROPE'S SHARED CULTURAL HERITAGE

Europe's unparalleled architecture shows that ideas have always flowed freely across the continent. Builders, traders, businessmen, pilgrims and mercenaries – as well as visionaries – have constantly been on the move.

The terracotta roof-tiles of the Romans colour all the Mediterranean's fashionable playground resorts. Italians built many of Poland's churches. Normans put up castles in northern Greece and southern Italy. German woodcarvers left their marks on Spanish choir stalls. Dutch masters followed the Hansa traders to the Baltic and a visitor would be hard-pressed to tell the difference between 17th-century houses in Gdansk, Bremen and Amsterdam.

The great architectural movements of Romanesque, Gothic, Renaissance, Baroque and Neo-classicism touched all of Europe. In the 19th century, France's art nouveau was Germany and Austria's *Jugendstil*, Italy's *Stile Liberty* and Spain's *Modernismo*.

Europeans see their cultural heritage as a social responsibility. Public spending on the arts in France is 20 times that of the whole of the US, and French film-makers are subsidised by nearly 2 billion francs a year. No stage sets can match those in the state-backed German theatre, while Italy hosts the most prestigious art gathering in Europe, the Venice Biennale.

palities of irrevocably ancient borders straight out of a 1940s Hollywood script in which the princes would usually be played by the likes of Stewart Granger.

Europe has some enjoyably eccentric corners but it cannot be accused of being insular. It has been shaped and honed over the centuries by neighbouring cultures.

Wider influences

Vikings came down from the north, sailing up to Paris and round into the Mediterranean, scattering a little of their language on their way, and giving fundamental lessons in rape and pil-

lage. Later, both the Swedish and Russian empire builders came knocking at the gates.

In the east the Ottoman Muslims held sway until the 19th century when Greece and Bulgaria re-emerged as countries after many centuries of occupation. At their height, the Turkish Ottomans pushed the Austro-Hungarian empire back to Vienna.

After the death of the prophet Muhammed, a missionary zeal swept Arab tribes up through Spain to Poitiers, not far from Paris. It swiftly subsided back into Spain where their caliphate produced not just an enormously rich culture and architecture in Córdoba and Granada, but affected the whole Spanish language to such an extent that a rousing roar of "*olé!*" may, some historians have suggested, be a remnant of a rallying call for "Allah!"

Modern-day links

A fast and integrated road system makes communications between the countries easier than ever before. Germany's *autobahns* are the densest network of roads in the world. The railway system is entirely integrated, and high-speed trains are in regular service, particularly in France where the service is modelled on airline techniques. Given Europe's overcrowded air space and airports, it is frequently faster to get around by train than by plane.

There is, in short, no difficulty in travelling the length and breadth of the world's second smallest continent (Antarctica is the smallest), which has proved to be quite unbeatable in its ambitions. In the past 500 years it had a good try at conquering the entire world, but the chief signs now of its glorious colonial past are its specialist restaurants: Algerian couscous in France; Indonesian rice tables in Holland, and Brazilian restaurants in Lisbon.

Role reversal

In recent years it has been Europe's turn to be colonised, by multinationals and big business from America and Japan. McDonald's hamburger houses are now ubiquitous, and no European city is without *sushi* restaurants. France even permitted Disneyland, Paris, and Japanese work practices have penetrated the most entrenched European labour markets.

Many residents of those former colonies and outposts return to Europe in search of their distant roots. Many names can be traced to places. Some are fortunate enough to know immediately where their ancestors came from: for example, those whose family names end "-*ian*" are from Armenia. Walt Disney's family was "d'Isigny" (from Isigny in Normandy). The late French historian Ferdinand Braudel could point to remote mountain valleys or city shopkeepers' alleyways as the place of origin of other family names. They can provide an excuse for character and temperament, too – one more thing Europe has to answer for. ❑

LEFT: catching a little performance art in Breitscheidplatz, Berlin.
RIGHT: France's biggest US import, Disneyland.

Decisive Dates

2000–1450 BC: Minoan civilisation, centred on Knossos in Crete.

1450–100 BC: Mycenaean civilisation, based at Mycenae in the Peloponnese.

800–500 BC: Archaic period. Athens and Sparta emerge as major city states.

750 BC: Rome, an Etruscan trading post, said to have been founded by Romulus and Remus.

509 BC: Rome becomes a republic.

490–450 BC: Greek wars against Persia.

450–338 BC: Classical period. Parthenon built.

Flowering of Greek literature and philosophy. Rome gradually takes over all Italy.

338–323 BC: Macedonia's Philip and Alexander the Great create unprecedented empires.

323–146 BC: Hellenistic period.

218 BC: The Carthaginian army attacks Rome, unsuccessfully.

146 BC: Greece falls to Rome.

48 BC: Death of Pompey the Great in civil war with Julius Caesar.

48 BC: Pax Romana spreads throughout Europe and Mediterranean, but declines within 200 years.

AD 330: Constantine, the first Christian Roman emperor, establishes an eastern capital in Constantinople.

AD 527: St Benedict founds the first monastic order, at Monte Cassino, southern Italy.

6th–7th centuries: Slavs settle in Balkans.

AD 714: Spain conquered by North African Muslims.

AD 800: In Rome, Charlemagne, a Frankish leader, is crowned Holy Roman Emperor.

11th century: Romanesque architecture, characterised by simple vaulting and rounded arches, evolves. Pisa Cathedral, Italy, and Church of the Apostles, Cologne, are good examples.

1072: French Normans (descendants of the Vikings) conquer Sicily.

1096: First Crusade against Muslims in the Holy Land; 500,000 join up.

12th century: Gothic architecture , identified by pointed arches and flying buttresses, becomes prevalent. Chartres Cathedral, France, and St Stephen's Cathedral, Vienna, are prime examples.

1150–70: First universities founded.

1283: Dante Alighieri begins writing in Florence, establishing Italian language.

1286: The papacy moves from Rome to Avignon.

1325–1495: The Renaissance is initiated by Filippo Brunelleschi, architect of the Florence Duomo, and exemplified by Giotto, Michelangelo and Leonardo da Vinci.

1347–51: Black Death sweeps the continent, killing one-third of the population.

1337–1453: Hundred Years' War between France and England results in Joan of Arc's martyrdom and England losing all claims to French territory.

1415: Czech heretic Jan Hus is burned at the stake.

1450: First printing press invented by Johannes Gutenberg in Germany. Bible is printed five years later.

1453: Ottoman Turks capture Constantinople and Byzantine empire falls.

1478: The Inquisition is established in Spain.

1492: Moors driven out of Spain; Jews expelled. Christopher Columbus arrives in the Americas.

1503: Leonardo da Vinci paints *Mona Lisa*.

1506–1626: St Peter's built in Rome, involving Michelangelo, da Vinci, Raphael and Bernini.

1519: Portuguese navigator Fernando Magellan circumnavigates the world.

1543: Poland's Nicolas Copernicus publishes theory that the earth revolves around the sun.

16th century: The Reformation in Northern Europe is a move against the corruption of the Church of Rome. 1517: Martin Luther nails his 95 points to Wittenberg church door. 1536: John Calvin establishes Presbyterian church in Switzerland.

1572: Protestant Huguenots purged in St Bartholomew's Day Massacre in France.

1579: The United Provinces established, founding the Netherlands.

1618–46: Thirty Years' War: initially a Protestant revolt against Catholicism.

1633: The Inquisition forces Italian scientist Galileo to renounce his Copernican belief that the earth revolves around the sun.

1643–1715: Louix XIV, creator of the Palace of Versailles in France, exemplifies a phase of absolute monarchy and the divine right of kings.

1755: Earthquake destroys Lisbon.

17th–18th centuries: Baroque architecture is a rich style, using gold, marble and mirrors to show off wealth and power. The palace of Versailles and Zwinger Palace in Dresden are good examples.

18th century: Age of Enlightenment. Toleration is urged by the French writer Voltaire and others. The practice is preached by Austro-Hungarian empress Maria Theresa, "the Mother of the Nation" (1717–80). Mozart plays at her court.

1792: The French Revolution. Louis XVI and Queen Marie Antoinette are guillotined.

1796–1815: Napoleon Bonaparte of France invades Austria, Italy, Spain, Portugal and Russia. He is defeated at Waterloo in modern Belgium.

Late 18th–19th centuries: Romanticism looks back to more idyllic times and inspires nationalist movements, encouraging local languages (Catalan, Provençal) and customs.

1822: Greece declares independence.

1848: Popular revolutions throughout Europe.

1861: Kingdom of Italy set up after Austrians ejected from the north, Spanish from the south.

1870–71: Franco-Prussian war, Paris besieged.

1874: First Impressionist exhibition held in Paris.

1885: First petrol engine vehicle made by Karl Benz.

1912–13: Balkan Wars result in most of European Turkey being divided up.

1914–18: World War I. War of attrition fought in northern France and Belgium. It results in the break-up of the Ottoman and Austro-Hungarian empires and the formation of new countries, including Yugoslavia and Czechoslovakia.

1922: Mussolini and 25,000 Fascist Blackshirts march on Rome.

1936–39: Spanish civil war. First mobilisation of troops by air. Francisco Franco becomes dictator.

1938: Adolf Hitler invades Austria.

PRECEDING PAGES: prehistoric cave painting from Lascaux, France. **LEFT:** Florence's great literary genius, Dante Alighieri. **RIGHT:** Louis XIV, the Sun King and absolute ruler of France.

1939–45 World War II. France, the Netherlands, Belgium, Yugoslavia, Albania and Greece occupied by Germans and Italians. Allied landings in Normandy and southern Italy lead to end of the war. Many German cities destroyed. Europe is divided between Western and Soviet spheres of influence.

1956: Hungarian revolution supressed.

1958: European Common Market set up.

1961: Berlin Wall built by the Russians.

1968: Student unrest throughout Europe. Czechoslovakian reforms of the "Prague Spring" are crushed by Soviet Union.

1974–75: Dictatorships in Greece, Spain and Portugal end.

1978: Poland's Cardinal Wojtyla becomes Pope John Paul II, first non-Italian pope for 400 years.

1989: Berlin Wall comes down. Eastern Europe begins to build democratic institutions.

1991: Hostilities break out in Yugoslavia. Slovenia, Croatia, Bosnia-Herzegovina and Macedonia subsequently declare their independence.

1992: Border controls between European Union (formerly EC) countries theoretically end.

1994: Channel Tunnel links France with Britain.

1998–99: Thousands of ethnic Albanians are driven out of Serbian province of Kosovo.

2000: Millennium celebrations throughout Europe.

2002: The Euro is adopted by all EU states apart from Denmark, Sweden and the UK. ❏

BEGINNINGS

Centuries of domination by the Greeks and Romans
eventually gave way to the turbulence of medieval Christendom

Europa, so legend has it, was the beautiful daughter of the king of Phoenicia, who was carried away by the god Zeus to the island of Crete. There she bore him three sons, including Minos, after whom the Minoan civilisation was named. It is more likely that the name Europe comes from the Assyrian word "*ereb*", the land of darkness and the setting sun ("*asu*", or Asia, was the land of the rising sun), but it is not such a romantic story.

Early civilisations

The Minoans flourished between the Middle and Late Bronze Ages, roughly 2000–1450 BC. We take this for granted now, but it was only about 100 years ago that their civilisation was discovered and the remains of their palaces, such as the most famous one at Knossos in Crete, were excavated, their layout and wall paintings suggesting a relatively sophisticated way of life – at least for the ruling classes.

The Minoans were superseded – and no one has yet discovered how or why – by the Mycenaeans, whose civilisation on mainland Greece was also unearthed only in the late 19th century. They appear to have been dominant for some 300 years, until about 1100 BC and, again, it is unclear why such a strong and wealthy civilisation should have been toppled, although outside attack and internal dissent undoubtedly played a part. Whatever the reasons, their demise plunged the Greek world into a dark age which lasted until the beginning of what historians call the Archaic period (800–500 BC).

This was the age of the polis or city-state, of which Athens and Sparta emerged as the most powerful, and which gave us two words in common usage today: tyrant – a leader who seized power from the ruling nobility by means of a military coup – and oligarchy – a tightly knit group who took control or had an unduly strong influence on the government.

The Persian Empire was the greatest threat to Greek security, a threat which culminated in the Persian Wars of 490–450 BC, which are now remembered chiefly for the great Athenian victory at Marathon, and the heroic defeat at Thermopylae. Although Athens and Sparta combined forces to vanquish the Persians, during the classical period that followed, it was

Athens which became most powerful.

This was the age of the great Athenian statesman Pericles, when Plato sat at the feet of Socrates before writing *The Republic*, on which much of Western philosophy is based. It was the period when the Parthenon was built, democracy was developed, when Sophocles wrote *Oedipus Rex* and Euripides created *Medea*.

This golden age came to an end when Athens and Sparta wrestled for power during the long drawn-out Peloponnesian War, weakening both sides and allowing Philip of Macedon to step into the breach. By 338 BC Philip had united the Greek city-states and, when he was assassinated two years later, his son

---

LEFT: Greek statue from the Early Cycladic II era.
RIGHT: detail from a fresco on Santorini.

Alexander the Great (356–323 BC) took over. Although only 20 years old, he was already a seasoned soldier, as well as a pupil of the great philosopher Aristotle.

Alexander's incursions into Persia were cut short when he fell ill and died in Babylon at the age of 32. Squabbling broke out among hopeful successors and Alexander's kingdom was split into three: Egypt, Asia Minor and Macedon-Greece. In all of these, and the many smaller kingdoms, Alexander was revered as a god. This was known as the Hel-

THE GREAT WARRIOR

In the 13 years of his short rule Alexander the Great succeeded in conquering the entire Persian Empire, amassing an empire of unprecedented size and wealth.

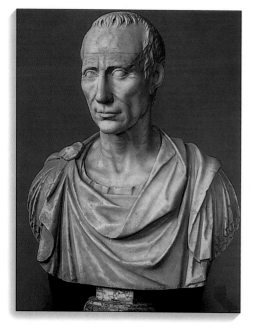

lenistic period, from the Greek word Hellenistes, meaning one who imitates the Greeks.

One thing that was imitated, or continued, was the concept of cities as political, commercial and social centres. Alexander had founded cities, named after himself, wherever he went – there were at least seven Alexandrias in the Hellenistic world and one Bucephalia – named after his favourite horse.

Trade and agriculture flourished in hte Hellenistic world, but competition and war between the kingdoms finally allowed the Romans to take control. Macedon was the first to go, in 167 BC, and Greece followed in 146 BC while Egypt held out until 31 BC.

Every Italian knows the story of Romulus and Remus, the twins abandoned on a river bank and brought up by a she-wolf, and that Romulus killed his brother, and founded Rome on the banks of the Tiber in about 750 BC. Archaeologists agree that there was a settlement here at that time and that it grew into a flourishing city, but it is most likely that it was established as a trading post by the Etruscans, a highly civilised people who were also skilled craftsmen and metal workers. The Etruscans ruled Rome until 509 BC, when Tarquin the Proud was ousted and a republic set up.

Roman rule

Over the next two centuries Rome conquered the rest of the Italian peninsula and in 241 BC took Sicily from the North Africa-based Carthaginians in the First Punic War. The Second Punic War began in 218 BC when Hannibal, a Carthaginian general, came up through Spain and France and made his famous crossing of the Alps with a huge army and a number of elephants. Hannibal was defeated, however, and after that there was no stopping the Romans: within less than a century they had conquered Carthage and Greece and were in control of the whole Mediterranean area.

During these years the rich grew richer but the poor, ousted from their menial jobs and thrown off their land to be replaced by the slaves their masters imported from conquered provinces, grew more discontented. Social unrest, coupled with military threats from all over the empire, exposed the ruling class as corrupt and incompetent and led to civil war. Gnaeus Pompeius Magnus (Pompey the Great, 106–48 BC) restored order, forming a Triumvirate with Marcus Crassus and Julius Caesar. But when Crassus died, civil war flared again. Pompey was killed in Egypt and Caesar returned to Rome in triumph.

It was short-lived. A group of senators conspired against him and, ignoring a soothsayer's warnings about the Ides of March, Caesar was stabbed to death in the senate chamber in 44 BC. His assassins did not long outlive him. Brutus and Cassius committed suicide after defeat in Macedonia and Mark Antony died at the side of Cleopatra, the Egyptian queen, after being decisively defeated by Octavian, Caesar's heir, at the Battle of Actium.

Fortunately, Octavian, who was granted the title Augustus (the revered one), was a wise man and a strong ruler. Handling the upper classes with tact and pleasing the masses with bread and circuses, he presided over a period known as the Pax Romana – the Roman peace – in which trade and agriculture prospered, and art and literature flourished, producing such great writers as Virgil and Horace.

A succession of emperors, after Augustus's death in AD 14, soon undid all his good works. Tiberius, Caligula and Nero were among the

Byzantine Empire, was to prove much stronger, lasting for another thousand years.

The spread of Christianity

By the end of the 4th century Christianity had spread throughout the Empire. At the end of the sixth century, Pope Gregory I sent missionaries to northern Europe to convert the heathens, and others followed their example.

But the Western Empire was disintegrating and Germanic tribes were moving in to fill the power vacuum: the Visigoths in Spain, the Ostrogoths in Italy and the Franks (who have bequeathed their name to France and Frankfurt),

best-known and most eccentric villains, and they were followed by a series of weak or wicked rulers. Anarchy grew as the empire declined. In AD 286 Diocletian divided the unwieldy mass into two, the eastern and western empires. His successor Constantine, the first Christian emperor, established an eastern capital in Constantinople (Istanbul) in 330. Rome was sacked by Visigoths in 410 and the last Roman emperor deposed in 476, but the Eastern Empire, which became known as the

LEFT: marble bust of Gaius Julius Caesar (c. 101–44 BC), one of the great generals of history.

ABOVE: Cicero asks Rome to unite against Cataline.

CHARLEMAGNE (742–814)

On Christmas Day in Rome, in the year 800, Charlemagne was crowned Emperor of the West by Pope Leo III. He consolidated his empire, building many palaces and churches and promoting Christianity. His court at Aix-La-Chapelle (Aachen) was an important centre of learning.

The title of "Holy Roman Emperor" was later inherited by the Austro-Hungarian Habsburgs but, as the French writer Voltaire pointed out, it was neither holy, nor Roman, nor an empire, and was finally abolished by Napoleon.

Charlemagne's own dynasty did not survive the divisions of lands made by his heir, Louis the Pious, and power slid into the hands of the German aristocracy.

ruled over Gaul. It was the Franks who were to prove most powerful. Their leader Charlemagne, founder of the Carolingian dynasty, conquered the lands now known as Italy, Hungary, Germany and the Lowlands.

Racial melting pot

There were huge movements of people all over Europe during these years. Lombards advanced through Italy in the 6th and 7th centuries, Slavs settled in the Balkans, Muslims from North Africa attacked Spain, conquering most of the peninsula by 714, and Arab raids on Constantinople threatened the security of the Eastern

Empire. Despite this, the empire imposed Orthodox Christianity on the Russian and Bulgar peoples, and its power waned only during the 11th century, when Turks overran Asia Minor and the Normans occupied southern Italy.

The Normans were descendants of the Vikings, who had been granted land in northern France early in the 10th century after repeated incursions into the Frankish kingdoms. They were soon integrated with the French nobility and strong enough to conquer England and sweep southwards, occupying southern Italy and seizing Sicily from the Arabs. Roger the Norman was crowned in Palermo in 1130 and, although Norman rule lasted barely 60 years, wonderful examples of the fusion of Arabic and Norman architecture still remain on the island.

The Crusades

At the end of the 11th century rumours spread through Christendom that the Ottoman Turks, who had held Jerusalem since the 7th century, were making life difficult for Christian pilgrims and in 1096 the First Crusade set out to liberate the Holy City. Although the Crusaders were initially successful, the Muslims retained the city and the next three centuries saw a succession of crusades, which despite occasional gains, were ultimately defeated.

A huge mythology has grown up around the exploits of the Knights Templars and the Hospitallers, the members of military monastic orders who led the crusades, and the defeat of Saladin and the capture of Richard the Lionheart are the stuff of heroic fairy tales. In fact, although there was genuine religious zeal at first, there was also avarice and self-interest.

MEDIEVAL ECCLESIASTICAL ARCHITECTURE

During the Middle Ages styles of ecclesiastical architecture spread rapidly across Europe, partly because of the movement of pilgrims, who carried new ideas with them, and partly because some of the great monastic houses, such as Cluny in Burgundy, ruled strings of monasteries stretching right across the continent.

Byzantine architecture had spread from Constantinople in the east, and many examples of its domed churches can be seen in Greece. The Romanesque style – so-called by a 19th-century French art historian because it used the rounded, classical arch and had solid grandeur which resembled that of the architecture of Rome – appeared

everywhere during the 11th and 12th centuries. There are many pure Romanesque churches still standing, scattered throughout Italy, France and Spain.

Gothic followed Romanesque, its great churches and cathedrals expressing a new airiness and grace, typified by pointed arches, vaulted ceilings, flying buttresses and numerous windows. The cathedral at Chartres, southwest of Paris, is an impressive example of early Gothic, from the middle of the 12th century.

Most of the surviving Gothic architecture is in Italy, such as the magnificent Doge's Palace in Venice, the Palazzo Vecchio in Florence and the Palazzo Pubblico in Siena.

The Muslim world was less successful in holding on to its lands in Spain than it was in the east, although the *reconquista*, the reconquest, was a slow process. The Christian kingdoms of Castile and Aragon gained ground during the 11th century, and the fabled hero El Cid won Valencia from the Moors in 1094. Portugal was founded as a Christian kingdom in 1139 by diverted Crusaders, but it took another century before the Muslims were ousted from the whole peninsula, apart from the Emirate of Granada,

VOYAGE OF DISCOVERY

Patronised by Ferdinand and Isabella of Spain, Columbus (1451–1506) made several sea voyages, hoping to reach India. Instead he discovered South America.

contemplation, self-denial and learning. St Benedict had laid down the rules for monastic life at Monte Cassino in Italy in AD 527.

In the Dark Ages that followed the fall of the Western Roman Empire, the only culture that survived in any form was in the monasteries. Except in Italy, where there was always some secular education, all learning and literacy was acquired in monastic schools. The monasteries were also the recipients of gifts of land and money from the wealthy, who hoped to lay up

which remained a part of Islam until 1492, when Ferdinand and Isabella, the Catholic monarchs, succeeded in uniting the country under their rule. In the same year Columbus set sail for the Americas.

The spread of learning

It would be difficult to over-emphasise the importance of the Christian church. As the religion spread across the continent, missionary communities had been founded as centres of

treasure in heaven. They therefore became not only large landowners but patrons of the arts, which is why most buildings, paintings and sculptures that survive have religious themes.

During the 12th century, monasteries lost their monopoly on education, and secular schools were set up. By the century's end, universities had been established in Oxford, Paris and Bologna. By the 13th century, most members of the upper class, of both sexes, were able to read, even if they could not write.

Inspired by the 14th-century Italian poet, Petrarch, scholars began to read Greek and Roman texts, and went on to re-examine man's role in the world. These ideas, known as human-

LEFT: Arab court painting.
ABOVE: Pope Urban II dedicates a high altar at Cluny, France, in 1095.

ism, spread throughout Europe and one of their most important proponents, the Dutch scholar Erasmus (1466–1536) also called for reform of the Church. In 1450 Johannes Gutenberg had set up his printing press in Mainz and the works of Erasmus, among others, reached a wide audience.

Revolt of the masses

For most people in Europe in the 14th century, the ideas behind humanist thought were not very important. They were occupied with trying to survive under circumstances even more dire than usual – the Black Death, the impact of which was enormous. Initially, land lay idle for lack of labour, food was scarce and prices rose sharply. In the long term the lack of manpower became a bargaining tool for the surviving peasants and contributed to the end of serfdom.

Under the feudal system, large landowners had received service from smaller ones, a system which spread from the monarch down to the lowliest peasant. At the top of the scale, knights would owe "knight service" to their masters and would have to fight when called upon. At the lower end, humble plot owners would have to work on their masters' land as well as on their own. After the plague this system gradually collapsed and peasants were able to take over some of the untended land.

Contributing to the unrest were royal demands for taxes to finance long drawn out wars, such as the Hundred Years' War. This was a power struggle between the English and French kings for territory in France, which actually lasted from 1337 to 1453, interrupted by a 28-year truce. It was a war littered with famous battles and heroic deeds, most importantly the leadership and martyrdom of Joan of Arc, burned at Rouen by the English as a heretic in 1431, and later canonised. The English were eventually defeated, leaving the aptly named Charles the Bold (1467–77) the undisputed ruler of what was now France.

ism, spread throughout Europe and one of their most important proponents, the Dutch scholar Erasmus (1466–1536) also called for reform of the Church. In 1450 Johannes Gutenberg had set up his printing press in Mainz and the works of Erasmus, among others, reached a wide audience.

ism, spread throughout Europe and one of their most important proponents, the Dutch scholar Erasmus (1466–1536) also called for reform of the Church. In 1450 Johannes Gutenberg had set up his printing press in Mainz and the works of Erasmus, among others, reached a wide audience.

The Church's stability was also under attack from the emergence of several heretical groupings. The Cathars, or Albigensians, in the south of France had been destroyed early in the 13th century by a combination of conversion – led by St Dominic who founded the Dominican order – and brute force at the hands of Crusaders, diverted from expeditions to the Holy Land, to stamp out heresy closer to home.

But during the time of the Great Schism, two other heresies appeared: the Lollards, inspired by the English scholar John Wyclif, rejected both the authority of the pope and the doctrine of transubstantiation; and the Hussites, led by

widely disseminated. Martin Luther, a German monk who led the attack on abuse of Church power, was excommunicated but his ideas spread rapidly and many Lutheran churches were established after the Peace of Augsburg (1555) gave individual princes the right to decide the religion of their subjects.

John Calvin was the other great leader of the Reformation. His influence spread throughout Holland, Hungary, Poland and parts of Germany as well as his native France where his followers, known as Huguenots, were involved in the 16th-century Wars of Religion. Their strength lessened after thousands of them were

the Czech Jan Hus, whose beliefs were similar to those of Wyclif and who flourished for another two decades after their leader was burned at the stake in 1415.

The Reformation

All these ideas, and more, were to re-emerge and bring about the Reformation in the following century. The new printing presses rolled out copies of the scriptures, and the pamphlets issued by the new movements' leaders were

killed in 1572 during the St Bartholomew's Day Massacre, but they obtained toleration for their views under the Edict of Nantes.

The Catholic Church did not take all this lying down. The Jesuit order was founded by a zealous Spaniard, Ignatius Loyola, whose name is inextricably linked with the Inquisition, the organisation responsible for investigating and stamping out heresy. Paranoia about any unorthodox beliefs led to the witch hunts which swept Europe during the 16th and 17th centuries.

Decades of religious dissent eventually erupted in the Thirty Years' War (1618–48), sparked off by a Protestant revolt in Prague against the Habsburg emperor Frederick II. ❏

LEFT: Joan of Arc, burnt in Rouen as a heretic in 1431.
ABOVE: portrait of John Calvin, the Huguenots' leader.
RIGHT: an officer cadet in the Thirty Years' War.

CONQUERORS OF THE WORLD

The eclipse of Europe's great empire and the rise of nationalism

provided the conditions for the Renaissance in art

From the 15th century, expansionist aims took over from religious ones. Spain resumed its on-going war with the Netherlands, the king of Sweden invaded Germany, and France took up the cudgels against her old enemy, the Habsburg Empire. The main conflict ended with the Peace of Westphalia (1648), which granted Protestants freedom of worship, but by this time about a third of the population of some German states had died, due to warfare, disease or famine.

An empire in decline

War between Spain and France rumbled on for another decade, but these were years of Spanish decline. Spain and Portugal had established the first great colonial empires, based on the early voyages of discovery by such explorers as Vasco da Gama and Christopher Columbus. Spanish power, consolidated by Ferdinand and Isabella's reconquest of the country, had been given a further boost when the Habsburg Charles V of Austria came to the Spanish throne and, in 1519, was elected Holy Roman Emperor, an event viewed with some alarm by the ruling House of Bourbon in France.

Charles's empire, he said, was so vast that it was one over which "the sun never set". Habsburg tombstones were inscribed AEIOU, meaning *Austria est emperare orbi universo* (All the earth is subject to Austria), and there were few who would have disagreed – at least in public. When Charles abdicated he bequeathed all the Habsburg lands, except those in Austria itself, to his son Philip II of Spain, who went on to add the Portuguese empire to his own after the death of the king of Portugal in battle in 1578. With gold and silver flooding in from the New World to fill the national coffers, this seemed to many in Spain to be a true golden age.

Spectacular successes were followed by miserable failures. Wars with France, the continued battle for independence by the Protestant Netherlands, and the defeat of the Armada by the English navy (1588), all proved extremely expensive. When recession hit the Americas in the early 17th century and the flood of silver dwindled to a trickle, it was clear that the balmy

days were over. Catalonia revolted when asked to shoulder some of the costs of empire, and Portugal followed suit. Although Catalonia was soon recovered, Portugal remained independent and the battle for supremacy over the Netherlands was finally lost.

This is not to say that the Spanish Empire was not worth having. When the last of that branch of the Habsburgs died out and the French Bourbon monarch Philip V took the throne, Charles, Archduke of Austria, was sufficiently alarmed by growing French power to take up arms in the War of the Spanish Succession (1701–13). It was a conflict which nearly brought the Spanish and French economies to

LEFT: detail from a Japanese screen (*c.* 1593) commemorating the arrival of Portuguese traders.

RIGHT: *The Cannon Shot* (*c.* 1660) by Dutch painter Willem van de Velde.

their knees but when it ended, with the Treaty of Utrecht in 1713, it confirmed the right of the Bourbon king to the Spanish throne.

Artistic patronage

Meanwhile, wonderful things were happening in the field of artistic endeavour during these centuries. The Renaissance began in Florence, spread to other Italian cities such as Venice and Rome, then northwards through Europe. The humanist interest in classical art forms made artists aware that Europe had a cul-

> ### THE MEDICI DYNASTY
>
> Cosimo de' Medici (1389–1464) and his grandson Lorenzo (1449–92) were grand dukes of Tuscany. The family also produced four popes and two queens of France.

tural past and there were wealthy patrons prepared to finance its rebirth.

The powerful Medici banking family, who controlled so much that happened in Florence, were dominant in promoting art in the city, but it was the wool trade that financed some of the greatest paintings, sculptures and architectural gems the world has ever known. Florence had grown rich on wool and its wealthiest merchants, members of the Arte della Lana, or wool guild, not only provided the money which had made their city Europe's financial capital by the end of the 14th century, but also sponsored works of art.

The results of such patronage were spec-

tacular. Donatello was commissioned to work on many of the city's civic projects, Giotto designed the campanile for the new cathedral and Uccello made early experiments with perspective in his painting. From Venice sprang Leonardo da Vinci, the archetypal Renaissance man – a scientist, mathematician and philosopher as well as an artist.

In the north of Europe Albrecht Dürer changed the status of woodcuts and engravings from craftwork to an important art form. Hieronymus Bosch painted mythical monsters and Pieter Bruegel's rural scenes were a landmark in the shift from religious and allegorical themes to secular subjects.

In the late 15th and early 16th centuries the hub of the Italian Renaissance moved from Florence to Rome, as the papacy poured money into the reconstruction and embellishment of the city. Among the artistic riches this produced are Michelangelo's *Pietà* and *The Last Judgement* in the Sistine Chapel, Raphael's cartoons, also created for the Sistine Chapel, and Bramante's classical architectural designs.

Later in the 16th century Palladio, who based his work on the great public buildings of ancient Rome, created a style which was emulated all over Europe.

Mannerism grew out of the Renaissance, producing such masters as the goldsmith Cellini, the Venetian artists Titian and Tintoretto, as well as the dramatic work of El Greco in Spain, and an architectural style that was so much admired by the French king François I that he used it in the construction of his château at Fontainebleau.

Baroque art

The reaction to Mannerism was the florid baroque style of the 17th century, exemplified in Italy by Guido Reni and the sculptor Bernini, in Spain by Velázquez, who won the lifelong patronage of Philip IV, but most famously of all by the Flemish painter, Rubens. The Dutch school of painting also flourished in the 17th century, stimulated by a wave of national self-confidence following the Netherlands' deliv-

LEFT: *Cosimo I* by Vasari, from the ceiling of Florence's Palazzo Vecchio.
RIGHT: Botticelli's *Judith*, from Florence's Uffizi Gallery.

erance from Spanish rule and its success as a trading nation. The domestic scenes painted by Vermeer and the works of Rembrandt were among the most important of the School's prolific output.

Enlightened despotism

From the ideas of the Enlightenment – the late 17th- and early 18th-century intellectual movement that was based on reason and tolerance – sprang the seemingly contradictory notion of enlightened despotism. Catherine the Great of Russia was influenced by its ideas when she began her programme of reform and Emperor

Joseph II of Austria's attempt to abolish serfdom appears to have had a humanitarian basis, although he may well have been more strongly influenced by the ideas and example of his mother, Maria Theresa (1717–80). Known as "the mother of the nation", she is said to have taken a personal interest in her subjects and opposed injustice.

The court of Maria Theresa had welcomed the child prodigy, Wolfgang Amadeus Mozart, but it was not until the year after her death that the 25-year-old musician left his home town of Salzburg to seek his fortune in Vienna. A few years later he was joined by Joseph Haydn, who

THE ABSOLUTE POWER OF LOUIS XIV

The 17th century in Europe was the age of absolute monarchy, a system under which kings dismissed any idea of consultation and held tightly to the reigns of government, believing that God had granted them a divine right to rule. Louis XIV was the most famous and flamboyant of the absolute monarchs. The concept is neatly summed up in his famous phrase *L'état c'est moi* ("I am the State").

His ideas of personal control may have been influenced by the enormous power wielded by ministers – Cardinal Richelieu and Cardinal Mazarin – during his father's reign and his own regency. He asserted his authority over the Church and created a standing army to reinforce his

secular powers, and to fight against Spain and the Holy Roman Empire. Nobles were obliged to attend the newly glorified Palace of Versailles where the king could keep an eye on them, and Louis' most able minister, Colbert, who some believe to have been the power behind the throne, created a strong navy, reorganised the tax system, set up academies of science and arts and centralised the unwieldy bureacracy.

Although harvest failures, continuous wars, and court extravagance undid much of his good works, France was still strong enough to impress and frighten other European nations at the time of Louis' death in 1715.

had been born humbly in nearby Rohrau in 1732 and was now middle-aged and famous. In the 1790s the young Ludwig van Beethoven (1770–1827) also arrived in the capital, his unprecedented powers of musical expression making Vienna the musical centre of an increasingly culture-conscious Europe.

The French Revolution

Music was not uppermost in the minds of the French in the late 18th century. The government was bankrupt, largely due to costly intervention in the American War of Independence. The poor were angry about the disproportionate share of the taxes they were obliged to pay. The bourgeoisie were resentful of the privileges of the aristocracy, and there was growing criticism of absolutism.

Louis XVI's attempt to raise taxes and reduce privileges led to the formation of a National Assembly, the establishment of a commune in Paris, peasant revolts and the abolition of feudalism. The Declaration of the Rights of Man – *Liberté, Égalité, Fraternité* – was proclaimed in 1789 and a new constitutional government organised. Louis was eventually forced to accept the constitution and for a while it seemed that a bloodless revolution had achieved its aims.

THE ENLIGHTENMENT

During the reign of Louis XV a group of French thinkers known as the *Philosophes*, inspired by the scientific discoveries of Sir Isaac Newton and the thinking of the English empirical philosopher John Locke, began to disseminate the ideas of the Enlightenment.

They believed that traditional explanations of the universe and man's place in it could no longer be taken for granted and that truth and meaning could only be discovered through reason and experience. Voltaire's dictum, "I may disagree with what you say but I will defend to the death your right to say it," encapsulates the movement's ideals and concern for toleration.

This apparent success was not welcomed by other European rulers, who feared that France's revolutionary ideas would spread across their own countries. Austria and Prussia invaded France in 1792, Britain a year later. These attacks engendered paranoia: conspiracy theories abounded and more than 1,000 suspected counter-revolutionaries were executed. France was declared a republic and Louis XVI and his queen, Marie Antoinette, were guillotined.

Revolts by those opposed to the Revolution broke out at home. The moderates in the new government – the Girondins – were overthrown by the Jacobins, and the Committee of Public Safety, led by Maximilien Robespierre, was set up. The subsequent "Reign of Terror" left thousands dead and only ended when Robespierre himself became one of its victims. The new power group, the Directory, ended the bloodletting, but was only able to keep the peace with the aid of the army and this increase in military influence led, in 1799, to the coup of 18 Brumaire (the Revolution had introduced a new calendar, and Brumaire was the new name for November).

Napoleon Bonaparte

The coup was led by Napoleon Bonaparte and, after serving as Consul for four years, he abolished the republic and was declared emperor, heading a military dictatorship which reversed most of the reforms achieved by the Revolution before the Terror.

Napoleon had won his stripes fighting against the Austrians in Italy. Despite subsequent defeat at the Battle of the Nile, he was still strong enough to be a hero at home, to compel Austria to accept French dominance in Italy, and to emerge the apparent victor of the Peace of Amiens in 1802.

It was a fleeting peace. Britain declared war again the following year and defeated the new emperor's fleet off Cape Trafalgar in 1805. It was to be his last defeat for some years: against a coalition of Britain, Austria, Russia and Naples, Napoleon seemed invincible, notching up victory after victory, causing the downfall of the Holy Roman Empire and winning the support of Austria after his second marriage to an Austrian princess.

Small in stature, grand in his designs and one of the most brilliant generals Europe has produced, Napoleon became too greedy for his own good. His disastrous defeat in the snows of Moscow in 1812, which only one-tenth of his army survived, was compounded by his long-running conflict in Spain – the Peninsular War. Having handed the Spanish throne to his brother in 1808, he spent the next five years fighting aggrieved Spaniards and their British allies before his defeat by the Duke of Wellington at Vitoria and an allied army at Leipzig in 1813. When Paris subsequently fell he was exiled to the Mediterranean island of Elba. He staged a comeback the following year but the combined forces of Prussia and Britain brought him down at Waterloo (in modern Belgium), and he was shipped off to distant St Helena, in the South Atlantic. Louis XVIII was restored to the French throne.

When the victorious allies sat round the table at the Congress of Vienna, their main aims were to stop France ever being so dominant again and, of course, to gain as much for themselves as they could. Austria kept Venice, which had previously been independent, Russia gained most of Poland, and the Netherlands became a new kingdom.

The rise of nationalism

The most dominant man around the table may well have been Metternich, Austrian prince and statesman who spent the next three decades attempting to stem the rising tide of nationalism both in Austria and abroad.

Nationalist sentiments, far from being extinguished, were strengthened by opposition and in 1848 popular revolutions broke out all over Europe. The first revolt, in Paris, inspired others in Italy and throughout the Austrian Empire, as Croats, Czechs and Hungarians demanded recognition as independent ethnic states. Optimism was high and initial gains were made, but the overthrow of the Orléans monarchy and

LEFT: Delacroix's *Liberty Leading the People* captured the spirit of revolutionary France.
RIGHT: Napoleon Bonaparte crosses the Alps.

proclamation of the Second Republic in France led not to democracy or liberalism but to the establishment of the Second Empire. The expulsion of Austrian rulers from northern Italy and Spanish Bourbons from the south turned out to be short-lived, and independence in other parts of the Austro-Hungarian Empire was soon crushed.

Eastern powers

Further east, the Ottoman Empire did not remain untouched by demands for self-determination and it was here that nationalism had one of its first successes. In 1822 a newly

formed National Assembly declared Greece an independent state.

After Russian intervention in response to Turkish atrocities, Britain and France pitched in, sunk the Turkish fleet in Navarino Bay and, together with Russia, guaranteed Greek independence in 1830. Otto of Bavaria was drafted from the stock of German royalty to give the nation suitable status, a practice followed by other emergent nations.

Fear of Russian encroachment was a dominant theme in Europe in the middle of the 19th century, particularly when it involved control of the entrance to the Black Sea, the so-called "warm water port". It did not take a great deal of political acumen to realise that the Russian doctrine of Pan-Slavism, by which Russia assumed the role of protector of smaller Slav nations who were struggling for independence, only came into play when it furthered Russia's territorial interests.

Elsewhere – in Poland, for example – nationalist movements were quickly put down. Russia was also quick to intervene in the Hungarian Revolution in 1848 and this, together with its occupation of Balkan territories in 1853, contributed to the outbreak of the Crimean War, a chaotic and mismanaged affair in which half a million men died.

The Risorgimento

The foreign power which governed most of the Italian peninsula was that of Austro-Hungary, whose chief statesman, Prince Clemens Metternich, once described Italy as "only a geographical expression". Although the peninsula had never been one nation, a unification movement

THE ROMANTIC MOVEMENT

Romanticism swept through the European continent's artistic circles, beginning at the end of the 18th century and continuing for much of the 19th century. A period of cultural renaissance, it was, in part, a way of trying to make sense of the world after the enormous social dislocations and upheavals brought about by the French and American revolutions; in part, a reaction against the physical ugliness created by the Industrial Revolution.

The Romantic movement also embodied a rejection of the rationalism which had characterised the Enlightenment. Instead, spontaneity, subjectivity and individualism came to the fore. Romantics harked back to a Golden Age: for

some, it was classical Greece, for others, the medieval world of courtly love and chivalry.

In France, Rousseau idealised the "noble savage"; in Germany, Goethe and Schiller extolled spiritual freedom and the beauty of nature; literature and the local language was rediscovered and extolled in Catalonia and Provence. Beethoven's Pastoral symphony was a deeply romantic work and composers such as Dvořák and Tchaikovsky were influenced by folk music and legends.

Idealisation of the past and the search for ethnic origins blended smoothly with the political aspirations of people refusing to live under the yoke of foreign powers.

known as the *Risorgimento* (Resurrection) now pressed for one. The *Carbonari* were unsuccessful in uniting the 13 separate states under Italian rule, but Camillo Cavour, the prime minister of Piedmont, ejected the Austrians from northern Italy in 1859.

The following year Guiseppe Garibaldi, Italy's best-known and most colourful freedom fighter, took southern Italy from the Spanish Bourbons. The new Kingdom of Italy was formed in 1861, although Vatican territory remained under French control until 1870.

OTTO VON BISMARCK

Bismarck was well known for his ruthlessness and cunning; one of his maxims was: "Nothing should be left to an invaded people except their eyes for weeping."

tria's defeat at Sadowa in 1866. Finally he engineered a war with France, the Franco-Prussian War of 1870, which he won with little difficulty, enabling him to grab the border territories of Alsace and Lorraine and unite the whole of the Germanic area under Prussian control.

In Paris, the Prussian invasion led to the establishment of the socialist Paris Commune, modelling itself on the Jacobin-dominated Assembly of 1793. The Commune was brutally put down, the death toll was enormous, and all the

Prussian supremacy

In Germany, the situation was even more complicated, and the fact that the 39 separate states became one unified country in 1871 was mainly due to the political skill of the Prussian prime minister Otto von Bismarck. His "blood and iron" policy involved allying Prussia with Austria against Denmark over the control of Schleswig and Holstein.

Bismarck then provoked a short, sharp war with his former ally, which ended with Aus-

LEFT: Johann Wolfgang von Goethe (1749–1832), champion of German Classicism.
ABOVE: Garibaldi fighting the French in 1849.

revolutionary elements were subsequently imprisoned or exiled, which did great damage to hopes for socialism in France for several years to come. Despite this, Karl Marx may have been right in regarding it as "the dawn of a new era", for socialist parties soon developed throughout the rest of Europe.

In the newly united Germany, the Social Democratic Party was formed in 1875, although Bismarck soon forced it underground. Socialist parties of various hues were formed in Austria, Belgium, Italy and Switzerland during the 1880s and early 1890s, by which time the German party re-emerged and became dominant among European parties of the left.

Sharing the spoils

Russia, which would be the first country to embrace state socialism, was, at this stage, still troubling the other European powers by her encroachments into the Balkans. At the Berlin Congress of 1878 Russia's possession of the Caucasus was confirmed and she was given control of Bessarabia. Bulgaria was declared an autonomous province, and Serbia, Montenegro and Romania all had their independence confirmed, while Bosnia-Herzogovina exchanged Turkish for Austro-Hungarian control.

The Berlin settlement was not satisfactory. The Ottoman Empire remained "the sick man of Europe" and complicated relations between the six Great Powers that existed now that so many disparate states had been unified. These powers – Great Britain, France, Italy, Germany, Russia and Austro-Hungary – were also rivals for overseas colonies. Between 1870 and 1914, they carved up most of Africa and the Pacific between them.

Rivalries within Europe and the overseas colonies led to the alliance system. Germany, Austro-Hungary and Italy formed the Triple Alliance, while Russia, France and Great Britain became partners in the Triple Entente. This system led inexorably to World War I.

NEW MOVEMENTS IN ART

The French Impressionist movement emerged in the 1860s and was to have an enormous impact on subsequent artists. In an effort to move away from the precise draughtsmanship of earlier art and to depict the visual impression of the moment, the Impressionists began to paint straight from nature, using free, loose brushwork.

Scorned by the official Paris Salon, Monet, Renoir, Degas, Pisarro and others held their own exhibition in 1874, followed by another seven such breakaway exhibitions during the next dozen years.

The Post-Impressionists, the most celebrated of whom were Cézanne, Gauguin and van Gogh, emphasised strong colours and powerful emotions in their work. They were followed by the Fauves (literally "Wild Beasts"), led by Matisse and Derain.

In Austria the Vienna Secession, led by Gustav Klimt, was another rebellion against conventional art forms. From the Secession emerged not only Klimt's erotic images, but the disturbing work of the Expressionist artists Egon Schiele and Oskar Kokoschka, and *Jugendstil*, the Austrian version of art nouveau.

The fluid forms of art nouveau glorified European cities in the early years of the 20th century, and can be seen at their most fantastic in the work of Gaudí in Barcelona.

Technological age

The people of Europe, meanwhile, were having fun exploring their countries and the continent on the new railways: learning to ski in the Alps and bathing in the Mediterranean Riviera.

New developments in the visual arts were reflected in music and literature. Claude Debussy was composing prolifically and Eric Satie was creating his playful, idiosyncratic music. "Realist" writers such as Emile Zola, Anton Chekhov and Henrik Ibsen forced their readers to face sometimes unpalatable truths.

The end of the 19th and beginning of the 20th century was also a period when tech-

Moves towards democratic forms of government had also been made in the industrialised countries by the turn of the century, including the rights to free speech and freedom of the press. Trade unions had been given full recognition in France by 1884 and in Germany soon after Bismarck's death in 1890.

Universal suffrage

These two countries also gave all men the right to vote in 1871, although women had to wait a lot longer – until 1918 in Germany and until the end of World War II in France. In Switzerland, women did not win the right to

nology was making huge strides. Guglielmo Marconi constructed the first radio in a Bologna attic in 1894. The Paris-Orléans railway was electrified in 1900, the same year that Count von Zeppelin's dirigible made its first flight and nine years before Louis Blériot piloted an aircraft across the English Channel. Karl Benz had produced his first petrol-engined Motorwagen in 1885 and just 10 years later motoring was well enough established for the 1895 Paris-Bordeaux road race to be run.

LEFT: the Berlin–Potsdam railway, c. 1850.
ABOVE: an early 19th-century view of wealthy Europeans at leisure in Monte Carlo.

vote until 1971, although universal male suffrage had been introduced in 1874. Belgium and Spain followed suit in the 1890s, although Portugal, Italy and the Austro-Hungarian Empire lagged behind.

Immunisation and improved sanitation were increasing life expectancy rates and slums were being cleared in most major cities. Bismarck initiated a social security system, offering insurance payments for sickness, accident and old age, and during the 1880s most other European countries introduced some or all of these benefits. All in all, unless one was very poor, life in Europe was not too bad, comparatively at least, in the first years of the 20th century.   ❑

MODERN TIMES

*All-out war tore Europe apart twice in the 20th century. New institutions mean that
today's battles are mostly economic – but the Balkan states remain in turmoil*

World War I, which was sparked off by the Austrian Archduke's assassination at Sarajevo, produced carnage on a scale never before imagined. An estimated 20 million people died before the Armistice was signed on 11 November 1918. This, it was said, had been the war to end all wars, and the Fourteen Point Peace Plan put forward by the American President Wilson at the Treaty of Versailles and subsequent treaties signed with Turkey and Austro-Hungary were supposed to lay the foundations for a lasting peace. In fact, they did the opposite. The old empires of Germany, Russia, Austro-Hungary and Turkey were broken up and the map of Europe completely redrawn.

New divisions

Alsace and Lorraine were returned to France, a new Polish state was created, with the Danzig Corridor giving it access, through German land, to the sea. Czechoslovakia also became an independent state and was awarded Bohemia and Moravia, which had been part of the Austrian Empire. Hungarian-controlled land went towards the formation of Yugoslavia, while Trieste, Istria and the south Tyrol were ceded to Italy. The Ottoman Empire had to relinquish much of the land it held in the Middle East, but an attempt to occupy part of Turkey itself provoked a revolt led by General Kemal Ataturk.

These divisions of land caused a great deal of bitterness and resentment. Even more doomed to failure were the restrictions imposed on the defeated German nation. The Rhineland was occupied by Allied troops, the Saarland governed by an international commission, Germany's overseas colonies were put under the control of the newly created League of Nations, re-armament was forbidden and the size of the army strictly limited. Most painful of all were the crippling financial reparations demanded

---

LEFT: the blood-spattered uniform of Austrian Archduke Franz Ferdinand.

RIGHT: an artist's impression of the Archduke's assassination at Sarajevo by a Serb nationalist.

by Britain and France. They were never fully paid but they contributed to the near collapse of the German economy and engendered huge resentment, which Adolf Hitler was able to manipulate during his rise to power.

The 1920s and 1930s were decades of totalitarian regimes and a great deal of hardship due

to the severe economic recession of the worldwide Depression. At the same time, the newly created states in Eastern Europe were bedevilled by nationalist tensions.

Political instability

In Poland, a coup in 1926 left the country a virtual dictatorship under Marshal Pilsudski. In Hungary, there was a fleeting period of communist control, and a much longer one under Romanian occupation. Ethnic arguments between Croats, Serbs and Slovenes in Yugoslavia culminated in the murder of King Alexander by a Croat separatist in 1934. Czechoslovakia was the most successful: under the much respected President Thomas Masaryk democracy survived into the mid-1930s, but in the German Sudetenland a strong national socialist party dominated the latter part of the decade.

In Greece, the interwar years saw constant rivalry between republicans, led by Venizelos, and royalists, loyal to King Constantine. When the monarchy was restored, in 1935, after a period of republicanism, the king could rule only with the backing of General Metaxas, a virtual dictator.

In the Iberian peninsula, Portugal, a republic since the overthrow of the monarchy in 1910, came under military control in 1926, and the

dictatorship of Antonio Salazar, who was to rule for the next 36 years, began in 1932. In Spain a period of military rule by General Primo de Rivera, and the abdication of King Alfonso XIII in 1931, left a shaky republic, torn with dissent between left and right. In 1936, a military revolt led by Francisco Franco initiated a civil war which lasted for three years, with Franco's nationalists supported by Germany and Italy, the republicans by the Soviet Union and an International Brigade of volunteers.

Franco's forces eventually defeated the republicans in 1939. He took control of a demoralised country, its people near starvation, and ruled at the head of a Falangist (neo-fascist) government until his death in 1975.

The rise of fascism

The first fascist party had arisen in Italy, where Benito Mussolini manipulated fears of communism to gain support and, in 1922, marched on Rome with his 25,000 Blackshirts. King Victor Emmanuel III reluctantly asked him to form a government, and four years later Mussolini declared himself Il Duce, the leader of the Italian people.

Savagely repressing his opponents, he embarked on massive programmes of public works, forged links with the German Nazi party and, in 1935, in an attempt to build an empire, invaded Abyssinia. Emboldened by the fact that the League of Nations, the body formed to prevent war, simply imposed a few economic sanctions, he walked into Albania four years later.

In Germany, Adolf Hitler also used the fear of communism, which was rife in the years following the 1917 Bolshevik Revolution in Russia, to win widespread support for his National Socialist party. He was also able to exploit the resentment felt by the German people over the terms of the Treaty of Versailles, the effects of which were further compounded by the economic crisis of the Depression after the 1929 Wall Street Crash in the United States.

The weak Weimar Republic could not survive and in 1933 Hitler became chancellor of Germany. When President von Hindenburg died the following year, Hitler established himself as Führer ("the leader"), banning opposition parties, granting draconian powers to the Gestapo, and initiating against Germany's Jewish population the increasingly repressive measures which would culminate in the holocaust.

In 1936 Hitler reoccupied the Rhineland and two years later, with the connivance of the pro-Nazi Austrian Chancellor Seyss-Inquart, invaded Austria and proclaimed the Anschluss, the union of the two countries.

Later that year, at the Munich Conference, Britain and France capitulated to Hitler's demands and allowed him control of the Sudetenland, but the "peace in our time", which the British prime minister Neville Chamberlain hoped this would ensure, lasted less than a year. Hitler seized the rest of

A SHAMEFUL EPISODE

In 1937 the town of Guernica in northern Spain entered history as the first place to be bombed from the air, an event immortalised in Picasso's painting *Guernica*.

Cologne and Dresden, which the Allies had relentlessly bombed. Warsaw's historic streets were faithfully recreated, but in most places new buildings were erected alongside old, changing the character of many towns – although, in the process, often providing better living conditions.

In Greece, civil war between monarchists and communists raged for four years. Spain, ostracised by the allied powers because of its support for Hitler, suffered years of severe hardship, its *noche negra*, or black night.

Czechoslovakia, signed a non-aggression pact with the Soviet Union, then invaded Poland. It was the end of appeasement and the beginning of World War II, in which Germany, Italy and, later, Japan, took on the world.

Aftermath of war

When the conflict finally came to an end in May 1945, Europe embarked on the long, costly process of putting itself together again. Shattered cities had to be rebuilt, particularly

LEFT: Hitler crossing the Czech border in 1939.
ABOVE: war-time devastation after bombing raids in the Polish capital, Warsaw.

In Eastern Europe, the USSR was allowed to keep within its sphere of interest all the areas occupied by the Red Army when the conflict ended. By the end of the decade, all these states had Soviet-dominated governments – although Yugoslavia and Romania soon installed their own brand of communism.

Germany was divided in two, and the allied powers given zones of occupation in Berlin. In 1948 tensions between the powers resulted in the Soviet Union blockading the city and subsequent discontent in the Eastern zone, due to marked differences in living standards, led the Russians to build the Berlin Wall in 1961, a potent symbol of repression in post-war Europe.

Hungary also learned the meaning of repression in 1956, when an uprising, designed to overthrow communist rule, was brutally suppressed by the Soviet Union and its leader, Imre Nagy, executed. The Iron Curtain, as Britain's former prime minister Winston Churchill called it, was firmly drawn across Europe, and global conflict was replaced by the Cold War.

Mass tourism

In Western Europe, the hardship and austerity of the post-war years faded and people began to enjoy more leisure and more mobility. The existence of annual paid holidays and disposable

chalets and cable cars and threatened by the ecological impact of the seasonal crowds. By the 1990s, weekend city breaks within Europe were commonplace through cheap flights, high-speed trains and fast motorway links.

Closer European ties

The idea of a European identity was slowly growing during these decades. The European Economic Community was born in 1958, with France, Belgium, Luxembourg, Italy, West Germany and the Netherlands as its members. Britain, Ireland and Denmark joined in 1973. Spain, Portugal and Greece also moved closer

income, and the growth of commercial airlines and car ownership, all contributed to the birth of the package holiday industry. During the 1960s sleepy fishing villages in Spain and Greece turned into bustling resorts, where bikini-clad northern Europeans rubbed shoulders with black-clad Mediterranean grandmothers and high-rise hotels overshadowed whitewashed cottages. It brought prosperity to poverty-stricken areas, as well as customs and values that may not have been so welcome.

Skiing, a sport for the many, instead of just for the rich, came a little later than sun-seeking, but soon the mountainous areas of Switzerland, Austria, Italy and France were peppered with

STUDENT UNREST

An awareness of the wider world that came with developments in mass media, and in particular the daily footage showing America's involvement in the unpopular war in Vietnam, led to a questioning of values in the 1960s, especially among students and young people.

Student unrest swept across Europe and the US, beginning with the student protest in Paris in May 1968, which brought France to the verge of civil war. In the same spirit of defiance came the Prague Spring, when students backed the reforming leader Alexander Dubcek against Czechoslovakia's Moscow-oriented regime. Their peaceful revolution was crushed by Soviet tanks.

to the rest of Europe during the mid-1970s, after all three ceased to be dictatorships. By 2000 a European-wide currency, the euro, was more than just a dream.

In Portugal, a left-wing military coup overthrew the heirs of Salazar, but attempts at Marxist government failed and there were democratic elections in 1976. In Greece the military junta was overthrown in 1974, and a new constitution adopted. Following the death of Franco in Spain in 1975 the monarchy was restored and a new constitution declared. After a failed military coup, Spain became a democracy and Juan Carlos a popular king.

Walesa was awarded the Nobel peace prize later that year. Just six years later, in 1989, elections defeated the Communist party and put a Solidarity prime minister in office.

But by then, the whole face of Eastern Europe was fast changing. In the USSR, Mikhail Gorbachev's policies of *perestroika* and *glasnost* led to more openness in government, and the end of the Brezhnev Doctrine, which had given the Soviet Union the right to intervene in the affairs of all the Warsaw Pact countries. These concessions were rapidly seized throughout Eastern Europe. One by one, the former satellite states renounced communism.

Polish solidarity

Democracy was also in the air in Poland in the early 1980s. *Solidarnosc* (Solidarity) an independent trade union, came to prominence in the Gdansk dockyards. The demands made by the unions frightened the authorities, who imposed martial law and arrested their charismatic leader, Lech Walesa.

However, after secret talks between the Polish leader, General Jaruzelski, and the Polish-born Pope John Paul II, martial law was lifted.

LEFT: jubilation at Pink Floyd's "The Wall" concert in Berlin on 21 July 1990.
ABOVE: Dubrovnik under fire in 1991.

In Czechoslovakia, a new government was formed under the playwright Vaclav Havel; and in Hungary, as in most of the other states, a democratic, multi-party government was formed. In Germany, the Berlin Wall came down, amid international rejoicing, in November 1989, and the divided country was reunited.

But poverty followed democracy in Eastern Europe, power struggles continued, racism resurfaced, and the peoples of the Balkans again suffered vicious warfare. Europe seems to be a cauldron that refuses to cool. But the very heat of its history, its conflicts and turmoil, have all been part of the process of creation and destruction that has built this continent. ❑

EUROPE FROM A TO Z

These cultural snapshots, from Architecture to Zeitgeist,

serve as an introduction to this panoply of nations

Just why is Europe such a magnet for travellers from elsewhere in the world? What makes it so different from "home"? In 1888 James Bryce provided one answer, writing in *The American Commonwealth* that "life in one of the great European centers is capable of an intensity, a richness blended of many elements which has not yet been reached in America... In whatever country of Europe one dwells, one feels that the other countries are near, that the fortunes of their people are bound up with the fortunes of one's own, that ideas are shooting to and fro between them."

Times change, of course, but the love-hate relationship between America and Europe, born of close historical ties, still provides the most accessible mirror in which Europeans can view themselves through an outsider's eyes. Henry James called the continent "the great American sedative" and Ralph Waldo Emerson claimed: "We go to Europe to be Americanized." James Baldwin, writing in 1961, took a more balanced view: "Europe has what we do not yet have, a sense of the mysterious and inexorable limits of life, in a word, of tragedy, and we [Americans] have what they surely need: a sense of life's possibilities."

To many people, therefore, Europe is much more than a living museum, a lengthy list of monuments to be ticked off as a dutiful obligation: it is a continent whose variety and density of culture can always surprise and often enrich the inquiring visitor. On the following pages, we focus on some of the quirkier aspects of Europe which may confound the first-time visitor, from kissing customs to queueing conventions, from centres of corruption to temples of gastronomy, from driving habits to swearing skills.

This alphabetical analysis does not explain everything that goes on either in public or behind closed doors between Paris and Prague. But it may shed light on some of the shadier areas of an assortment of societies known to the rest of the world for their curious customs, mild eccentricities and irresistible fascination. ❏

PRECEDING PAGES: glittering gala at Milan's 200-year-old La Scala opera house.
LEFT: Caravaggio's *Bacchus* raises a weary glass to the good life.

Architecture

A tourist in a new city often takes a dutiful interest in its ancient cathedrals and palaces, But Europe also has exciting and contentious public buildings that arose in the past 100 years.

The starting point is the Bauhaus Museum in Dessau. The Bauhaus design school, begun by Walter Gropius, set the pace in the 1920s and 1930s. Interest was added by the Swiss architect Le Corbusier, whose designs included the modular Unité d'Habitation in Marseille using units proportional to the human figure.

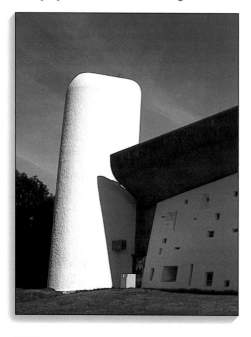

LE CORBUSIER'S MASTERPIECE

The little town of Ronchamp in Alsace-Lorraine is home to one of Europe's most famous post-war buildings: Le Corbusier's Chapel of Notre-Dame-du-Haut, which he designed to replace another church here that was destroyed during World War II. Unconstrained by a geometric framework, the design is dominated by curves, with walls and roof sloping at irregular angles, and windows of varying proportions placed haphazardly along the walls. Le Corbusier's unique vision was a deliberate gesture against the right angle and straight line, and was intended to reflect the forms of its hilltop setting and the natural features of the surrounding landscape.

In the reparations of the 1950s and the boom of the 1960s, architectural heroes emerged, such as Giovanni Ponti, who designed the radical Pirelli tower block in Milan that looks down over Ulisse Stracchini's elegant white Central Station of 1931. Josep Lluis Sert, a Spaniard who followed Gropius into the chair of architecture at Harvard University, designed the Maeght gallery in St-Paul-de-Vence in the south of France, and the Miró Foundation in Barcelona, a short walk from the rebuilt 1929 Pavilion of Mies van der Rohe, first director of the Bauhaus.

Among many architects involved in revamping or building new museums in the 1980s was the American Richard Meier, who designed the first of his "white refrigerators" in Frankfurt to house the Museum of Crafts and Allied Arts.

Barcelona was a showcase for the world's architects during the 1992 Olympic Games. Among the contributors were Sir Norman Foster, who went on to redesign Berlin's Reichstag, and America's I.M. Pei, who designed the Louvre pyramid, just one of the *Grands Projets* begun during the boom years of the 1980s when Europe changed the shape not only of museums, but also of business districts, obsolete docklands and industrial sites. Cities have become ambitious, attracting state-of-the-art architects to design new museums and refresh older ones. Many – such as the Guggenheim in Bilbao – are in danger of becoming more interesting than the collections they house.

Beaches

Europe has two shores, sea and ocean, and their characteristics are distinct. The wide stretches of Atlantic and North Sea beaches are churned up by two tides a day, which can discolour the water and shift the sand. In the more saline, tideless Mediterranean, the beaches are spread out between small rocky coves, where the water can be stunningly translucent. Of course, there is pollution and contamination, but to discourage it the European Union hands out annual Clean Beach awards.

The Atlantic's rollers are for surfing. Guincho in Portugal has a reputation among the windsurfing nomads, as does Tarifa, southwest Spain. The cooler North Sea end of this bracing coast, in Germany and the Dutch Frisian islands, is where many German naturists bare themselves to the sandpapering winds and billowing seas. But tidal waters can be a hazard, especially where the shore is flat and the twice-daily tide becomes speedy, cutting off cliffs and causeways at a frightening pace. At Mont-St-Michel in northern France the tide is one of the fastest in the world, covering 40 km (25 miles) in six hours, and the difference in height between high and low tides can be 15 metres.

The Mediterranean, on the other hand, is rather safe, but its coast and its unexpected winds still make it a rugged place. Typically, the coast is where mountains come down to the sea, and the coves are backed with dunes and

Corruption

"In the Mediterranean culture," argues Franco Ferrarotti, professor of sociology at Rome University, "stealing is not considered a serious offence, especially if you do it with manual dexterity. Corruption, if it does not entail physical offence to the persons involved, is rather considered a fine art. The same thing applies to lying, which is considered very serious in the Protestant countries. Here it is considered an expedient, part of a way of life."

Traditionally in Italy, says Ferrarotti, corrup-

umbrella pines. Many resorts have half a dozen beaches for a choice of amenities and perhaps a choice of uses: family, nude, gay; or they may be colonised by a single nationality.

The popularity of such sandy stretches as Italy's crowded lidos around Rimini on the Adriatic, prompted some resorts to import sand. The impressive 6-km (4-mile) beach at Benidorm, Spain's most notorious package-holiday destination, was established with sand shipped in from Morocco, and is still regularly topped up.

LEFT: Le Corbusier's Notre-Dame-du-Haut at Ronchamp, France.
ABOVE: *boules* on the beach.

tion was excused as a human weakness – provided one eventually delivered the goods. "Now two things have gone wrong. First, the order of magnitude of the corruption. Second, corruption no longer produces. You may accept 5 per cent more on the cost of a highway but in the end you get the highway. But if you have to pay 30 per cent more and then you don't get anything at all, well, that's too much."

The attitude reached all levels of society. As the writer Umberto Eco put it: "The Italians knew who you needed to see for a favour and how much it cost. They knew how to get out of a traffic fine, how to find an easy little job with a letter of recommendation, how to win a contract without difficult competition. In short, it suited people well enough, so they held their noses and voted."

Eventually, though, the smell (and the cost of bribery) became just too great. A series of anti-mafia trials began, and even Giulio Andreotti, who had headed as many as seven of Italy's short-serving governments, faced a string of corruption charges.

The rest of Europe had few grounds for complacency. The French and Spanish governments were rocked in the 1990s by public-sector corruption scandals, gangs from Eastern Europe brought large-scale racketeering to the newly

hearse than an ambulance, yet Germany's roads are among the safer highways of Europe. Greece tops the league table for road deaths, followed by Portugal, France and Spain. The reason is that Germany's drivers, though impatient, are disciplined, and you can be fined for making an insulting gesture to another motorist.

Italians, by contrast, reflect in their driving style their anarchic attitude towards authority in general. Horns are blasted habitually and ineffectually whenever traffic stops, overtaking is instinctive, and anyone foolish enough to stop as a light turns red is likely to find several disbelieving drivers crashing into him. The phil-

united Germany, and the entire European Commission resigned in March 1999 following allegations of fraud and mismanagement.

Driving

Linger too long in the outside lane of a German *autobahn* and your rear-view mirror will soon reflect the flashing headlights of a Porsche or BMW bearing down on you at 240 kph (150 mph). Germany's love of speed usually triumphs over demands for a blanket speed limit on its *autobahn* system. When an accident occurs, of course, you're more likely to need a

osophy was summed up by the reaction of some Italians when a seat-belt law was passed: such restraints being incompatible with their macho outlook, they tried to fool police by wearing tee-shirts with a seat-belt printed across the front. Spanish driving, it's said, reflects the culture's obsession with death. French pride interprets overtaking as insulting behaviour, while Swiss drivers are awfully proper.

Whatever the truth of such stereotypes, the first-time visitor to Europe should bear two things in mind. One is that driving styles are generally geared to getting from A to B as fast as possible. The second is that mixing driving and alcohol carries very severe penalties.

European Union

Just after World War II, which left the continent devastated, Britain's wartime leader, Sir Winston Churchill, declared: "We must build a kind of United States of Europe." Throughout history, visionaries from Caesar and Charlemagne to Napoleon had tried to unite Europe, usually by force. In 1950 a French businessman, Jean Monnet, proposed a route dictated by economic self-interest: by pooling coal and steel resources Europe's industrial powers could more effectively compete in world markets.

the Euro was adopted with a great fanfare by all the EU member states apart from Denmark, Sweden and the UK, whose people remained deeply sceptical about its benefits.

Unlike the United States, however, the EU has no common language or culture and, when times get tough, its individual members, far from uniting to solve problems, become more nationalistic. Tariff barriers may have disappeared within the Union, but mental barriers remain. In reality, Europe's nations are still warring, but now their warriors are the battalions of officials and politicians who face each other across the floors of the EU's assemblies.

The resulting Coal and Steel Community developed into the European Economic Community (the Common Market) in 1957. Most border controls were removed in 1992. As it grew to its current 15-nation membership (Austria, Belgium, Denmark, Finland, France, Germany, Greece, Ireland, Italy, Luxembourg, the Netherlands, Portugal, Spain, Sweden and the UK), it changed its name to the European Union and gained greater aspirations, among them the single currency. On 1 January 2002,

LEFT: a mean driving machine outside Hotel du Lac in the resort town of Bellagio on Italy's Lake Como.
ABOVE: the celebrated French chef Paul Bocuse.

Food

France remains the shrine at which gourmets worship. One reason is that, for all the elaborate, sophisticated dishes concocted over the centuries – a delight for their sheer inventiveness in the use of herbs, spices, creams, cheeses and wines – the French also know the job of ingenious simplicity.

The *charcuterie* are delicious; these include cold pork cuts and sausage such as *rosette de Lyon*, ham from Auvergne or Bayonne, and *rillettes*, a rich cold mince of pork or goose-meat cooked in its own fat. *Terrine* is the generic

French name for *pâté*, prepared in an earthenware dish from pork, rabbit, goose, duck, or chicken livers, or fish such as salmon and pike.

Refrigeration techniques have made it safe to eat oysters at any time of the year, but the best are still served from September to April. Mussels are great served *marinière* in a white wine sauce drunk like soup. The best snails come from Burgundy. Frogs' legs taste like garlic-seasoned veal.

A favourite fish is sea bass (called *loup de mer* on the Mediterranean and *bar* on the Atlantic), poached or grilled with fennel (*fenouil*). Red mullet (*rouget*), sole, sea bream (*daurade*) and turbot are other favourites. Trout (*truite*) can be sautéed in butter (*meunière*) or with almonds (*aux amandes*).

Beef steak is popular nationwide: thick *Chateaubriand* fillet, juicy *entrecôte*, tender *tournedos* fillet wrapped in bacon, and the more resilient *bavette*. Leg of lamb is *gigot*.

Outstanding poultry dishes include *poulet à l'estragon* (chicken roasted in a tarragon sauce) and duck roasted not only *à l'orange* but also with cherries, peaches, fresh figs, turnips or olives. Increasingly popular is the *magret* or *aiguillettes* of duck, fillet slices from the breast roasted to a rare deep pink.

Regional dishes abound. Provence favours garlic, herbs, tomatoes and olives in preparing roast chicken and lamb chops. Marseille's pride and joy, *bouillabaisse*, is a fish stew of racasse, red mullet and sea perch with spiny lobster, crab and other shellfish stewed in a saffron-spiced sauce.

Burgundy's great gastronomic offering is *boeuf bourguignon*, a beef stew simmered for hours in red wine with whole baby onions, mushrooms and bits of bacon.

The southwest, from Perigord to the Pyrenees, defeats the diet-conscious with its goose and duck specialities such as the truffle-studded *pâté de fois gras* and the roast *confit d'oie* (goose) or *de canard* (duck) that has been slowly cooked in its own fat.

Gestures

Giving a thumbs-up sign will signify approval in most countries – but not in Greece, where it is a vulgar insult, equivalent to raising the middle finger elsewhere. Flick your ear with a forefinger in Italy and you could be suggesting someone is homosexual. Jerking your forearm up and slapping your other hand into the crook of the arm would be an insult in most of Europe – although elsewhere in the world the gesture is regarded as a sign of sexual appreciation.

Make a ring with your thumb or index finger and most Europeans will interpret it as meaning OK, but others will see it as Zero or worthless, and a Greek could be referring to a bodily orifice.

A shrug can convey different things, depending on whether it is accompanied by moving the shoulders, raising the eyebrows or pursing

---

SAY "CHEESE"

When it comes to French cheeses, one can only recall General de Gaulle's remark about the impossibilty of uniting a country capable of producing 324 different kinds of cheese.

Classic cheeses are given *appellation d'origine* labels, which are as prestigious as those accorded to wine. Their names are often derived from nobility: the pungent fermented cheeses with white or yellow skin such as Camembert, Brie, Coulommiers, Pont L'Evêque; the blues of Roquefort, Fourme d'Ambert and Auvergne; the ripe and creamy Epoisses; the hard but piquant Cantal; and the goat cheeses of Valençay or Corsica.

the mouth. Is someone resigned? Indifferent? Helpless? It's sometimes hard to tell.

In France, mouth movements are important. This is partly because nine of the 16 French vowels involve rounding the lips (compared with only five in German and two in English). The French are also great gesticulators, using their hands rather than their entire arms – but their repertoire is narrower than the Italians'.

The Italians have long been regarded as Europe's most expressive people. A wide variety of hand signals are used to convey agreement, surprise, delight, disgust, and gestures familiar to Homer can still be seen today.

but is strong in Germany, where scatalogical references appear even in children's riddles. Belgians, by contrast, are conservative about sex, so there are few sex jokes in Belgium. Really, there's only one thing regarded as funny throughout Europe: other Europeans.

Immigrants

Every year around 700,000 people seek asylum in Europe, but new laws in most countries mean their chances are increasingly slim. Since the Soviet system disintegrated and Yugoslavia

Humour

Language plays a large part in forming humour. Thus, while French lends itself to puns, Spanish doesn't. Much French wit, therefore, incorporates clever, sarcastic wordplay. On the other hand, there is a fine old tradition of slapstick in France, and the French have an earthy humour built around sex – though it's far from sexist.

Anal humour, however, is absent in France,

LEFT: body language speaks much louder than words in Naples. **ABOVE:** former East Berliners get their first taste of a united city.

broke up into warring factions, an influx of refugees has combined with high unemployment to revive racial antagonism as an ugly reality of life. In just one year (1992), 440,000 immigrants, mostly from Yugoslavia, some from Romania and Bulgaria, settled in Germany, which had one of the most liberal immigration laws in Europe. The following year, when unemployment in the recently reunited country reached 6 million, the rules were tightened up. Meanwhile, serious attacks on immigrants had left 17 dead and 2,500 injured.

In Belgium, Turks and Moroccans have been the objects of attack by the Flemish Vlaams Blok party, as much anti-French as anti-Islam.

They represent Flemish speakers who want a separate, break-away state.

In France, the National Front, led by the charismatic Jean-Marie Le Pen, rose on a tide of racist feelings against Muslim and African immigrants when Le Pen gained 15 percent of the votes in the 1995 French presidential elections. In Italy, where the Adriatic shores are constantly patrolled for Albanians escaping the turmoil of their own country, the neo-fascist Italian Social Movement has gained influence, while a group called the Ultras interrupts football matches with racist outbursts.

Especially disturbing has been the continuing

attacks on Jews, whose cemeteries and synagogues are vandalised – even in liberal Holland. Do some people, pessimists wonder, ever learn anything from history?

Jet Set

Sometimes one simply has to have the sun, and only the Caribbean will do. But, for much of the year, the curious coterie of pop singers, film stars, millionaires, aristocrats and royalty (real and ersatz) who constitute the international "glam clan" can find an acceptable venue in Europe. After checking out the Paris fashion

shows in January, it's off to the ski slopes of Klosters or St Moritz in February. After a short break, perhaps, for a southern-hemisphere safari, it's off in May to Monaco to see the Grand Prix and say hello to the Rainiers. In June, Britain beckons with Royal Ascot, the Henley Regatta and Wimbledon. Then, pausing to take in the Paris summer collections, one can follow the English in July as they head for their villas in Tuscany (which has become so English that it's been dubbed Chiantishire).

And so it continues… yachting in Cap Ferrat, villa parties on Patmos (the only really exclusive Greek island), the Prix de l'Arc de Tri-

omph (you don't have to own a racehorse), and sundry charity balls in grand locations. Like all heavenly bodies, the jet set like to have their fixed orbits.

Kissing

Latin has three words for "kiss", distinguishing between a kiss of friendship on the cheek, a kiss of affection on the mouth and a lover's kiss on the mouth. The Roman tradition lives on, for people around the Mediterranean are more spontaneously intimate than their northern cousins: they sit closer together, they touch more, they stand closer together when talking, and everyone seems to cheek-kiss enthusiastically.

In Germany, men seldom kiss the cheeks of other men, and personal space is assiduously protected. Hand-shaking is more common, but usually only when meeting someone by appointment. In France, it is common to shake hands with someone each time you meet and depart, even if you meet them several times a day.

But few generalisations are reliable. The Italians are supposedly the most tactile Europeans – yet, although two men will touch frequently when talking (perhaps to deter the other person from interrupting), and even guide each other round a corner while walking, there is noticeably less touching between the sexes. Even married couples are less likely to walk along hand in hand than they are in Denmark or Austria. Could it be that Italian men regard hand-holding as a sign of submissiveness?

Lavatories

Can the character of a nation's toilets give a clue to the nature of its people? Proponents of the theory would point to the Germans, whose humour is sometimes seen as tending towards the anal and whose toilet bowls often incorporate a shelf on which, before flushing, one may inspect one's faeces for tell-tale signs of potential ill-health.

Multinational manufacturing has largely eroded the varieties of bathroom fittings that once added extra spice to travelling. Modern coin-operated cabins have replaced most of Paris's old pissoirs, which enabled a gentleman to relieve himself while continuing a conversation with his companion outside. In rural France, though, you can still find some old "hole in the ground" toilets which compel you to squat – a healthy posture, many claim.

It's not unusual to find restaurants with toilets used by both men and women, and many public toilets for men have female attendants.

And what of hygiene? A survey by one roller-towel manufacturer recently revealed that 27 percent of Europeans failed to wash their hands after using the lavatory. Another market

research finding claimed that only 19 percent of French men and 32 percent of French women take a bath each day and only 5 percent wash their hair every day, and that more than half the population goes to bed without cleaning their teeth. But they spend 50 percent more on fresheners than Italians. When Germany was united, West Germans were found to wash their hair twice as often as East Germans. The Spanish bathe least, but they use lots of fragrances.

What can all this mean? One view is that the French regard body odours as quite natural and fear that eliminating them might reduce sexual appeal. Many French perfumes, therefore, are

designed to accentuate natural odours, rather than to conceal them.

Monarchies

Hereditary kings and queens have shown remarkable endurance in an age so concerned with the spread of democracy. One country, Spain, even restored its monarchy in 1975 and, despite predictions that he would be known as "Juan Carlos the Brief", the king is still on the throne, his reputation hugely enhanced by his successful appeal to the armed forces to avert an attempted military coup in 1981. Likewise,

LEFT: the lovers' kiss in Sicily and the mafia kiss that can spell death.
RIGHT: King Juan Carlos of Spain.

none of Europe's other six major crowned heads – or indeed less weighty rulers such as Prince Rainier of Monaco or Prince Hans Adam of Liechtenstein – looks imminently set to join the ranks of the jobless.

Most European monarchs are tolerated because they have no real power, and are valued mainly for providing a sense of continuity and a useful focus for ceremonial. The Swedish monarch is probably the most powerless, playing no part whatsoever in the parliamentary process. The Norwegian, Danish and British monarchs could theoretically appoint prime ministers in the event of an electoral deadlock. The Dutch, although

permitting their queen a great deal of power in theory, allow her almost none in practice.

In 1993, the Belgians removed King Baudouin's right to approve the appointment of a prime minster. He died soon afterwards, childless, and his younger brother Albert, who had been something of a playboy, found himself unexpectedly king at the age of 59. The monarchy was still valued as an institution, however, because it seemed virtually the only glue holding together the Dutch and French-speaking halves of a politically divided country. In contrast with Britain, whose royal family increasingly resembles the cast of a soap opera, Belgium does not permit its media to comment

on the king; indeed, one lawyer who said that the king's Christmas message to his people was boring was charged under an 1846 law of committing "outrage to royalty".

Long live the king! And long live pragmatism!

Nature

From the eagles' eyries of the snowy alps to the lizard sunbeds of the Spanish sierras, Continental Europe supports a vast range of animal habitats. Hunting is widely permitted, and migrant birds must dodge the bullets of Italians and Spaniards who will eat anything that flaps a wing. The big-game hunters are the Germans, who like wild boar and are enthusiastic chasers of wolves and bears in the newly accessible Eastern Europe.

Boar are popular in much of Europe and in the shooting season (roughly from November to February) they are hunted, along with ducks. In France and Portugal, huntsmen dress in bright liveries, blow their bugles and give chase on horseback after foxes.

Many countries have special animals. In France, there are the long-horned black cattle of the Camargue, at the delta of the Rhône where flamingoes flock. Southern Italy has water buffalo, from which mozzarella cheese is made. Switzerland has the Chamois mountain goat, Spain the Moorish gecko, a lizard.

There is the occasional viper or adder, but in the main Continental Europe is a safe place for wild things and creepy-crawlies. Even the small brown scorpions found around the Mediterranean seem too lazy to bite. But occasionally a jellyfish in the Mediterranean will sting as fiercely as a bee.

Oath-making

The Romance languages lend themselves particularly well to cursing and swearing. Italy, being a Catholic country, often combines imprecations and blasphemy: common examples are *Porco Dio!* (That pig of a god) and *Madonna puttana!* (That whore of a virgin Mary).

Spain also embraces blasphemy. Hostia! (Holy bread) is mild enough; more extreme is *Me cago en todos los Santos*, which means "I defecate on all the Saints."

In Germany excrement crops up readily: Scheiss can express frustration or be an insult. The equivalent in French (*merde*) is not insulting, merely a much-used expression indicating mild annoyance

Punctuality

The closer you get to the Mediterranean, the slower the pace of life becomes. People even walk less fast. Partly it's a matter of adapting to a hot climate, partly it's a reflection of the attitude that time serves people rather than the

Queues

It has been said of the Englishman that, even if he is alone, he forms an orderly queue of one. This attitude is not one that is widely shared by his continental neighbours. In affluent Switzerland, they'll form a line too, on the rational basis that this is the most efficient way for everyone to be served quickly and fairly.

In Italy, however, the free-for-all prevails: standing in an orderly line would be regarded as both an imposition and a stifling of personal initiative. Sociologists devote learned works to

other way round. To be late for an appointment in Germany, Belgium, Austria or Switzerland would be regarded as rude, or at least inconsiderate. In Greece or Spain, by contrast, nobody is expected to show up on time. Indeed, being *very* late may even be a sign of status.

In France it is not done to discuss business at a business lunch until at least the first course has arrived; this restraint shows you know the value of friendship, not to mention food and wine, and that you are a more rounded person.

LEFT: brown bears in the Bavarian Forest National Park, southeast Germany.
ABOVE: for some, queueing comes naturally.

drawing parallels between such anarchic behaviour and attitudes towards government (especially disrespectful in Italy, France and Spain).

Robbery

Most of the world's 300 million tourists a year don't get robbed or mugged. Nevertheless, the ancient tradition of highway robbery lives on in Europe, and visitors should take precautions.

Amazingly, the oldest tricks still find gullible victims. A Vespa-riding pickpocket in Rome will snatch a handbag without even slowing down. A young man in Barcelona will offer to take your photograph for you and make off with your camera as soon as you hand it over. In Benidorm, men pose as porters and steal luggage. In Greece, men are invited into a bar, find themselves buying drinks for a number of friendly women, and then are presented with an exorbitant bill.

Importing a cunning ruse from Florida, French gangs steal cars and use them on a quiet stretch of autoroute to ram the back of a foreign-registered car, making it seem accidental. When the victim pulls over to inspect the damage, the gang relieves him and his family of their valuables – and maybe steals his car as well.

The French have a name for the villains: "*les pirates de la route*". But their advice to potential victims is the bleak suggestion that they add a new phrase to their vocabulary; "*Prenez l'argent*" (Take the money).

Status

Nothing could be further from the informal way in which Americans greet people they scarcely know than the formality that is preserved in many European countries. Germans in particular put great emphasis on titles and can be seriously offended if they are not addressed

properly. As the psychologist Carl Jung once observed: "There are no ordinary human beings, you are 'Herr Professor' or 'Herr Geheimrat', 'Herr Oberrechnungsrat' and even longer things than that."

Two colleagues with much the same job status can work in the same office for 20 years and still address each other as "Herr Vogel" and "Frau Schmidt". They would feel very uncomfortable, they will tell you, using first names. The advantage of such formality is that it distinguishes acquaintances from friends, and when a friendship is finally cemented by the adoption of first names, it is a memorable occasion, usually celebrated with a few drinks.

Another method by which status is delineated is in the choice of second-person pronoun. All the main European languages except English (which dispensed with "thou" in the 17th century) have two words for "you": the familiar form (*tu* in French, *du* in German) and the formal version (*vous* in French, *Sie* in German). Again, the move from the formal to the familiar is a signal that amity has become camaraderie. In a business environment, the decision to switch is usually initiated by the person with superior status.

Such distinctions were one of the problems faced by East Germans when the country was reunited. Under communism, they had as comrades been encouraged to address one another by the familiar *du*; now, as they come to terms with the complexities of capitalism, *Sie* is making a comeback.

Television

Switch on a TV set anywhere in Europe, turn down the sound, and you'll be amazed at how difficult it is to identify which country you're in. Here are the familiar news pictures of famine in Africa, here are the inane game shows, here is a self-satisfied political figure trying to look sincere, here is the agonised expression of the soap-opera heroine, here is... surely not *Casablanca*? Turn up the volume and you may be treated to the sound of Humphrey Bogart speaking fluent French, or John Wayne dubbed into Dutch.

Many TV stations in Europe still operate under some loose form of government control, but the growth of satellite broadcasting has shifted most channels' agendas to the ruthlessly commercial question of how to gain and keep the biggest audiences. The temptation is often to go for slick, affordable and popular American series – some private French channels came close to devoting half their air-time to US programmes – but resistance has been growing at the extent of this "cultural imperialism" being pumped through millions of cathode-ray tubes. Since the US accounts for 80 percent of the movies released in Europe, the fear is a real one.

WEATHERING THE STORM

Wherever you are in Europe, a high rainfall in July, say, does not mean that it rains all the time: there may simply be thunderstorms. But it's still best to pack your brolly.

unseasonal." Which is no consolation at all. The following statistics, therefore, although no guarantee of anything, may dispel a few myths.

The driest month in Berlin is March, and the wettest July and August. In Munich, the driest is December and the wettest June and July. Being near the Alps, southern Germany has colder, snowier winters than the north, but sharp winds from Russia can make northern Germany seem pretty arctic.

Confirming the wisdom of seeing Paris in the spring, rainfall is least in March and April. It's

Umbrellas

Except in parts of the Mediterranean in high summer, these are more often used in Europe to fend off rain than sun. The essence of the weather, however, is its unpredictability: the character of winter or summer will vary wildly from one year to another and a favourite sympathetic comment from locals as you shelter from a cloudburst or hailstorm is: "It's very

LEFT: French chic – but do they call each other "tu" or "vous"?
ABOVE: the best use for brollies.

highest in August. In Marseille, July is the driest month; the wettest are October and November. The mistral wind can bring unseasonably cold weather to the south of France in spring.

In Brussels, it rains most in July (thanks partly to thunderstorms) and December, least in March and May. Winters are wetter in the south and hill fogs occur frequently. The Netherlands has a similar climate. It rains most in July and August, least in March and April.

In Italy it rains least in the extreme north of the mainland and in Sicily and Sardinia. Rome can expect least rain in July, most in November. Venice can expect least in January, with the heaviest downpours in November.

Mountainous Switzerland, affected by weather from both the Atlantic and eastern Europe, is notoriously changeable. The driest months in Zurich are March and December, the wettest June and July. Austria has a similar climate. Most rain falls on Vienna in July, the least in January. Greece is rightly known for its sunshine. But rainfall is heavy when it happens, which it does most notably in December. The driest months are July and August, when you can expect virtually no rain at all.

It's a mistake to assume that all of Spain has a Mediterranean climate; the Pyrenees give the north quite a different weather pattern. Most

rain falls on Madrid in April and December, least in July. In Palma, Majorca, hardly any rain falls in July; October is the wettest month. Coastal Portugal is at the mercy of the Atlantic. It's dry in both Lisbon and Faro in July and August, but wet in December and January.

Vendetta

Although Italy's mafia get the headlines for their acts of vengeance, most of their murders are motivated more by economic gain than personal grievance. For a cold-blooded interpretation of the Biblical "eye for an eye" principle,

few have been able to match the Corsicans.

The tradition began centuries ago when the islanders retaliated against their Genoese conquerors by killing a soldier for every Corsican killed by the occupiers. The Genoese would respond and the constant retaliation meant that whole clans were wiped out.

When France annexed the island in 1769, its rigorous penal code seemed too weak to the passionate Corsicans, who demanded the blood of a crime's perpetrator when family honour was at stake. A man marked by the curse of the vendetta might take refuge in the island's thorny undergrowth, but he would know that death was only a matter of time.

Prosper Mérimée, the poet who created *Carmen*, based his novella *Colomba* on a tribal drama of this kind. Balzac, Dumas and Maupassant also carved for the Corsican vendetta a place in history.

Nowadays, although *vendetta corse* is still written on penknives in the island's souvenir shops, the vendetta manifests itself less in killing than in the destruction of property: the supermarket that gets burnt down the day before it's due to open, for instance, because it provides unwanted competition in a seaside resort. And, as always, the perpetrators can still be sure that the ancient code of silence observed by their fellow-citizens will protect them.

Wine-making

In California or Australia, the combination of an equable climate and close scientific control can ensure that wines from a particular estate vary little from year to year. In Europe, by contrast, wines are at the mercy of the continent's capricious weather: one year a wine may be classed as truly great, the next year the same slopes will produce at best a mediocre vintage. Such uncertainty adds interest.

French wine comes from eight main areas: Bordeaux, the most important; Burgundy in the east; Tourraine, including the Loire Valley, in the west; the Rhône Valley from Lyons to Avignon; the Champagne area around Rheims and Epernay; Alsace, along the left bank of the Rhine; the Jura mountains; and Languedoc in the south. Bordeaux produces a high proportion of the world's greatest wines, and Burgundy whites remain fashionable (and therefore expensive).

Italy makes prodigious amounts of wine, from the Alpine valleys down to the tip of Sicily. It tends to be lighter than French, and lacks the depth, but fine wines come from Chianti, Orvieto, Soave and Valpolicella.

Spain's wines have greatly improved in recent years. Many are now world-class, although the best known are still Riojas from the north. Germany produces some splendid wines, especially hocks; these white wines from the Rhineland can be either sweet or dry.

> **WIT IN ALL LANGUAGES**
>
> Charles V's claim that he spoke Spanish to God, Italian to women, French to men, and German to his horse sparked a tradition of jokes at other Europeans' expense.

are the comedians, the Italians are the defence force, the Frenchmen dig the roads, the Belgians are the pop singers, the Spanish run the railways, the Albanians cook the food, the Portuguese are the waiters, the Greeks run the government, and the common language is Dutch.

As so often, jokes are a means of voicing inadmissable opinions. Thus the French and the Dutch make fun of the Belgians. Northern Germans mock the laziness of southern Germans, who in turn deride the stupidity of north-

Xenophobia

If colonising an island, it was said in 1790, a Spaniard would first build a church, a Frenchman a fort, and a Dutchman a warehouse. In 1820, Lord Byron claimed that French courage was based on vanity, German courage on phlegm, Dutch courage on obstinacy, and Italian courage on anger. The modern version of the stereotype game is to define hell as a place where the Germans are the police, the Swedish

erners. Both northern and southern Germans ridicule their new compatriots from the former East Germany. Copenhageners will make fun of somebody from Jutland. Belgium's Flemings and Walloons joke about each other.

Images, like fashion, are subject to change. Thus the idea of the Germans as aggressive and authoritarian emerged only in the mid-19th century; previously, Machiavelli, a shrewd observer of human nature, had described them as peace-loving and rather timid.

Nicknames, mostly inoffensive, are subject to the whims of language. In Great Britain, sauerkraut-eating Germans naturally became known as Krauts and didn't appear to mind

LEFT: nosing out a good vintage. **ABOVE:** there are good neighbours – and less good neighbours.

being compared to pickled cabbage. In the same way, spaghetti-munching Italians were christened Spags. How the French turned into frogs is less obvious: the term may have derived from their eating habits, but it could equally have originated from the three leaping toads portrayed on the coat of arms of the ancient Frankish kings (later replaced by the fleur-de-lys).

The term *dago*, on the other hand, is regarded as offensive by Spaniards, Portuguese and Italians. The reasons can't be found in its innocent origins (the Spanish *Diego*, meaning James), and it was originally innocuous.

for a new type of craft, dubbed the "mega-yacht" – fully crewed private vessels over 36 metres (120 ft) long.

Riviera harbours are open to anyone wishing for a closer look at the lifestyles of the rich and famous. Between the Italian border at Menton and the port of Marseille 235 km (127 nautical miles) to the west there are 130 of these harbours, totalling over 52,000 moorings. French Riviera ports shelter a third of the world megayacht fleet of about 3,500 yachts. Yachting occupies 1,500 local businesses, including many small craftsmen and tradesmen, and provides 6,000 jobs, not including crew.

Yacht Watching

Luxury yachting has always been part of the Riviera legend but in recent years it has become a fully-fledged industry that is now vital to the economy of the region. Nowhere else on earth is there so much extravagant floating real estate in one place.

While some harbours – like Cannes or St Tropez – see the traditional *pointu* fishing boats go happily about their business alongside sleek and shining luxury vessels, there are many new ports designed exclusively for private yachts. These have made the Riviera the world centre

Famous names still frequent Riviera ports but, except in a few cases (terrorism and tax-man *oblige*), with cautious discretion. Some flamboyant owners, however, make no secret of their possession and the name of a yacht is often a clue to the ownership.

If a taste of the seafaring life sounds tempting, a used 18-metre (60-ft) displacement model can be had for about £1 million. If you want something with a bit more speed or cabin space you should be thinking in the neighbourhood of £3 million. Today, yachts worth more than £20 million are not at all uncommon and you should count on 10 percent of the boat's value as the cost of annual upkeep.

Chartering offers a cheaper solution for those on a budget and the American dollar is the trading currency. For about $4,000 a day you can hire a modest yacht, but if you plan on sailing farther afield or throwing large parties on board you'll need a bigger model at up to $20,000 a day.

These prices include the yacht itself and the crew but not berthing fees, fuel, food or drink. On the Côte d'Azur more than anywhere else, a yacht truly is a hole in the water you throw money into.

MILLENNIAL MADNESS

Cities throughout Europe spent millions as they competed to produce the most glittering celebrations and fireworks at the dawn of the third millennium.

good and the mood in Europe is pretty glum. On the political front, confidence in leadership has plummeted. On the economic front, unemployment, prices and taxes are all too high. On the home front, immigration, corruption, inner-city blight, poverty and crime all threaten social cohesion.

Internationally, a logical conclusion couldn't be found to the alarming deterioration of the former Soviet Union. The vicious civil war fought in 1991 on Europe's doorstep in the former Yugoslavia,

Zeitgeist

The 20th century was popularly called the American Century. The 21st, pundits predict, will belong to Asia. So where does that leave Europe? Will the world echo the words of the American writer F. Scott Fitzgerald, who exclaimed in 1921: "God damn the continent of Europe. It is of merely antiquarian interest"? Or will the new millennium give the old world a new impetus? The preliminary diagnosis isn't

LEFT: yachts on the Riviera. **ABOVE:** tomorrow's world – the geodesic dome at La Villete, Paris.

and the ethnic cleansing of thousands of Albanians from Kosovo in the last years of the 2nd millennium produced similarly controversial solutions from the rest of Europe.

But that isn't the whole story. More people than ever before are educated, affluent, in good health, and able to enjoy a remarkable range of leisure pursuits. Better communications have made them aware of the problems around them to a greater extent, making them more likely to demand more of their own leaders. Sometimes it takes an outsider to point out the silver linings on the dark clouds: the millions of tourists who descend on Continental Europe each year are prepared to do just that. ❏

ΑΓ. ΑΘΑΝΑΣΙΟΣ Λ.Μ. 49

Κ.105

·ΗΛΙΑΣ·Λ·

PLACES

*A detailed guide to Europe's top destinations, with principal
sites clearly cross-referenced by number to the maps*

There is something reassuringly familiar about the continent of
Europe. Its snowy mountains and its beaches, its Roman
remains and its cathedrals, its vineyards and cafés are all places
that have figured in books and films. Yet there is such a quantity of
architecture and art to absorb, so many acres of countryside to
explore, so much good food to try, so many vintage wines to taste,
that nobody can know it all. What follows is a full flavour of Continental Europe: 15 countries that cover the land mass from Cabo de
Roca, the westernmost point of Portugal, to Greece, abutting the
borders with Asia in the east.

Getting around the continent is no problem. Cities are linked by
road and rail, and airports are busy round the clock. Although in
theory the borders between most members of the European
Community were removed in 1992, the reality is that checkpoints
remain in force, even though they often seem redundant and
uniformed officers turn their backs on cars passing through. Crossing
borders to former Eastern European countries will be more formal.

There are few places that are not used to visitors all the year round.
Springtime is the time of wildflowers, which cover the Alps and
carpet the meadowlands. In summer many people gather in the
playgrounds of the Mediterranean: most crowded are Rimini on the
Adriatic coast, the French Riviera and Spain's Costa del Sol, but
there are always empty beaches to seek out, on the Atlantic coast,
perhaps, or among Greece's myriad islands. In the autumn the
vineyards of France, Italy, Spain and the Rhine in Germany redden
and the grapes are gathered in, often amid celebrations. In winter
the snowy Alps attract skiers to Austria, Switzerland and France,
and there are winter sports in Italy and Spain, too.

Any time of year is a good time to visit Europe's cities, which are
among the most exciting in the world, a mix of architectural styles,
usually starting around grand cathedrals and spreading out to modern
business centres and suburbs, catering for people with an infinite
variety of tastes from all over the world. ❑

PRECEDING PAGES: driving sheep in the Schnals Valley, South Tyrol; rooftops
of Florence, Italy; fishing boats, Greek Islands.
LEFT: gathering grapes in Alsace, France.

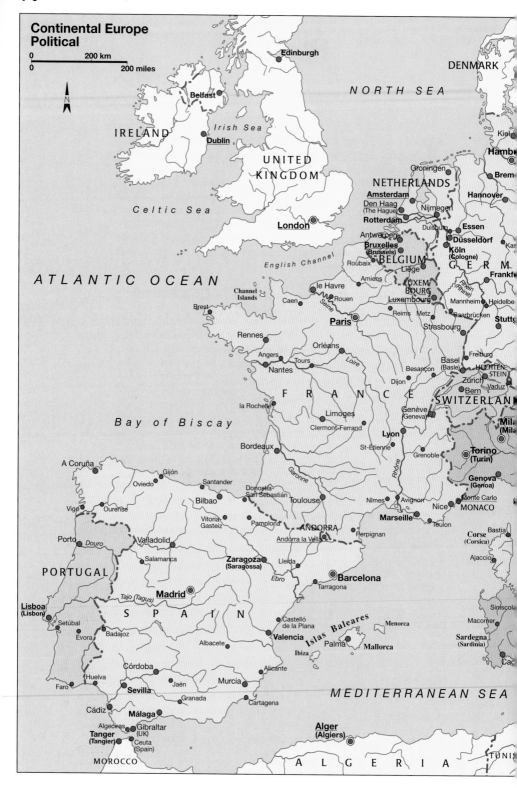

Continental Europe
Political

0 — 200 km
0 — 200 miles

N

Edinburgh

DENMARK

NORTH SEA

Kiel

Belfast

Hamb

IRELAND

Irish Sea

Groningen

NETHERLANDS

Brem

Dublin

UNITED
KINGDOM

Amsterdam
Den Haag
(The Hague)

Nijmegen

Hannover

Celtic Sea

Rotterdam

Duisburg

Essen

Antwerpen

Düsseldorf

London

Bruxelles
(Brussels)

Köln
(Cologne)

Kas

BELGIUM

Liège

G E R M

English Channel

Roubaix

Frankf

Amiens

LUXEM-
BOURG

le Havre

Rhein
(Rhine)

Channel
Islands

Caen

Rouen

Luxembourg

Metz

Mannheim

Heidelbe

Brest

Seine

Reims

Saarbrücken

Paris

Strasbourg

Stutt

Rennes

Orléans

Basel
(Basle)

Freiburg

LIECHTEN-
STEIN

Angers

Tours

Loire

Besançon

Zürich

Vaduz

Nantes

F R A N C E

Dijon

Bern

SWITZERLAN

la Rochelle

Genève
(Geneva)

Mila
(Mila

Bay of Biscay

Limoges

Lyon

ATLANTIC OCEAN

Clermont-Ferrand

St-Étienne

Grenoble

Torino
(Turin)

Bordeaux

Rhône

A Coruña

Gijón

Santander

Oviedo

Donostia-
San Sebastián

Toulouse

Nîmes

Avignon

Nice

Monte Carlo

Genova
(Genoa)

Garonne

Bilbao

Marseille

Toulon

MONACO

Vigo

Ourense

Vitoria-
Gasteiz

Pamplona

ANDORRA

Perpignan

Corse
(Corsica)

Bastia

Porto

Douro

Valladolid

Andorra la Vella

Ajaccio

Salamanca

PORTUGAL

Zaragoza
(Saragossa)

Lleida

Ebro

Barcelona

Madrid

Tarragona

Lisboa
(Lisbon)

Tajo (Tagus)

S P A I N

Setúbal

Évora

Badajoz

Albacete

Castelló
de la Plana

Valencia

Islas Baleares

Menorca

Sinisco

Macomer

Córdoba

Palma

Mallorca

Sardegna
(Sardinia)

Faro

Huelva

Jaén

Murcia

Alicante

Ibiza

Cac

Sevilla

Granada

Cartagena

MEDITERRANEAN SEA

Cádiz

Málaga

Algeciras

Gibraltar
(UK)

Tanger
(Tangier)

Ceuta
(Spain)

Alger
(Algiers)

MOROCCO

A L G E R I A

TUNIS

FRANCE

This is Europe's oldest country and its culinary heart. Its varied landscapes produce superb food and wine

France likes to think of itself as the most essential component in Europe. Foreigners think so, too. It is the place people overseas often think of first when they come to the continent, and the place many businesses initially sound out to see if it would be suitable for starting up European operations. Its attractions are well known: it has the world's best food, best wine, finest domestic architecture and a people who know how to dress.

Its popularity is undeniable: the population of 57 million is just about the same as the number of visitors who arrive every year. France is Europe's largest country (not counting European Russia) and the world's fourth richest country. Its population is spread thinly through a remarkably diverse landscape covering 547,000 sq km (211,200 sq miles), and even on major roads wayside towns and villages can seem deserted. But rural France is the real France. The French are proud of their agricultural heritage and their farmers are respected as much as the food they produce.

France is also Europe's oldest nation and, give or take the occasional small border shift, it has existed roughly in its present form since the 15th century. The nation's boundaries are largely natural ones, with the English Channel to the north, the Atlantic to the west, the Pyrenees and the Mediterranean to the south and the Alps, the Jura mountains and the Rhine to the east. These all contrive to make the French almost insular and, as a result, the overwhelmingly Catholic people are not as cosmopolitan as other European countries which have more openly shared borders. Accordingly, some visitors find them cool and uninterested in foreigners. (This is not borne out by a poll which showed 82 percent of French people would be happy to act as guides for tourists.) In spite of its insularity, this nation has had immense cultural influence on the rest of the world, and the existence of several minority languages within the country – Breton, Basque, Catalan, Alsace German and Italian – show the variety that lies within its borders.

Among the country's riches, the châteaux of the Loire stand out, buildings whose cost and craftsmanship could never be matched today. But French culture stretches through all the arts, especially to film, which is why the annual festival at Cannes is the most important event in the cinema industry's year, an event which highlights the country's stunning Riviera. Most of all, however, when thoughts turn to France, they turn to Paris, a vibrant city of 9 million people, whose name has become synonymous with everything chic. ❑

PRECEDING PAGES: Villandry in the Loire Valley; checking out the *menu touristique*.
LEFT: a wine farmer from Bordeaux.

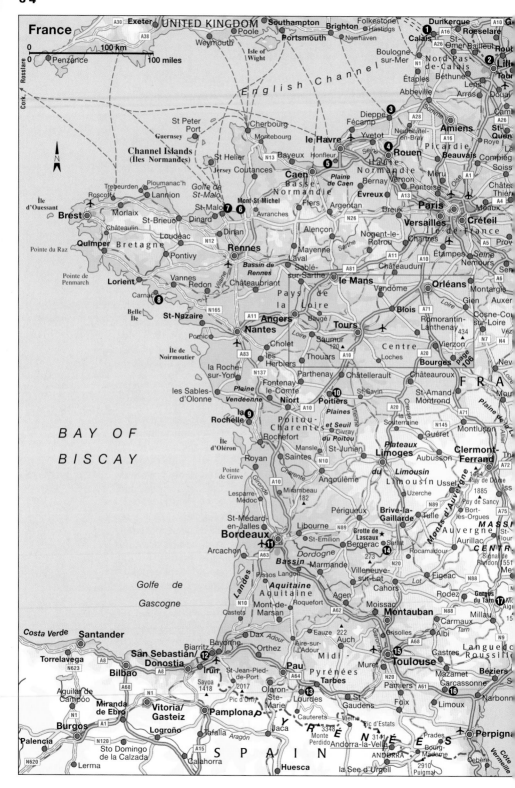

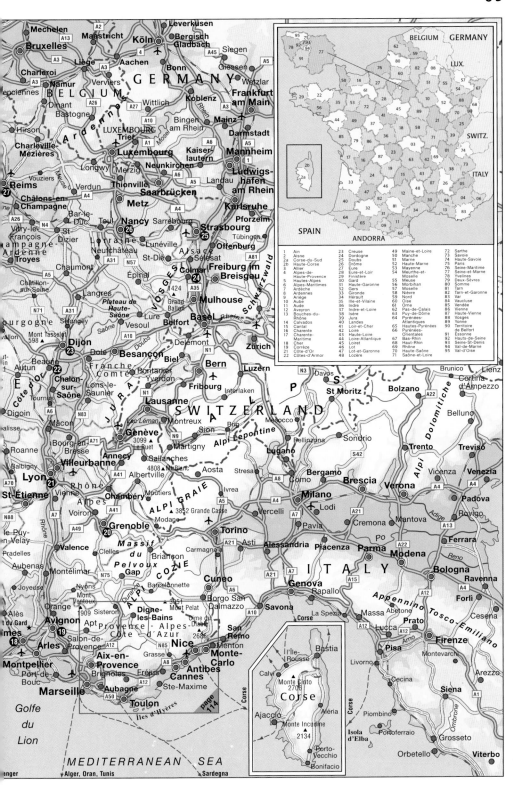

1	Ain	23	Creuse	49	Maine-et-Loire	72	Sarthe
2	Aisne	24	Dordogne	50	Manche	73	Savoie
2a	Corse-du-Sud	25	Doubs	51	Marne	74	Haute-Savoie
2b	Haute-Corse	26	Drôme	52	Haute-Marne	75	Paris
3	Allier	27	Eure	53	Mayenne	76	Seine-Maritime
4	Alpes-de-Haute-Provence	28	Eure-et-Loir	54	Meurthe-et-Moselle	77	Seine-et-Marne
5	Hautes-Alpes	29	Finistère	55	Moselle	78	Yvelines
6	Alpes-Maritimes	30	Gard	56	Meuse	79	Deux-Sèvres
7	Ardèche	31	Haute-Garonne	57	Morbihan	80	Somme
8	Ardennes	32	Gers	58	Moselle	81	Tarn
9	Ariège	33	Gironde	59	Nièvre	82	Tarn-et-Garonne
10	Aube	34	Hérault	60	Nord	83	Var
11	Aude	35	Ille-et-Vilaine	61	Oise	84	Vaucluse
12	Aveyron	36	Indre	62	Orne	85	Vendée
13	Bouches-du-Rhône	37	Indre-et-Loire	63	Pas-de-Calais	86	Vienne
14	Calvados	38	Isère	64	Puy-de-Dôme	87	Haute-Vienne
15	Cantal	39	Jura	65	Pyrénées-Atlantiques	88	Vosges
16	Charente	40	Landes	66	Hautes-Pyrénées	89	Yonne
17	Charente-Maritime	41	Loir-et-Cher	67	Pyrénées-Orientales	90	Territoire de Belfort
18	Cher	42	Loire	68	Bas-Rhin	91	Essonne
19	Corrèze	43	Haute-Loire	69	Haut-Rhin	92	Hauts-de-Seine
20	Côte-d'Or	44	Loire-Atlantique	70	Rhône	93	Seine-St-Denis
21	Côtes-d'Armor	45	Loiret	71	Haute-Saône	94	Val-de-Marne
22		46	Lot	48	Saône-et-Loire	95	Val-d'Oise
		47	Lot-et-Garonne				
		48	Lozère				

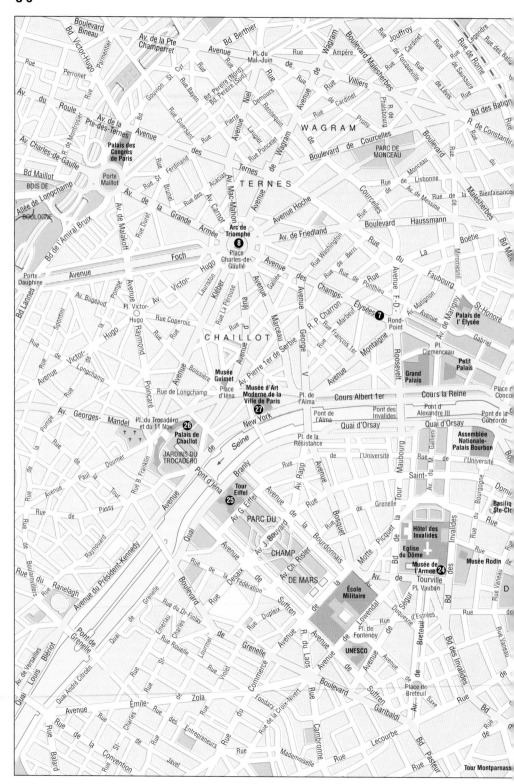

Paris

0 ___ 500 m
0 ___ 500 yds

PARIS

Its grand architecture and reputation for high living, fine cuisine and haute couture combine to make Paris the most glamorous of all European capitals

Map on pages 86–7

Paris may at first appear a really cosmopolitan city but it has maintained its quintessentially French character despite the invasion of American fast-food chains and the proliferation of Anglicisms in the French language, creating an idiom called *Franglais*. From the *clochards* sheltering in the subway stations, to the crêpe makers and the *bouquinistes* (open-air book sellers) along the Seine, Paris offers a plethora of sights, sounds and smells.

Altogether, downtown Paris covers a circular area of 105 sq km (41 sq miles) and is bounded by the recreational parks of the **Bois de Vincennes** to the east and the **Bois de Boulogne** to the west. The city is divided into 20 districts called *arrondissements*, each with its own distinct character. The lower numbers up to nine designate the oldest districts of the city. *La ville de Paris*, which is the city proper (population 2.2 million), is surrounded by a belt of communities called the *banlieue* (suburbs) totalling about 8½ million people.

Early settlements

The origins of Paris are concentrated on the Île de la Cité, the largest of the two odd-shaped islands in the middle of the Seine. Here, Celtic fishermen called *Parisii* founded a village in the 3rd century BC, which they named *Lutetia* – "a place surrounded by water". In 52 BC, during his Gallic War, Julius Caesar conquered the settlement. More invasions came from Germanic tribes; the strongest of them, the Franks, made Paris their capital in the 6th century. In the 10th century Hugo Capet ascended the throne as the first of the Capetian monarchs and made Paris a medieval centre of culture and learning.

The Renaissance monarchs were responsible for creating what today constitutes the classic beauty of Paris: some of the major streets, charming squares, the Louvre Palace with the grand Tuileries Gardens and the first stone bridge across the Seine, the Pont Neuf. Sun King Louis XIV moved the capital to Versailles in the late 17th century but Paris continued to prosper, luxury trades adding to the prestige of the city. The overthrow of the *ancien régime* by the legendary storming of the Bastille prison on 14 July 1789 was followed by the rise and fall of Napoleon Bonaparte, who left Paris the Arc de Triomphe and other great Neo-classical monuments.

The modern era

In the middle of the 19th century the urban planner Baron Haussmann laid out his *grands boulevards*. The Bois de Boulogne and Bois de Vincennes, the railway stations and the Opéra were also on his drawing board when the military defeat in the Franco-Prussian War of 1870–71 brought down the Second Empire of

LEFT: dusk in the romantic city.
BELOW: puppy love.

*When the Germans
retreated from Paris
in August 1944,
Hitler ordered the
bridges over the
Seine to be blown up.
But the commandant
in charge saved the
city for future
generations by
disregarding his
instructions.*

Napoleon III. The *belle époque* came to an abrupt end in 1914 when World War I broke out and the advancing Germans shelled Paris. However, they never got into the city as they did in World War II when Paris was occupied for more than four years.

The post-war era again changed the face of Paris and successive presidents have left their marks on the city. André Malraux, Minister of Culture under the presidency of Charles de Gaulle, began a large-scale programme to whitewash the facades of the capital. The **Pompidou Centre** was built under President Pompidou in 1977 and President Mitterrand left his mark with the **Grande Arche**, a giant rectangular office block in the **La Défense** quarter to the west of the city, and the glass pyramid entranceway to the Louvre, built by I.M. Pei.

A city tour

The right bank and the left bank of Paris grew up with a separate and distinct social tradition which still prevails today. The right bank has retained its established role as the mercantile centre. Here are the banks, swanky department stores, posh airline and government offices and the *Bourse*, the pompous stock exchange. The left bank, on the other hand, has been the domain of the intellectual community.

BELOW: La Grande
Arche, La Défense.
RIGHT: modern
Houdini outside the
Pompidou Centre.

A tour of Paris may begin from any of its major landmarks. Those eager for an introductory panoramic view usually head for the Basilique du Sacré-Coeur on the heights of Montmartre or the Eiffel Tower by the river, two of the classic vantage points. Others set out for the Place de l'Opéra to explore the *grands boulevards*, the *mondaine* shops along the Faubourg St-Honoré or the beautifully colonnaded Rue de Rivoli. Departing from the right bank, it may be equally

tempting to take a stroll along the Champs-Élysées. You can either walk down from the Arc de Triomphe or walk up from the Louvre, farther east.

Map on pages 86–7

World-class museums

The **Louvre** ❶ (open Wed–Mon; entrance charge) is the largest art museum in the world (see pages 98–9), although it was originally built as a medieval fortress to protect the River Seine. One of the most dramatic features of the major on-going renovation of the Louvre is the Richelieu wing with its two splendid light-flooded sculpture courts. The *Mona Lisa* also now has her own room.

From the Louvre to the Place de la Concorde extend the **Jardin des Tuileries** ❷, some of the best examples of typically French-styled formal gardens where trees, plants and decorations are carefully laid out in a pattern. The small **Jeu de Paume** has temporary exhibitions and on the opposite (river) side of the Tuileries, the **Orangerie** offers regular retrospectives of 19th- and 20th-century artists. (Métro: Palais Royal, Louvre and Tuileries.)

A luscious portrait by Renoir at the Orangerie gallery.

The grand glass-and-iron *belle-époque* railway station of Quai d'Orsay, just across the river, has become one of the city's great art museums, the **Musée d'Orsay** ❸ (open Tues–Sun; entrance charge). It has a major collection of late 19th-century works, particularly by Delacroix and Ingres, as well as paintings by the Impressionists, Monet, Manet, Renoir, Cézanne and Van Gogh.

The Jardin des Tuileries opens to the **Place de la Concorde** ❹, a vast square that occupies a bloody chapter in French history. In 1793 it became the site of executions where Marie Antoinette and Louis XVI, among others, met their fate on the guillotine. In 1795 peace returned to the square, today one of the hubs of Parisian traffic, which rushes past the oldest monument to be found in the

LEFT: Louvre and Champs-Élysées.
BELOW: the Galerie d'Apollon.

A guard stands to attention outside the Palais d'Élysée.

BELOW:
Montmartre artists,
Place du Tertre.

city: the 55-foot (17-metre) Obelisk of Luxor. Dating from 1300 BC, it was taken from the Temple of Rameses in Egypt and shipped as a gift to Paris in 1836. (Métro: Concorde.)

From the Tuileries, **Rue Castiglione** leads north to **Place Vendôme** ❺, the queen of all squares in Paris. Shaped like an octagon, it is lined by 17th-century buildings which house some of the city's most exclusive stores, specialising in perfume, fashion and jewellery. In its centre towers a 44-metre (144-foot) column with bas-reliefs of bronze from 1,200 cannons captured in 1805 from the Austrians at the Battle of Austerlitz.

A pseudo-Greek temple stands out prominently from its position at the junction of the **Grands Boulevards** and the end of **Rue Royal**, leading from Concorde. Napoleon dedicated this monument to the glory of his Grand Armée. Better known as **La Madeleine** ❻, it has served as a church since 1842. Opposite the church along the Boulevard de la Madeleine is a flower market. (Métro: Place de la Madeleine.)

Famous promenade

Continuing west from the Place de la Concorde, you immediately enter the **Champs-Élysées** ❼. The lower stretch to the Rond-Point is a broad avenue lined with horse chestnut and plane trees. It makes an attractive promenade and has a little park if you need to rest, north of which lies the presidential **Palais d'Élysée**. Between the Rond-Point and the **Arc de Triomphe** ❽ the Champs-Élysées takes on a different character. It becomes an elegant and prestigious avenue of smart shops and luxury boutiques. Walking up the Champs-Élysées gives a magnificent view of the monumental Arc de Triomphe.

Built between 1806 and 1836, this impressive monument stands 50 metres (165 feet) high and 45 metres (148 feet) wide. The Arc is noted for its frieze of hundreds of figures each 2 metres (6 feet) high and its 10 sculptures. The names of the major victories between the Revolution and the First Empire (military defeats are omitted) are inscribed under the arch, and the Tomb of the Unknown Soldier lies beneath. The eternal flame, scene of patriotic ceremonies, is rekindled every day at 6.30pm. The 284 steps to the top (there is also an elevator) give access to a spectacular view down the Champs-Élysées and to La Défense. In 1970 the Place de L'Étoile was officially named Charles de Gaulle after France's late resistance leader and state president. (Métro: George V and Étoile-Charles de Gaulle.)

Bohemian quarter

The district of **Montmartre**, the haunt of writers and artists until early in the 20th century, is still one of the liveliest spots after dark. This area is often regarded as the birthplace of modern art since Rousseau, Utrillo, Renoir, Gauguin and others spent the early part of their careers here late in the 19th century.

Known locally as *La Butte*, it was once unspoiled bohemian, and songs and comedies flowed from the dim cafés. Later, Montparnasse on the left bank took over as the artistic and literary centre. At the **Place du Tertre**, however, some of Montmartre's former reputation lives on. Street artists dominate the scene, offering tourists caricatures or Parisian townscapes.

Incongruously set in Montmartre is the virginal-white **Basilique du Sacré-Coeur** ⓿. Perched on a hill, its Byzantine cupolas are as much a part of the city skyline as the Eiffel Tower; when the lights are turned on at night, Sacré Coeur resembles a lit wedding cake. It can be reached by walking up 250 steps or by taking a funicular railway.

At the foot of Sacré Coeur, along **Boulevard de Clichy**, is **Pigalle**, the traditional entertainment quarter of Paris. It is symbolized by the neon-red windmill sails of the **Moulin Rouge** cabaret, home of can-can dancing since the days of Toulouse-Lautrec. Here, too, were once the dimly lit cabarets where the legendary Edith Piaf, the "Sparrow of Paris," sang. Lining the side streets of **Place Pigalle** ⓾, the *belles de nuit* (beauties of the night) beckon for clients while touts try to lure strangers to a "real Parisian private party". The **Folies-Bergères**, about 2 km (1 mile) south on Rue Richer, offers much the same fare as the Moulin Rouge.

Into the Marais

If you walk along nearby Rue La Fayette you will emerge at the gloriously romantic **Opéra de Paris** ⓫, designed in 1875 by Charles Garnier and enclosed by a triangle of Haussmann's *grands boulevards*. Inside, the majestic staircase and rich marble decorations evoke swirling gowns, tuxedos and top hats.

Before crossing the Boulevard Sébastopol and entering the area known as the **Marais**, visit the sprawling multi-storey shopping complex of **Forum des Halles** ⓬, filled with cinema halls, boutiques, galleries and restaurants. To the

Map on pages 86–7

TIP

It's worth going inside the Opéra de Paris just to see the magnificent ceiling painted by Surrealist Marc Chagall in 1964.

BELOW: looking down the Champs Élysées to the Arc de Triomphe.

A poster advertises the Picasso Museum. Although Spanish, Picasso lived and worked in Paris for many years.

east of the historic markets off Boulevard de Sébastopol looms the giant cultural machine of the **Pompidou Centre** ⑬ (the Centre Nationale d'Art et de Culture Georges Pompidou, to give it its official name; open Wed–Mon; entrance charge). Built between 1972 and 1976 by the architects Renzo Piano and Richard Rogers (winners among 681 competing designs), the futuristic structure with its multi-coloured piping and tubing resembles an oil refinery rather than a museum. It was refurbished in 1997–99 and reopened on 1 January 2000, continuing with off-beat exhibits centred on its contemporary art collection.

East of the Pompidou Centre is one of the city's most charming quarters and home to some of the finest mansions to be found in Paris. The Marais was originally swampland but became a fashionable residential district in the 17th century. Rue de Thorigny leads to the **Musée Picasso** ⑭ (open Wed–Mon; entrance fee) in the beautifully restored Hôtel de Salé. The paintings, drawings and sculptures inside the museum cover the artist's long and prolific career.

In the same neighbourhood is the old Jewish quarter of Paris and a splendid little square that is the city's oldest. The 63 houses of **Place des Vosges** ⑮, with arcades, were deliberately built to look symmetrical. The writer Victor Hugo (1802–85) once lived here and his house at No. 6 is a museum.

The Left Bank

In the very heart of Paris, the Seine River divides to embrace **Île de la Cité** and **Île St-Louis** ⑯. Traditionally a residence of Paris gentry, the latter has remained a patch of tranquillity in this fast-paced city. Neighbouring Île de la Cité is cluttered with historic landmarks, the most celebrated being the **Catédral Notre-Dame** ⑰ (open daily; free). This magnificent example of Gothic ecclesiastical architecture is simply stunning viewed from any angle. It was purportedly built on the grounds of a Gallo-Roman temple that was first replaced by a Christian basilica and a Romanesque church. The construction of the cathedral itself began in 1133 and work was only completed in 1345.

Also on Île de la Cité is the **Conciergerie** (open daily; entrance charge), once part of the Royal Palace where the warden of the kings used to live. This massive building is a beautiful sight at night when its arches are illuminated. During the French Revolution in 1789, it served as a prison for those awaiting the guillotine. Guided tours take you through the courtyards to Marie Antoinette's private cell, the kitchen and the guardroom.

The **Palais de Justice**, housing the present Paris law courts, was built on the same spot that over centuries served as the administrative quarters of the ancient Roman government and the early kings. In the courtyard is **Sainte Chapelle** ⑱, a Gothic chapel with magnificent stained-glass windows built in the 13th century by the saintly King Louis IX. (Métro: Cité, Châtelet.)

South of the river

From the Île de la Cité, the **Pont St Michel** leads to the left bank straight into the **Latin Quarter**. It earned its name from the dominance of Latin-speaking stu-

BELOW: floor show in the Latin Quarter.

dents who attended the nearby Sorbonne university. East of **Boulevard St-Michel**, its main thoroughfare, the Latin Quarter is threaded with numerous narrow alleys such as **Rue de la Huchette**, a twisting lane of Greek restaurants, kebab corners, jazz spots and cinemas. A mini Chinatown with Chinese and Vietnamese restaurants and food stalls has sprung up.

Where Boulevards St-Michel and **St-Germain** meet is **Musée de Cluny** ⓳ (open Tues–Sun; entrance charge), housing the ruins of the Roman baths. The building also contains the exquisite tapestry of *La Dame à la Licorn* (The Lady and the Unicorn). Walking down Boulevard St-Michel and turning to the left into Rue Soufflot, you arrive at the **Panthéon** ⓴. Built as a church to fulfil Louis XV's pious vow after he recovered from an illness, the Panthéon has, since 1791, served as a shrine to France's most outstanding citizens.

On the opposite side of Boulevard St-Michel stretches the spacious **Jardin du Luxembourg** ㉑. These gardens are popular with students whiling away time between classes, and children are thrilled by the adventures of Guignol (the French equivalent of the Punch and Judy Show) which are featured in the gardens' **Théâtre des Marionettes**. (Métro: St-Michel, Odéon, Luxembourg.)

In the evening and late into the night the **Rive Gauche** becomes even more animated as crowds of people promenade along Boulevard St-Michel and Boulevard St-Germain, which leads from the **Pont de la Concorde** further east into the Latin Quarter. The open-air terraces of restaurants and cafés in the area are popular venues for people to sit for a drink and to soak in the ambience. Next to the pre-Gothic church of **St-Germain-des-Prés** ㉒ are two cafés that have been elevated to the rank of institutions: the **Café Aux Deux Magots** and the **Café de Flore**. (Métro: Mabillon, St-Germain-des-Prés.)

Detail from La Dame à la Licorn *tapestry at the Musée de Cluny.*

BELOW: the celebrated Café Aux Deux Magots.

LEFT BANK RENDEZVOUS

Café Voltaire (1 Place de l'Odéon), named after its most industrious regular, was the place where the famous 18th-century writer used to meet fellow philosopher Diderot to discuss their Enlightenment theories. The tormented 19th-century poets Verlaine and Mallarmé traded Symbolist ideas here and, much later, the American writers Hemingway and F. Scott Fitzgerald extolled the café's "sudden provincial quality".

Writers between the two world wars spent many impassioned hours at their favourite tables in Le Procope (13 Rue de l'Ancienne-Comédie). After World War II, artists, writers and musicians converged on the Left Bank, making it the centre of the intellectual and artistic world.

Existentialist philosopher and writer Jean-Paul Sartre and his lover Simone de Beauvoir consolidated the highbrow reputation of Aux Deux Magots (6 Place St-Germain-des-Prés) in the 1950s. The café is reputed to serve the best hot chocolate in Paris. The art deco Café de Flore (172 Boulevard St-Germain) was another favourite haunt of Sartre's. At times, the Café de Flore was like a classroom, with Sartre writing at one table and de Beauvoir at another.

Today, it is politicians who tend to congregate – at Brasserie Lipp, just across the road.

TIP

Queues for the Eiffel Tower can be up to two hours long in summer, so get there early. A lift from the second level is the only means of reaching the top.

Heading south into **Rue des Rennes** and then changing into **Boulevard Raspail**, you pass into the **Quartier de Montparnasse**, which replaced Montmartre as the centre of bohemian life early in the 20th century. Artists, writers, poets and revolutionaries, among them Lenin and Trotsky, flocked to live here. After World War I, American expatriate writers of the "Lost Generation", such as Hemingway, F. Scott Fitzgerald and Henry Miller, joined the locals who used to congregate in famous literary cafés like Le Dome, La Rotonde, Le Sélect or the huge dining halls of La Coupole.

All these celebrated places are now surrounded by an air of nostalgia since Montparnasse has undergone extensive urban renewal in the past two decades. Many of the quarter's artist studios and small hotels have been demolished and the huge **Tour Montparnasse** ㉓ symbolises the region's changing identity as a business centre. (Métro: Vavin, Raspail, Montparnasse.)

Back to the Seine

The gilded **Dome des Invalides** faces the right bank from across Pont d'Alexandre III. Immediately beneath the vast cupola rests Emperor Napoleon I, whose body was transferred here from the island of St Helena in 1840. It is encased in seven separate sarcophagi, the exterior one being made of precious red marble. The church is surrounded by the Hôtel des Invalides, built by Louis XIV as a hospital to shelter 7,000 disabled soldiers. Today the building houses the **Musée de l'Armée** ㉔ (open daily; entrance charge), featuring arms, uniforms and trophies from France's military past.

BELOW:
the Eiffel tower, a symbol of Paris.

Just a few steps away at No. 77 Rue de Varenne, the former studio of sculptor Auguste Rodin (1840–1917) is now the **Musée Rodin** (open Wed–Mon; entrance charge). Some of the artist's best and most famous works are here, both inside the museum and outside in the garden.

To the west of the Invalides is the École Militaire – the French Military College. It is fronted by a former parade ground, Champs de Mars, which leads to the **Tour Eiffel** ㉕ (open daily until 11pm; entrance charge). Named after its creator Gustave Eiffel (who had designed the structure for New York's Statue of Liberty), the tower was designed as a temporary istallation, slated to be dismantled in 1910, 21 years after its inauguration at the Paris World Fair. But since it proved its value as a wireless tower it remained intact, and of course it is now synonymous with Paris. From its top platform, 267 metres (800 ft) above ground, there is a view in a radius of about 48 km (30 miles) on a clear day.

Opposite the Eiffel Tower on the right bank is the **Palais de Chaillot** ㉖, dating from the International Exposition of 1937. It is host to several museums and the national film library, **Cinémathèque Français**, which shows four films daily. Close by on Avenue du Président Wilson, the Palais de Tokyo contains the underrated **Musée d'Art Moderne de la Ville de Paris** ㉗, with works by Picasso, Matisse, Modigliani, Soutine and Dufy, among others (open Tues–Sun; entrance charge). (Métro: Invalides, Varenne, Trocadéro, École Militaire.)

Around the city

The most sumptuous of all castles in France is the **Château de Versailles** (open Tues–Sun; entrance charge; tel: 01-30 84 74 00). Not to be missed, it is a mere 21 km (13 miles) away from the capital. Versailles was remodelled from an original manor farm by Louis XIII, who used to hunt in the surrounding woods. He had the farm converted into a rose brick-and-stone château. This was expanded by Louis XIV, the Sun King, who took 50 years to create a palace that was so magnificent that it was copied all over Europe.

Versailles served as capital of France on various occasions and, in its heyday, had a court population of 20,000. The palace itself housed 5,000. It was a royal residence until the Revolution of 1789.

Inside, the tour takes you through the King's Apartments and the 70-metre (233-ft) Hall of Mirrors. Outside in the park, which was designed by André le Nôtre, are the smaller royal residences of the **Grand Trianon** and **Petit Trianon**, as well as Marie-Antionette's make-believe village of **Hameau**.

Northwest of Paris, on the Seine, is the house and garden of **Giverny** (open Apr–Oct: Tues–Sun; entrance charge; tel: 02-32 51 28 21) created by Claude Monet who lived there until his death in 1926. Beautifully restored, it has become a popular tourist spot, particularly the Japanese garden where the lilies, so famously painted by this premier Impressionist, still blossom.

A bigger attraction, though of different appeal, is **Disneyland Paris** (open daily until 11pm; entrance charge), the US entertainment empire's first foothold in Europe, which opened with a great fanfare in 1992. It is located at Marne-la-Vallée, 32 km (20 miles) east of Paris. Although it got off to a rocky financial start, it initially attracted more than twice as many visitors as the Louvre. ❑

Map
on pages
86–7

TIP

Two- or three-day passports to Disneyland, available either at the gate or from the Disney Store or Virgin Megastore on the Champs-Elysées, are an economical way to visit the attraction.

BELOW: the Château de Versailles.

TREASURES OF THE LOUVRE

The largest palace in Europe, the Louvre has assembled an incomparable collection of old masters, sculptures and antiquities

One of the world's greatest museums, the Louvre is immense in scale; the size of its collections (well over 200,000 pieces) and the crowds that invariably throng its galleries (5 million visitors each year) make it one of the more challenging Parisian sights. It is impossible to try to see everything in one visit, although many people manage to cram in the edited highlights during one morning. This, however, does little justice to the wealth of exhibits, which range from European sculpture and painting to antiquities, decorative arts and objects.

HISTORY OF THE COLLECTION

The Louvre's collection was built up through patronage, gift-giving, requisition and other methods of appropriation. François I (*pictured above*, by Jean Clouet) was a Renaissance king who amassed a superb array of mostly Italian contemporary and classical works, and patronised artists such as Leonardo da Vinci. Louis XIV similarly made patronage a royal duty and added to the collection. Nationalisation of most French works of art after the Revolution led to the Musée de la Règpublique being opened to the public in 1793. The greatest contribution to the museum was made by Napoleon I, who brought back the spoils of his various campaigns. Louis XVIII acquired works including the Venus de Milo, but in 1848 the Louvre once again became the property of the State.

▷ THE BATHERS

It is thought that Fragonard painted this canvas in the 1760s following his first trip to Italy. Fragonard was greatly influenced by Rubens in his use of colour, the fullness of his figures, and the painting's sensual and joyous theme was enhanced by the use of scumbles and glazes. Donated in 1869, the canvas is today part of the museum's comprehensive collection of European painting.

△ OBJETS D'ART

This 13th-century reliquary of St Francis of Assisi is one of the fabulous items found in the eclectic department of Objets d'Art.

▷ ANTIQUITIES

During the 18th and 19th centuries, antiquities were seen as the greatest art form, although the Louvre's core collection contains pieces which belonged to François I.

◁ DYING SLAVE

One of a pair of sculptures by Michelangelo, thought to represent the Arts, held captive by Death, after the death of Pope Julius II, a great arts patron.

CASTLE, PRISON AND PALACE

The Louvre building, thought to be named after an area where wolves were hunted, has been enlarged and remodelled by French rulers for more than 800 years. The first building on the site was Philippe-Auguste's 12th-century fortified castle, known popularly as the "Tour de Paris", which contained the state treasury, archives and the royal storeroom. It also served as a prison. As medieval Paris grew, and the monarchy established other residences, the Louvre's importance declined.

In 1527, François I commissioned a Renaissance palace – the first example of French Classical architecture – to replace the château. By the end of the 17th century there was hardly an original stone left standing. The buildings surrounding the Cour Carrée predate 1715, and comprise the oldest parts of the building. In the 19th century, Napoleon I added the Galerie du Nord, and the buildings which flank the north and south sides of the Cour Napoleon date from the time of Napoleon III. The most recent addition to the Louvre's landscape is I.M. Pei's dramatic glass pyramid, which has become the museum's 20th-century emblem.

FONTAINEBLEAU SCHOOL

...is 16th-century painting of ...e Duchess of Villars and ...abrielle d'Estrée, attributed ...the School of Fontaine-...eau, is a fine example of the ...en popular portrait genre. It ...ows the two sisters taking a ...th. The Duchess, in a ...mbolic gesture, is ...nouncing the future birth of ...r sister's child, the ...egitimate son of Henry IV.

TOMB OF PHILIPPE POT

...star of the collection of ...ropean sculpture is this ...usual late 15th-century ...ece by Antoine le Moiturier. ...ilippe Pot was the Great ...neschal of Burgundy, an ...ficial of considerable rank. ...s imposing tomb, which ...as formerly in the Abbey of ...teaux, shows him dressed ...armour, being carried on a ...ield and supported by eight ...eeping figures dressed in ...ourning garb.

▽ SARCOPHAGUS OF THE RECLINING COUPLE

Standing more than a metre high, this painted terracotta sarcophagus is one of the most impressive of the museum's Etruscan treasures. It depicts in detail everything from the folds of the garments to enigmatic smiles. The base of the sarcophagus is a couch, used by guests at an Etruscan banquet.

AROUND FRANCE

Every region of France has something distinctive to offer; the majestic châteaux of the Loire Valley and sun-drenched beaches of the Mediterranean coast are just two of the highlights

Map on pages 84–5

France has an admirable network of road, rail and air transport that makes for quick and efficient travel. The expansion of the *autoroute* (motorway) system has been accelerated in recent years. It runs from the north coast to the south and provides access to the southwest and the east by going round rather than through Paris. The link from Calais to Marseille via Reims makes the journey from north to south around 11 hours. The greatest asset of the French road network is the superlative quality of its clearly signposted secondary roads.

The railways have a reputation for being the best in Europe. The trains are punctual, clean and fast. The 300-kph (186-mph) TGV (*Train à Grande Vitesse*) has cut the four-hour journey from Paris to Lyon by half. The lines also run to Calais, Le Mans and Tours, and a TGV Med service is underway to Marseille. The two lines will link up, giving a straight-through run from the Channel Tunnel to the Côte d'Azur. TGV lines are also planned to Italy and Spain.

First ports of call

Visitors arriving by sea via the English Channel might like to stretch their legs in the port towns before continuing the journey inland. **Calais ❶** is distinctly shabby and soulless but in **Parc St Pierre** you'll find the famous bronze statue by August Rodin of the *Burghers of Calais* who, in 1346, offered their necks to Edward III, the English king, if he would spare the city. He spared both. In **Boulogne**, the 13th-century ramparts of the picturesquely cobbled upper town (*ville haute*) make an interesting walk. A good overall view of the town and harbour can be had from the top of the belfry of the town hall. A little inland, **St Omer's Basilique Notre-Dame**, begun in 1200 and completed in the 15th century, is a triumphant union of Romanesque and Gothic styles, the jewel of Flanders' ecclesiastic architecture.

Close to the Belgian border is **Lille ❷**, the capital of French Flanders. It is distinguished by its welcoming Flemish atmosphere and richly restored civic buildings, in particular the grand 17th-century **Vieille Bourse** (Old Stock Exchange) and Louis XIV's imposing fortified citadel – a massive star-shaped construction of 60 million bricks that demanded the labour of 2,000 bricklayers.

To the south are **Arras** and **Amiens**, the former famous to the English for the tapestries through which Hamlet stabbed old Polonius, and to the French as the home town of revolutionary leader Robespierre. It is worth a visit today for its lively squares and marketplaces, most notably Place des Héros, Grand-Place and Place du Tertre. The 13th-century Gothic cathedral at Amiens is the largest in France, and even more miraculous for having survived the bombardments of

LEFT: flying the flag in Burgundy.
BELOW: Breton women in native costume.

TIP

Rouen Cathedral is illuminated at night until 1am. If you are staying nearby it's worth lingering in town to have dinner and view the spectacular silhouette.

two world wars. Its masterpiece is the intricate wooden carving of the 16th-century choirstalls. Back on the coast, between Boulogne and Dieppe, is the favourite seaside resort of **Le Touquet**. It was once known as "Paris-Plage", promising a touch of city sophistication at the seaside, but now has an air of faded gentility.

Normandy

Dieppe ❸, on the Normandy coast, is the most attractive of the ports serving the Channel crossings, dealing good-humouredly with a huge volume of English day-trippers while still managing to retain its influx of French holiday-makers. The **Boulevard du Maréchal Foch** offers a pleasant promenade along the the extensive pebble beach. The liveliest part of town, however, is around the **Place du Puits Sale**, where you will find the renowned Café des Tribuneaux.

Inland you should visit the superb abbey ruins in **Jumièges**, consecrated in 1067 to celebrate William's conquest of England. **Rouen ❹**, capital of upper Normandy, is cherished by the French as the place where Joan of Arc was burned at the stake. The 11th- and 12th-century **cathedral** is only one of several splendid monuments in this great medieval city and port on the River Seine.

Further west along the Calvados coast are some lovely resorts and historical ports, the most picturesque of which is **Honfleur ❺**. The **Musée Eugène Boudin** (open mid-Mar–Sep Wed–Mon 10am–noon, 2–6pm, Oct–mid-Mar 2.30–5pm, Oct–mid-Mar weekends 10am–noon, 2.30–5pm; entrance charge) attests to the town's popularity with painters – Corot, Courbet, Monet and Dufy. **Deauville**, with its casino and fashionable discos, is the queen of Channel resorts, retaining much of the elegance that made it a name in the *belle époque*.

BELOW:
rue Damiette
and St-Ouen
abbey, Rouen.

THE FATAL SHORE

The north of France, flat and defenceless as Belgium, has been the poignant arena for countless invasions, its place names sounding like a litany of battlefields.

Dunkirk is famous for the providential evacuation of 140,000 French and 200,000 British troops in May 1940. From the lighthouse or the Watier locks, you can see where it happened. The English remember glorious Crécy and Henry V's Agincourt (Azincourt in French), while the French prefer to remember Bouvines, an important victory over an Anglo-German alliance in 1214.

Other battles, whether ending in victory or defeat, soaked the fields of Flanders and Picardy, the plateau of the Ardennes and the banks of the Somme and Marne in blood. There are impressive monuments to Canadian troops at Vimy (north of Arras), to the Australians at Corbie (east of Amiens) and to the Americans at Bellicourt (south-west of LeQuesnoy), while British cemeteries of World War I are found mostly in Belgium.

However, the traveller in Normandy is constantly reminded of the colossal effort that went into the rebuilding of the towns and cities destroyed by fighting – Caen, Le Havre, Rouen, Avranches, Dunkerque and Boulogne have all been lovingly reconstructed from the rubble.

Map on pages 84–5

The beaches of the **D-Day landings** of 6 June 1944 – Omaha, Utah, Gold, Juno and Sword – are also to be found along the Calvados coast. The most important exhibition commemorating "Operation Overlord" is located at **Arromanches**. In the bay the remnants of the former artificial Mulberry harbour peek out of the water. The huge concrete construction, comprising a breakwater and piers, was towed across the Channel and installed off Arromanches in order to land supplies for the Allied forces.

A swig of the fine local Calvados apple brandy might be advisable before braving the Atlantic winds along the Cotentin peninsula, where the wild Norman conquerors came from. **Caen** is the capital of lower Normandy and was the home of William the Conqueror before he moved to England. He and his wife Mathilde left two fine abbeys, *aux Hommes* and *aux Dames,* west and east of the city centre. Caen was flattened in the 1944 Battle of Normandy; in 1988 the impressive **Musée pour la Paix** (Peace Museum; open Feb–Dec: daily; entrance charge) opened in the town.

In the **Centre-Guillaume-le-Conquérant** (open daily; entrance charge) at **Bayeux**, 28 km (17 miles) northwest of Caen**,** hangs the highly celebrated and exquisite tapestry, stitched in 1067, depicting the events surrounding William of Normandy's conquest of England in 1066.

The 70-metre (230-ft) Bayeux Tapestry is, in fact, not a tapestry at all but a fine example of medieval English embroidery. It was probably made in Canterbury, southeast England.

Mont-St-Michel

Probably the most dramatic ecclesiastical building in all France, indeed one of the wonders of the Western world, is **Mont-St-Michel ❻**, in a bay at the bottom of the Cotentin peninsula. The **abbey** (open daily; entrance charge), built between the 11th century and the 16th century, makes a strong impression when seen

BELOW: majestic Mont-St-Michel.

The menhirs (standing stones) at Carnac are 1,000 years older than the pyramids but were aligned with extraordinary anatomical accuracy.

from a distance. It stands at the summit of an island-rock, 75 metres (250 ft) above the sea, and is reached by road along a dyke. Try to be there at high tide.

Brittany

Jaques Cartier set off from the ancient port of **St Malo** ❼ on the 16th-century voyage which led to the discovery of Canada. Much of the town was rebuilt after its almost complete destruction during World War II, but you can still walk all around the town on top of the ramparts and get a fine view aross the estuary towards **Dinard**, one of Brittany's most successful resorts.

But Brittany is appreciated most for the beauty of its craggy coastline. The pink granite rocks of the Corniche Bretonne run from **Ploumanac'h**, via **Tregastel**'s excellent swimming beach, to **Trebeurden**. The Bretons maintain their own Celtic language and customs, most notably the Pardons, religious processions which still see local people in their rich regional dress. Their ancient Celtic origins can be seen in the extraordinary stone circles such as those at **Carnac** ❽, where 3,000 giant stones were laid out by their ancestors for some form of worship. The dolmens and tumuli are thought to mark burial sites.

A tour of the Loire Valley

Brittany's largest city, **Nantes**, is the point at which the River Loire meets the tidal estuary that takes it to the Atlantic Ocean. The celebrated valley of the River Loire has been praised as the garden of France and has been described as a melting pot of the Celtic, Roman and Nordic civilisations. Most of all, however, it was the home of kings and princes who have left a splendid mosaic of châteaux, recognised as among the finest in the world.

Maps:
France 84
Loire 106

Writers such as Rousseau, Voltaire and Molière have also been seduced by the valley's gentle life. Jean Rabelais, lusty poet of the French Renaissance, was born here, as was Honoré de Balzac, the great social historian and genius of the French 19th-century novel.

From Paris, a tour of the Loire Valley usually begins in **Gien** or **Orléans 🅐**, an hour's drive west of the capital. The Loire proper, rising on Mont Gerbier de Joncs in the Massif Central is, at 1,015 km (634 miles), the longest river in France. The soul of Orléans, a modern city whose heart was bombed out during World War II, lives on in the cult of Joan of Arc; it was here that she successfully resisted the English army before being burned at the stake at Rouen. The site where she stayed in 1429 has become the **Maison Jeanne d'Arc** (3 Place Général de Gaulle; open Tues–Sun; entrance charge), where scenes from her life are re-created. Each year on 7 and 8 May her triumphant entry into the city is celebrated as the greatest event in its history. At the choir of the present cathedral the pious virgin delivered her prayers of thanks, and at **Place du Martroi** she can be seen in bronze, riding out to battle.

Jeanne d'Arc, the maid of Orléans.

Châteaux of the Loire

Beaugency 🅑, 18 km (11 miles) south of Orléans, has an 11th-century dungeon, 12th-century abbey, Renaissance town hall and charming bridge. From here, the road leads on to the very heart of château country. Altogether, the Loire region has about 3,000 castles of various periods. To visit all of them would take a lifetime. The oldest ones, such as the castle of **Loches**, began life as fortified towers and served as shelters during the strife-torn Middle Ages; the latest ones, such as the opulent palace of **Cheverny**, were designed for comfort

BELOW: the château of Tanlay.

*Medieval sailors
bringing a cargo of
salt down the Loire.*

rather than for defence, serving as pleasure grounds for the aristocracy during the age of absolutism. The châteaux built between the 15th and the mid-16th centuries rank as the apogee of the Renaissance.

The crown of France belonged by that time to the house of Valois so the Loire Valley consequently became known as the country of the Valois. The first Valois to seek refuge here was Charles VII in 1418. Then Dauphin (heir to the throne) of France, he had been driven out of Paris by the Duke of Burgundy who supported the claims of Henry IV of England to the French crown during the Hundred Years' War with England. In 1429 the war took a miraculous turn when Jeanne la Pucelle, an 18-year-old peasant girl from Lorraine, appeared at the castle of Chinon, west of Tours, which was then the seat of the royal court. She revealed to the Dauphin that divine voices had told her to aid him in the reconquest of his legitimate throne. The girl became France's national heroine, Joan of Arc, and proved her divine mission by her stunning military feat three months later at Orléans.

The first château to be seen when entering the Loire Valley from Orléans is **Chambord ⓒ** (open daily; entrance charge; tel: 01-54 50 40 00), a fantasy palace that bewitched even the most blasé of the Venetian ambassadors to the court of France. The building is a gigantic stairway on which wings have been grafted. The stairway, with its double turn, is the structure's pivot. It soars to the roofs, and offers an unmistakable symbol of the power of the French king. Everything about Chambord is colossal, but François I, who built it, spent only 40 days there, Henri IV never came near it and Louis XIII dropped in but once. The court stopped coming in 1684, which meant that nobody troubled to complete the enormous structure. A *son et lumière* show celebrates its past glories.

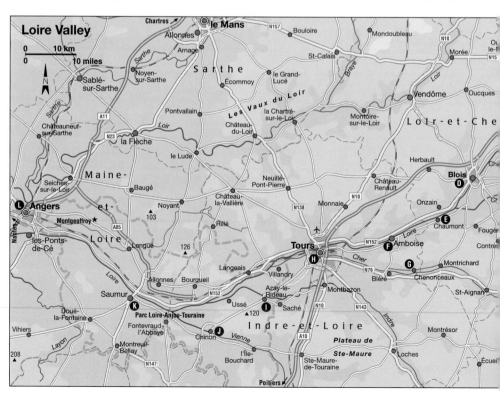

Blois D, which has France's most frequented château (open daily; entrance charge) after Versailles, is next along the valley. Without fortifications, opening on the Louis XIII wing, it has the look of a grand bourgeois dwelling offering peace, prosperity and ornament. As a vestige of its earliest years, Blois has kept its ramparts facing the Loire. Its tower of Foix provides a superb panorama over the river and suburbs.

The château at **Chaumont E** (open daily; entrance charge), on the left bank of the Loire, lies in a setting that the Prince de Broglie transformed into a veritable pastiche of the Arabian Nights. Further west, on the opposite bank, is **Amboise F**, whose château (open daily; entrance charge), once the home of Louis XI, Charles VIII, Louis XIII, François I and Habsburg Emperor Charles V, is considered one of the finest. Much of the palace has disappeared but what is left still offers a striking contrast between the "Italianate" modifications of Charles VIII and the old medieval fortress. Renaissance master Leonardo da Vinci is buried in St Hubert's Chapel.

Jewel of the Renaissance

There is no clash of style about **Chenonceaux G** (open daily; entrance charge; tel: 02-47 23 90 97), which achieves a perfect harmony in its Renaissance architecture. Anchored like a great ship in the middle of the River Cher, south of Amboise, and surrounded by broad fields, Chenonceaux is a work of feminine grace, a delicate jewel set in a green casket.

It was the preferred home of Diane de Poitiers, "the eternally beautiful" ravishing mistress of Henri II, and of cruel Marie de Medici, bitter enemy not only of her husband Henri IV, but also her son Louis XIII. Chenonceaux was famous

Map on pages 106–7

BELOW: Château de Villandry, seen from the ornamental gardens.

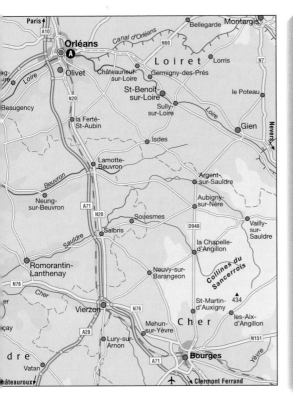

for its festivities. One of the first was the triumphal celebration on 1 March 1560 for François II and his young wife Mary Stuart. Today, the parties are all but forgotten, though there is still magic in the great classical gallery on a bridge of five arches creating a lovely reflection in the waters of the river.

Amboise and Chenonceaux are on the eastern edge of the region called the Touraine, which has the lively university town of **Tours** ❽ as its capital. The medieval quarter, centred on **Place Plumereau**, is a showcase of Gothic architecture. About 23 km (14 miles) southwest of Tours is **Azay-le-Rideau** ❾, (open daily; enrance charge; tel: 02-47 45 42 04), a small château of exquisite proportions partly built over the River Indre. This "multi-faceted diamond..., mounted on pillars, a maske of flowers" as it was described by Balzac, is the quintessence of the Touraine's architecture. Not far away is the **Château de Villandry** and its famous 16th-century garden (open daily; entrance charge).

Ruined château fort

Chinon ❿, 20 km (12 miles) southwest of Azay, once consisted of three different fortresses. Some of the mighty fortifications as well as parts of the moat are left. A length of wall with a high Gothic chimney-piece remains from the **Grand Logis**, the hall where the court witnessed the unerring judgement of Joan of Arc when she recognized the Dauphin despite his disguise as a humble courtier. One of the castle's towers was called Agnes Sorel after the mistress of Charles VII. In contrast to Joan of Arc, who was canonized in 1920, Agnes Sorel stands little chance of being worshipped as a saint. Her sins were so many, it is said, that her confession gave time for the priest's staff to be planted in the earth and turn into a holy tree.

In the 17th century Chinon once more became a centre of French politics when Cardinal Richelieu, first minister of France, took over the castle. His family abandoned it to become the grand ruins that can be seen today.

Beyond Chinon is **Saumur** ⓚ, where the surrounding woodlands are rich in mushrooms and, in this wine country where the whites are pre-eminent, the local pride is the red Champigny and sparkling Saumur. The town's medieval castle houses the **Musée des Arts Décoratifs** and **Musée du Cheval** (Horse Museum; both open Apr–Sept: daily; Oct–Mar: Wed–Mon; entrance charge), the latter tracing the long history of the horse in France. As God's companion, the horse was also regarded in Gallo-Roman mythology as an embodiment of God Himself, echoes of which are to be found in local traditions. At the end of July, the *Carrousel* festivities include impressive demonstrations of dressage and horsemanship. In Saumur itself the **Musée du Champignon** (open Feb–Nov: daily; entrance charge) offers guided visits to the underground galleries where mushrooms are cultivated. The road from Saumur to Angers follows the riverbank, past compact white villages worth a stop for local delicacies.

At Ponts-de-Cé, a road leads north to **Angers** ⓛ, town of the good King René, Duke of Anjou and of Provence. In the old town there are many fine specimens of Renaissance houses, most notably the **Logis Barrault** (housing the fine arts museum with some noteworthy works by Watteau, Chardin and Boucher), and the **Hôtel de Pincé** (also now an art museum devoted to Greek, Etruscan, Chinese and Japanese works). But pride of place among Angers' art treasures must go to the tapestries in the château, particularly the *Tenture de l'Apocalypse*, 70 pictures from a 14th-century work. The château itself is a splendid example of a medieval feudal fortress.

The Atlantic coast

Travelling south of Angers towards **la Rochelle** ❾ on the Atlantic coast you will come to a mysterious region of swampland and woods, the national park of **Le Marais Poitevin**. Beter known as La Venise Verte – Green Venice – it consists of 15,000 hectares (37,000 acres) of lush, green countryside threaded with 1,450 km (900 miles) of waterways. At Coulon, 11 km (7 miles) west of Niort, local boatmen await tourists with their long forked poles, *pigoulles*.

The gracious port town of La Rochelle is famous for Cardinal Richelieu's ruthless siege of the Protestant population in the 17th century – the Protestants are still there. Today it's a favourite port of call for yachtsmen and the houses of the old town have retained their 17th- and 18th-century charm, particularly along the Rue du Palais. **Tour St Nicolas** and **Tour de la Chaine** face each other across the sheltered 13th-century port where nightly a huge chain was drawn across to keep ships out.

Inland, the regional capital of **Poitiers** ❿ is one of the oldest cities in France. The church of **Notre-Dame-la-Grand**, in the town centre, has a magnificent, richly sculpted Romanesque facade and 12th-century frescoes in the vault of the

*Maps:
France 84
Loire 106*

In 1627 Cardinal Richelieu laid siege to the Huguenot stronghold of La Rochelle. When the 15-month siege ended, only 5,000 of the 28,000 inhabitants were still alive.

BELOW: the Renaissance palace at Chambord.

The Bordeaux wine region covers 135,000 hectares (333,585 acres). Red wines are produced in the Médoc, Saint-Emilion and Pomerol vineyards to the north, while white wines such as Graves and Sauternes are made further south.

choir. The church of St-Hilaire-le-Grand is the oldest in Poitiers, with parts dating to the 11th century.

Celebrated wine region

The essence of **Bordeaux** ⓫, France's fifth largest city and sixth largest port, is to be found along the Avenue Allées de Tourny. At one end is the **Grand Théâtre**, a Neo-classical monument of symmetrical columns and arches, while on the river side opens the gravelled Esplanades des Quinconces, the name referring to the arrangement of the trees. In between is the **Maison du Vin**, an indispensable stop for documentation on the different Bordelais vineyards and, in particular, those open to the public, where Médocs, Margaux and Pauillacs can be tasted in wine cellars. Nearby is the charming small town of **Saint-Emilion**, which provides a closer look at the vineyards.

Where the vineyards give out to the south of Bordeaux, the beach takes over. The immense, fine sand beach at **Arcachon** is circled by some of Europe's highest dunes. **Les Landes**, sweeping southwards for 240 km (150 miles), is the largest forest in France yet entirely artificial, created to retain the coastal sands.

Biarritz ⓬, cherished resort of Emperor Napoleon III and his wife Eugénie, Bismarck and the Prince of Wales (before he became Edward VII), gives a sense of France's old-style grandeur.

In the heart of the town are the **Promenades**, where steep cliffs fall to the ocean. Romantic alleys shaded by tamarisk trees lead to the **Rocher de la Vierge** (Rock of the Virgin), from which point the entire Basque coast can be admired. Biarritz is famous for its outrageous waves, and some of Europe's most important surfing competitions are held here.

BELOW:
Biarritz beach.
RIGHT:
St Emilion bar.

The French Pyrénées

Extending from the Atlantic Ocean to the Mediterranean Sea, the Pyrénées form a massive and continuous chain along the Spanish border. It is possible to hike their entire length, along the **GR10** trail (which could take up to two months), but the same trail also offers several shorter trips into the highest mountains.

Nestled in a valley at the foot of the highest Pyrénéan mountain is the picturesque old town of **Lourdes** ⓭, one of the most important Catholic shrines in the world. Unfortunately the area surrounding the shrine itself is woefully lacking in charm or aesthetic appeal, although this does not deter the thousands who crowd the town in search of miracles and healing.

Southwest France

The southwest is also the rugged countryside of the **Auvergne**, the rolling valley of the **Dordogne** and the succulent cuisine of the **Périgord**, to be tasted in such picturesque towns as **Sarlat** ⓮ or **Cahors**. Sarlat is a bustling market town that could be the stage for a film set in the Renaissance, the church and episcopal palace creating a breathing space among the interlacing streets that run between the sculpted facades. The Black Madonna on the altar of the **Chapelle de Notre-Dame** (open daily; free) at **Rocamadour**, 25 km (16 miles) east of Sarlat, has been a focus for Christian devotion since 1166. An accretion of crypts and chapels cluster against the cliff, and a path of the Stations of the Cross leads up to the shrine. The **museum** (open daily; entrance charge) has an important collection of 12th–14th-century treasures.

North of Sarlat, in a short stretch of the Vézère Valley between Montignac and Les Eyzies, is the **Grotte de Lascaux**, the world's most astonishing collection

Map on pages 84–5

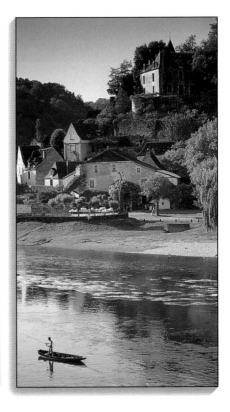

BELOW: tranquillity at Limeuil in the Dordogne.

PREHISTORY AT LASCAUX

Closed off in prehistoric times, the Grotte de Lascaux was not rediscovered until 12 September 1940 – during the search for a dog which had disappeared down a hole. Due to the preoccupations of World War II and ensuing hardships, crowds only started flocking to the site some years later.

When an astute official learned in 1963 that a green fungus was growing over the paintings the cave was immediately closed while restoration was still possible. In compensation a partial copy, called **Lascaux II**, has been created with great skill and care in the adjacent quarry, and is open to the public (obtain tickets in advance from the Montignac office; open Feb–June & Sept–Dec: Tues–Sun; July–Aug: daily; entrance charge).

Lascaux is just one of almost 200 prehistoric sites in the Dordogne. Most of the world-famous paintings, in black, yellow and red, are thought to date from the Aurignacian period, between 30,000–20,000 BC. They cover the walls and roofs of the cave and represent a number of animals including bulls, cows, deer, bison and horses. Lascaux II has reproductions of many of the paintings, notably a rare human figure visible only with difficulty in the original cave because it is inside a well.

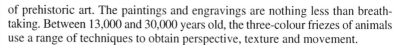

The medieval fortress of Carcassonne dominates the surrounding plains.

of prehistoric art. The paintings and engravings are nothing less than breathtaking. Between 13,000 and 30,000 years old, the three-colour friezes of animals use a range of techniques to obtain perspective, texture and movement.

Further south, the capital of the central southwestern lands of the Languedoc is **Toulouse** ⓯, which brims with character and civic pride. It has a massive red-brick fortress-church, **St-Sernin**, and impressive 16th- and 17th-century mansions in the old town district, also built of the region's red brick. Its museums are rich in Romanesque sculpture. Today it is the hi-tech capital of France, home of the Airbus and Concorde.

Towards the Mediterranean

Halfway beween Toulouse and the Mediterranean Sea along what was once the border with Spain is the fortified town of **Carcassonne** ⓰. There is no medieval monument like it in Europe. Its uniqueness lies in its two sets of intact fortifications. The first ramparts were built by the Romans in the 3rd and 4th centuries AD. They were later improved on in the 13th century under St Louis, for fear of Spanish invasion. The two sets of walls rendered the city absolutely impregnable during the Middle Ages. Nearby is **Castelnaudry**, home of a famous French stew. Approximately 50 km (30 miles) north on the banks of the river Tarn is **Albi**, best-known today as the birthplace, in 1864, of the painter Toulouse-Lautrec. The old episcopal palace now houses the **Musée Henri de Toulouse-Lautrec** (open Apr–Sept: daily; Oct–Mar: Wed–Mon; entrance charge), which contains the most complete collection of his work.

BELOW: Provence in full bloom.

While the Tarn at Albi is wide and majestic as it meanders westward, 100 km (60 miles) to the east the magnificent **Gorges du Tarn** ⓱ begin, the river carving extraordinary canyons through steep limestone cliffs. The Détroits (the straits), the most impressive section of the gorges, start from the town of Le Rozier. Here the river is only a few metres wide, with the cliffs towering more than 300 metres (1,000 ft) above. Just a few kilometres upstream of Les Vignes, where the river widens, is the **Point Sublime**.

Roman remains

Crossing over into the region of **Provence**, the 2,000-year-old Roman amphitheatres at **Nîmes** ⓲, **Orange** and **Arles** still echo with thundering hooves when summer bullfights draw enormous crowds to these former gladiatorial arenas. Twenty km (12 miles) north of Nîmes is one of the great engineering and aesthetic achievements of Roman antiquity, the **Pont du Gard** aqueduct (open daily; entrance charge), which spans half a mile over the river Gardon. It carried 20,000 cubic metres (26,000 cubic yards) of water daily to the town. The view from the top tier of arches is breathtaking.

The lively town of **Avignon** ⓳ offers a great summer theatre festival in and around its superb **Palais des Papes** (open daily; entrance charge). This 14th-century edifice was built at a time when the popes found Rome too dangerous to stay in. Its silent cloisters, cavernous halls and imposing ramparts are a delight to explore. In contrast, the famous bridge ("*l'on y danse, tous en rond*") now only reaching halfway across the River Rhône, is a disappointing four-arch ruin. (In fact, the people didn't dance on it as the French song says, but underneath it.)

North of Avignon, **Orange** lies at the northern tip of Provence and was a favoured resort for the Romans when it was a colony of their empire, with a population four times the size of its present-day 25,000. The Roman theatre, graced by a statue of Emperor Augustus, is regarded as the most beautiful amphitheatre of the classical era. Surrounding Orange, the area of the **Vaucluse** is richly fertile. The fascinating ruins at **Vaison-la-Romaine** provide a glimpse of the private side of Roman life in some well-preserved houses of 2,000 years ago. **Mont Ventoux** has a view over the whole of Provence down to Marseille and the Mediterranean or clear across to the Swiss Alps. One of the great attractions of this mountain region is the **Fontaine-de-Vaucluse**, where the underground River Sorgue suddenly springs into sight in a spectacular setting of grottos.

The region's most picturesque site of ancient Roman life is **Arles**, which, besides its fine amphitheatre and arena, has the fascinating necropolis of Les Alyscamps in a lovely setting. The tree-shaped promenade of Les Lices creates a relaxed atmosphere for the many open-air cafés. Van Gogh famously lost his sanity here, in the sun-dappled cafés and neighbouring heat-swirled fields.

Provençal life

Coming east again, **St-Rémy-de-Provence** is a delightful market town surrounded by vineyards, olive groves and almond trees. **Aix-en-Provence Ⓐ**, serenest of university towns, with its wonderful arcade of plane trees across the Cours Mirabeau, is the intellectual heart of Provence. Zola grew up in the

---

Maps:
France 84
Area 114

Arles is the gateway to the Camargue, a wild place of lagoons, rice fields and cowboys. In summer thousands of flamingos congregate on the lagoons, turning the water pink.

LEFT: lavender fields in Provence. **BELOW:** café concerns in Languedoc.

Tempting restaurant sign in Marseille, where seafood reigns supreme.

city along with his friend, the painter Paul Cézanne. One of the best ways to see Aix is by taking the Cézanne trail, following a free leaflet from the tourist office. **L'Atelier Paul Cézanne** (open daily; entrance charge) preserves the artist's studio and house – his cape and beret hang where he left them.

South of Aix, **Marseille ❸** is France's oldest and second largest city. Founded by Greek traders in 600 BC, the gateway to the Mediterranean, the Orient and beyond has been a bustling port for centuries. Today the **Vieux Port** has a colourful fish market and many seafood restaurants. The streets around **La Canebière**, Marseille's most famous thoroughfare which leads from the port, are the liveliest in the city, especially in the evening.

Between Marseilles and Toulon, the shore is distinguished by Les Calanques, steep-sided fjords carved out of cliffs, best viewed by boat from **Cassis ❸**. This chic resort of restored houses with a popular golden beach is famous for its fragrant white wines which tantalises the palate with savours of rosemary, gorse and myrtle – the herbs that cover these hills.

The Côte d'Azur

The sun-drenched Côte d'Azur meanders lazily from **Toulon ❹**, home to France's Mediterranean naval fleet, to the Italian border along rocky lagoons and coves. An amphitheatre of limestone hills at Toulon screens the deep natural harbour, one of the Mediterranean's most attractive. Modern **Hyères ❺**, east of Toulon along the coast, is made up of a *vieille ville* and a newer area of modern villas and boulevards with date palms. This was once an ancient and medieval port, but it is now 4 km (2 miles) from the sea. Hyères was the first "climatic" resort on the Côte d'Azur, its sub-tropical climate encouraging sailing, scuba-

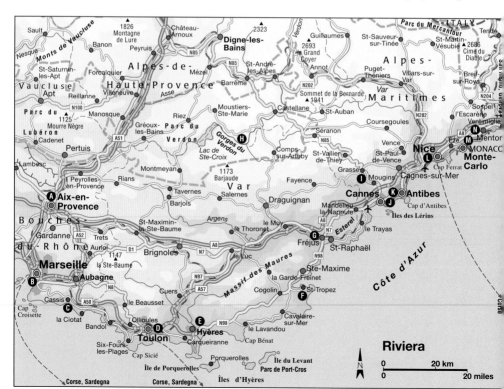

Riviera

0   20 km

0   20 miles

diving, wind-surfing and water-skiing. Within the old town, entered via its 13th-century gate, is the **Place Massillon**, where there is a food market every day that is especially good for Arab and Provençal specialities.

The once-tiny fishing village of **St-Tropez** receives up to 10,000 visitors in summer, becoming a sort of Mediterranean extension of Paris, with all that this implies for parking and prices. French painters and writers had discovered it by the late 19th century; some of these early paintings, showing the village in its unspoiled state, are on display in a converted chapel, the **Musée de l'Annonciade** (open Wed–Mon; entrance charge).

The plateau town of **Fréjus** **G**, like Hyères, used to lie on the sea. Its name derives from *Forum Julius*; it was founded by Julius Caesar in 49 BC as one of the important trading centres of Transalpine Gaul. Important Roman ruins here include the 10,000-seat arena where Picasso used to watch bullfights.

Alpine retreat

For fewer crowds and more countryside, head north into the hills to the **Gorges du Verdon** **H**, France's Grand Canyon. The Verdon cuts through limestone cliffs which plunge to the torrent 600 metres (2,000 ft) below. From here stretch the Alpes de Haute Provence, a wild, barren landscape leading up into the French Alps. Heading back to the coast, stop off at **Grasse** **I**, where there have been perfume distilleries since the 16th century. The **Musée International de la Parfumerie** (open June–Sept: daily; Oct–May: Wed–Sun; entrance charge), housed in an elegant 18th-century mansion, relates the history of perfume manufacture. You can also see a remarkable collection of perfume bottles and smell the perfumed plants themselves in a rooftop greenhouse.

Hermès label at the Musée International de la Parfumerie.

BELOW: the palm-fringed beach at Cap d'Antibes.

Modern sculpture at the Fondation Maeght.

BELOW: *Venus sculpture by Renoir at Cagnes-sur-Mer.*

The International Film Festival held each May in **Cannes ❿** is one of the highlights of an annual chain of events that attracts a set of celebrities few other cities of its size in the world could take in their stride. Kings and queens of all kinds and persuasions, sheikhs, film stars, emperors and the fabulously wealthy are all grist for a mill that has been grinding since Lord Brougham, the Lord Chancellor of England, was stranded in Cannes in 1834 because of an outbreak of cholera in Nice, where he was headed for a winter holiday. It pleased him so much that he built a house on the side of **Mont Chevalier** and encouraged other British aristocrats to do the same. **Le Suquet** is the ancient quarter around Mont Chevalier. At dinner hour in the high season, elegant women in pearls and Parisian evening gowns and gentlemen in tuxedos emerge on to the streets, perhaps from a yacht anchored in the old harbour, and struggle up **Rue St-Antoine** to the fashionable restaurants for which the Suquet is noted.

Dinner will almost certainly be followed by a stroll along the luxurious **Boulevard de la Croisette** for the magnificent views of Le Suquet silhouetted against **La Napoule Bay**, with the chunky red hills of the Esterel in the background.

Antibes ⓚ and **Cap d'Antibes** face Nice and St Jean-Cap-Ferrat across the Baie des Anges (Bay of Angels). Here the magnificent yacht harbour rests at the foot of an enormous brick citadel built in the 16th century to protect the infant town from assaults by Barbary pirates. The Château Grimaldi on a terrace overlooking the sea, originally a 12th-century building but much reconstructed in the 16th, is now home to the **Musée Picasso** (open Tues–Sun; entrance charge). It contains a remarkable collection of more than 50 works painted by Picasso during his stay here in 1946, including major works such as *La Joie de Vivre* and *Antipolis Suite*.

A LEGACY OF ART

Painters have been especially fascinated by the Côte d'Azur because of its unique sunlight. The quality of the light is due largely to the Mistral, a cold, dry, strong wind that often blows in from the Rhône Valley, sweeping the sky to crystal clarity, enriching colours and deepening shadows. Earlier art of the south of France, from naive *sandos* to Roman and Greek remains, also provided the inspiration for 20th-century artists.

Matisse, Picasso, Dufy and Chagall were all devoted to the region, and the products of their fidelity are displayed in museums and private collections along the Riviera.

Pablo Picasso spent 27 creative years on the Côte d'Azur, more than half of them at **Vallauris** behind Cannes, where he established a ceramics studio, the Madoura Pottery, where copies are still sold. At the village of **Biot** between Nice and Cannes, the **Musée Fernand Léger** (open Wed–Mon; entrance charge), shaded by cypress and olive trees, houses hundreds of works by the artist, who contributed to the creation of Cubism.

Auguste Renoir spent the last 12 years of his life at **Cagnes-sur-Mer**, where his home, **Maison Les Colettes** (open Wed–Mon; entrance charge), remains exactly as it was when he died.

Artists' enclave

Matisse's **Chapelle de Rosaire** (open Tues, Thur, Sat, Sun; entrance charge) at Vence, northeast of Grasse by the D2210, is considered his masterpiece, a finely tuned synthesis of architectural elements, the most important being stained glass and the white walls on which their coloured light falls. The artist gave it much of his time between 1948 and 1951.

Directly south of Vence, the walled town of **St-Paul-de-Vence** was discovered by artists in the 1920s. They patronised **La Colombe d'Or** café, now an exclusive hotel and restaurant with a priceless collection of works originally donated by visiting artists. St-Paul itself is a perfectly formed hill village with a vista of villas and cypresses as far as the eye can see but its popularity means that its narrow winding main street becomes jammed wih visitors.

Just outside the village the **Fondation Maeght** (open daily; entrance charge) occupies a white concrete and rose brick structure designed by the Spanish architect J. L. Sert. The collection includes 20th-century paintings by Braque, Bonnard, Kandinsky, and Chagall, and several outdoor sculpture areas with works by Giacometti, Calder, Miró, Arp and others.

Map on page 114

The Fondation Maeght – a shrine to 20th-century art.

Winter haven of the British

"The English come and pass the winter here to take the cure, soothe their chronic spleens and live out their fantasies," wrote an observer of the budding Anglo-Saxon social scene in **Nice ❶** in 1775. They have been doing it ever since in increasing numbers, and justifiably take credit for establishing this city as the centre for touring the Riviera. At one time it took 15 hazardous days to cross the 1,300 km (800 miles) between London and Nice by train and ferry, the latter mostly across raging seas if contemporary commentators are to be believed. Nevertheless, by 1787, at least 115 wealthy British families had established a summer colony that marked the first blush of an enduring love affair between the English and Nice.

The Promenade des Anglais, the striking waterfront dual carriageway embellished with flowerbeds and palm trees, was originally built in 1822 by the English for easier access to the sea. Queen Victoria enjoyed her morning constitutionals along that coastal path on several occasions before the turn of the 20th century, after which time she was carried along in her famous black-and-red varnished donkey cart.

Today, the promenade skirts the pebbly Mediterranean waterfront, bedecked with luxury hotels, high-rise apartment blocks and trendy cafés. A short stroll away are the narrow winding alleyways of the **vieille ville** (old town) where the visitor gets a salty taste of medieval Provençal lifestyles, heightened by aromas of garlic, wine and pungent North African spices emanating from a succession of *couscous* parlours.

A diminishing number of plain but traditional restaurants around the flower market on the **Cours Saleya** specialise in *soupe de poissons*, and *bourride*, a native variation of *bouillabaisse*, is usually available too. *Aioli*, a rough local mayonnaise made with olive oil and crushed garlic, is traditionally served with salted codfish on Fridays.

BELOW:
flower market on the Cours Saleya in Nice.

Poster advertising the Musée Oceanographique in Monaco.

North of the old town is the **Musée Chagall** (open Wed–Mon; entrance charge), containing many of the artist's drawings and all his bronzes. The building was specially designed to house his masterpiece, *Messages Bibliques* – 17 monumental paintings depicting scenes from the Old Testament. There are also three stained-glass windows depicting *The Creation* and a 6-metre (20-ft) mosaic of Elijah in his fiery chariot.

The remains of an amphitheatre, capable of seating 4,000 spectators, and three public baths dating from the Roman occupation have been uncovered at **Cimiez**, an exclusive residential quarter of Nice, located 1.6 km (1 mile) northeast of the city centre. The archaeological treasures taken from the site are housed nearby in a 17th-century villa. In the same building the **Musée Matisse** (open Wed–Mon; entrance charge), has an extensive collection of paintings, sculpture, engravings and ceramics by the artist.

A paradise for gamblers

Many people have experienced those heady days when they get the feeling that they're worth a king's ransom. **Monte Carlo**, the ritzy resort of the principality of Monaco, is the place to put it all to the supreme test. The sumptuously decorated gaming rooms of the world's most famous gambling **Casino** are open to visitors, as is the Las Vegas-style gambling hall at the nearby **Loews Hotel**. Today's visitors seem to prefer the more relaxed atmosphere of the Loews, but Monaco's social butterflies still flutter around the famous *belle époque* wedding-cake-style Casino and its neatly trimmed gardens and terraces. The western section, the building's oldest, was built in 1878 by the same architect who designed the stately Paris Opera House. The centre section, a tiny 529-seat rococo-styled theatre, is the home of the **Monte Carlo Opera**, which was the first to sing Wagner's *Tristan and Isolde* in French. At the **Foyer de la Dance** the Ballet Russe de Monte Carlo of Sergei Diaghilev performed its controversial *avant-garde* premieres in the early years of the 20th century.

There is also the justly famous Monte Carlo National Orchestra which has premiered works by Berlioz, Ravel and Massenet. In July and August, it gives concerts at the doll's-house palace of Prince Rainier, a crenellated, part-Moorish, part-Italian Renaissance castle perched on a 61-metre (200-ft) rocky promontory jutting nearly 800 metres (half a mile) into the sea. Visitors can tour the state apartments and throne room, and the court of honour, which sports an arcaded and frescoed gallery.

Famed principality

From there, the charming ancient quarter of **Monaco** Ⓜ, tinted with Provençal pink, orange and yellow hues, is at hand. It surrounds the neo-Romanesque cathedral, which prizes its paintings by Louis Brea, the 15th-century Nice School's most renowned artist. The aquarium located in the nearby **Musée Oceanographique** (open daily; entrance charge) is one of the finest and best kept in Europe, and along with the tropical gardens, which contain a remarkable collection of different species of cactus, and grottos decked

BELOW: the view from St Martin's Gardens to Fontvieille, Monaco.

with stalactites and stalagmites, attracts more than 1 million footstrong visitors a year. A climb of 558 steps is required to view the grottos properly, so be sure to arrive wearing suitable footwear.

From the days of its early Genoese rulers, the principality of Monaco has survived as a political curiosity on the map of Europe. It exists under the protection of France but has remained a mini-monarchy of the Grimaldi family, with its own tax privileges, national licence plates and coat of arms. This tiny principality of less than 1.5 sq km (1 sq mile) and a population of 30,000, has lived down its reputation as a sunny place for shady people. Today, it dotes instead on tourists – the raw material of its biggest industry. Prince Rainier III, who hit the headlines when he married the American film star Grace Kelly and who now lives somewhat in the shadow of his headline-grabbing daughters, the princesses Caroline and Stephanie, is a no-nonsense administrator of the Casino and works hard to maintain Monaco's year-round lustre.

When photographers want to capture the full panorama of Monaco on film they trudge to the tiny village of **La Turbie**, situated behind the principality's yawning harbour. Here are the remains of one of the most impressive, yet little known Roman monuments, the **Alpine Trophy**.

In 6 BC Rome commemorated the final subjugation of the warriors of the Alps region by raising an enormous stone trophy where it could be seen from both directions far along the Aurelian Way (which ran from Rome to the Rhône). The impressive 35-metre (114-ft) Doric colonnade is still standing and the list of conquered tribes making up the inscription to Caesar Augustus has survived.

Perched villages

La Turbie is but one of a myriad of peasant villages which, during the Middle Ages and before, sprouted like eagles' nests on mountain peaks. Inaccessible and often enclosed within a protective stone barricade and fortified gate, the villages and their villagers have often shunned outsiders. But many of the more picturesque communities, such as Eze, Peille, Roquebrune and Gourdon, tolerate and even welcome tourists.

Eze, the best known because it is near the sea, is easy to reach and offers a splendid panoramic overview of much of the Côte d'Azur from its 470-metres (1,550-ft) elevation. It has an intriguing history of pirate assaults and Moorish massacres that can be traced back to the 1st century, when a colony of Phoenicians unnerved their Roman neighbours by consecrating a temple to their god Isis. The Romans quickly and violently replaced it with a monument more to their liking and religious persuasion. Perhaps this is what caught the imagination of Friedrich Nietzsche, who was inspired in Eze to write *Thus Spake Zarathustra*. Eze is noted today for the crumbling ramparts of its 14th-century castle.

Close to the Italian frontier, the 17th-century town of **Menton**  is probably the warmest winter resort on any French coast and offers one of the most typical townscapes in Provence. In the narrow, twisting, vaulted streets overhead balconies jut out over the alleyways until they almost bump balustrades.

Map on page 114

BELOW: tropical gardens at Eze.

L'Hôtel-Dieu in Beaune, which hosts its famous wine auction on the third Sunday in November every year.

To the Rhône valley

A scenic highway (N85) traces Napoleon's journey after he landed on French shores in 1815 following his Elba exile, and is known as the Route Napoleon. It begins at Cannes and goes through Grasse and on to **Grenoble** ㉓. The birthplace of Stendhal, author of *The Red and the Black*, Grenoble is the undisputed capital of the French Alps and was given a boost when it hosted the Winter Olympics in 1968. The best view of the city can be had from the **Fort de la Bastille**, which was built in the 16th century and strengthened in the 19th.

France's third-largest city, **Lyon** ㉑, lying on the Rivers Sâone and Rhone, is where southern France begins and it is a "must" for gourmets. Get here in the morning for the open-air market on the Quai Victor-Augagneur (and take side-trips to the gastronomic temple of Paul Bocuse at nearby Collonges).

Lyon is Europe's historic silk capital, and its history can be seen in the intriguing **Musée Historique des Tissus** (Cloth Museum; 34 Rue de la Charité; open Tues–Sun; entrance charge). The newly restored **Musée des Beaux Arts** (Palais St Pierre, 20 Place des Terreaux; open Wed–Sun; entrance charge) ranks next in importance to the Louvre, with an impressive collection of French and European paintings. The old neighbourhoods of **St Jean** and **Croix-Rousse** have some fine Renaissance houses linked by strange underground passages unique to Lyon, known as *traboules*.

Burgundy wine route

BELOW: glorious countryside around Clos de Vougeot, Burgundy.

Beaune ㉒ has been at the heart of the Burgundian wine trade since the 18th century, and the auction of the Hospices de Beaune in **L'Hôtel-Dieu** (open daily; entrance charge), a charity hospital historically supported by wine produced on land donated by benefactors, is still the high point in the local wine calendar. Under its spendid multicoloured roof, the long ward of the hospital contains the original sick beds. The halls off the courtyard house a collection of art work and tapesty, crowned by a magnificently detailed painting of the *Last Judgment* by Rogier Van der Weyden.

The undisputed capital of Burgundy is **Dijon** ㉓, and the wine country tour from Dijon down to Beaune goes through such illustrious "labels" as **Gevrey-Chambertin**, **Nuits-St-Georges** and **Clos de Vougeot**. The monumental **Palais des Ducs**, where the 14th- and 15th-century Dukes of Burgundy rest in grandiose tombs, is in Dijon's busy city centre. The oldest part of the palace houses the **Musée des Beaux Arts** (open Wed–Mon; entrance charge), one of the finest in France with French, German and Italian statuary and paintings from the 14th to 18th centuries.

Approximately 45 km (28 miles) northwest of Dijon, the **Abbaye de Fontenay** (open daily; entrance charge) makes for a welcome moment of peace in its 12th-century cloisters. Intended to be piously modest, without ornament of any kind, the bare paving stones and immaculate columns acquired, in the course of time, a look of grandeur.

West of here, set high on a hilltop, **Vézelay** is one of Burgundy's most spectacular monuments. The majestic **Basilique Ste Madeleine** was founded in the

9th century as an abbey; the presence of Mary Magdalene's supposed relics here made Vézelay a place of pilgrimage.

In the Jura mountains of Franche-Comté east of Dijon, the town of **Besançon** nestles in a sweeping curve of the River Doubs. The 16th-century **Palais Granville** was the aristocratic home of the Chancellor to Spanish Habsburg Emperor Charles V. The town also has an impressive 70-dial astronomical clock in the cathedral and a formidable 17th-century citadel built for Louis XIV's eastern defences.

Alsace-Lorraine

Lorraine and Alsace have been historic bones of contention between France and Germany. Here after World War I the French built the Maginot Line, an impressive line of fortifications along their eastern border. Unfortunately it was never used, for the Germans simply went round it.

Belfort owes its glory to its successful resistance against the Prussians in 1870, commemorated by the monumental lion designed by Auguste Bartholdi, creator of New York's Statue of Liberty. **Colmar ㉔** has a quiet but irresistible charm; its 16th-century houses are the very essence of Alsatian tradition. Most cherished of its treasures is Mathias Grünewald's celebrated Issenheim altar painting in the **Musée d'Unterlinden** (open daily; entrance charge).

Strasbourg ㉕ is Alsace's dignified capital and the headquarters of the European Parliament. The River Ill encircles the lovely old town where Goethe was a happy student in 1770. The graceful cathedral, with its intriguing asymmetrically erected steeple, is as inspiring as ever, particularly for its central porch and the stained-glass rose window above.

On the way from Alsace to Lorraine, stop at **Ronchamp** to admire Le Corbusier's striking chapel Notre-Dame-du-Haut, a landmark of 20th-century architecture *(see page 52)*. The mountain ridge of the **Vosges** embraces a charming countryside of forests, orchards and vineyards, among which the villages of **Riquewihr** and **Kaysersberg** are true medieval gems.

Nancy ㉖, capital of Lorraine, is graced by a beautifully harmonious main square, the 18th-century **Place Stanislas**, its palatial pavilions flanked by magnificent gilded wrought-iron gates. In the older town, the renovated houses of the Grande Rue lead to the Port de la Craffe, whose two towers and connecting bastion are impressive reminders of earlier fortifications. Along the way, the Palais Ducal houses the **Musée Historique Lorraine** and the **Ecole de Nancy**, the epitome of Art Nouveau (both museums open Wed–Mon; separate entrance charges).

Champagne

Reims ㉗ marks the start of the royal road as far as Vertus, the **Route de Champagne**. The kings of France were crowned in this city's magnificent **Cathédrale Notre-Dame**. The stained glass is superb, from the 13th-century **Rose Window** to the 20th-century windows by Chagall. The name of the region has become the generic term for sparkling wine, but genuine champagne comes only from this area. ❑

Map
on pages
84–5

The "méthode champenoise" consists of starting and controlling a second fermentation in the bottle, after careful blending of wines from different vines, by adding a sugary liqueur.

BELOW: Champagne maker displays his product.

BELGIUM

Although one of the smallest countries in Europe,
Belgium is pleasantly rich in art, history – and food

If they don't dally, drivers can cross Belgium in two hours. Zooming along highways lit with yellow sodium lights at night, rolling through deserted and drab industrial towns, they can reach the far border unaware that only a few miles away, off the beaten track, lie picturesque, medieval villages and towns that are among the best preserved in Europe.

This small country of 30,500 sq km (11,780 sq miles) has a population of 10 million people and 3½ million racing pigeons. French-speaking Walloons inhabit the south and Flemings, whose language most closely resembles Dutch, live in the north. In spite of a common interest and a small domain, they are not as neighbourly as they might be and rivalry exists between the two parts.

The country has all the ingredients for an agreeable visit: attractive beaches, lonely mountains, rivers, lakes and, towards the east, forests. Because of its relative flatness, cycling is easy and a popular hobby as well as a profession, and the heroic race ace Eddy Merckx had both Walloons and Flemings rooting for him.

Belgium also has some beautiful medieval towns, such as Ghent, Bruges and the diamond capital, Antwerp, which, with their canals and cobbled streets, are easy to explore. There is also an exceptional number of good museums housing, among other things, the works of the great Flemish painters who are a key to the story of European art. Finally (though many would say primarily) there is the cuisine which, Belgians will tell you, surpasses even that of France. Thousands of non-Belgian bureaucrats assigned to Economic Union or NATO posts in Brussels are especially grateful that the food is so good.

Although it has a distinctive flavour of its own, the country has in turn been ruled by Spain, Austria, France and Holland. It also has its own royal family, acquired in 1831 with Leopold of Saxe-Coburg who kicked off the dynasty, today headed by Albert II and his Italian-born wife Paola. Belgians are good at pageants and some of the most colourful festivals in Europe take place here. With luck, the visitor will arrive to find the flags flying high. ❑

PRECEDING PAGES: medieval Bruges, the "jewel of Flanders"; the Grand-Place, Brussels.
LEFT: masked carnival.

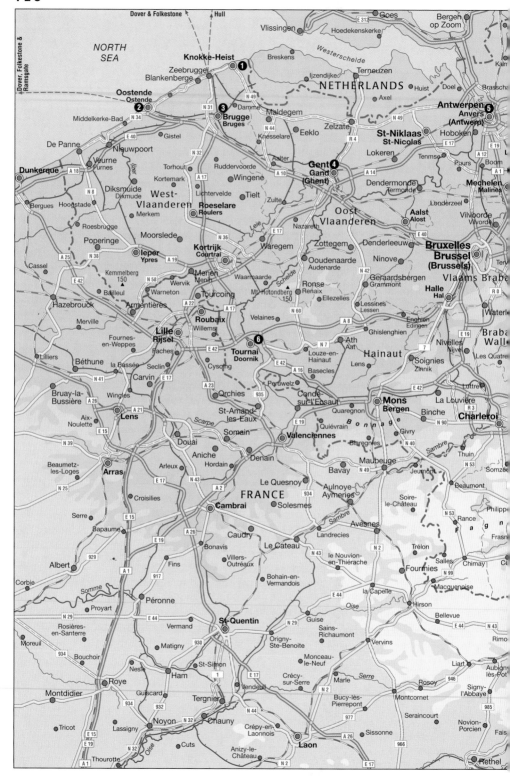

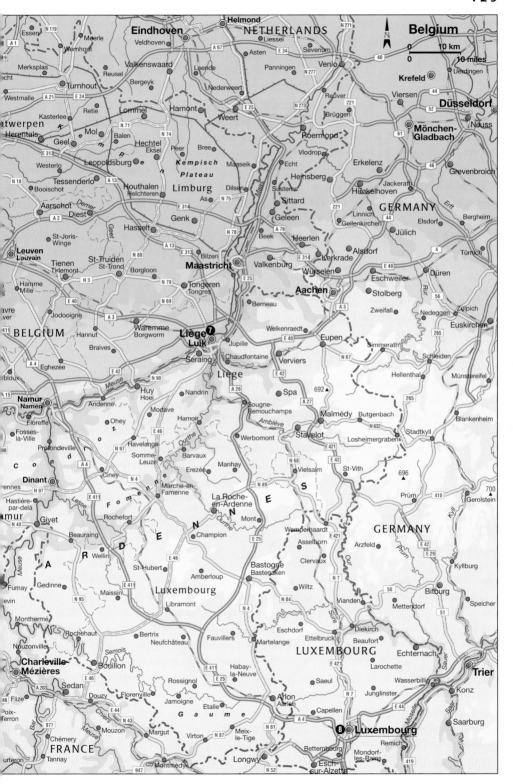

Belgium

10 km
10 miles

NETHERLANDS

Belgium

Essen · N 119 · Meerle
Wernhout
A 1
Merksplas · Reusel
Turnhout
Westmalle · A 21 · E 34
Kasterlee · Retie
twerpen · Mol · Balen · N 71
Herentals · Geel
Westerlo
Tessenderlo · A 13
Booischot
Aarschot · Demer · Diest
A 2
St-Joris-Winge
Leuven · Louvain
Tienen · St-Truiden · St-Trond
Tirlemont · N 3
Hamme · Mille
E 40
Jodoigne
avre · Hannut · Braives
ver
411 · **BELGIUM**
A 4
Eghezée
bloux
15 · **Namur** · **Namen**
Floreffe
Fosses-la-Ville
Profondeville
88 · Dinant
rennes · N 97
Hastière-par-delà
mur · Givet
N 40
Beauraing · Wellin
A · R
Fumay · Gedinne
evin · N 95 · Maissin
Monthermé
Rochehaut
Nouzonville
Charleville-Mézières
Sedan · Douzy
Flize · A 203
Poix-Terron
Chémery · Tannay
FRANCE
urteron

Helmond
Eindhoven · Veldhoven · Liessel
A 67 · Asten · E 34 · Sevenum
Valkenswaard · Leende · Panningen · N 277 · Venlo
Bergeyk · Nederweert
Lommel · Hamont · Weert · E 25
Peer · Bree
Hechtel · Eksel
Leopoldsburg
Kempisch · Maaseik · Echt
Plateau
Houthalen · Dilsen
Helchteren · As · N 75 · Susteren
Limburg
E 314
Genk · Geleen
Hasselt · N 78 · Beek · Heerlen
A 13 · E 313 · Bilzen · Valkenburg · E 314
Maastricht
Borgloon · N 79 · E 25
Tongeren · Berneau
Tongres · N 69
Waremme · Liège 7
Borgworm · Luik · Jupille · E 40
Seraing · Chaudfontaine
E 42 · Liège · E 42
N 90
Huy · Nandrin · A 26 · Spa
Hoei · Andenne
Ohey · Modave · Sougne-Remouchamps
z · Harmoir · Amblève
E 46 · Werbomont · Stavelot
Havelange · Barvaux
N 97 · Somme-Leuze
Ciney · Erezée · Manhay
N 4 · Marche-en-Famenne · Vielsalm
Lesse · E 411 · La Roche-en-Ardenne · N 89
Rochefort · Mont
Champion · E 25 · Wemperhaardt
E 46 · Asselborn
St-Hubert · Bastogne · Bastenaken
Amberloup · Clervaux
E 411 · **Luxembourg** · Wiltz
Libramont · N 4 · Vianden
Bertrix · Eschdorf · Diekirch
Neufchâteau · Fauvillers · Martelange · Ettelbruck · Beaufort
Bouillon · **LUXEMBOURG** · Echternach
E 46 · Rossignol · Habay-la-Neuve · Saeul · Larochette
Florenville · E 25 · Wasserbillig
Jamoigne · Etalle · Junglinster
G a u m e · Arlon · Aarlen · Capellen · E 44
Margut · Virton · Meix-le-Tige · N 81 · 8 Luxembourg
Mouzon · N 43 · N 87 · Bettembourg · Remich
Montmédy · Longwy · Esch-sur-Alzette · Mondorf-les-Bains
N 52

Roermond
Vlodrop
Echt
Maas · Heinsberg
Sittard · Linnich
Geleen · Geilenkirchen
Kerkrade · Alsdorf
Würselen
Aachen · Stolberg
Zweifall · Nedeggen
Welkenraedt · Eupen · Simmerath
Verviers · N 67 · Schleiden
Hellenthal
692 · 265
Malmédy · Butgenbach
N 632 · Stadtkyll
Losheimergraben
E 421 · E 42
St-Vith
696 · Prüm · 410
700 · Gerolstein
GERMANY
Arzfeld · E 42 · E 29
N 7 · Kyllburg
Vianden · 50 · Bitburg · Speicher
Mettendorf · 51
Sûre · Sauer
Konz
Trier
Saarburg

N 271
Krefeld
Viersen · 44
52 · **Düsseldorf**
Brüggen · 221 · Neuss
N 273 · **Mönchen-Gladbach** · Grevenbroich
61 · 46
Erkelenz
Jackerath
Hückelhoven
GERMANY · Erft
221 · 44 · Elsdorf · Bergheim
Jülich
4 · Türnich
Eschweiler · Düren
A 3 · 56
Zülpich
Euskirchen
265
Münstereifel
Blankenheim
40 · N

Belgium · Kempisch · Plateau · Limburg · Fomenne · ARDENNE · Condroz · Luxembourg · Gaume

BRUSSELS

In the "capital of Europe" office blocks in tinted glass squat beside Gothic churches, and Art Nouveau masterpieces are wedged between tenement blocks

Map on page 132

Here north and south, the Teuton and the Latin represented by the Dutch-speaking Fleming and the French-speaking Walloon, have been fused by hook and by crook into the Bruxellois – Europe's first urban hybrid. As befits a bilingual city, the street signs are in French and Flemish. Brussels' origins go back to a fortified castle built in the 6th century on a little island in the River Senne, one of the tributaries of the Schelde. It was first mentioned in 966 under the name of *Bruoscelle* (meaning settlement in the marshes) in a chronicle of Emperor Otto I. It flourished as a trading centre along the route from Bruges to Cologne and became politically important when Duke Philip the Good of Burgundy made it his capital in the 15th century.

Shortly after, Charles V turned it into the capital of the Spanish Low Countries, later to be dominated by the Austrians, the French and the Dutch. The independence movement of 1830 against the Dutch finally gave the country its own identity. With the progress of parliamentary democracy, the Belgian monarchy today plays a representative and ceremonial role, along the lines of their English cousins, though far less aloof.

Historic core

The heart of Brussels is the **Grand-Place ❶**. Belgians call it the most beautiful square in the world and many visitors agree. Here, every day except Monday, a flower market is held and once a year the square is carpeted with flowers. Brussels' markets are famous and everything can be found on their stalls, from the local lace to caged birds. Seven alleys lead into the Grand-Place and its spectacle of lavishly decorated Flemish-Baroque Guild Houses. Dating from between 1695 and 1699, the facades appear to have been stamped from the same mould. Each one is different, however, yet blends harmoniously with the others.

Dominating the Square is the **Hôtel de Ville ❷** (Town Hall) with a 15th-century Gothic spire. It climbs into the sky like the minaret of a mosque. Inside, fine tapestries decorate the walls. After a lengthy renovation, the spire has been cleaned and regilded, with the old statue of St Michael (the city's patron) replaced by a new copy.

Opposite the Town Hall is the **Maison du Roi** (King's House), though no king ever lived there. Behind it begins **Ilot Sacré**, the labyrinth of alleys and arcades dotted with pubs, boutiques and restaurants. Outside, crabs, shrimps, mussels, shellfish, sea urchins, squid and cuttlefish are laid out extremely appetizingly on ice and framed with lemons and parsley. Inside, the flame of an open fireplace in winter, or a cool fan in summer, provides a welcome.

LEFT: Grand-Place.
BELOW: Manneken Pis.

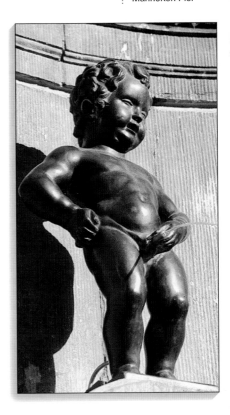

Brussels beer sign.

Brussels' leading exponent of Art Nouveau was Victor Horta (1861–1947). He pioneered the concept of total design, creating furniture, carpets and wall decorations as well as the overall design of a building.

Legendary duke

For centuries the people of Brussels have shown a particular affection for **Manneken Pis ❸**, the bronze statuette of a little boy relieving himself into the fountain at the corner of **Rue de l'Etuve** and **Rue de Chêne**, in the city centre. It incarnates the irreverent spirit and humour of the Bruxellois.

Legend claims he represents Duke Godfrey III. In 1142, when only a few months old, the baby duke was brought to the battlefield at Ransbeke and his cradle was hung from an oak to encourage the soldiers, dejected by his father's death. At the decisive moment, when his forces were about to retreat, the young duke rose in his cradle and made the gesture reproduced later at the fountain. This, so legend goes, encouraged his troops to victory. However, a rival legend maintains that the statuette commemorates the little boy whose action inadvertently extinguished a time bomb intended to blow up the Town Hall.

Going down the Rue au Beurre from the Grand-Place you come to the **Bourse**, the city's Stock Exchange, a Neo-classical building dating from 1873. Here the business heart of Brussels throbs. From the end of the bustling **Petite Rue des Bouchers** in the Ilot Sacré, it is only a stone's throw to the exclusive glass-roofed shopping arcades of the **Galeries Saint-Hubert**.

The Upper City

The monumental **Cathédral St-Michel ❹** (open daily; free) rises majestically on the hillside between the Upper and Lower City. It was built from the 13th to the 15th century, and recent excavations have only just revealed the Romanesque crypt. The stained glass within the cathedral is particularly fine; the west window offers a remarkable depiction of *The Last Judgement* from 1528.

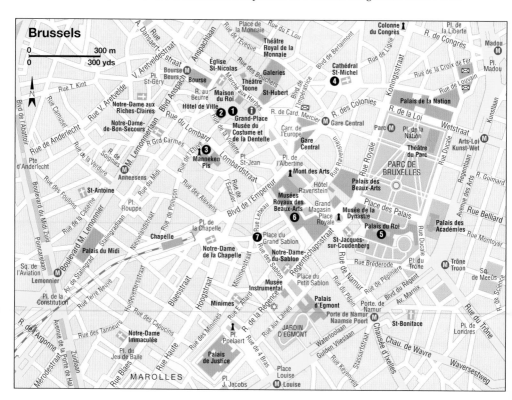

Crossing the elegant **Parc de Bruxelles** brings you to **Place Royale**, which had a facelift in the 1990s. The square is bordered by **Saint-Jacques-sur-Coudenberg**, a graceful Neo-classical church inspired by a Roman temple, and the newly restored Art Nouveau **Old England** department store. The dignified but dull **Palais du Roi ❺**, just off the square, was built in 1820, almost a century after an earlier royal household burned down. This is where King Albert II conducts his official business.

Place du Musée

Adjoining Place Royale are the **Musées des Royaux des Beaux-Arts ❻** (open Tues–Sun; entrance charge), Belgium's finest collection of art treasures. The well-designed and interconnected collections are distributed between the **Musée d'Art Ancien** and the **Musée d'Art Moderne**. The former has a superb collection of Flemish and Dutch masters from the 15th to the 19th centuries, including works by Rembrandt, Hals, Rubens, van Eyck and Hieronymus Bosch. The latter, with modern paintings and sculpture from the 19th and 20th centuries, is centred on a well of light which illuminates the eight underground storeys. Highlights are masterpieces by Belgian Surrealists Magritte and Delvaux, as well as works by Ensor, Permeke and the Flemish Expressionists.

From here, the Rue de la Régence leads to the **Place du Grand Sablon ❼** which, with its magnificent High Gothic church of **Notre-Dame-du-Sablon**, marks the location of a number of antique shops. The **Place du Petit Sablon**, surrounded by 48 bronze statuettes representing traditional trades, is opposite. Further south is the **Palais de Justice** (Law Court), its courts and 103-metre (337-ft) cupola occupying an area bigger than St Peter's Square in Rome. ❑

Map on page 132

In 1999 a new **Magritte Museum** *opened in the artist's former home in Jette, North Brussels (135 Rue Esseghem; tel: 323-449 6614), with a permanent collection of his work.*

BELOW: bird market in the Grand-Place.

ROYAL GLASS CITY

The Royal Domain lies in the outlying district of Laeken, to the north of Brussels. The magnificent botanical gardens and greenhouses have earned the domain the title of "glass city". Although the Château Royal is not open to the public, the domain is crowded with curious monuments and memorials. Leopold II extended the palace and embellished the park with two oriental follies, a Chinese pavilion, with a priceless collection of oriental porcelain, and a Japanese pagoda (both open Tues–Sun).

But the crowning glory of the park was the creation of the **Serres Royales**, the Royal Greenhouses, in 1875 (open for one week in late Apr–early May). Attributed to Alphonse Balat and the young Victor Horta, they present an architectural treasure comprising a huge central dome, topped by an ironwork crown and flanked by a secondary chamber, cupolas, turrets and vaulted glass tunnels.

To the northwest of the park is the **Atomium**, a gigantic model of an iron molecule. This curious monument was designed by André Waterkeyn, a professional engineer, for the World Exhibition in 1958, its dynamic frame symbolising the potential of Belgian industry in the postwar period. Visitors are conveyed around the structure by escalators inside the tubes connecting the nine spheres.

AROUND BELGIUM

Map
on pages
128–9

*A country with two languages and two clashing cultures,
Belgium is far from predictable. But its people have
an infectious taste for the good things in life*

Brussels●

Belgium is not, as some would have it, a "pancake", except along its 65-km (40-mile) coastline washed by the North Sea. A wide ribbon of golden sands begins at **Knokke-Heist ❶** on the Dutch border and stretches down to **De Panne** on the French frontier. The shallow beaches are safe but more suited to family holidays than water sports. They are perfect for ball games and the spectacular hybrid known as sand-yachting. The biggest and best known of the nine coastal resorts is **Oostende ❷**, where the ferries from Britain disgorge their cargoes next to a romantic fishing and yacht harbour.

The best of the Flemish towns lie at varying distances off the road on the leisurely drive from Oostende to the capital, Brussels *(see pages 130–133)*. The route runs alongside shipping canals, lazy rivers and rolling hills, past moors, heaths and lakes and through fir and pine woods. The countryside of **Kempen** is dotted with churches. The peal of bells is a commonplace sound in Flanders.

Preserved medieval city

Bruges (Brugge) **❸**, the *grande dame* of the cities of Flanders, serves as a window on to Belgium's history. Miniature bridges over its delightful canals, gabled houses and verdant lawns have helped the city to retain a medieval atmosphere reminiscent of the time when it was one of Europe's greatest trade centres and held to be one of the most beautiful cities in the world. Bruges declined as the reputation of its rival, Antwerp, increased. Having never spilled over its 13th-century fortifications, the city, with its magnificent Gothic **Stadhuis** (Town Hall) and medieval cloth hall with an 88-metre (300-ft) **Bell Tower** (open daily; entrance charge), has become a kind of museum. By the Town Hall is the **Basilica of the Holy Blood**, containing a reliquary carried in a procession through the city on Ascension Day.

Bruges is also famous for its Flemish art. Some of the finest paintings of the Flemish school are exhibited at the **Groeningemuseum** (open Apr–Sept: daily; Oct–Mar: Wed–Mon; entrance charge), among them Jan van Eyck's controversial portrait of his wife, with the astonishingly high coiffure, and his *Canon Van Der Paelen* kneeling before the Virgin. Michelangelo's *Virgin and Child* is another prized exhibit. The newly restored **Memlingmuseum** (open daily; entrance charge) is a medieval hospice containing graceful and radiant works by the Flemish Primitives.

Five km (3 miles) north of Bruges nestles the little village of **Damme**, where white windmills stand on green meadows beside tree-flanked canals. **Wingene**, 16 km (10 miles) south of Bruges, is noted for its biennial September beer festival which commemorates the 16th-century painter Pieter Bruegel.

LEFT: Basilica of the Holy Blood, Bruges.
BELOW: musician in Liege.

Rubens' "Descent from the Cross" in Antwerp.

Try the self-guided Rubens and van Dyck walks around Antwerp (tel: 03-255 10 13 for details).

BELOW: canal trip in historic Bruges.

Ghent (Gent) ❹ is the city of 200 bridges and criss-crossing canals. The old medieval centre is dominated by the church of Saint Nicholas, with its Gothic belfry and 52-bell *carillon* (a mechanical bell-ring device). Next to the flamboyant Town Hall is **St-Baafskathedraal** (St Bavo's Cathedral; open Mon–Sat; entrance charge), which houses the Van Eyck brothers' masterpiece, *The Adoration of the Holy Lamb*, known as the Ghent altarpiece.

The road to Antwerp leads past **Mechelen**, the city of belfries and carillons and home of Belgium's only school for bellringers. At the church of Our Lady of the Dijle is the Rubens masterpiece *The Miraculous Catch of the Fishes*, and at St-Janskerk is another Rubens, *The Adoration of the Magi*.

City of diamonds

Antwerp (Antwerpen) ❺ is Europe's third largest port. At one time, its maritime traffic – 100 ships a day and 2,000 barges – surpassed even that of Venice in its heyday. But the city lost its leading role as a trade centre in the 17th century when, under Spanish rule, its wealthy merchants fled to Holland to escape the Inquisition. The home of Peter Paul Rubens (1577–1640), Antwerp has become the centre of Flemish art and culture. The **Kathedraal** (open daily; entrance charge) is Belgium's biggest and most magnificent religious building. The art collection at the **Koninklijk Museum voor Schone Kunsten** (Royal Museum of Fine Arts; open Tues–Sun; entrance charge) covers hundreds of years of Flemish art – both classical and modern. Antwerp was known as the "City of Diamonds" for its role as the cutting and trading centre of the world's diamond industry. The **Provincial Diamond Museum** (Lange Herentalsstraat 31) offers a glimpse into the world of hot rocks and diamond cuts.

WATERLOO

The road south from Brussels leads to a location where a watershed in European history took place: **Waterloo**. On 18 June 1815, just south of this small town, the combined Prussian and British forces imposed the final defeat on Napoleon Bonaparte after his escape from Elba.

From the town it is about 3 km (2 miles) to the site of the battle. During the nine-hour carnage 55,000 soldiers died, 32,000 of them French. The vast battlefield is now tranquil farmland and the only reminder of the battle which changed the face of Europe is the lofty memorial standing on **Butte de Lion** (Lion Mound; open daily; entrance charge). The butte rises to a height of 45 metres (147 ft), and is surmounted by a 28-tonne lion. The view from the top is extensive, and most of the tactical sites of the battle can be picked out across the landscape.

Napoleon spent the night of 17 June in a farmhouse south of the battlefield at Le Caillou. The farmhouse now houses the **Musée Provincial du Caillou** (open Tues–Sun; entrance charge), containing mementos relating to the battle and the Emperor's life. Back in the town, souvenirs and T-shirts all bear the image of Napoleon, who has been immortalised by the locals. There are no souvenirs of the Duke of Wellington, nor of the Prussian Marshal Blücher.

Southwest of Brussels is the royal residence and capital of medieval France, **Tournai ❻**. It is famous for its five-towered Romanesque cathedral of **Notre Dame**. The **Musée des Beaux-Arts** (open Wed–Mon; entrance charge) has many examples of modern art as well as paintings by Rogier van der Weyden and Rubens. **Mons**, east of Tournai, is another venerable Wallonian city. Its **Singe du Grand-Garde**, a little cast-iron monkey, supposedly brings luck if kissed.

The Ardennes

Namur, known as the Gateway to the **Ardennes**, is dominated by a huge rocky peak which is the site of a 17th-century citadel accessible by cable car. The green woods of the Ardennes, the hills where some of the great battles of World War II took place, lie to the south. The most famous confrontation occurred during the winter of 1944–45 at **Bastogne** where outnumbered US forces held out against a German counter-offensive in what has become known as the **Battle of the Bulge**. The offensive cost the lives of 77,000 American soldiers and their sacrifice is commemorated at the **Mardasson Liberty Memorial** and a nearby museum commonly referred to as "Nuts" – the reply the American commander General McAuliffe gave the Germans when asked to surrender.

In the eastern corner of Wallonia, near the German border, is **Liège ❼**, birthplace of one of Belgium's famous sons, Georges Simenon, creator of the Maigret detective series. This city of craftsmen has established a wide reputation for Val-St-Lambert crystal, exquisitely designed jewellery and quality sporting guns. The **Musée d'Art Moderne** (open Tues–Sat; entrance charge), in the Parc de la Boverie, has an impressive collection of painting and sculpture from 1850 to the present, including works by Chagall, Ensor, Gauguin, Magritte and Picasso. Internationally recognised as one of the best museums of its kind, the **Musée d'Armes** (open Wed–Mon; entrance charge) contains 12,500 different weapons.

North of Liège is the province of Limburg, a pleasant agricultural region where **Tongeren** is the oldest town in the country, founded by the Romans in the 1st century AD.

Luxembourg past and present

In the extreme southeast of Belgium is the Province of Luxembourg, a rugged region of forests and valleys whose capital, **Arlon**, an old Roman settlement, is the site of a beautiful castle and an archaeological site. The local **Luxembourg Museum** (open Mon–Sat; entrance charge) contains Roman remains of great importance. Tombstones from the 2nd century depict life before the advent of Christianity.

This region of the Ardennes was the western part of the **Grand Duchy of Luxembourg** before it became part of Belgium. The eastern part of the Grand Duchy is now Europe's smallest independent nation, Luxembourg. The capital, called **Luxembourg ❽**, like the state (the total population is approximately 305,000), was once an important fortress called "The Gibraltar of the North". It is now the seat of several European Community bodies and an international banking centre, thanks to its low taxes. It is also the smallest member of NATO. ❑

Bouillon, in the southern Ardennes, has a spectacular setting in the plunging valley of the River Semois, and has Belgium's finest medieval castle (open daily; entrance charge).

BELOW: hirsute humour.

THE NETHERLANDS

*The picturesque Dutch landscapes seen in paintings
by the Old Masters are a timeless reality*

The Netherlands is a small country. Stretching over 15,892 sq miles (41,160 sq km), more than half of its area lies below sea level and almost one fifth is covered by lakes, rivers and canals. Building dykes, barriers and dams is a full-time occupation and no other nation is so acutely aware of the dangers of global warming. While the country is flat, a lush greenness is everywhere and the skies are sometimes filled with the silvery lumines-

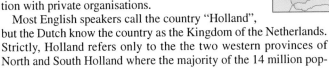

cence so distinctive in classic Dutch landscape paint-ing. Of more than 10,000 windmills that once helped pump the land dry and featured so prominently among the favourite subjects of artists, about 1,000 remain. They are now regarded as national monuments and have been restored by the government in co-opera-tion with private organisations.

Most English speakers call the country "Holland", but the Dutch know the country as the Kingdom of the Netherlands. Strictly, Holland refers only to the the two western provinces of North and South Holland where the majority of the 14 million pop-ulation lives.

The capital, Amsterdam (pop: 750,000), is in this region, along with Rotterdam, Europe's largest port, and the administrative capti-tal of The Hague (Gravenhage, or Den Haag in Dutch), where the European Court of Justice sits. The venerable university town of Leiden is here, as well as Delft, famous for its blue pottery, and Edam, famous for its cheese.

The 10 provinces that make up the rest of the country are surpris-ingly varied. Zeeland in the south is a region of islands, peninsulas, sandy coastlines and bird-filled marshes which a series of huge bar-riers prevent from flooding. The Catholic southern provinces have a more flamboyant architecture and wooded hills. Heath, woodlands and orchards mark the northern provinces and in Drenthe, in the northeast, the wilder landscape is dotted with megaliths.

The dense network of interurban train or bus services offers a swift, comfortable means of transport in the cities while a car or even a bicycle is a good idea for the country. Exploring this varied country is made easier by the network of tourist information centres (known by the initials VVV), which are found in virtually every town. As well as handling bookings for accommodation and entertainment, they are an excellent source of local information.   ❑

PRECEDING PAGES: windmills lining the Kinderdijk; the Netherlands' favourite form of transport.
LEFT: selling fresh fish at Bunschoten.

Netherlands

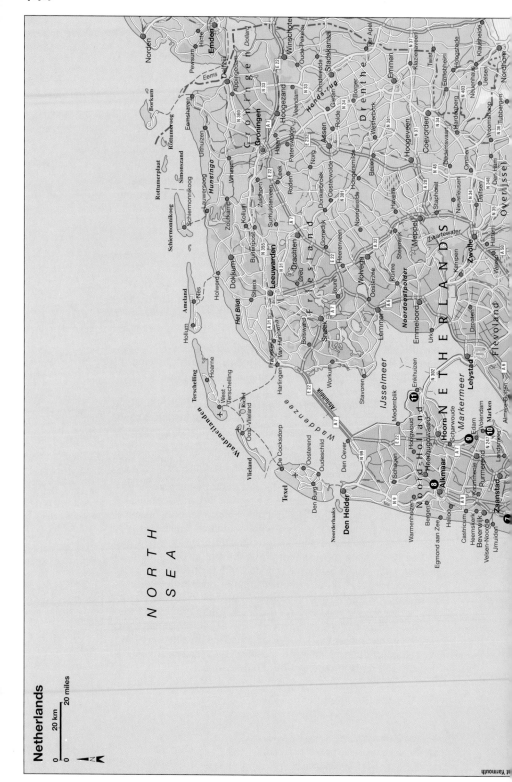

AMSTERDAM

This "city of museums" has the vitality of a modern metropolis while keeping a satisfying sense of age and continuity, plus a sense of fun

Map on page 148

T he first impression of Amsterdam may be its museum-like quality. Indeed, 6,700 buildings in the core of the city are protected monuments, virtually intact from the Golden Age of the 17th century, during which time the city rose to spectacular wealth, political power and cultural heights. Amsterdam's navy dominated an era when prosperity depended on ships opening trade routes to the West and East Indies. Profits from these ventures provided funds for the growth of a compact city built around a dam that had been placed on the Amstel River in the 13th century. Historic models for the modern Dutch character are common-sense merchants and businessmen, rather than inaccessible monarchs and ethereal clerics. The city's monuments tend to be private houses rather than imposing public buildings.

Amsterdam, as a museum, is not at all stale. Here one can find a gourmet Indonesian rice table dinner, a lively and safe night life, Europe's largest selection of antiques, some world-famous cheeses, the great paintings of the Golden Age (especially Vermeer, Rembrandt, and Frans Hals), extensive sidewalk café-idling and some exquisite flowers. To see all this requires only a good pair of walking shoes.

LEFT: Zuiderkerk.
BELOW: a Dutch woman of Indonesian extraction.

Amsterdam's horseshoes

A good point to begin is at the indispensable **VVV** (the Dutch Tourist Information Office) opposite the **Centraal Station ❶**. From here, the main street, **Damrak**, leads to the **Dam**, a large square that is the hub of the canals and also the site of **Koninklijk Paleis ❷** (Royal Palace; open June–Sept: daily; also Easter & Oct school holidays; entrance charge). Built in 1665 on 13,659 piles, it is now used for diplomatic receptions, with parts of it open to the public. Also situated in the square is the **Nieuwe Kerk ❸** (New Church), dating from 1400, where the Dutch monarchs are crowned. The fine interior may be admired during concerts held throughout the year. Follow Warmoesstraat from Dam square to the **Oude Kerk ❹** (Old Church), Amsterdam's oldest building and the best preserved of all its churches. The 13th-century tower is still intact, and some of the stained-glass windows date from the 16th century.

Amsterdam, built on a design of expanding horseshoe canals that fit one within the other, is unlike other cities. On a map, with the railway station at the top, the smaller numbers for canal streets begin at the upper left-hand corner and then become progressively larger as the canal swings down and then up to the right hand corner. Among more than 1,000 bridges, the **Magere Brug** (Slender Bridge), dating from 1670, is one of the more notable.

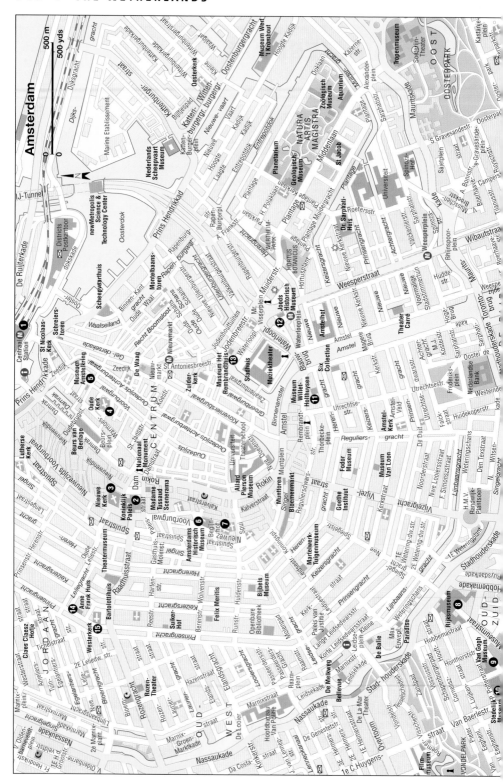

Map on page 148

The **Museum Amstelkring** ❺ (Oudezijds Voorburgwal 40; open daily; entrance charge) contains the finest of the city's "clandestine" churches, concealed within a 17th-century merchant's house. After the Alteration, when Amsterdam became officially Protestant, Catholics were forced to worship in secret. The top floors of three gabled houses were linked to form two galleries with space for up to 400 worshippers.

Once the city orphanage, **Amsterdams Historisch Museum** ❻ (Nieuwezijds Voorburgwal 359; open daily; entrance charge) chronicles the city's history and development with paintings, furniture and cleverly juxtaposed artefacts. Highlights include *het groei carte* ("growth map"), which traces Amsterdam's growth over the centuries, and the 16th-, 17th- and 18th-century group portraits of the civic guards. The adjoining **Begijnhof** ❼ is Amsterdam's finest almshouse court and one of the city's most spiritual enclaves. Reached through a number of inner courtyards, it comprises a series of brick and stone gabled houses built between the 14th and 17th centuries to house the Begijntjes, a lay Catholic sisterhood. *Het Houten Huys*, at No. 34, is the oldest house in Amsterdam, built in around 1460.

TIP

Take a tour of the canals by boat to get a sense of what the city was like before modern roads were built. Boats depart from several embarkation points opposite Centraal Station, along Prins Hendrikkade, the Damrak and Rokin.

BELOW: exhibit in the Stedelijk Museum.

An abundance of art

It is a quarter-hour walk from the Dam to the redeveloped **Museumplein** and the **Rijksmuseum** ❽ (open daily; entrance charge; tel: 020-674 7000), the repository of much of Amsterdam's great art from the first half of the 17th century. Among more than a million art objects the star attractions must be the incomparable Dutch Masters, notably Rembrandt, Jan Vermeer, Frans Hals, Jan Steen, Pieter de Hooch and Jacob van Ruisdael. Vermeer's paintings include his deeply felt and quiet works of everyday events such as *Young Girl Reading* and *A Maidservant Pouring Milk*. Rembrandt is well represented with, among many others, *The Jewish Bride*, *Syndicate of the Drapers*, and *The Nightwatch*, a group portrait which dominates the Gallery of Honour on the top floor.

From the Rijksmuseum it is a short walk to the **Van Gogh Museum** ❾ (open daily; entrance charge; tel: 020-570 5200). The permanent collection focuses on Van Gogh's painting, and the artist's development can be traced from the haunting animalism of his early *Potato Eaters* to the swirling hallucinogenic brilliance of his later *Sunflowers*. A new wing was added in 1999 and is used for changing exhibitions. Its strikingly modern design, incorporating a titanium roof and wall, is by Japanese architect Kisho Kurokawa.

The **Stedelijk Museum** ❿ (open daily; entrance charge; tel: 020-573 2911) displays work from the mid-19th century to the present. Exhibitions from the permanent collection change constantly, but artists such as Chagall, Braque, Matisse and Mondrian are represented, as are works by contemporary artists like Jan Dibbets, Ren Daniels and Stanley Brouwn. Major restoration work is planned during 2001–2, including the addition of two new wings.

To the west of the Museumplein the **Vondelpark** offers a refuge for joggers, cyclists and dog-walkers. In summer there are lively conerts and dance events.

The popular Anne Frank Huis, where Anne began her diary in 1942.

BELOW:
strolling in Damrak.

A tour of the Jewish Quarter

Leidseplein plunges you back into the lively humanity of Amsterdam. This square is a busy tram intersection and buzzes both night and day with street performers and a plethora of bars, nightclubs and cinemas.

Walking through the open-air museum of Amsterdam's architecture doesn't, unfortunately, reveal anything of the insides of the canal houses. A good opportunities to see behind the buildings' facades presents itself along **Herengracht**. At the **Museum Willet-Holthuysen** ⓫ (Herengracht 605; open daily; entrance charge), you can see the interior and furnishings of a 17th-century canal house. Coal magnate Pieter Holthuysen left the house to his daughter Sandrina and her husband Abraham Willet in 1858. The luxurious house is full of the paintings, glass and silver that the couple collected.

Cross over the Amstel via the Blauwbrug, then follow Nieuwe Amstelstraat to reach the **Joods Historisch Museum** ⓬ (Jonas Daniel Meijerplein 2–4; open daily; entrance charge), a complex of four former Ashkenazic synagogues which opened as a museum in 1987. Exhibitions trace the spread of Judaism throughout the Netherlands, culminating in the devastation of World War II and the Holocaust. In 1945 the nearby **Zuiderkerk** (South Church) was turned into a temporary morgue for Jews killed in Nazi raids.

At No. 4 Jodenbreestraat is the **Museum Het Rembrandthuis** ⓭ (open daily; entrance charge), where the artist lived from 1639 to 1660. The mansion contains 250 of his drawings and etchings, including various self-portraits and portraits of his wife, Saskia.

For an insight into life in Amsterdam during the Occupation visit the **Anne Frank Huis** ⓮ (open daily; entrance charge) at No. 263 **Prinsengracht**. This

CAFÉ LIFE

The Netherlands has a long café tradition. Some claim that the first bar opened its doors in Amsterdam in the 13th century when two men and a dog in a boat drifted ashore on the marshy bamks of the (then) river IJ. By the 17th century there were countless taverns in the city.

Traditional brown cafés (so-called because walls and ceilings have turned brown from age and smoke) are identified by dark, cosy, wooden interiors. The only sounds are the buzz of lively conversation and the tinkle of glasses. Coffee is generally brewed, not machine made, and if you fancy a snack to go with your beer or spirit, there is usually a plate of olives or cheese. These cafés define the Dutch word *gezelligiheid*, which means a state of cosiness or conviviality. This is where locals come for a few beers after work, to play cards, engage in political debates and tell tales. Two of the best brown cafés are **De Tuin** (2e Tuindwarsstraat 13) in the Jordaan to the northwest of the city, and **'t Doktertje** (Rozenboomsteeg 4) near the Begijnhof.

The more elegant and sylish grand cafés serve lunch and desserts and tend to have high ceilings, more light, reading tables and a variety of music. If you are in search of high culture, call in at the **Café Americain** (Leidseplein 28) to luxuriate in Art Nouveau splendour.

is where the teenager and her family hid from the Nazis in World War II, until they were caught and sent to their deaths at the Bergen-Belsen concentration camp. This moving and popular museum underwent renovation and expansion in 1999; it now includes a bookshop, café and resource centre, and visiting conditions have been much improved, as has the interpretation of Anne's diary.

The **Westerkerk** ⑮ nearby dates to 1630. It was renovated in 1990 and is the city's finest church, a masterpiece in Dutch Renaissance style.

Red lights and bright lights

Amsterdam has a low crime rate and is a relatively safe place, even after dark. At night the roads along the canals are lit and make for engaging routes to walk along. The Slender Bridge, also lit up at night, is one of Amsterdam's loveliest sights. The bawdy **Zeedijk** section of the city, where prostitution is an open and government-sanctioned activity, is Amsterdam's contribution to the world's oldest profession and provides an eye-opening diversion for any visitor.

On balmy nights the outdoor cafés along the Rembrandtsplein and Leidseplein throb with life. Disco, jazz and folk music flourish in small clubs. The **Melkweg** entertainment complex (Lijnbaansgracht 234) is the prime location for a blend of African bands, "alternative" discos and world music, while **Paradiso** (Weteringschans 6) offers more mainstream music along with unknown up-and-coming bands.

Amsterdam's famous music hall, the **Concertgebouw** (Concert Hall), to the south of Museumplein, offers a range of musical performances from the city orchestra to rock concerts.

Amsterdam's markets

Shopping in the city is easily done on foot and there are many intriguing stores tucked down side streets. The **Kalverstraat** is the busiest shopping street in the city and **P.C. Hooftstraat**, near the Leidseplein, is one of the most elegant. Amsterdam is a centre of the European antique market and **Spiegelstraat** and **Nieuwe Spiegelstraat** (leading to the Rijksmuseum) house more than 20 antique shops. Asian antiquities, old Dutch tiles, Art Deco objects, Russian icons and pewter are just some of the specialities here. The city is also a leading centre for the cutting, polishing, and mounting of diamonds. **Coster Diamonds**, near the Rijksmuseum, offers an interesting diamond workshop tour and shop.

Amsterdam is justly famous for its open air markets. The most elaborate is the **Waterlooplein** market in the heart of the Jewish Quarter, selling clothing, jewellery, wood carvings and bric-a-brac. The **Albert Cuypmarkt** in the south of the city is another lively outdoor market with a wide variety of food and merchandise, including fish, poultry, cheese, fruit and vegetables as well as clothes. It is an especially good place to sample a Dutch delicacy – raw herring with chopped onion. Watching a native eat a herring reveals how it should be done. The **Bloemenmarkt** on the Singel is still one of the best places to go for fresh cut flowers, and also sells bulbs and tubers. ❑

Map on page 148

Map on page 148

TIP

Indonesian restaurants abound in Amsterdam and can offer good value meals. The *rijsttafel* (rice table) is a tasty variant on the sweet and sour theme, consisting of a large bowl of rice and perhaps 15 condiment dishes of meat, fish, fruits, nuts and vegetables.

BELOW: horse-drawn carriage at Koninklijk Paleis.

AROUND THE NETHERLANDS

The historic cities of the Randstadt give way to North Holland's old fishing communities and the former royal hunting forests of Gelderland

Map
on pages
144–5

L ess than 99 km (61 miles) from Amsterdam is **Den Haag ❶** (The Hague), home of the royal family and also the seat of the Dutch Parliament and of many foreign embassies. In the **Vredespaleis** (open Mon–Fri; entrance charge), a Neo-Gothic structure donated by Scottish-American Andrew Carnegie, sits the International Court of Justice of the United Nations. The Hague, with a population of about half a million, is the third largest city of the Netherlands, often referred to as "Europe's largest and most elegant village" because of its pleasant residential character.

The historic centre was built around the **Binnenhof**, the Inner Court of the castle of the counts of Holland. The 13th-century **Ridderzaal** (Knights' Hall; open Mon–Sat; entrance charge), is now only used for ceremonial purposes. Behind the Ridderzaal a gateway leads to the **Mauritshuis** (Korte Vijverberg 8; open daily; entrance fee), where the Royal Cabinet of Paintings has a choice collection of Flemish, Dutch and German Old Masters. Among the treasures in this handsome building are such outstanding works as Rembrandt's *The Anatomy Lesson of Dr Tulp* and Vermeer's *View of Delft*. Wandering through the Mauritshuis, you are inevitably struck by the impressive views of the **Hofvijver**, all that remains of the castle moat. A pleasant walk around the lake brings you to **Schilderijengalerie**, also known as Galerij Prins Willem V (open Tues–Sun; entrance charge), the oldest picture gallery in the Netherlands with a packed collection of Dutch Old Masters.

An eclectic collection of modern painting and decorative art is on display at **Haags Gemeentemuseum** (Stadhouderslaan 41; open Tues–Sun; entrance charge), built by H.P. Berlage, the founder of Dutch modern architecture. The museum is renowned for both early and late works by Piet Mondrian as well as its collections of Delftware and musical instruments.

The seaboard

Holland's oldest bathing resort on the North Sea is **Scheveningen ❷**, which now forms a suburb of The Hague. The promenade is dominated by a modern pier and the *belle-époque* architecture of the **Kurhaus** hotel. All year Scheveningen offers fresh air, a choice of sports and entertainment and a fashionable casino staffed by 200 croupiers. At the **Scheveningen Sea Life Centre** (open daily; entrance charge) you can walk through an underwater tunnel to experience life on the seabed without ever getting wet.

The traditional role of the Netherlands as a maritime trading nation is illustrated by the port city of Amsterdam and the world's busiest harbour at **Rotterdam ❸**. The volume of containerised freight shipped out from here, the barge traffic chugging up

LEFT: Keukenhof at the height of the bulb season.
BELOW: traditional costume in Marken.

Skilled artisan at work in Delft.

BELOW: enjoying the sun in Edam.

the River Rhine (Rhein) into Germany, and the shipbuilding and ship repairing is stunning. The entire harbour can be explored from the vantage point of an excursion boat, complete with a guide pointing out the sights in four languages.

Another vantage point from which to view the harbour and the city is the **Euromast** (open daily; entrance charge). The observation tower with a height of 185 metres (600 ft) is the landmark of modern Rotterdam. During the German invasion of May 1940, the historic centre of the city as well as the harbour suffered heavy damage from a bombing raid. That's why Rotterdam today appears as the most modern city of the Netherlands.

The **Museum Boymans van Beuningen** (open daily; entrance charge), standing on the edge of the **Museumpark** on the west side of the city centre, houses one of the best art collections in the Netherlands. Its permanent exhibitions include Flemish masterpieces by Hieronymus Bosch and Pieter Bruegel the Elder, Rembrandt's tender portrait of his son Titus, and 19th- and 20th-century canvases by Monet, Van Gogh, Kandinsky, Magritte and Dalí.

Just 26 km (16 miles) west of Rotterdam lies **Hoek van Holland** (Hook of Holland) ❹, the traditional ferry harbour which has become part of the greater port of Rotterdam. The car and rail ferries leave from here for Harwich on the east coast of England (from where it is an hour's journey by rail to London).

University town

Leiden ❺ is a likeable university town, full of cafés and student bookshops. The **Stedelijk Museum De Lakenhal** (Oude Singel 28–32; open Tues–Sun; entrance charge), occupying a 17th-century canal-side cloth hall, traces the history of the town and also stages temporary exhibitions of modern art.

An extensive collection of archaeological finds from the Netherlands, ancient Greece, Rome and Egypt are displayed at the **Rijksmuseum van Oudheden** (Rapenburg 28; open daily; entrance charge). The centrepiece of the collection is the mysterious floodlit Temple of Taffel, which was presented to the Dutch people by the Egyptian government

The pleasant, picturesque town of **Delft** ❻, midway between the Hague and Rotterdam, has changed little over the centuries. In the Middle Ages it was a weaving and brewing centre but an explosion of the national arsenal in 1645 destroyed much of the medieval town. The distinctive blue-and-white pottery for which the town is famous was developed from majolica introduced by Italian potters in the 16th century. Tours of local factories are available, where you can also buy reasonably priced Delftware.

Lovers of classical Dutch painting should not miss a trip to **Haarlem** ❼, the provincial capital of North Holland. Here, in the **Frans Hals Museum** (Groot Heiligland 62; open daily; entrance charge), one can study the incisive group portraits that Frans Hals painted of the Dutch at a time when the nation was at the height of its economic and political power.

He shows the faces with a marvellous complexity of character. Each is a bundle of motives, a worldly person possessed of few illusions, sometimes cynical but often ingenuous. The uniqueness of Haarlem's Frans

Hals Museum extends beyond this superb collection. The structure itself, a Dutch Renaissance building begun in 1608, was designed as a home for old men. Later it became an orphanage, and in 1913 the museum was established. Artists in Hals' immediate milieu are also represented.

Map on pages 144–5

Cheese market

North of Haarlem is **Alkmaar ❽**, a pleasant old town with tree-lined canals and a traditional cheese market, held every Friday morning in summer, The town of **Edam ❾**, 22 km (14 miles) northeast of Amsterdam, was once an important whaling town but is now famous for its round cheeses, which are produced by farms on the fertile Beemster and Purmer polders. Edam cheeses can be bought in the 16th-century Waag (weigh house) on Waagplein.

The Zuiderzee used to be a part of the North Sea, before a dyke built in 1932 transformed it into a freshwater lake, the present-day **IJsselmeer**. **Volendam ❿**, on the western shore of the lake, was a Catholic village, and nearby **Marken** was its Protestant counterpart. Residents of both towns have their distinctive costumes, now worn largely for the benefit of visitors who are drawn here by the old-world character of the two towns.

The Zuiderzee's history is vividly presented at the **Zuiderzee Museum** in **Enkhuizen ⓫** (open Apr–Oct daily; entrance charge). Traditional fishing boats and pleasure craft are displayed in a waterfront Dutch Renaissance building (the Binnenmuseum), while the outdoor museum (the Buitenmuseum) can only be reached by boat. Its focus is a reconstruction of old fishing communities, made up of around 130 buildings rescued from the towns around the Zuiderzee, some of them shipped intact across the IJsselmeer.

BELOW: inland sea of the IJsselmeer.

At the flower auctions in Aalsmeer.

Tulipmania

In the early 17th century, newly acquired bulbs from Turkey produced a "tulip-mania" which swept the country. The tradition of bulb production and flower growing has flourished ever since. Worldwide distribution by air from Schiphol was introduced in the 1950s. Today, 36 countries buy 4 billion Dutch bulbs each year. A visitor can enjoy this floral world by touring the flower regions west of Amsterdam in the blooming time – the 28-hectare (70-acre) wooded park of **Keukenhof** just outside Lisse is one of the most spectacular.

Alternatively, you can go to the flower auctions held daily in **Aalsmeer** ⓬ 10 km (6 miles) south of Amsterdam, where flowers grown under glass are sold. From the public balcony one watches the carts of flowers being brought in and the 2,000 buyers sitting below. A huge clock-like bidding wheel starts with a price higher than expected and then swirls around slowly to a lower bid.

City of churches

BELOW: Drenthe's timeless byways.

Utrecht ⓭ is one of the oldest cities in the Netherlands, founded by the Romans in AD 47 to protect an important crossing on the Rhine. The **Oudegracht** (old canal), lined with brick quays and cavernous cellars that now house restaurants and bars, winds its way through the city. The **Domtoren** (cathedral tower) is one of the architectural marvels of the Gothic age. Built between 1321 and 1383, it rises to an ethereal octagonal lantern 112 metres (376 ft) high.

All that remains of the **Domkerk** (open daily; free), begun in 1254, are the choir and transepts – the nave came crashing down during a freak hurricane in 1674. The skyline of Utrecht was once a mass of spires, though many of the city's other churches were also toppled by the hurricane.

The Veluwe

Bounded in the north by the former Zuiderzee coastline, the Veluwe is dominated by wild heather, pines, heathland and sand dunes. The main attraction of this popular holidaying area is the **Nationaal Park De Hoge Veluwe** (open daily; entrance charge). Once royal hunting territory, it still has miles of forests that are rich in wildlife.

At the centre of the park is the exceptional **Rijksmuseum Kröller-Müller** (open Tues–Sun; free with park entrance ticket), a striking glass-walled structure housing a magnificent collection of 278 of Vincent Van Gogh's paintings and drawings as well as works by other modern European masters such as Mondrian, Seurat, Redon, Braque and Picasso. A fabulous sculpture park in the grounds has pieces by, among others, Rodin, Moore, Paolozzi and Hepworth.

Royal hunting lodge

The town of **Apeldoorn** ⑮, to the north of the Veluwe, is nothing to write home about, but just outside is one of the loveliest of Dutch palaces, **Paleis Het Loo** (open Tues–Sun; entrance charge). It was built by William III, Stadholder of the Netherlands and King of England and Scotland, in 1692 as a hunting lodge, and generations of the House of Orange used it as a summer palace. The interior and gardens, now restored to their former opulence, constitute a museum tracing the history of the House of Orange-Nassau.

Arnhem ⑯, south of the Veluwe, will always be associated with the Allied paratroopers who landed here in September 1944 in an attempt to invade Germany and end the war. At the beautifully kept **Oosterbeek War Cemetery**, 8 km (5 miles) west of Arnhem, lie the remains of 1,748 Allied troops. ❑

Map on pages 144–5

TIP

The best way to explore the Nationaal Park De Hoge Veluwe is on one of the hundreds of white bikes that visitors can borrow for free.

BELOW: souvenir shop in Volendam.

COUNTRY PURSUITS

Though the Netherlands is the most densely populated country in Europe, it has beautiful countryside. The coastline is a 290-km (180-mile) stretch of sandy beaches with some 55 seaside resorts. Off the north coast is a string of five islands, called the **West Friesians**, which can only be reached by boat from the naval port of **Den Helder**.

Zeeland, a cluster of islands linked to the mainland by dykes and dams, is Holland's sunniest spot, with beaches, nature reserves and cycle trails. A fitting destination for the naturalist, the bird watcher or the photographer is **Drenthe** which, after Zeeland, is the least populous Dutch province. An abundance of wild flowers and picnic areas, set amid the small lakes called *vennen*, allure the traveller.

The provincial capital of **Assen**, a two-hour train ride from Amsterdam, is the starting point for a day or more of driving or cycling through the 300 km (170 miles) of bike trails and numerous back country roads. The prehistoric stone burial mounds called *hunebedden* are scattered throughout this northeastern province and are worth a visit. The largest of the 51 sites is at **Borger**. Witnessing these large boulder burial houses (or "giant beds", as the word translates), which Stone Age or Bronze Age people built to commemorate their dead, is an awesome experience.

GERMANY

*The cities are strong in culture, but it's the picturesque villages
and countryside that linger in the memory*

Germany is the financial and industrial powerhouse of Europe.
But behind the skyscrapers and beyond the industrial ribbon of
the Rhur, castles and countryside remain romantic and alluring.
East and west may have unified when the Berlin wall came down in
November 1989, but the land the country occupies today is still made
up of peoples of greatly differing origins and characters. At the two
extremes are the sombre upright Prussians of the north,
personified in the spike-helmeted Bismarck, and the
jolly Bavarians of the south who are represented in
lederhosen and chamois hats swilling foaming tankards
of beer. In between is the Swabian who lives in a neat
cottage and keeps his carefully washed Mercedes in a
garage, the Ruhrgebiet miner who keeps pigeons in the
colliery loft, and the Lower Saxony cattle farmer who
warms his damp days with glasses of schnapps.

They are bound together by many common elements, of politeness and punctuality and also an enjoyment of each other's company. An old saying runs: "One German makes a philosopher, three
Germans make a club." And it is true that throughout the country
people love forming and joining non profit-making clubs, for hob-
bies, for sports, for charities or neighbourhoods, electing presidents,
treasurers, secretaries and committees.

The difference between east and west is marked in the cities. Urban
areas that came under the influence of the east have grown up in
dull slabs, though many of those in the west also had to be substantially rebuilt after World War II. The 21st century presents an opportunity to visit Germany's eastern cultural centres – Potsdam, Dresden
and Weimar – once more, as well as unspoilt coasts.

It is easy to travel to any spot in Germany. The major cities have
airports, but it is just as practical to travel by the intercity trains
which link some 50 cities every hour, and the high-speed ICE trains
have reduced travel time dramatically.

For a country that produces some of the world's most prestigious
cars, it is not surprising that the road systems are good. But Germany's 13,600 km (8,500 miles) of motorway make the network one
of the densest in the world and summer visitors should be prepared
for delays. If the *autobahn* pace becomes a bit nerve-racking, the
secondary roads, which lead from one picturesque village to another,
offer an alternative. You may arrive at a small country festival, which
shows that Germans are good at organising their fun, not just at the
explosive springtime Carnival in the Rhine or the October beer
festival in Munich, but at any time of the year. ❑

PRECEDING PAGES: Berlin's Brandenberg Gate; a thirsty gathering at Munich's
Oktoberfest.
LEFT: biker with attitude.

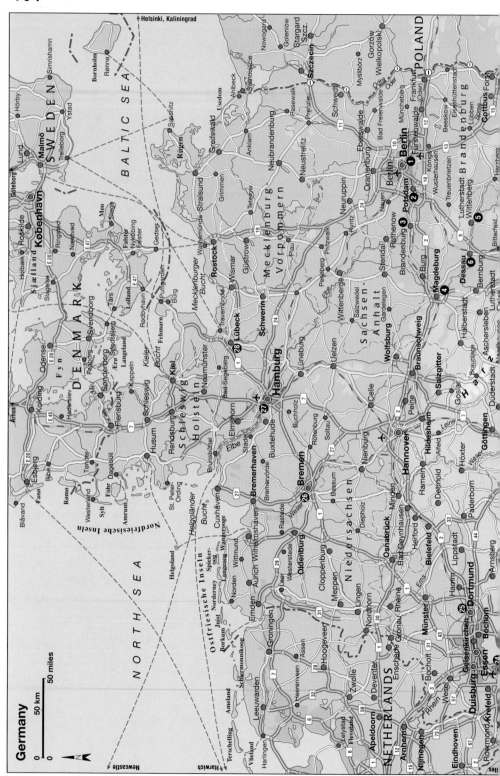

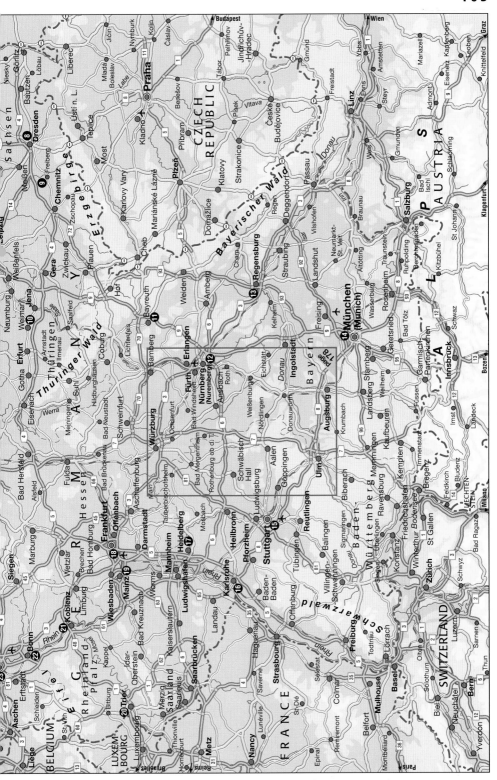

BERLIN

*Germany's government has returned to its pre-war home.
The reunited city has responded by rediscovering the excitement
that first made it one of Europe's most vibrant capitals*

Map on page 168

Berlin

Germany's re-established capital is once more a single city, but it still remains to its inhabitants a divided place. Virtually nothing is left of the Wall, but the division between the two halves of the city is a psychological scar that has yet to heal. It will take time, too, before the city finds architectural harmony: the flashy west, particularly around the famous Kurfürstendamm shopping street, contrasts with the more sombre former east, where there is much building in progress, not least to take account of the new spaces required to house the Bundestag (parliament) which will return to a refurbished Reichstag beside the Brandenburg Gate.

But the east, which encompassed Berlin-Mitte, the old city centre, is by no means a poor relation. Beyond the Brandenberg Gate is the elegant **Unter den Linden** boulevard, which has begun to usurp the position held by the Ku'damm as *the* street for taking a stroll, while **Friedrichstrasse** is busily making up for lost years by becoming the smart business address. And one of the liveliest districts in the city is **Schenenviertel**, further east.

There are many ways of getting around the city. The centre is not large and the public transport system is easy to use, but one of the best ways to get an idea of the place is by boat. Regular trips encircle the city, passing through Tiergarten, the city's popular park, going around the monumental buildings on **Museum Island** in the former east, and travelling down the River Spree.

LEFT: coffee break on the Ku'damm.
BELOW: strolling on Unter den Linden.

A decadent street

Usually known as the Ku'damm, **Kurfürstendamm**, which means "The Electors' Road", only emerged 100 years ago. From the 16th century it was a broad track leading out to the country, serving as a bridle path for the electors who rode out from the royal palace in the direction of Grunewald to go hunting.

Only with Germany's rapid industrial expansion in the late 19th century did the street begin to take shape. Inspired by the Champs Élysées in Paris, Bismarck decided that he wanted just such a boulevard for the new capital of the *Reich*. Building work proceeded in "Wilhelmenian" style: generous, ornate and even florid; truly representative of the age. Proverbial Prussian frugality suffered its heaviest defeat at the hands of the Kurfürstendamm.

By the 1920s the Kurfürstendamm had become the place where everything considered bohemian was on offer. The most famous meeting-place was the Romanische Café, situated where the austere Europa-Center now stands. In 1933 all the colourful goings on were abruptly halted and, with the victimisation of Jews, the traditional centre of entertainment had become the stage for a *danse macabre*.

TIP

If you want to do some
shopping and also
want to get away from
the Ku'damm's large
international chain
stores, try the little side
roads. Bleibtreustrasse
and Schlüterstrasse, in
particular, offer a large
choice of boutiques.

The street was all but wiped from the map in World War II but, during the post-war years, it became a symbol of Western prosperity and acquired a dazzling night life. It was significant that on the night following the collapse of the Wall, it was to the Ku'damm that most East Berliners flocked.

Shopping options

At the eastern end of Ku'damm is **Breitscheidplatz** with the ruins of the **Kaiser-Wilhelm-Gedächtniskirche** (Memorial Church) ❶ and its blue-glazed rebuilt version. Since 1983, particularly in the summer, all sorts of people have tended to gather around the **Wasserklops**, a huge fountain created by the sculptor Schmettau which stands next to the **Europa-Center** ❷. This modern shopping complex is one of the tallest buildings in Berlin. A lift takes visitors to a viewing platform some 20 storeys up, from which there is a fine view of the city. Inside, meals are overpriced and a casino tries to emulate Monte Carlo: it is a good place to head for when it's raining, but only when you're prepared to splash out. More stylish is **KaDeWe**, the "Store of the West" on the adjacent **Wittenbergerplatz**, Berlin's Harrods.

In the side streets, called **Off-Ku' damm**, are some of the better restaurants, cafés and pubs. The city has more than 8,000 places to eat and drink, more than any other city in Germany. Entertainment of a cultural nature can be enjoyed in the evening by booking seats for the **Schaubühne** ❸ on Lehniner Platz. Originally in Kreuzberg, this theatre made a name for itself through the brilliant productions of its director, Peter Stein. Although this is one of the city's best theatres, since moving into its technically perfect new site, performances have tended to lack their former experimental vivacity.

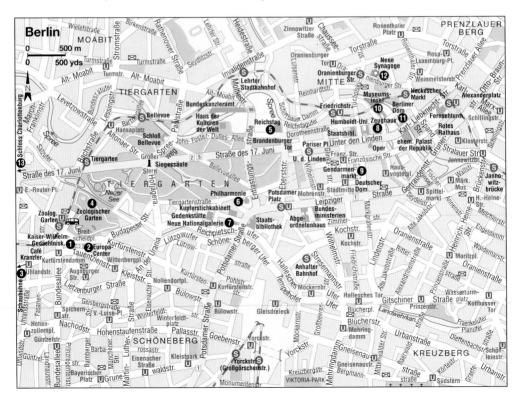

Map on page 168

Breathing space

The city is surrounded by many lakes and open spaces, such as the **Grunewald** forest to the west, where there are lakes and bathing beaches. In the middle of the city is the 212-hectare (525-acre) **Tiergarten**, a wonderful park where many Berliners spend time at the weekends. The **Zoologischer Garten** (Zoo; open daily; entrance charge) ❹ is just west of the Tiergarten. It is one of the largest zoos in the world and home to around 14,000 animals. Its aquarium houses more than 8,000 fish.

In the centre of the park is the 67-metres (223-ft) Victory Column, built in 1873 to commemorate the Prussian victory over the Danes nine years earlier. From here there is a grand view down to the **Brandenburg Gate**. On the north side of the gate on the edge of the park is the **Reichstag** ❺, built in the 19th century in Italian Renaissance style, which has taken its place once more as home of the national parliament. Its dome, destroyed in the famous fire of 1933 and left ruined during the post-war rebuilding, has been redesigned.

On the south side of the Tiergarten is the **Philharmonie** concert hall ❻ made famous by its conductor, the late Herbert von Karajan, and the **Musikinstrumentenmuseum** (Museum of Musical Instruments; open Mon–Sat; entrance charge), with more than 2,500 instruments. The **Neue Nationalgalerie** ❼ (New National Galerie; open daily; entrance charge) in Tiergarten has Realist, Impressionist and other modern works. It was completed in 1968 after designs by Ludwig Mies Van Der Rohe (1866–1969) of the Bauhaus movement, and there is a separate **Bauhausmuseum.**

At the entrance to Berlin's zoo.

BELOW: the revamped Reichstag building.

Historical centre

The Brandenburg Gate leads on to Under den Linden and the centre of the city, **Berlin-Mitte**. Since its inauguration in 1791, the Gate has been a symbol of the fate of Germany. Napoleon marched through it on his triumphant way to Russia, and slunk round it on his humiliating retreat. The Quadriga, the goddess of victory on her chariot drawn by four horses on top of the Gate, was stolen in 1806 but brought back in triumph by Marshal Blücher eight years later.

Barricades were erected at the Gate during the German Revolution of 1848. Kings and emperors paraded here. The revolutionary crowds of 1918 streamed through it on their way to the palace to proclaim the republic. The Nazis also staged their victory parades through the Brandenburg Gate but, following their downfall in 1945, Soviet soldiers hoisted the Red Flag on the Quadriga. Following the construction of the Berlin Wall, the entire area around the monument was cordoned off, both from the east and the west. After the collapse of the Wall, the Gate became a symbol of the hopes and expectations of a united Germany.

The most Prussian of Berlin's streets is undoubtedly the **Unter den Linden,** which leads from the Brandenburg Gate towards the heart of old Berlin. Strolling down this elegant boulevard today, the ambience of the old metropolis is almost tangible. On the left of the street going east are the monumental buildings of the **German State Library** and the **Humboldt**

Daniel Libeskind's acute-angled Jewish Museum (9–14 Lindenstrasse, Tues–Sun 10am–8pm, free, tel 2599 3410) contains an extensive collection of artefacts and artworks relating to German Jews.

BELOW: life on Kurfürstendamm.

University. Berlin-Mitte is more than just royal Berlin. It is also fascist and socialist Berlin. It was opposite the university, the old Opern Platz, now renamed Bebel Platz, where the Nazis burnt more than 20,000 books in 1933. The **Forum Fridericianum**, round this square, is graced with structures from every epoch. There is the baroque **Zeughaus** ❽, the old arsenal, decorated with 22 warriors' death masks, which is now the **Deutsches Historisches Museum** (open Thur–Tues; entrance charge), with exhibits from the Middle Ages to reunification in 1990. The **Deutsche Staatsoper** (Opera House) was conceived in classical style, but has been renovated and rebuilt so many times that it now bears little resemblance to the original edifice. Behind it is **St Hedwig's Cathedral**, which is based on the Pantheon in Rome.

In the Nikolai District the **Church of St Nicholas**, Berlin's oldest edifice dating from the 13th century, was rebuilt during the 1970s in exemplary fashion, but the buildings around the church square were converted into doll's houses, into a Berlin "Disney World".

Schinkel's legacy

The imposing classical structures conceived by the 19th-century architect Karl Friedrich Schinkel (1781–1841), which transformed the city into "Athens on the Spree", testify eloquently to the fact that Berlin once ranked among the most beautiful European cities. It is open to debate which of Schinkel's buildings is the most beautiful. Some maintain that it is the **Schauspielhaus** (theatre) on the **Gendarmenmarkt** ❾. Framed by the German Cathedral and the French Cathedral, the entire square is an aesthetically perfect ensemble. Others point to the **Neue Wache** near the university on Unter den Linden as being Schinkel's

Map on page 168

most complete work. It was his first building in Berlin, and it certainly possesses the harmony of classical simplicity. In GDR days, soldiers of the People's Army goosestepped in front of the Neue Wache, which served as a memorial to the victims of fascism and militarism. As the Central Memorial of the German Federal Republic, its role has now changed to commemorate the victims of both world wars.

Museum Island

A third favourite candidate for Schinkel's masterpiece is the **Altes (Old) Museum** on **Museumsinsel ❿** (Museum Island; all museums open Tues–Sun 10am–6pm; entrance charges). This is, indeed, his most impressive building. Inside and out it was entirely designed to serve its purpose, namely to display works of art. But then the whole Museum Island is, in both form and content, an extraordinary artistic ensemble. It takes more than an afternoon to visit the **Altes** (Old) and **Neues** (New) **museums**, the **Alte Nationalgalerie** (Old National Gallery), the **Pergamon Museum** and the **Bode Museum**. Their treasures from antiquity are wonderful. Chief among them is the Altar of Zeus (180–160 BC) from Pergamon in Turkey, which gave the museum its name. It also has the throne room facade from Nebuchadnezzar II's Babylon and the tiled market gate (604–562 BC) from Miletus. The Bode Museum has Egyptian and Graeco-Roman collections.

Berlin Cathedral **⓫** is a monument to the Wilhelmenian expression of splendour. The nearby equestrian statue of Frederick the Great looks beyond the Television Tower, which dominates everything on Alexanderplatz, to the Palace of the Republic. Originally built in 1866, the **Neue Synagoge ⓬** in Oranienburger Strasse was rebuilt after being bombed in World War II. It served the largest Jewish community in Europe, who lived around the synagogue in the **Scheunenviertal** district to the north of Museum Island. This has once more become one of the liveliest areas of the city, with a thriving art scene and many bustling cafés and restaurants.

Art collections

Art lovers will wish to visit the **Kulturforum** on Potsdammer Platz (open daily; entrance charge), whose Painting Gallery has examples of every Western art movement up to 1800 and includes work by Canaletto, Caravaggio, Giorgione, Mantegna, Rafael, Rubens and Titian. The Prints and Drawings Collection is the finest in Germany, with many works by Dürer and Rembrandt. The centre also has an arts library, a Gallery of Applied Arts and a copperplate etching museum.

The finest house in the city is the baroque **Charlottenburg Palace ⓭** (open daily; entrance charge) to the west of the centre. Originally built in 1695 as a country house for Sophie Charlotte, Queen of Prussia, it was elaborated in the 18th century. The Historical Rooms have been fully restored and the New Wing built under Frederick the Great contains more paintings by Jean-Antoine Watteau than any other gallery outside France. In the palace grounds are the **Museum of Antiquity** and the **Egyptian Museum**. ❏

TIP

The English-language Info-Line, tel: 2090 5555, has details on the museums on Museum Island, as well as information on special exhibitions, opening times and entrance fees.

BELOW: Berlin Cathedral from the Spree Canal.

AROUND GERMANY

From the sparkling vineyards of the Rhine to the fairytale castles of the Romantic Road, Europe's leading industrial nation has a rich variety of historic sites

Map on pages 164–5

Berlin

Visitors to **Berlin ❶** *(see pages 167–171)* should also take in **Potsdam ❷** and **Sanssouci** (open Tues–Sun; entrance charge), the palace which Frederick the Great designed himself in 1744. Here he patronised the arts and entertained his famous guest, the French philosopher Voltaire. Today tourists flock to Sanssouci, which has 12 gloriously decorated rooms and a 290-hectare (717-acre) adjacent park. Left of the main alley the gold of the **Chinese Tea House** reflects the sunlight. At the end of the long path is the **Neues Palais** (New Palace), a typical example of royal architecture, which was the home of Frederick the Great's household and guests towards the end of his reign. Nearby there is the impressive **Charlottenhof Palace**, designed and built in classical style by Schinkel for Friedrich Wilhelm IV, as were the atmospheric **Roman Baths**. The Renaissance-style **Orangery** is on the other side of the park.

Through the Harz

The journey from Berlin through Saxony-Anhalt to Leipzig is a series of contrasts. In the Harz, the picture-book landscape is one of half-timbered houses and fine Romanesque buildings. The industrial present takes over in Halle, while Leipzig is clearly a busy city currently being rebuilt after decades of neglect. **Brandenburg ❸**, straddling the river Havel, flourished in the 14th and 15th centuries as a centre for trade and the manufacture of cloth, but its importance declined followed the rise of Berlin as the residence of Friedrich Wilhelm, the Great Elector. Today, the townscape is dominated by the steel industry but some gems, such as the Cathedral, remain. Medieval in origin, it was transformed into a Gothic basilica in the 14th century but still has some medieval stained-glass windows.

Magdeburg ❹, the capital of Saxony-Anhalt, is easily the biggest inland port in eastern Germany. The city suffered extensive damage during World War II but many Romanesque buildings survive, including **Unser Lieben Frauen Kloster** (Monastery of Our Lady, 1064–1160), which now serves as a concert hall.

Approaching **Lutherstadt Wittenberg ❺** from the west the first impression is of the **Schlosskirche**, whose dome looks like a well-fitting crown. It was to the door of this church, on 31 October 1517, that Martin Luther posted his 95 Theses against the Catholic practice of indulgences, which eventually led to the Reformation.

The Bauhaus school

Dessau ❻, on the main route between Berlin and Leipzig, was home to the Bauhaus school of architecture from 1925 until the Nazis put a stop to it in 1932; in 1977 the town reopened the **Bauhaus Build-**

LEFT: Heidelberg from the Philosophenweg. **BELOW:** Bavarian national costume.

Decorative plaster-work in the Church of St Nicholas, Leipzig.

BELOW: the Zwinger Palace, Dresden.

ing as a museum (open Tues–Sun; entrance charge). Other examples of Bauhaus architecture around the town incude the old labour exchange on August-Bel-Platz designed by Gropius, the Bauhaus housing estate with the Cooperative Building in the Törten district, and the Meisterhäuser in Elbert-Alee.

Dessau's heyday was in the time of Prince Leopold Friedrich Franz von Anhalt-Dessau (1740–1817), who surrounded himself with artists, poets and architects and established an English-style country park at **Scloss Wörlitz**. Over 800 varieties of trees are planted among winding paths, canals, artificial lakes and antique sculptures. The art collection here includes works by Averkamp, Rubens and Canaletto. The grounds are dotted with various buildings, such as an Italian farmstead, a Greek temple, a Gothic folly and a palm house.

With the founding of its university in 1409, **Leipzig** ❼, already an important trading centre, also became a cultural enclave, attracting such influential students as philosophers Leibnitz and Nietzsche, and the poet Goethe. The latter named Leipzig "Little Paris", and with a population of just under 500,000 it was the second largest city of the former GDR. In 1930 the population was around 700,000, but the division of Germany hit the city hard. Today the streets are fast returning to their former elegance. The exquisite interior of the **Church of St Nicholas**, begun in the 12th century, is testament to the city's former wealth. The **Church of St Thomas**, home of the Thomaner Choir, was founded in around 1212 and assumed its late-Gothic form in the 15th century. At first the choir consisted of only 12 boys who sang at the Mass, but soon they went on to sing at church and state ceremonies. Johann Sebastian Bach (1685–1750) became choirmaster and organist in 1723 and wrote most of his motets for this choir. More can be learnt about Bach's life in the **Bach Museum** (open Tues–Thur; entrance charge).

The most beautiful city in Germany

Dresden ❽ will forever be associated with the devastating bombing campaign of 14 February 1945, when almost the entire city centre was destroyed. A great deal of rebuilding has been done since then, however, to restore the city's epithet of "most beautiful city in Germany". In 1485 the Albertine succession, the Saxon line of the ruling Wettin family, elevated Dresden to royal status. No visitor should miss the **Zwinger Palace**, a masterpiece of German baroque built between 1710 and 1732. The original design was based on the orangery at Versailles, but the complex of pavilions, galleries and gardens grew to take up an enormous area. The **Gemäldegalerie Alte Meister** (Old Masters' Art Gallery; open Tues–Sun; entrance charge) is the most important of several galleries in the complex, holding 2,000 works of art, including *Sistine Madonna* by Raphael and Rembrandt's *Self portrait with Saskia*.

The **Albertinum** close by was built as an armoury but is now home to a variety of collections. The most famous is the **Grünes Gewölbe** (Green Vault; open daily; entrance charge), with jewellery, precious stones and paintings belonging to the Saxon princes. Further collections include the **Galerie Neuer Meister**, with 19th-century masterpieces by Gauguin and Caspar David Friedrich, the **Sculpture Gallery** (ancient and modern pieces) and the **Coin Collection**.

Dresden's environs are no less appealing than the city itself. A visit to **Pillnitz Palace** (open Wed–Mon; entrance charge), the opulent summer residence of Augustus the Strong (1670–1733), makes a pleasant day trip. With its sweeping pagoda-like roofs, it is an important example of the Chinese style so fashionable at the time. A large collection of camellias imported from Japan in 1770 provides a riot of blossom in the spring.

Map on pages 164–5

TIP

To get a feel for the city of Dresden, take a trip on the Elbe in one of the excursion boats (Sächsischen Dampfschiffahrtsgesellschaft, Terrassenufer 2; tel: 0351-5023877).

LEFT: ancient sculpture in the Albertinum.
BELOW: the Zwinger Palace in Dresden.

Goethe and Schiller still dominate the cultural landscape of Weimar.

The mountain range bordering the Czech Republic to the southwest of Dresden is known as the Erzgebirge (Ore Mountains), where minerals such as lead, tin, silver and iron ore have been extracted since the 12th century. The silver mining town of **Freiberg ❾** was the richest town in Saxony until the 15th century, dwarfing even Dresden and Leipzig, and some of the town's buildings, such as the 15th-century town hall and cathedral, still display its former wealth.

In the footsteps of Goethe

Further west is **Weimar ❿**, the natural starting point for any journey across the Thuringian Forest. From the mid-18th century Weimar was the hub of German cultural life. Goethe (1749–1832) became privy councillor of the duchy of Saxony-Weimar-Eisenach 1775, and later served as education minister and director of the Weimar theatre, where he came into contact with playwright and poet Friedrich Schiller (1759–1805) with whom he shared a close friendship.

Weimar is home to **Goethe's House** (open Tues–Sun; entrance charge), containing his 6,500-volume libary, as well as his **Gartenhaus** (Summer house) and the **Schillerhaus** (open Mon–Wed; entrance charge), each effectively portraying the daily lives and work of these great men of literature. The **Kunstsammlungen zu Weimar** (Weimar Art collections; open Tues–Sun; entrance charge) are housed in the **Stadtschloss** (castle) and include paintings by Lucas Cranach the Elder, Tintoretto and Caspar David Friedrich.

Undulating, thickly forested hills, narrow river valleys and rounded mountain tops combine to form the unique quality of the **Thuringian Forest**. Goethe himself enjoyed the natural surroundings of this region, and today's hikers will be in good company if they follow the **Rennsteig** – the famous 168-km (105-mile) long-distance ridge path that crosses the whole area. The route also passes the Grosser Inselberg (916 metres/3,000 ft), only the fourth-highest mountain in the region but the one offering the best views.

BELOW: deep forest in Thuringia.

Bavaria

South of Weimar, the attractive and ancient town of **Arnstadt** was the home from 1620 of the Bach family. The most famous of them, Johann Sebastian, was the organist from 1703–7 in the church which today bears his name. Further south still, the town of **Bayreuth ⓫** in Bavaria is associated with another musician and composer – Richard Wagner, who built an opera house here in 1876. Every year it is the setting for the Wagner Festival, from 25 July to 28 August. The old, free imperial city of **Nürnberg** (Nuremberg) ⓬ was devastated by bombs during World War II but has been faithfully restored so that much of its old charm remains. From the 12th to the 16th century it was regarded as the unofficial capital of the Holy Roman Empire of German Nations. The river Pegnitz divided the **Old City** into the Sebalderstadt in the north and the Lorenzerstadt in the south, both surrounded by a sturdy 13th-century defensive wall with 46 fortified towers – the landmarks of the city.

The oldest parts of the enormous **Kaiserburg** (Imperial Castle), built on sandstone crags high above the old city, date to the 11th and 12th centuries.

Between the 15th and 17th centuries, the city attracted artists and scientists such as Albrecht Dürer, Adam Krafft and Veit Stoss. The **Albrecht Dürer House** (open Tues–Sun; entrance charge), near the castle, is now a museum. The **Hauptmarkt** (main market) is the site of Nuremberg's famous annual Weihnachtmarkt (Christmas market), while at the Kornmarkt the **Germanisches Nationalmuseum** (open Tues–Sun; entrance charge) was founded in 1851 and has a huge collection of artefacts devoted to German arts and culture, some dating back to pre- and early history. A less celebrated chapter in Nuremberg's history was written by the Nazis, who held rallies here between 1933 and 1938.

Maps:
Germany
164–5
Local 178

The Romantic Road

The popularity of the Romantic Road, the name given to the route from **Würzburg** Ⓐ in the north to Augsburg east of Munich and Füssen near the Austrian border, attracts many visitors. Despite massive Allied bombing in March 1945, Würzburg's long history of rule by successive prince-bishops still gives it a majestic appearance.

Start your tour of the city at the **Residenz**, built in 1720–44 by Balthasar Neumann and ranked as one of the finest baroque palaces in Europe. The impressive stairwell extends right up the two-storey building and is crowned by a single concave vault 30 metres (100 ft) long by 18 metres (59 ft) wide. More renowned than the vault itself is the **ceiling fresco** painted by the Italian artist Giambattista Tiepolo, who was summoned to Würzburg in 1750 to create the largest painting in the world. Tiepolo, depicted the Gods of Olympus and allegories of the four continents known at the time. The Tiepolo paintings in the Kaisersaal allude to the marriage between Emperor Frederick Barbarossa and

BELOW: Würzburg.

TIP

Take a steamer along the Main to Veitshöchheim (7 km/ 4 miles), where you can visit the baroque palace with its beautiful rococo gardens, once the summer residence of the Würzburg bishops. The steamers leave Würzburg at the landing stage close to the Alten Kranen.

Beatrix of Burgundy in the year 1156. Miraculously, the frescos survived the allied bombing of 1945 unscathed. After a tour of the interior, take time to stroll in the **Hofgarten** behind the Residenz, with its fine wrought-iron gates and beautiful baroque group of figures.

From the Residenz follow the Hofstrasse to Kiliansplatz and the Romanesque **Cathedral**, which was rebuilt after its destruction in 1945. The **Shönborn Chapel**, one of Balthasar Neumann's most important works, contains the shrine of the prince-bishops of Shönborn. Cross the Main river by the Alte Mainbrücke (Old Main Bridge) and follow the steep path up to the **Festung Marienberg**. Founded in 1201, the massive rectangular fortress encloses a courtyard and the 13th-century keep as well as the Renaissance fountain and the Church of St Mary. Between 1253 and 1719, the prince-bishops used it as a stronghold to keep the ever-more powerful townsfolk at bay. During the Peasants' Revolt of 1525, the lower classes attempted to take the fortress by burying explosives under its walls. After 1631, when the city was taken by Gustav Adolf of Sweden during the Thirty Years' War, the fortress was extended and began to take the form of the building seen today, with its baroque facades and the Fürstengarten (princes' garden).

One of the main attractions of the fortress is the **Mainfränkisches Museum** (Apr–Oct Tues–Sun 10am–5pm, Nov–Mar 10am–4pm), whose exhibits include a remarkable collection of statuary by the woodcarver and sculptor Tilman Riemenschneider (1460–1531), who came to Würzburg from his home in the Harz Mountains in 1483 and rapidly rose to fame in Franconia. Such was his popularity that he was elected Würzburg's mayor in 1520, However, during the Peasants' Revolt he supported the peasants against the prince-bishop Konrad von Thingen. When they were ultimately defeated at the Marienberg fortress, he was imprisoned and tortured. He died a broken man in 1531. On a hill to the south of the fortress is the **Käppele** (little chapel) which was designed by Balthasar Neumann as a pilgrimage church in 1748.

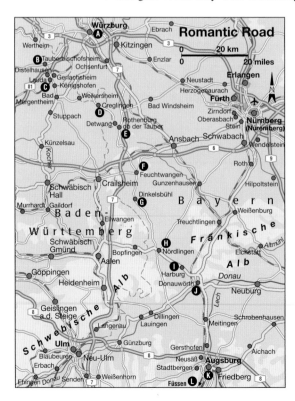

The Romantic Road passes through **Tauberbischofsheim ⓑ** ("home of the bishop"), where St Boniface founded a convent in 725 and **Lauda ⓒ**, which for centuries has been the hub of a wine-producing region. A 16th-century house at Rathausstrasse 25 has a **museum** dedicated to wine and local history (open Apr–Oct: Sun; entrance charge). What may be regarded as Riemenschneider's greatest achievement can be admired in **Creglingen ⓓ**, whose Herrgottskirche (Church of Our Lord) has his carved altarpiece dedicated to the Virgin.

One of the best preserved medieval towns in Germany is **Rothenburg ob der Tauber ⓔ**, whose special status as a free imperial city from 1274 provided the basis for its prosperity. Its streets converge like the spokes of a wheel from the city walls to the central

Map on page 178

market place and the **Rathaus** (Town Hall) which, with its Renaissance archway and baroque arcades, is a rich mix of architectural styles. Its 55-metre (180-ft) Gothic tower affords the best view of the town's maze of red-tiled roofs. The medieval churches of Rothenberg are rich in ecclesiastical art, the pride of the town being the **Helig-Blut-Altar** (Altar of the Holy Blood) in St-Jakobs-Kirche (Church of St James), commissioned from Riemenschneider in 1501–5. The **Plönlein** area in the centre of town is the prettiest part of Rothenberg and one much favoured by photographers.

South to Augsburg

In summer the Romanesque cloisters of the Stiftskirche in **Feuchtwangen F**, the next stop on the Romantic Route, serve as a stage for excellent open-air theatre. **Dinkelsbühl G**, a little further south, can only be entered through one of its four main gates. Here, every year in July, the historical play known as the **Kinderzeche** and a colourful parade commemorate the Thirty Years' War (1618–48), when the town was under siege by Swedish forces.

From the tower of St George's Church in **Nördlingen H** there is a panoramic view of the 99 villages of the **Rieskrater**, a crater formed 15 million years ago when a meteorite struck the earth's surface at a speed of around 70,000 km (40,000 miles) per hour. The impact created a wall-like formation of rock and earth about 13 km (8 miles) in diameter. The modern **Rieskratermuseum** (open Tues–Sun; entrance charge) has a multimedia show which explains the very specific geological history of the crater. Continue on through **Harburg I**, the setting for one of Germany's oldest castles, and **Donnauwörth J**, home of the Käthe Kruse dolls which have been manufactured here since 1910.

TIP

Don't miss the Museum of the Third Dimension in Dinkelsbühl's Old Mill. Here holograms, three-dimensional art and other illusionary features will startle your eyes and stun your mind.

BELOW:
Rothenburg, on the Romantic Road.

The Fuggerei

The medieval trading city of **Augsburg** Ⓚ grew to a commercial centre and episcopal seat at the crossroads of the important routes linking Italy and the centre of Franco-Carolingian power. By about 1500 it was among the largest cities in the German-speaking world. The wealthy Fuggers banking family was responsible for the extraordinary social housing settlement of the **Fuggerei** (1516), where for a peppercorn rent poor Catholic senior citizens can rent a small home. The town has a wealth of artistic treasures, including the Renaissance City Hall, with onion-domed towers and magnificent **Goldener Saal** (Golden Hall; open daily; entrance charge). The Romanesque-Gothic Cathedral is the home of precious works of art, including valuable altar pictures and the oldest known glass windows in Germany (dating from around 1130).

Neuschwanstein Castle (open daily; entrance charge) near **Füssen** Ⓛ was built by Ludwig II in 1869–86 and was a total anachronism even then. Its sole *raison d'être* was that of a glorified stage set. In the **Sängersaal**, the "Minstrels' Hall" which forms the centrepiece of the fairytale castle, Ludwig staged performances of scenes from the opera *Tannhäuser*.

The 2,000-year-old city of **Regensburg** ⓫, at the northernmost point of the river Danube, was largely undamaged during World War II. There is a fine view from the **Steinerne Brücke** (Stone Bridge), a masterpiece of medieval engineering, 310 metres (1,017 ft) in length. The river is lined by stately mansions, over whose roofs tower the spires of St Peter's Cathedral, the most impressive Gothic structure in Bavaria. Away to the north, the landscape of heavily-wooded Bavarian Forest extends as far as the Czech border and is a great place to get away from it all and enjoy the wide open spaces.

BELOW:
Neuschwanstein.

Capital of Bavaria

Duke Henry the Lion, who preceded the Wittelsbachs, performed a historic function 800 years ago when he put a new bridge across the Isar River for the transport of salt shipments from the mines in Bad Reichenhall to Augsburg. **München** (Munich) , the town that grew up around the bridge, took its name from the occupants of a nearby monastery. The city was originally called Mönchen (Little Monk) and its symbol is still a childlike monk, the *Münchner Kindl* (The Munich Child).

Maps: Germany 164–5 Local 178

Drinking from a giant tankard at the Oktoberfest.

While the Wittelsbachs had a Munich residence from the early 1500s, it was not until the 19th century that the city, under the reign of Ludwig I and Ludwig II, acquired a reputation as a centre for the arts and sciences. Much of this was due to ambitious and flamboyant architectural projects, but the city and its schools also attracted leading scientists, artists and writers. Today, Munich claims to publish more books than any other city except New York, although **Schwabing**, the traditional artists' and intellectuals' quarter, has increasingly been taken over by boutiques and tourists.

In many ways, the whole city remains a sophisticated village. Women in *dirndls*, the traditional Bavarian-Austrian rural woman's dress, sip afternoon coffee in chic cafés while men in green *loden* coats, originally woven for shepherds, drive sports cars. Country women in ankle-length dresses sell medicinal herbs from wicker baskets at the bustling **Viktualienmarkt** right in the city centre, where you can also buy the finest French cheese and wine.

Visitors come from around the world to look at the **Asamkirche** (a Catholic church built by the Asam brothers) and other baroque extravaganzas as well as the ultra-modern headquarters of the **Bavarian Motor Works** (BMW), shaped

BELOW: Munich's town hall.

MUNICH'S BEER GARDENS

By five o'clock on a hot summer's afternoon, you can find most of Munich's population sitting out under the chestnut trees in one of the city's beer gardens, hoisting a *Mass* (a litre mug) of beer, polishing off a *Hendle* (roast chicken), and lingering until late into the night, when lights festooned in the branches light up the area like a stage set.

Class barriers are unknown here. A group of rowdy punks may be seated between a group of middle-aged men in *Tracht* and three elegantly coiffed ladies in Jil Sander ensembles, at a single table. Self-service is the rule and standing in line is part of the beer garden experience. Not that you have to buy all your food: many families come with picnic baskets loaded with radishes, cheese, cold cuts, bread, and even a checkered tablecloth, just picking up beer to complete the meal.

In Munich, beer gardens come in all shapes and sizes. While the classic brass band still oom-pahs away from the Chinese Tower in the **English Garden**, jazz sets the tone at the popular **Waldwirtschaft** in Grosshesselohe, south of Munich. And while little **Max Emmanuel Brauerei** in Schwabing still concentrates on traditional specialities like spare ribs, **Mangostin**, in the south of town, offers a range of Asian dishes along with the beer and *Wurst*.

*Mechanical figures
dance for the crowds
in the tower of
Munich's town hall.*

like an automobile cylinder. Visitors flock to the scientific and technological **Deutsches Museum** (German Museum; open daily; entrance charge), situated on an island in the Isar River. It includes a replica of a coal mine and a planetarium, as well as numerous exhibits from the worlds of engineering, seafaring and flight. To see everything would take days.

Munich's two famous art museums, the **Alte** and **Neue Pinakothek** (both open Tues–Sun; entrance charge), are situated to the west of the centre, as is **Königsplatz**, with its fine museum of ancient Greek and Roman sculptures, the **Glyptothek** (open Tues–Fri; entrance charge). The Alta Pinakothek exhibits works of European masters from the 14th–18th centuries, with an emphasis on the Dutch and Flemish schools; its collection of Rubens paintings is perhaps the finest in the world. The adjacent Neue Pinakothek has 400 paintings and sculptures from the Impressionist to Art Nouveau and Symbolist movements.

Munich's festival

The Theresienwiese is the site of the world-famous **Oktoberfest**; it is dominated by a statue personifying Bavaria in the form of an Amazonian woman. The traditional beer halls and restaurants are conveniently located in the centre of the city in an area framed by the Hauptbahnhof, Karlsplatz, the Rathaus (City Hall), the Residenz and Odeonsplatz. Nearby are the **Hofbräuhaus** (the former court brewery's beer halls). The **Hofgarten** (Court Garden) on Hofgartenstrasse is near the Residenz's small rococo gem, the **Cuvilliés Theatre**. The historic rooms of the **Residenz** (Royal Palace; open Tues–Sun; entrance charge) are worth a tour; and you should try to be at the **Rathaus** (Town Hall) at 11am to view the daily performance of the mechanical figures in the tower.

BELOW: costume
parade at the
Oktoberfest.

A must outside the city is **Schloss Nymphenburg** (open Tues–Sun; entrance charge), the summer residence of the Bavarian princes and kings, which now houses a porcelain factory and the famous **Schönheitsgalerie** (Gallery of Beauty) with paintings of 24 women including Lola Montez, the beautiful Irish mistress of Ludwig I. The park is laid out on the French pattern and includes the **Amalienburg** hunting lodge, considered a masterpiece of European rococo.

Stuttgart and the Black Forest

The whole length of road from the ancient university town of **Freiburg** to **Stuttgart** ⑮ winds along small river valleys through an area of outstanding beauty. Tourists have been coming to the **Schwarzwald** (Black Forest) since the 18th century, attracted by the contrast of the Rhine Plain and the mountains rising some 1,200 metres (4,000 ft) above it. The forested slopes ascending above the picture-postcard valleys provide extensive possibilities for walking. Grouse and pheasant, buzzards and hawks, deer, foxes and badgers populate the more remote areas.

Stuttgart has the highest per capita income of any city in Germany, due in part to its manufacture of Mercedes cars. Opulence was displayed differently by the rich and powerful in earlier times, as evidenced by the 16th-century Altes Schloss (Old Palace) and 18th-century Neues Schloss (New Palace) on Schiller-platz. Well worth a visit outside the city centre are the **Daimler-Benz-Museum** (open Tues–Sun; entrance charge) in the district of Untertürkheim, and the **Porsche Museum** (open daily; entrance charge) in Stuttgart-Zuffenhausen.

Map on pages 164–5

Down the valley to Heidelberg

Although the spa tradition of **Baden-Baden** goes back to Roman times, it was not revived until 1838 when Jacques Benazet opened his **Casino**, a luxurious fun palace, in the Kurhaus. It suddenly became fashionable again to visit Baden-Baden. The existence of **Karlsruhe ⓰**, further north, is entirely due to the palace which Margrave Karl Wilhelm of Baden-Durlach had built around 1715. Most of its attractions are found around the palace, which houses the **Badisches Landemusueum** (Baden State Museum; open daily; entrance charge). The **State Majolica Museum** (open daily; entrance charge), with a display of faïence pottery, the **Staatliche Kunsthalle** (open daily; entrance charge), containing one of the best displays of European painting in southern Germany, and the **Botanical Gardens** (open Sun–Fri; entrance charge) are all nearby.

High above the picturesque lanes of **Heidelberg ⓱**, the ruins of the **Castle** (open daily; guided tours; entrance charge) rise majestically. Several million people visit the castle every year, making Heidelberg one of the most popular destinations in Germany. The city's location on the edge of the Odenwald Forest, where the Neckar reaches the Rhine Plain, make it, for many people, the epitome of German Romanticism. Beneath the castle, the six arches of the **Alte Brücke** (Old Bridge) span the river. Its 13th-century gate is topped by baroque spires and leads to **Philosophenweg** (Philosopher's Way), a mountain promenade along **Heiligenberg**. The most interesting part of the castle is the Otto-

Heidelberg's castle complex, with its fortifications, domestic quarters and palaces, took 400 years to complete, so the building styles evolved all the way from 14th-century Gothic to baroque.

BELOW: a student society's ultra-conservative members.

The Lorelei legend tells of a beautiful siren who lured unsuspecting Rhine boatmen to their deaths on the rocks.

Heinrich Wing, which houses the **Deutsches Apothekenmuseum** (German Apothecary Museum; open Apr–Oct: daily; Nov–Mar: Sat & Sun; entrance charge), a collection of furniture, books, medical instruments and medicine bottles of all shapes and sizes.

Frankfurt

Germany's financial centre on the River Main, **Frankfurt** ⑱ has developed into a pulsating metropolis, thanks to its location at the intersection of important road, rail and air traffic routes. The new cathedrals of the world of finance – the skyscrapers housing international banks and financial corporations – create a dramatic skyline which epitomises the power of this bustling city.

Yet the glass of soaring modern buildings reflects the Gothic tower of Frankfurt's cathedral; apple-wine pubs stand at cobblestone-street level in **Sachsenhausen**, the Bohemian quarter; paintings by Rubens, Rembrandt, Dürer and Holbein are in the art museums. The new museum quarter on and around the Schumankai is the most exciting in Germany. It includes the decidedly modern **Museum für Kunsthandwerk** (Museum of Applied Arts; open Tues–Sun; entrance charge), and the **Städelsche Kunstinstitut**, one of Germany's most famous art galleries, which has paintings from the 14th century to the present.

The **Römer** (open daily; entrance charge), the city's town hall, is a collection of three Neo-Gothic buildings and includes the church where the Holy Roman Emperors were crowned. The **Goethehaus** (open daily; entrance charge) at Grosser Hirschgraben 23–25 is where Johann Wolfgang von Goethe, Germany's greatest poet, was born in 1749. The River Main slices through the city, on its way to join the Rhine, which runs north through Germany's wine land.

The Rhine and Moselle

Not far from the confluence of the Main and the Rhine lies the ancient city of **Mainz** ⑲, founded in 38 BC. In AD 747 St Boniface made it the seat of an archbishop, whereby the city became the centre of Germanic Christendom. Mainz's most famous son is undoubtedly Johannes Gutenburg (*c.* 1397–1468), the inventor of printing. One of his 42-page Latin Bibles can be seen in the **Gutenberg Museum** (open Tues–Sun; entrance charge), along with old printing apparatus and a replica of the master's workshop.

Almost due west from here, in the heart of the Moselle valley, is **Trier** ⑳, the oldest city in Germany, founded in 16 BC by Caesar Augustus. Dominated by the well-preserved **Porta Nigra**, the huge Roman gate, the city is a treasure chest of ruins and relics, and many residents dabble in archaeology. It is said that, to store potatoes safe from winter's frost, the people simply dig down to the Roman mosaics. The **Rheinisches Landemuseum** (open Tues–Sun; entrance charge) has a wealth of Roman treasures, including mosaics, sculpture, glass and coins. The fortress-like **St Peter's Cathedral**, one of Germany's oldest churches in the Romanesque style, bears witness to Trier's Christian Middle Ages.

At **Koblenz** ㉑, the Moselle, perhaps Germany's loveliest river, joins the Rhine. Where two great wine rivers meet stands an impressive monument known as das Deutsches Eck (the German Corner). On the opposite side of the river, high on the edge of a ridge, lies **Ehrenbreitsein**, a 13th-century fortress that has controlled this key area and changed hands several times between the French and Germans. Above the Pfaffendorf Bridge, with the Moselle on the left and the Rhine on the right, is the famous **Wine Village**. It was built as a replica of a wine-producing village, complete with authentic vineyards and typical half-timbered houses from the most celebrated German wine-growing regions.

The route to Cologne

With the fall of the Berlin Wall, the city of **Bonn** ㉒ returned the function of German capital to Berlin. Before it was chosen as the seat of the Federal Government in 1949, the major claim to fame of this sleepy city was as the birthplace of Ludwig van Beethoven (1770–1827). But, thanks to its **Museum Mile**, Bonn still has a lot to offer, including the **Kunst- und Austellungshalle** (Art and Exhibition Hall), the **Kunstmuseum** (Museum of Art) and the **Alexander Koenig Museum** (Zoological Museum; all museums open daily; entrance charges). Exhibits at the **Beethovenhaus** (open daily; entrance charge) include the piano made specially for the composer in Vienna.

Köln (Cologne) ㉓ is a much livelier city with a population of about one million. It is not only famous for its twin-spired cathedral, exuberant Mardi Gras celebrations and religious processions, but also the courage with which it was rebuilt after being reduced to rubble during World War II. The spirit of Cologne is embodied in its mighty **Dom** (Cathedral) and the **Severinsbrücke** (Severinsbridge), a unique construction across the Rhine, supported by only

Map on pages 164–5

The idyllic Moselle Valley is the best known of Germany's wine-producing areas. Winningen, Zell, Bernkastel-Kues and Piesport are typically picturesque towns and villages along the route.

BELOW: at work in the vineyards.

Cologne is highly acclaimed for its theatre and music. Carnival here in April is celebrated with gay abandon and plenty of local Kölsch beer.

one off-centre pillar. The Cathedral, considered the greatest Gothic church in Christendom, contains the remains of the Wise Men of the East, the paintings of Stephan Lochner and a feeling of immense space and lofty aspirations that have an awesome effect on the visitor. Begun in 1248, its twin spires, each 157 metres (515 ft) high, were not built until 1842–80, during an era when heady ideas and monuments were in vogue.

The city also has some excellent museums. The **Römisch-Germanisches Museum** (open daily; entrance charge) contains priceless treasures and offers an insight into the city's Roman past. The museum was built over the world-famous **Dionysos Mosaic**, which was discovered during construction work on an air-raid shelter. The 2nd-century masterpiece covers an area of 70 sq metres (84 sq yds) and consists of more than 1 million ceramic and glass components.

Detour to **Aachen**, one of Germany's oldest cities and the favourite residence of Charlemagne, who is buried in the Münster (minster) there, before visiting **Düsseldorf ㉔**, 40 km (25 miles) to the north of Cologne. Düsseldorf's trademarks, the **Schlossturm** tower and the **Church of St Lambert**, with its characteristic slightly crooked spire, stand directly on the Rhine. Take a stroll along the Uferpromenade, the pedestrianised space between the river and the bustling old town – a square mile packed with pubs and restaurants. The city has a reputation as a centre for the arts; the **Kunstammlung Nordrhein-Westfalen** (State Art Collection; open Tues–Sun; entrance charge) on Grabbeplatz has 20th-century works by artists ranging from Picasso to Lichtenstein and a comprehensive collection of works by Klee.

Dortmund ㉕, on the eastern edge of the Ruhr, is at the top of the German brewing league. Indeed, more brewing goes on here than in any other city in

BELOW: Cologne, dominated by its Gothic cathedral.

Map on pages 164–5

Europe, including its rival to the south, Munich. All is explained in the **Brauerei Museum** (Brewery Museum; open Tues–Sun; entrance charge).

On the trail of the Brothers Grimm

The picturesque Weser Valley, further east, picks up the trail of the **Fairytale Road** which leads from **Hanau**, the birthplace of Jacob and Wilhelm Grimm, to Bremen. Riverside meadows, spruced-up towns and villages, castle ruins and Renaissance palaces lead you to believe that, just as in the fairy tale of *Sleeping Beauty*, time actually could stand still here. **Hameln** (Hamelin), midway along the route, quite rightfully calls itself "the city of the Weser Renaissance". The **Rattenfängerhaus** recalls the famous story of the *Pied Piper of Hamelin*, and every Sunday in summer a play depicting the legend is performed in front of the **Hochzeithaus** (Wedding House).

The old Hanseatic town of **Bremen** ㉖ is the oldest German maritime city, although its modern deep sea port of **Bremerhaven**, 57 km (35 miles) further north, was founded in the 19th century. The Bremen Town Musicians, a dog, a donkey, a cat and a rooster, from the story by the Brothers Grimm, stand near the **Rathaus** (Town Hall). The cavernous cellar beneath this building is famous for its Gothic vaults, and houses a restaurant serving all the wines of Germany.

Heading for the beach.

Maritime Hamburg

Hamburg ㉗ is Germany's second largest city (population 1.7 million), and a major port, although it is 110 km (66 miles) from the sea. Water has always been the lifeblood of the city. Cargo ships ply the River Elbe to unload bananas and venison, carpets and spices, teak and automobiles, cameras and computers. One of the most charming areas is the **Speicherstadt**, the old warehouse district, and the best way to see it is on a narrow boat cruise.

BELOW: Hamburg's seafaring tradition.

Hamburg's red-light district, the **Reeperbahn** and adjacent **Grosse Freiheit** and **Herbertstrasse**, may be Europe's raunchiest but the area is well-policed and the tourist office takes pains to tell visitors which clubs are reputable. The more elegant side of Hamburg can be seen by strolling from the Railway Station into the city centre. Just to the north of the station is the **Kunsthalle** (Art Gallery; open Tues–Sun; entrance charge), with a magnificent collection of paintings and sculpture from the 13th to the 20th centuries, including works by Andy Warhol and Joseph Beuys. On the other side of the station is one of the world's largest and best *Jugendstil* (Art Nouveau) collections, in the **Museum für Kunst und Gewerbe** (Museum of Arts and Crafts; open Tues–Sun; entrance charge).

Lübeck ㉘, on the Baltic Sea, was for 250 years the undisputed commercial metropolis of the Holy Roman Empire, and by 1356 it was the most powerful of all the towns in the Hanseatic League. It is now a prime port for ferries to Scandinavia. **Travemünde** in Lübeck Bay has been its up-market beach resort since the 19th century. The chubby **Holstentor** (Holsten Gate), one of the few remaining sections of the city wall, leads to the old town, which contains Lübeck's seven Gothic brick churches. ❑

FESTIVE TRADITIONS, LOCAL COLOUR

Germany's old traditions live on in a range of colourful festivals, from the parades of Carnival and the Oktoberfest to town and village celebrations

Düsseldorf, with its glittering boutiques and skyscrapers, is a modern urban centre. But visit during Carnival and this world is turned on its head, with parades and revelry and a complete suspension of everyday rules. Even in this cosmopolitan metropolis, the originally pagan tradition of Carnival lives on.

Germany works hard and plays hard. Moreover, local festivals underline the very different characters and customs of the individual German states, which weren't confederated until 1871. It's a long way from the showy, Las Vegas-style parades of the Carnival in the Rhineland to the grim masks of a *Fastnet* in the Black Forest.

Some festivals commemorate specific historic events, such as the Dinkelsbühl *Kinderzeche*, in which the town's children march out and plead with the Swedish army to spare their homes (*see page 179*). The world-famous Oktoberfest in Munich dates back to the celebration of Ludwig I and Princess Therese's wedding in 1810. There are many more beer – and wine – festivals all over the country. Strong on tradition, too, are the *Schützen-feste* (*above*), the celebrations of the local shooting associations.

▷ **IN A WHIRL**
More than just a beer drinker's extravaganza, Munich's Oktoberfest is also a fair with amusement park rides – great fun for kids.

△ **HERITAGE PRESERVED**
Dating back to the Middle Ages, the ubiquitous *Schützenfeste* have become festivals of local costumes and mores.

△ **STREET PARTY**
In most of Southern Germany, Carnival time is known as *Fasching*. The colourful proceedings in Munich constitute a massive street party.

▷ **FASTNET FACE**
In the Black Forest area, the heathen Alemannic origins of Carnival, here called *Fastnet*, are evident in the carved wooden masks.

▷ **WEDDING GROUP**
In 1475, some 10,000 people attended the wedding in Landshut of Duke Ludwig the Rich's son, George, to the Polish princess Jadwiga.

CHRISTMAS MARKETS

The smell of Glühwein wafts around stalls selling *Lebkuchen* (gingerbread) and Christmas ornaments, while carol singers make joyful sounds from the balcony of the town hall. Christmas markets are one of the highlights of the year.

The *Christkindlmarkt* has its roots in the Reformation, when Catholic saints' days were abolished and children were left without presents on 6 December, St Nicholas' Day. To compensate, it was said that the Christ Child (*Christkind*) brought gifts on the night of his birth. The markets sprang up to meet the demand for gifts, and became a popular tradition. Having flourished during the early 19th century they were almost forgotten until their rediscovery in the 1930s. The most famous *Christkindlmarkt* is the one at Nuremberg (*above*) with a local school child appearing as the market's namesake.

◁ **FEAST OF FOOLS**
At Carnival time, the *Rosenmontag* parades in Mainz and Cologne, the day before Shrove Tuesday, are nationally televised. Carnival kings and queens reign over the festivities.

▷ **SUN, MOON AND STARS**
On 11 November children commemorate St Martin's Day by parading through the streets bearing homemade candlelit lanterns and singing traditional songs about the charitable saint.

◁ **CELEBRATIONS**
Five centuries on, the Landshut Wedding is re-enacted every four years in a sumptuous pageant.

▷ **BLAST OFF**
Although it culminates on Shrove Tuesday, Carnival begins on 11 November at 11.11am.

SWITZERLAND

Landlocked at the very heart of Europe, the country's
most treasured possession is its unique landscape

The letters CH carried on Swiss cars stand for Confederatio Helvetica. The Helvetii were a Celtic tribe crushed by Julius Caesar, and Helveticus was for five centuries the Roman name for what is now western Switzerland. The source of the word Switzerland comes from Schwyz, one of the three cantons which formed the original union at Rütli on Lake Lucerne in 1291. Today there are 23 members of the confederation and the cantons are divided into those that speak French, German and Italian.

Switzerland is only a small country, about the same size as the Netherlands but with half the population, and its largest city, Zürich, has only 706,000 people. About 1 million of its 6.3 million inhabitants are foreigners, half of them guest workers from Italy. The country is famed for its banking, neutrality and Swatch watches, and it works hard to maintain its independence: every fit male is armed and spends a number of days training each year until the age of 50. The only remnants of the *Reisege*, mercenaries who fought in Europe's wars for four centuries, are the Swiss Guard at the Vatican.

Eastern Switzerland and the lowlands, with blossoming orchards and lush meadows, are best in spring. Summer visitors head for the lakes. Autumn can be enjoyed in the vineyards of the Valais or the Vaud, in the larch forests of the Engadine and the southern valleys of the Grison, or in the Ticino where even in October the days seem to be longer and the fog thinner than in much of the rest of Switzerland. Finally, winter provides endless possibilities through the entire Alpine region, for skiing, or simply enjoying the beautiful, chocolate-box snow scenes.

In contrast to tourists of the past, who were compelled to explore the still undiscovered Alpine country of Switzerland on foot, on the backs of mules, or in coaches with little if any suspension, today's travellers have an astonishingly thorough and comprehensive traffic system at their disposal. Thanks to the many and varied means of travel available – whether rail, bus, cable railway, or boat – it is very tempting simply to leave the car at home, and to get to know really large areas of the country in a relatively short time. Every railway station in Switzerland can provide detailed information about these types of round-trip, and combination tickets for various different types of transport are available everywhere.   ❑

PRECEDING PAGES: Lake Thun in the Bernese Oberland; Swiss cheesemaker.
LEFT: traditional female dress in Apenzall, a German-speaking area.

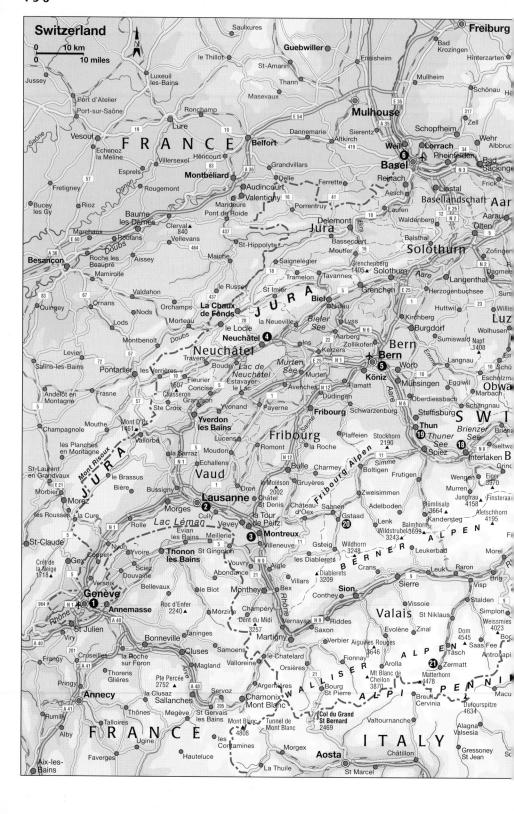

Switzerland

0   10 km
0   10 miles

AROUND SWITZERLAND

The shores of Lake Geneva and the Bernese Alps beyond them are the cradle of tourism, not just in Switzerland but in all of Continental Europe

Map on pages 196–7

Bern

The first tourists were British, and connections between Britain and this part of Switzerland are everywhere. Lord Byron's *The Prisoner of Chillon* was set in a castle on the shores of Lake Geneva, and Sir Arthur Conan Doyle's fictional creation Sherlock Holmes was to end his successful career at Reichenbach Falls in the **Bernese Oberland** at the hands of the infamous Professor Moriarty, the "Napoleon of Evil". Sir Arthur also wrote about skiing in Switzerland and started an influx of British skiers that continues up to this day.

The earliest package tours to the continent were arranged by Thomas Cook's of London, the world's oldest travel agency. The first one, in 1863, was from London to Lake Geneva and the Bernese Oberland.The group travelled by train and channel boat to Paris, where they changed trains for the 17-hour ride to Geneva. From there they went up the **Rhône** to **Sion** and then to **Interlaken** and the region around **Lake Lucerne**.

Victorian restraints were thrown to the winds. The gentlemen dared to wear knicker-bockers with their tailcoats and top hats, and a snowball fight erupted in one of the passes. Giggling ladies protected themselves with their parasols and one gentleman lost his glass eye in the snow. The group also travelled by boat, stagecoach and mule.

LEFT: Zermatt, in the shadow of the Matterhorn. **BELOW:** amateur actors portray William Tell and his son.

Winding roads

Modern means of transportation and tunnels such as the one through **Mont Blanc** make it much easier to get into and out of Switzerland. Travel around the country has also improved and even some of the most remote areas are accessible. Direct distances between various villages and towns are short but can be greatly increased by winding mountain roads.

For travellers with time, the postal service's (PTT) national bus system is to Switzerland what the Greyhound is to the US. Curving through the highest parts of the land and through scenic valleys, these regularly scheduled buses provide a good way of seeing rural Switzerland. There is also an excellent national rail network linking all major towns and cities. The finely graded climate of the country ranges from sub-tropical warmth to Arctic cold in the Alpine peaks above 4,000 metres (12,000 ft). The range of climates results in an equal variety of vegetation – from fertile plains in the lowlands to mountain pastures and vineyards.

Driving a car in Swiss cities is no less hectic than in other European cities. In country areas, farm vehicles and military convoys on manoeuvres slow down and even stop other traffic. Occasionally, two-way mountain roads seem barely wider than a goat path. Most Alpine passes are closed all winter; those that aren't can be crossed only by cars equipped with snow chains.

Mountain trains and cablecars take skiers and sightseers up the **Kleines Matterhorn**, **Jungfrau**, **Corvatsch** and other peaks. The Swiss continue to improve this system. They already have Europe's highest railway and the Alps' longest aerial cableway. The world's highest subway, the Metro-Alpin, 3,500 metres (11,500 ft) up in **Saas Fee** in the canton of Valais, makes year-round skiing possible. Among the various means of transportation, railways and funiculars stay on the ground at all heights, cable cars and lifts do not. Anybody with a bad head for heights should ask about routes before journeying into the mountains.

Around Lake Geneva

Local music-making.

Genève ❶ (Geneva) is at the westernmost tip of **Lac Léman** (Lake Geneva), which is fed by the River Rhône. Here is the westernmost point of Switzerland; the city is surrounded by France on three sides. It has a panorama of water, mountains, parks and flowerbeds, and its elegant villas lining the lakeshore and multi-coloured sails out on the water create a truly cosmopolitan impression.

Many of the well-known sights are found right where the River Rhône leaves Geneva. The **Jet d'Eau** (Water Fountain) out in the harbour can send a dazzling plume of white foam 145 metres (475 ft) into the air. The first bridge to span the Rhône is the **Pont du Mont-Blanc**. From here and from the **Quai du Mont-Blanc**, on the right bank, one can enjoy (on clear days) an unobstructed view of **Mont Blanc**, the highest peak in Europe at 4,807 metres (15,771 ft). The Geneva Casino is located on the Quai du Mont-Blanc under the Hilton hotel.

The **Jardin Anglais** (English Garden) and flower clock are here (on the left bank), while a little further on is **Ile Rousseau**, a place for literary pilgrims. The French philosopher Jean-Jacques Rousseau liked to stroll on the island, which

BELOW:
Geneva Cathedral.

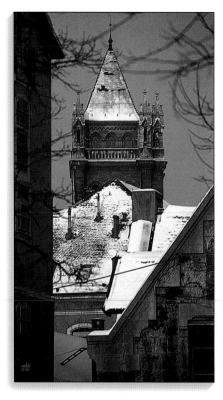

LANGUAGES AND LIFESTYLES

Travelling through Switzerland clearly reveals how the linguistic and cultural background, predominantly German, French or Italian, influences everything, especially food, architecture and lifestyle.

About two-thirds of the Swiss are German-speaking. They speak *Schwyzerdütsch*, a German-Swiss dialect that is used at all social levels. Even fluent German speakers have difficulty understanding this heritage from Alemannic tribes, and its regional and local variations.

French has worked its way into Swiss-German, too, so that people say *merci vielmals* for "thank you very much". Menus use German for some dishes, French for others, and *Schwyzerdütsch* for the items that you should try. The languages in the French and Italian areas of the country are more or less identical to those spoken in France and Italy.

The German area extends from the French-speaking west all the way east to the border with the pocket Principality of Liechtenstein and with Austria. Language divisions do not always follow the borders of the cantons. Basel, Zürich and St Gallen in the north, and Bern, Lucerne, Zermatt and Davos are all part of the German-speaking region. The Italian Swiss are found primarily around Lago Maggiore and in parts of Grisons in the southeast.

can be reached by a footbridge from the **Pont des Bergues**. Behind the English Garden, crossing the Rue de Rive – Geneva's main shopping street – numerous steep, narrow lanes lead to the **Vieille Ville** (Old Town), with picturesque streets and squares. Don't miss the **Place du Bourg-de-Four** and the **Cathédrale de St Pierre**. Down from the far side of the Old Town is Reformation Wall, in the Parc des Bastions, which commemorates some of the key figures of Protestantism including John Calvin, John Knox, Oliver Cromwell and the Pilgrim Fathers.

Geneva is the capital of Swiss watchmaking. The **Musée de l'Horlogerie** (Clock Museum; daily May–Sep 10am–noon; Oct–Apr Mon–Fri 10am–noon, 2–6pm; entrance charge) displays timepieces, enamelled watches and music boxes dating from the 16th century.

Map on pages 196–7

Protestant work ethic

As the city of Calvin (1509–64), Geneva figures prominently in the history of the Protestant Reformation. He inspired the city to turn to Protestantism in 1536, and made it the "Protestant Rome", promulgating his doctrine of rigid morality, the sovereignty of God and predestination. He closed the theatres, banned dancing and the wearing of jewellery, and considered food and drink to be necessities and not sources of enjoyment.

Calvin's influence was not entirely negative. It can be argued that it was he who made it such an international city. Protestant refugees flocked in from England, France and Italy, giving Geneva a cosmopolitan air. Calvin also made the city a centre of French learning, founding an academy that evolved into the university. And since there were no recreational activities, the people of Geneva had no choice but to work and accumulate wealth.

Calvin's strict Protestant ethic forbade the wearing of jewellery, which resulted in Geneva's jewellers turning to clockmaking instead.

BELOW: park and lakeside, Geneva.

European headquarters of the United Nations, Geneva.

As the city of Jean-Jacques Rousseau (1712–78), Geneva was the wellspring of many of the ideas that led to the French Revolution of 1789. Rousseau's social theory of the equality of man caused the whole Western world to rethink the notion of aristocratic government. He not only laid the groundwork for the French Revolution, but also sparked the Romantic movement in literature and the arts. The city and locality of Geneva became a place of ideas because of him. The French philosopher Voltaire was also a Genevan by adoption, and Romantic writers such as Lord Byron were drawn to the area.

Geneva is important today because of its role as the headquarters for many international organisations and the seat of diplomatic conferences. The **Palace of Nations** was built between 1929 and 1936 for the League of Nations, the predecessor to the UN, and is now its European headquarters. Several other UN subsidiary organisations, including the International Labour Organisation (ILO) and the World Health Organisation (WHO), are based in Geneva.

The city has a surprisingly small population of 450,000 – less than Switzerland's other main city, Zürich. Yet Geneva is linked in the public mind with the struggle for peace and brotherhood of man. It is from this that it derives its own unique stature.

The lakeshore

Lake Geneva is shared between France to the south and Switzerland to the north. The Swiss side is known as the **Vaud Riviera** and the name is appropriate. The mountains protect the area from north and east winds, giving it a mild climate with 2,000 hours of sunshine a year. There is little rain and a temperature that rarely falls below 5° C (40° F), even on winter nights. The lakeside towns and villages are lined with well-tended flower-beds and trees. Behind them neat vineyards cloak the foothills of the Jura and face the snow-capped Alps across the lake. A ferry service – extensive in summer – links the towns around the lake, including Evian and Yvoire on the French side.

A string of pretty towns and villages lines the lakeshore between Geneva and the eastern end of the lake, just beyong Montreux. **Coppet**, with its picturesque main street and small château – the **Villa of Madame de Staël** – is the first of these. Exiled from Paris by Napoleon for her liberal ideas, Madame de Staël continued to entertain the literary figures of the day, including Byron, at her salons in Coppet. Further along, **Nyon**, founded by the Romans, clings to a steep hillside. This attractive town, with winding streets and plane tree-lined lakeside promenade, ample cafés and shops, makes for a good stop. The **Château de Prangins**, 2 km (1 mile) east of Nyon, is a strikingly beautiful 18th-century building and now home to the recently opened **Swiss National Museum** for the French-speaking part of the county. The extensive collection details Switzerland's 18th- and 19th-century history. In the grounds, the 18th-century kitchen garden has been faithfully re-created.

Lausanne ❷, the "second city" of French Switzerland, midway between Geneva and Montreux, enjoys a sheltered, sunny spot on the southern slopes of steep

terraces and gorges. The city is the capital of Vaud and has a population of 290,000. The old quarter goes by the name of **La Cité** and is the location of the medieval **cathedral** which has the most impressive exterior in Switzerland. The International Olympic Committee has its headquarters in the city, and an Olympic Museum down on the quayside at **Ouchy**. In summer, this lakeside area attracts a cosmopolitan crowd for boating and other water sports. Opposite Lausanne on the French side of Lake Geneva is **Evian les Bains**, a fashionable spa with mineral springs.

Czars and festivals

The region of **Montreux-Vevey** lies along the lakeside highway near the south-eastern end of Lake Geneva. While on a visit, the mother of Czar Alexander II wrote: "I am in the most beautiful country in the world."

The czars are gone and **Montreux ❸** is now seeking to attract a different kind of international clientele. Only 72 km (45 miles) away from Geneva International Airport, it has built a conference and exhibition centre and mounts international festivals such as the Golden Rose TV Festival, Montreux International Jazz Festival and the Montreux Classical Festival. The town spreads along 6.5 km (4 miles) of lakeshore, making it the biggest resort on Lake Geneva. The pre-World War I glitter may have faded but the beautiful natural setting remains. The lush green hills still slope down to the lake, with the mountain peaks in the background. Flowers bloom easily in the unusually mild climate.

The literary set of the 18th and 19th centuries could not stay away. Rousseau set his 1761 novel, *La Nouvelle Héloïse,* in the village of **Clarens**, now part of Montreux. Voltaire arrived, followed shortly by Lord Byron, who put Montreux

Map on pages 196–7

Byron visited the Château de Chillon in 1816 and carved his name on the pillar to which he believed the Swiss clergyman Bonivard had been chained. The graffiti is still there, protected by glass.

BELOW: lakeside Château de Chillon.

The symbol of Bern. Legend says that Duke Bechtold of Zähringen hunted down a bear in the area just after establishing the town in 1191.

BELOW: tram outside the Rathaus in Basel.

on the itinerary of British tourists for the next 150 years. Charles Dickens, Leo Tolstoy, Hans Christian Andersen and Fyodor Dostoevski are some of the other literati who came. The best-known resident of nearby **Vevey** was Charlie Chaplin, who is buried here; there is a monument of his derby hat and cane.

About 1.6 km (1 mile) west of Montreux is the **Château de Chillon** (open Nov–Feb 10am–4pm, March and Oct 9.30am–5pm, April–Sep 9am–6pm; entrance charge). It was built by one of the dukes of Savoy in the 9th or 10th century and expanded in the 13th century to its present appearance. The building has large dungeons into which critics and plotters against the dukes were tossed. One of these was a clergyman from Geneva named François de Bonivard, who spent six years at Chillon before being freed in 1536 when the Bernese conquered this area.

Home of Gruyère

The Montreux-Vevey area provides a starting point for several excursions such as the one to the cheese-making town of **Gruyères**, home of the light yellow, very rich Gruyère cheese. A model dairy farm shows the cheesemaking process (samples provided) and there is a short film.

The Gruyères district is idyllic. In addition to the famous cheese, it produces country ham, cream, strawberries and chocolate (there is a Nestlé plant in nearby Broc). The medieval town of Gruyères has only one main thoroughfare – a wide cobblestone area from which cars have been banned and which is lined with traditional buildings. This street, which leads up to a **castle**, is liberally planted with flowers. The hilltop location of this community ensures that it won't grow any larger.

At the foot of the Jura mountains

Historians would like to know more about the Raurici, the ancient warriors who once populated the forests and valleys of the Jura. Despite a lot of archaeological finds, no one actually knows how large an area they covered. The **Haut Jura Neuchâtelais**, part of a mighty system of mountains 780 km (500 miles) in length, can be reached from **Neuchâtel ❹** itself, at the bottom end of the largest lake lying wholly in Swiss territory. The town was founded in the 11th century by the Counts of Neuenburg, who turned the **château** above the town into a mighty fortress. There are also some fine museums here, in particular the **Musée d'Art et de l'Histoire** (open Tues–Sun 10am–5pm; entrance charge), which has a large collection of old clocks and watches and other antiquities.

Bern ❺ (population 325,000) is the national capital of the Swiss Federation and also known as the town of bears, which is translated as *Bearn* in the local dialect. There are automated metal bears on the *glockenspiel* at the **Zeitglockenturm** and bears in the zoo. The old city is located on what the Bernese call a "peninsula", a sharp bend in the **River Aare**, with bridges heading off to the "mainland" in three directions. After a disastrous fire in 1405, the town was rebuilt with locally quarried sandstone, and the result is impressive. Gothic sandstone buildings, with elaborate bay windows, overhanging gables and red geraniums in window boxes, are ubiquitous as are squares with flower-decked fountains. There are more arcades (6 km/4 miles of them) than in any other city of Europe. The Florentine **parliament building** and a number of banking houses face each other on the same square.

Map on pages 196–7

Where three countries meet

Switzerland's second biggest economic centre after Zürich is **Basel ❻** (population 405,000), which is one of the largest ports on the Rhine and an important centre of the chemical industry. It also houses the **Zolli** (Zoo; Mar–Apr/Sep–Oct 8am–6pm, May–Aug 8am–6.30pm, Nov–Feb 8am–5.30pm; entrance charge), Switzerland's largest zoo, and plays a leading role in the international arts and antiques trade.

Nearly all the sights of the city are in what local people call **Grossbasel**, the Old Town which rises steeply from the Rhine's right bank. Among the striking Gothic buildings are the impressive **Rathaus** (town hall) and the 12th-century cathedral. Basel has no fewer than 36 museums catering for every taste. Auguste Rodin's *Les Bourgeois de Calais* welcomes visitors to the most prestigious of these at the **Museum of Art** (open daily; entrance charge). This, the oldest art collection in the world, has an outstanding selection of 19th- and 20th-century art, including works by Gauguin, Van Gogh, Picasso, Chagall, Klee, Max Ernst and Kandinsky. Hans Holbein the Younger and Arnold Böcklin, a native of the city, are also well represented. To the north of the Old Town, The **Dreiländereck** (Three Country Corner) is something of a novelty. By walking around a marker there, you are able to pass in a matter of seconds through Switzerland, France and Germany – all without having to show a passport.

BELOW:
the quays in Zürich.

Zürich

Tucked in between high hills on the north end of Lake Zürich is the country's largest city, **Zürich ❼** (pop: 946,000), also one of the world's key financial centres. The region here is not yet part of the Alps but part of the Mittelland (Midland), a wide strip of land that cuts across Switzerland from the northeast to the southwest. The River Limmat divides the **Altstadt** (Old Town) between the **Hauptbahnhof** station on the west side and **Limmatquai**, a riverside promenade, on the east. **Bahnhofstrasse**, one of Europe's most elegant shopping streets, runs south from the Hauptbahnhof parallel to the river. Price tags, if any, suggest a city of millionaires – which is what many of the city's population are.

The city has some architectural gems, notably the Romanesque-Gothic **Grossmünster**, with twin towers, cut down to size somewhat after an 18th-century fire. At the nearby **Kunsthaus** (open Tues–Sun; entrance charge) on **Heimplatz** you can race through two millennia of European art history at one of Switzerland's largest galleries. The labyrinthine **Swiss National Museum** (open Tues–Sun; entrance charge) just north of Hauptbahnhof has Roman relics, cultural artefacts from the Middle Ages, heraldic shields, and rooms furnished in the styles of the 15th to 18th centuries. On the west bank of the Limmat is the rococo **Zur Meisen**

It was at Uri, on Lake Lucerne, in 1291 that William Tell, the country's national hero, was forced to shoot an apple off his own son's head. Needless to say, the arrow was true and the boy was spared.

Guildhall, a jewel-box of a building, alongside the slim Gothic grandeur of the **Fraumünster**, and also **St Peter's** church, with an eye-catching clockface.

Lucerne

The French name, **Lucerne**, leaves the visitor totally unprepared for the very German character of this city of about 180,000. Far better to use the same name as the locals: **Luzern ❽**. The covered **Kapellbrücke** (Chapel Bridge), built in 1333 and reconstructed after a serious fire in 1993, is Lucerne's best-known landmark. It has a distinctive red-tile roof and its interior is lined with gabled paintings which glorify the martyrs and heroes of the region. A few hundred yards further upstream a second medieval bridge with a small chapel crosses the **River Reuss**, which feeds **Vierwaldstättersee (Lake Lucerne)**. **Spreuerbrücke** (Spreuer Bridge) is made of wood and has a gable roof. The gable ends are decorated with paintings of Caspar Meglinger's famous *Totentanz* ("Dance of Death").

Lucerne's medieval ambience is enhanced by its breathtaking surroundings: a big mirror-like lake criss-crossed by paddle steamers, flanked on either side by the two mountain giants of the **Rigi** and **Pilatus**. The crystal blue waters meeting the mountain faces are reminiscent of Norwegian fjords. Boat cruises stop at various points from where cable cars lead up to the surrounding peaks. You can walk up from the village of **Vitznau** to the peak of the Rigi in about four hours. The alpine panorama is splendid, stretching 300 km (nearly 200 miles) in every direction. The cog-wheel railway on the Pilatus, with a 48 percent gradient, is one of the world's steepest. Yodelling, flag-throwing and alphorn concerts, once a genuine part of the regional folklore, are kept alive for tourists.

Lucerne is also known as the place where German composer Richard Wag-

BELOW: Lucerne's Kapellbrücke.

ner wrote *Die Meistersinger, Siegfried* and *Götterdämmerung,* three of his major works. He lived in Lucerne between 1866 and 1872 in an early Victorian mansion on the Tribschen peninsula which is now the **Wagner Museum** (open 10am–noon & 2–5pm Tues–Sun mid-March–end-Nov; entrance charge). This was where Wagner had his illicit rendezvous with Cosima von Bülow, the daughter of Franz Liszt. When Cosima's husband learned about the trysts he divorced her, whereupon she became Wagner's wife.

Each year in August and September, Lucerne is host to the **Internationale Musikfestwochen** (International Music Festival Weeks). A popular feature of the music festivals are outdoor serenades at the **Löwenplatz.** The acoustics of the water and rock and the soft illumination of the colossal lion carved from a cliff combine to provide an enchanting nocturnal experience.

The town of **Schwyz** ❾, on the other side of Lake Lucerne, gave its name to the country. Switzerland's most important document – the Swiss Charter of 1291 – is housed in the **Bundesbriefmuseum** here. Close to the centre, the wonderfully preserved 17th-century mansion, **Ital-Reding-Haus,** tells the story of the rich families who supplied foreign courts and countries with the town's most famous export – mercenaries – in the 17th and 18th centuries.

Lake Constance

Eastern Switzerland is relatively unexplored but the area around the broad expanse of **Bodensee** (Lake Constance) ❿, with vine-covered slopes, orchards, meadows and historic towns and villages, is a scenic oasis scarcely equalled anywhere else in Switzerland. The city of **St Gallen** ⓫, the largest in eastern Switzerland, can be reached quickly by motorway from Zürich or inter-city

Map on pages 196–7

The road from Lucerne to Bern passes through the valley of the river Emme, home of the famous Swiss Emmental cheese.

BELOW: library at the monastery of St Gallen.

THE POWER OF ST GALLEN

The baroque monastery area of St Gallen bears magnificent witness to the final flourishing of one of Europe's most important abbeys, its history stretching back more than 12 centuries. In AD 612, an Irish itinerant monk named Gall built a wooden chapel and a cell, in which to live and sleep, here in the Steinach Valley, which at that time was still thickly overgrown with forest. In 747 a Benedictine monastery was erected on the site, but this was replaced in the 9th century by an abbey complex which subsequently became a great centre of ecclesiastical power.

In the 15th century it developed into a self-contained state ruled by prince-abbots. Their reign continued until 1798, when the monastery was disbanded by the French, but in 1847 its minster was elevated as the cathedral of the newly formed diocese of St Gallen.

The abbey seen today was freely modelled on Caspar Mosbrugger's famous plan of 1721, now kept in the rococo abbey library. The library, nave and rotunda were built in 1755–67 by Peter Thumb, and the new choir with the twin-towered facade was added in 1761. The abbey houses an important collection of rare manuscripts, including the famous *Folchart* and *Golden Psalters*, from AD 864–872, and the *Evangelium Longum* from around AD 900.

The majestic Matterhorn.

train. It originally developed from a monastery precinct now dominated by the baroque **cathedral** (open daily; entrance charge). The city also contains a series of exceptionally successful baroque facades, particularly the **Zum Greif** house (22 Gallusstrasse) and the **Haus zum Pelikan** (15 Schmiedgasse).

In a quiet corner on the Swiss-Austrian border, next to the cantons of St Gallen and Grisons, lies **Liechtenstein** ⑫. This independent *Fürstentum* (principality), which uses Swiss currency, is left over from the Holy Roman Empire and occupies only 158 sq km (61 sq miles) between the River Rhine and the Vorarlberg mountains.

The Graubünden Alps

Chur ⑬, the capital of the Graubünden, is the oldest town in Switzerland, having been settled by the Celts 5,000 years ago. The old part of town is exceptionally beautiful when snow lies on the mighty roofs of the Gothic **Town Hall**, the **Bishop's Palace** and the Romanesque **Cathedral**, which contains a magnificent late Gothic carved High Altar.

Anyone who wants to cross the passes in Graubünden has to take the route through the narrow gap formed by the Bündner Herrschaft and Chur, via either **Lenzerheide** and **Tiefencastel** or **Landquart** and **Klosters**, to **Davos** ⑭. Davos's fame lies principally in the **Parsenn** – which provides 200 km (125 miles) of its total of 320 km (200 miles) of piste leading into the valley below. But the winter resort, *par excellence*, has to be **St Moritz** ⑮. It all began in 1864, when Johannes Badrutt, who built St Moritz's Kulm Hotel, invited some English summer guests to spend the winter here. In 1880 Europe's first curling tournament took place here, and in 1884 the first toboggan-run was built. Nowadays, the most popular activity is hang-gliding down to the **St Moritzer See**.

To escape the bustle of the town and lake, take the route down the right-hand side of the valley up to **Maloja**, which leads across wooded, sheltered slopes through an idyllic landscape with wonderful views of Lake Silvaplana below; continue past the foot of the **Corvatsch**, considered by many to be the best mountain for skiing in the world.

The Ticino

In the **Ticino** it is still possible to find seemingly endless and wonderfully quiet valleys filled with sunshine and sub-Alpine vegetation, although they may be just a few kilometres from noisy motorways and railways. Predominantly mountainous, the region has two great lakes at the foot of the Alps where the Ticino borders on Italy: **Lago Maggiore** and **Lago di Lugano**.

In recent years, **Lugano** ⑯ has developed a new banking quarter. The rapid construction in the town has spared a few arcaded alleyways; the **Cathedral of San Lorenzo,** on the steep slope between the railway station and the lower part of town, has also survived. Its facade is a masterpiece of Lombardy Renaissance. With the **Museo d'Arte Moderna** and **Museo Cantonale d'Arte**, where modern art can also be seen (both museums open Tues–Sun; separate entrance charges) in the Villa Malpensata, Lugano has made a

BELOW: savouring the Alpine sun.

name for itself as a city of the arts. The **Villa Favorita** (open Apr–Nov: Fri–Sun; entrance charge), just east of the Old Town, contains paintings from the collection of Baron Thyssen-Bornemisza. Since 1993, when a large part of the collection went to Madrid *(see page 348)*, works of American and European artists from the 19th and 20th centuries have been on show at the Favorita.

Locarno ⓱ and the numerous small villages on the banks of Lago Maggiore can claim to enjoy the mildest climate in the Ticino. This has encouraged tourism to the extent that there is a perpetual coming and going around the lake area, and the consequent increase in traffic has become almost unbearable. The 14th-century **Castello Visconti** now houses the **Museo Civico** and an archaeological musuem. **Ascona** is one of the most ancient settlements on the lake, and the houses along the promenade are a reminder that fishermen once lived there.

The Bernese Oberland and the Valais

There are 51 mountains over 4,000 metres (13,000 ft) high in the chain formed by the Valaisan and Bernese Alps, which lie between the Rhône Glacier and Lake Geneva. The town of **Interlaken** ⓲, full of splendid hotel buildings, serves as a reminder of the health-spa-oriented lifestyle of the upper classes of Victorian Europe. **Thun** ⓳, considered the gateway to the Oberland, is dominated by its castle, perched on a steep hill above the town. The 12th-century keep, with its four corner towers, is reminiscent of a Norman castle.

The route to Montreux passes through the mountain resort of **Gstaad** ⓴, where high society from all over the world meets up in the winter months. Further south in the Valais region, **Zermatt** ㉑, the skiing and mountaineering mecca, lies at the foot of the most famous peak in the Alps, the Matterhorn. ❏

Map on pages 196–7

South of Interlaken are the classic valleys and peaks of the Jungfrau region – the ultimate destination of those first tourists on Thomas Cook's original excursion.

LEFT: the Davos-Parsenn skiing area.
BELOW: jewellery shopping in Davos.

AUSTRIA

*Combining alpine scenery with Mozart and Strauss, the
country is hard to beat when it comes to romance*

The opening words of Austria's national anthem are "Land of
mountains..." and that is exactly what this 84,000 sq km
(32,000 sq mile) country is. For centuries these uplands were a
bugbear, making life hard for the farmer. John Gunther, a traveller in
the 1930s, remarked: "The chief crop of provincial Austria is the
scenery." That scenery, combined with some of the best skiing in
Europe, is now the country's highest earner, and the
year-round tourist industry accounts for the largest
slice of the national economy.

Nestled among the wild Alpine scenery are hundreds of mountain lakes and idyllic watercourses
which are especially attractive in summer. The gentle
charms of the Salzkammergut and the Carinthian Lake
District are underlined by the majestic backdrop of
mountains. To the east, the foothills of the Alps gradually peter out in the Vienna woods, reaching right up to the suburbs
of the capital. Vienna, once the seat of the Babenberg dynasty, was
for 600 years the centre of one of Europe's superpowers, the Austro-
Hungarian Empire. It is a beautiful city today, and it houses a wealth
of treasures. Salzburg, on the north side of the Alps, is equally romantic, and has become almost a theme park for its most esteemed inhabitant, Wolfgang Amadeus Mozart.

Every period of European cultural development is reflected in
Austria. Romanesque, Gothic, Renaissance and baroque buildings are
scattered across the land. Statues, frescoes, ceiling and wall paintings
document more than 1,000 years of often turbulent history.

Austrians are known for their courtesy and hospitality, but they
have their regional differences. The inhabitants of the eastern
provinces reveal a mixture of German and Slavic characteristics. In
Salzburg and the Tyrol the people have more affinity with Bavarians.
The natives of Vorarlberg in the west are of Alemannic and Rhaetian
descent, and are related to the inhabitants of the Engadine and Upper
Rhine. Half its borders lie against eastern European countries: the
Czech and Slovak republics, Hungary and Slovenia, which make it
feel at the centre of the changing new world. For the visitor, however,
it still looks very much like the old world. ❑

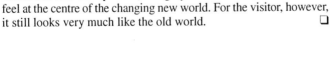

PRECEDING PAGES: Salzburg by night; beside the Grundlsee, in the Salzkammergut.
LEFT: looking towards the Sonnenspitze.

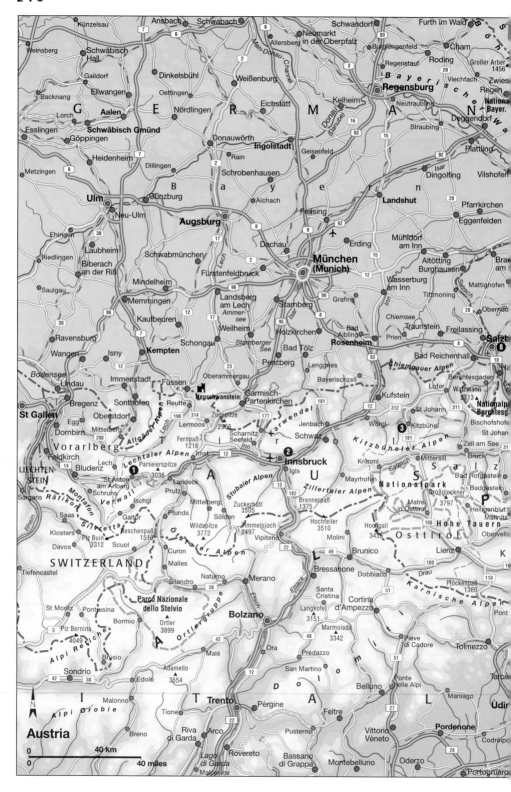

Künzelsau Ansbach Schwabach Schwandorf Furth im Wald Böh

Weinsberg Schwäbisch Hall 7 6 9 Neumarkt Allersberg in der Oberpfalz Burglengenfeld 93 Cham

Gaildorf Dinkelsbühl Weißenburg 2 Regenstauf Roding Großer Arber 1456

Backnang Ellwangen Oettingen 3 Viechtach Zwies 20 Regen

Lorch **G Aalen** Nördlingen Eichstätt **Regensburg** Neutraubling **Bayer.**

Esslingen **Schwäbisch Gmünd** Donauwörth Kelheim Straubing Deggendorf **N** Wa

Göppingen Rain **Ingolstadt** Geisenfeld 16 93 15 Plattling 92

Heidenheim 7 Dillingen Schrobenhausen 2 Isar Dingolfing Vilshofen

Metzingen 8 Günzburg Aichach y e n Landshut 20 Pfarrkirchen

Ulm Neu-Ulm Freising 92 Eggenfelden

Ehingen 30 **Augsburg** 8 9 Erding Mühldorf am Inn Altötting Bra am

Riedlingen Laubheim Schwabmünchen Dachau 15 Burghausen

Biberach an der Riß Fürstenfeldbruck 2 **München (Munich)** 12 Wasserburg am Inn Mattighofen

Saulgau Mindelheim 96 Landsberg am Lech 99 Grafing 8 Tittmoning Obern

Memmingen 12 Kaufbeuren 17 Ammer- see Starnberg 95 8 Chiemsee Traunstein Freilassing 20

30 Schongau Weilheim Holzkirchen Bad Aibling **Rosenheim** Prien 8 **Salz**

Ravensburg 7 Kempten Starnberger See Bad Tölz Penzberg Lenggries Bad Reichenhall 10

Wangen Isny 12 Bodensee Immenstadt Füssen Oberammergau Bayerischzell Chiemgauer Alpen Berchtesgaden Watzmann 2713 Nationalpark Berchtesg.

Lindau Bregenz Sonthofen Reutte 314 Garmisch-Partenkirchen 181 Kufstein Lofer

St Gallen Egg Oberstdorf 198 177 Zugspitze 2966 Scharnitz Seefeld Schwaz Wörgl Kitzbühel St Johann Bischofshofen

Dornbirn Mittelberg 200 Lermoos Fernpaß 1216 Inn Jenbach Schwaz Kitzbüheler Alpen St Johan Zell am See 31

Feldkirch Vorarlberg Imst 12 Innsbruck Krimml Mittersill Bruck

LIECHTEN-STEIN 14 Bludenz Lech Parseierspitze 3036 Landeck Igls Stubaier Alpen Mayrhofen Zillertaler Alpen Nationalpark Bad Hofgastein Badgastein

St Anton am Arlberg Schruns Prutz 13 182 Brennerpaß 1375 Großglockner 3797 Heiligenblut Mallnitz

Sargans Rätikon Verwall Ischgl Mittelberg Zuckerhütl 3505 Matrei in Osttirol 108 Hohe Tauern Obervella

Saas Galtür Pfunds Sölden Wildspitze 3772 Timmelsjoch 2497 Hochfeiler 3510 Hoangall 3438 Osttirol

Klosters Piz Buin 3312 Scuol Curon Ötztaler Alpen Vipiteno Molini Lienz K

Davos Malles 22 L 49 Brunico 100

SWITZERLAND Naturno Merano Bressanone Dobbiaco Drau 110

Tiefencastel Silandro 38 Santa Cristina Cortina d'Ampezzo 51 Plöckenpaß 1360 Karnische Alpen Pont

St Moritz Pontresina Bormio Parco Nazionale dello Stelvio Ortler 3899 Langkofel 3151 Marmolada 3342 48 Pieve di Cadore Tolmezzo

3 Piz Bernina 4049 Alpi Retiche Brusio Ortlergruppe 42 Malé Ora Predazzo 51 Ponte nelle Alpi Tarpe

Sondrio 42 38 Edolo Adamello 3554 12 San Martino Belluno Maniago Udi

Alpi Orobie Malonno I T **Trento** Pèrgine Feltre 27 Pordenone

Austria Tione 22 Vittorio Vèneto Codrèipo

0 40 km Breno Riva di Garda Arco Pusterno Bassano di Grappa Montebelluno Oderzo 28

0 40 miles Lago di Garda Rovereto Portogruaro

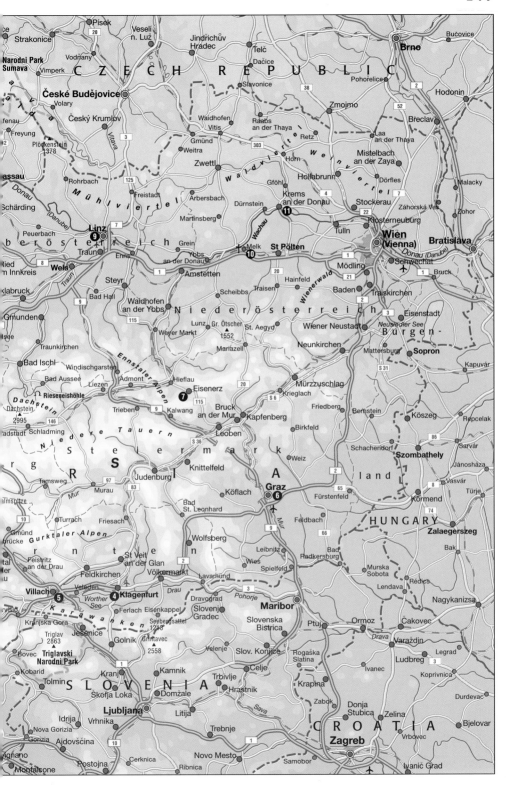

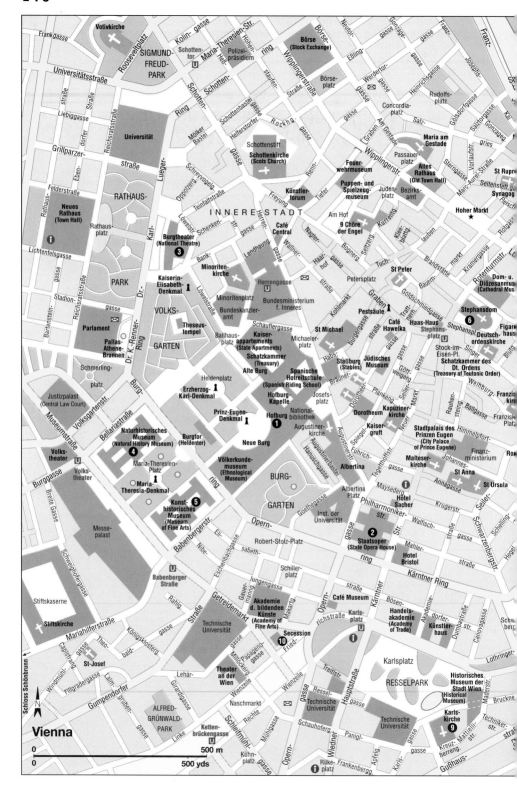

Vienna

0   500 m

0   500 yds

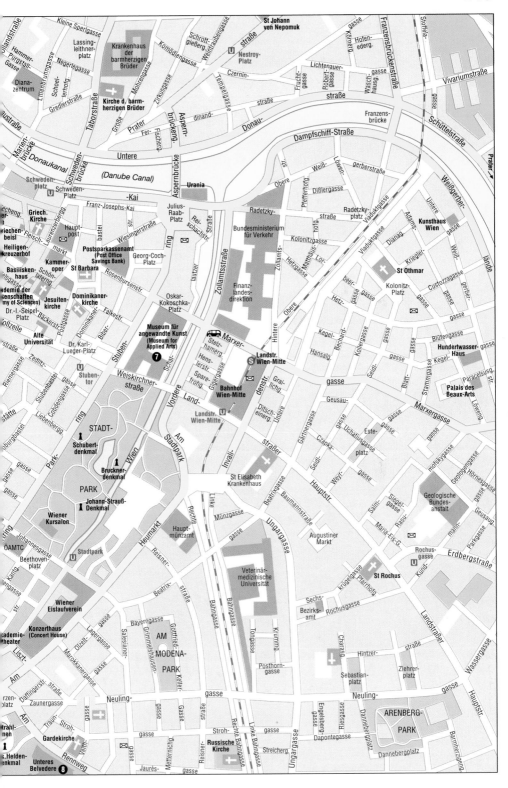

VIENNA

The capital of the former Habsburg Empire gave the world the waltz, and has been home to some of the world's great composers

Map on pages 218–9

Vienna

Vienna is an easy city to get to know, not because nobody ever gets lost in its maze of streets and passages (they do), but because the Viennese themselves have a reputation for being courteous and helpful. The diversity of people here can be traced directly to the far-flung Habsburg Empire; Vienna was the seat of the ruling family for almost 650 years. Situated in the Danube Valley, it was first settled by the Celts around 400 BC, and known as *Vindonbona*.

Austria's capital of 1.6 million people lies on the eastern edge of the country where East meets West and has always been something of a bulwark. It was recognised by Europe as the saviour of Christendom when it finally repelled the Turks in 1683. For centuries, all manner of ideas were fomented and flourished among the city's cultural palaces and cafés. Art and music, theatre, medicine and psychology found the ideal climate in which to grow. Vienna has been home to some of the great composers, from Haydn to Beethoven to Schoenberg; and to some equally great architects from the historicist Heinrich von Ferstel to Otto Wagner, founder of the Viennese *Jugendstil* (Art Nouveau) movement. Today Vienna serves as a neutral meeting ground for diplomats of all political persuasions. It is the seat of OPEC (Organization of Petroleum Exporting Countries) and the third seat of the United Nations (after New York City and Geneva).

LEFT: Viennese Fiakers – traditional horse-drawn open carriages.
BELOW: equestrian statue at the Hofburg.

Building for glory

The Habsburgs were great builders. At the heart of the old town they erected the **Hofburg** ❶ (Imperial Palace), a town itself within the city, which was "always being built but never finished." Construction began about 1220, but it was enlarged and renovated right into the 20th century. The **Neue Burg** (open Wed–Sun; entrance charge) wing as it now stands was completed just 10 years before the collapse of the Habsburg Empire; it houses collections of musical instruments, armour and weapons, the **Ephesos Archaeological Museum** and the **Ethnological Museum**.

The oldest part of the Hofburg is the **Schweizerhof** (Swiss Court). A chapel was added next, then the **Amalienhof**, the **Stallburg** (stables), the **Imperial Apartments**, the **Chancellery**, the **Spanish Riding School**, the **Albertina** and the **National Library**, all of which open on to lovely courts and gardens.

Notable collections housed in the Imperial Palace are the **Collection of Court Porcelain and Silver** (open daily; entrance charge) and the **Imperial Treasury** (open Wed–Mon; entrance charge). The treasury contains the bejewelled crown of the Holy Roman Empire, which was founded in 800 by Charlemagne and lasted until 1803, when it was broken up by Napoleon. The crown, symbol of German kings and emperors, was carried from 1273 on by the Habsburg

rulers, a role which made them one of the most influential dynasties in the political affairs of Central Europe. Among other exhibitions from the time of the Habsburg emperors is the **Albertina** (closed for renovation), which has a remarkable collection of watercolours, prints and drawings, including works by Albrecht Dürer, Michelangelo and Rubens.

The Vienna Ball season closes every year on the last Thursday in February with the glamorous Opera Ball at the Staatsoper. The event attracts guests from all over the world.

The all-white baroque confection of the **Spanische Hofreitschule** (Spanish Riding School; open Mar–Jun & Sept–Oct for performances; see tourist board leaflet for how to obtain tickets) dates from the 17th century when Emperor Karl VI introduced the Spanish court ceremonial in Vienna. The Lipizzaner horses, originally a Spanish breed, were first raised in Lipizza (later part of Yugoslavia) and then in the Styrian town of Piber. It is a unique experience to watch the white stallions perform the delicate steps of the *haute école* of riding to the music of classical dances such as the gavotte, quadrille, polka and waltz.

The magnificent Ring

Vienna has hundreds of palaces, large and small, but the biggest building spree the city has ever seen was the **Ring**. This wide avenue, 57 metres (187 ft) across, follows the line of fortifications which stood until Emperor Franz Joseph ordered the ramparts razed in 1857. Architectural competitions were launched and the city received a brand-new face. Standing at the centre of the Ring, and the first of the buildings to be completed in 1869, is the **Staatsoper ❷** (Opera House). The Viennese ridiculed the Romantic-Historicist style as it was being built and, stung by the criticism, one of its architects hanged himself.

BELOW: performing at the Spanish Riding School.

It remained for the prolific architect Heinrich von Ferstel to set the traditional tone of the Ring with the **Votivkirche** (Votive Church), built in gratitude for the failure of an assassination attempt against Franz Joseph in 1853. The church is Neo-Gothic down to the last detail and later buildings in the vicinity were adjusted to fit the style.

Von Ferstel's other Ring building is the **University**, built in the Italian Renaissance style. The soaring architecture continues around the circle with the **Rathaus** (Town Hall), built in imitation Gothic, and **Parliament** building in Hellenistic style. The **Burgtheater ❸**, just steps from the University, was built in the shape of a Greek lyre, but its acoustics were so poor that it had to be reconstructed 10 years later. The "House on the Ring" is justifiably considered the most significant theatrical stage in the German-speaking world. The convex arch of the central tract is particularly impressive, and the spreading wings on either side house the staircases leading to the boxes.

Museum Quarter

Both the **Naturhistorisches Museum ❹** (Natural History Museum, open Wed–Mon; entrance charge), with a wide-ranging collection of dinosaur skeletons, human skulls, gemstones and Iron and Bronze Age items, and the **Kunsthistorisches Museum ❺** (Fine Arts Museum; open Tues–Sun; entrance charge) are also Italian Renaissance. They stand across the Ring from the Neue Burg and its parks. The Fine Arts Museum contains the fourth-largest collection of paintings in the world, among them works by Dutch, Flemish, Italian and Spanish masters such as Rembrandt, Vermeer, van Eyck, Rubens, Titian and Velázquez. There are also fine collections of European sculpture and decorative art, as well as Greek, Roman, Oriental and Egyptian antiquities.

Map on pages 218–9

The Stephansdom

On the other side of the Hofburg complex lies **Stephansplatz**, Vienna's most famous square and also the city's bustling centre. The south tower of **Stephansdom** ❻ (St Stephen's Cathedral) gives a fabulous overview of the city: climb the 343 steps to the watchman's room and you are rewarded with a dramatic view of the heart of the city. As an alternative, an elevator ascends the unfinished north tower of the cathedral as far as *Pummerin* (Boomer), a copy of the giant bell which was destroyed in World War II. The original *Pummerin* was cast in 1711 from cannons captured from the Turks. Habsburg marriages took place in St Stephen's cathedral (*Steffl* to the Viennese), following their habit of acquiring territory through marriage instead of war whenever possible. And here in the catacombs are the urns containing the entrails of the Austrian emperors.

In front of the asymmetrical Steffl is the smart shopping centre of Vienna, the pedestrian zone including the **Graben** and **Kärntnerstrasse**. The latter continues on the other side of the Ring as **Mariahilferstrasse**, where the large department stores can be found. The area behind St Stephen's is called **Old Vienna** because it best retains the air of the past, though it is not actually the oldest quarter. A jumble of building styles from the 16th and 17th centuries in the network of narrow lanes are well preserved. In **Bäckerstrasse** and **Schönlaterngasse**, in particular, there are many bars and restaurants which are often thronged with people until the early hours of the morning.

From here, stroll down Wollzeile to the Stubenring, and cross over to the **Museum für angewandte Kunst** ❼ (Museum of Applied Arts; open Tues–Sun; entrance charge). Renovated in 1993, this enormous building is the repository for fine Austrian furniture as well as porcelain, textiles, glass and jewellery from around the world. The varied interior decoration of the exhibition rooms adds a splendid extra dimension.

Upmarket Belvedere

Between the Applied Arts Museum and the Belvedere Palace lies the **Stadtpark**, laid out in 1862 and the most extensive patch of green in the vicinity of the Ringstrasse. The ancient trees are reflected in the ponds and River Wien, which is flanked by a string of pavilions and a promenade adorned with statuary.

The **Belvedere** ❽ (gardens open daily; museums open Tues–Sun; entrance charges), a palace of sumptuous proportions, was built between 1714 and 1723 for Prince Eugene of Savoy, who routed the Turks in 1683. In fact, it is really two palaces, the Upper and Lower Belvedere, joined by terraced gardens. The former houses the **Österreichische Galerie des 19 and 20 Jahrhunderts** (Austrian Gallery for 19th-century and 20th-century Art), including a memorable Gustav Klimt collection; the Lower Belvedere houses the **Barockmuseum** (Museum of Baroque Art), while the

BELOW: the Stephansdom.

The Prater: Vienna's pleasure gardens.

Orangery next door displays Gothic and early Renaissance masterpieces in the **Museum Mittelalterlicher Kunst** (Museum of Medieval Art).

Going back in the direction of the city centre you'll come to Karlsplatz, and the splended baroque **Karlskirche ❾**. Regarded as the finest ecclesiastical baroque building in the city, it was pledged by Charles VI during an epidemic of plague in 1713, started by Johann Fischer von Erlach and completed by his son, Joseph Emanuel. Its unique design includes a magnificent green cupola, twin triumphal pillars with spiral reliefs, and exterior belfries.

Tucked in between the Karlskirche and the Opera house, at Friedrichstrasse 12, is the *Jugendstil* **Secession Building ❿** (open Tues–Sun; entrance charge). It was designed by Joseph Maria Olbrich as a showcase for the Secession movement's artists such as Schiele, Kokoschka and Klimt, whose *Beethoven Frieze* (1902) covers three interior walls of the building.

Excursions from the city

A look at a map of Vienna shows that it is laid out in concentric circles. The **Innenstadt** (Inner City), also known as I. Bezirk (first district), is enclosed by the Ring and the Donaukanal. On the other side of the Ring is the **Vorstadt**, the part of the city that grew up outside the fortifications. It is surrounded by another ring road – the Gürtel. Outside the Gürtel come the suburbs, little villages such as Grinzing, Nussdorf, Gumpoldskirchen and Severing, and their rural wine taverns called *Heurigen*.

BELOW: Johann Strauss, playing his violin.

The woods and meadows between the Danube and its canal to the east of the city enclose the **Prater** (open Apr–Oct: daily; entrance charge), once a playground of emperors but opened to the public as a park in 1766 by Emperor

MUSIC UNTIL DAWN

Vienna loves music, and musicians of every kind thrive in Vienna. In the **Burgkapelle** (Chapel of the Imperial Palace), the *Wiener Sängerknaben* still sing Mass on Sundays; the Vienna Boys' Choir was organised 500 years ago by Emperor Maximilian, but it is now a private group.

Waltzes by Johann Strauss and Franz Lehár are especially popular at Carnival season, when the elegant balls continue until dawn. Then there are the great composers like Haydn, Schubert, Mozart, Mahler, Bruckner, Schoenberg and others. Traces of them can be found in many streets throughout Vienna.

Among the houses which have been turned into small museums or memorials are: the house where Haydn wrote his *Creation* (Haydngasse 19); the apartment where Mozart spent the happiest years of his life (Figaro House, Domgasse 5); the places where Schubert was born (Nussdorferstrasse 54) and where he died (Kettenbrückengasse 6).

Beethoven had more than 25 different addresses. In 1800, he moved to Heiligenstadt in the 19th district of Döbling. It was here at Probusgasse 6, today the **Beethoven Museum** (open Tues–Sun), that he wrote his Heiligenstädter Testament, a moving document in which he revealed his desperate feelings about his growing deafness.

Joseph II. Its landmark is the *Riesenrad* (open daily), a giant Ferris wheel that arcs to a high point of nearly 65 metres (213 ft). Notices above the cabin windows help to identify important landmarks in the city. There are also a Planetarium, miniature railway, tennis courts, bicycle hire shops and a swimming pool in the park, as well as the 5-km (3-mile) **Hauptalle** for strolls and picnics.

Exploring Vienna can be followed with a trip along the Danube, although its waters are disappointingly brown. Boats operate from April to mid-October and make various journeys including day-trips to Bratislava, just inside the Czech Republic, or an overnight run to Hungary's capital, Budapest *(see pages 249–251)*. The city subsides into the **Vienna Woods**, where the Alps end – or begin – at the edge of the Hungarian Plains.

Serene residence

A short distance beyond the confines of the Ringstrasse and the inner city lies the **Schloss Schönbrunn** (open daily; entrance charge), the imperial summer residence. The site of the palace is the **Schöner Brunnen** (Beautiful Fountains), spacious grounds where Leopold I wished to build a palace to rival Versailles. Because of financial difficulties, his plans did not come to fruition and it was not until 1743 that Empress Maria Theresa employed Nikolaus Pacassi to build the palace we see today.

Schönbrunn contains 1,200 rooms, 45 of which are open to the public. Notable among these are a selection of private rooms used by Maria Theresa, including the Breakfast Room and Vieux-Lacque Room, and various ceremonial and state rooms. In the grounds are the baroque Zoo, the English Garden and Palm House, and a coach museum displaying the coronation coach of Karl VI. ❑

Map on pages 218–9

BELOW: Schönbrunn palace and gardens.

AROUND AUSTRIA

With two-thirds of the country taken up by the Alps,
Austria is the place for winter skiers and summer hikers.
Salzburg and Innsbruck make good centres to stay

Map
on pages
216–7

Vienna

Austria is a land of peaks and valleys, high roads and mountain passes, ski slopes and Alpine meadows that fall away eastward to the Hungarian plains. The spectacular scenery, friendly people, good food and well-developed resorts have earned Austria a deservedly high reputation around the world. Where farmers once eked out a living during the short summers, well-established hotels and restaurants have sprung up. A vast network of lifts and cable cars lace the mountainsides taking visitors, winter and summer, to the high playgrounds.

The birthplace of downhill skiing

The **Arlberg** mountain region, straddling the border of the Tyrol and Vorarlberg provinces, is considered the cradle of Alpine skiing. Here Austrian skiers refined the Scandinavian sport to suit their own steep slopes and founded a system of teaching. Hannes Schneider gave the first ski lessons to tourists in 1907 in **St Anton am Arlberg ❶**, a village that has grown into a first-class ski resort. Others include **Kitzbühel** and **Ischgl**, whose slopes lead into Switzerland, and **St Johann** and **Seefeld** in Tyrol – usually sleepy villages whose population is greatly outnumbered by winter visitors.

LEFT: Wilten church.
BELOW: the National Games at Taxen-bach in the Alps.

The **Tyrol** is the best known of the ski regions but good skiing is by no means limited to that province. Next to Vorarlberg is the **Montafon Valley**, gateway to the Silvretta High Alpine road, with 3,312-metre (10,863-ft) **Piz Buin** towering in the background. The Montafon was the site of Austria's first ski championships after World War II, and the story is told of the local official who wanted to provide good food for the participants in the event. He managed to acquire two cows, even though meat was severely rationed at the time. The people dined well but the official spent six months in jail for his hospitality. Montafoners are descended from the Rhaeto-Romansch civilisation, as their dialect, place names and complexions attest.

The Tyrol and the Vorarlberg reach like an arm between Germany to the north and Switzerland and Italy to the south; it is no wonder that the Montafon folk so closely resemble the Engadine Swiss, and the Tyroleans are hard to tell from their Bavarian cousins.

Innsbruck

Just as the Tyrol juts between countries, the province of **Salzburgerland** juts into the Tyrol and touches the Italian border, for practical purposes cutting the East Tyrol district off from its provincial capital, **Innsbruck ❷**. (The connecting section of country was chopped off and passed to Italian control in 1919.)

The city had its golden age as the residence of the House of Habsburg in the 15th and 16th centuries, and reached its prime under the reign of Emperor Maximilian I (1493–1516). Trade and manufacturing flourished, as well as architecture. Many of the city's landmarks hail from this period.

A tour of the Old Town

Innsbruck's Old Town is oval-shaped and constitutes a precious assembly of medieval architecture. It is bordered by the **River Inn** and the streets of **Marktgraben, Burggraben** and **Herrengasse**. Almost every street offers a view of the peaks of the "**die Zweitausender**" ("Two Thousand") nearby. The narrow lanes in the centre have been turned into a pedestrian precinct, allowing visitors to stroll without hindrance past the pergolas, oriel windows, painted facades and stucco ornaments. Another way of viewing these architectural treasures is by hiring one of the horse-drawn carriages that wait on Rennweg, in front of the **Tiroler Ländestheater** (Tirolean Provincial Theatre).

In somnolent mood, Innsbruck.

Herzog-Friedrich-Strasse leads straight into the heart of the Old Town to **Goldenes Dachl** (Little Golden Roof), a magnificent oriel built around 1500 in the late Gothic style. It was added to the **Neuer Hof** (New Palace) in commemoration of the betrothal of Maximilian I and Maria Bianca Sforza, daughter of the duke of Milan. The decorative alcove, adorned with 3,450 gilt copper shingles, served as a box for spectators watching tournaments and plays in the square below. It is Innsbruck's best known landmark.

Herzog-Friedrich-Strasse is famous for a string of medieval houses among which **Trautsonhaus**, built during the transition from the Gothic to the Renaissance period, and **Katzunghaus**, with its unique reliefs on the balcony dating back to 1530, are especially noteworthy. Another landmark is the 56-metre (180-ft) **City Tower** built in 1360 as a watchtower against fire. There is a 33-metre (110-ft) gallery, which has a magnificent view of the whole town and the mountains. The sights include the **Ottoburg**, a residential tower on the embankment built in 1495, and the **Burgriesenhaus in Hofgasse**, which Duke Siegmund built in 1490 for his court favourite Niklas Haidl, a 2.4-metre (7 ft 10-inch) giant.

BELOW: the mountains around Innsbruck.

In the opposite direction through Pfarrgasse is Domplatz (at the rear of Little Golden Roof). It is the location of Innsbruck's **Parish Church of Sankt Jakob**, which, with its twin towers, represents a splendid example of baroque architecture. A copy of *Mariahilf* ("Our Lady of Succour") by Lukas Cranach the Elder adorns the high altar.

Renaissance building boom

No other place in Austria conveys such a vivid impression of 16th-century architecture as the eastern part of the Old Town. The 15th-century **Hofburg** (Royal Palace; open Mon–Sun 9am–5pm; entrance charge) was rebuilt from 1754 to 1776 in late rococo style. One highlight of the guided tours is the **Riesensaal** (Giant's Room), a two-storey stateroom with rococo stucco-work and portraits of the Imperial family. The **Hofkirche** (Royal Church) houses the **mausoleum of Maximilian I**, although he was actually buried in

Wiener Neustadt near Vienna. Twenty-eight of his forebears and contemporaries, all cast as larger-than-life bronze statures, stand guard around the grave.

To the east of the Royal Church, in an old Franciscan monastery, is the **Tiroler Volkskunstmuseum** (Tyrolean Folkcraft Museum; open Mon–Sun 9am–5pm; entrance charge), which contains 20 rustic interiors from various periods as well as furniture, folk costumes and other folk art exemplifying the creativity of the native Tyrolean people.

Leading to the south from Herzog-Friedrich-Strasse is Innsbruck's principal thoroughfare, **Maria Theresien Strasse**, where **Anna Saule** (St Anne's Column) commemorates 26 July 1703, St Anne's Day, when the Bavarian troops forced the inhabitants out of Innsbruck during the War of the Spanish Succession (1701–14). Leopoldstrasse, to the south, leads both to **Stiftkirche Wilten** (Wilten Abbey Church), founded in 1138 by the Premonstratensians, and to the **Wiltener Basilika** (Wilten Basilica), built in 1755 on the foundations of a previous building. The abbey church as it stands today was completed in 1670. It is regarded as one of the loveliest churches of the early baroque period in Austria and the Basilica ranks highly as an example of rococo.

The former residence of Archduke Ferdinand, **Schloss Ambras** (Ambras Castle), lies 3.2 km (2 miles) southeast of the city. Today the castle is a museum housing a substantial art and armour collection from the 16th century. In the age of chivalry, Innsbruck was a proper jousting place where the cream of Europe's knights used to gather for their games and tournaments to seek the favour of the young ladies of the castle.

Olympic legacy

In 1964 and 1976 Innsbruck hosted a different kind of games: the Winter Olympics. An imposing legacy of the games just outside the city in front of Bergisel is the **Olympic ski jumps**, with a stadium seating 60,000 spectators. Also remaining from the games is the **Olympic ice stadium** (open all year) and an artificial bob sleigh at **Igls**, a popular holiday resort a short distance outside the city.

The reputation of **Kitzbühel** ❸ as a chic winter sports centre dates from the triple Olympic victory in 1956 of local boy Toni Sailer – the "Kitz Comet". The famous **Hahnenkamm** races, in the mountains to the west of the centre, and the **Kitzbüheler Horn** to the east, also ensure that the Kitzbühel skiing area attracts top enthusiasts from all over the world. In summer, the relatively tame Kitzbühel Alps afford an extensive range of mountain walks; for those who prefer it steeper, rockier and more challenging, there are the vast limestone peaks of the **Wilder Kaiser**. The best starting point for a mountain walk is **St Johann**, the scattered village lying in the valley between the Kitzbüheler Horn and the Wilder Kaiser.

The East Tyrol and the provinces of Salzburgerland and Kärnten (Carinthia) converge at the **Grossglockner**, the highest point in Austria at 3,797 metres (12,457 ft). At its foot glistens the **Pasterze glacier**. The best view of both mountain and glacier is from **Franz-Josef-Höhe**, a spur at the end of one branch of

Map on pages 216–7

Innsbruck is the gateway to a variety of ski areas in the Tyrol region. The Stubbai Alps, southwest of the city, are easily accessible; Neustift, at 1,000 metres (3,300 ft) above sea level, is perhaps the best known resort.

BELOW: on the Grossglockner alpine road.

Grossglockner Road. The road is one of the great Alpine highways which snake across Austria's mountain ranges. It begins at **Bruck** and ends at the mountaineering town of **Heiligenblut**.

Klagenfurt and Lake Wörther

A faster scenic route linking north and south is the **Tauern Autobahn** (motorway), where two large tunnels cut the travel time between Salzburg and the Carinthian capital, **Klagenfurt ❹**. Today it is hard to imagine that this region of lakes and rivers, majestic mountains and secluded valleys was once rough marshland. Legend tells of a winged dragon that once struck terror into the hearts of local inhabitants. Its statue is immortalised as the emblem of Klagenfurt, standing in the middle of the Neuer Platz, where most of the lovely houses date from the 17th century.

The house **Zur Goldenen Gans** (the Golden Goose), listed in records of 1489, was originally planned as an imperial residence, and the town has a number of important historical buildings. The **Landhaus**, dating from the 16th century, displays 665 coats of arms, while the Palais Porcia and Town Hall also date from the 16th century. There are also no fewer than 22 castles within a radius of a few miles. On the **Magdalensberg** lies the site of the largest archaelogical excavations in Austria – a Nordic-Roman town, with an open-air museum and display rooms (open mid-Apr–mid-Oct 9am–7pm; entrance charge).

Lake Wörther, lying beside Klagenfurt, is the largest lakeside bathing area in Europe. In spite of its depth of 85 metres (275 ft) in places, the water temperature can reach 28°C (83°F) – a fact which makes it irresistible to swimmers. Numerous resorts adorn the shores of the lake, including **Krumpendorf**,

BELOW: transporting winter fodder.

Pörtschach, Veleden and Maria Wörth. A further attraction beside the lake is Minimundus (open Apr–Oct: daily; entrance charge), where there are more than 150 replicas of famous buildings, a miniature railway and a harbour with model ships. Carinthia possesses a total of 1,270 lakes, which provide excellent beaches, sports facilities and amenities in idyllic surroundings to suit all tastes.

Villach ❺, a chic and historic town, lies at the centre of the Carinthian lake district. The Romans built a fort and a bridge over the Drava here during the first century, constructing paved roads as they did so, and the town became the economic and cultural centre of Carinthia in the 16th century. Paracelsus spent his youth here and described the healing powers of the springs which were to move Napoleon to rapturous enthusiasm. Even today, the warm waters offer relaxation and healing to guests from all over the world in the cure and bathing centres.

Styria

Further east is Graz ❻, the capital of Styria and the second largest Austrian city, with a population of 240,000. The Italian influence on the architecture of the city is unmistakable, notably the Town Hall, the late Gothic Franciscan Church (1520) and the Renaissance-style Landhaus. Other architectural jewels include the Castle, Old University, Cathedral and numerous baroque palaces. The Arsenal (open Apr–Oct: daily; entrance charge), on the south side of the Landhaus, is one of the finest in the world, with 15th-century suits of armour, two-handed swords, shields, muskets, guns and rifles all on view. The Schlossberg, the dolomite rock 470 metres (1,550 ft) high, can be ascended by funicular or on foot. It is crowned by the Clocktower (28 metres/90 ft high and with a clock dating to 1712) and has become the city landmark, visible for miles around.

Map on pages 216–7

*Some 40 km (25 miles) west of Graz lies the **Piber Stud Farm**, where the Lipizzaner stallions for the Spanish Riding School in Vienna are bred (daily tours are available).*

BELOW: Altausee, Salzkammergut.

Geranium-bedecked window in Salzburg.

Austrians regard Styria as the "Green Province" of Austria. This second-largest Austrian province includes Alpine topographical forms – perpetual ice and deeply cut ravines – as well as extensive expanses of forest which slowly give way to gently rolling ranges of hills skirting the lower Hungarian plains.

The town of **Eisenerz** ❼ lies in a wild, romantic valley basin at the mouth of the Krumpentala and Trofeng valleys. It is also the centre of an ore-mining region and has a well-developed infrastructure for tourists: camp sites, climbing school, fitness circuit, footpaths and a lake for bathing. The **Erzberg** (1,470 metres/4,810 ft) rises high above the valley floor and is still in use as an open-cast iron ore mine. Eisenerz is the ideal starting point for tours up the Erzberg (guided tours twice daily from May to October).

Salzburg

Many towns in Austria are blessed with splendid churches, squares and ornamental fountains; in none but **Salzburg** ❽, however, do they enjoy such a vibrant, cosmopolitan atmosphere and such magnificent surrounding scenery. The birthplace of Wolfgang Amadeus Mozart (1756–91), Salzburg is one of the most visited towns in Austria, especially during the annual festival in tribute to the composer in January. The annual summer Music Festival also bears Mozart's indelible stamp. His birthplace at **Getreidegasse** No. 9 is now a museum (open Mon–Sun 9am–5.30pm; entrance charge) with many mementos of his life, including his violin.

Traditionally the summer festival of operas and concerts opens with Hugo von Hofmannsthal's *Jederman* (*Everyman*), a morality play performed in the open **Domplatz** (Cathedral Square).

BELOW: at Mozart's birthplace in Salzburg, and, **RIGHT**, the piano in his studio.

The **Mönchsberg** and the **Burgberg** – the two mountains within the city boundaries – still stand sentinel over the narrow alleys of the **Old Town**, with their tall, narrow merchants' houses, hidden arcaded courtyards, baroque-domed churches, palaces and spacious squares of the prince-bishops' quarter. Clinging to the side of Mönchsberg, and dominating the old town, is the fortress of **Hohensalzburg** (open for guided tours daily; entrance charge), a symbol of the powerbase that shaped so many chapters in the city's history. Archbishop Gebhard began its construction in 1077, and the castle was continuously expanded until the 17th century. One particularly interesting item is a monumental porcelain tile stove dating from 1501 in the Golden Room.

Map on pages 216–7

The Wachau

The **Brucknerhaus**, which opened in 1974 in **Linz ❾**, is the location of the annual Bruckner Festival. Anton Bruckner (1824–96), "God's musician", as he was dubbed, is a great favourite among Austrian people. The Danube flows through the town that boasts Austria's most modern port. It is an industrial city, but pretty in spite of that, especially around the **Hauptplatz** (the main square). A Holy Trinity column stands in the centre, and among the buildings surrounding the square are the **Council House**, built in 1513, and the **Old Cathedral** (Jesuit Church) with its twin spires.

The Danube River meanders across the north of Austria, past woods and fields, through cities, in the shadow of churches and abbeys. The spectacular Benedictine **Abbey of Melk ❿**, its side facade some 340 metres (1,115 ft) long, is poised in all its baroque splendour on a promontory, and gives a fine view of the river and its valley. Apricot blossoms and Richard the Lionheart, the waves of the Danube, castles, fish and wine are all aspects of this charming river region known as the **Wachau**. **Dürnstein** is probably the region's most popular village and enjoys one of the most beautiful situations. At the end of the 12th century, Richard the Lionheart, King of England, was captured on his return from a crusade and languished in the dungeons of Dürnstein castle. Blondel, his faithful minstrel, set off to find him and eventually struck up the first bars of Richard's favourite song beneath the impregnable fortress. Soon afterwards, Richard was released following payment of a huge ransom by the English (the money was used to finance the construction of Vienna's first city wall).

A few miles downstream is **Krems an der Donau ⓫**, the "Model Town for the Preservation of Historical Monuments". The town lies nestled among terraced vineyards, clinging to the bank of the Danube. Every visitor to the Wachau should taste the region's fine wines and, in particular, its apricot brandy. The entire valley is full of apricot trees. During spring, the blossom turns the countryside into a spectacle of great beauty.

The river continues past the villages of the **Vienna Woods**, such as Heiligenkreuz, where there is a gem of a Cistercian abbey, and Soos, a classic wine-growing village. Further on from here, the Vienna High Road affords a magnificent view of the capital ❑

BELOW: in the mountains near Salzburg.

EXCURSIONS TO THE EAST

Cities such as Prague, Warsaw, Kraków and Budapest have become firmly established on the tourist map

When the "iron curtain" was drawn back in 1990 the traveller in Continental Europe could once more discover the great cities that had shaped its history. In the Czech Republic the glittering city of Prague, its centre largely untouched in communist times, immediately attracted many visitors. Those travelling to Poland make their way to Warsaw and, more often, to Kraców while to the south Europe's great river, the Danube, could be followed to Budapest, the capital of Hungary.

The attraction of these cities is not just their novelty. Many retain the magnificent architecture and characteristic cafés, which evoke the 19th-century cultural flowering, though the tragedies of the 20th century are also not far away. There are the haunts of Kafka, Conrad, Mozart, Chopin, Dvořák and Liszt. This is, after all, the home of the original Bohemians and the gypsy violin. And although McDonald's hamburgers have arrived, a visitor to these countries is rewarded with a glimpse of a different and sometimes fast disappearing way of life.

Just a look at the map is a reminder that these cities have always been central to mainstream European history and culture. They fall in a cluster between Berlin and Vienna. Prague is no further east than Naples; Warsaw and Budapest are due north of Italy's heel. From Prague it is little more than an hour's drive to the German border, and barely twice that south to Austria's capital, Vienna, which history has treated as a next-door neighbour. From Vienna you can hitch a ride on a slow boat down the Danube to Budapest and find that coffee houses are not confined to the Austrian capital.

Prague, Vienna and Budapest were the jewels in the Austro-Hungarian Empire's crown. All of them were profoundly affected by the break-up of the former empires at the end of World War I when history once more shifted their borders. Poland, on the other hand, suffered the vagaries of history under the changing fortunes of Lithuanian, Prussian and Russian empires.

Communist town planning tended to leave the hearts of cities alone, and each of them have well-preserved cores; Warsaw's historic main square has been entirely rebuilt. This makes them ideal places for brief visits, as everywhere is accessible on foot. ❑

PRECEDING PAGES: Prague's Tyn church, seen from the old town hall; Bugac horseman from Hungary.
LEFT: Rynek Old Town, Warsaw.

PRAGUE

Prague used to be known as the "Five Towns", now the historic districts of Hradčany, Malá Strana, Staré Město, Nové Město and Josefov, the Jewish Quarter

Map on page 242

Princess Libussa was the mythical beauty reputed to have summoned an unsuspecting plough-hand, still wearing his boots, to found Bohemia's Přemyslid dynasty, starting with good King Wenceslas I (903–35). This version of events overlooks the fact that the shadowy historical figure of one Samo, the victor over the Avars in about 620, established his capital at Vysehrad, a short distance away. By the 14th century Prague was the grandest city in Europe, a marvel of Gothic architecture. Three centuries later, Prague was embellished with the finest baroque buildings of the age.

Hradčany and Prague Castle

High on the west bank of the Vlatva River is **Hradčany** and **Prague Castle ❶**, the seat of political power from the 12th century. After a fire in 1541, the castle was rebuilt in full Renaissance splendour. The original architects were Master Matthew of Arras, whom Pope Clement recommended, and after his death in 1352 a young Swabian named Peter Parler, who was also a sculptor and wood-carver. Together they produced **Katedrála su. Vita ❷** (St Vitus's Cathedral, open daily 9am–5pm; free) and the Charles Bridge. The main entrance to the castle complex is on **Hradčanské náměstí**, or Castle Square. Entry through the gate, guarded by Titans which are 1912 copies of 1768 originals, leads to a series of courtyards. Off the second of these is the **Obrazána Pražského hradu** (Castle Gallery, open Tues–Sun; entrance charge), with a collection of works by Rubens, Titian and Tintoretto that once belonged to Charles I of England.

The third courtyard is dominated by the towering Gothic spires of **St Vitus's Cathedral**. Construction started in 1344 on top of the remains of 10th- and 11th-century churches, and was completed only in 1929. The Wenceslas' Chapel, its walls studded with semi-precious stones and ancient frescoes, survived the fire. The ring on the door is reputed to be from an earlier church in which St Wenceslas was murdered by his brother Boleslav in 935. It is said he clung to this ring as life ebbed away. His tomb and relics are in the chapel; his statue, by Peter Parler's nephew, is dated 1373. The principal royal mausoleum is in the centre of the cathedral (before the high altar).

To one side of the cathedral, behind a deceptively modest entrance, is the great **Vladislav Hall**, part of the **Old Royal Palace** (open Tues–Sun; entrance charge). The hall gives access to the Statthalterei (council room), where the Protestant nobles gathered in 1618 to remonstrate with Catholic councillors. A certain Count Thurni suggested that the two Catholic ringleaders, Councillors Martinic and Slavata, be thrown out of the window.

LEFT: Charles Bridge and Prague Castle by night.
BELOW: shop front in Nové Město.

*A puppet makes music
on Charles Bridge.*

Across the square behind the cathedral is **Bazilika su. Jiří** (St George's Church) and **Monastery**, whose towers are relics of 970. It contains early and baroque Bohemian art. Beyond is the **Zlatá ulička** (Golden Lane), a row of small houses built into the castle walls after the 1541 fire and now lively with antique and book shops. It is worth returning to the square at the main entrance to see the baroque **Arcibiskupský palác** (Archbishop's Palace), the **National Gallery** (open Tues–Sun; entrance charge) in the Sternberg Palace and the **Museum of Military History** (open Apr–Nov Tues–Sun; entrance charge) in the Schwarzenberg (formerly Lobkovicz) Palace. A lane leads to the **Loreto** church ❸, the gift of a Czech noblewoman who believed that the miraculous transfer of the Holy House of Nazareth to Loreto in the 13th century saved the Italian town from the infidel. She commissioned the Loreto as a copy for the city of Prague in 1626. The church has a monstrance, the "Sun of Prague", set with 6,222 diamonds.

The **Strahovský klaster** (Strahov Monastery) ❹, the oldest in Bohemia, sits on the slopes of Petřín Hill, outside the fortifications. It houses the **Museum of National Literature** (open Tues–Sun: entrance charge), established 800 years ago and now with examples of almost the complete literature of Western Christianity.

Malá Strana

The main road through Malá Strana (Little Quarter) to Charles Bridge is **Mostecká**, flanked by mansions built after the 1541 fire. The most impressive is **Valdaštejnský palác** ❺ (Waldstein Palace, 1623–45), with an **art gallery** (open Tues–Sun; free) and **gardens** (open May–Sept: daily; free) where concerts are staged. **Su. Mikuláše** ❻ (St Nicholas' church, open Apr–Sept daily; Oct–Mar: Sat & Sun; free), a baroque masterpiece, divides Malá Strana's main square in two.

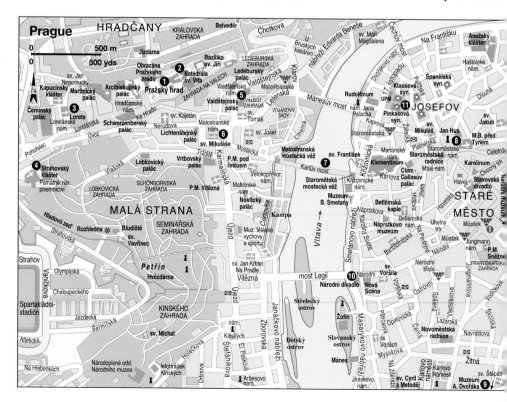

The Old and New towns

Karluvmost ❼ (Charles Bridge) links the castle and Malá Strana to the **Old Town** (Staré Město), and is a tourist attraction in its own right. **Celetná Street**, once on the royal processional route that filed through the Old Town and across Charles Bridge up to the Hradˇcany, is now closed to traffic and lined with coffee bars and wine cellars. It enters the delightful **Staročm stské námě stíl ❽** (Old Town Square) and adjacent Little Square, the latter famous for the astronomical clock on the **Staroměstská radnice** (Old Town Hall; open Tues–Sun; entrance charge), a row of colourful Gothic and Renaissance buildings established in 1338.

Wenceslas Square is a broad and sloping boulevard that links the Old and **New Town** (Nové Město); it is enclosed by the uninspiring but vast neo-Renaissance **Národní muzeum** (National Museum). Villa Amerika, built in 1720 at Ke Karluva 20, houses the **Muzeum A. Dvořáka ❾** (Dvořák Museum; open Tues–Sun; entrance charge), with memorabilia relating to the great 19th-century Czech composer. The magnificently restored **Národní divadio ❿** (National Theatre; box office tel: 2490 1448) is on the river.

Josefov

Parizska or Maislova streets lead to the **Jewish Quarter**, the oldest in Europe, dating to at least the 10th century. The **Old-New Synagogue** was built about 1270; the **Old Jewish Cemetery** nearby presents the extraordinary sight of more than 12,000 graves crammed into layers one on top of another. Its history is told in the **Jewish State Museum ⓫** housed in the **Pinkasová Synagogue** (open daily; entrance charge), which contains the names of the 77,000 Bohemian and Moravian Jews murdered by the Nazis. ❑

Map on page 242

Wenceslas Square is an entertainment in itself. This is where everyone congregates and people-watching is accordingly fruitful.

BELOW: pedestrians in Prague's Old Town Square.

WARSAW AND KRAKÓW

Poland bridges two cultural spheres. Warsaw and Kraków, its two great cities, are amalgams of the past, present and future

Map on page 246

Warsaw

Krakow

Warsaw is divided by the River Wisła (Vistula), and it is the meticulously recreated left bank that is of most interest to visitors. The centre of the Old Town is the 13th-century **Rynek Starego Miasta** (Old Town Market Square) **1**. It's always bustling with street-traders and people visiting the square's numerous cafés, bars, restaurants, galleries and shops. Beautifully recreated burghers' houses, dating from the 15th and 16th centuries, line the square, each with individual architectural features. The **Muzeum Historyczne st Warszawy** (Warsaw History Museum; open daily except Mon; entrance charge) is at No. 28. Numerous exhibits and a film presentation detail the city's history and evolution. Also set within a burgher's house at No. 20 is the **Muzeum Literatury im A Mickiewicza** (A Mickiewicz Literature Museum; closed Sat; free). Leaving the Old Town Market Square along Swiętojańska leads to **Katedra Św. Jana** (St John's Cathedral) **2** (closed Sun). Warsaw's oldest church, and the largest church in the Old Town, the cathedral was rebuilt after World War II in the original 14th-century style.

Swiętojańska culminates at Plac Zamkowy (Castle Square), dominated by the reconstructed **Zamek Królewski** (Royal Castle) **3** (closed Mon; ticket office Swiętojańska 2). A castle was first established here in the 13th century as the residence of the Mazovian dukes. From the end of the 15th century it became the royal residence, as well as the seat of the *Sejm* (Parliament). Between the two World Wars, the castle was the president's official residence. The interiors of the castle are largely 18th-century, with most of the works of art and furniture either original to the castle or donated by museums and private collectors. Adjoining the royal castle, but also offering a different experience, is **Pałac Pod Blachą** (Plac Zamkowy 2; closed Mon; entrance charge). This baroque palace has a rare collection of rugs. Plac Zamkowy also features Warsaw's oldest monument, **Kolumna Zygmunta III Wazy** (Zygmunt's Column) **4** erected in 1644, in which the king is depicted bearing a sword and a large cross (reflecting his counter-reformatory stance). This square also marks the beginning of the so-called **Trakt Królewski** (Royal Route), a favourite stroll for Varsovians and a good way to see numerous historic sights with almost no visual interference from modern buildings. Extending along Krakówskie Przedmieście, the Royal Route continues along Nowy Świat and Aleje Ujazdowskie, past Łazienki Park and ends at Wilanów Palace. Walking to Wilanów is unrealistic, but a stroll with café breaks en route should get you to Łazienki Park.

At Krakówskie Przedmieście 68 is **Kościół Św. Anny** (St Anna's Church) **5** (open daily). The earliest sections are late 15th-century Gothic, though the

LEFT: old Warsaw.
BELOW: Catholicism is still strong in Poland.

Taking a ride on a Warsaw tram.

TIP

Take bus No. 116, 122 or 193 to the beautiful Łazienki Park and Palace on the Lake. Tel: 625 7944 for guided tours.

BELOW: the Royal Castle, Warsaw.

church was refashioned several times. Continuing along Krakówskie Prze‹ mieście, decorative railings delineate a small square with lawns and flow‹ beds featuring the **Pomnik Adama Mickiewicza** (Adam Mickiewicz Mon‹ ment) dating from 1889, the centenary of the poet's birth. Another grand Ne‹ classical building is **Pałac Namiestnikowski ❻** (Namiestnikowski Palace; n‹ open to the public) established as the residence of the Polish president in 199‹ At Krakówskie Przedmieście 26–28 is **Uniwersytet Warszawski ❼** (Warsa‹ University; open daily), several imposing buildings which serve as lecture hal‹ set amid courtyards and greenery, have a distinguished provenance. Pl‹ Bankowy leads to **Ogród Saski** (Saxon Gardens) ❽, Warsaw's first public ga‹ dens, opened in 1727. At the edge of the gardens, on Plac Piłsudkiego is **Gr‹ Nieznanego Żołnierza** (Tomb of the Unknown Soldier). Consecrated in 192‹ it includes urns from battlefields in which Polish troops fought, as well as fro‹ the graves of Polish officers murdered by the Red Army in Katyń.

Kraków: Poland's intellectual and cultural city

Formerly the capital of Poland, Kraków has immense beauty, which is readi‹ accessible within the pedestrianised **Old Town**. The heart of the city, the **Ryn‹ Główny** (Main Market Square) is always busy with locals and tourists. At th‹ centre of the market square is the **Sukiennice ❶** (Cloth Hall; open daily). Ori‹ inally a covered market with stalls, shops and warehouses, the current Renai‹ sance facade was designed by Giovannia Maria of Padua between 1556–6‹ The **Wieża Ratuszowa ❷** (Town Hall Tower; closed Mon) provides fine vie‹ of the immediate area and includes a museum detailing the city's evolutio‹ The tiny Romanesque **Kościół Św. Wojciecha ❸** (St Adalbert's Church; op‹

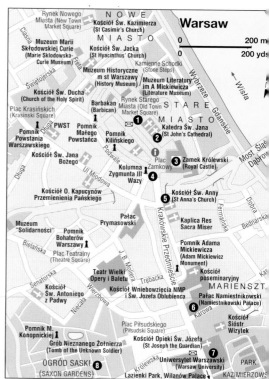

daily) dates from the 11th and 12th centuries, and features ornate interiors while the imposing, twin-towered **Kościół Mariacki ⓓ** (St Mary's Church; open daily) was built from the 14th–16th centuries and has an incredible late-Gothic altar piece. Every hour a trumpeter plays the *"hejnał"* from the taller of the two church towers, which originally served as a warning against attack by the Tartars. Taking Floriańska street from the market square leads to **Dom Jana Matejki ⓔ** (Jan Matejko's House; closed Mon), Poland's greatest historical painter. Matejko was born and subsequently worked here and the house retains the original interiors. The street culminates at **Brama Floriańska** (Florian's Gate) **ⓕ**, the Old Town's only remaining gateway, and features a section of the city wall together with four fortified turrets dating from the 14th century. The wall is hung with pictures by local artists. The **Muzeum Szołayskich ⓖ** (Szotayski Museum; pl Szczepański 9; closed Mon) has a collection of paintings and sculpture up to 1764, much of it taken from churches around Little Poland.

On Grodzka is the city's earliest baroque church, **Kościół Św. Piotra i Pawła ⓗ** (St Peter and St Paul's Church; open daily) and, at the end of the street, you have an inspiring view of the **Wawel ⓘ** (Royal Castle; closed Mon), built on a limestone hill rising above the Wisła (Vistula) River. Serving as the royal residence between 1038 and 1596, this complex of buildings includes medieval defensive walls and towers, the royal castle, royal cathedral, treasury and armoury. The castle's perfectly proportioned, three-storey arcaded courtyard, from which the castle extends along four wings, is one of Europe's finest examples of Renaissance architecture. Stanisław Wyspiański wrote about Wawel: "Here everything is Poland, every stone and fragment, and the person who enters here becomes a part of Poland." ❑

Maps on pages 246 & 247

Kraków's Jewish quarter, Kazimierz, is centred on Szeroka. Much of the film "Schindler's List" (based on the life of Oskar Schindler) was shot in and around Kraków.

BELOW: Kraków's market square.

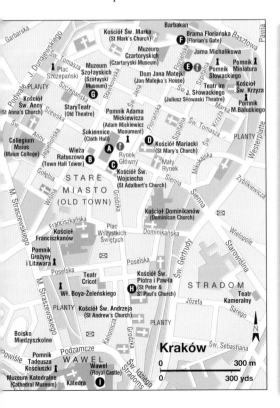

Kraków

0	300 m
0	300 yds

BUDAPEST

The thermal springs of the "Queen of the Danube" were exploited in Roman times, but the essence of the modern city stems from the wealth of the Austro-Hungarian Empire

Map on page 250

Budapest

A lthough Budapest straddles the River Danube, the first bridge linking Buda on the west bank and Pest on the east was not built until the 1840s. Buda, Obuda (Old Buda) and Pest became a single city in 1872, and other bridges followed. However, they were all blown up during World War II and the **Chain Bridge** did not reopen until 1949.

Buda looks older than Pest, but it was in fact started only after the destruction of Pest by the Mongols in 1241.The present boulevards were mostly laid out at the beginning of the 20th century. It was on one of the hills on the Buda west bank that in 1046 the worthy Swiss Bishop Gellert presumed to preach Christianity to unreceptive locals and for his pains was stuffed into a barrel studded with nails and launched down the hill into the river. The hill named after him provides an excellent panorama, one that conveys the vastness of the plain beyond the city and the way the Danube arcs through it.

Castle Hill

Bela IV's plans for the new town of Buda in the 13th century began with a **Castle (Vár) ❶** on Castle Hill to protect the civilian quarter to the north of Gellert Hill. A stormy future lay ahead. The city got off lightly in the Turkish conquest of 1526 – the decisive battle was fought at Mohacs – but not in the subsequent recapture in 1686. The Turks then turned the churches into mosques and gave the city a certain Oriental air.

After the Turks were ousted, the ruined city was rebuilt in the late-baroque fashion of the times, the best examples of which are the **University Church**, the **Zichy Manor** and **Silk Factory** in Obuda, and **St Anne's Church** in Batthyany Square. The restoration of the monarchy in 1867 led to a second wave of celebratory building in which the castle was transformed into a royal palace.

The destruction of almost everything that stood on Castle Hill as the Germans made their last stand in 1944 at least gave archaeologists a chance to poke about in the rubble, and this brought to light evidence of the great names of Hungarian history: the Arpads, Angevins, Mathias Corvinus and all. These remains were cleverly integrated in the reconstruction of the palace, which now houses the **Budapest Historical Museum**, the **Magyar Nemzeti Galéria ❷** (Hungarian National Gallery; open Tues–Sun, Mar–Nov 10am–6pm; Dec–Feb 10am–4pm; entrance charge), with a valuable collection of Hungarian paintings, and the **Ludwig Museum**, a gallery of contemporary art.

Castle Hill, which has a tunnel through its bowels, can be reached by a funicular railway from **Clark Adam Square** at the end of the Chain Bridge. The

LEFT: the bridge linking Buda and Pest.
BELOW: folk band on a city street.

Steep medieval alleyway in the Castle Hill district.

several streets on the top of the hill, linked by narrow passages, are now closed to private cars and have a fairground atmosphere. Beautiful **Bécsi kapu tér** (Vienna Gate Square) is named after **Vienna Gate**, one of the oldest entrances to the castle. Just to the west, in Kapisztrán tér, is the **Hadtörténeti Múzeum ❸** (Museum of Military History; open Tues–Sun, Jan–Sept 10am–6pm; Oct–Dec 10am–4pm; entrance charge), where the exhibits are mostly concerned with the Hungarian uprising of 1848 against Austria and Russia.

Mátyás tenplom (Mátyás Church) ❹, also known as the Church of Our Lady (and for a while an important Turkish mosque), is generally known by the name of the Hungarian king and hero Mathias Corvinus (1443–90). As one's eyes adjust to the gloom, a magnificent interior emerges. The murals depict the lives of the Hungarian saints and among the sarcophagi are those of Bela III (1173–96) and his wife Anne of Châtillon, transferred from Szekesfehervar.

A short distance from the church is the **Halászbastya** (Fishermen's Bastion), designed by Frigyes Schulek in Neo-Romanesque style at the beginning of the 20th century and named after the medieval fishermen's town which stood below.

The Pest side

The fitting way to enter Pest on the east side of the river is to walk the 600 metres across the **Széchenyi Lánchíd** (Chain Bridge) ❺. **Roosevelt tér** (Roosevelt Square) is on the other side, the Neo-Renaissance **Academy of Sciences** having been founded by the former. The **Corzo**, running south, is a pedestrian promenade leading to **Vigado tér** (Vigado Square) where, in the **Concert Hall**, all the musical giants seem to have performed at one time or another. The roll-call begins with Brahms and Liszt.

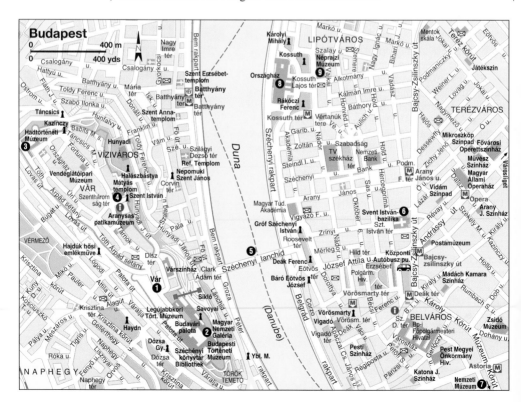

Parallel with the Corso is **Váci utca**, Budapest's smartest shopping street with, at one end, the **Budapest market**, an amazing 19th-century building with soaring metal columns, high walkways and ramps. Just to the north of Vörösmarty Square is the Neo-Romanesque **Szent István bazilika** (St Stephen's Basilica) **❻**, completed in 1905, to which a steady stream of Hungarian Catholics make the pilgrimage to see the right hand of St Stephen. The church interior was decorated by the best-known Hungarian painters and sculptors of the time. Nearby is the **Állami Operaház** (Opera House), decorated with statues of famous European composers.

The **Nemzeti Múzeum ❼** (National Museum; open Tues–Sun, Mar–Oct 10am–6pm; Nov–Feb 10am–5pm; entrance charge) holds the Apostolic Crown of St Stephen and the coronation insignia. Since the fall of communism, it has been restored, and the magnificent heritage it contains has been reorganised. Close to the museum is the **Great Synagogue**, identifiable by its onion dome. The huge **Országház** (Parliament) **❽** was built between 1880 and 1902 to a design by Imre Steindl. There are 10 courtyards, 29 staircases and 27 gates behind the 268-metre (879-ft) facade, with 88 statues of Hungarian leaders and generals. Tours of the magnificent interior are given several times a week. Opposite, housed in the Palace of Justice, is the impressive **Neprajzi Múzeum ❾** (Ethnographic Museum; open Tues–Sun, Mar–Oct 10am–6pm; Nov–Feb 10am–4pm; entrance charge), with Hungarian folk art from the 17th to the 20th centuries.

Close to the **Városliget** (City Park) is the **Fine Arts Museum** (entrance charge), designed in 1906 in the style of a Greek temple. It includes Italian Old Masters, Dutch, Spanish and English works from the 15th–18th centuries, Impressionist paintings, and European sculpture from the 19th and 20th centuries. ❑

Map on page 250

*Budapest's **City Park** (Városliget) is a popular recreation area containing **Vajdahunyad Castle**, in a hotchpotch of architectural styles, on an island in the middle of a lake.*

BELOW: a popular spa hotel in the centre of Budapest.

ITALY

Italian art and architecture draws the visitors, as does its reputation for good food and wine

The traveller in Italy will frequently have the feeling of *déjà vu*, for many of its landmarks are well known and many of its medieval towns and city centres look as if they have been built as copies of Renaissance paintings. But the traveller will not feel alone: in summer the major attractions, such as Rome, Florence and Venice, are a heady mix of heat, noise and tourists, and if possible visitors should come at other times of the year.

Italy is also a lively, modern country (Milan is the fashion centre of Europe) and the pace, particularly on the roads, can be fast. The cities are all best explored on foot. If you are driving, head for the Centro Storico (historic centre) or Duomo (cathedral), and find a *parcheggio* to park.

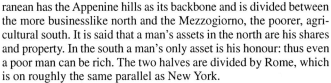

The 301,000 sq km (116,500 sq mile) Italian boot which dips its toes into the middle of the Mediterranean has the Appenine hills as its backbone and is divided between the more businesslike north and the Mezzogiorno, the poorer, agricultural south. It is said that a man's assets in the north are his shares and property. In the south a man's only asset is his honour: thus even a poor man can be rich. The two halves are divided by Rome, which is on roughly the same parallel as New York.

Modern life has stamped even small villages with a bar and a large population of motor-cycle-riding youths. Every town has its Duomo, but how different is the austere Romanesque cathedral of Apulia from the lavish baroque of the one in Turin. Every town has at least one piazza: in the South they are crowded with men smoking and playing cards; in the North, the men are still there, but so are the women and the tourists.

There are few idle pastimes more rewarding than observing Italians going about their lives. They are past-masters at showing off, at preserving *la bella figura*. Both their public and social life is intricate and intriguing. Governments lurch from one crisis to another and scandals regularly invade public lives, usually in the form of corruption and the Mafia. And while women visitors may find young men oppressively predatory, a woman's role is crucial at home. "No Italian who has a family is ever alone," wrote Luigi Barzini in *The Italians*. "He finds in it a refuge to lick his wounds after defeat, or an arsenal and a staff for his victorious drives." ❑

PRECEDING PAGES: Florence's skyline at dusk; traditional costumes at the Quintana Festival.
LEFT: Venice's carnival is noted for its striking but slightly sinister masks.

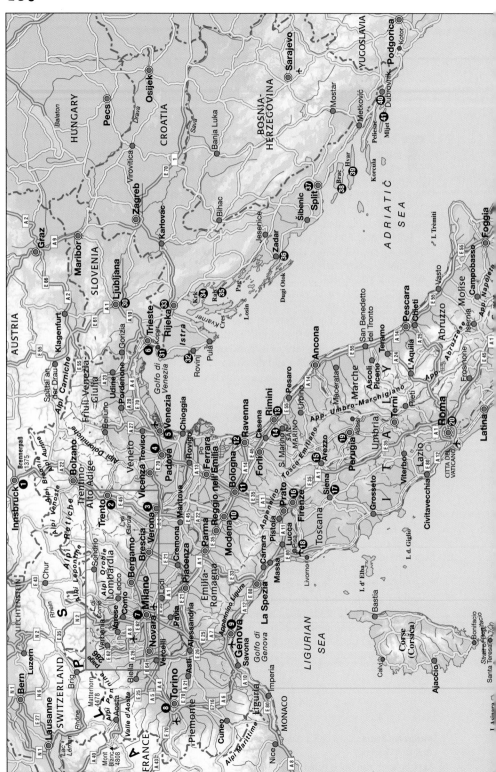

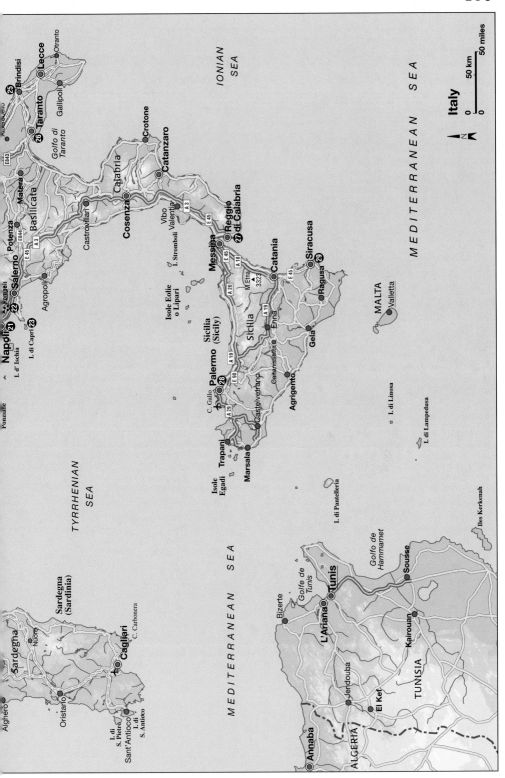

Italy

0 50 km
0 50 miles

N

MEDITERRANEAN SEA

TYRRHENIAN SEA

IONIAN SEA

MEDITERRANEAN SEA

Ponziane

Alghero

Sardegna Sardinia

Sardegna (Sardinia)

Nuoro

Oristano

I. di S. Pietro
I. di Sant'Antioco

Cagliari

C. Carbonara

Alberobello

Brindisi 25

Lecce

Orranto

Taranto 26

Gallipoli

Golfo di Taranto

Crotone

E843

Catanzaro

Calabria

E844

A3

Matera

Basilicata

Potenza

E45

A33

Castrovillari

Cosenza

Vibo Valentia

I. Stromboli

A3

Reggio
di Calabria 27

E45

Salerno 22

Napoli 21

Pompei

I. d' Ischia

I. di Capri 23

Agropoli

Isole Eolie o Lipari

Messina

E45

A20

A18

M.Etna
3323

Catania

E45

Siracusa 29

Ragusa 29

Sicilia (Sicily)

A19

Enna

A19

Caltanissetta

Gela

C. Gallo

Palermo 28

E90

A19

Castelvetrano

A29

Agrigento

Trapani

Marsala

Isole Egadi

I. di Linosa

I. di Lampedusa

MALTA

Valletta

I. di Pantelleria

I. di Lampedusa

Bizerte

Golfe de Tunis

Tunis

L'Ariana

Golfo de Hammamet

Sousse

Kairouan

Annaba

ALGERIA

Jendouba

El Kef

TUNISIA

Iles Kerkenah

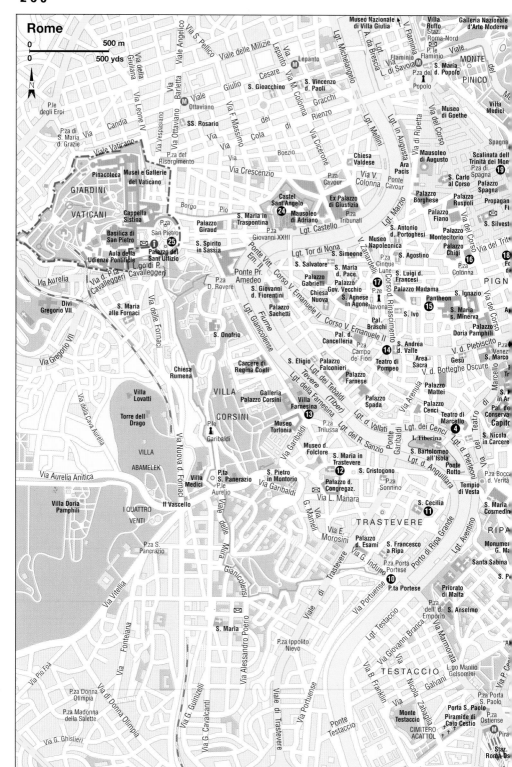

Rome

0 ———— 500 m
0 ———— 500 yds

N

P.le degli Eroi

P.za di S. Maria d. Grazie

Via della Giuliana

Via Leone IV

Via Candia

Via Angelico

Via S. Pellico

Viale Angelico

Viale delle Milizie

Via Vespasiano

Via Ottaviano

Via Barletta

Giulio

Cesare

Viale

Via F. Massimo

Viale

Lepanto

Via M. Colonna

SS. Rosario

S. Gioacchino

S. Vincenzo d. Paoli

Gracchi

P.za del Risorgimento

Via Crescenzio

dei

Cola

di

Rienzo

Via Cicerone

Boezio

Pio

Borgo

GIARDINI VATICANI

Pinacoteca

Musei e Gallerie del Vaticano

Cappella Sistina

Basilica di San Pietro

Aula della Udienze Pontificie

Palazzo del Sant'Uffizio

L.go di P.

Via d. P.ta Cavalleggeri

P.za San Pietro

Palazzo Giraud

S. Maria in Traspontina

Castel Sant'Angelo **24**

Mausoleo di Adriano

S. Spirito in Sassia

Ponte Vitt. Em. II

S. Giovanni d. Fiorentini

Via Aurelia

Divi Gregorio VII

S. Maria alle Fornaci

Via delle Fornaci

S. Onofrio

P.za D. Rovere

Ponte Pr. Amedeo

Corso V. Emanuele II

Palazzo Gabrielli

Chiesa Nuova

Palazzo Sachetti

S. Salvatore

S. Simeone

S. Maria d. Pace

Gov. Vecchio

S. Agnese in Agone

Lgt. Tor di Nona

Lgt. Castello

P.za Cavour

Ponte Cavour

Lgt. Marzio

Museo Napoleonica

Cinque Lune

P.za Navona

Pal. Braschi

Pal. d. Cancelleria

Teatro di Pompeo

Campo de' Fiori

S. Eligio

Palazzo Falconieri

Palazzo Farnese

Carcere di Regina Coeli

Chiesa Rumena

Via Gregorio VII

Via della Cava Aurelia

VILLA LOVATTI

Torre dell Drago

VILLA ABAMELEK

Via Nuova d. Fornaci

VILLA CORSINI

Galleria Palazzo Corsini

P.le Garibaldi

Villa Farnesina **13**

Lgt. dei Tebaldi

Lgt. della Farnesina

Fiume Tevere (Tiber)

Lgt. Sanzio

Museo Torlonia

Museo d. Folclore

S. Maria in Trastevere **12**

Villa Doria Pamphili

I QUATTRO VENTI

Il Vascello

Villa Medici

P.le Aurelio

P.ta S. Panerazio

S. Pietro in Montorio

Palazzo di Congregaz. **10**

Via Garibaldi

Via L. Manara

S. Cristogono

Via G. Mameli

Via E. Morosini

Palazzo d. Esami

TRASTEVERE

S. Francesco a Ripa

Via G. Induno

Via di Trastevere

Viale di Trastevere

S. Cecilia **11**

P.ta Portese **10**

Via Portuense

Via delle Mura

Giancolense

Via Alessandro Poerio

P.za Ippolito Nievo

S. Maria

Via G. Guinizelli

Via G. Cavalcanti

Via Vitellia

Via Fonteiana

Via Aurelia Antica

Via Pio Foà

P.za Donna Olimpia

P.za Madonna della Salette

Via di Donna Olimpia

Via G. Ghisleri

Ponte Testaccio

Viale di Trastevere

Via Portuense

Lgt. Testaccio

TESTACCIO

Via Nicola

Via B. Franklin

Monte Testaccio

Via Galvani

Via Zabaglia

L.go Manlio Gelsomini

CIMITERO ACATTOL

Piramide di Caio Cestio

Porta S. Paolo

P.za Porta S. Paolo

P.za Ostiense

Staz. Roma-Os

Pira

Museo Nazionale di Villa Giulia

V. A. da Brescia

Villa Ruffo

Staz. Roma-Nord

Galleria Nazionale d'Arte Moderna

Via Michelangelo

Via Flaminia

Flaminio

Viale

MONTE PINICO

P.le Flaminio

Lepanto

L. di Savoia

Lgt. M.

Popolo

P.za del Popolo

Villa Medici

Lgt. Mellini

Chiesa Valdese

Ara Pacis

Lgt. in Augusta

Lgt. di Ripetta

Via del Corso

Museo di Goethe

Spagna

Scalinata del Trinità dei Mon

P.za di Spagna **19**

Ponte Cavour

Mausoleo di Augusto

S. Carlo al Corso

Palazzo Borghese

Palazzo Ruspoli

Palazzo Spagna

Propagan Fi

S. Antonio d. Portoghesi

Palazzo Fiano

S. Silvest

S. Agostino

Palazzo Montecitorio

S. Luigi d. Francesi

Palazzo Madama

Palazzo Chigi

Via del Corso

Via del Tri **18**

16 P.za Colonna

Pantheon

S. Ivo

Zanardelli

Corso d. Rinascimento

S. Andrea d. Valle **14**

Gesù

S. Ignazio

Via del Corso

S. Maria s. Minerva

Palazzo Doria Pamphili

V. d. Plebiscito

V. d. Botteghe Oscure

P.za Venez

S. Marco

Area Sacra

Palazzo Mattei

Palazzo Cenci

Lgt. dei Cenci

Teatro di Marcello **4**

Marcello

Via Arenula

Palazzo Spada

l. Tiberina

S. Bartolomeo all'Isola

Ponte Rotto

Tempio di Vesta

Lgt. d. Anguillara

Lgt. di Pierleoni

S. Maria Cosmedin

RIPA

Santa Sabina

S. Nicola in Carcere

Capit

Pal. d. Conserva

Pal. in Ar

S. in Ar

Tr

S. Marco

P.za Bocca d. Verità

P.ta Portese

S. Sonnino

Via Portuense

P.ta Portese

S. Anselmo

Priorato di Malta

P.za dell'Emporio

S. Anselmo

Lgt. Aventino

Monumer G. Ma

S. P

Via Giovanni Branca

Via Marmorata

A

P. Ce

P.za Porta Ostiense

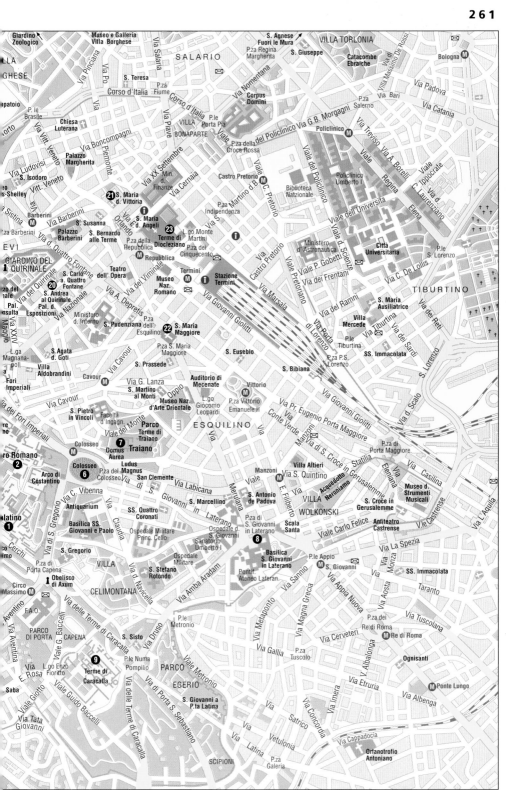

ROME

Follow in the footsteps of emperors and saints, discovering the monuments and churches that mark Rome as the capital of Italy and the ancient world

Map on pages 260–1

Rome

Byron described the pastoral ruins of **Palatino** (Palatine Hill) ❶ in the following lines: *Cypress and ivy, weed and wallflower grown/ Matted and mass'd together, hillocks heap'd/ On what were chambers, arch crush'd, column strown/ In fragments, choked up vaults, and frescos steep'd/ In subterranean damps…* This still stands as an accurate description of the place that serves as the best introduction to Rome. It was here, the story goes, that Romulus and Remus were brought up by a wolf in a cave and, as if to show that there is more to myth than mere legend, archaeologists have discovered traces of Iron-Age huts that date back to the 8th century BC.

The easiest way to reach Palatine Hill is by way of a gentle stroll from the **Foro Romano** ❷ (Forum; open daily until 1½ hours before sunset; Sun until 1pm; special night viewings in summer; entrance charge), ancient Rome's commercial and political centre. In the fading light, and with some imagination, the stark columns and ghostly white blocks of weather-beaten marble take on flesh and life. The Forum emerges for a few minutes again as the magnificent civic and religious centre of the world. And if there are pieces missing the blame must be placed on successive popes, and the noble families of Rome who, for more than a millennium, have used the Forum as a convenient quarry to provide stones for their palaces.

LEFT: inside St Peter's.
BELOW: the she-wolf, symbol of Rome.

The foreground is dominated by the eight surviving columns of the **Tempio di Saturno** (Temple of Saturn) but the star attraction is the **Arco di Settimio Severo** (Arch of Septimius Severus), built in 203 after the emperor had just conquered the Parthians and made Mesopotamia a new province of Rome.

The Capitoline Hill and the ghetto

Another city landmark is the **Capitolino** (Capitoline Hill) ❸, home to the **Palazzo dei Conservatori** and the **Palazzo del Museo Capitolino** (open Tues–Sat & Sun am; entrance charge) and their superb collections of art. On the western side of the Capitoline Hill lies Rome's old ghetto, near the ruins of the **Teatro di Marcello** ❹. Jews first came to Rome as slaves but their skills were quickly appreciated and it was not until the 16th century that a pope ordered all Jews in the city to live inside a high-walled enclosure. You will still find kosher food here, and the impressive synagogue on Lungotevere dates from the 1870s.

Not all sightseeing in Rome involves ancient buildings. The best of the contemporary city and a good place to head for is the **Piazza Venezia** ❺. This is where the main streets of the city meet, a fact that is quickly and perilously acknowledged when trying to cross one of them: "Hurry as we may, we are blocked by a surging crowd… If that load of marble overturns

Sculpture of Constantine II.

BELOW: the Colosseum.

on to the crowd, what will be left of their bodies?" So wrote Juvenal in the first century and he didn't have to contend with the cars and scooters.

One side of the square is dominated by **Palazzo Venezia**, a palatial Renaissance building that served as the headquarters of Benito Mussolini, Italy's dictator from 1922 to 1945. It is a magnificent edifice, built in 1455 for a Venetian cardinal who later became Pope Paul II, and the central balcony is where Mussolini stood and addressed adoring crowds in the 1930s. It now houses a fine collection in its **Museo del Palazzo di Venezia** (open Tues–Sun am only; entrance charge), ranging from early Renaissance paintings, and sculptures by Bernini and Algardi, to tapestries and arms and armour. Despite this, the museum has not attracted the attention it deserves.

Around the Colosseum

The **Colosseo ❻** (Colosseum; open Mon–Sat until 1½ hours before sunset; Sun till 1pm; entrance charge) rises like a huge battleship cast in stone, making it easy to see how it could hold up to 55,000 spectators in its heyday in the first and second centuries AD *(see pages 272–3)*. To create space for the building of the Colosseum, Vespasian had drained the lake of the **Domus Aurea (Golden House) ❼**, a palace built by the tyrannical emperor Nero after the fire in AD 64.

The conflagration which destroyed much of the city was thought to have been ordered by Nero who, according to Tacitus, then "set up as the culprits and punished with the utmost refinement of cruelty a class hated for their abominations, who are commonly called Christians." The Golden House was not discovered until the Renaissance, when artists such as Raphael were excited by the finds that were revealed from the ruins.

From the Colosseum, Via di San Giovanni in Laterano opens up into the **Piazza di San Giovanni** in **Laterano** ❽, where a cluster of important buildings stand. Pride of place goes to the magnificent **Basilica San Giovanni in Laterano**, seat of the popes until the schism in 1309, when they moved to Avignon. It has an imposing facade by Alessandro Galilei and a breathtaking baroque interior by Borromini. The nearby **Scala Santa** attracts the pious, with a door at the top of stairs that leads to the Sancta Sanctorum, the private chapel of the pope.

The biggest baths in the world

Via Amba Aradam leads from the square and turns into Via Druso before reaching another large junction over which loom the **Terme di Caracalla** ❾ (Baths of Caracalla; open Tues–Sat till 6pm, till 3pm in winter; till 1pm Sun and Mon; entrance charge).

Many baths had been built by previous emperors but Antoninus Caracalla was determined to relegate them all to history when construction began in AD 212 on the largest baths Rome had ever seen. Holding up to 1,500 bathers at a time, the baths continued to function until the Goths invaded two centuries later and vandalised the aqueducts that supplied them with water.

Roman baths were a place for social, physical and intellectual pursuits, with stories of less salubrious activities arising from the sessions of mixed bathing. Rich patrons came here with their slaves but the poor masses were not excluded. The poet Shelley composed his great *Prometheus Unbound* (1820) on a visit to the ruins of the baths and the cultural associations with the place are evoked each summer when operas are mounted here.

Map on pages 260–1

TIP

Taking a picnic into the Forum or Palatine is not officially allowed but, as long as you are discreet and leave no litter behind, there should be no problem.

BELOW: Constantine's Arch.

Facade mosaics at
Santa Maria in
Trastevere, showing
Mary, Christ and
10 lamp-bearing
women.

Across the Tiber

Trastevere, from *trans Tiberim* ("over the Tiber"), used to mark the beginning of Etruscan territory but over the centuries it has developed into a lively working-class district of Rome. It is home to a number of affordable restaurants as well as the **Porta Portese** ❿, where a popular flea market bursts into life every Sunday morning. There is an astonishing variety of objects for sale, from old furniture, fake icons, ethnic bric-a-brac to the usual array of luggage, clothes and fashion items. Do not even think about paying the first price that is quoted for anything and expect at least a 30 percent discount.

There are two churches of note in Trastevere. **Santa Cecilia** ⓫ is dedicated to the patron saint of music who was martyred in AD 230, with a church being founded on the site of her execution. The artistic highlight is a fresco of *The Last Judgement* by Pietro Cavallini, dating from the late 13th century, reached through the adjoining convent entrance. The other church, **Santa Maria in Trastevere** ⓬, is one of the oldest in Rome and its foundation is credited to Pope Callixtus I in the 3rd century. The chief attractions of any visit are the mosaics, especially those by Cavallini depicting the life of the Virgin, and the authentic medieval character of the church.

Raphael's touch

BELOW and **RIGHT:**
scenes from
Rome's authentic
"village life".

A little way to the north of these churches, and close to the Tiber, is the **Villa Farnesina** ⓭ (open Tues–Sat am only; entrance charge) dating from the first decade of the 16th century and built for a wealthy banker who gloried in the appellation of "The Magnificent". The villa contains a number of noted works of art, including a fresco by Raphael and his assistants depicting the legend of

Cupid and Psyche. In the Galatea room there is a superb painting by Raphael, with the ceiling decorated with astrological scenes, and in the bedroom is Sodoma's erotic painting *The Wedding of Alexander and Roxanne*.

On the other side of the river **Sant'Andrea della Valle** ❶ has achieved fame because Puccini made the setting of the first act of his *Tosca* but it is worth a visit in its own right. The splendidly restored facade self-consciously celebrates the baroque style and the richly decorated interior is just as impressive. Two popes are buried inside but the major attraction is the gorgeous dome, the second-largest in the city after St Peter's, with frescos painted by Domenichino and Lanfranco. There was intense competition between these two painters, and because Lanfranco won most of the commission his jealous rival is said to have tried to murder him.

The **Pantheon** ❶ (open Mon–Sat; Sun till 1pm; free) was built as a temple in 27 BC, first restored by the emperor Domitian in AD 80 and by Hadrian in the second century. The early Christian emperors kept it closed, along with other buildings that proclaimed their paganism, and it was finally converted into a church in the 7th century. The architectural wonder of the building is its massive dome, which has a single hole at the very centre of the coffered ceiling providing the only light. The building of such a structure was an ambitious undertaking; a wooden framework was used to support the tons of masonry that were incorporated into the building, and the total weight was distributed among a set of supporting arches that are built into the walls.

The entrance to the church is under a porch supported by 16 granite columns and, once you are inside, the sense of wonder is palpable. The geometrical proportions are such that the diameter is equal in size to the overall height. In 1520

Map on pages 260–1

TIP

Museum opening times in Rome, perhaps more than anywhere else, are subject to change. It's always a good idea to check with the tourist office before planning your day.

BELOW: catering for a sweet tooth.

ROME AND THE BAROQUE

The baroque movement (1600–1750) was born in Rome, and nurtured by papal campaign to make the city one of unparalleled beauty "for the greater glory of God and the Church". One artist to answer the call was Caravaggio (1573–1610), whose early secular portraits of sybaritic youths revealed him to be a painfully realistic artist. His later monumental religious painting entitled *The Calling of St Matthew*, in San Luigi dei Francesi, shocked the city by setting a holy act in a contemporary tavern.

The decoration of the interior of St Peter's by Gianlorenzo Bernini (1598–1680) was more acceptable to the Romans: a bronze tabernacle with spiralling columns at the main altar; a magnificent throne with angels clustered around a burst of sacred light at the end of the church; and, for the exterior, the classically simple colonnade embracing the piazza (1657).

Bernini's rival was Francesco Borromini (1599–1667), whose eccentric designs were the opposite of Bernini's classics. Many of Borromini's most famous designs hinge on a complex interplay of concave and convex surfaces, which can be seen in the undulating facades of San Carlo alle Quattro Fontane, Sant'Ivo, and Sant'Agnese in Piazza Navona (1653–63).

Detail from Bernini's "Fontana dei Fiumi" in Piazza Navona.

the artist Raphael, following his own wish, was buried inside the Pantheon. His tomb is decorated with a Madonna by Lorenzetto.

To the east of the Pantheon the Via del Corso, once the main route out of Rome and known as the Via Lata (Broad Way), is lined with shops and the **Piazza Colonna** ⓰ at the junction with another main shopping street, Via del Tritone. The central 30-metre (100-ft) column in the square dates from the second century and was built in honour of Marcus Aurelius and his defeat of barbarian tribes from the Danube. The column consists of 28 drums of marble, and when it was restored in the 16th century the pope had the emperor's statue taken off the top and replaced by one of St Paul.

Fountains and the Spanish Steps

There are so many churches and historical sites and sights in Rome that a prudent visitor needs to guard against culture fatigue setting in prematurely. It makes sense to intersperse such visits with a good dose of contemporary street life, and the **Piazza Navona** ⓱, west of the Pantheon, will fit the bill. This pedestrianised square lies at the heart of the city; its pavement restaurants, cafés and *gelaterie*, though none too cheap, are a great place for people watching. There is certainly no shortage of churches, temples, museums and historic buildings around the square but there is also a buzz of people, visitors as well as city residents, and it is a grand place to soak up some atmosphere and feel that you are in a great world city. More ritzy is the **Via Vitt. Veneto**, Rome's Hollywood Boulevard, which is reached along Via Tritone from Via del Corso. It became synonymous with *La Dolce Vita* (the sweet life) after Federico Fellini's film of that name. The pavement cafés are still there, along with white-aproned

BELOW:
the Spanish Steps.
RIGHT: relaxing in
the Piazza Navona.

waiters and bumper-to-bumper traffic. Another meeting point is the **Fontana di Trevi** (Trevi Fountain) ⓲ on the other side of the Via del Tritone, one of many splendid aquatic sculptures in the city. But perhaps the most famous meeting place is the **Scalinata della Trinità dei Monti** (Spanish Steps) ⓳, which lead up from the **Piazza di Spagna** to the church of the **Trinità dei Monte**, where Mendelssohn listened to the famous choir of nuns who could be heard but not seen. They take their name from the residence of the Spanish ambassador in the square. Everyone gathers here to watch the world go by, just as they have done for several centuries. The **Keats and Shelley Museum** (open Mon–Sat; entrance charge) is in the house where the poet John Keats died in 1852; Henry James stayed at the Hotlel Inghilterra; Goethe lived nearby at No. 20 Via del Corso, where there is a museum devoted to his travels in Italy.

Map on pages 260–1

The masterwork of Gianlorenzo Bernini

To the east of Via del Corso, **Sant'Andrea al Quirinale** ⓴, on Via del Quirinale, is reckoned by many to be the finest example of the work of Bernini (1598–1680), the baroque genius who, more than any other artist, has left his personal mark on Rome. The interior decoration of this church is supreme justification for the high estimation in which Bernini is held; every inch is covered with gilt and marble, and *putti* ascend the walls as if in a cloud of smoke. The church was built for the Jesuits but there is nothing spartan about the rooms of St Stanislas Kostka, a Polish saint who is celebrated in rich marble by Pierre Legros.

Another exemplary example of Bernini's work may be seen by heading off in the other direction to **Santa Maria della Vittoria** ㉑, in Largo Santa Susanna (off Via XX Settembre). Here you will discover one of the artist's most ambi-

BELOW:
the Trevi Fountain.

Map on pages 260–1

tious undertakings, the *Ecstasy of St Theresa*. This depiction of the 17th-century Spanish mystic, St Theresa of Avila, evokes for many visitors a sense of sensual ecstasy rather than the physical pain that might seem more appropriate. It is perhaps as well to bear in mind, however, St Theresa's own description of her feelings when God sent an angel down to pierce her with an arrow: "The pain was so sharp that I cried aloud but at the same time I experienced such delight that I wished it would last for ever."

Another church to visit, but by no means the last church in Rome, is **Santa Maria Maggiore ㉒**, which manages to combine a variety of architectural styles more successfully than any other church in the city. The basilica was built in the 5th century, the marble floor and the bell tower are medieval, the ceiling is unmistakably a product of the Renaissance, while the twin domes are pure baroque. The manner in which it all manages to hang together stylistically is quite astonishing, but it does and to a remarkable degree. Inside the church there are stunning mosaics from the 5th century.

An emperor's baths and Tosca's grand finale

To the north of the Santa Maria Maggiore is a secular institution, the **Terme di Diocleziano ㉓** (Baths of Diocletian; open Tues–Sun am only; entrance charge). Built in AD 306, these were the largest baths in the city, welcoming up to 3,000 bathers at a time. Michelangelo created the Santa Maria degli Angeli, near Piazza della Repubblica, from the *tepidarium* of the baths. Unfortunately, the church was changed radically in the 18th century and bears little mark of Michelangelo's genius, although there is a remarkable fresco inside by Domenichino.

If you are crossing the Tiber on the **Ponte Sant' Angelo** on your way to the Vatican, what you see before you is not the dome of St Peter's but the massive medieval walls of the **Castel Sant' Angelo ㉔** (open daily, except 2nd and 4th Tues of each month; entrance charge). It started life as a mausoleum for the emperor Hadrian in AD 139 but has been adapted many times since, and there are more than 50 rooms inside charting the varied history of the place. If time is short, seek out the frescos by Perin del Vaga and Pellegrino Tibaldi that play little tricks with the eye in the style of a 16th-century Magritte. But if you do nothing else, make your way to the castle's terrace where there are exceptional views all around and which provide the scene this time of the last act of Puccini's *Tosca*.

From Castel Sant' Angelo, Via della Conciliazione leads to **St Peter's** via **Piazza San Pietro (St Peter's Square) ㉕**. The square is famously packed on particular religious holidays when the pope appears on the balcony to address and bless the vast crowds. When the square was begun by Bernini in 1656 the effect he intended for his grand colonnades which sweep into an embrace (some say a claw) of St Peter's church was quite different from what is experienced today. His idea was to surprise the pilgrim visitor with a sudden view of the basilica, but when the Via della Conciliazione was built in the 1930s it provided a distant view of the church and so now acts as the monumental approach to St Peter's. ❏

BELOW: view from Castel Sant' Angelo.

The Vatican

Rome and the Vatican have lived for more than one and a half millennia in symbiosis, not always perfect, not always happy, but always mutually rewarding. Rome is where the Church gained its martyrs, where the emperor Constantine made Christianity the predominant religion in AD 337. In return, the Vatican eventually gave Rome another empire, a spiritual and a political one, at times almost as powerful as the worldly one lost to the barbarians.

Vatican is the name given to a hill on the right bank of the Tiber. There the emperor Nero completed a circus which Gaius had built and adorned with an obelisk brought from Egypt (the one which now rises in the middle of St Peter's Square). Early Christians were tortured here and the emperor Constantine gave the land to the church where, over the grave of St Peter, who had been martyred in the Nero persecutions in AD 64, a place of worship was built that developed into the vast complex to be seen today. St Peter's Church is the largest in Christendom, and some 700 million Catholics are governed from this walled-in hill known as Vatican City.

There is plenty to see and do, beginning perhaps with the purchase of some Vatican stamps and the posting of a card from the Vatican post office or a climb up the 244 stairs to the top of St Peter's Dome. As you enter St Peter's, on the right, Michelangelo's *Pietà* still enthrals, as it first did in 1499 when the artist finished it at the age of 25. Since being vandalised in 1972, the marble sculpture has been enclosed by glass. Further up the nave is the bronze statue of St Peter, its toe worn away by the countless kisses of unhygienic but pious pilgrims. A highly ornate baroque canopy by Bernini dominates the nave above the Papal Altar where only the pope may conduct mass.

You will, in all probability, want to visit the **Vatican Museums** (open winter: Mon–Sat am only; summer: Mon–Fri till 4pm, Sat till 1pm; entrance charge) but don't try to pack in too much. What should not be missed is the

Cappella Sistina (Sistine Chapel), with walls covered in frescos by Botticelli (*Temptations of Christ*, with the devil disguised in the habit of a Franciscan monk, and *Punishment of the Rebels*), Ghirlandaio (*Calling of St Peter and St Andrew*) and Perugino (*Handing over the Keys to St Peter*), and its ceiling painted by Michelangelo between 1508 and 1512.

Michelangelo worked alone on the ceiling from a specially designed scaffold and the controversial restoration work of the 1980s has allowed a new generation of visitors to appreciate some of the skill and passion that went into the work. The only subject matter that is not from the Bible's Old Testament is the Classical Sibyls and they only get a nose in because of the highly suspect story that they prophesied the birth of Christ.

"All the world hastened to behold this marvel and was overwhelmed, speechless with astonishment," the 15th-century art historian, Vasari, wrote of Michelangelo's handiwork. The validity of the judgment may help sustain your patience as the queue to enter the chapel slowly makes its way forward. ❑

RIGHT: appreciative crowd at a papal audience, Vatican City.

THE COLOSSEUM: BREAD AND CIRCUSES

"While the Colosseum stands, Rome shall stand; when the Colosseum falls, Rome shall fall; when Rome falls, the world shall fall."

The Venerable Bede's 8th-century prophecy has been taken to heart and the Colosseum shored up ever since. The ancient amphitheatre is the city's most stirring sight, a place of stupendous size and spatial harmony. The Colosseum was begun by Vespasian, inaugurated by his son Titus in AD 80, and completed by Domitian (AD 81–96). Titus used Jewish captives from Jerusalem as masons. The Colosseum had 80 numbered, arched entrances, allowing over 50,000 spectators to be seated within 10 minutes. "Bread and circuses" was how Juvenal, the 2nd-century satirist, mocked the Romans who here sold their souls for free food and entertainment.

FALL AND RUIN

With the fall of the empire, the Colosseum fell into disuse. During the Renaissance, the ruins were plundered to create churches and palaces all over Rome, including Palazzo Farnese, now the French Embassy. Quarrying was only halted by Pope Benedict XIV, in the 18th century, and the site consecrated to Christian martyrs. The Colosseum was still neglected on the German poet Goethe's visit in 1787, with a hermit and beggars "at home in the crumbling vaults". In 1817 Lord Byron was enthralled by this "noble wreck in ruinous perfection", while Edgar Allan Poe, another Romantic poet, celebrated its "grandeur, gloom and glory".

During the Fascist era, Mussolini, attracted to the power which the Colosseum represented, demolished a line of buildings to create a clear view of it from his balcony on Palazzo di Venezia. An ambitious restoration programme was undertaken to make the Colosseum fit for Holy Year in the year 2000.

△ **ALL AT SEA**
Renaissance historians believed that, in ancient times, Roman arenas were sometimes flooded to stage mock naval battles, but there is scant evidence to suggest such a display ever took place in the Colosseum.

▽ **GLADIATORIAL COMBAT**
The price of failure: the Gate of Life was reserved for victorious gladiators, with vanquished gladiators doomed to the Gate of Death.

△ **BEHIND THE SCENES**
From the higher tiers stretch views down to the arena and a maze of passages. The arena was encircled by netting to prevent beasts escaping. The moveable wooden floor was covered in sand, the better to soak up the blood. Below, the subterranean section concealed the animal cages and sophisticated technical apparatus, from winches and mechanical lifts to ramps and trap doors.

▽ SOCIAL STRATA

Although supremely public, the Colosseum was a stratified affair. The podium, set on the lowest tier, was reserved exclusively for the emperor, senators, magistrates and Vestal Virgins. Above them sat the bourgeoisie, with the lower orders restricted to the top tier, and the populace on wooden seats in the very top rows.

◁ IMPERIAL COINAGE

Bearing the head of Emperor Vespasian, the coin depicts no grape-sucking degenerate but a professional soldier who consolidated Roman rule in Britain and Germany and was a popular military commander. As the founder of the Flavian dynasty and emperor between AD 69 and 79, he set in motion the construction of the stadium.

◁ ROMANTIC ROME

This 18th-century view by Giovanni Volpato reflects the nostalgic sensibility of the Romantic era. Visitors on the Grand Tour were beguiled by the ruins bathed in moonlight or haunted by the sense of a lost civilisation. In Byron's words, "Some cypresses beyond the time-worn breach/Appeared to skirt the horizon, yet they stood/Within a bowshot – where the Caesars dwelt."

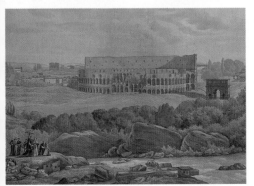

ENTERTAINMENT FOR THE MASSES

The Roman appetite for bloodshed was legendary, with the barbaric *munera*, or blood sports, introduced as a corrupt version of Greek games. The animals, mostly imported from Africa, included lions, elephants, giraffes, hyenas, hippos, wild horses and zebras. The contests were also a way of eliminating slaves and proscribed sects, Christians and common criminals, political agitators and prisoners of war. Variants included battles involving nets, swords and tridents, mock hunts and freak shows with panthers pulling chariots or cripples pitted against clowns. Seneca, Nero's tutor, came expecting "fun, wit and some relaxation" but was dumbfounded by the butchery and cries of: "Kill him! Lash him! Why does he meet the sword so timidly?"

In AD 248, the millennium of the founding of Rome was celebrated by contests involving 2,000 gladiators and the slaying of tame giraffes and hippos as well as big cats. Although convicted criminals were routinely fed to the lions, Christian martyrdom in the arena is less well documented. However, St Ignatius of Antioch, who described himself as "the wheat of Christ", was dutifully devoured by lions in AD 107. Gladiatorial combat was banned in AD 404, while animal fights ended in the following century.

FLORENCE

One of the world's great artistic centres, packed with aesthetic masterpieces, the city is the essential destination for students of Renaissance art and architecture

Map on page 276

Florence and the Renaissance are almost synonymous. No city in Italy has produced such an avalanche of genius: Leonardo da Vinci, Michelangelo, Dante, Brunelleschi, Donatello, Machiavelli, Botticelli, Fra Angelico, Fra Filippo Lippi, Ghirlandaio, Giotto, Ghiberti, Uccello. No city has so reshaped modern thought and art, nor gathered within its walls such a treasure of local art and architecture. Florentines ushered in the Renaissance and took the arts to heights not even the Greeks had attained.

Magnificent cupola

The famous **Duomo** ❶ (cathedral; open daily; free) lies at the heart of Florence. Its dome, a free-hanging cupola designed by Brunelleschi, has astonished architects and builders for centuries. Florentines refer to it as *Il Cupolone*, the dome of domes. A seemingly endless stairway leads to the lantern gallery where Brunelleschi's building secret is revealed: there are "two" mutually supporting domes, one shell inside the other. It's worth climbing the 285 steps to the top of the **Campanile** (belltower; open daily; entrance charge) beside it for intimate views of the cathedral dome and roofline. The octagonal **Battistero** (Baptistry; open daily; entrance charge) close by, with its celebrated bronze doors by Ghiberti, dates in part to the 7th century.

LEFT: the Duomo.
BELOW: Neptune's Fountain.

The man who perhaps best symbolises both the greatness and the parochialism of this city was Michelangelo Buonarroti (1475–1574), who supposedly never washed and always went to bed in his long gaiters. He was, like many Florentines of his time, thrifty and endowed with a dose of insolence, which prompted Pope Clement VII to write that one had to ask Michelangelo to sit down immediately or else he would do so anyway, and leave others standing.

A firm republican, Michelangelo mourned the public burning in 1498 of the Florentine Dominican friar Girolamo Savonarola, who had ruled Florence from 1494 to 1497. Savonarola denounced the sins of the pope and corruption in the church and, during the Lent Carnival of 1497, organised the "Bonfire of the Vanities", a massive conflagration of books and works of art deemed to be indecent or frivolous. His administration ended when, on the orders of the pope, he was arrested, tortured, hanged and burned. On the **Piazza della Signoria** ❷ a plaque on the spot pays tribute to this popular orator.

After midnight, when the city is asleep, a ghostly spectacle appears in this piazza. "The Great White Man", Ammannati's imposing Neptune, climbs from his fountain, walks across the piazza and talks to his friends. Florentines believe he is really the river god Arno, famous for spurning the love of women.

A detail from Botticelli's "St John and the Angels" in the Uffizi.

Florentines have believed for centuries that spirits are imprisoned in their marble statues. They believe that the spirits begin to move and talk as soon as the **Uffizi ❸** (open daily; entrance fee), one of the world's greatest art galleries, closes down at night. The galleries were built as offices (*uffizi*) alongside the **Palazzo Vecchio** (Town Hall) and the collection is arranged chronologically so you can trace, almost in textbook fashion, the development of Florentine art from 13th-century formal Gothic to the Mannerist period of the 16th century. From here it is a short step to the **Bargello ❹** (open daily; entrance charge), a museum devoted to sculpture and applied art where you can see works by Donatello, Michelangelo, Cellini and Giambologna.

From the Uffizi you can walk across the **Ponte Vecchio ❺**, the historic bridge across the River Arno which dates in its present form from 1345. Some of Italy's finest silver jewellery is made and sold in kiosks lining the bridge and there is always a throng jostling to see it. In boutiques in the old city, a tradition of leather goods and textiles still flourishes.

Home of the Medicis

On the other side of the bridge, the forbidding-looking **Palazzo Pitti ❻**, the home of the Medici Grand Dukes in the middle of the 16th century, now houses a number of museums containing art treasures. If you visit only one, make it the **Palatine Gallery** (open daily; entrance fee) where you can admire portraits by Titian, and Rubens' renowned *The Consequences of War* (1638). On the same side of the Arno is the church of **Santa Maria del Carmine** (open Wed–Mon; entrance charge), where the Brancacci chapel contains Masaccio's fresco cycle on *The Life of St Peter*, one of the great works of the early Renaissance.

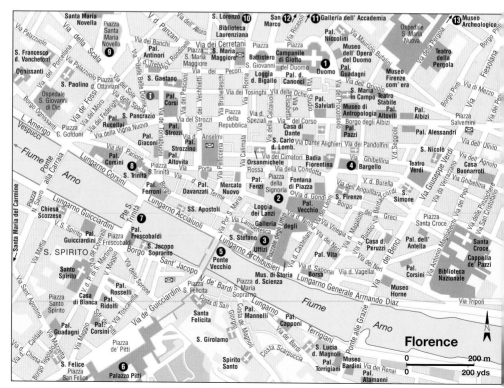

Florence

Back by the River Arno, the **Ponte Santa Trinità ❼** had a miraculous rebirth after being blown up by retreating Nazis in 1944. After World War II the city launched a frenetic search for the missing head of "Spring", a vital member of the Four Seasons quartet guarding each end of the bridge. It was found at the bottom of the River Arno and, in a noisy procession, taken back to the bridge.

The bridge is named after the nearby church of **Santa Trinità ❽**, famous for its frescoes by Ghirlandaio depicting the life of St Francis against a recognisable Florentine background. The area north of the church, around the Palazzo Antinori, has some expensive restaurants but there are budget alternatives in the nearby **Piazza Santa Maria Novella ❾**. The church of **Santa Maria Novella**, which you can see from the square, has more frescoes by Ghirlandaio and Paolo Uccello's celebrated *Universal Deluge*, a painting that itself fell victim to heavy floods in 1966 but which was not damaged beyond recognition.

Affordable shopping possibilities fill the streets around **San Lorenzo ❿**, an excellent place to hunt for presents and souvenirs. Market stalls pop up most days of the week. Find time for a visit to the northeast of this area where one of the most famous works of world art, Michelangelo's *David*, is on display in the **Galleria dell'Accademia ⓫** (open daily; entrance charge). Worth considering, if your patience is challenged by the length of the queue, is a visit instead to the nearby convent of **San Marco ⓬** (open daily; museum open Tues-Sun; entrance charge), where the heavenly paintings and frescoes of Fra Angelico are on view. Angelico entered a Dominican monastery near Florence as a young man and began to paint soon afterwards. By way of contrast, pagan Egyptian and Etruscan art is on show at the **Museo Archeologico ⓭** (open daily; closed alternate Sun and Mon; entrance charge).   ❑

The Florentines discovered perspective and painted the first nudes of the Renaissance. The first humanist, Petrarch, was born here, and Tuscan scholar Boccaccio initiated literary criticism and wrote the first modern love story.

BELOW:
Ponte Vecchio.

VENICE

For a millennium the Republic of Venice repelled unwelcome invaders. Now the city built on water embraces a tidal wave of tourists – on its own terms

Map on page 280

S ometimes, in the morning, when the mist still lingers over the lagoon and the water cannot be seen, only heard, one may be forgiven for thinking that Venice is not real, that it is really only a *fata morgana*, an illusion that will dissolve in time and space. Nothing in Venice is ever quite what it seems. The placid lagoon is in reality gnawing at the foundations, having already gobbled up all but 30 of the 490 islands that existed a thousand years ago. The *palazzi* with their glistening, gilded facades are like slums at their rear ends. Yesterday's Venetians defended their city for 986 years with bluff, bluster, cunning and masterly diplomacy – and then let it fall without a blow. The city itself, once the bazaar of the world and the centre of cosmopolitan life, today is no more than a vast cavernous museum with only echoes of its former splendour.

The republic reached its peak in 1203 with an act of treachery as wicked as it proved expedient. In exchange for allowing the Crusaders to use his port, the blind Doge Enrico Dandolo, a man of enormous size and appetite, persuaded the flotilla of 500 ships to ransack Constantinople, capital of Byzantium, the eastern Roman empire which had been founded after the sack of Rome. It had become the richest city in the world and its power and seafaring influence had long been a thorn in the side of Venice.

In 1203, the pious Crusaders sacked Constantinople, murdering the city's inhabitants. As booty, Venice was awarded the legendary "quarter and a half of a quarter" of the eastern Roman Empire. Her sailors carried off to Saint Mark's Square Constantinople's finest monuments, among them the Quadriga of Horses from the emperor's box at the Hippodrome and the Ikon of Nikopoeia. Venice became the chief depository of Byzantine art.

Souvenirs for the first tourists

When a number of well-to-do tourists started to arrive in the 18th century, a Venetian school of skilled "view" painters sprang up. Giovanni Antonio Canal became the dominant figure. Later known as Canaletto (1697–1768), he was mostly absorbed in meeting foreign demands for souvenir views and pressure upon him was such that he was ultimately forced to work largely from drawings or even from other artists' engravings. This was the Venice fascinated and haunted by the amorous exploits of Casanova, the Venice Lord Byron praised as being (next to the East) "the greenest island of my imagination", a place he loved so much that he swam the 3.5-km (2-mile) Grand Canal from end to end.

Today Venice is supposed to be sinking, and in winter planks are needed to cross **Piazza San Marco ❶**, but the orchestras play on, a little out of tune maybe,

LEFT: Canaletto's vision of 18th-century Venice.
BELOW: symbol of the city.

Venice

0 ——————— 300 m

0 ——————— 300 yds

a little shabby even, but determined to see the Grand Old Lady dance to her grave. The square is still invaded by entertainers and café orchestras. Napoleon, seeing the gossiping multitudes and lavish decor for the first time, called it "the finest drawing room in Europe." Wagner sat at the famous Caffè Florian, still the best place for a coffee on the Piazza; Thomas Mann brooded here in the early 20th century and wrote *Death in Venice*; and Ernest Hemingway guzzled six bottles of wine a night here while he wrote some of his best prose.

Be sure to visit the **Basilica di San Marco** ❷ (open daily; entrance charge for Sanctuary, Pala d'Oro and Treasury) to see gold-backed mosaics, carved galleries and the bones of Saint Mark, stolen from the Middle East. Wander through the oriental **Palazzo Ducale** (Doge's Palace, open daily; entrance charge), where the Doge lived more like a puppet than a ruler. Behind the palace is the **Ponte dei Sospiri** (Bridge of Sighs), where prisoners from the Palace who crossed to the dungeons drew their last breath of free air.

A striking feature of the square is the soaring **Campanile**, a replica of the original tower that collapsed in 1902. Inside, a lift ascends 100 metres (330 ft) for a sweeping panorama of the city. At the lagoon end of the square is the wharf dominated by two columns bearing Saint Theodorus and the Lion of Venice. Where pleasure boats today set out for a trip around the lagoon, merchant ships used to ride at anchor. V*aporetti* (water buses) and speedboat taxis stop here, with the remaining gondolas from the flotilla that was once 20,000 strong.

Map on page 280

Along the Grand Canal

The **Canale Grande** (Grand Canal) is the Champs Elysées of Venice; along its winding 3.5-km (2-mile) route stand 200 palaces and seven churches. At times this unique waterway is as congested as an urban road. Polished mahogany speedboats jostle for space with the *vaporetti*. Dodging in and out between them are the freight barges, the postman's barge, the milkman, the debt collector, the tourist gondolas, the gondolas training for the annual race down the canal, and the flat-bottomed barges that ferry pedestrians across it. The Grand Canal was one of Europe's largest ports until the 16th century when the Portuguese navigator Vasco da Gama found a new sea route to the Indies around the Cape of Good Hope. The discovery ruined the overland spice traffic which had filled Venetian treasuries with revenue far greater than the income of the papacy or the empires of the time.

The energetic row their own boats (a sport known as "water jogging") in the style of the gondolier. Their black-lacquered gondolas, half rowed, half punted with a viola-shaped oar, were multi-coloured until 1562 when the City Council decreed that they all had to be black. This, the city fathers claimed, was the proper colour for the vehicles of a serious city.

At this southern end of the Grand Canal, **Santa Maria della Salute** ❸ squats like a fat dove. The church was built in the 17th century by the city's fathers in gratitude for the deliverance of Venice from the plague. A short distance away, on the same side of the canal, is the **Palazzo Venier dei Leoni** ❹ (open Wed–Mon; entrance charge), home to the Guggen-

BELOW: a water taxi – an essential part of life in Venice.

A modern-day gondolier.

BELOW: the Campanile and Doge's Palace.

heim Collection of modern art. Classical Venetian art – Bellini, Giorgione, Titian, Tintoretto – is housed not far away in the **Galleria dell'Accademia** ❺ (open daily; entrance charge). A great admirer of Venetian painting, the poet Robert Browning (1812–89) died in the palace of the **Ca' Rezzonico** ❻, which is now a museum of baroque art (open Sat–Thur; entrance charge).

Grand canal-side palaces

On the other side of the canal, the **Palazzo Corner Spinelli** ❼ is a fine example of the early flowering of the Renaissance spirit in Venice; it can be compared with the **Palazzo Grimani** ❽ on the other side of the next side canal, which represents a final Renaissance flourish from the master Sanmicheli. Up ahead is one of Venice's most famous sights, the **Ponte di Rialto** ❾, built in the late 16th century to replace an original wooden structure that had collapsed. The area around the original bridge was known simply as the Rialto and in its day was the Wall Street of Europe. Venetians still go to the Rialto every day, to shop in its popular stores and the market on the western bank.

Venice's most famous palace, the **Ca' d'Oro** ❿ (Golden Palace), stands at the first landing stage beyond the Rialto. It was here that Shakespeare set up Desdemona, the wife of Othello, and Shylock lived nearby according to the bard's *Merchant of Venice*. Further up, on the same side of the canal, is the **Palazzo Vendramin-Calergi** ⓫, designed by Mauro Coducci and another superb Renaissance creation. This is the last major building before the railway station, **Ferroviaria S. Lucia** ⓬.

The area to the north of the Grand Canal, between the railway station and the Palazzo Vendramin-Calergi, is **Cannaregio** and the **Ghetto**. Its name comes

from an iron foundry (*getto*) that once stood here, in an area where only Jews worked and lived in the 16th century.

The area of **San Polo** that lies within the large bend of the Grand Canal is home to the **Scuola Grande di San Rocco ⑬** (open Mon–Fri; entrance charge) which is visited primarily for its works of art by Tintoretto (1518–94). They include *The Crucifixion*, which inspired the American novelist Henry James to exclaim: "Surely no single picture in the world contains more human life, there is everything in it including the most exquisite beauty."

Map on page 280

Castello and the islands

The eastern section of the city, **Castello**, has charm of its own, and a good place to begin a visit is the **Campo Santa Maria Formosa ⑭**, a congenial work-a-day market square. The elegant church is worth stepping inside to admire Palma il Vecchio's *St Barbara and Saints*. Further north, but still very much in Castello, the **Campo Santi Giovanni e Paolo ⑮** is another delightful square, enlivened by the imposing statue of the mercenary Bartolomeo Colleoni and the regal, Gothic church of **Santi Giovanni e Paolo**. Very different in style is the baroque church of the **Gesuiti ⑯** near Fondamente Nuove, the main ferry departure point for the northern islands. The church's visually arresting interior is impressive; the prize work of art is Titian's *Martyrdom of St Lawrence*.

The island that can be seen from the quayside is the sombre **San Michele** which, with its dark cypress tress, is the lagoon's famous cemetery island. Further north, **Murano** has become the island of the glass blowers. Its inhabitants developed a technique for making the fragile, almost air-thin Murano glass which has become a trademark all over the world. ❑

BELOW: San Michele island.

AROUND ITALY

In a tour of Italy, the northern lakes and the rolling Tuscan landscape soothe the spirits, while the Bay of Naples and the sun-drenched island of Sicily promise excitement

Map on pages 258–9

The majority of travellers crossing the Alps from Austria into Italy use the **Brenner Pass ❶**; its alpine landscape of wooden chalets and onion-domed churches is more German than Italian. The people in this region of Italy are South Tyroleans and the majority speak German, while their cuisine is Austrian and their manners Teutonic. Fiercely independent, they have been granted a measure of autonomy by the Italian government. The Brenner Highway runs past castles, fortifications and independence monuments to medieval **Trento ❷** which has a Romanesque **cathedral** and the **Castello del Buonconsiglio** (open Tues–Sun; entrance charge), with exhibitions of local art. The highway runs south from Trento and close to **Verona ❸**, the gateway to Italy, and the city in which Romeo and Juliet are said to have lived and loved. **Juliet's House** (open Tues–Sun; entrance charge), at 23 Via Cappello, is a real medieval townhouse of the kind the fictional Juliet could have inhabited. To the east of Verona, a highway leads to the lovely city of **Padova ❹** (Padua), the setting for Katherine's challenge to the male order in Shakespeare's *The Taming of the Shrew*.

From Padua it is a short hop further east along the highway to **Venezia ❺** (Venice, *see pages 279–283*), and the Adriatic coast. Italy's "Adria" begins at **Trieste ❻**. The city has been subjected to constant ownership disputes, none of which bothered James Joyce when he arrived in the city in 1905. He thought his stay would be a short one but Trieste became his home for 10 years. The city retains a feel for the past; and with one of the largest piazzas anywhere in Italy, the **Piazza dell'Unità d'Italia**, there is space aplenty to watch life pass by.

Back at Verona, the A4 highway speeds westwards to **Milano ❼** (Milan) and its 4 million inhabitants, which make it Italy's biggest city. It is also the most industrialised city, a bastion of Italian fashion, a citadel of music (La Scala Opera House) and noted for its cathedral, the biggest Gothic construction in Italy. Milan, **Torino ❽** (Turin) and **Genova ❾** (Genoa) form Italy's industrial triangle, the largest concentration of industry in the country. Turin, Italy's first capital, was the seat of the royal house of Savoy which, under Victor Emanuel, became the Italian royal family. The city bristles with stuffy statuary around its **Palazzo Reale** (regular guided tours Tues–Sun 9am–6pm; tour charge).

Genoa, the ancient sea republic near the chic resort of **Portofino**, on the Italian Riviera, is still the country's busiest port. Between the three cities trucks shunt goods back and forth on a network of highways. Roads are the most popular means of transport in Italy; Italians, who have produced some great names in sports cars (FIAT in Turin, Ferrari in Modena), are passionate drivers, though railways are cheaper.

LEFT: the church of Assisi.
BELOW: traditional Italian womanhood.

The Lakes

Italy's Lake District is made up of five major lakes and the most westerly one is **Lago Maggiore** ⒶⒶ (Lake Maggiore), with the spry settlement of **Stresa** Ⓑ on its western shore. Readers of Hemingway's *A Farewell to Arms* will particularly want to see Stresa but every visitor should enjoy a stroll around the gardens of the **Villa Pallavicino** (open Mar–Oct: daily; entrance charge) or a quick trip by car to the top of **Monte Mottarone**, from where there is a panoramic view of the town, the lake and the surrounding Alps. A longer scenic drive may be enjoyed by taking the road south to **Arona** Ⓒ, with superb views of lakes and islands along the way.

Boatman for hire at the Italian Lakes.

Lago di Lugano Ⓓ (Lake Lugano) lies mostly in Switzerland and Swiss currency is more common than the lira around the tiny eastern part of the lake that juts into Italy. The most visually stunning of the lakes is undoubtedly **Lago di Como** Ⓔ (Lake Como), 31 km (19 miles) long and 5 km (3 miles) wide at its broadest point. The Alps enclose the lake to the north and skiers enjoy unparalleled views as they whoosh down the glaciers of the mountains. Fine views of the lake may be enjoyed by non-skiers from the relaxing little town of **Como** Ⓕ.

It takes about an hour to drive up the eastern side of Lake Como to the small town of **Bellágio** Ⓖ so consider an alternative mode of transport by taking a slow cruise on the regular boat service from Como. Either way, the journey is worthwhile, for Bellagio has the most inclusive views of Lake Como and there is another splendidly relaxing villa and garden at the **Villa Carlotta** (open mid-Mar–Oct: daily; entrance charge). The most attractive destination along the southeastern spur of Lake Como is **Lecco** Ⓗ, home to some eye-catching frescos in the city's Basilica.

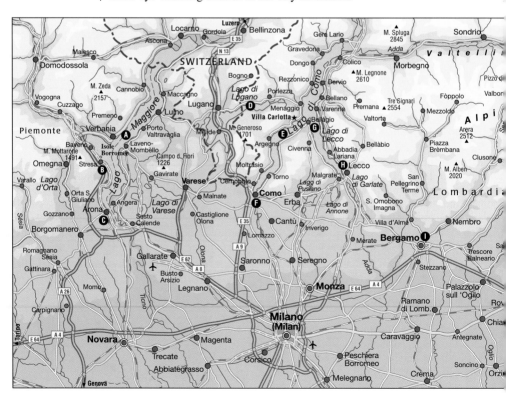

Bergamo ❶ is a colourful and soothing town to the southeast of Lecco with a number of attractions. Discerning art lovers make their way to the understated **Accademia Carrara** (open Wed–Mon; entrance charge) to view works by Mantegna and Bellini, while a funicular takes visitors to the old part of the town.

East of Bergamo lies **Lago d'Iseo ❶** (Lake Iseo), where Monte Isola (Mountain Island) occupies the centre of the lake and dominates the view. The city of **Brescia ❸** lies southeast of the lake and there are a number of small but important museums here. The **Museo Romano** (open Tues–Sun; closed 12.30–3pm; entrance charge) occupies the site of a Roman temple, remains of which are on display. The next phase in the town's cultural history is celebrated in the **Museum of Christian Antiquities** (open Mon–Sat; closed 12–3pm and Sat pm), while the **Museo delle Armi** (open Tues-Sun; closed 12.30–3pm; entrance charge) specialises in antique weapons from medieval times onwards.

The largest of the Italian lakes, and the most popular, is **Lago di Garda ❹** (Lake Garda). Water sports and sailing draw in visitors while a reminder of an unhappy chapter in Italy's history is to be found in the resort town of **Gardone Riviera ❿**. Gabriele d'Annunzio, the poet and enthusiastic patriot famous for his daring aerial reconnaissance over Vienna in 1918 and later an ardent supporter of Mussolini, was given a home here by the dictator. The house, **Il Vittoriale** (open Tues–Sun; entrance charge) and its estate are a shrine to d'Annunzio's dreams of Italian imperialism. His famous plane is suspended from the ceiling of the auditorium. Neighbouring **Salò**, a charming lakeside resort, is synonymous with the notorious wartime Republic of Salò, where Mussolini made his last stand. On a tip of land at the southern end of Lake Garda the ancient town of **Sirmione ❹** is a good place to while away an hour or two.

Map on pages 286–7

TIP

Lecco is a good base for hikers. It also has excellent rail connections with Milan and Bergamo.

BELOW: the town of Bellagio on Lake Como.

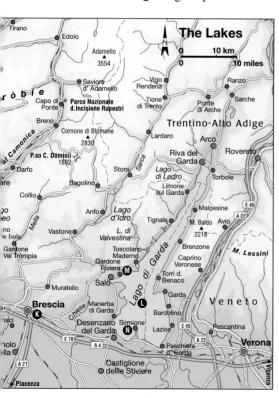

The Po Valley

South of Verona begins the great Italian plain in the Po Valley, cut by irrigation channels and shivering with ghostly poplar trees. This fertile region between Milan in the west and Rovigo in the east is Italy's larder as well as its fruit and vegetable garden. The Brenner Highway links up with the Autostrada del Sole (the Sun Motorway) near **Modena** ⑩. This 1,200-km (780-mile) artery, beginning at Milan, runs the length of the peninsula down to Reggio di Calabria on the Strait of Messina at Italy's toe. A far more ancient road, the Via Emilia, was built by the Romans and it still runs through the centre of Modena with the city's most illustrious sight, the Romanesque **Duomo** (cathedral), sitting grandly alongside the road. The **Biblioteca Estense** (open Mon–Sat; free) in the **Palazzo dei Musei** (open Tue–Sun; entrance charge) has a 15th-century copy of Dante's *Divine Comedy* and a superb set of illuminated manuscripts.

Part of the Via Emilia linked Modena with the historic city of **Bologna** ⑪, where there is plenty to see and some excellent restaurants to sample in between visits to the grand squares of **Piazza del Nettuno** and **Piazza Maggiore** and the various "leaning towers". The story goes that two aristocratic families expressed their rivalry by competing to build the tallest tower in the city. One of the towers is now only 48 metres (157 ft), having been shortened for safety reasons in the 14th century, but still leaning more than 3 metres (10 ft). The other tower stands to its full height of 97 metres (318 ft) and leans more than 1 metre (3 ft). Bologna's famous university, attended by the great lyric poet Petrarch (1304–74), among other luminaries, is now dotted all around the city but its official centre is the 16th-century **Palazzo Poggi**. The **Pinacoteca Nazionale** (open Tues–Sun; entrance charge) nearby includes works by Raphael and Perugino.

BELOW:
Piazza Maggiore, Bologna's main square.

If you are travelling down the east coast on the A14 Adriatic Highway don't overlook the port town of **Ravenna** ⓬ where the churches have dazzling mosaics. The finest are in the 6th-century basilica of **San Vitale** (open daily; entrance charge). These world-class mosaics owe their existence to the rule of Justinian who made Ravenna his capital after reconquering parts of Italy from the barbarians who had overrun Rome. Opposite the cathedral is the baroque church of **San Francisco**, where Dante is buried.

Map on pages 258–9

The Adriatic

Sandy beaches stretch unendingly down the coast south of Ravenna. **Rimini** ⓭ is the Adriatic's principal resort. Hedonistic pleasures apart, it has its own cultural attractions in the medieval town 2 km (1 mile) from the beach. Chief of these is the Renaissance edifice, the **Tempio Malatestiano** (open daily; free), built around 1450 for Sigismondo Malatesta, an evil *condottiere,* and condemned by the pope as a "temple of devil worshippers". The adjoining square, the Piazza Tre Martiri, site of a Roman forum, owes its name to three partisans who were executed here by the Nazis in 1944.

Barely half an hour's drive inland from Rimini lies the world's smallest republic – **San Marino** ⓮. This mini-country has just 18,000 inhabitants and was made famous by its fierce independence and the variety of its stamps (which, together with tourism and farming, provide the main revenue). Small it may be, but since the 5th century San Marino has managed, with wile and guile, to maintain its sovereign status, while other republics on the peninsula have lost theirs. In 1861 Abraham Lincoln accepted honorary citizenship of the republic, though this did not prevent the Americans from bombing it during World War II

LEFT: on the beach in Rimini.
BELOW: fresh fish at Comacchio.

when Germans troops were in occupation. The capital, also called San Marino, has just over 3,000 residents, and it is run by its Grand Council, whose 60 members are elected every five years. Women were given the right to vote and the right to hold public office in 1960 and 1973 respectively. To the west of San Marino stands the hill-top fortress of San Leo, a conspicuous sight that attracts thousands of visitors annually. The 18th-century alchemist Cagliostro was imprisoned here and his reconstructed cell can be visited.

Tuscany

Heading south from Bologna towards Rome on the Autostrada del Sole the town of **Arezzo** ⓕ offers worthy relief from the rigours of the highway. The chief attraction lies in Piero della Francesca's frescos depicting *The Legend of The True Cross* in the church of **San Francesco** (open daily; free), but the town's **Museo Archeologico** (open daily 10am–2pm; entrance charge) and **Anfiteatro Romano** just south of town are also worth a visit.

Tuscany, neat, regimented and functional, resembles its capital, **Firenze** (Florence) ⓖ *(see pages 275–7)*. The farmland has a linear pattern and is edged by hedgerows. The pointed cypresses, the tall "males" and dishevelled "females", are planted with geometrical exactitude, picketing the hills, delineating borders, flanking gateposts, dividing plots of land or simply giving shade to a crop. The houses, rectangular and frugal like the inhabitants, stand on conical hills or, like soldiers on parade, along well-planned streets.

During the Renaissance Tuscan cities were carefully planned with bylaws to ensure everything matched. No house had a wrong colour, wrong window, wrong shape, height or width. The houses of the Tuscans are inward-looking,

bristling against entry. They have been compared to safe deposit boxes, a fortification in which possessions can be defended.

The narrow lanes and alleys that do so much to evoke the medieval flavour of **Siena** ⑰, which lies at the geographical heart of Tuscany, are mercifully free of traffic but finding a place to park close to the central square, the **Campo**, is no easy feat. But the Campo is one of the finest squares in Italy, a great place to enjoy a drink at one of the many pavement cafés. If you are not here on 2 July or 16 August, just imagine the scene on those days when horses and their riders charge around the square in one of the wildest horse races in the world. The stake is a simple piece of cloth, Il Palio. A colourful procession of pages, knights, flagtossers and men-at-arms, dressed in 15th-century costumes, opens the spectacle. Riding bareback, the riders risk life and limb.

The square is also home to the **Museo Civico** (open daily; entrance charge), which has two frescos by Simone Martini as well as Ambrogio Lorenzetti's *Allegory of Good and Bad Government*. The facade of Siena's Gothic **Duomo** (open daily; free) is a festival of green, pink and white marble, while the interior is decorated with a series of black-and-white geometric patterns.

Saving Pisa's Leaning Tower

The Leaning Tower of **Pisa** ⑱ was begun in 1173, but almost immediately began to tilt because the alluvial subsoil was unable to take its weight. In 1989 the tower was closed because of the increasing tilt (measured at 5.5 metres/18 ft from the vertical). After more than a decade under wraps, it has been stabilised and is once more open to the public. Pisa is also one of Italy's great cities of art. The old maritime republic, once a flourishing sea port on the River Arno's

Map on pages 258–9

The Leaning Tower of Pisa – continuing to defy gravity.

BELOW:
Palio race in Siena.

Chianti grapes ripening in the Tuscan sunshine.

estuary, was an ally of the Normans during their conquest of Sicily, and its ships carried the First Crusade to the Holy Land, a journey that gave Pisa trading posts in the East. Pisa's links with Hohenstaufen Emperor Frederic Barbarossa gave it a leading position in Tuscany during the 12th century, which ended with the city's defeat by Genoa in 1284. In 1406 it was taken by Florence after a long siege. During World War II the city was badly damaged but faithfully reconstructed. The **Campo dei Miracoli** (The Field of Miracles), containing the Baptistry and Cathedral beside the Leaning Tower, is the main area of interest in the town. The Islamic influence on the architecture of the baptistry and cathedral is what makes these buildings so distinctive, a legacy of the Pisan merchants who established important trading links with North Africa and Moorish Spain.

The N222 from Siena leads through the Chianti Way to **Chianti** itself, rolling hillsides of small vineyards of the *fattorie* (wine estates) which produce this classic Italian wine.

Umbria

To the east of Tuscany is the province of Umbria and its capital, **Perugia ⑲**. The city reflects the bellicose side of a region where the martial and the mystical are inextricably intertwined, where the harsh oak and the gentle olive grow on the same hillside and where the shepherd cuts the sheep's gullet then plays the flute to mourn it. Perugia's churches were never completed in the same generation since the citizens were too busy with wars, feuds, pillage and murder. In this barbed hilltop fortress the "divine" Raphael studied under the great Pietro Perugino, who squandered his impressive talent on making copies of his most popular works just for the money.

BELOW: fresco of St Francis in the Basilica di San Francesco.

ST FRANCIS OF ASSISI

The picture-postcard town of Assisi in Umbria, flower-decked and wood-smoke scented, draws tremendous crowds, who come to experience something of the spiritualism of the Franciscan order, founded by the town's most famous son, Francis of Assisi.

Born Giovanni Bernadone in 1181, Francis embraced asceticism at an early age, and by 1219 had a brotherhood of 5,000 monks. The main tenets of the original Franciscan order were poverty, chastity and obedience; in particular, Francis repudiated the decadence of the Catholic church, posing a challenge to the worldliness of the papacy. On his return from preaching in the Holy Land, Francis is said to have received the marks of the *stigmata*, and was canonised in 1228, two years after his death.

Construction of the two-tiered **Basilica di San Francesco** began in the mid-13th century. The **Basilica Inferiore** (Lower Basilica; open daily; entrance charge) was built around the saint's crypt and commemorates Francis's modest life with frescos by Simone Martini and Cimabue. The **Basilica Superiore** (Upper Basilica), containing Giotto's famous fresco cycle of *The Life of St Francis*, was damaged in the 1997 earthquake and has recently been undergoing restoration.

A legacy of the earthquakes that rocked Perugia in 1997 is that some of the historic buildings, especially churches, have still not been reopened to the public. What can be seen, however, are works by many of Umbria's most noted painters in the **Galleria Nazionale dell'Umbria** (open daily; closed first Mon of month; entrance charge). Fra Angelica and Piero della Francesca are both well represented. To reach the gallery walk down the Corso Vannucci from the city's main square, the Piazza IV Novembre, and look for the **Palazzo dei Priori**, the town hall, on the right hand side.

Map on pages 258–9

The Bay of Naples

On the road south of **Rome ㉑** (*see pages 263–71*) the Bay of Naples will draw you in, just as it has the Phoenicians, Greeks, Romans, Goths, Vandals, Saracens, Turks, Normans, Germans, Spaniards, French and British. **Napoli ㉑** (Naples), despite its hopeless overcrowding, unemployment and crime rate, continues to exert a fascination that makes itself felt in a palpable buzz that energises the city. Down the centuries her troubles have been great, but so have her charms. They still are. A Neapolitan thief will relieve victims of their valuables with a smile and a politeness that will make it quite painless. If porters, taxi drivers, merchants and vendors cheat a little they do so while raining down titles such as "Dottore", "Professore", "Generale" and "Your Excellency".

Founded by Greek colonists who named it "Neapolis" (the New City), the city was once part of Magna Graecia, the ancient Greek colonies. It was captured by the Romans in 326 BC, they enriched the settlement with temples, gymnasiums, aqueducts, hippodromes, arenas and numerous catacombs outside the city. It became the favourite residence of many of the emperors and this is where the infamous Nero made his stage debut.

BELOW:
the Bay of Naples.

After the fall of the Roman Empire Naples became a Byzantine dukedom in the 7th century, and early in the 12th century it fell to the feudal Norman Kingdom of Sicily. Since then European monarchies have converted it into the flourishing capital of a kingdom, inhabited by a people who quickly learned to adjust to the whims of their foreign rulers. Wily, ingenious, devious, roguish yet loyal and proud, they are sons of a city where politics and business are a blend of Machiavellian realism and Byzantine intrigue. In this atmosphere laws were never taken too seriously; after all they were made by foreign bosses to benefit themselves and rob poor Neapolitans. A quarter of a million Neapolitans live, directly or indirectly, from smuggling, chiefly cigarettes.

The **Duomo** of Naples is sandwiched between family apartments in the northern part of the historic centre. In its crypt rests the relic Neapolitans treasure most: a phial containing the blood of Saint Januarius (San Genaro) who was martyred in AD 305. The blood must liquefy and boil three times a year – on the first Saturday in May, on 19 September and on 16 December – if Naples is to escape disaster. The Vatican has eliminated San Genaro from the official list of saints, but liquefication ceremonies remain the highlights of the Neopolitan ecclesiastical year. If the miracle is slow in happening and the blood refuses to liquefy,

Proving the bikini isn't so modern: a detail from a Roman mosaic found at the Villa Romana on the island of Sicily.

BELOW: Sorrento on the Amalfi coast.

then Neapolitans have their own ways of coaxing the saint into action: in fact, the cursing of San Genaro became so coarse that the Archbishop of Naples has banned swearing in church.

A good place to begin a tour of Naples is the **Castel Nuovo**, not far from one of the city's tourist offices, where a stupendous Triumphal Arch still stands in commemoration of Alfonso I's defeat of the French in the 15th century. From outside the castle the Via San Carlo leads the way to Italy's largest opera house, the **Teatro San Carlo**. All the tourist offices dispense a visitors' magazine, *Qui Napoli*, which is updated monthly with details of the concerts and operas taking place within its hallowed walls. The acoustics for which the early 18th-century theatre is so renowned are said to owe something to the numerous clay pitchers that were inserted between its walls after a fire in 1816.

Under the volcano

The eyes of the people living on the Bay of Naples are imperceptibly drawn every day towards the giant sentinel who stands ominously above them to check and comment on his mood. They refer to him simply as "he", never as Vesuvius. The height of the cone is 1,280 metres (4,200 ft), but it varies after each eruption. He last erupted in 1944 and his "vomit" (as the locals call it) is still scattered in a vast slag heap around the crater. His lava became the fertile Vesuvian soil where the finest vines and olive grow, the main reason why peasants for thousands of years have stubbornly clung to the precarious slopes.

His most famous explosion occurred in 79 BC at a time when everyone thought he was extinct, when woods brimming with wild boar covered his very summit. Spartacus and his rebellious slaves withdrew into these woods to escape the first punitive expeditions of the Roman legions. The eruption, elaborately described by Pliny the Younger, buried the flourishing cities of **Herculaneum** (open daily; entrance charge; tel: 081-788 1243) and **Pompeii** ❷ (open daily; special night openings in summer; entrance charge; tel: 081-861 0913) under the mountains of ashes and brimstone. The life and last drama of these cities, preserved in volcanic ashes, came to light over the past century when archaeologists dug them from their airtight tomb. The imprints and skeletons help make this one of the most impressive ancient monuments in the world. Excavators found the bones of a rich man, his fingers still clutching the keys to the treasure chests his slaves carried behind him. A thief, one hand still on a stolen purse, is nailed against the wall with his victim. Wine stands on tables, bread lies in the oven. The skeleton of an aristocratic lady is found in the sleeping quarters of a gladiator. Graffiti proclaims love and engages in obscenities and political baiting.

The tour groups that congregate at Pompeii can prove dismaying at the height of the tourist season and a visit to the lesser-known Herculaneum is one way of dealing with the problem. Although the town was never animated by the commercial buzz that made Pompeii so lively and diverse a community in its heyday, there is still plenty to see. Well-preserved frescos decorate the **Casa Sannitica** and the **Casa**

dell'Atrio Mosaico, and Herculaneum is also a convenient starting point for an early evening ascent of Mount Vesuvius. Buses leave regularly from the city of Ercolano, which nestles just below the volcano.

Many of the finest finds of old Pompeii have been taken for exhibition to the **Museo Archeologico Nazionale di Napoli** (open 8am–10pm daily; entrance charge). These exhibits include the spectacular mosaics on the mezzanine floor and should not be missed on any account. Many of the finest formed a border around the gigantic portrayal of the Battle of Issus, where Alexander the Great defeated the Persians, and the battle scene itself can be admired in a separate room of the museum. Try also to give yourself enough time to admire the Roman copies of Greek sculptures that are housed here.

Capri and the Amalfi coast

The island of **Capri** ❷ is easily reached by ferry or hydrofoil from Naples or Sorrento. The remains of **Tiberius's Villa** (open daily; entrance charge) here, reached by bus from the town of Capri, are one of the chief attractions. Tiberius chose the island as his retirement home in AD 27 and, while he may or may not have organised rural orgies on the island, the story has certainly not diminished Capri's appeal. Even more popular as a destination on the island is the **Grotta Azzurra** (Blue Grotto), a cave on the water's edge. Its strange light has made it the most visited attraction on this coast after Pompeii.

Opposite Capri lies **Sorrento** and the start of the attractive, twisting Amalfi coast, which dips into pretty fishing villages such as **Positano** and **Amalfi** itself, once so powerful it had its own pope, and reaches the beautiful clifftop village of **Ravello**, where the American writer Gore Vidal has long had a home.

Map on pages 258–9

BELOW: looking out to the Bay of Capri.

*Waiter serving
pasta at a Sicilian
restaurant.*

Apulia: the heel of the boot

From south of Naples it is possible to drive, via Potenza, to the Adriatic coast of Italy where Puglia forms the heel and spur of Italy's boot. **Bari ㉔**, originally an ancient Greek colony, is the main commercial centre of this corner of Italy but there is a wonderful absence of modernity in the warren of narrow streets and dazzling white houses in the ancient half of the city.

Two sights worth seeking out are the church of **San Nicola**, with fine medieval treasures, and the **Pinacoteca Provinciale** (open Tues–Sun am only; entrance charge), which has a surprising number of minor masterpieces that include Vivarini's *Annunciation*. Around **Alberobello**, 50 km (30 miles) south-east of Bari, round peasants' huts called *trulli* are distinctive.

The coastal road from Bari continues to **Brindisi ㉕**, where a column marks the end of the Via Appia, the first and greatest of the ancient roads that lead to Rome. Most visitors to Brindisi today are arriving or departing on one of the ferries that ply the route to and from Greece.

Taranto ㉖, on the instep of Italy's boot and founded by Spartan navigators in 706 BC, became the largest city in the Magna Graecia, the Greek empire in Italy. Its **Museu Nazionale** (open daily; entrance charge) is the second most important archaeological museum in southern Italy after Naples'.

And so to Calabria, at the foot of the boot, and **Reggio di Calabria ㉗** from where ferries to Sicily depart. The first Greek settlers made the sea journey from Sicily in the 8th century BC and the most celebrated evidence of this early contact between the two great civilisations of the ancient world only came to light in 1972. It was then that some fishermen happened to discover two colossal Greek statues thought to have gone down with a Greek ship. These star-

BELOW: basking
in the sunshine.
RIGHT: Sicilian
street life.

tling statues are deservedly the chief exhibits in the **Museo Nazionale della Magna Graecia** (open daily; closed 1st and 3rd Mon of month; entrance charge).

Map on pages 258–9

Sicily

The fertile island of **Sicilia** (Sicily) has always been at the confluence of the Mediterranean world, serving as a springboard for ambitious conquerors. It is best seen by road: though the ever-smouldering volcano Etna provides the most dramatic single vantage point. Around the central town of Enna, the countryside is one rolling plain of golden cornstalks. **Palermo** ㉘, Sicily's capital, is a turbulent place, famous both for its Mafia connections and for some wonderful architecture. The **Palazzo dei Normanni** was originally a Norman palace and is now the seat of the Sicilian parliament. It is home to the **Cappella Palatina** (open Mon–Fri, and Sat am; free) and from here guided tours of the adjoining **Sala di Re Ruggero** are possible. Just along the north coast is the pretty seaside town of **Cefalù**, with a surprisingly impressive 12th-century Duomo.

Siracusa ㉙ (Syracuse), one of the most important Greek colonies, is on the other side of Sicily and should not be missed by anyone with an interest in ancient history. A cultural capital, it attracted Aeschylus whose play, *Women of Etna*, was possibly first staged at the great amphitheatre that still stands. The theatre, the **Teatro Greco**, is one of the finest examples in the ancient Greek world. It holds up to 15,000 spectators and during the months of May and June evocative performances of classical plays take place here.

Off Sicily's northeastern tip are the **Isole Eolie** (Aeolian islands), where the Greeks believed the god Aeolus kept the winds imprisoned. Now a holiday resort, the scattered islands include **Stromboli**, which spews lava into the night. ❑

BELOW: unspoilt beach and old town of Cefalù, Sicily.

THE BALKAN COAST

*The Adriatic coast of the former Yugoslavia is a slice
of eastern Europe with a Mediterranean flavour*

The Balkan coast has recovered from the turmoil of the early 1990s to re-emerge, albeit slowly, as one of Europe's most attractive and unspoilt shores. To the north lies Slovenia, curling up beside Italy and Austria and offering just 47 km (29 miles) of beach. To the south, against the Albanian border, is Montenegro, with 140 km (80 miles) of seaside centred on the Gulf of Kotor. In between, Croatia takes the lion's share of the Adriatic shore, including Dalmatia and the historic town of Dubrovnik. Its 1,600 km (1,000 miles) of coastline, 1,100 islands, 500 ports and 50 marinas make this sailing area a close second to the Mediterranean islands of Turkey and Greece.

The Mediterranean flavour of this eastern European shore can be seen in such habits as the afternoon siesta in summer, and the locals dressing up for evening strolls on the promenades. If the towns seem familiar, it is because this area once belonged to the Venetian empire, which built Italianate ports and named Montenegro after its black mountains. The food, too, has fallen to outside influences: pasta from Italy, strüdel from Austria and ghoulash from Hungary. But wine and fruit brandies drunk during the day and before meals are definitely local.

The language, too, is quite different. If the spelling of Slovene and Croatian, both south Slavonic languages, looks intimidatingly short on vowels, don't worry too much. English, German and Italian are frequently understood in the main resorts. The languages are similar. *Zdravo* means "hello" in both, *ne* means "no" and *hvala* means "thank you". But in Slovene *ja* is "yes" and *prosim* is "please"; in Croatian these are *da* and *molim*. The people of both countries are courteous; they are careful to dress well, wishing to be associated with western Europe, and brook little argument in relation to their part in recent troubles. As in many former communist states, religion now plays an important role in daily life, and around 75 percent of Slovenians and Croats are Roman Catholic. They are fortunate to have a variety of attractive Romanesque, Renaissance and baroque churches in which to worship. ❏

PRECEDING PAGES: Dubrovnik Old Town.
LEFT: the port town of Korcula, Croatia.

SLOVENIA AND THE CROATIAN COAST

Least affected of the emergent nations during the break-up of Yugoslavia, these areas are beginning to attract tourists again. In the meantime, this is where to go to avoid the crowds

Map on pages 258–9

Heading into **Croatia** (Hrvatska) from **Trieste** brings you briefly into **Slovenia** (Slovenija). This small country of 20,000 sq km (7,725 sq miles) and 2 million people is green and pastoral with an alpine backdrop; baroque castles and tranquil lakes stretch east to the Hungarian border. It has some 50 ski resorts, mainly in the Julian Alps and the Pohorje Massif, and provides good cycling and horse-riding country. In 1580 the Austrian Archduke Charles established a stud farm at Lipizza for the Spanish Riding School in Vienna *(see page 232)*. Today visitors can watch and ride the famous Lipizzaner horses at the 310-hectare (770-acre) stud farm in what is now called **Lipica**, just over the border from Trieste.

Slovenia's capital, **Ljubljana** ㉚, lies an equal 90 km (55 miles) from the Austrian border and from the sea. A sociable pedestrianised central square, Presernov trg, connects the new town with the old. Here are the architectural flourishes of the 19th and 20th centuries which embellished such traditional meeting places as the Central Pharmacy. Across the river the Old Town, where the daily market is held, curves round the wooded Castle Hill, rebuilt after an earthquake in 1511. The tower and ramparts have good views across the town.

Devoid of large beaches to mop up the visiting Italians, Germans and Austrians, the resorts on the country's small slice of coast soon fill up in summer. But the attractiveness of the former Venetian towns remain. **Koper** ㉛ has a fine 15th-century arcaded Loggia in the main square, and the small cobbled streets of **Piran** make it Slovenia's most attractive resort. The **Maritime Museum** here is in a fine 17th-century palace (open Apr–Jun: daily; entrance charge). **Primorska**, the neighbouring resort, has Slovenia's sandiest beaches, and is the most built up of the country's resorts. A nearby curiosity is the bleak, abandoned medieval salt pans at Secovlje, stretching to the Croatian border.

Into Croatia

The coastal strip of Croatia, backed by the Karst mountains, is one leg of the country: the other leg, the lowland basin where the capital **Zagreb** is situated, runs due east beneath Slovenia and Hungary. All told, Croatia is nearly two-and-a-half times as big as Slovenia, both in size and population, and it makes up approximately half of the former Yugoslavia.

The coast, full of coves and pine-backed small beaches, begins at the pear-shaped peninsula of ancient Istra. Halfway down its west coast is the laid-

LEFT: Hvar town square, Croatia.
BELOW: a Lipizaner horse in Lipica.

Dressing up in traditional Croatian costume.

back medieval town of **Rovinj** ② where colour-washed stone houses are perched in steep wooded terraces, interspersed by low-rise hotels and surrounded by a necklace of more than a dozen verdant islands. Here, too, it's all very Italian, with narrow streets, *piazzas* and *piazzettas*. The 18th-century **Cathedral of St Euphemia** is impossible to miss and well worth a visit, if only to admire the baroque tomb of the martyred St Euphemia. There is an active fishing quay, and the **Rovinj Aquarium** (open Easter to mid–Oct: daily; entrance charge) displays a fine variety of the busy marine life that lurks beneath the dazzling waters of Istra.

Pula, towards the tip of the peninsula, is an important naval base with few beaches and in an unremarkable setting, but it is worth visiting for its Roman remains, which include a magnificent 1st-century amphitheatre overlooking the harbour. The main road continues around the tip of the peninsula and up the east coast to **Rijeka** ③ and the Gulf of Kvarner. Rijeka cannot compete with the resort facilities of Istra or the attractions waiting further down the coast, but its location on the main coastal highway and the railway line makes it a major transport hub. There is the added bonus of hopping on to one of the ferries that run throughout the year between Rijeka and Dubrovnik; however, because they leave in the early evening there is little to see until you reach Split.

From Rijeka the coastal road runs down to Dalmatia with tempting offshore islands along the way. **Krk Island** ④ is reached by a monstrous concrete bridge which has allowed ease of access and a frenzy of building, but there is a pleasant little beach at its southern tip and Krk town has an appealing medieval flavour. **Rab Island** ⑤ is particularly appealing, easily reached by bus from Rijeka or boat from Krk Island, and with a relaxed atmosphere that is attracting a growing number of visitors. Croatian devotion is reflected by the number of old churches, the Romanesque cathedral, the 12th-century monastery of St Anthony and a convent of Benedictine nuns.

BELOW:
the theatre in Split.

Historic Dalmatia

Dalmatia, which occupies the rest of the Adriatic coast all the way to Dubrovnik, is packed with historic towns and beach resorts and produces the country's best wine as well as a most hospitable climate and landscape that is hard to distinguish from the best the Mediterranean can offer. First stop is likely to be **Zadar** ⑯, full of old churches and museums, and with a twice-weekly ferry service to and from Venice during the summer months. The best of the churches to visit is **St Donatus**, built as it is over Roman remains, and exuding charm on sultry summer evenings when concerts of Renaissance music take place. A **Museum of Church Art** (open daily; free) is directly opposite in the monastery, crammed full of relics, antiquities and devotional paintings.

The Roman emperor Diocletian settled in **Split** ⑰ at the end of the 3rd century AD, recognising it as a perfect retirement setting, and the ruins of his fortified palace dominate the harbour. You can wander through the excavated halls, the pretty peristyle and the impressive vestibule. The mausoleum that was built to accommodate Diocletian is now a cathedral, ironic in view of the ferocious persecution of Christians unleashed by the emperor, and the church tower can be climbed (there is an entrance charge) for views over the town. Split has a number of worthwhile museums, including the **Meštrović Gallery** (open Tues–Sat, Sun am; entrance charge), with a fine collection of contemporary art, and a **Museum of Archeology** (open Tues–Sun 10am–1pm). As evening draws in, the harbour-side road in front of the palace ruins, with the tourist office at its west end, lights up with pavement cafés. During the day, the harbour is busy with ferries shuffling to and from the Dalmatian islands, and a boat ride down to Dubrovnik is a highlight of a visit to Croatia.

Island delights

Brac Island ❸ is the third largest Adriatic island and its popularity with European holidaymakers is facilitated by a small international airport. Tucked away on the south coast, nestling under lush pine forests, Bol is the best-known resort settlement. Its quaint promenade has the usual array of shops and cafés and a miniature railway connects the tourist hotels. Be up early to bag a space on the nearby 630-metre sandbar that projects for half that distance into the crystal clear sea – the extraordinary **Zlatni Rat** (Golden Horn) beach – though the local pebbly beaches are less crowded and one of Dalmatia's many nudist beaches is close by. The island's small capital town is **Supetar**, hardly the most idyllic-sounding name but with attractive beaches protected from coastal winds.

Known as "the Madeira of the Adriatic" and basking in the renown of being voted one of the world's ten most beautiful islands by *Traveller Magazine*, **Hvar Island** ❸ is stunningly beautiful, lush with pine woods, olive trees and lavender plants that leave a permanent scent in the unpolluted air. Tourists are

Map on pages 258–9

TIP

A serious contender for the best Croatian dish is black rice risotto with squid, coloured by ink, and served with fresh Parmesan and a glass of Postup.

BELOW: Hvar town and harbour.

Map on pages 258–9

zipped here in two hours from Split airport, but once on the island it would be a shame to rush. The medieval atmosphere of Hvar town is best appreciated by meandering through the back streets, seeking out the Franciscan monastery and its collection of Venetian paintings, or the ruined Dominican monastery with fine views over the bay. Even better views are enjoyed from the hilltop 16th-century Venetian fortress, best climbed to after the heat of the day has run its course. Dusk also brings musicians to the steps of Hotel Slavija to conjure up a Venetian mood and there are lively clubs and discos in the vicinity.

Dubrovnik: a complement to Venice

Those who wish to see heaven on earth should come to Dubrovnik.

– GEORGE BERNARD SHAW, 1929

Historic **Dubrovnik** ⑩ owes its past to its location: the last safe port before the sea opens up into the wide expanse of the Ionian and Mediterranean waters. An independent Republic of Ragusa until Napoleon invaded in 1806, Dubrovnik complemented Venice on the world trade route and its wonderfully preserved old town centre is eloquent testimony to a long-departed era. Time-washed stone houses, unostentatiously catching the bright light, cobbled squares and ancient, clay-roofed buildings have been saved by an ambitious UNESCO restoration programme following devastating bombing in 1991–2, during which two-thirds of the town's ancient buildings were hit.

Cars make a mercifully small impact inside the city walls and strolling through the narrow streets and the pedestrian promenade is reassuringly safe. The Dubrovnik Summer Festival starts in mid-July and runs for a month with indoor and outdoor performances of music and drama. Part of the cultural attraction of the city and the nearby islands is the rich variety of traditional seafood dishes. Lobster risotto, the glass or two of *grk* or *maraština*, eel stew, and Dalmatian smoked ham are all worth seeking out on the menus of the various restaurants on Prijeko Street.

BELOW:
Dubrovnik Place, in the Old Town.

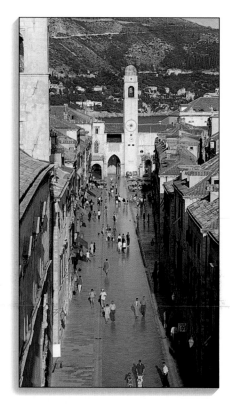

Excursions from the city are easy to arrange. There is an hourly ferry service in summer to the national park on **Lokrum Island**, where there is a nudist beach and the ruins of a medieval monastery. **Mljet Island** ⑪ has a more impressive national park – an island ferry departs from Dubrovnik every afternoon except Sunday. Of the two saltwater lakes on the island, the larger one of **Veliko** has its own tiny island of St Mary. Small taxi boats chug out to its 12th-century Benedictine monastery, which has been converted into a restaurant.

There is plenty to do on Mljet: bicycles are available at most of the hotels and there are many bathing beaches close to the resort hotels that dot the island. A 20-km (12-mile) bus ride south of Dubrovnik reaches the small resort town of **Cavtat**. Its comfortable old-world character, which attracts British visitors particularly, sits easily alongside modern hotels, bars and pavement restaurants.

Beyond Cavtat lies **Montenegro** and the stunning **Bay of Kotor**. Medieval **Kotor**, at the head of the bay at the foot of the 1,770-metre (5,800-ft) sheer wall face of Mount Lovcen, makes it seem like the world's end. An earthquake in 1979 affected Montenegro's coastal towns. Recent politics in neighbouring Albania have also helped to keep the tourists away. ❑

Albania

Europe's last unspoilt lands must lie among the wilderness of Albania, a country so long kept in the dark, and now so impoverished and lawless that tourists give it a wide berth. With the help of specialist tour operators, however, intrepid travellers can get to some of its sites, which helps to complete the story of the classical world as well as showing the social conditions of a traditional Mediterranean life. A visit to Albania may be the last chance to see the living history of the Balkans.

Lord Byron described the country as "a shore unknown, which all admire but many dread to view" and a glimpse of the rugged country from an aeroplane window does conjure up a fearsome prospect. In these highlands, which rise up like great storm clouds, one can feel the spirit of this land of mountain men with dark moustaches, white felt hats and ancient rifles slung across their shoulders.

But from the moment you arrive in Albania you are the object of intense but respectful interest. The Albanian people's hospitality is the remnant of one of the ancient laws, the *kanum*, part of an unwritten constitution derived from the ancient Illyrians, from whom Albanians claim their descent.

Not much larger than Slovenia, it has a population of around 3 million, which lives mainly on the central plain that stretches for 200 km (125 miles) along the Adriatic coast. In the 1990s, in the mess left after the fall of the last Stalinist dictator, Enver Hoxha, who had been in power since the end of World War II, many tried to board boats to sail the 100 km (60 miles) to southern Italy.

Tirana, the country's capital, is centred on Skanderberg Square, overlooked by the dull slab of the Tirana Hotel. Skanderberg is Albania's great national hero who brought independence between 1443 and 1468, which was than lost again 1912. His equestrian statue is at the end of the Martyrs of the Nation avenue which leads toi the Datji Hotel, where much of the city's unofficial business takes place. The city has historical and archaeological museums.

Albturist, the national tourist authority, organises tours to various places of interest. Most towns have museums and other attractions. Firmly on the tourist route is Darrës, the country's principal port, where there is a Roman amphitheatre.

The old ruling elite favoured Saranda, south of Darrës in the middle of Albania's "riviera", where they built exquisite wooden villas among the fruit groves beside fine sandy beaches. The nearby ruins of Buthrotum are thought to have been built by the Trojans. Girokastër, in the south, has been designated a "museum town". Its older houses have been preserved and architecturally it retains a marked Greek character, with steep streets leading to an old citadel.

Much of Albania's archaeology and ethnographic richness still has to be discovered by the west, and bird watchers, botanists, hikers and mountaineers, as well as simple sun seekers, all have treats in store as the country opens up. ❏

RIGHT: the Mosque of Etham Bey in Skanderberg Square, the centre of Tirana.

GREECE

*History, drama, politics, philosophy: the words as well
as their concepts have their roots here*

Modern Greece, which emerged in the 19th century from 500 years of Ottoman rule, lies in a rocky pile of peninsulas and islands at the bottom of the Balkans in the eastern Mediterranean, with a language and landscape redolent of its pre-eminent place in the history of the western world. There are several fertile plains, in Thessaly on the mainland and in the Peloponnese, the southern half of the country split from the mainland by the Corinth Canal. But, by and large, the country presents a rugged landscape that makes life hard: Greece is the poorest member of the Economic Community. To the north, the 132,000-sq km (51,000-sq mile) country borders the Balkan flashpoints of Albania, the former Yugoslavia province of Macedonia, Bulgaria and, for a few last miles, its former master, Turkey. Just over Turkey's border is Istanbul, Constantinople, capital of Byzantium and centre of Eastern Orthodox Christianity, to which the Greek Orthodox church subscribes. That is where Asia begins.

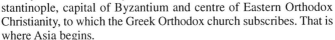

Around these rugged lands are the familiar names of the city states which vied for supremacy in the eastern Mediterranean more than 2,000 years ago: Corinth, Sparta, Mycenae, Thrace, Athens. And here are Delphi, the Parthenon and Mount Olympus, still haunted by the ancient gods.

It is easy to fall in love with Greece – its beauty is self-evident. Travellers return time after time, for the mirror-smooth Aegean Sea shimmering in the still of the morning, for the *kafenía* with their rickety tables offering some shade from the blistering afternoon heat, and for the silvery olive groves where the cicadas drone at evening time. It is a land for connoisseurs and explorers, with an ancient inheritance that remains relevant to this day. The Acropolis in Athens, the oracle sites at Delphi and the ruins of Olympia are places of unique importance in western culture.

Greece is not a hard place to find one's way around. The adventurous will take a boat from Athens' port of Piraeus and explore the delights of just a few of the hundreds of islands the gods tossed into the Aegean and Ionian seas. ❑

PRECEDING PAGES: the sun sets over the Temple of Poseidon; changing the guard at the Tomb of the Unknown Soldier in front of the parliament building in Athens.
LEFT: island cottage industry.

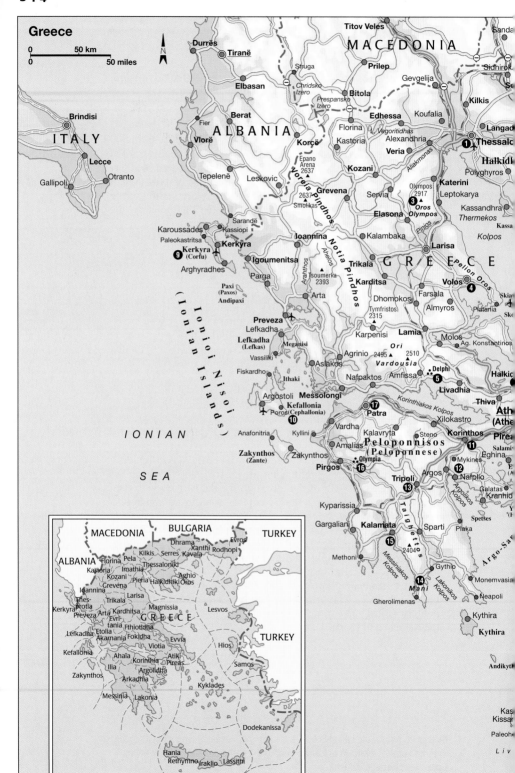

Greece

0 — 50 km
0 — 50 miles

ITALY

Brindisi
Lecce
Gallipoli
Otranto

Titov Veles
MACEDONIA
Durrës
Tiranë
Struga
Prilep
Sanda
Sidhirok
Se
Elbasan
Chridsko
Izero
Prespansko
Izero
Bitola
Gevgelija
Kilkis
Edhessa
Koufalia
Langad
Berat
Fier
Florina
L. Vegoritidhas
Alexandhria
Thessalo
ALBANIA
Korçë
Kastoria
Alexandhria
Halkidi
Vlorë
Veria
Aliakmonas
Polyghyros
Epano
Arena
2637
Kozani
Olympos
2917
Katerini
Tepelenë
Leskovic
Grevena
Servia
Oros
Leptokarya
2637
Smolikas
Kassandhra
Sarandë
Elasona
Olympos
Thermekos
Karoussades
Kassiopi
Ioannina
Kalambaka
Pinios
Larisa
Kassa
Kolpos
Paleokastritsa
Notia
Kerkyra
G R E E C E
9 **Kerkyra**
(Corfu)
Igoumenitsa
Trikala
Pelion Oros
Arghyradhes
Parga
Itsoumerka
2393
Karditsa
Volos
4
Skia
Paxi
(Paxos)
Andipaxi
Arta
Dhomokos
Farsala
Almyros
Platania
Sko
Ori
Tymfristos
2315
Lamia
Molos
Ag. Konstantinos
Preveza
Lefkadha
Karpenisi
Lefkadha
(Lefkas)
Meganisi
Agrinio
2495
2510
Vardousia
5 **Delphi**
Halkic
Vassiliki
Fiskardho
Ithaki
Nafpaktos
Amfissa
5
Livadhia
Argostoli
Messolongi
Korinthiakos Kolpos
Thiva
Kefallonia
(Cephallonia)
17 **Patra**
Xilokastro
Ath
Poros
10
Korinthos
(Athe
Anafonitria
Kyllini
Vardha
Kalavryta
Steno
11
Pirea
Amalias
Peloponnisos
(Peloponnese)
Salami
Eghina
Zakynthos
(Zante)
Zakynthos
Mykines
12
Nafplio
Galatas
16 Olympia
Pirgos
Kranhid
Tripoli
Argos
Argolikos
Kolpos
13
Kyparissia
Spetses
Gargaliani
Kalamata
Sparti
Plaka
Methoni
15
2404
Gythio
Monemvasia
Mani
Neapoli
14
Gherolimenas
Kythira
Kythira
Andikyth

Ionioi Nisoi
(Ionian Islands)

I O N I A N

S E A

Taighettos
Argo-Sar
Messiniakos
Kolpos
Lakonikos
Kolpos

MACEDONIA
BULGARIA
TURKEY
Dhrama
Xanthi
Rodhopi
ALBANIA
Kilkis
Serres
Kavala
Evros
Florina
Pela
Thessaloniki
Kastoria
Imathia
Kozani
Pieria
Aghio
Grevena
Halkidhiki
Oros
Ioannina
Larisa
Thes-
Trikala
protia
Kerkyra
Magnissia
Lesvos
Arta
Kardhitsa
Preveza
Evri-
tania
Fthiotidha
Lefkadha
Etolia
Akarnania
Foklidha
Evvia
Viotia
Hios
Atiki-
GREECE
Kefallonia
Ahaïa
Pireas
Korinthia
Samos
Ilia
Argollidha
Zakynthos
Arkadhia
TURKEY
Kyklades
Messinia
Lakonia
Dodekanissa

Kas
Kissar
Paleoh
L i v

Hania
Rethymno
Iraklio
Lassithi

ATHENS

The power and beauty of the ancient Greek empire breathes through this muddle of a modern city, overlooked on every street by the pinnacle of classical architecture: the Parthenon

Map on page 318

Athens

The English novelist John Fowles described Athens as a mass of dice scattered across the Attica plain. It certainly isn't the prettiest of European cities: look down from Mount Pendhéli and you'll appreciate the full extent of its architectural sprawl, with block after block of characterless, uniform cement buildings. Combine this visible chaos with the hooting traffic and *néfos* (heavy sulphurous smog) that chokes the centre and is bleaching and eating away at its monuments, and you might be tempted to head straight for a ferry to the islands.

But be patient with Athens: catch the Parthenon when the crowds are thinnest, link arms with the locals for a spot of Greek dancing, strike up conversation in an *ouzería* over all things political (a perennial Greek conversation piece), or barter over a pair of sandals in Pláka, and this muddle of a city will grow on you.

Acropolis

The **Acropolis** ❶ (or "upper city") rises some 60 metres (200 ft) above the city. Viewed from the streets beneath, it has a presence that makes all else in Athens fade into insignificance; your reward for the climb to the top is a strip of blue sea edged with grey hills marking the horizon. Best time to visit is early morning in summer or early afternoon in winter.

Star attraction of the Acropolis is the **Parthenon** (Virgin's Chamber), the crowning glory of Pericles' giant public works programme in the 440s BC (open summer: Mon–Fri 8am–6.30pm; Sat–Sun 8.30am–2.30pm; winter: Mon–Fri 8am–4.30pm; Sat–Sun 8.30am–2.30pm; entrance charge, but free on Sunday). Opponents said the statesman was dressing up the city as a harlot, but when you catch a glimpse of the temple's faintly golden marble columns you will not begrudge him his extravagance. Note how the columns incline slightly inwards and not a single structural line is straight, testament to the mathematical genius of its architect Phidias.

Conservation work has made the Parthenon the most beautiful it has been in modern times. Hundreds of blocks of its masonry have been removed to replace the rusting iron clamps inserted in the 1920s with non-corrosive titanium, and restorers have collected about 1,600 chunks of its marble scattered over the hilltop.

Further up the Acropolis, the Erechtheion is an elegant temple completed in 396 BC, a generation after the Parthenon. The Caryatids (nymphs) now supporting the columns are copies, but the originals are well worth a visit in the Acropolis Museum.

Roped off on what was at one time the citadel's southern bastion is the small, square temple of Athena Nike, completed in 421 BC. According to legend, it

LEFT: the Acropolis.
BELOW: many Athenians bring their chairs outside to sit sociably on the pavement.

The Erechtheion is said to be the site where Poseidon left his trident marks, and where Athena's olive tree sprouted.

stands on the spot where Theseus's father, King Aegeus, threw himself to his death on seeing a black-sailed ship approaching. Theseus had promised to hoist a white sail on his return if he succeeded in killing the Minotaur in Crete, but carelessly forgot.

The sculptures that Lord Elgin (British ambassador to Greece at the end of the 18th century) did not sell to the British Museum can be viewed in the **Acropolis Museum ❷** (open Mon 11am–6.45pm; Tues–Fri 8am–6.45pm; Sat–Sun 8.30am–2.30am; entrance charge, but free on Sunday). For an idea of the ancients' image of beauty, take a close look at the *kórai*: you can still make out the traces of make-up and earrings, and the patterns of their crinkled, close-fitting dresses.

In the shadow of the Acropolis

On the south approach to the Acropolis lies the **Theatre of Dionysus ❸** (entrances on Leofóros Dionissíou Areopagítou and above the Herod Atticus theatre; open daily; entrance charge). The marble seating tiers date from around 320 BC and later, but scholars agree this is where the plays of Aeschylus, Sophocles, Euripides and Aristophanes were staged at the Festival of Dionysia during the 5th century BC. They were major annual events, enjoyed by some 15,000 citizens who were given the day off to attend.

Farther along Dionissíou Areopagítou, the **Theatre of Herod Atticus ❹** was built in the 2nd century and dedicated to the memory of his wife. Here, from the ranks of its steep, concentric, semicircular rows of seats, you can gain a modern-day taste of the atmosphere and occasion of the ancient Greek plays, which are re-enacted annually during the Athens Festival of Music and Drama.

On the other side of the Acropolis, extending southeastwards, is the ancient

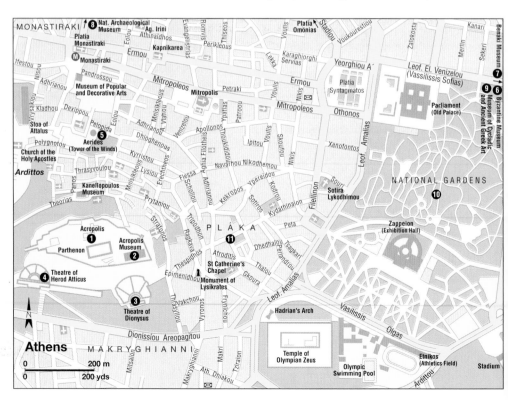

Agora, marketplace and centre of Periclean public life. Its focal point is the **Stoa of Attalus**, an impressive two-aisled colonnade nearly 122 metres (400 ft) long. To its east stands the **Tower of the Winds** (Aerides) ❺, one of the few monuments that survive from a building programme undertaken in the 2nd century by the philhellene Roman Emperor Hadrian. Looming over the remains of the Roman Agora, it served in its day as a public clock and weathervane.

Modern Athens

Athens' heart lies within an almost equilateral triangle defined by Omonia Square (Platía Omónias) in the north, Monastiráki in the south and Syntagma Square (Platía Syntagmatos) to the southeast. No cars are permitted in this area (except for down three small streets), which means it has taken on a new lease of life. Ermóu, once a traffic-clogged mess, is now a long pedestrian walkway with reinvigorated shops, enlivened by buskers and pushcarts.

Syntagma is bounded on all sides by big-name hotels, travel agencies, international airlines, banks, restaurants and cafés buzzing with small talk. It bears a smart western look, with Gucci, St Laurent and Chanel vying for custom. A beer can cost double what you'd pay in Pláka, but it's worth it to watch the Athenians at work and at play.

Less than a mile away is Athens' Northern pole, Omonia Square, filled with hawkers peddling anything from wristwatches to rice pudding. Here you can savour a Greek coffee in some of the largest *kafeneía* (coffee houses) in the country – this is a very male preserve, however, and women enter bravely.

Running parallel between these two squares are the main shopping streets of Stadiou and Odós El Venízelou (Panepistímiou), with department stores, neat

Map on page 318

TIP

Due to staff shortages, opening hours for sites and museums in Athens are liable to change without notice. To be sure of getting in, visit between 9am and noon.

BELOW: relaxing after a tour of the antiquities.

*Stylised sculpture
from the Museum of
Cycladic Art.*

BELOW: Athens'
flea market.
RIGHT: in the
Turkish district.

shopping arcades and cinemas. Kolonáki Square is where the Athenian jetset heads for clothes and shoes.

Everything is sold in Monastiráki, from kitsch through gawdy, mass-produced tourist trinkets to traditional leatherware and copperwork. Head into the narrower streets of the Flea Market off Monastiráki and you step back into an almost pre-industrial era. Bargaining is expected and relished.

Museum notes

Athens is well endowed with museums. The **Byzantine Museum** ❻ houses a brilliant array of icons and church relics from the 13th to the 18th centuries; the **Benáki Museum** ❼ an eclectic collection of Greek treasures from all periods, including jewellery, costumes and two icons attributed to El Greco (both open Tues–Sun; entrance charge).

The **National Archaeological Museum** ❽ is a fantastic storehouse of Greek art (open daily; closed Mon am & Sat/Sun pm; entrance charge, but free on Sunday and public holidays). Here you will see many of the most famous antiquities: Agamemnon's mask, found by Schliemann at Mycenae; the lifelike equestrian bronze of Emperor Augustus; the bronze of Poseidon poised to throw his trident; plus many well-preserved and colourful frescoes. Visit early morning for a quiet, private view of these wonders.

The highlight of the **Museum of Cycladic and Ancient Greek Art** ❾, also known as the Goulandrís Museum (open Mon & Wed–Sat, entrance charge, but free on Sat) is a unique collection of 230 slim, stylised Cycladic idols in white marble. These figurines, dating to 3200–2000BC, fascinated such artists as Picasso, Modigliani and Henry Moore. Many bowls and vessels are also on display.

Head for the hills

A saving grace of Athens is that there are easy – and visible – ways out of the sprawl, noise and grime. Take the funicular railway up **Mount Lykavittós** for spectacular views (every 20 minutes in summer, 8am–10pm, from Ploutárhou Street, near Platía Kolonáki) and upmarket eateries and cafés. The **National Gardens** ⓾, a jungly haven for birds, cats and deer, are a stone's throw from the Byzantine and Benáki Museums (*see above*). To the whirr of cicadas lovers meet, old men meditate, businessmen wolf sandwiches and hitchhikers sleep.

Not particularly green, but certainly an oasis is **Pláka** ⓫, the old quarter clustered at the foot of the Acropolis. Gone are the garish nightclubs and discos; with houses repainted and streets tidied up, this city "village" is pleasant for a wander.

For true greenery and fresh air, **Mount Hymettus**, 5 km (3 miles) east and much loved by bees, offers tranquil views over the city. **Mount Párnitha**, just over an hour northwest, is a dark wilderness of fir trees. About 5 miles (8 km) out of town, **Daphne Monastery** is a curious mix of Gothic and Byzantine. As well as being a peaceful, windswept spot spared of coachloads of tourists, its interior is decorated with magnificent, highly colourful 11th-century mosaics.

But if you make no other excursion from Athens, it must be to **Cape Sounion** (buses run half hourly from the bus station). Teetering on top of a hill bashed by the sea is the **Temple of Poseidon** (open Tues–Sun), probably the most evocative ancient temple and, with 16 out of 34 columns remaining, one of the best preserved. Look out for a touch of poetical licence on the nearest column to the entrance: Lord Byron scratched his name here in 1810. On a clear day you can see Cyclades islands to the southeast and the Peloponnese to the east. Bathed in the glow of sunset, you can appreciate why Byron loved Greece so dearly. ❑

Map on page 318

TIP

If you stay at the Hotel Aegon or at one of the campsites on the beach, you can enjoy the Temple of Poseidon in Byronic solitude. You'll need to book ahead, though.

BELOW:
Mount Lykavittós seen from the Academy, University and National Library complex.

AROUND GREECE

*Greece's ancient monuments bear testimony to
the vast empire that, at its height, stretched from Italy to
India. The islands also offer paradise – and beaches galore*

The largest town in the north of the Greek mainland, and the second largest in the country, is **Thessaloníki ❶**. Founded in 316–315 BC by the Macedonian king Kassander, the town rose to prominence under the Romans, boosted by its position on the Via Egnatia between Rome and Byzantium. A dozen Byzantine churches survive here, the earliest examples being clear adaptations of colonnaded Roman basilica, which were in turn descended from Greek temples. The town's **Byzantine Museum** (open daily; entrance fee) has a collection of Byzantine secular and sacred art – top-notch icons, pottery, jewellery, coins – housed in the Lefkós Pýrgos (White Tower) by the waterfront. Macedonian, Hellenistic and Roman finds from the region are displayed in the **Archaeological Museum** (open daily; entrance charge), including the magnificent treasures of the royal tombs of the Macedonian king, Philip II.

On the furthest east of the three fingers of land that stretch down from Thessaloníki into the Aegean Sea is **Mt Áthos ❷**, one of the country's stunning monastery sites founded by St Athanesios in AD 963. There are 20 surviving monasteries, the most spectacular being **Símonos Pétra**, built into a sheer cliff with vertiginous drops on three sides. Females are still completely banned from the site, and the Byzantine process of obtaining an entry permit is designed to deter all but the most determined male pilgrims.

To the south, where Macedonia stretches down into Thessaly, **Olympos** (Mount Olympus) **❸**, home of the ancient gods, rises to a snow-capped 2,917-metre (9,750-ft) summit, the highest point in the country. From here, Zeus would let fly with his thunderbolts, and in the wooded hills beneath lived the half-man, half-horse Centaur.

South to Delphi

Further south the busy modern port of **Vólos ❹** is one of the fastest growing industrial centres in the country – but there is a lovely promenade along the quay, and the harbour seems more like an island harbour than a big city port. Vólos has a long history, dating back to Neolithic times (about 4600–2600 BC); the **Archaeological Museum** (open Tues–Sun; entrance charge) is worth exploring.

On the southern slope of **Mount Parnassus**, terraces rise to the sanctuary of **Delphi ❺**, site of antiquity's most revered oracle. Nestled in a natural stone amphitheatre, it was for many centuries the holiest place of all for the Greeks, who believed that here, where Zeus's two eagles had come together, the divine and the earthly touched at the "navel of the earth".

The first site you will notice is the **Castalian Spring** (open daily; free). Across the road is the **gymnasium** area, with a long straight track and a round

LEFT: Meteora's mountaintop monastery.
BELOW: Greek Orthodox priest.

bath. The main site is the **Sanctuary of Apollo** (open daily; entrance charge). Most of the ruins are Roman, but inside the sanctuary there are earlier monuments. The zigzag ascent known as the **Sacred Way** meanders among temples, statue bases, *stoas* and treasuries bearing the *ex-votos* (offerings made in pursuance of a vow) of the devoutly grateful Athenians, Arcadians and many more. The Doric **Treasury of Athens** is the only one intact, having been rebuilt in 1904 with much of the marble of the original structure of 490 BC.

The **Temple of Apollo** seen today was the sixth built on the site, in the 4th century BC. The god Apollo, son of Zeus and Leto, was associated with the finer things in life: music, art, philosophy, law, medicine, archery – and prophecy was his main function here.

The small **theatre** above the Temple of Apollo seats 5,000 people, has marvellous acoustics and a wonderful view over the sanctuary. The **stadium**, 200 metres (650 ft) long, stretches above the theatre in a state of fine preservation. In its heyday it hosted the Pythian Games in honour of Apollo, and its 12 tiers of seats accommodated 7,000 spectators.

Évvoia (Euboea)

Scattered across the three Greek seas – the Aegean, Mediterranean and Ionian – are more than 1,400 islands, all chips off the mainland mountain block. As these are such an integral part of Greece, nobody should leave without visiting at least one. **Évvoia**, Greece's second-largest island (after Crete) is just off the coast of mainland Greece, looking like a large jigsaw puzzle piece just slightly out of position. The island's main town, **Halkídha** ❻, is now an industrial town, but the **kástro** with its mosque and church of **Aghía Paraskeví** are worth

BELOW: Delphi's Temple of Apollo.

visiting, as is the Archaeological Museum in the new town. **Erétria** to the south is a crowded summer resort town where the ferries land from Skála Oropoú on the mainland. In general, the southern part of the island is drier and less green. The east coast is mountainous, with rocky shoulders dropping down to the sea.

Map on pages 314–5

Sporades and Saronic Gulf islands

On the Aegean side of the mainland are the Sporades, reached from Volos. Most popular is **Skiáthos** ❼, which combines greenery with good beaches. The island has beaches for all occasions, not least because some among the supposed 60 will always be sheltered whatever the direction of the wind. **Koukounariés** is the most photographed, a scythe of golden sand with clear ink-blue sea. Nightlife is lively on this island, and the lights are brightest and tackiest at **Papadhiamántis**. But hire a moped or car and you can head for the roads looping up the mountains, to tranquil monasteries and stunning views.

Southwest of Athens, there is a handful of islands in the Saronic Gulf. The closest is **Eghina** (Aegina) ❽, about a half-hour ferry ride from Pireas. By far the most interesting ruins to be found here are those of the Doric temple of the goddess of Aphaía, couched in a tranquil mountain setting surrounded by pine woods. If it looks familiar, it should, as it served as a model for the Parthenon. It is one of the best-preserved island temples. **Ydhra** (Hydra), about three hours out of Pireas, is barren (except for the colourful harbour). The island has no ultra-modern tourist complexes, nor even a road, so it is ideal for barefoot bohemians. The touristy dock area is to be avoided. A mule ride to the monasteries serenely situated 300 metres (980 ft) in the mountains provides fine views of the bustling half-moon harbour.

BELOW: Arcadian beehives.

Ionian islands

The islands off the west coast of Greece in the Ionian Sea are wet and green, and unlike the typical parched rocky outcrops in the Aegean. The largest and best known is **Kérkyra (Corfu) ❾**, which lies just off the mainland and is around 10 hours from Athens by public transport. Its inhabitants have been welcoming visitors since Odysseus was received so warmly by Princess Nafsicaa.

Although the island is a popular tourist spot, often overcrowded at Róda, Astrakeri and Sidáro and the old harbour at Kassiópi, it is big enough to keep some spots hidden. Further down the west coast, **Paleokastrítsa** is a busy resort, comprising a series of beautiful bays embraced by ancient jagged rocks and a backdrop of dramatic greenness. Corfu is an idyll that inspired both Lawrence Durrell, the English poet and novelist, and his brother Gerald, the naturalist.

Kefalloniá ❿ is the most mountainous of the Ionian islands. **Mount Énos**, at 1,628 metres (5,340 ft), is the highest mountain on these islands, and covered in Cephalonian fir trees. The west coast below Argostóli has some wonderful beaches beginning at **Lássi** and continuing all the way down the coast. The beautiful beach of **Myrtosá** is on the east side of the Gulf of Myrtos but the island's most famous resort is the small port of **Fiskárdho**. There are some beautiful small beaches all around this northern part of the island.

Zákynthos is another island of green mountains and plains, stunning beaches and both good and bad tourist developments. The long white sands of **Laganás Bay** have an agglomeration of hotels, restaurants and discos, while the development at Laganás itself is relatively new. The beaches on this island defy superlatives. The southern peninsula below Zákynthos Town past **Argási** has some wonderful stretches along the east coast, culminating at **Yeráki**.

Fragrant citrus fruit, introduced by American advisers after World War II, is widely grown in Greece.

BELOW: gypsy girl.

The Peloponnese

Driving over from Attica (Attikí), it is easy to miss the little isthmus – riven by the Corinth Canal – joining the Peloponnese (Pelóponnisos) to the mainland. Ancient **Corinth**, 4 km (2½ miles) southwest of modern **Kórinthos** ⑪, could not help but prosper through the domination of trans-Isthmian haulage in pre-canal days. The Hellenistic city was razed in 146 BC by the Romans but refounded a century later as capital of Greece. What remains is the most complete imperial Roman town plan in Greece (site open daily; entrance charge).

The wide tollway to Trípoli forges southwest from modern Kórinthos. The old highway enters the Argolid plain at modern **Mykínes**, a village devoted to citrus and tourism; adjacent stands the ancient fortified palace complex of **Mycenae** (open daily; entrance charge). German scholar Heinrich Schliemann excavated here between 1874 and 1876, relying on little other than intuition and the literal accuracy of Homer's epics. Greek archaeologists had already revealed the imposing **Lion Gate** of the citadel, but the rich tomb finds Schliemann made, now in the National Archaeological Museum of Athens *(see page 320)*, amply corroborated Mycenae's Homeric epithet "rich in gold".

The road across the Argolid plain divides at Árgos. Just south of the modern town sprawl the ruins of **ancient Argos**, one of the oldest Greek settlements; most notable is the huge, steeply raked **theatre** (open all hours; free). From here, walk up to the Frankish castle atop Lárissa hill, site of the ancient acropolis, for far-reaching views. The upmarket resort of **Náfplio** ⑫ is overawed by **Akronafpliá**, four separate fortresses of various ages just overhead, plus the sprawling, early 18th-century **Palamídhi**, enclosing seven self-contained bastions. Just under 900 steps lead up from the Old Town to the summit

Map on pages 314–5

BELOW: shepherd and his flock in the Máni – a peaceful scene that belies the area's belligerent history.

Trípoli ⓭, capital of Arkadhía province, has little of interest for tourists. Further south lies the ancient Spartan heartland of Lakonía, and the **Máni** ⓮, an arid, isolated region and the last part of Greece to espouse Christianity. In medieval times, poor farmland and a fast-growing population spurred banditry and vendettas between clans.

Kalamáta ⓯ has only just recovered from a devastating earthquake which left half the population homeless; despite subsequent emigration, it is still the largest town hereabouts, with an attractive seafront, some lively, untouristy tavernas and its famous shiny black olives to recommend it. A pleasant coastal drive northwards leads to the ancient site of **Olympia** ⓰. The sanctuary here was in use for two millennia as a religious and athletic centre; of all the Hellenic competitions associated with shrines, the Olympic Games were the most prestigious. The most salient monuments are the **Palaestra** training centre, the **workshop of Phidias**, the archaic **Hera temple**, the enormous **Zeus temple**, and the **stadium**, with its 192-metre (630-ft) running course and vaulted entrance (open daily; entrance charge). On the north coast is **Patra** ⓱, Greece's third-largest city and principal port for ferries to Italy and select Ionian islands, although it has little to offer as a holiday retreat itself.

The Cyclades

Further out in the Aegean Sea are the **Cyclades**, the quintessential Greek islands where island hopping tourism is at its spontaneous best. Inter-island boats and flights are frequent and reasonably priced. There are 24 inhabited Cyclades, each singing a different Siren song. **Mykonos** ⓲, still dazzling after half a century of concentrated tourism, basks among whitewashed windmills and little

BELOW: the bay at Paleokastrítsa, Corfu.

churches. Here the chic crowd still set about the serious business of beach and bar life. Despite the thousands who pour off the ferry on to **Páros** ⑲ every summer, its inhabitants manage to keep the island surprisingly Greek. The gleaming white buildings, overflowing with pot plants, narrow alleys and small tavernas give this place a village feel; and Páros is so fertile that vineyards, olive plantations and citrus groves abound. As well as the beaches, the capital **Parikía** has the beautiful Byzantine Ekatontapyliani Church and to the west is the Valley of the Butterflies, aflutter with black and yellow moths in summer.

Náxos ⑳ is the Cyclades' most magnificent island, due to its mountainous terrain interspersed with fertile orchards and vineyards – and it's the cheapest. **Hóra**, its capital, is a labyrinthine chaos of Venetian homes and castle walls, post-Byzantine churches, Cycladic to medieval ruins and garden restaurants. But it is only in the past 10 years that Náxos has become known for its beaches. During the first week in August the Dionysia festival features folk dancing, food and retsina aplenty.

Probably the best known of the Cyclades is **Thira** (Santoríni) ㉑. With its sheer cliffs looming, reddish-brown and bare of plants, around a crater, this island has a sinister air borne of its turbulent geographical history. Ever since its volcano erupted in the second century BC, sinking its centre into the sea, Santoríni has been steeped in myth: it was linked with the legends of Atlantis (the city lost to the sea) by the ancient Greeks, and even recently was credited with being haunted by vampires. But though the island has some of the most remarkable excavations at **Akrotíri**, displaying a skeletal vignette of life in the 5th century BC, it is to its beaches, chi-chi cafés and nightlife that visitors are drawn. Unfortunately, the island's charms are now more Shirley Valentine than Platonic.

Map on pages 314–5

TIP

Some of the best beaches on Naxos include Yeórhios (most popular), Aghía Ánna (partly nude), Mikrí Vígla (good taverna) and Kastráki (blissful solitude).

BELOW: colourful houses of Kálymnos, the island to the north of Kós.

*A four-legged
inhabitant of Crete,
soaking up the
sunshine.*

Knossós – centre of Europe's first civilisation

Kriti (Crete) ❷, the largest of Greece's islands, is claimed by many to be the most authentic. It certainly offers something for everyone. Its ancient ruins are the major magnet: the Minoan palace of **Knossos** (open daily; entrance charge) takes visitors back to a culture 3,500 years ago. Though purists bemoan its lack of authenticity, the brightly painted frescoes in the reconstructed royal palace, villa and city are a vivid revisit to the legend of Minos, the king who imprisoned the Minotaur, the human-bovine child of his wife Pasiphae, in a labyrinth.

To appreciate it fully, you should first pay a visit to the island's outstanding **Archaeological Museum** (open daily; entrance charge). Among the 1,300 rooms of the main palace were the sacred and the commercial: lustral baths for holy ceremonies, store rooms for agricultural produce, workshops for metallurgy and stone-cutting.

But this is just one of Crete's many faces. There are also Greek, Roman and Venetian remains for which many tourist authorities would give their eye teeth; dozens of monasteries; the 18-km (11-mile) **Gorge of Samariá**; glorious mountains to the south, honeycombed with caves; and hundreds of Byzantine churches, many housing rare frescoes with the distinctly Cretan elongated figures. Homer's "island of 100 towns" could also be called an island of 100 beaches, some simply a place to beach a boat, others vast tracts of unspoilt sand and azure sea.

The Dodecanese

In the far southeast of the Aegean off the coast of Turkey are the **Dodecanese**: though their name implies there should be 12, there are in fact 14. The largest,

Rodhos (Rhodes) **❷❸**, named after its abundance of rock roses, is swamped with tourists almost year round. But hire a car, jeep or powerful motorbike and head for the east coast and you can still explore deserted beaches, remote monasteries and castles perched above citrus groves.

Rhodes is a historical patchwork, the legacy of ancient Greeks, crusading knights, besieging Ottomans and colonial Italians. **Mandhráki** harbour, guarded today by twin bronze deer atop imposing columns, is said to be where the Colossus once stood. The island's stunningly preserved medieval walled town is justifiably much visited. A list of its star sites – from the Palace of the Grand Masters to the cathedral and pebble-stoned Street of the Knights – does it no justice. Just wandering the warren of narrow streets, through arches and side alleys amid brightly painted houses, is a cultural delight.

Map on pages 314–5

Kós

The second-largest Dodecanese island in population, **Kós ❷❹** is also third-largest in size, after Rhodes and **Karpathos**. An earthquake in 1933 devastated most of Kós Town, but gave Italian archaeologists a perfect excuse to excavate comprehensively the ancient city. Hence, much of the town centre is an archaeological park, with the ruins of the **Roman agora** (the eastern excavation) lapping up to the 18th-century **Loggia Mosque** and the millennial **Plane Tree of Hippocrates**. In the southern excavation stand an *odeion* and the **Casa Romana**, a restored Roman villa with more mosaics and murals (open Tues–Sun; entrance charge). The most scenic and sheltered beaches are in the far southwest of the island, and have names like "Banana" and "Magic"; at nearby **Ághios Stéfanos**, twin 16th-century basilicas are among several early Christian monuments. ❏

LEFT: the Palace of Knossós, Crete.
BELOW: drying an octopus.

THE ISLANDS IN BLOOM

The Greek islands are at their most bountiful in spring and early summer, when every hillside and valley is decorated with glorious colour

Greece in spring is a botanist's dream and a gardener's despair. Some 6,000 species of wild plant grow in Greece and the islands, and in the spring (March to May) visitors may enjoy a magnificent cornucopia of flowers and fragrances.

Hillsides resemble giant rock gardens, while brilliant patches of untended waste ground outdo northern Europe's carefully tended herbaceous borders with ease. Winter rains, followed by a bright, hot, frost-free spring, produce a season's flowers compressed into a few, spectacular weeks before the summer's heat and drought become too much. By late May or June the flowers are over, the seeds for next year's show are ripening, and greens are fading to brown to match the tourists on the beaches.

SUMMER SURVIVAL

Except in the cooler, higher mountains, most plants go into semi-dormancy to survive the arid summer. The first rains of autumn, which could be in early September, but may be late November, tempt a few autumn bulbs into flower but also initiate the germination of seeds – plants that will grow and build up strength during the winter in preparation for the following spring when their flowers will again colour in the waiting canvas of the hills and valleys.

The richness and diversity of the flora are due in part to the islands' location between three continents – Europe, Asia and Africa – partly to the Ice-Age survival in temperate Greece of pre-glacial species, and partly to the wonderful variety of habitats. Limestone, the foundation of much of Greece, is a favoured home for plants, providing the stability, minerals, water supply and protection they need.

▷ **THE HILLS ARE ALIVE**
Sunshine, colour and quantity mark the spring flowering of the islands, as here in the mountains of Crete in mid-April.

△ **A GOOD REED**
Not bamboo – but it has similar uses. The giant reed (*Arundo donax*) can even be made into pan-pipes.

▽ **CUP OF MANY COLOURS**
Ranunculus asiaticus is an unlikely buttercup, with poppy-sized flowers in shades of white, pink, orange, red – and occasionally yellow.

▽ **SCARLET MEMORIAL**
The startling reds of *Anemone coronaria* mark the arrival of spring and in myth represent the spilt blood of the dying Adonis.

▽ **HANDY BUSH**
The long flowering period of the native oleander makes it popular in gardens and as an ornamental roadside crash-barrier.

BEETLES, BEES AND BUTTERFLIES

The profusion of flowers and plants provides food for an equal profusion of insects. Butterflies are conspicuous from spring to autumn, including the lovely swallowtail (*above*) whose colourful caterpillars feed on the leaves of common fennel. Its larger, paler and more angular relative, the scarce swallowtail, despite its name, is even more abundant.

Look for clouded yellows and paler cleopatras, reddish-brown painted ladies and southern commas, white admirals, and a myriad of smaller blue butterflies.

Butterflies, bees and day-flying hawkmoths tend to go for flowers with nectar, while beetles and flies go for the pollen. Some bugs even use the heat accumulated in the solar cup of many flowers in order to warm up their sex lives.

The leaves of plants feed armies of insect herbivores, which themselves are eaten by more aggressive insects. Some of the omniverous Greek grasshoppers and crickets are as happy munching through a caterpillar, or even another grasshopper, as the grass it was sitting on.

◁ FIRE FENNEL
According to legend, fire was brought to earth by Prometheus hidden in the smouldering stem of a giant fennel (*Ferula communis*).

▽ NATURAL FOOD
Wild artichokes are painfully spiny to prepare for the pot, but their flavour is much prized by Greek country folk over the spineless cultivated variety, and their market price increases accordingly.

«Las Señoritas de Avignon».

SPAIN

A relaxed atmosphere, plenty of sun, and towns with a medieval flavour all help give Spain its attraction

Continental Spain covers about four-fifths of the Iberian peninsula, Europe's southwest corner lying on the sunny side of the Pyrenees. The other fifth belongs to Portugal and a few square miles at its extreme tip is Gibraltar which belongs, somewhat contentiously, to Great Britain. Spain is divided into 50 provinces, one of which is the Balearic Islands in the Mediterranean, while two cover the Canary Islands in the Atlantic. With an area of 505,000 sq km (195,000 sq miles), the country is Europe's second largest after France.

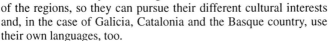

Spain is inhabited by a mix of peoples, from the industrious Barcelonans, whose history is mixed with that of their neighbours over the border in France, to the fiesta lovers of Seville and the south, who were moulded by the Moors during their 500-year occupation. Semi-autonomy has been granted to a number of the regions, so they can pursue their different cultural interests and, in the case of Galicia, Catalonia and the Basque country, use their own languages, too.

From the wet Atlantic coast in the north, which has often been compared to Scotland, to the ski slopes of the Sierra Nevada and the incomparable beaches of its popular *costas,* Spain is a country of great contrasts. It is the most mountainous country in Europe after Switzerland and much of its landscape is breathtakingly vast. It is a land of illusion: in the clear, bright air the windmills on the horizon seem close enough to touch, and nearly every journey is longer than it appears on the map. It has thousands of romantic castles and a number of splendid cities where old town quarters seem straight from the Middle Ages.

At the heart of the central plateau, or *meseta,* which covers 40 percent of the country, is Madrid. Deliberately established as the capital, it is as far from the country's celebrated seaside as you can get. On the other hand, rival Barcelona, Spain's second city, is the largest metropolis on the Mediterranean. Both these exciting cities are explored in the following chapters.   ❏

PRECEDING PAGES: windmills of La Mancha; young men show off their courage in a Pamplona bull ring.
LEFT: an early mural by Picasso.

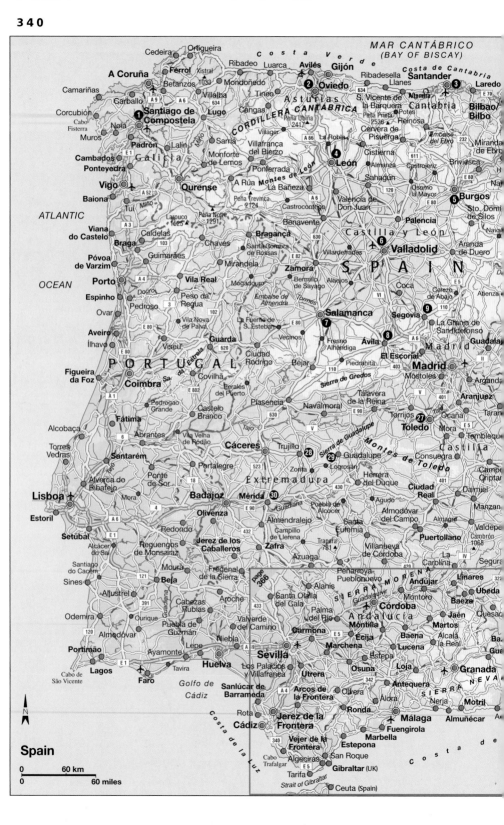

Spain

0   60 km
0   60 miles

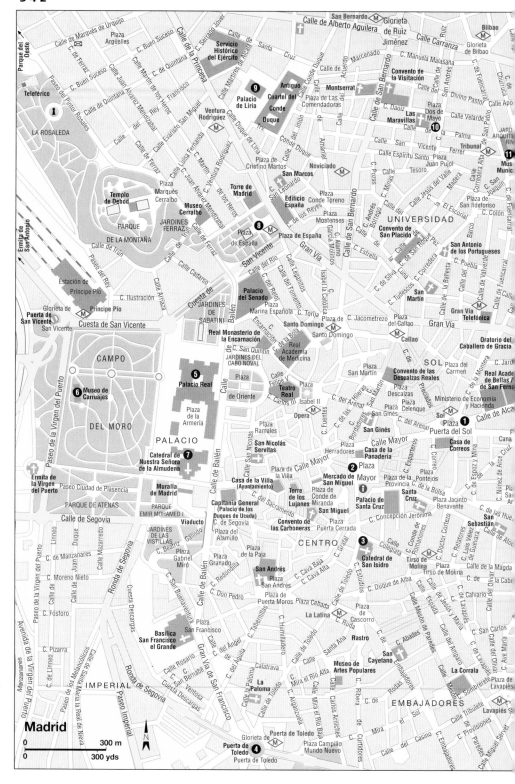

Madrid

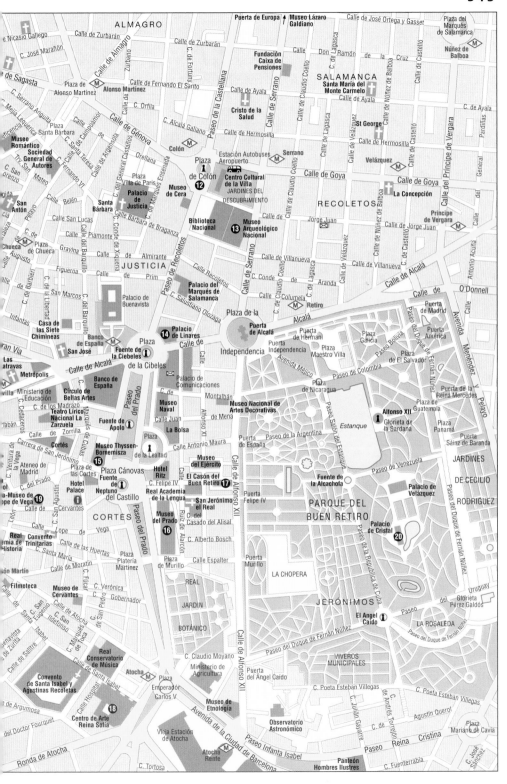

MADRID

*Europe's loftiest capital has some splendid monuments
from its regal past, and a lively population that
like to stay out late*

Map
on pages
342–3

Madrid

Madrid is the geographical centre of mainland Spain. It lies as far from the sea as one can get. At 655 metres (2,150 ft) above sea level, it is the highest capital in Europe, with a population of 3.2 million (over 4.5 million counting the hinterland). Situated on the central plateau surrounded by mountains, it has not only been climatically sheltered from maritime influences, but culturally and socially insulated as well.

In the 10th century the future capital of Spain was a Moorish fortress named Majerit which, a century later, was captured by Alfonso VI, king of Castile. In 1561, during Spain's Golden Age of empire, Philip II moved his residence here from nearby Toledo and proclaimed Madrid his new capital. Except for the brief period between 1601 and 1607 when Philip III moved to Valladolid, it has remained the capital ever since. In 1808, the French invaded Spain and installed Joseph Bonaparte, Napoleon's brother, on the Spanish throne. The city rose in rebellion. In his paintings *Dos de Mayo, 1808* and *Tres de Mayo, 1808*, in the Prado Museum, Goya chronicles the gruesome street battles and reprisals that cost more than 1,000 lives. The resulting Peninsular War, known in Spain as the War of Independence, brought British troops under the command of the Duke of Wellington to Spain's side and the conflict dragged on until 1814, when the French were finally defeated.

LEFT: Madrid's
Royal Palace.
BELOW: Cervantes
memorial.

The city was again besieged in November 1936, three months after General Franco's Nationalist uprising against the Republican government. The central post office sustained 155 direct hits from Nationalist artillery fire but the city did not succumb until 28 March 1939. Franco remained in power until his death in 1974, when King Juan Carlos was returned to the Spanish throne.

Echoes of empire

Most of Madrid's sightseeing attractions are intimately linked with its history as a royal residence and centre of a vanished empire. The oldest part of the city is the area between the Palacio Real (Royal Palace, also known as the Palacio de Oriente) and the Paseo del Prado. It embraces the Plaza Mayor, the Puerta del Sol and the Morería (the old Arab quarter). By and large, this area is still as it was at the beginning of the 17th century. On a map it is readily distinguished by its chaotic arrangement of narrow streets.

The heart of this area is **Plaza Puerta del Sol ❶** (Gate of the Sun), the site of a city gate which disappeared in the 16th century. Today it is Madrid's Times Square, where metropolitan subway and bus lines, as well as national highways, converge. Madrid revellers gather there to tick off the final seconds of the old year and usher in the new with the tradition of *las*

BELOW: at the
Rastro flea market.

uvas, the grapes. The idea is to swallow one with each stroke of the midnight clock – a tough task after having imbibed a little of the juice of the *uva.*

In its younger days the **Plaza Mayor ❷**, a square just to the west surrounded by 17th-century town houses, saw tournaments and bullfights, political gatherings, book burnings, and an occasional hanging or *auto da fé.* With the passing of time it has become the scene of such pastimes as coin and stamp fairs on a Sunday morning, theatrical productions in summer, and an odd bazaar or fiesta hoopla. Once the epicentre of *madrileño* life, the Plaza Mayor has come to be an important focal point for visitors. More than one tourist tryst has been faithfully kept at the statue of Philip III. In spring the square blossoms with outdoor cafés, and throughout the year it is often graced by itinerant artists and street musicians.

Southwest of the Plaza Mayor is an intricate maze of narrow streets whose names are frequently indicated on *azulejo* (decorated tile) plaques. This is the **Morería**, surviving soul of Moorish Madrid. Between the Plaza Mayor and the Royal Palace are many quaint, domesticated plazas, staircased streets and balconies bulging with flowers.

Castizo and the Rastro market

The gloomy 17th-century former cathedral of **San Isidro ❸** where bones of Madrid's patron saint lie, is beside Calle de Toledo on the edge of the **Castizo neighbourhood**, perhaps the most characteristic area of old Madrid, extending eastwards from Calle de Atocha. This is where the traditions of craftsmanship, architecture, food and fiestas have been preserved best. The most popular event in the neighbourhood is the **Rastro**, the animated Saturday and Sunday flea market. If you're hoping to find a bargain, arrive before 11am, and watch out for pickpockets. The former fish market at **Puerta de Toledo ❹** on the south side has been turned into an area of upmarket shops.

The **Palacio Real ❺** (Royal Palace, open daily; closed Sun pm; entrance charge) is off the pretty Plaza de Oriente, home of the **Teatro Real** (Royal Theatre). Built between 1738 and 1764 by Italian architects in an imitation French style, the Royal Palace is not much to look at from the outside, but inside it is overwhelming. Sumptuous and elegant, it is without doubt one of the most splendid palaces in Europe. Though it has more than 2,000 rooms, only a dozen or so are open to the public. The highlights are the apartments of Charles III, the Salas Gasparini, the throne room and the dining room. King Juan Carlos and Queen Sophia do not live here but they frequently use the palace for receptions and gala banquets. The inner courtyard has statues of the Roman emperors Trajan, Hadrian, Theodosius, and Honorius, all born in Spain. There is a good view of the palace from the Campo del Moro, the park behind it, though the **Museo de Carruajes ❻** (Carriage Museum) here has been closed. On the south side of the palace is the **Catedral de Nuestra Señora de la Almudena ❼**, consecrated by John Paul II in 1995, 110 years after it was begun.

The centre of the west end of Madrid, at the end of the Gran Via, is the **Plaza de España ❽** where larger-than-life statues of Don Quixote and his faithful servant Sancho Panza ride into the sunset. Just to the north of the Plaza is the **Palacio de Liria ❾** (address written requests for a visit to: Don Miguel, Calle de Princesa 20, 28008 Madrid), the magnificent 18th-century home of the Duchess of Alba, with an outstanding collection of furniture and paintings.

To the east, **Plaza Dos de Mayo ❿**, commemorating the date of fierce fighting here during the Napoleonic wars that was captured on canvas by Goya, is the centre of the city's counter-culture. The district, **Malasaña**, is the place to enjoy the city's nightlife; in the evenings its music bars and cafés come to life.

The **Museo Municipal ⓫** (open Tues–Sun, closed Sat and Sun pm and weekday pm in Aug; entrance charge) on nearby Calle de Fuencarral is in a former poorhouse which has an ornate late baroque facade. Among its attractions are Goya's *Allegory of the City of Madrid*, an exquisite 1830 model of the capital, and photographs going back to 1850.

A few blocks to the east is the **Plaza de Colón ⓬**, where there is a statue of Columbus on a neo-Gothic column. On the east side of the square is the **Centro Cultural de la Villa**, with theatre, concert hall and exhibition space. Alongside the plaza is a monolithic Hellenic structure enclosing the **Museo Arqueológico Nacional ⓭**. Among its exhibits are three outstanding displays: the *Dama de Baza*, a realistic goddess figure of the 4th century; the gold-crafted regalia of the Visigothic kings; and, in an underground gallery outside in the garden, a faithful reproduction of the cave paintings at Altamira (*see page 358*).

At the other end of the Paseo de Recoletos is the Plaza de la Cibeles and the **Palacio de Linares ⓮** (open Tues, Thur, Fri 9.30–11.30am, Sat, Sun 11.30am–1pm; entrance charge), a centre for Latin American studies. Guided tours reveal a fantastic 1870s interior and walls groaning with gold leaf, silk and marble.

Map on pages 342–3

The archway in the Plaza Dos de Mayo, in commemoration of those killed in the 1808 uprising against the French.

BELOW: two *madrileñas* peck outside the Café Gijon.

The Infanta Margarita in Velázquez's "Las Meninas".

Art treasures

From the Plaza de la Cibeles, Paseo del Prado leads to Madrid's great art treasures. First there is the **Museo Thyssen-Bornemisza ⓯** (open Tues–Sun 10am–7pm; entrance charge) in the **Palacio Villahermosa**. The collection, bought from Baron Thyssen-Bornemisza in the 1990s for £230 million (US$372 million) is notable for its 17th-century Dutch old masters, 19th-century North American paintings and 20th-century Russian and German Constructivist paintings.

The main art event of the city lies opposite. The **Museo del Prado ⓰** (open Tues–Sat 9am–7pm, Sun 9am–2pm; entrance charge) contains more than 6,000 paintings, including nearly all the collections of Spain's former royal families. If time allows for only one brief visit it should include Francisco de Goya (1746–1828). His work is represented in its full range and shines at its brilliant best on its home turf. No one who has seen the Prado's Goyas can fail to feel that he or she has been privy, however briefly, to the most intimate musings of the Spanish soul. A first visit should also include the works of Spain's other celebrated artists Diego Velázquez (1746–1828) and El Greco (1541–1614), although El Greco is seen to better advantage in his adopted home town of Toledo *(see page 364)*. Among the works of Velázquez not to be missed are *Las Meninas* (The Maids of Honour), *Las Handeras* (The Spinners), and *Los Borrachos* (The Drunkards). Entry to the Prado includes a visit to the museum's annexe, the **Casón del Buen Retiro ⓱**, which houses the collection's 19th-century work and once displayed Picasso's *Guernica,* an allegory of the bombing of a village in northern Spain by the Nationalists during the Civil War. In 1992 it was moved to a new showcase for modern art, the **Centro de Arte Reina Sofia ⓲** (open Wed–Sat 10am–9pm, Sun 10am–2.30pm; entrance charge) just

BELOW: in the Museo del Prado.

off the Paseo del Prado. Formerly the city hospital, the building has been dramatically renovated to house works by Spain's masters Dalí and Miró, as well as Picasso. It also has a lively programme of contemporary exhibitions.

La Casa-Museo de Lope de Vega ⑲ at 11 Calle de Cervantes, not far from the Prado, is the former home and now museum of the dramatist Lope de Vega (1562–1635). Miguel Cervantes, creator of Don Quixote, died in the house at No. 2 in 1616. He was born in 1547 in the nearby town of Alcalá de Henares, but later came to live in Madrid.

Parks and other escapes

For a peaceful respite from sightseeing, Madrid offers several pleasant parks, particularly **El Retiro**, the city's most popular park and a lively meeting place. Fountains, statues and the delicate **Palacio de Cristal ⑳** (open Tues–Sun; entrance charge) still give the Retiro the air of a royal garden. The royal summer retreat, the **Real Palacio de Aranjuez** (open Tues–Sun 10am–6pm; guided tours only; entrance charge), made famous by Rodriguez's Guitar Concerto, is 45 km (27 miles) south of the capital. Stuffed with portraits and porcelain, its attraction lies in its setting in 300 hectares (740 acres) of gardens.

El Escorial (open Tues–Sun 10am–5pm, closed public holidays; entrance fee) 50 km (30 miles) northwest of Madrid, is the monstrously grandiose fantasy of Philip II. Part palace, part monastery, part church and part pantheon, the king had it built in honour of San Lorenzo, on whose feast day (10 August) in 1557 the Spanish won an important victory over the French at St Quentin. In a country that has always built its cathedrals and monuments in an overwhelming way, El Escorial remains in a class of its own. ❏

Map on pages 342–3

TIP

For many, the most interesting part of El Escorial is its Library. With 50,000 volumes and manuscripts, it is said to rank second only to the Vatican's collection in quality, and contains the writings of Alfonso the Wise, St Augustine and Santa Teresa.

BELOW: the austere facade of El Escorial.

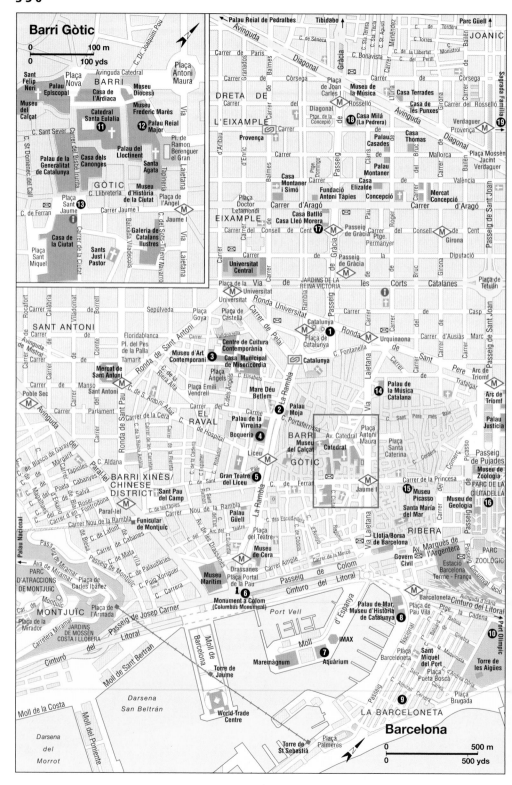

Barri Gòtic

0	100 m
0	100 yds

Sant Felip Neri
Plaça Nova
Avinguda Catedral
BARRI
Palau Episcopal
Casa de l'Ardiaca
Museu Diocesà
Museu del Calçat
Catedral Santa Eulalia **11**
Museu Frederic Marès
12 Palau Reial Major
C. Sant Sever
C. de St Domenec del Call
Palau del Lloctinent
Pl. de Ramon Berenguer el Gran
Palau de la Generalitat de Catalunya
Casa dels Canonges
Santa Agata
GÒTIC
C. Llibreteria
Museu d'Història de la Ciutat
Plaça de l'Àngel
Plaça Sant Jaume **13**
Carrer Jaume I
C. de Ferran
Casa de la Ciutat
Plaça Sant Miquel
Sants Just i Pastor
Galeria de Catalans Illustres
Baixada Viladecols
C. del Sots-Tinent Navarro

Plaça Antoni Maura
C. Dr. Joaquim Pou

Palau Reial de Pedralbes
Tibidabo
Parc Güell
JOANIC
Avinguda
C. de Sèneca
C. Sta Tecla
C. de Sant Agustí
C. de Tòrdera
Granados
Balmes
Diagonal
Gràcia
C. Bonavista
C. de la Llibertat
C. Monistrol
C. de Torres
C. del Perill
Bailèn
Carrer de Paris
Carrer
de
Còrsega
Plaça de Joan Carles I
Museu de la Música
Casa Terrades
Còrsega
DRETA DE
Carrer
del
Rosselló
Casa de les Punxes
Carrer del Rosselló
Sagrada Família
L'EIXAMPLE
Diagonal
Ptge. de la Concepció
18 Casa Milà (La Pedrera)
Avinguda
Girona
Verdaguer
19
Provença
Casa Thomas
Diagonal
d'Arbau
d'Enric
Provença
Palau Casades
Casa Montaner
Plaça Mossèn Jacint Verdaguer
Balmes
Carrer
Mallorca
Palau Montaner
Casa Montaner i Simó
Fundació Antoni Tàpies
Casa Elizalde
Concepció
València
EIXAMPLE
Plaça Doctor Letamendi
Carrer d'Aragó
Mercat Concepció
d'Aragó
Casa Batlló
Casa Lleó Morera
17
Carrer del Consell de Cent
Passeig de Gràcia
Consell
Girona
de Cent
Passeig de Sant Joan
Universitat Central
Girona
Permanyer
Diputació
Plaça de la Reina Victòria
Via
de
les
Corts
Catalanes
Plaça de Tetuàn
Plaça Universitat
M Universitat
Ronda
Universitat
Ronda
Casp
M Urquinaona
Carrer d'Ausiàs Marc
SANT ANTONI
Carrer
Sepúlveda
Plaça Goya
Plaça de Castella
Carrer de Pelai
Plaça de Catalunya **1**
M Catalunya
Arc de Triomf
M Arc de Triomf
Floridablanca
Pl. del Pes de la Palla
Valldonzella
Centre de Cultura Contemporània
Catalunya
Pere
Palau de la Música Catalana
Tamarit
Casa Municipal de Misericòrdia
C. Fontanella
Trafalgar
Mercat de Sant Antoni
Museu d'Art Contemporani **3**
Plaça Àngels
Plaça Emili Vendrell
Mare Déu Betlem
Carme
BARRI
Plaça Antoni Maura
Palau Justícia
M Poble Sec
Sant Antoni
Carrer del
Plaça
Palau Moja **2**
Catedral
Plaça Santa Caterina
Passeig de Pujades
EL RAVAL
de Hospital
Palau de la Virreina
GÒTIC
Museu de Zoologia
PARC DE LA CIUTADELLA
Boqueria **4**
Museu del Calçat
Jaume I
M
BARRI XINÈS/ CHINESE DISTRICT
Liceu **M**
Gran Teatre del Liceu **5**
Carrer de Ferran
Museu Picasso **15**
Museu de Geologia **16**
Sant Pau del Camp
M Paral·lel
Palau Güell
La Rambla
RIBERA
Santa Maria del Mar
Funicular de Montjuïc
Plaça del Teatre
Museu de Cera
M Drassanes
Carrer de la Mercè
Llotja/Borsa de Barcelona
Av. Marquès de l'Argentera
PARC ZOOLÒGIC
PARC D'ATRACCIONS DE MONTJUÏC
Palau Nacional
Museu Marítim **6**
Plaça Portal de la Pau
Govern Civil
Estació Barcelona Terme - França
Avinguda d'Icària
M
Barceloneta
Monument a Colom (Columbus Monument)
Passeig de Colom
Passeig
del
Litoral
Cinturo del Litoral
MONTJUÏC
Palau de Mar Museu d'Història de Catalunya **8**
Plaça de Pau Vila
Port Olímpic **10**
Plaça de la Mirador
IMAX
Port Vell
Aquàrium **7**
Sant Miquel del Port
Torre de les Aigües
Torre de Jaume I
Moll
Maremàgnum
Moll de Barcelona
Barceloneta
Plaça d'Andreu d'Ibèria
Darsena San Beltrán
World Trade Centre
9
LA BARCELONETA
Plaça Brugada
Darsena del Morrot
Moll de la Costa
Moll del Ponent
Torre de St Sebastià
Plaça Palmeres

Barcelona

0	500 m
0	500 yds

BARCELONA

*Almost half the population of Catalonia lives in Barcelona,
Spain's second city and one of the most vivacious
and stimulating places in Europe*

Map
on page
350

Barcelona

Madrid

The heart of Barcelona is **Plaça de Catalunya ❶**, an open space just beyond the inland medieval wall that was knocked down to build the Eixample (expansion) in the 1850s. Seven thoroughfares converge on the square, which hides a main station and a tourist information point. The square is the centre of political demonstrations, particularly on National Day, 11 September, and the latest statue is to Francesc Maciá, the brief president of the Catalan Republic of 1931.

The Rambla

The Plaça de Catalunya connects the elegant 19th-century Rambla de Catalunya with **La Rambla ❷**, Barcelona's most famous street, which heads 1,200 metres (¾ mile) down to the port. The Rambla is in five parts. The Rambla Canaletes is named after a drinking fountain where Barça football supporters meet. Next comes the Rambla dels Estudis, taking its name from the former university and known as the Rambla dels Ocells (rambla of the birds). Canaries, parakeets and other exotic birds are encaged in its stalls. Behind the Rambla dels Estudis in the working-class Raval district is the shockingly modern **Museu d'Art Contemporani ❸** (MAC, open daily; entrance charge) designed by the American architect Richard Meier. Its changing exhibitions of sculptures and installations seem secondary in attraction to the building itself.

BELOW:
Miró mosaic
in La Rambla.

From the Rambla dels Ocells the twitter of birds gives way to the kaleidoscope of flowers in the Rambla de Sant Josep or Rambla de les Flors, overlooked by the imposing Palau de la Virreina (1778). Built for the Viceroy of Peru, it is now the property of the city, which has installed a bookshop and gallery spaces.

Just beyond is **La Boqueria ❹**, or the Mercat de Sant Josep, a food emporium of iron and stained glass built in 1835 and containing all the best food Catalonia has to offer, from mushrooms and truffles to bright fruits, neat piles of vegetables and shimmering fish. Shop before 10am for the best bargains, and try the small bars, such as La Garduña, at the market's edge. Outside the market, coloured pavings by Joan Miró in the middle of the Rambla mark the Plaça Boqueria, a former place of execution just outside the city gates.

The **Gran Teatre del Liceu ❺** on the Rambla dels Caputxins is one of Europe's great opera houses, which has risen from the ashes of a devastating fire in 1994. Opposite is the Cafe de l'Opera, a delightful period café, said to have been a haunt of Casanova.

Beside the opera, Carrer Nou de la Rambla leads to **Palau Güell** (open Mon–Sat; entrance charge), gloomiest of Gaudí's buildings, bristling with dark metalwork. Ten years earlier, in 1878, Gaudí designed

Outside the Santa Eulàlia Cathedral in the Barri Gòtic.

BELOW: Port Vell and the Museu d'Historia de Catalunya.

the lampposts in **Plaça Reial**, opposite Carrer Nou. With classical, arcaded facades, cafés, restaurants, palm trees and a central fountain, this is one of the most exciting squares in the city.

The Rambla Santa Mònica is the last wide stretch of promenade before the sea. At weekends craft stalls give this traditionally low-life end of the Rambla an innocent air. The Rambla terminates in front of the 50-metre (160-ft) **Monument a Colom ❻** (Columbus Monument), built in 1888 by Gaietà Buigas and sitting on a traffic island. A lift takes visitors to the top for a grand view over the city and waterfront. Barcelona's seafaring activities can be appreciated with a visit to the **Museu Marítim** (open Tues–Sun; entrance charge), housed in the impressive 13th-century Reial Drassanes (Royal Shipyards) close by.

At the end of his first American voyage, Columbus came ashore on the steps in front of his statue, where the Golondrinas (pleasure boats) now give trips round the harbour and to the Olympic port. The port authority building lies beside the steps. The jetty over to the right is the Moll de Barcelona, site of the World Trade Centre and the terminal for cruise liners are located.

After this brief interruption, the Rambla continues as the Rambla del Mar, a walkway out over the harbour to shops and restaurants, IMEX cinema and the **Aquàrium ❼** (open daily; entrance charge), where visitors walk through glass tunnels to see creatures of the deep. The only remaining industrial building on the north side of the port is the warehouse designed by the modernist architect Elies Rogent and now turned into the Palau de Mar, where the **Museu d'Història de Catalunya ❽** (open Tues–Sat, Sun and hols am only; entrance charge) tells the story of the region. Behind it is the fishermen's quarter of **La Barceloneta ❾**, a night-time haunt of good small bars and fish restaurants.

Barceloneta is also the start of the city's 6-km (4-mile) beach, which leads past Nova Icària, the former Olympic Village, to the **Port Olìmpic ❿**, dominated by twin towers and lined with popular restaurants.

The Barri Gòtic and royal city

The Gothic Quarter is Barcelona's old city, begun by the Romans and still darkly medieval, with thick walled buildings, narrow lanes and heavy doorways. The **Cathedral of Santa Eulàlia ⓫** is built near the high point of Mons Taber, selected by the Romans for their settlement. To the right of the main entrance of the cathedral is the Romanesque Capella de Santa Llúcia, dating from 1268. Inside, to the left of the main entrance, a tablet commemorates the baptism here of the natives Columbus brought back with him from America. The cloisters are not to be missed. This shady quadrangle surrounds a garden of ferns, tropical plants, soaring majestic palms and a family of geese which has lorded it here for centuries.

Behind the cathedral and cloisters is a network of alleys and courtyards. Carrer Condes, on the left, leads to the **Museu Frederic Marès** (open Tues–Sat, Sun am; entrance charge), an eccentric museum in part of the former **Palau Reial Major ⓬** (open Tues–Sun; entrance charge), palace of the count-kings of Barcelona-Aragon. The palace faces on to the **Plaça del Rei**, the heart of royal Barcelona looked down on by the tall

Map
on page
350

rectangular watchtower of Martí I (the Humanist), last of the 500-year dynasty of Counts of Barcelona. On the outer side of this intimate square is the 15th-century Palau Clariana Padellàs, entrance to the **Museu d'Història de la Ciutat** (open Tues–Sat and Sun am; entrance charge). The main reason for visiting the city museum is to see the layout of extensive Roman streets and walls uncovered beneath the Plaça Real. Beyond the museum, a flight of steps leads to a reception hall and the 36-metre (120-ft) **Saló de Tinell**, built in 1370. Used as a throne room, and by the Inquisition, this impressive space is where Ferdinand and Isabella greeted Columbus on his return from America. To the right of the hall is the 14th-century royal **chapel of Santa Àgata**, which has a fine altarpiece, *Retrat del Conestable*, by Jaume Huguet (1414–92).

Between the Cathedral and Plaça del Rei is **Plaça Sant Jaume ⑬**, the city's political hub, with the **Palau de la Generalitat de Catalunya**, the seat of Catalonia's government, on one side and the **Casa de la Ciutat**, home of the city council, on the other. The Palau de la Generalitat opens up on St George's Day, 23 April, the patron saint of the city. Behind the Generalitat building was the medieval **Jewish quarter** or Call, which occupied the streets between Carrer del Call and Carrer Banys Nous. A Hebrew inscription on the wall of No. 1 Carrer Martlet dates from 692. The Jews were forced from the city in 1424.

La Ribera and the Picasso Museum

La Ribera lies on the far side of Via Laietana, the 19th-century thoroughfare. Towards the top on the right is **Palau de la Música Catalana ⑭**, a fine Modernist concert hall designed by Domènech i Montaner in 1908. It has a magnificent tiled facade and its interior is equally impressive. La Ribera is penetrated

There are an estimated 6 million Catalan speakers in Spain and, though Catalan is the first language in schools, the many immigrants to the region ensure that Spanish is still universally used.

BELOW:
the Palau de la Música Catalana.

by Carrer Princesa and its noblest street is Carrer Montcada. Palau Berenguer d'Aguilar, built in the 15th century by Marc Safont, is one of a string of elegant mansions that crowd this narrow lane, and it has become the home, with the adjoining Palau Castallet, of the **Museu Picasso** ⑮ (open daily; entrance charge). The museum has a collection of around 3,000 of Picasso's works, including some ceramics. Many are from his early years when he was a student in the city and they show what a competent and precocious draughtsman he was. Pride of place goes to *Las Meninas*, 58 paintings based on Velázquez's originals in the Prado in Madrid.

Carrer Montcada leads into Passeig de Born, and **Santa María del Mar**, the finest church in the city, built in one harmonious hit, between 1329 and 1384.

Beyond La Ribera lies the 34-hectare (85-acre) **Parc de la Ciutadella** ⑯. The Catalan Parliament sits here in the former arsenal, which is also occupied by the **Museu d'Art Modern** (open Tues–Sat, Sun am; entrance charge), a fine gallery of 19th- and 20th-century Catalan painters. The 30-hectare (75-acre) city **zoo** (open Tues–Sat, Sun am; entrance charge) covers the south side of the park, and beside it is a fountain with *Dama del Paraigues*, a captivating sculpture of a young woman beneath an umbrella, by Roig i Soler.

In 1926 the great Modernist architect, Antoni Gaudí i Cornet, was fatally run down by a tram. Taken for a tramp, he was put in the local hospital's "paupers' ward".

The Modernist city

Catalonia's distinctive art nouveau, called Modernism, flowered among Ildefons Cerdà's 19th-century Eixample. It was his grid plan, in which the corners of the squares were clipped off, that provided the platform for the city's newly enriched industrialists to show off. The best examples lie within the Quadrat d'Or, the golden square, centred on the fashionable **Passeig de Gràcia**, which leads up from the Plaça de Catalunya. **Casa Lleó Morera** ⑰ at No. 35 is by Domènech i Montaner (1850–1923), perhaps the purist of the Modernist practitioners, and from here you can obtain a ticket to visit the main Modernist sites.

No. 41 is **Casa Amatller**, a beautiful, eclectic building by Josep Puig i Cadafalch (1867–1967), beside the more excessive work of its neighbour, **Casa Batlló**, by Antoni Gaudí i Cornet (1852–1926), a glazed and undulating building typical of the movement's greatest exponent. The three buildings are known as the Mançana de Discòrdia, the "block of discord".

Further up the Passeig de Gràcia, on the right, is Gaudí's best-known civic work, **Casa Milà** ⑱, known as La Pedrera, (the Stone Quarry), an eight-storey apartment block devoid of straight lines and topped with sinister chimneys nicknamed *espanta-bruixes,* "witch scarers".

After he finished La Pedrera, Gaudí devoted himself exclusively to his most famous work, the **Sagrada Família** ⑲, reached along Carrer de Provença, which runs beside La Pedrera. He finished only the crypt and the Nativity facade with three doorways to Faith, Hope and Charity. Work continues to complete the ambitious project, which will eventually be 27 metres (87 ft) longer than Barcelona's old cathedral and twice the height. Gaudí spent his last 10 years living, unpaid, in a hut on the site, abandoning the house he

BELOW: the stunning Sagrada Família.

had lived in at **Park Güell**. This pleasure garden, originally designed as a housing project, is 15 minutes' walk from Lleseps metro station on the outskirts of the Collserola hills and has good views of the city.

Map
on page
350

Pedralbes

Count Eusebi Güell, Gaudí's industrialist patron, had a country estate at Pedralbes, and, in 1919, a year after his death, his manor house was turned into a palace for visiting royalty. **The Palau Reial de Pedralbes** (metro to Palau Reial) houses the **Museu Ceràmica** (open Tues-Sun; entrance charge), an excellent collection of pottery and kitchenware going back to the 8th century. On the inland side of the estate is the exquisite **Reial Monastir de Pedralbes** (open Tues-Sun; entrance charge), one of the jewels of the city (FCG to Reina Elisenda, then a 10-minute walk). This collection of buildings includes the monastery church where its founder, Queen Elisenda, wife of Jaume II, is buried. Inside, the Santa Maria convent looks much as the nuns left it. Their dormitory is now given over to the **Thyssen-Bornemisza Collection** of some 70 religious paintings, mostly from Italy.

TIP

For a day out from Barcelona, visit the Montserrat monastery 45 minutes inland. This spectacular setting is home of La Moreneta, the Black Virgin, Catalonia's most revered shrine.

Montjuïc and Tibidabo: hilltop playgrounds

Montjuïc, the 213-metre (700-ft) hill overlooking the port, has been the city's playground since it was laid out for the International Exhibition of 1929, and it would take several days to get round it all. The austere **Palau Nacional** houses the **Museu d'Art de Catalunya** (open Tues-Sun; entrance charge). This is an exemplary collection, particularly of Catalan Romanesque art from remote churches in the Pyrenees. Catalan Gothic art is also well represented. Modern art is to be found in the **Fundació Joan Miró** (open daily; entrance charge), in a stylish white building, built by the painter's friend, Josep Lluís Sert in 1975, eight years before the Catalan painter's death. The most ambitious project for the 1929 Exhibition was **Poble Espanyol**, a "village" comprising buildings that display the architectural differences of the various regions of Spain. This is a popular place to visit: its nightlife of bars and restaurants, and flamenco dancing in the Àvila towers, makes the place lively till dawn. On the top of the hill, above the 1992 Olympic complex, is the **Castell de Montjuïc**, which has a small military museum and spectacular views from its battlements over the port.

BELOW: funfair at Tibidabo.

From here you can also see the city's other hilltop playground, **Tibidabo**, among the Collserola hills at the back of the city (FCG to Avenido Tibidabo, then Tramvia Blau bus and cable car). It has an amusement park not unlike Montjuïc's, a museum devoted to mechanical toys and a church, the Sagrat Cor, to take you above the 500-metre (1,640-ft) summit where, on a rare clear day, you might be able to see the mountain of Montserrat, the snow-capped Pyrenees – and even Mallorca.

The last word in heights, however, must go to Norman Foster's nearby communications tower, the **Torre de Collserola**, a vertiginous needle with a glass viewing panel 115 metres (337 ft) above-ground. ❑

AROUND SPAIN

Most visitors head for Spain's famous beaches – but cities such as Segovia and Mérida have significant Roman remains and in the south is the Oriental legacy of the Moors

Map on pages 340–1

The northwest of the country, jutting out into the Atlantic beneath the Bay of Biscay, is "Green Spain", one of the wettest regions of Europe, where Atlantic winds are driven on to the mountainous coast and rainfall averages up to 250 cm (100 inches) a year. This area was least touched by the Moorish incursion and from its inhospitable mountains the reconquest of the peninsula, under the ancient dynasties of Asturias and Navarre, began. This was also one of the first "tourist" destinations in Spain, to **Santiago de Compostela ❶**, after the apparent discovery of the tomb of St James, patron of Spain, in AD 812. The present cathedral dates from 1075 and remains the goal of pilgrims who walk many miles to reach the saint's shrine. Consecrated in 1211, the handsome Romanesque building faces on to the Praza do Obradoro where the grand Hostal de los Reyes Católicos, begun in 1501 under the order of Ferdinand and Isabella as an inn and hospital for pilgrims, is now an elegant hotel.

Pilgrims from England sometimes reached Santiago by sailing to **A Coruña**, Galicia's principal city and port in the northwest corner of the country where white buildings with characteristic enclosed glass balconies (*miradores*) line the seafront. The city's showpiece is the Torre de Hércules, a lighthouse from Roman times. The coast west and south of Coruña towards the **Rias Baixas** is wild and fjord-like. At **Cabo Fisterra**, pilgrims once came to see what they thought was literally the end of the world. **Padrón** and **Pontevedra** are pleasant towns by the coast and the island of **A Toxa**, surrounded by mussel rafts, is at the heart of the holiday haunts, while **Vigo** maintains the largest fishing fleet in Europe. Galicia's earthy wildness is confirmed in the remains of Celtic settlements, *castros*, and in its wailing bagpipes. It is one of the poorest regions of Spain, and the grain stores, *hórreos*, attest to its grip on the past, while its white wines, such as Riberia and Albariño, produced around **Cambados**, are greatly sought after.

LEFT: the flamenco tradition.
BELOW: the Picos de Europa.

Asturias and the Costa Verde

The **Corderilla Cantabrica** is a high range of mountains that cuts Asturias and Cantabria off from inland Spain. The coastal drive along the Costa Verde winds over cliffs and through valleys, arriving at picturesque fishing ports such as **Luarca**. This is a land of cider, and the apple brew is poured from fizzy heights in the cider bars around the country. Inland, the capital, **Oviedo ❷**, is a treasure house of pre-Romanesque architecture, the finest in Spain. Part royal palace, part church, **Santa Maria del Naranco** dates from Ramiri I in the 9th century, and nearby San Miguel de Lillo and San Julián de los Prados should also not be missed. The first king of Asturias was Pelayo, who began the reconquest in 722 by defeating the Moors at **Covadonga** in what is now the **Parque Nacional de los Picos de Europa**, the most spectacular mountain region of Spain. Entry points are at **Potes** and **Cangas de Onis** and a cable car rises 800 metres (2,625ft) from **Fuente Dé**, giving heavenly views.

The Cantabrian coast has a variety of resorts. There are sandy beaches at **Laredo** and around **Santander ❸**, the principal city and port, which was ravaged by fire in 1941 but now sits serenely between the green hills and blue sea. **Santillana del Mar** is a picturesque medieval village; nearby at **Altamira** is the "Sistine chapel" of cave art, which dates from 13,000 BC. The bison, deer, boar and horses painted on the ceilings in ochres, manganese oxide, charcoal and iron carbonate are the largest known group of prehistoric polychrome figures in the world. Access to the cave is severely restricted but a **museum** (open daily; entrance charge) gives a flavour of the finds.

Cable car at Fuente Dé in the Picos de Europa.

BELOW:
the spectacular mountain region of Picos de Europa.

Castilla y Léon

When the reconquest of the peninsula began, the Christian Spaniards came down out of the hills of Asturias on to the inhospitable depopulated *meseta,* where winters are cold and summers baking hot. Here they built fortified castles, *castiles,* to push their frontier forward. The first two cities to be created in this new land of Castilla (Castile) were León and Burgos, both on the main route from the Pyrenees to Santiago de Compostela, and both given Gothic cathedrals. **León ❹**, formerly politically connected to Galicia, has a particularly fine cathedral with 1,800 sq metres (20,000 sq ft) of wonderful stained-glass windows, yet its construction is fragile and no one is sure quite how it still manages to stay up. Even more impressive is the **Basilica de San Isidoro** (open daily; free), which has delightful ceiling frescoes of the seasons, and the adjoining **Panteón Real**, where some 20 monarchs are entombed.

Burgos ❺ is the home of the great vanquisher of the Moors, Rodrigo Díaz de Vivar (1043–99), known as El Cid, whose tomb lies in the cathedral. But the great treasures of this town are to be found in the **Real Monasterio de las Huelgas** (open Tues–Sun; entrance charge), founded in 1187 by Alfonso VIII and surprisingly decorated with Moorish patterns, as are the clothes, still in fine repair, worn by the medieval monarchs and their families. Southeast of Burgos is the **Monasterio de Santo Diomingo de Silos** (open daily; free), famous for its cloisters and chart-topping community of chanting Benedictine monks.

The Christian reconquest spread across what until 1983 was called Old Castile, and while many Castilian villages are ancient, they still have an outpost feeling and cannot be described as quaint. **Valladolid ❻**, a rambling town with elaborate churches. The **Museu Nacional de Escultura** (open Tues–Sat and Sun am; entrance fee), is a crash course in Spanish Renaissance architecture. **Salamanca ❼**, on the other hand, is very much a part of cultural Spain. Its university was founded in 1218, though the Inquisition put paid to its reputation as a haven for new ideas and thinkers. The philosopher and novelist Miguel de Unanumo brought it brief glory before the Civil War, and it has again begun to take its place at the forefront of Spanish literary life. It has three universities, and its **Plaza Major**, designed by Churriguera, is magnificent both for architecture and for ambience. **Ávila ❽**, 113 km (70 miles) northwest of Madrid, has been compared by poets to both a coffer and a crown. The highest city on the peninsula, it is sealed within its perfectly preserved medieval walls 10 metres (33 ft) high, with 88 round towers and nine fortified entrances.

Closer to Madrid is **Segovia ❾**, whose charms are evident at first sight. It fills up with *madrileños* every weekend who come to admire the Roman **aqueduct** and fairytale **Alcázar**, and feast on the cuisine for which the province is famous. The Alcázar (open daily; entrance charge) is a child's dream of a castle. The most interesting rooms are the Sala de Reyes, containing wood carvings of early Castilian, Leonese and Asturian kings, and Sala del Cordón, decorated with a frieze of the Franciscan cord. The arduous climb up to the Torre de Juan II is rewarded by sweeping views of the Segovian countryside.

Rioja, the Basque Country and Aragón

To the east of Burgos lies **Rioja**, Spain's best-known wine country. Its reputation was made in the 19th century by the Marqués de Riscal and the Marqués de Murriertta, who returned from exile in Bordeaux to emulate methods they had encountered in France, using oak barrels to age the wines. Their wineries still operate, in **Elciego** and **Logroño ❿** respectively, and there are now 350 wine houses in the 500 sq-km (200 sq-mile) region. The main town, **Haro**, has the bacchanalian Batalla del Vino on 29 June, when everyone is drenched with wine.

Rioja is on the southern edge of the ancient kingdom of Navarre, now shared with France and the Pais Vasco, the Basque Country, where the language

Map on pages 340–1

BELOW: *encierro* during the Fiesta de San Fermín, Pamplona.

(Euskera) is impenentrable, the men strong as oxes and traditions live on in games and sports, such as *jai-allai*. Its capital is **Vitoria** ⓫ (Vitoria-Gasteiz), built on a high point. The *miradores* on the old houses around its main square, **Plaza de la Virgen Blanca**, are typical of the northern coast. The main port of the Basque country is **Bilbao** ⓬ (Bilbo), a grey city squeezed into the banks of the Nervión, which was pitched into dazzling fame when the **Museo Guggenheim de Arte Contemporáneo** (open Tues–Sun; entrance charge), a shining "metallic flower" designed by the Californian architect Frank O. Gehry, opened in 1997. Shockingly modern, it is set by the river and has changing exhibitions, though most people come to see the building itself.

Basque food is one of the wonders of Spain, and there are many places along the coast where the seafood is fresh and delicious. **San Sebastian** ⓭ (Donostia) is queen of the resorts, with great restaurants, a bar-hopping old quarter and dozens of private, all-male eating societies.

Pamplona ⓮ (Iruña), former capital of the kingdom of Navarre, was made famous beyond Spain by Ernest Hemingway, who came to see the running of the bulls which he wrote about in *The Sun Also Rises* (1926). The event still takes place each year with a wild, week-long festival starting on the eve of San Fermín (6 July) and culminating in the *encierro*, when bulls run through the streets to the ring. There are often serious accidents among the dare-devil participants.

The **Monasterio de Leyre**, southeast of Pamplona, was Navarre's 11th-century spiritual centre and pantheon for its kings. It is a beautiful Romanesque building with a fine vaulted crypt, consecrated in 1057. Recently restored by Benedictines, whose chants can be heard, it now includes a hotel. Further east, in the land-locked region of Aragón, is **San Juan de la Peña** (open Apr–Sept: Tues–Sun; Oct–Mar: Wed–Sun; entrance charge), wedged between enormous boulders under a sheer rock cliff. It was built for Sancho Ramirez (1063–94) and contains tombs of early Aragon kings. Just to the north is **Jaca** ⓯, the first capital of Aragon, which today has a lively music bar scene and dreams of hosting a Winter Olympics. Jaca is a good centre for exploring the lovely valleys in the central Pyrenees. The Aragón capitals crept south as the reconquest soldiered on: after Jaca came Huesca, then **Zaragoza** ⓰, a venerable town which was knocked about in the Napoleonic Wars. It has two cathedrals; **Nuestra Señora del Pilar** has 11 distinctive domes and a cupola painted by Goya, a native of Aragón. More impressive is the **Aljafería**, built in the 11th century by the ruling Moorish king.

BELOW:
church of Sant Andreu at Salardú in the Vall d'Aran.

Catalonia

Aragón was united with the neighbouring House of Barcelona in the 12th century, but the seafaring Catalans fiercely guarded their independence, their rights and their language. A further variance on their language is Aranese, spoken in the **Vall d'Aran**. Cut off every winter until 1948, when a tunnel was built through the mountains, this lovely valley around the town of **Vielha** ⓱ supports unique butterfly life and is a popular ski centre, notably at **Baqueira-Beret**, a haunt of Spain's royal family. Catalan is also the offi-

Map on pages 340–1

cial language of **Andorra** , the anomalous 468 sq-km (180 sq-mile) principality ruled jointly by the Counts of Foix (a title now devolved to the president of France) and the Bishop of La Seu d'Urgell. The upper reaches of the principality are pleasing and remote but the roads leading to Andorra la Vella can be hell during holidays, weekends and August. **La Seu d'Urgell**, on the other hand, is a sleepy old mountain town with 12th-century cathedral, 13th-century cloister and an excellent collection of Romanesque art in its episcopal museum.

Catalonia's Pyrenean valleys are notable for their stunning Romanesque churches with tall bell towers, such as Sant Climent de Taüll in the Boí Valley, just south of the **Parc Nacional de Aigüestortes**. A masterpiece of Romanesque carvings can be seen on the facade of the former monastery of Santa Maria in **Ripoll** ⓳, a sheep town with an excellent folk museum. Ripoll monastery was founded in 888 by Guifré el Pilós, first count of Barcelona, and the town has been called "the cradle of Catalonia". At the nearby monastery of **Sant Joan de les Abadesses**, where Guifre's daughter was abbess, there is an exquisite Romanesque calvary in the church.

The Costa Brava and Dalí

Brava means wild or rugged, and this coast, running some 90 km (60 miles) from the French border to **Blanes**, just short of Barcelona, twists and turns around coves and over cliffs in one of the most celebrated shores of the Mediterranean. This was where the Romans first arrived on the peninsula, to subjugate the people. They made a base at **Empúries** in the Bay of Roses, where the Greeks already had a trading settlement with the indigenous Iberians. The site includes the remains of the Greek harbour wall. On the north side of the bay is

Catalonia was Spain's most important centre for Romanesque painting, which shows the Byzantine influence. Its ritualistic figures are almost expressionless, even when they undergo horrifying martyrdoms.

BELOW: view over Aiguablava on the Costa Brava.

Girona cathedral, dominating the steep streets of the town.

Cap de Creu and Spain's easternmost mainland town, **Cadaqués** ㉛. This is the St Tropez of the coast, with galleries and boutiques in steep cobbled streets. The painter Salvador Dalí lived at **Port-Lligat**, just to the north, and **Casa-Museu Salvador Dalí** (open Easter–Oct: Tues–Sun; entrance charge), the two fishermen's houses he famously made his home, are now visitable. It is a strangely enchanting place. A Dalí route takes in the castle he bought inland at Puból, and the town of **Figueres**, where the **Teatre-Museu Dalí** (open Tues–Sun; entrance charge), his museum in the old town theatre, is one of the most popular in Spain.

There is an old-fashioned, family air to many of the resorts on the coast, particularly the more intimate coves and beaches such as **Aiguablava**, **Tamariu**, **Calella de Palafrugell** and even **Tossa de Mar**. The larger resorts of **Roses**, **Platja d'Aro**, **Palamós**, **Lloret de Mar** and **Blanes** have spread along sandy beaches and are brighter and brasher, catering for a younger, night-owl crowd.

The main town for the Costa Brava is **Girona** ㉑, some 20 km (12 miles) inland. It is attractively sited beside the River Onyar, where bridges lead to a Rambla and steep cobbled streets heading for a cathedral with the widest nave in Christendom. An archaeological walk follows the old town walls, which were breached in an heroic siege in the Napoleonic Wars. At the heart of the old town a former Jewish quarter has been opened up.

Tarragona and the Costa Daurada

BELOW: the Monestir de Poblet.

Sitges ㉒, 45 minutes on the train from Barcelona, is an eternally elegant resort, popular for Sunday lunch and also for gays, who dominate the outrageous pre-Lent carnival. The sandy beaches of the Costa Daurada continue past the wine

town of **Valafranca del Penedès** to **Tarragona ㉓**, the major provincial town of Roman Tarraconensis, where an amphitheatre, beneath the Balcó de Europa at the end of the Rambla, overlooks the sea. Its Roman walls have massive stones and there is a museum of archaeological finds. Its cathedral is built on the site of a Roman Temple and Arab Mosque. Inland is the **Monestir de Poblet**, grandest of the "Cistercian Triangle" of monasteries. Founded in 1151 and several times despoiled, it contains royal tombs from the 12th to 14th centuries.

Near the resort of Salou, south of Tarragona, is **Port Aventura**, one of the biggest theme parks in Europe (open Easter to Oct: daily; entrance charge). The Costa Daurada ends at the rice-growing delta of the Ebro (Ebre), Spain's largest river, which fans out into the sea to create an important habitat for flamingoes and other bird life. There is an information centre in **Deltebre**.

Map on pages 340–1

The Romans founded Valencia in 138 BC and it became known as a retirement area for old soldiers, who enjoyed the year-round mild climate.

Valencia and the Costa Blanca

Valencia ㉔ lies in the most fertile farmlands of Spain. The country's third largest city is known for its oranges and the sensational conflagration that ends the city's Las Fallas fiesta on 19 March. Ceramics are also a speciality and there is some lovely tile work to be seen in the city as well as at the **Museo Nacional de Cerámica**. One of the city's most handsome buildings, the 15th-century commodities exchange, La Lonja, is now a concert and exhibition venue, and a modern vibrancy is reflected in galleries of contemporary art.

Many resorts on this varied coast, such as **Dénia** and **Altea**, have attractive old towns; **Peñiscola** is a memorable "tail" of land with a fortified community at its tip, surrounded by the sea. But it is **Benidorm**, with a fine sandy beach and acres of high-rise hotels, that has given the area its package-holiday reputation.

BELOW: looking out from the medieval castle in Tortosa, southern Catalonia.

Alicante (Alacant) ❷❺ is the Costa Blanca's main city, with a port and airport, and it has a fine, palm-lined esplanade. In the town hall is a metal disc, which is the marker for all measurements above sea level around Spain. Near Alicante is the extraordinary plantation at **Elche** (Elx) of more than a quarter of a million palms, said to have been planted by the Phoenicians. A 5th-century BC stone bust of a priestess, La Dame de Elche, found here, is one of the nation's great treasures; it is now in Mardrid. Away from the coast, both Valencia and Murcia are mountainous. One of the most picturesque upland areas is **El Maestrazgo** (Maestrat) where crags and flat-topped summits form a backdrop to stout medieval towns such as **Morella**.

Toledo and Castilla-La Mancha

One of Spain's most dramatically sited towns is **Cuenca** ❷❻, where the Casas Colgadas (Hanging Houses) teeter on the edge of a cliff over the River Huéscar. One of them contains the **Museu de Arte Abstracto**, with works by the Catalan Antoní Tapies and the Basque Eduardo Chillado (open Tues–Sun; entrance charge). Further inland are the plains of **La Mancha**, made famous by Don Quixote. Windmills remain at **Consuegra**, which in late October has a festival of saffron, one of the world's most expensive spices, introduced to Spain by the Arabs. It is an essential ingredient of *paella*.

The former capital of Spain and still its spiritual heart lies on a bend on the River Tajo 70 km (45 miles) south of Madrid. **Toledo** ❷❼ has many claims to fame: damascene metalwork, El Greco and an old town that is listed as a UN World Heritage site. The city's cathedral has a venerable history, and was a centre of Christianity before the Moors arrived. Richly embellished, it has a

BELOW:
a typical windmill, mistaken by Don Quixote for a giant.

THE QUIXOTE TRAIL

A tour of central La Mancha is an opportunity for fans of *Don Quixote* to trace key points in various chapters from Miguel Cervantes' novel – the world's first bestseller, published in 1615. El Toboso, on the N-301 between Albacete and Ocaña, was the village of Dulcinea, Don Quixote's fantasised true love for whom he was so quick to risk all. Casa de Dulcinea (open Tues–Sun; entrance fee), thought to be the house of the woman on whom Cervantes modelled his damsel, has been restored to its 16th-century appearance. The town hall has copies of *Don Quixote* in some three dozen languages. Puerto Lápiz, 20 km (12 miles) southeast of Consuegra, matches Cervantes' description of the inn where Don Quixote was sworn in as a knight errant. The line of windmills nearby at Campo de Criptana look as if they might be the ones Quixote mistook for giants, their flailing sails "attacking" the deluded knight tilting at them. The Cueva de Montesinos near San Pedro lake in the Lagunas de Ruidera valley is the cave where our hero was treated to elegiac visions of other bewitched knights and of his beloved Dulcinea. The nearby village of Argamasilla de Alba is a firm candidate for the place where it began: "Es un lugar de la Mancha…" – There is a place in La Mancha…

good picture collection in the sacristy. But the town's other worshippers are well represented: Visigothic crown jewels can be seen in the **Iglesia de San Roman**; and there are two synagogues, one of which contains a Sefardic museum. El Greco lived in the Jewish quarter from his arrival in the city in 1517 till his death in 1614. The **Casa-Museo de El Greco** (open Tues–Sun; entrance charge) contains several of his works. One of the dominating buildings in the town is the **Alcázar**, mainly 16th-century but dating back to the time of El Cid. It was the object of a protracted siege in the 1936–39 Civil War and today contains an army museum.

Extremadura, land of the conquistadores

West of Madrid is **Extremadura**, one of the least visited parts of Spain, which provided many adventurers for the New World. Francisco Pizarro, conqueror of Peru, was born in **Trujillo** ㉘, where his statue adorns the Plaza Major. His brother, Hernando, built the Palacio del Marqués de la Conquista (open daily; free) opposite the statue. The facade has a bust of Francisco Pizarro and his wife, Inés Yupanqui, sister of the Inca emperor Atahualpa.

Many Catholics make their way to the **Monasterio de Guadalupe** ㉙ to see the Guadalupe Virgin, who exercises her influence not just in Spain but also in the Americas where more than 100 cities are named after her.

Southwest of Guadalupe is **Mérida** ㉚, capital of Lusitania, the Roman's western Iberian province. Roman history is scattered all over the town; the impressive theatre is still used for summer drama festivals, and the **Museo Nacional de Arte Roman** (open daily; entrance charge), designed in 1988 by Rafael Moneo, has the largest collection of Roman artefacts outside Italy.

Map on page 340–1

TIP

South of Toledo is the Parque Nacional de Cabañeros, reached via the C-401 and C-403. You can take a guided tour of the park in a four-wheel drive vehicle, during which you may well see wild boar, stag and imperial eagles.

BELOW: Toledo: city and Alcázar.

The sultry south

Named al-Andalus by its Arabic conquerors, Andalucia, the province of the south, is the soul of Spain. Warm, sleepy, polite, proud, vibrant, it is the country's most populace province, with 6 million people in an area the size of Portugal. Under Moorish dominion in the Middle Ages, it had one of the most highly developed civilisations in Europe. Until the Reconquest of Granada by the Catholic monarchs Fernando and Isabel in 1492, Andalucia had rarely been united under one ruler. Internecine strife among *emirs* and *taífas* of Córdoba, Jaén, Granada and Seville undermined Moorish domination until the increasing pressure of Spain's northern Christian kingdoms ultimately vanquished it. Today its coast is the most cosmopolitan in Europe.

Taking a leisurely ride through the streets of Seville.

Seville (Sevilla) **Ⓐ**, capital of Andalucia and the country's fourth-largest city, is the dazzling setting of Byron's *Don Juan*, Bizet's *Carmen* and Rossini's barber. The cities two finest buildings face each other across the Plaza del Triunfo in the central Santa Cruz district. On the north side is the **Cathedral** (open Mon–Sat 11am–5pm, Sun 2–4pm; entrance charge), Europe's largest, where Christopher Columbus has a highly figurative tomb. The adjoining Moorish belltower is known as the **Giralda**, after the weathervane (*giraldillo*) at the top, and from here there are good views of the city. God and Muhammad have been worshipped on the same sites in the south. The cathedral was built on an earlier mosque; Muslim worshippers would wash their hands and feet in the fountain of the **Patio de los Naranjos**, the orange orchard cloisters.

On the south side of the square is the **Reales Alcázares**, the Royal Palace (open Tues–Sat 10.30am–5.30pm, Sun 10am–1pm; entrance charge). Like the cathedral, it has excellent Mudejar designs, in particular its patios and beauti-

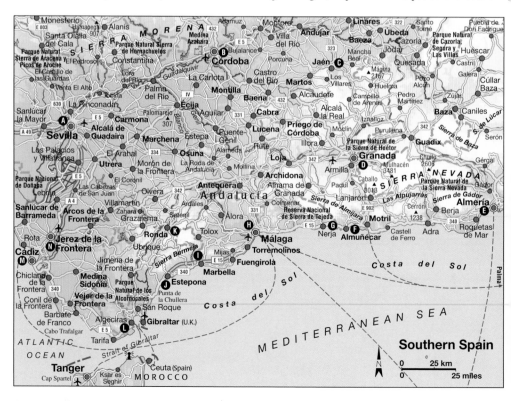

ful Ambassadors' Hall, which are fantasies in filigree. The former palace of the Almohads was redesigned by Pedro I in 1344 after the city's conquest. From here Isabel sent Columbus and other navigators to the New World, their ships sailing down the River Guadalquivir. The dockyards were to the south, in El Arenal district, where the fine 18th-century bullring can be found. Beside it is the Prado de San Sebastián, where pavilions are set up for the brilliant April Feria, when everyone dresses to the nines and lets down their hair in a confluence of Andalusian stereotypes: wine, bulls, horses and flamenco.

Córdoba ❸, smaller and less flamboyant than Seville, was the city of a brilliant Caliphate, and its Great Mosque, the **Mezquita**, dating from Abd al Rahman in the 8th century, is one of the splendours of Moorish Spain (open Mon–Sat 10am–6pm, Sun 3.30–7pm, 5pm in winter; entrance charge). Take a walk in the Jewish quarter beside the mosque for an idea of how the medieval city must have been; the area includes the remains of a 14th-century synagogue.

To the east is Jaén province, a massive, undulating area of 150 million olive trees. Its capital, **Jaén** ❸, perched above the western plain with its back to the sierras, has a massive cathedral, fine Arab Baths and hilltop Moorish castle which is now a parador. The nearby town of **Baeza**, an architectural gem of Renaissance buildings, was the home of Spain's great 20th-century poet Antonio Machado (1875–1939). Úbeda is also an elegant Renaissance gem.

The jewel of Moorish Spain is the **Alhambra** (open daily; combined entrance charge for the Alhambra, Alcazaba and Palacio Generalife) in **Granada** ❸. Picturesquely set at the foot of the snowy Sierra Nevada, this was the last stronghold of the longest-running kingdom of the Moors, and the home of Spain's great poet and playwrite Federico García Lorca (1898–1936). No amount of

Map on page 366

TIP

Córdoba is noted for the crafts of silver filigree and stamped leather. In the 16th and 17th centuries it was the fashion for all walls and seats to be covered with leather, properly embossed, tooled, tinted and gilded.

BELOW: the Salón de los Embajadores, in the Alhambra.

A white town in the hills near Ronda.

description can prepare the visitor for the Alhambra's exquisite architecture, which is the epitome of Moorish imagination and artistry. The royal residence is highlighted by the **Patio de los Arrayanes** (Patio of the Myrtles) and **Patio de los Leones** (Patio of the Lions). The adjoining Palacio Generalife, dating from 1250, was the summer palace of the sultans – cool and green and full of restful pools and murmuring fountains. In summer an International Festival of Music and Dance is held in the grounds. The conquerors of the Moors, Catholic Monarchs Ferdinand and Isabel, share a mausoleum in the Capilla Real. The **Alcazaba** (castle), at the western end of Alhambra Hill, is a 9th-century Moorish citadel with grand views over the city.

Across the **Sierra Nevada**, where **Solynieve**, at 2,100 metres (6,890 ft), is the southernmost ski resort in Europe, lies **Almería** ❺, a harsh landscape tamed by a massive modern agricultural business.

Costa del Sol

At the western end of the Sierra Nevada the white villages on the mountain slopes of Las Alpujarras lead down to the coast. The climate at **Almuñécar** ❻ is warm enough for exotic fruits to grow, causing this to be labelled the Costa Tropical. To the west is **Nerja** ❼, on cliffs above sandy coves. A series of prehistoric caves were discovered here in 1957 and summertime concerts are held in the largest one.

Málaga ❽ is the capital of the Costa del Sol, a bustling town visited by cruise liners. This was the port of the city of Granada, and its Moorish castle, the 11th-century **Alcazaba** (open daily; entrance charge) was built inside the extensive Roman fort beside an amphitheatre. Phoenician, Roman and Moorish arte-

BELOW: poolside at the Costa del Sol.

facts are displayed in the **Museu Arqueológico** inside. Picasso spent his early childhood in the town and a new **Picasso Museum** has opened in the Palacio de Buenavista in Calle San Augustin not far from the Picasso Foundation in the Casa Natal de Picasso (open Mon-Fri; free). Some of his early sketches are in the **Museo de Bellas Artes** (open Tues–Sun; entrance charge), which also has paintings by Murillo and Zubarán.

The Costa del Sol has its densest population between Málaga and Marbella, and reaches a down-market low at **Torremolinas**, which was a poor fishing village until it was "discovered" in the 1960s. It is now grotesquely overgrown with hundreds of bars and overhead walkways. Coastal traffic is heavy in summer all along the coast through **Fuengirola**, where high-rise hotels and apartment blocks pack the water's edge all the way to **Marbella ❶**. Between Marbella and the flashy marina **Puerto Banús** is the Golden Mile, playground of celebrities, sheikhs, millionaires, royalty and bullfighters, though Marbella's old town remains attractive. **Estepona ❷**, the most westerly of the Costa's swollen fishing villages, has avoided too many high-rises.

Inland the contrast is stark. The countryside grows wilder towards **Ronda ❸** and the "White Towns", with dazzling communities such as **Grazalema**, **Ubrique**, **Zahara** and **Jimena de la Frontera**. Ronda itself is a bustling town on a rocky bluff with sheer walls falling dramatically away on three sides and concealing one of the oldest bullrings in Spain.

Gibraltar and the Costa de la Luz

Gibraltar, Britain's anachronistic enclave in Spain, can be freely entered. With pubs and policemen, its 7 sq km (3 sq miles) is a strange placewarp. Its rock, looking out across the narrow strait, joins the Mediterranean to the Atlantic. The ugly industrial town of **Algeciras ❹** is the boarding point for ferries to **Tanger** (Tangier) and the Spanish North African enclave of Ceuta.

West of Gibraltar the tidal Atlantic washes the **Costa de la Luz**. The wind and waves make the whole coast, particularly around **Tarifa**, a sailboard haunt. After the discovery of the Americas, **Cádiz ❺** became the wealthiest port in Europe. The town has a safe harbour and is known for its seafood, as well as for flamenco artists. Its grand cathedral contains the tomb of the native composer Manuel de Falla, and the Oratorio e la Santa Cueva has scenes from the New Testament painted by Goya. Inland from Cádiz is the rolling landscape of The Sherry Triangle, centred on **Jerez de la Frontera ❻**. The city also has a strong horse breeding tradition, and its May Horse Show follows on the heels of Seville's April Feria.

Sanlúcar de la Barrameda, beyond beaches of golden sand north of Cadiz, is known for its light dry sherries. It looks across the mouth of the Guadalquivir to the dunes and marshlands of the **Parque Nacional de Doñana**, one of the country's principal nature reserves. The imperial eagle and Spanish lynx are among its rarer inhabitants. Organised tours in four-wheel-drive vehicles start from the Visitors' Centre at **El Acebuche** (book ahead: tel: 959-43 04 32). ❑

Map
on page
366

TIP

While in Marbella, make a point of visiting the 17th-century Iglesia Santa María de la Encarnación, the town's main church, from where a signpost leads to the Museo del Grabado, devoted to contemporary art.

BELOW:
riding out at Jerez de la Frontera.

AMONG THE CASTLES OF IMPOSSIBLE DREAMS

Imperious, impervious, fantastic, steeped in history and dripping romance – it's no wonder that castles in Spain are an unattainable dream

Castile is the high, arid heart of Spain, Castilian is the country's spoken language. Both derive their names from *castillo* (castle), the building that for years was the most dominant feature of this part of Spain. Castile was where the first significant advances were made against the Moors, a Wild West of adventurers and pioneers. Frontiers were marked along the Duero, Arlanzón and Ebro rivers where there were no walled cities, monasteries or manorial estates to run to in times of trouble. Strongholds were established about 100 years after the Moorish conquest, notably under Fernán Gonzáles (910–970), first Count of Castile, and over the next 400 years of fighting, castles appeared all over the countryside.

MOORISH CASTLES

The Moors were great castle builders, too. At Berlanga de Duero the Moors constructed a fortress with a massive curtain wall and drum towers with a commanding view (*pictured above*).

As the lands became safer, castles were adopted as glorified homes. The Fonseca family's Castillo de Coca in Segovia, for example, displays some fine Mudéjar military architecture, but it was never intended to be put to the test.

After the Moors had been driven out in 1492, castle building was forbidden, but by then some 2,000 had altered Spain's landscape forever.

△ **CASTILLO DE GUADALEST**
Alicante's eyries have commanding views. The coast needed protection from pirates.

◁ **PONFERRADA**
On the pilgrim route to Santiago de Compostella, Ponferrada was run by the Knights Templar.

◁ **SEGOVIA ALCAZAR**
The castle where Fernando and Isabel were proclaimed is the ultimate fairytale fortress. It stands on an 80-metre (260-ft) rocky outcrop.

△ **TORRE DE HOMENAJE**
Segovia's keep has unusual candlestick-and-snuffer towers. This was the residential and social hub of the castle.

ARISTOCRATIC LODGINGS

The picture above is of the interior of the parador at Zamora, a 15th-century castle and former home of the counts of Alba y Aliste on the banks of the Duero. The word parador (from the Arabic *waradah*, meaning "halting place") had been in use for many centuries before 1928 when the government instigated this chain of state-run hotels in restored historic buildings. Designed to be no more than a day's journey apart, there are around 90 altogether. They are all relatively inexpensive and have a reputation for good service and good food. As a matter of policy, they have always served the best local dishes, and even if you don't stay in one, they are worth a visit for a meal, or a coffee, just to have a look around.

△ **PEÑAFIEL**
One of a number of early Castilian castles built on the banks of the Duero, Peñafiel dates from the 10th century, but is mostly 15th-century.

◁ **VALENCIA DE DON JUAN**
The most arrogant castle in León, Valencia de Don Juan has high walls and lofty towers looming above the River Esla, near Coyança.

▽ **CASTILLO DE SANTA CATALINA**
This 13th-century castle in Jaén was built by Ibn-al-Ahmar, who ceded it to Ferdinand III in 1245 in return for control of Granada. The castle is now a parador.

PORTUGAL

*Europe's most westerly country is underpopulated,
tranquil and full of impressive scenery*

Tucked in the corner of the continent, nobody passes through Portugal because, really, there is nowhere else to go. It is a land on the edge, "where land ends and sea begins" as the 16th-century epic poet Luís Vaz de Camões put it. At the western periphery of Europe, it is also caught between traditional living – fishing and farming – and the technology that has made the world smaller, more integrated, more complex.

Although in many ways Portugal has a Mediterranean feel, its light is more limpid and its shores are washed clean by the Atlantic tides. The cosmopolitan nature of the country is evident everywhere: nearly 2 million returned from former colonies when they were granted independence in the mid-1970s. Many headed for the countryside rather than towns, and Lisbon, the capital, has a comparatively small population of one million – out of a total population for the country of around 10 million.

Both the towns and the country are easy to get around even if Portugal was the last country in Europe to build motorways: the main one that links Lisbon with the second city of Oporto, to the north, was not opened until 1991. The Portuguese are enthusiastic drivers and, as rush-hour shows, few choose public transport, even when it is as quaint as the funiculars and trams of Lisbon. There are surprisingly few roads altogether in the country and a typical full-size road map shows the smallest lanes. The mountainous regions of the centre and north are hard work, but there never seems any reason to rush. On the northern Costa Verde, vistors can step back in time by taking a ride on one of several preserved steam train lines.

The country covers 92,100 sq km (35,550 sq miles) and its land borders Spain, of which it was part only up until the 12th century: their languages, the languages of South America, are surprisingly different. Portugal benefits from Spain's gift of three important rivers. In the north are the Minho and the Douro, which transport picturesque barges carrying barrels of port (fortified wine) down to Oporto. Lisbon lies on the Tagus, south of which is the Alentejo and the popular coast of the Algarve. The cities have a distinct flavour, and the people savour their differences. "Coimbra sings, Braga plays, Lisbon shows off and Oporto works" is one way the Portuguese people sum them up. ❑

PRECEDING PAGES: main street in Monsaraz; fishermen on Mira beach.
LEFT: a Coimbra University student with the red ribbons of the law school.

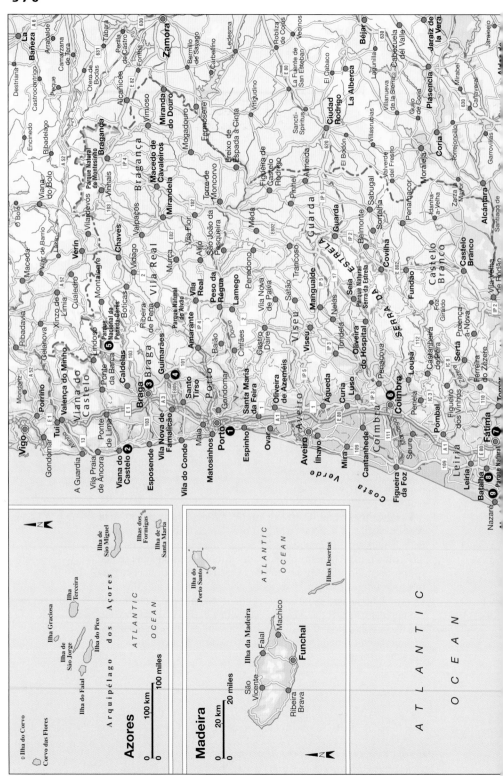

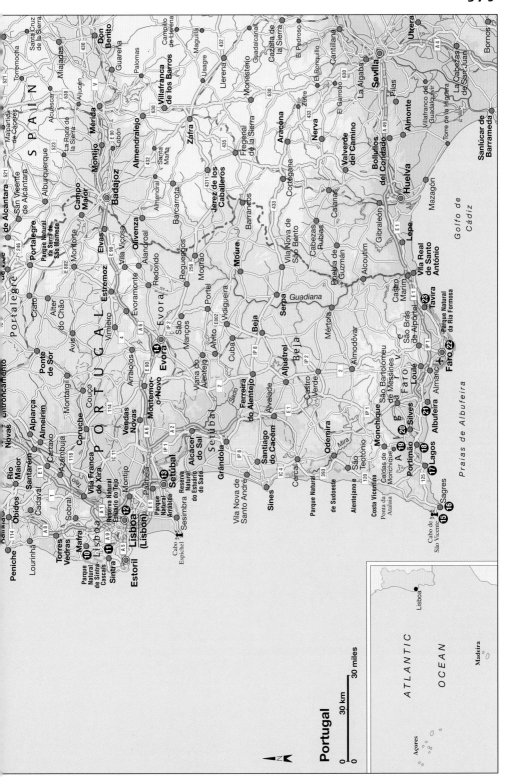

Portugal

0   30 km
0   30 miles

ATLANTIC

OCEAN

Lisboa

Açores

Madeira

LISBON

Map
on page
382

*Its population of just 1 million inhabitants gives Lisbon
the feel of a big town rather than a major city;
nevertheless, it is truly cosmopolitan*

L isbon is one of Europe's smallest capitals, but bristles with the evidence of former empires from Brazil to Macao. The town is set on the right bank of the River Tejo (Tagus), facing south, and is spread over seven hills, which have a number of *miradouros*, terraces and viewing points which look down over the city's rooftops. One such is the **Castelo de São Jorge ❶**. Originally Roman, this was where the Moorish governor had his residence until 1147 when the Moors were driven out and it became the Portuguese royal palace, occupied and embellished by Dinis I (1279–1325) and Manuel I (1495–1521). When the palace moved down to the river, it became a fortress, then a barracks. Ten towers and sturdy walls remain, surrounded by a moat.

The area around the castle, the **Alfama**, is the oldest part of the city, where lanes and tramlines meander up and down hill and some of the alleys are so narrow two people can barely pass. One such is Rua de São Pedro, where fisherwomen sell their daily catch or eat fresh fish in the tiny front rooms that pass as restaurants. The **Sé ❷** (cathedral) is in this part of town, a solid structure fronted by two crenellated towers and a fine rose window. Inside is the font where St Anthony of Padua, the city's unofficial patron saint, was christened in 1195. The relics of St Vincent, the city's official patron saint, are displayed in the treasury. Opposite is **Sant Antonio de Sé**, a small church which was built over the room where St Anthony was born.

Regal square

The royal residence was transferred from the castle to the waterside at what is now the **Praça do Comércio ❸**, known locally as Terreiro do Paço (Palace Terrace), after the 16th-century palace that stood here and received waterborne visitors in sumptuous barges. The palace was just one of the casualties of the 1755 earthquake that reduced most of the city to rubble. The massive rebuilding in the aftermath was undertaken by the Marquês de Pombal, the autocratic prime minister who didn't bother to wait for the rubble to be cleared away, but just rebuilt the new city on top. The Neo-classical pink arcades of this square are typical "Pombaline Lisbon". In the centre is a statue by Machada de Castro of José I, the monarch during Pombal's administration. The statue is by Machada de Castro, Portugal's best-known sculptor. On 1 February 1908 in the northwest corner of this square, Carlos I and his heir Luís Felipe were assassinated in an open landau.

Two years later a republic was declared from the balcony of the 19th-century **town hall** in the Praça do Municipio, a short stroll away to the west of the square. At its centre is a twisted column with a banded sphere, a typical Manueline architectural device and

LEFT: trams make sightseeing a treat. **BELOW:** blooms for sale in Rossio.

Taking a break at the Cervjaria de Trinidade in the Chiado shopping centre.

the symbol of the city. The central archway leads through to the **Baixa**, the downtown shopping district, a lively few blocks of old shops, tea houses and restaurants, as well as a delightful little cinema. Its Rua do Ouro and Rua da Plata, Gold and Silver Streets, give a flavour of the times when precious metals arrived from the New World.

Up on the west side of the Baixa is the **Bairro Alto**, reached by steep lanes, a funicular or the Santa Justa Lift, a whimsical iron structure designed by the French engineer Gustave Eiffel, who gave Paris the Eiffel Tower. This immediately arrives at the **Chiado**, the smart shopping centre, which was badly damaged in a major fire in 1988. One of the city's major department stores was lost in the fire. A smart new hotel is rising from the ashes.

The 18th-century earthquake demolished the monastery of **Carmo ❹**, and left its church, then Lisbon's largest, roofless, as it is today. It also brought down the facade of the pretty little church of **São Roque**. This is a treasurehouse of gold and marble, lapiz and amethyst, and each of its eight chapels is a delight. The St John the Baptist chapel was made in Rome, blessed by the pope, transported to Lisbon in three ships and is said to be the costliest chapel in the world.

The Bairro Alto is full of restaurants and nightspots, and *fado*, the famous Portuguese song, can be heard in its rawest as well as its most commercial forms. The city's opera house, the Italianate **Teatro de São Carlos**, built in 1792, is also here. An evening out may well start at the **Solar de Instituto do Vinho do Porto ❺**, the Port Wine Institute in Rua São Pedro de Alcântara, a bar with a club-like atmosphere which serves a large selection of ports, red and white. The *miradoura* opposite has a grand view across the Baixa to the castle. The Gloria funicular leads back down to the Praça de Restauradores and the neo-

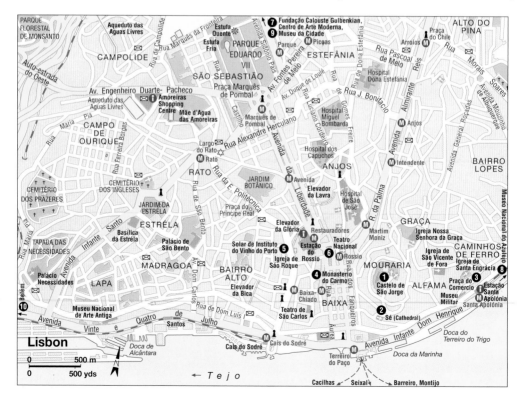

Manueline Rossio station, where suburban trains run to Benfica and Sintra, the first place to think of for an out-of-town excursion (*see page 387*). **Rossio** was once the city's main square where bullfights, carnivals and and *autos da fé* took place. Today, entertainment is confined to the **Teatro Nacional** (National Theatre) , built in 1840. The two large fountains in the square were brought from Paris in 1890. Today they are surrounded by colourful flower stalls.

Beyond Restauradores is the Avenida da Liberdade, the city's grand avenue where airline offices and banks line the roadside. At the top, in a square named after him, is a statue to Pombal, looking down on all he created.

Millionaire's museums

Lisbon's other benefactor was Calouste Gulbenkian, the Armenian oil magnate who was hounded out of Britain during World War II and settled in neutral Lisbon. His gift to the city is the **Fundação Calouste Gulbenkian** , the city's principal culture centre with a large general collection and a museum of modern art. This is above the Pombal statue beside Parque Eduardo VII, where there are two fine botanical houses.

To the east of the city, just beyond the Alfama, is the **Museo Nacional do Azulejo** , a museum dedicated to Portugal's principal native art, highly coloured glazed tiles. The museum is in the splendid Madre de Deus church. The **Museu da Cidade** , the City Museum, is in the Palacio Pimenta at Campo Grande, a fine manor built during the reign of King João V (1706–50). The city's other main museums are the **Museu de Arte Antiga** near the river to the west of the town, and the **Coach** and **Maritime museums** even further west, in Belém . The Coach museum is housed in the former Royal Riding School.

Although Belém (Bethelehem) is 5 km (3 miles) west of the centre of town, no visit to the city should exclude it. This is the Lisbon of the navigators, the visionaries and the soldiers of fortune. On the flat land beside the river is the **Torre de Belém**, the city's enduring landmark. It was built in 1521 to defend the harbour called Restello which used to be here and which was at the navigators' point of departure.

In 1497, at the start of his epic voyage to India, Vasco da Gama prayed in a small chapel beside the Restello, built by Henry the Navigator. The chapel was levelled shortly afterwards and in its place arose the spectacular **Mosteiro dos Jerónimos** and its church of **Santa María**.

Manuel I ordered the building in 1502 and it is a perfect symbol of the extravagant Age of Discovery. The apogee of the unique Portuguese Manueline style, the huge monastery buildings and cloisters are laced with nautical motifs, particularly the armillary sphere.

Beyond Belém the river widens into the ocean. On the same bank are the resorts of **Cascais** and **Estoril**, 30 to 45 minutes from Cais do Sodré station on Lisbon's waterfront. This is the former "Coast of Kings", which several of this century's deposed European monarchs chose for exile. They smart resorts have good restaurants and nightlife. Cascais caters more for the under-30s; Estoril has elegant residential areas. Both are within commuting distance of the city. ❑

Map
on page
382

TIP

Walking is the best way to see the city, but there is a good transport system of trams (*eléctricos*), buses, taxis and lifts (*elevadors*). Avoid the inevitable traffic jams by using the efficient Metro system.

BELOW: the Marquês de Pombal surveys the Avenida de Liberdade.

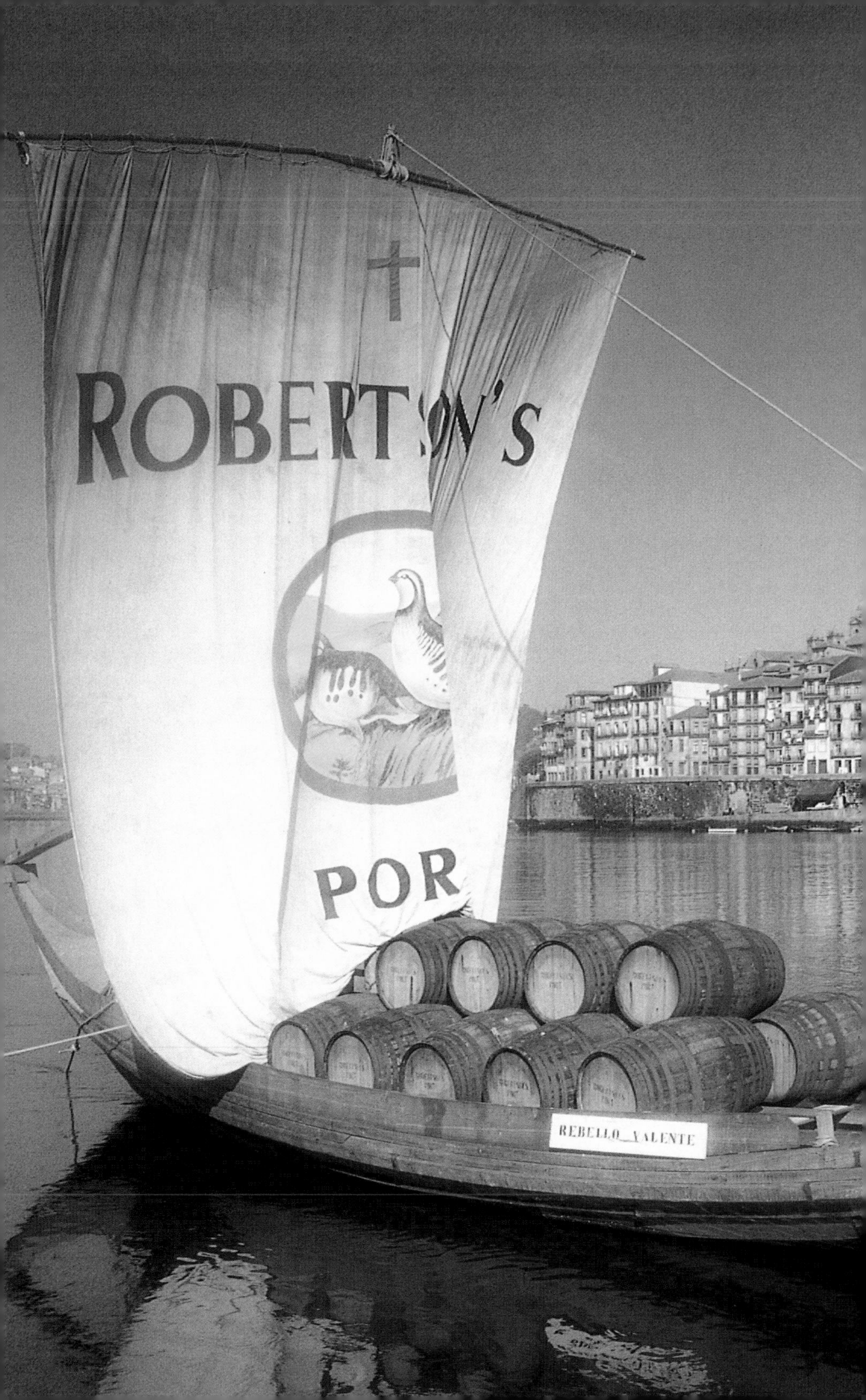
POR
REBELLO VALENTE

AROUND PORTUGAL

This is the land of sad songs called "fados", and the place from which two great navigators, Vasco da Gama and Ferdinand Magellan, set sail to discover new worlds

Lisbon

P ortugal takes its name from its second city, **Porto** (Oporto) ❶, which has become synonymous with its fortified dessert wine. Majestically sited on rocky cliffs overlooking the River Douro, it was originally two cities each side of the river's mouth: Portus on the right bank, Cale on the left. And, when Alfonso Henriques united the country in the 12th century, he called his new kingdom Portucalia. Oporto is a stern and sober town of granite church towers and narrow streets and its baroque treasures must be hunted out. The **Church of São Francisco** in Praça do Infante Dom Henrique should be seen for its baroque splendour, while the **Salon de Arabe** in the Palacio de Bolsa is a remarkably opulent neo-Moorish reception hall. Up the hill from the stock exchange, wines can be tasted at the **Solar do Vinho do Porto** or at any of the 60 or so port wine lodges in **Vila Nova de Gaia** on the south side of the Dom Luís I Bridge. The **Cais de Ribera** on the riverbank is the liveliest part of the city, where small shops and restaurants are built into the old city wall.

Night-times are quiet and young people tend to head for the Foz de Douro suburb, older people to the coastal resort of Espinho, where there is a casino and nightclub. When festivities are on the calendar, however, the town livens up. At the **Alameda das Fontainhas**, a square overlooking the Dom Luís I Bridge, people sing and dance round bonfires, drink *vinho verde*, the refreshing, slightly sparkling local wine, and feast on roast kid and sardines.

The Green Coast

The green wine lands of the Duoro and the Minho rivers colour the whole coast, giving it its name, the **Costa Verde.** The main resort town north of Oporto is **Viana do Castelo** ❷, where the splendid Basilica of Santa Luzia looks over the sweep of sandy beaches.

Minho's capital, **Braga** ❸, is the former seat of powerful bishops. Its baroque **Sé** (cathedral) was built in the 12th century by Henri of Burgundy and his wife Dona Teresa, whose tombs are in one of the richly decorated chapels. A famous church in the vicinity is the **Bom Jesús do Monte** (5km/3 miles from Braga), an important place of pilgrimage. An imposing flight of 19th-century steps leads up to the church entrance (564metres/1,850ft), but you can drive up or take the venerable funicular railway.

Just to the south is **Guimarães** ❹, the first capital of Portugal, with a 10th-century castle (open Tues–Sun; entrance charge) and church of Our Lady of the Olive Tree, which has a Romanesque cloister and good museum. The massive granite Paço do Duques, the Palace of the Dukes of Bragança, can also be visited.

In the far north west is the **Trás-os-Montes**, the most remote district in Portugal, where life was so

LEFT: port barges in Oporto.
BELOW: making port barrels in Vila Nova de Gaia.

Colour in Coimbra.

BELOW:
the Igreja de Jésus.

harsh in post-war years that people emigrated to become peasant farmers in the Portuguese colonies in Africa. On its edges is the 70,000-hectare (173,000-acre) **Peneda-Gerês National Park ❺**, which has a series of lakes and is a popular destination for all kinds of water sports.

Seat of learning

To the south of Oporto, perched on a hill overlooking the River Mondego, is the university town of **Coimbra ❻**. The tangle of narrow streets at the heart of the old town leads to the Pátio das Escolas, reached through the 17th-century Porta Férrea. Behind the statue of João III, who gave his palace to the university, is a magnificent view of the river below, and in the far corner is the library, one of the most beautiful in the world, with ceiling frescoes and intricately decorated ladders. Luis de Camôes (1524–80), Portugal's greatest poet, was a student here, and the traditions of the university go back centuries. Every spring there is the week-long Queima das Fitas, the "burning of the ribbons", when students ignite the ribbons they wear on their sleeves to show what faculty they belong to. University graduates also have something of a monopoly on the local *fado,* which is more serious and intellectual than the *fado* sung in Lisbon, and to show their approval the people in the audience are not supposed to clap but merely to clear their throats.

One of the country's greatest traditions is the pilgrimage at **Fátima ❼**, situated between Coimbra and Lisbon. On 13 May 1917 three shepherd girls had a vision of the Virgin, who appeared in a glow of light over an oak tree. She asked them to pray for the peace of the world and promised to return on the 13th day of each month until October. Those are the days which have been celebrated since, and thousands come from all over the world to visit the basilica that has been built beside a colonnaded square in which up to 1 million people have congregated during visits by the pope.

Tomar, east of Fátima, is a delightful town with many good points, including the castle and former headquarters of the Knights Templar in Portugal and the splendid Convento do Cristo, a UNESCO World Heritage site. **Batalha ❽**, 20 km (12 miles) west of Fátima, has a beautiful Gothic abbey, in the Santa Maria da Vitória monastery, an unmistakable landmark beside the Lisbon-Oporto motorway. The ornate facade hides a simple, elegant interior. Tombs in the Founder's Chapel include João I and subsequent members of the Aviz ruling dynasty. Others, in the "Unfinished Chapels", include that of Prince Henry the Navigator (1394–1460), patron of the country's great explorers. The cloister is built in Portugal's elaborate Manueline style, named after the monarch who benefited most from South American riches. Its typical flourishes include nautical fantasy and, the symbol of Portuguese knowledge and power, the armillary sphere. Most striking of all are the **Capelas Imperfeitas**, the Unfinished Chapels, which suffered when the royal coffers ran low.

At **Alcobaça**, just to the south, is Portugal's largest church in a Cistercian Abbey, another UNESCO World Heritage site. Fine medieval stone carvings tell the tale of Pedro I who exumed his skeletal queen, crowned her and made his nobles kiss her hand. On the coast is **Nazaré** (Nazereth) ❾, a timeless fishing village where fishermen wear stocking caps, women wear petticoats and the colourful boats are hauled up the beach by oxen. In summer, holidaymakers' brightly-striped canvas tents create the romantic atmosphere of a Moorish battle camp.

Around Lisbon

Near Lisbon is **Mafra** ❿, which started life as a Capuchin monastery and was expanded into something more palatial by João V. A craft school was established as a result of the building works, and among its teachers was Joaquim Machado de Castro. The resultant limestone facade is 220 metres (720 ft) long, and behind it is a church which shows off Portugal's wonderful marble, as well as six statues of saints from Italy in Carrara marble. But the high spot of the building is its beautiful baroque library of 35,000 books, including the first editions of Camões' *Os Lusíadas* and the earliest edition of Homer in Greek.

Mafra is the site of the church of Santo André. Pedro Hispano was priest here before he was elected Pope John XXI in 1276 – the only Portuguese pope in the history of the Vatican.

Mafra is a good place to visit from Lisbon, but **Sintra** ⓫, 25 km (15 miles) northwest of the city, is a must. It has captivated everyone who has been there. At its height is the **Royal Palace**, used by Portugal's monarchs for 600 years. It was built by King João I at the end of the 14th century and extended by Manuel I in the 16th century, and it has Portugal's finest *azulejos* (tiles), which cover its Arab and Swan halls and the chapel. Beautifully situated, the palace is floodlit at night and there is often a *son-et-lumière* performance in summer.

Another royal residence is at **Queluz**, an 18th-century small-scale Versailles in a rather dull town 14 km (9 miles) west of Lisbon. Among the interior's gilt and glass is a magnificent throne room, used for a season of concerts. A ferry ride across the Tagus from the city of **Lisboa** (Lisbon) ⓬ leads to the industrial

BELOW: the Unfinished Chapels, Batalha.

heartland of **Setúbal** ⓭, which is worth negotiating for the Church of Jesus. This was an early work of Boytec, master of the Jeronimos monastery. There are some good primitive paintings in the museum.

Alentejo is the "land beyond the Tejo" – in other words, south of the River Tagus. This is the flattest part of the country, one-third of it covered by parched planes of oak woods and olive groves. Its main town is **Evora** ⓮, an ancient city which had its time of brilliance as a favoured residence of the kings of Burgundy and Avis dynasty; its sites, from Roman Temple of Diana to cathedral and university, are worth a day's excursion.

The Algarve

The south-facing 150-km (95-mile) southern coastal strip of Portugal is very different from the rest of the country. Its architecture is Moorish, its vegetation is almost sub-tropical and the sea temperature in winter rarely falls below 15°C (59°F). In the 1970s it began to take off as a tourist destination, served by the increasingly busy airport at Faro. Time-share villas and apartments and second homes began surrounding the towns and springing up as isolated "property resorts". But there are still unspoilt villages and beaches to go with the infrastructure of golf courses, casinos, water sports and other tourist necessities.

Algarve is from the Arabic *el gharb* meaning "the west". Its western extremity is **Cabo de São Vicente** ⓯, described as *o fim do mundo*, "the end of the world". It is a wild corner, where the wind has bent almond trees double. Europe's strongest lighthouse, which can be visited, has 3,000-watt bulbs and can be seen 96 km (56 miles) away. Along this coast the red earth rises in cliffs of impressive height, reaching 150 metres (500 ft) at **Tôrre de Asp**.

Five km (3 miles) east of Cape St Vincent at the lobster-fishing port of **Sagres** ⓰, Henry the Navigator (the Infante Dom Henrique, 1394–1460) established a school of navigation, where Vasco da Gama, Christopher Columbus and many other explorers acquired their skills. The school was housed in the Forteleza, the huge, severe-looking fortress, rebuilt in the 17th century, and the 39-metre (130-ft) compass rose Henry used to make his calculations is laid out in stone. Henry's interest in Sagres helped open up an area cut off from the rest of the country. The **Caldeirão** and **Monchique** mountain ranges stretching behind it had seen to that, while in the east the River Guadiana provided a border with Spain.

In the exciting whirl of adventure in the 16th century, as riches were being brought back from the east, the port of **Lagos** ⓱ was filled with caravelles, and it was here that the first slave market was established in Europe. The town has a good natural harbour which the Romans used, and in Moorish times it was a trade centre with Africa. The palace of Dom Henrique has become the local hospital and crenellated defensive walls guard the harbour now used by fishing boats. A specially delightful church is the Igreja de Santo António. Its rich, gilt baroque interior has earned it the name of the "Golden Chapel". Near the town are a number of grottoes which can be explored by boat.

Game fishing centre

From Silves the River Arade slips down to the sea at **Praia da Rocha**, the best-known and longest-established resort on the coast. The wide sandy beach is backed by a clifftop promenade lined with villas and hotels. The resort was started at the beginning of the 20th century by the wealthy people of **Portimão** , an attractive old fishing port 3 km (1½ miles) up the estuary which has become the busiest and biggest city on this western stretch of the coast. *Carinhas*, horse-drawn coaches, take tourists between the two places. Portimão is a good shopping centre, and the tuna and sardine catches can be sampled in its many restaurants, such as the Lanterna, where smoked swordfish is a speciality and its fish soup is claimed to be the best on the coast. *Caldeirada*, a fish chowder, is often on restaurant menus, as is *cataplana*, a dish of clams and meat. Game fishing cruisers can be hired at Portimão, or visitors can just go along to watch. This is said to be the last part of Europe where game fishing is still possible. The reefs where the sharks hunt are 20 km (12 miles) offshore, about two hours out. Blue and copper sharks lie in wait, as does the tasty *mako* – the sharp-nosed mackerel shark. **Ferragudo** on the eastern side of the River Arade, with a fine fort overlooking the estuary, is a centre of windsurfing and surfboarding.

Caldas de Monchique ⑲, a spa town in the hills behind the coast, makes a change from the cosmopolitan resorts. The water is supposed to have healing properties, but people also come to buy bottles of *Medronho*, a spirit distilled from the strawberry tree, *Arbutus uneda*, which blossoms all around the spa. In the town of **Monchique** the Carmen convent has good views over the coast.

In between is **Silves** ⑳, which as *Chelib* was the Moorish capital of the region. Then it was on a navigable part of the River Arade. Chelib was a cen-

Algarve has many spectacular beaches but Praia da Marinha, south of Porches, is one of the most photogenic. For a huge expanse of sand backed by colourful cliffs, try Falésia just west of Quarteira.

BELOW: peaceful harbour at Albufeira.

Map
on pages
378–9

tre for arts and learning, and at its height it had a population of 30,000. It fell to Sancho I of Portugal in 1189 after a six-week seige and from then on the monarchs took the title of "King of Portugal and the Algarve". Silves has a 13th-century cathedral with part of a Moorish mosque behind the altar, and its huge castle, a walled fortress with solid square Albarra towers, is one of the best Moorish buildings in Portugal. The earthquake of 1755 reduced most of the town to rubble and today the population has settled at 20,000. The **Cross of Portugal** is a 16th-century stone lacework cross on the Silves-Messines road just outside the town. South of Silves is **Lagos** a centre of wine growing, and the co-operative cellar is a good stopping-off point. Beside the main Estrada Nacional 125, 5 km (3 miles) east of Lagos near **Porches**, a town famous for its decorated pottery, is an Artisans' Village where local wines can be tasted.

The morning fish market is one of the attractions of **Albufeira ㉑**, a small fishing port with steep narrow streets and a tumble of whitewashed houses, topped with Moorish cupolas. But it has been overwhelmed by the biggest resort on the Algarve coast: it is now turned over entirely to tourism, with a number of fish restaurants around the fish market, and souvenir shops spilling out on to the main shopping street. The beach is crowded in high summer, but there are quieter beaches, such as **São Rafael** and **Olhos d'Água**, nearby.

BELOW:
the coast of Aljezur.
RIGHT: window
on the world.
OVERPAGE:
a Catholic cleric.

Regional capital

Albufeira is 36 km (22 miles) west of **Faro ㉒**, the finest town on the coast and the regional capital since the 18th century. The 1755 earthquake put paid to earlier buildings, but many fine baroque flourishes remain. The old town is inside what remains of its old walls and is approached through the 18th-century

Arco da Vila. Built on the site of a Moorish mosque, the Sé (cathedral) has a fine interior with a Renaissance misericordia and a lacquered organ. Among other notable churches are São Francisco, with a gilded interior, São Pedro, with good *azulejos*, and the curious Igreja do Carmo, which has a chapel decorated with human bones. The Archaeological Museum in a 16th-century convent has a good Roman collection, some of which comes from the ruins of Milreu in **Estói** 11 km (7 miles) north. The yacht basin in the centre of town shows how much Faro is linked to leisure and tourism. Some explore the islands and sandbars just off the coast which make up the **Parque Natural de Ria Formosa**, and from Faro spits continue towards the Spanish border.

The prettiest resort on the coast is the surprisingly unspoilt fishing village of **Tavira ㉓** 32 km (20 miles) east of Faro. The river Asseca on which it stands, crossed by a seven-arch Roman bridge, has long been silted up. Sparkling white with a castle, several churches, Moorish cupolas and lovely little gardens, it is the epitome of an Algarve town.

The country east of Tavira is little visited. The drive up to the hilltop castle at Castro Marim beside the River Guadiana gives a feeling of remoteness. The saltmarshes to the south are busy breeding grounds for storks and noisy black-winged stilts. ❑

INSIGHT GUIDES
TRAVEL TIPS

New Insight Maps

Maps in Insight Guides are tailored to complement the text. But when you're on the road you sometimes need the big picture that only a large-scale map can provide. This new range of durable Insight Fleximaps has been designed to meet just that need.

Detailed, clear cartography
makes the comprehensive route and city maps easy to follow, highlights all the major tourist sites and provides valuable motoring information plus a full index.

Informative and easy to use
with additional text and photographs covering a destination's top 10 essential sites, plus useful addresses, facts about the destination and handy tips on getting around.

Laminated finish
allows you to mark your route on the map using a non-permanent marker pen, and wipe it off. It makes the maps more durable and easier to fold than traditional maps.

The first titles
cover many popular destinations. They include Algarve, Amsterdam, Bangkok, California, Cyprus, Dominican Republic, Florence, Hong Kong, Ireland, London, Mallorca, Paris, Prague, Rome, San Francisco, Sydney, Thailand, Tuscany, USA Southwest, Venice, and Vienna.

INSIGHT GUIDES
The world's largest collection of visual travel guides

CONTENTS

Introduction

GETTING ACQUAINTED ..394
Time Zones 394
Climate 394
Vegetation & Crops......394
PLANNING THE TRIP 395
What to Wear 395
What to Bring 395
Visas & Passports........395
Health 395
Currency 396
Public Holidays...........397
PRACTICAL TIPS 397
Security & Crime 397
Weights & Measures ..397
GETTING AROUND 398
Air, Rail, Taxi, Car 398
Motoring Advice 399
WHERE TO STAY............399
ATTRACTIONS 400
SHOPPING 401
Clothing Size Chart......401
LANGUAGE....................401

France

Getting Acquainted 402
Paris Airports 402
The Channel Tunnel 403
Useful Addresses 404
Getting Around 405
Motoring Advice 405
Paris: Transport 406
Emergency Numbers ..407

Belgium

Getting Acquainted 408
Getting There 408
Tourist Information 409
Getting Around 409
Emergency Numbers ..409
Brussels: Transport......411
Brussels: Shopping......411

The Netherlands

Getting Acquainted 412

Getting There 412
Emergency Numbers ..412
Getting Around 413
Tourist Information 413
Amsterdam: Transport 415
Coach Tours 416

Germany

Getting Acquainted 417
Getting There 417
Emergency Numbers ..417
Getting Around 418
Tourist Information 418
Berlin: Transport..........420
Berlin: City Tours 421

Switzerland

Getting Acquainted 422
Getting There 422
Emergency Numbers ..423
Getting Around 424
Motoring Advice 424
Where to Stay..............425

Austria

Getting Acquainted 425
Getting There 425
Emergency Numbers ..426
Getting Around 426
Tourist Information 427
Vienna: Shopping 428

Budapest

Getting Acquainted 428
Getting There 428
Emergency Numbers ..429
Getting Around 430
Tourist Information 430
Sightseeing 430

Warsaw & Kraków

Getting Acquainted 431
Getting There 431
Emergency Numbers ..432
Tourist Information 432
Getting Around 432

Prague

Getting Acquainted 433
Getting There 433
Emergency Numbers ..434
Getting Around 434

Italy

Getting Acquainted 436
Getting There 436
Emergency Numbers ..436
Getting Around 437
Tourist Information 437
Rome: Transport..........438
Rome: Shopping..........439

Croatia

Getting Acquainted 440
Getting There 440
Emergency Numbers ..440
Getting Around 441
Climate 441

Greece

Getting Acquainted 441
Getting There 442
Tourist Information 442
Getting Around 443
Emergency Numbers ..444
Athens: Transport........444

Spain

Getting Acquainted 446
Getting There 446
Emergency Numbers ..446
Getting Around 447
Tourist Information 447
Madrid: Transport........449
Madrid: Shopping........449

Portugal

Getting Acquainted 450
Getting There 450
Medical Services 451
Getting Around 451
Lisbon: Transport 452

Getting Acquainted

In continental terms, Europe, at 10.5 million sq km (4 million sq miles) isn't especially large; only Australia is smaller. But it is very densely populated. Including the European portion of the Commonwealth of Independent States, its population is 670 million, giving an average of 64 people per sq km (167 people per sq mile). On average, 60 percent of the population is urban, rising to 95 percent in Belgium.

Continental Europe is surrounded by water on three sides: the west, north and south. Its coastline is very irregular: the many bays, peninsulas, inlets and islands combine to create a coastal length of 80,500 km (50,000 miles), longer than Africa's coast. The Alps form the most dominant physical feature and are the source of many major rivers.

The western and southern parts of Europe – which are effectively a peninsula of the greater land mass to the east – are characterised by many mountains, valleys, plateaus, and lowlands. Glacier movements during the last ice age (which ended less than 12,000 years ago) left much poorly drained land in the north and melting glaciers formed many lakes. The glaciers deepened the valleys and sharpened the peaks of the high mountains in the south, such as the Alps and Pyrenees. While the Alps rise to Mont Blanc's 3,404 metres (15,771 ft), much of the coastal Netherlands is below sea level, the water being held back by a complex system of dikes.

Climate

It is difficult to generalise about the weather across a continent, but using the Alps as a rough dividing line helps.

North of the Alps you can count on cold, damp winters with grey skies. Summers are mild and often rainy. The maritime climate in the west has moderate temperatures all year round. The North Atlantic Drift, a continuation of the Gulf Stream, keeps coastal areas mild. In parts of northwestern Spain, for example, the winter/summer variation might be no more than 10–18°C (18–32°F). Rainfall is fairly even throughout the year. The continental climate in the east and north has extreme differences between winter and summer, with temperatures falling well below freezing in mid-winter.

South of the Alps, it is a different story. The Mediterranean region has dry, hot summers, averaging 22°C (72°F) in July. But the winters are mild and quite rainy, with January temperatures averaging 8°C (46°F).

A fourth category, the mountain climate, is to be found in the Alps themselves. It is variable, with temperatures ranging from minus 4°C (25°F) in January to 16°C (61°F) in July.

Time Zones

Almost all of Continental Europe lies in the Central European Time Zone, which is Greenwich Mean Time (GMT) plus one hour and US Eastern Standard Time (EST) minus six hours. Greece is an exception, being two hours ahead of GMT and seven hours behind EST. All countries observe Daylight Saving Time, setting their clocks one hour ahead from the last weekend in March until the last weekend in September, with the exception of the Netherlands, which adjusts its clocks on the last Sunday in April and October.

Vegetation & Crops

Much of western Europe was once covered by deciduous forest, but most of it has been felled to facilitate farming. Most trees are hardwoods such as oak and beech. A deep layer of brown forest soil remains, making the region quite fertile. Most of the commercial forests are in Scandinavia.

In the Mediterranean area, the drought-resistant vegetation is mainly scrub evergreen, cypress, olive and low bushes. When the soil is reddish, it means it has a high iron content. In most western European countries, about half the land is arable. Wheat is a major crop, along with barley, oats and potatoes. Citrus fruits, olives and grapes are grown in the Mediterranean. Dairy farming is everywhere, but especially in Denmark and the Netherlands. Sheep and goats are grazed on hilly areas.

Fauna

There is an abundance of small mammals such as rabbits, squirrels, moles and hedgehogs. In mountain regions and northern forests, there are wolves and foxes. Deer are found in most forested areas. Common sea fish include cod, haddock, herring and mackerel. Tuna and sardines are found in the Mediterranean.

Minerals

Considerable quantities of coal and iron ore made the Industrial Revolution possible. The best quality coal lies in Germany's Ruhr, in northern France and in southern Belgium. Europe is no longer a significant producer of iron ore, though deposits are still found in Lorraine in northeastern France and in European Russia.

Good quantities of bauxite are mined in southern France and Hungary, and potash is found in France, Germany and Spain. Many other minerals, such as lead, zinc and copper, are mined in limited quantities.

Planning the Trip

Two cardinal rules for travellers: travel light and dress comfortably. Don't bring things you'll only wear once or clothes you wouldn't be comfortable in for up to 24 hours (sometimes it can be a long time between stops). In summer, cotton clothes with a light jacket or sweater will suffice. In winter, sturdy waterproof shoes, a warm overcoat and several layers will keep you cosy. A collapsable umbrella or a lightweight raincoat is always a good thing to carry along, and comfortable walking shoes are very important.

Throughout Europe, dress is informal except for an occasional evening out at the opera, theatre or a fancy restaurant. Women should also remember to dress respectfully when visiting churches or cathedrals, especially in Italy where those wearing shorts or bare-backed dresses will be refused entry. You may be asked to cover bare arms as well.

What To Bring

ELECTRICITY

The electric current used throughout Europe is 220 volts, 50 cycles alternating current, with the exception of some areas, particularly the rural parts of some Mediterranean countries where 110 volts is still in use. A 220-volt appliance plugged into a 110-volt socket won't do any harm but will result in low performance. A 110-volt appliance however, plugged into a 220-volt socket, may short-circuit or burn up. Therefore, travellers from the United States, Canada and parts of Southeast Asia will need adapters for their electrical appliances. Two-pin plugs are used nearly everywhere in Europe but can vary in shape so bring a variety of adapters along, or ask for a suitable adapter from your hotel.

Entry Regulations

VISAS & PASSPORTS

Visa requirements vary between nationalities and change from time to time so it is wise to check with your embassy or travel agent about current regulations. A valid passport is required by all Europe-bound travellers, with the exception of citizens of several European countries who only require a national identity card. Citizens of Canada, the United Kingdom, the Republic of Ireland, the United States, Australia and New Zealand do not require a visa for a stay of up to three months in any of the countries featured in this book. Citizens of Malaysia and Singapore require a visa to enter Greece. Children under 16 require no passport if they are entered in the passport of an adult travelling with them. For people over 16, a separate document is required. Visitors requiring a visa should consult the relevant embassy or consulate in their homeland. Passports should be kept in a safe, handy place – not in your suitcase – as they are needed when crossing borders, checking into hotels or changing money.

Customs

Precise customs formalities vary from country to country but as a general rule, non-European travellers coming to the countries in this book may import the following items duty-free:

All articles intended for personal use (clothing, luggage, toilet articles, photographic equipment and amateur cine cameras with film, camping and sports equipment, personal jewellery etc.) on the condition that they are re-exported and not intended for sale; food provisions required in transit; souvenirs, gifts and personal purchases whose total value does not exceed the limitations of the individual countries; 400 cigarettes or 200 small cigars (cigarillos) or 100 cigars or 500 grams of tobacco or proportionally equivalent mixed amounts. Residents of European countries and non-residents who have stopped over for more than 24 hours in any European country are allowed half the above. All travellers are allowed one litre of spirits containing more than 22 percent alcohol or two litres of sparkling or liqueur wine or any other beverage containing less than 22 percent alcohol and two litres of still or other wine; 50 grams of perfume; 0.25 litres of toilet water; 500–250 grams of coffee (depending on country) or 200–100 grams coffee extracts; 100 grams tea or 400 grams tea extracts.

Tobacco and alcoholic beverages are duty-free only for those over 17, and coffee only for those over 15.

Customs barriers do not exist between European Union members (see page 55 for list of members).

Pets

Dogs and cats brought into Europe will require a veterinary Certificate of Health in the language of the respective countries of entry, certified by an official translation agency or by the Embassy or Consular Office.

Health

Vaccinations

Inoculation certificates are only required of passengers coming from certain officially declared infected areas (normally selected African countries), or those who have been in these areas for over five days.

Within Europe, vaccinations are not normally necessary. North of the Alps is almost always free from diseases requiring vaccination, but southern Europe has had occasional instances of cholera, typhoid and hepatitis. If you want vaccinations against any of these, you need to arrange it with your doctor at least eight weeks before departure. If you have recently been to an area affected by yellow fever, you will need to acquire a vaccination certificate before you arrive in Continental Europe.

Food and Drink
Generally speaking, drinking and eating in the northern European countries is quite safe. In the Mediterranean countries however, some precaution is necessary. When in doubt, drink bottled water or tea and be careful to wash your hands whenever possible before handling food.

Hospital Treatment
Medical fees are high throughout Europe although you can get free emergency treatment in some countries (the Netherlands, for example). Nationals of the United Kingdom can receive free or partially free medical care through the reciprocal scheme of the European Union (EU), and must obtain form No. E111 from the Department of Social Security well before departure.

Emergencies
In emergencies, if you require an English-speaking doctor, dentist or pharmacist, a list is supplied by the American or British consulates and, sometimes, the local tourist office. At night, on Sunday or holidays, your hotel receptionist or the police can obtain this information for you. In several of the countries listed in this guide, pharmacies operate on a rota system for Sunday and night duty. They display signs indicating the location of the nearest open shop.

All countries maintain 24-hour emergency numbers for the police, fire brigade and ambulance services which can be found in phone directories and booths. These and other useful telephone numbers are listed in the individual entries for each country.

Travel Insurance
Taking out a comprehensive travel insurance policy to cover yourself and your property for the entire time you are away from home is strongly recommended. Such policies can include medical costs, loss or damage to baggage or property – including traveller's cheques and money – personal accident, third party liability and cancellation and curtailment fees which can result in substantial additional costs should you alter your plans. Make sure you have the kind of policy that provides you with instant money to get replacement clothing, luggage or camera, without having to wait months for a reimbursement.

Lost Property

If you lose your passport or have it stolen, report it to the police and then to the nearest embassy or consulate. They will issue you with a new passport or some emergency papers for immigration purposes. They will usually take a week or two to come through and will probably only have limited validity (extendable when you get home). Make sure you have your document number or better still, a photocopy of it (kept in a separate place) and extra passport photos as this will speed up the process considerably.

Currency

Customs
The countries mentioned in this book do not have a strict restriction on the amount of foreign currency brought in or out of the country. In some countries however, it is advisable to declare large amounts of incoming currency at customs if the same amount is to be exported. In the Euro zone unlimited amounts of local currency can be brought in and out; in the remaining countries there are certain limitations on import and export. (See individual chapters for specifics.) As all of this information is subject to alteration,

it is a good idea to check with your travel agent or bank before you depart.

Traveller's Cheques
Traveller's cheques are one of the easiest ways of carrying money while travelling and they have the added advantage of being fairly quickly reimbursed if lost or stolen. You are responsible for any cheques fraudulently cashed between the time of loss or theft and the time of notification, so it is important that such occurrences be reported immediately to the issuing office or to a representative agent abroad. Keep a record of the serial numbers separate from the cheques themselves and cross off each one as you use it. Fastidious record-keeping will expedite your reimbursement. In terms of easy cashing and refundability, American Express US$ traveller's cheques are your best bet; other currencies you could consider buying traveller's cheques in are British Sterling, Euros or Swiss Francs, all of which are usually easily negotiable for cash throughout Europe. Australian Dollar traveller's cheques are not easily convertible in Europe.

Credit Cards
Credit cards are generally cashable at all banks and accepted in most hotels and business establishments.

Changing Money
Since January 2002, the Euro zone includes the following European Union countries: Austria, Belgium, Finland, France, Germany, Greece, Ireland, Italy, Luxembourg, Netherlands, Portugal and Spain. This makes life easier for the European traveller, as the only currency you need for travelling through all these countries is the Euro. The only EU member states not participating are Denmark, Sweden and the UK. One Euro is roughly equivalent to a US dollar.

Throughout Europe, foreign currency and traveller's cheques can be exchanged at banks and exchange agencies during normal working hours. Outside these hours, and sometimes round the clock, currency can be exchanged at most major train stations, airports, seaports and frontier crossings. Currency can also be exchanged on board international trains and in some post offices with foreign currency departments. Money can be changed at major hotels (four- and five-star), travel agencies and some stores, usually at a much less favourable rate. When entering or leaving the Euro zone, try to use up coins before reaching the frontier, as they are often not exchangeable.

Public Holidays

Public holidays in Europe vary from country to country, within countries, from region to region and village to village. No list of public holidays could ever be complete, but below is a skeletal calendar of holidays celebrated by most of the countries listed in this book:

New Year's Day: 1 January
Easter Monday
Labour Day: 1 May
Ascension Day
Whit Monday
Assumption Day: 15 August
All Saint's Day: 1 November
Christmas Day: 25 December
St Stephen's Day: 26 December

Siesta: Because of the heat, most Mediterranean countries (Italy, Spain, Greece and the south of France) observe a siesta, which means that offices and shops are generally shut between 1 and 4pm. This is a firmly entrenched custom in this region regardless of the temperature, although sometimes the afternoon siesta is shorter in the winter months. Most shops and offices stay open until 7 or 8pm. Public transport runs fitfully, and some bars, tobacco shops and pharmacies operate through the siesta hours, although in low gear. Doctors and dentists normally honour the siesta, but emergency services still function. Please refer to each specific country for further details.

Getting There

BY AIR

Most visitors travel to Europe by air, either via London or direct to one of the continent's major international gateways, which include Amsterdam, Brussels, Frankfurt, Luxembourg, Paris, Rome and Zurich. Continental Europe has air links worldwide and is served by a wide choice of international carriers which run scheduled and charter flights.

If you fly from London, Heathrow and Gatwick airports provide daily connections to all major continental cities. Gatwick now has scheduled flights from more US cities than any other European airport, and receives charter flights.

The major international airport in most European countries is located in the capital city. Exceptions to this rule include Germany, where the main gateway is Frankfurt, and Switzerland, where travellers generally fly to Zurich or Geneva.

BY RAIL

Continental Europe can be reached from the Far East by the Trans-Siberian Railway via Moscow, with onward connections to Berlin, Paris and other cities. Trains and buses link Istanbul and the continent, travelling via Bulgaria and former Yugoslavia. Motorists can use the frontier crossings of Algeciras, Spain (from Morocco); the Channel Tunnel from London to Paris and Brussels; or the cities of Belgrade and Vienna (from points east).

BY SEA

Passenger ferry services depart from the British ports of Dover Harwich, Hull, Newhaven and Portsmouth to the Hook of Holland and Rotterdam in the Netherlands; Ostend and Zeebrugge in Belgium; Boulogne, Caen, Calais, Dieppe, Le Havre and Saint Malo in France; and Santander in Spain.

Practical Tips

Security and Crime

The usual traveller's precautions are recommended:
● Don't keep all money, credit cards or traveller's cheques in one wallet or purse; disperse them so one theft won't leave you totally penniless.
● Hold bags close and keep them fastened. Never leave them unattended.
● Have some form of identification in your wallet, because sometimes the thief will deposit your stolen wallet (minus the money, of course, but with all else intact) in a local mail box or drop it where someone might recover it. Immediately notify the local police station and your nearest consulate or embassy and see if it turns up. If you're in town long enough, check periodically at the main post office.

Weights and Measures

Continental Europe uses the metric system. Some useful conversion rates include:
1 gram (g) = 0.04 ounces (oz)
1 kilogram (kg) = 2.2 pounds (lb)
1 litre (l) = 1.76 pints (pt)
1 millimetre (mm) =
  0.39 inches (in)
1 metre (m) = 3.28 feet (ft)
1 kilometre (km) = 0.62 miles
8 kilometres = 5 miles
For a guide to comparative clothing and shoe sizes, look under *Shopping, page 401*.

Religious Services

Most tourist information offices can supply you with a list of English-speaking religious services or, for a small charge, you can get a full listing of English-language churches in Europe from The Commonwealth and Continental Church Society, 175 Tower Bridge Road, London SE1.

Tourist Information

All of the countries listed in this guide have intensive tourist information services. Their national tourist organisations, widely represented at home and overseas, provide information before you go and once you're there. The more popular destinations are usually supplemented with a city or a regional tourist office, which dispenses more detailed information about that specific area. They are the best places to obtain city and road maps, informative brochures, schedules of cultural programmes, sightseeing guides, hotel listings and weekly magazines, all of which are available in English. Addresses of these organisations are listed under individual countries later in this guide.

Embassies & Consulates

Foreign embassies and consulates are usually located in the national capitals but many foreign governments, especially those of the larger countries, maintain additional consulates or missions in other major European cities and touristic regions. These are invaluable if you lose your passport or encounter any other problems while travelling. In extreme cases, if you are without money, traveller's cheques or transport because of loss, theft or other damages, they can arrange for your passage home (usually the slowest and cheapest way) and will sometimes hold your passport as security on the loan.

Embassies and consulates are often listed in the literature distributed by the various tourist offices. When not, consult the telephone directory or refer to relevant sections in this guide.

Getting Around

Public Transport

BY AIR

Europe has such a dense network of airways interlinking all the countries in the continent that flying from country to country has long become a matter of ease and convenience. Airlines, both domestic and international, servicing these routes are innumerable. For more specific information, refer to chapters of individual countries.

BY RAIL

To move about in Europe, travellers have the choice of many types of trains – the high-speed TGV, the plush first-class TEE, the modern Intercities, Rapidos, Talgo or Corail trains. Those with more time to spare can use the regular trains that take a less direct, but usually a more picturesque route. Almost all of the major routes run night-trains.

The Eurail pass and the Eurail Youthpass, offered by the national railways of 16 western European countries (excluding Britain), are among the most economical ways of getting around in Europe, providing unlimited travel on all national railways and many private rail lines, steamers and ferry crossings. The Eurail pass entitles its holder to unlimited first-class travel within the validity period (from 15 days to 3 months). The Eurail Youthpass, available to travellers under 26 years of age, allows unlimited second-class travel for a period of one or two months. Both must be purchased before leaving

home through a travel agent or from one of the issuing offices in your country. For more information, contact offices of CIT Tours, French National Railways, German Federal Railways or Swiss Federal Railways.

BY TAXI

Taxis are abundant in the larger cities and can be hailed in the streets, booked by telephone, or obtained at taxi ranks, usually at railway stations, airports and near major hotels or shopping centres. Fares differ from place to place but in general they are significantly lower (and taxis scarcer) in the small towns. All official taxis are equipped with meters – beware of those that aren't; the taxi *pirati* in Rome, for example, charge two or three times the normal taxi rates for rides in their private cars. Supplements are charged for luggage, extra passengers and often for trips outside the city limits (the airport, for example). A tip of 10 percent or rounding up the fare is customary.

Private Transport

CAR RENTAL

You can book a car from major international car rental companies in offices all over Europe in all large towns and at airports and train stations. Most of them have one-way rental policies – rent it here, leave it there. If you want to rent a car for just a day or two, the cheapest deals are offered by the smaller local car rental firms, which advertise in local papers or can be found in the telephone directory (under *Autonoleggio* in Italy, *Location des Voitures* in France, and *Autovermietung* in Germany). The local tourist office can also supply the addresses of car rental firms. If you fly to Europe and want to hire a car at the other end, ask a travel agent about inclusive Fly-Drive offers, where the price of the air ticket includes free car hire, usually for one week.

Live it up!

Ride through the past in a trishaw and be welcomed into the future by lions.

For the time of your life, live it up in Singapore!
Explore historic back lanes and shop in malls of the future. Take part in a traditional tea ceremony at a quaint Peranakan house, then tee off for a birdie at one of our challenging golf courses.

Spice things up with some hot Pepper Crab and unwind in a world-class spa. Join a Feng Shui Tour to harness positive energy and later channel it into a night on the town. Come to Singapore and catch the buzz and excitement of Asia's most vibrant city.

Singapore

NEW ASIA

www.newasia-singapore.com

Holiday villas beyond indulgence.

BALEARICS ~ CARIBBEAN ~ FRANCE ~ GREECE ~ ITALY ~ MAURITIUS
MOROCCO ~ PORTUGAL ~ SCOTLAND ~ SPAIN

If you enjoy the really good things in life, we offer the highest quality holiday villas with the utmost privacy, style and true luxury. You'll find each with maid service and most have swimming pools.

For 18 years, we've gone to great lengths to select the very best villas at all of our locations around the world.

Contact us for a brochure on the destination of your choice and experience what most only dream of.

INTERNATIONAL
CHAPTERS

Toll Free: 1 866 493 8340
International Chapters, 47-51 St. John's Wood High Street, London NW8 7NJ. Telephone: +44(0)20 7722 0722
email: info@villa-rentals.com www.villa-rentals.com

MOTORWAYS

The whole of Continental Europe is intricately laced with an extensive network of main and secondary roads. European "E" Routes, easily distinguishable by the "E" preceding the road number, make up the motorway system and provide links between all major cities and some of the lesser known towns en route. Major motorways are lined with rest stops open 24 hours a day, providing maps, information and necessary facilities, as well as intermittent emergency telephones for breakdown services. Most countries have motorway tolls: Germany and Belgium are notable exceptions.

MOTORING ADVICE

No customs documents are required for the temporary import of a motor vehicle for personal use. Foreign driving licences and car registration papers issued abroad are recognised in many countries, although the motorist planning extensive travel in Europe should get an international driving licence. This can be done by applying to your local motoring organisation. Third party insurance is mandatory throughout Europe. Motorists who don't have this insurance will be obliged to take out a temporary policy at the border of each country entered. (This does not apply to rented cars.) International signs and symbols mark all roads and motorways, and traffic regulations are fairly standardized.

Driving while under the influence of alcohol carries stiff penalties in Europe and motorists with a blood-alcohol content of 0.8 percent or more are considered intoxicated. In some countries, *any* use of alcohol before or while driving is illegal and punishable by a fine.

Each country has at least one motoring club which usually operates breakdown services and which should be contacted for further information.

Rules of the Road

● Drive on the right, pass on the left (passing on the right is strictly forbidden).
● The wearing of safety belts by the driver and the front-seat passenger is compulsory as is the use of crash helmets by both the driver and the passenger on a motorcycle.
● Children under 12 years can sit in the front seat only if no other seats are available.
● As a rough guide, speed limits in built-up areas are 50–60 kph (31–37 mph) or as posted. On motorways they are 100–130 kph (62–80 mph) and 40–70 kph (25–43 mph) on dual carriageways (divided highways) – with the exception of Germany where there is no maximum speed limit on some *Autobahnen* (motorways) and very disciplined driving is therefore essential. Speed limits on all other roads are 80–100 kph (49–62 mph).

Where to Stay

Accommodation

Reservations

If your itinerary is more or less concrete, it's a good idea to reserve accommodation in advance, especially when travelling in the peak season (June–September). This can be done through a travel agent or, if you're flying, through the airline's hotel reservations department. The various national tourist offices can book your lodgings or provide you with a listing from which you can book directly. When writing to these offices for information, specify the region you plan to visit. Don't forget to enclose an International Reply Coupon, available at most post offices.

Although a bit inflexible (deposits can be forfeited or compensation demanded if reservations are cancelled), advance bookings save time and energy and prevent chaos when you first arrive at your destination. For the traveller without advance reservations, it's wise to check if there is any coming major event which could make accommodation hard to find. Local tourist information offices in major train stations and airports usually have hotel reservation services which, for a small fee, can book you a room on the spot.

Youth Hostels

These are widespread in Europe and provide one of the cheapest ways of keeping a roof over your head while travelling. You usually require a valid membership card which can be purchased at home before departure or on the spot. In most instances, addresses of youth hostels can also be acquired from the local tourist offices.

Attractions

Architecture

Europe has the world's richest variety of architectural styles, reflecting the cross-fertilisation of its many cultures.

GREEK & ROMAN

Greek architecture is characterised by the arrangement of posts and lintels, straight lines, fluted columns and pointed porticos. The difference between Ionic, Doric and Corinthian styles depends on the width of the columns in relation to their height and the shape and decoration of their capitals. One of the best-known examples of the Doric style is the Parthenon in Athens. The Erechtheum, also on the Acropolis, is Ionic. The Olympieum at Athens is Corinthian.

The arched vault is typical of Roman architecture. Out of this were developed cupolas and rotundas (rounded or elliptical structures). A fine example is the Parthenon, built by Hadrian between AD 120 and 124, and a Christian church in Rome known as Santa Maria Rotunda.

BYZANTINE

This style, which lasted from the 3rd to the 15th centuries, takes its name from the ancient Greek city of Byzantium, which later became Constantinople and is today Istanbul. Characteristic of the style are the pedentives (spherical triangles formed by intersecting arches) supporting a large dome. A good example is St Mark's in Venice.

ROMANESQUE

This style developed in central and western Europe after the Roman empire fell in AD 467. Romanesque buildings have a central area, aisles or galleries at the sides and a raised platform or an apse. Walls are heavy, doors and windows usually small and round-arched, and columns are short and stumpy. In place of columns, square or clustered piers are sometimes used to separate the nave from the aisles. Good examples are Pisa Cathedral in Italy and the Church of the Apostles in Cologne, Germany.

GOTHIC

This slender and more energetic style of building, reflecting the spiritual power of the Catholic Church, began around 1150. The pointed arch is one characteristic feature; the style is also marked by large arched windows made of coloured glass and usually depicting biblical scenes. The overall impression is of verticality and lightness. The Cathedral at Chartres is a splendid example of Gothic architecture at its best. Other examples are Notre Dame in Paris, Cologne Cathedral and the cathedral in Brussels.

RENAISSANCE

The basic idea of the Renaissance was a revival of the Roman standards combined with new materials and technologies. Florence was its birthplace and Filippo Brunelleschi, a metal worker by trade, was its initiator. If the aim during the Gothic period had been to strive towards heaven, the architects of the Renaissance strove to combine weight with elegance. Many of today's most famous buildings come from this period: the church of San Giorgio Maggiore in Venice, the Escorial in Madrid and the Ecole Militaire in Paris.

BAROQUE

An extension of the late Renaissance style, Baroque dominated during the 17th and 18th centuries. Starting in Rome, it travelled through Europe and adapted itself to different countries, reflecting not only their different climates, materials and technical know-how but also the gradual emancipation of various royal houses stemming from the Church. Baroque architecture, emphasising both richness and splendour, can also be seen as an indicator of the wealth and power of the aristocracy. Famous examples include Rome's Trevi Fountain, the Louvre in Paris, the palace and extensive gardens at Versailles, France and the Karlskirche in Vienna.

ROCOCO

This is a more playful and more florid variant of Baroque, and not to everyone's taste. This flamboyant style was prevalent in the late 18th century.

EMPIRE

Empire loosely describes the monumental, neo-classical style which arose in France from Napoleon's desire to recreate the grandeur and luxury of imperial Rome. The Chamber of Deputies in Paris exemplifies the style, which was exported to the United States in buildings such as Washington's Supreme Court.

ART NOUVEAU

Known as *Jugendstil* in Germany, *Sezessionist* in Austria and *Stile Liberte* in Italy, this was a short-lived and more decorative variant of the neo-classical style at the end of the 19th century. It decorates with a variety of motifs, exterior and interior, buildings that otherwise impress by solidity rather than sense of proportion.

Shopping

receive a refund, amounting to as much as 25 percent of the purchase price, either upon leaving the country or by mail at your home address.

Tax-free shopping at airports and aboard ships, available to those leaving the country or in transit, takes on a different form: the VAT is excluded from the purchase price, eliminating the need for refunds.

Prices

In the majority of European countries, fixed prices are normal. You should bargain only at stalls in flea markets and bazaars.

Tax Free Shopping

Many of the larger shops and department stores in Europe display the "tax-free" sign, which means that travellers from non-European Union (non-EU) countries can receive a refund of the Value Added Tax or sales tax (VAT) levied on the more substantial purchases intended for export outside the EU. By filling out a tax form available at the place of purchase, you can

Language

Language

In southern Europe, the *Romance* group of languages predominates, being found in France, southern Belgium, Spain, Portugal and Italy.

The *Germanic* group of languages predominates in Germany, Austria, Switzerland, the Netherlands and northern Belgium.

Slavic languages such as Russian, Czech, Slovak, Polish and Bulgarian dominate in eastern Europe.

Greece has a Hellenic language. Some old languages linger on among small groups; Bretons in northwestern France speak a variety of Celtic; Basque and Catalan are spoken on the Spanish-French border.

In France, three separate regional languages are spoken: Breton in Brittany, Basque in the southwest, and Catalan in Roussillon (Eastern Pyrenees). A form of German is also spoken in Alsace. The first foreign language taught in schools is English, but few people speak it outside of the tourist centres. As with much of Europe, even rudimentary attempts at the language will often break the ice for a continued conversation in English.

Clothing Chart

Women's Dresses/Suits

Continental	American	British
38/34N	6	8/30
40/36N	8	10/32
42/38N	10	12/34
44/40N	12	14/36
46/42N	14	16/38
48/44N	16	18/40

Women's Shoes

Continental	American	British
36	4½	3
37	5½	4
38	6½	5
39	7½	6
40	8½	7
41	9½	8
42	10½	9

Men's Suits

Continental	American	British
44	34	34
46	—	36
48	38	38

Continental	American	British
50	—	40
52	42	42
54	—	44
56	46	46

Men's Shirts

Continental	American	British
36	14	14
37	14½	14½
38	15	15
39	15½	15½
40	16	16
41	16½	16½
42	17	17

Men's Shoes

Continental	American	British
—	6½	6
40	7½	7
41	8½	8
42	9½	9
43	10½	10
44	11½	11

FRANCE

Area 543,965 sq km (210,026 sq miles).

Population Around 59 million.

Language Everyone in France speaks French, but regional languages still exist in Brittany (Breton), Alsace (Alsatian), the western Pyrénées (Basque) and the eastern Pyrénées (Catalan).

Time Zone For most of the year, France is one hour ahead of Greenwich Mean Time. When it is noon in France, it is 6am in New York.

Note that France uses the 24-hour clock.

Currency the Euro.

Electricity Generally 220/230 volts, but still 110 in a few areas. Visitors from the US will need a transformer for shavers, hairdryers and other equipment; visitors from the UK just need an adapter plug.

Weights & Measures France is metric for all weights and measures, although old-fashioned terms such as *livre* (about 1lb or 500g) are still used by many shopkeepers. For quick and easy conversion: 2.5cm is about 1 inch, 1 metre is about a yard, 100g is just over 4oz and 1kg is just over 2lb. A kilometre is five-eighths of a mile, so 80 km is 50 miles and 80 kpm is 50 mph.

Direct Dialling Dialling from the UK: 00 (international code) + 33 (France) + a ten-figure number that includes the area code.

Public Holidays: In addition to those holidays mentioned in the Introduction, France recognises Bastille Day (14 July) and Armistice Day (11 November).

Getting There

BY AIR

Several airlines operate to France from the UK, and deregulation means the choice is constantly changing.

Air France is the main carrier, with flights to Lyon, Toulouse, Paris, Nice and Strasbourg. **British Airways** flies from various destinations in the UK to Marseilles, Bordeaux, Toulouse, Nice, Lyons and Montpellier. **British Midland** also flies to Paris and Nice. **Ryanair** flies to Carcassonne and St-Etienne, and **Easyjet** to Nice.

Travellers from North America and elsewhere can get direct flights to Paris and major destinations, such as Nice and Lyon, via Air France and most national airlines. American Airlines, United Airlines, TWA and Delta also fly to France.

Internal flights are operated by Air France, Air Littoral, Air Liberté and AOM.

Paris Airports

Paris has two airports:
● **Roissy–Charles de Gaulle**, 23 km (15 miles) north of the city via the A1 or RN2, tel: 01 48 62 12 12.
● **Orly**, 14 km (9 miles) south of the centre via the A6 or RN7, tel: 01 49 75 15 15.

See *Getting Around* for information on travelling to and from (and between) the airports.

Rail Packages

Air France operates a rail package with flights available from 15 airports around the UK and Ireland (not Heathrow) to Paris, then onward by train to one of 3,000 stations. These inclusive tickets can also be combined with a 15-day France Vacances rail pass. Air France also has offices abroad offering advice and information on holidays in France.

Students

Students and young people can normally obtain discounted charter fares through specialist travel agencies in their own countries. In the UK, try: **Campus Travel**, 52 Grosvenor Gardens, London SW1W 0AG, tel: 020-7730 3402 for your nearest branch. Campus is part of the international group USIT, whose main US address is the New York Student Centre, 895 Amsterdam Avenue, New York, NY 10025, tel: 212-663 5435.

Useful numbers
In the UK
Air France
Tel: 020-8742 6600
Air UK.
Tel: 08705-074074
British Airways
Tel: 0345-222111
British Midland
Tel: 0345-554554
Easyjet
Tel: 08705-292929
Ryanair
Tel: 020-7435 7101
In France
Air France
Tel: 01 41 56 78 00
Air Littoral.
Tel: 04 67 20 67 20
Air Liberté
Tel: 01 49 79 23 00
AOM
Tel: 01 49 79 10 00
In the US & Canada
Air France New York.
Tel: 212-838 7800
Air France Los Angeles.
Tel: 310-271 66 65
Air France Montréal.
Tel: 514-288 42 64

BY SEA

There are several ferry services operating from the UK, the Republic of Ireland and the Channel Islands to the northern ports of France. All of them carry cars as well as foot passengers. The shortest crossing is between Dover and Calais, but cross-Channel services have been greatly undermined since the advent of much quicker Eurostar passenger trains and Eurotunnel vehicle trains, and competitively priced no-frills air carriers.

The Channel Tunnel

The Channel Tunnel offers fast, frequent rail services between Britain and France.

The **Eurostar** service offers high speed connections between London (Waterloo) or Ashford and Lille (2 hours) or Paris (Gare du Nord – 3 hours). Eurostar also operates high speed trains direct from London and Ashford to Disneyland Paris.

For Eurostar passenger services, tel: 08705-186186.

Le Shuttle is the name of the train service that takes cars and their passengers from Folkestone to Calais on a simple drive-on-drive-off system. The journey time through the tunnel is about 25 minutes. Reservations are not needed – you just turn up and take the next service, but during holiday periods there can be a long wait. The price of tickets varies, with travel at peak hours considerably more expensive than nighttime crossings. Le Shuttle runs 24 hours a day, all year round, with a service at least once an hour through the night.

For Eurotunnel car services, tel: 08705-353535.

BY RAIL

France has a fast, efficient rail network operated by the SNCF (Société Nationale des Chemins de Fer de France). Its much praised TGV programme offers comfortable express services via Paris and Lille to many destinations. For visitors travelling from Paris, the train is a comfortable way to reach any major destination in France, with most express services offering refreshments (and even play areas for young children). There are five main stations serving the provinces from Paris, so check which one you need before setting out. Car and bicycle hire is available at most main stations – as a package with your rail ticket if you prefer (details from French Railways).

Tickets and Information

Tickets may be booked for through journeys from outside France.

In the UK, tickets (including ferry travel) can be booked from most National Rail stations. Larger National Rail travel centres can supply details of continental services. Alternatively, contact Rail Europe/French Travel Service. As well as rail tickets, they can arrange ferry bookings, discounted tickets for young people or a *Carte Vermeil* for senior citizens, which gives a generous discount on tickets and Eurodomino rail passes (*see Rail Passes*). Lines are open Monday to Friday from 8am–8pm and Saturdays from 9am–4pm, tel: 08705 848 848. Be warned that these lines are usually very busy and a little patience is required.

SNCF has a central reservation office in Paris, tel: 08 36 35 35 35 (national info.) or 01 53 90 20 20 (Paris info).

Most French railway stations accept Visa and American Express.

Rail Passes

There are several rail passes available to foreign visitors. These must be purchased before leaving for France.

In the UK, a Eurodomino Pass offers unlimited rail travel in France on any 3, 5, or 10 days within a month. This can also be bought in conjunction with an Air France Rail Ticket (*see By Air*).

In the US, visitors have a wider choice of passes, including Eurailpass, Flexipass and Saver Pass. Call 212-308 3103 (for information) and 800 223 636 (for reservations). The France Rail 'n' Drive pass offers a flexible rail and car-rental package,

Similar passes are available in other countries, but the names of the tickets and conditions may vary.

Motorail

Motorail takes much of the strain out of driving long distances to your holiday destination while allowing you the freedom of being able to drive your own car once you've arrived.

Some services operate during the summer only from the channel ports e.g. Boulogne to Biarritz, Brive, Bordeaux, Toulouse, Narbonne; Calais to Nice; Dieppe to Avignon and Fréjus. Also useful for ferry users are the routes from Lille to Avignon, Brive and Narbonne. There are over 30 motorail routes out of Paris, some of which depart daily all year round. Tickets can be booked to include cross-channel ferries. In the UK, tel: 08702 415 415. Note that tickets cannot be reserved more than 3 months in advance.

BY BUS

Eurolines is a consortium of almost 30 coach companies, operating in France and throughout Europe. They operate services from London (Victoria) to many major French destinations. Some (such as Paris) are daily, others are seasonal and some have services several times a week throughout the year.

This is one of the cheapest ways of reaching France, and there are discounts available for young people and senior citizens. The ticket includes the ferry crossing (via Dover). National Express coaches have connections from most major towns in the UK that link up with the London departures.

For details contact Eurolines UK, 52 Grosvenor Gardens, Victoria, London SW1W 0AU, tel: 01582-404511; or in France at 28, Avenue du Général de Gaulle, 93541 Bagnolet, tel: 01 49 72 51 51.

BY CAR

Almost all the motorways in France are privately owned and subject to tolls (credit cards are usually acceptable). The trip from the northern ports to the south of France costs around £50 (US$84) in tolls one-way. The benefits of paying for the use of the motorway can be seen in the high standards of maintenance of the roads and the frequent rest areas, picnic sites and catering facilities.

Free motorway maps are often available at motorway service stations/cafeterias and are useful as they mark the position and facilities of all the rest areas on the route.

If speed is not of the essence and you intend to make the drive part of your holiday, follow the green holiday route signs (*bis*) to your destination – these form part of a national network of *bison futé* routes to avoid traffic congestion at peak periods. You will discover parts of France you never knew existed and are more likely to arrive relaxed. The first and last (*rentrée*) weekend in August and the public holiday on 15 August are usually the worst times to travel, so avoid them if you can. (For further details about driving in France, see *Getting Around.*)

Useful Addresses

United Kingdom and Ireland
Air France
● *UK*: 10 Warwick St, London W1R 5RA, tel: 020-8742 6600 (reservations).
● *Ireland*: 29–30 Dawson Street, Dublin 2, tel: 77 8272, or 77 8899 (for reservations).

French Government Tourist Office
178 Piccadilly, London W1V 0AL; tel: 0891-244 123, fax: 020-7493 6594; E-mail: piccadilly@mdlf.demon.co.uk Web site: http://www.franceguide.com

French Consulate
● *London*: 21 Cromwell Road, London SW7 2EN, tel: 020-7838 2000, fax: 020-7838 2001. *Visa section*: 6a Cromwell Place, London SW7 2EN, tel: 0891-887733.
● *Edinburgh*: 11 Randolph Crescent, Edinburgh EH3 7TT, tel: 0131-225 7954, fax: 0131-225 8975.

French Embassy
Commercial Department: 21–24 Grosvenor Place, London SW1X 7HU, tel: 020-7235 7080, fax: 020-235 8598.

Cultural department: 23 Cromwell Road, London SW7 2EL, tel: 020 7838 2055, fax: 020-7838 2088.

Monaco Government Tourist and Convention Office
3–18 Chelsea Garden Market, Chelsea Harbour, London SW10 0XE, tel: 020-7352 9962, fax: 020-7352 2103.

US and Canada
Air France
● *New York*: 666 Fifth Avenue, NY 10019, tel: 212-315 1122 (toll-free reservations tel: 800 237 2747).
● *Los Angeles*: 8501 Wilshire Boulevard, Beverly Hills, CA 90211, tel: 213-688 9220.
● *Montreal*: 979 Ouest Boulevard de Maisonneuve, Québec H3A 1M4, tel: 514-284 2825.
● *Toronto*: 151 Bloor Street West, Suite 600, Ontario M5S 1S4, tel: 416-922 3344.

French Government Tourist Office
● *New York*: 444 Madison Ave, NY 10022, tel: 212-838 7800, fax: 212-838 7855.
● *Chicago*: 676 North Michigan Avenue, Suite 3360, Chicago IL 0611-2819, tel: 312-751 7500, fax: 312-337 6339.
● *Texas*: Cedar Maple Plaza, 2305 Cedar Springs Road, Suite 205, Dallas, Texas 75201, tel: 214-720 4010, fax: 214-702 0250.
● *Montreal*: 1981 Avenue McGill Collège, Tour Esso, Suite 490, Montreal PQ, H3A 2W9, tel: 514-288 4264, fax: 514-845 4868.
● *Toronto*: 30 St Patrick Street, Suite 700, M5T 3A3 Ontario, tel: 416-593 4723.

France
Air France
119 Champs Elysées, 75384 Cedex 08, tel: 01 44 08 24 24; Central Reservations: tel: 01 44 08 22 22.

Maison de la France (French Government Tourist Office)
8 Avenue de l'Opéra, 75001 Paris, tel: 01 42 96 10 23, fax: 01 42 60 75 12.

Business Hours

Ordinary shops open around 9am and close at 7pm, but food shops normally open at 7.30 or 8am and don't close until 7.30 or 8pm. They close for lunch at about 1pm and reopen at about 3.30 or 4pm. Large department stores, supermarkets and hypermarkets stay open until 9 or 10pm for at least one night a week. Some shops close on Monday, others don't close at midday and those in major towns are also open on Sunday mornings.

Office Nationale des Forêts (Forestry Commission)
217 Rue Grande, 77300 Fontainebleau, tel: 01 60 74 92 10.

Practical Tips

Emergency Medical Services
Pharmacies (recognisable by the green cross) are open six days a week from 9am–noon and 2–7pm. Sunday and evening rotas are posted in all chemists' windows. The duty chemist is also officially on call at night – you will find a bell (*sonnette de nuit*) by his door. Doctors also have night and weekend rotas. They, and chemists, are listed in local newspapers under *Pharmaciens de Garde* and *Médecins de Garde.*

Tipping
The practice of adding 12–15 percent service charge to the bill is common in restaurants, hotels and cafés all over France. In such cases, there is no obligation to leave anything additional, although most people do, either rounding up the change or leaving around 1 Euro extra, depending on the size of the bill. Tip room service almost everywhere and wine stewards if they are helpful; taxi drivers usually get 15 percent.

Postal Services

Provincial post offices – Postes or PTTS – are generally open Monday–Friday 9am–noon and 2–5pm, Saturday 9am–noon (opening hours are posted outside); in Paris and other large cities they are generally open continuously from 8am–7pm. Exceptionally, the main post office in Paris is open 24 hours every day, at 52 Rue du Louvre, 75001 Paris.

Stamps may be purchased in post offices, cafés and newsagents. Post boxes are yellow, but at large post offices there are separate boxes for inland and foreign mail. You may receive or send money through the post office.

Telephones

The French telephone system has recently been overhauled so that all telephone numbers have 10 digits. Paris and Ile de France numbers begin with 01, while the rest of France is divided into four zones (North West 02, North East 03, South East and Corsica 04 and South West 05). Freephone numbers begin with 08 00; 08 36 numbers are charged at premium rates and 06 numbers are mobile phones.

There are two kinds of phone boxes in Paris from which you can make local and international calls: coin-operated phones, which are extremely difficult to find, and card-operated phones, which are replacing them. It may be difficult to find a telephone box that is working. Remember that you get 50 percent more call-time for your money if you ring 10.30pm–8am on weekdays and from 2pm at weekends.

A télécarte can be bought from kiosks, tabacs and post offices. Insert the card and follow the instructions on the screen: you can also dial from all post offices, which have both coin- and card-operated phones. To call long distance ask at one of the counters and you will be assigned a booth – you pay when your call is over. Cafés and tabacs often have public phones next to the toilets. They use coins or jetons, coin-like discs bought at the bar.

To call other countries from France, first dial the international access code (00), then the country code: Australia 61, UK 44, US and Canada 1. If using a US credit phone card, call the company's access number: Sprint, tel: 19 00 87; AT&T, tel: 19 00 11; MCI, tel: 19 00 19.

Useful numbers: operator services 13; directory enquiries 12.

Telegrams (cables) can be sent during post office hours or by telephone (24-hours); to send a telegram in English dial 05 33 4411; to send a telegram in French, tel: 3655.

Getting Around

By Air

Air France, with its associate company Air Inter, operates an intensive network of routes within France. Many fly from Paris but there are also cross-country air links such as between Nice and Toulouse, Lille and Bordeaux, and Lyons and Biarritz. A number of smaller airlines also offer good services to smaller locations.

By Rail

France has an excellent rail network operated by the SNCF (Société des Chemins de Fer Français), which runs trains to all parts of France and is linked to the European network. Trains have first- and second-class seats and supplements are only charged on the TVG or High Speed Train service during peak times and on the TEE, which is first-class only. Any rail ticket bought in France must be validated by using the orange automatic date-stamping machine at the entrance to the platform. Failure to do so incurs a surcharge. Carriages with "double decker" sections are for travellers who opt for scenic viewing . SNCF has a central reservation office in Paris, tel: (01) 45 65 60 60 and a telephone information service in English on: (01) 45 82 08 41; in French on: (01) 45 82 50 50. The SNCF office in Paris is at 10 Place de Budapest, 75436 Paris Cedex 09, tel: (01) 42 85 60 00, fax: (01) 42 85 63 78. Most railway stations accept payment by Visa and American Express.

By Road

France has a total road network of about 1.5 million km (930,000 miles), including over 4,828 km (3,000 miles) of motorway. Apart from the first few miles leading out of large cities, all motorways carry tolls. Be aware that French roads are usually very crowded in summer, in particular those that connect Paris to the Mediterranean and Atlantic coasts.

Information: For current road conditions, tel: (01) 48 94 33 33, for routes around France contact the Autoroute Information (Centre de Renseignements Autoroutes), tel: (01) 47 53 37 00.

Parking: This is increasingly difficult in towns; to park your car in zones bleues, special discs have to be displayed. They're obtainable free from tourist offices, tobacco kiosks, police stations, customs offices, garages and hotels.

Emergencies: On motorways, there are orange emergency telephones every 2.4 km (1½ miles).

Motoring Clubs: The Automobile Club National is the umbrella organisation of France's 40-odd motoring clubs. It will assist any motorist whose own club has an agreement with it. Contact it at 9 Rue Anatole-de-la-Forge, 75017 Paris, tel: 01-43 80 94 63, fax: 01-40 54 00 15.

Motoring Advice

- All cars must carry a red warning triangle and spare bulbs for headlights.
- After dark, motorists have the choice of using dipped headlights or parking lights, even in rainy weather.
- In some areas, horns may be sounded only in dire need.

Public Transport

Details of routes and timetables are generally available free of charge either from bus stations (*gare routière*), which are often situated close to rail stations, or from tourist offices. They will also give details of coach tours and sightseeing excursions which are widely available.

Waterways

Car ferries to Corsica, run in connection with SNCF rail services, sail from Marseille, Toulon and Nice. Cruises also operate on the Marne, the Canal du Midi and its extensions, and the canals of Brittany, Burgundy and the Camargue. One of the most pleasant ways of exploring a small corner of France is on board a narrowboat, or one of the other craft that can be hired on many of the country's navigable canals and rivers. Holidays on inland waterways range from a simple day, or half-day cruise, to piloting your own hired boat or enjoying the luxury of the so-called hotel barges, where you just sit back and relax while the navigation is all taken care of. Burgundy is particularly favoured as an internal waterway, the Canal de Bourgogne is the longest, connecting the river Yonne in the north to the Saone in the south.

Devotees of canal architecture can use the acqueduct at Briare. This masterpiece of engineering, whose foundations were laid by the engineer Eiffel's company, was built by Sully in the early 17th century and served as a prototype for all of France's later canal building.

Even if you have never navigated before, you will feel confident after minimum instruction (foreigners require no permit or licence).

Paris

Getting There

By Air
From Roissy/Charles de Gaulle Airport
Train: The quickest and most reliable way to get to central Paris, RER trains go direct from terminal 2 (Air France flights), or you can take the free shuttle bus (*navette*) from terminal 1. Trains run every 15 minutes from 5am to 11.45pm to Métro Gare du Nord or Châtelet.

The average journey time is 45 minutes.

Bus: The Roissy bus runs between the airport and Rue Scribe, near Place de l'Opéra from terminals 1 gate 30, 2A gate 10 and 2D gate 12. It runs every 15 minutes from 6am to 11pm and takes 45 minutes.

Alternatively, the Air France bus (to Métro Porte de Maillot or Charles-de-Gaulle Etoile) leaves from terminals 2A and 2B or terminal 1 arrival level gate 34. It runs every 12 minutes from 5.40am to 11pm.

Taxi: This is by far the most expensive but unquestionably the easiest solution. It can take 30 minutes to over an hour, depending on traffic. The cost appears on the meter, but a supplement is charged for each large piece of luggage, pushchair and animal.

From Orly Airport
Train: Take the shuttle from gate H at Orly Sud or arrivals gate F at Orly Ouest to the Orly train station. The RER stops at Austerlitz, Pont St-Michel and the Quai d'Orsay. It runs every 15 minutes between 5.50am–10.50pm and takes about 30 minutes to Austerlitz.

The Orlyval automatic train is a shuttle to Antony (the nearest RER to Orly). It runs every 5–8 minutes from 6.30am–9.15pm Monday to Saturday and 7am–10.55pm on Sunday, and takes 30 minutes.

Bus: The Orlybus (to Place Denfert-Rochereau) leaves from Orly Sud gate F or Orly Ouest arrivals gate D.

It runs every 10–12 minutes from 6am to 11.30pm.

Air France buses (to Invalides and Gare Montparnasse) leave from Orly Sud, gate J or Orly Ouest arrivals gate E. They run every 20 minutes from 6am to 11pm and take 30 minutes. Tickets are available from the Air France terminus.

Taxis: By taxi the journey to central Paris takes 20–40 minutes.

Between Airports
An Air France bus links Roissy/Charles de Gaulle and Orly every 20 minutes from 6am to 11pm.

By Rail
The main train stations in Paris are Gare du Nord (for British connections), Gare de l'Est, Gare d'Austerlitz, Gare Saint-Lazare and Gare de Lyon (for links with the Riviera, Spain and Italy).

Channel Tunnel
The 50-km (30-mile) Channel Tunnel enables fast, frequent rail services between London (Waterloo) and Ashford and Paris (Gare du Nord). Le Shuttle takes cars and passengers from Folkstone to Calais on a drive on, drive off service taking 25 minutes. Le Shuttle runs 24 hours a day, all year, at least once an hour. For details, tel: 08705 353535 (UK) or 03 21 00 60 00 (France).

By Sea
Ferries and Seacats from English ports are linked to the Gare du Nord by fast train from Calais or Boulogne and their fares are included in the cost of your ticket. Coach-boat-coach routes to Paris also exist from Victoria Station in London.

Practical Tips

Medical Services
Pharmacies with green crosses are helpful with minor ailments or finding a nurse if you need injections or special care. The Pharmacie Dhéry, 84 Champs-Elysée, tel: 45 62 02 41, is open 24 hours (Metro: George V). Two

Emergency Numbers

Police: 17
Ambulance: 15
Fire Brigade: 18
SOS-Help: Crisis hotline, tel: 47 23 80 80 from 3–11pm (subject to change). English spoken.

Lost credit cards:
- American Express, tel: 01 47 77 72 00
- Diners Club, tel: 01 49 06 17 50
- Carte Bleu/Visa, tel: 01 42 77 11 90.

private hospitals serve the Anglo-American community: American Hospital of Paris, 63 Bld Victor-Hugo, 92202 Neuilly, tel: 01 46 41 25 25; and the French-British Hospital of Paris, 48 Rue de Villiers, Levallois-Perret, tel: 01 46 39 22 22.
Doctor (SOS Médecins): Tel: 01 43 37 77 77 or 01 47 07 77 77.

Tourist Information

Paris's main tourist information office (Office de Tourisme de Paris/Bureau d'Accueil Central) is located at 127 Champs-Elysées, 75001 Paris (metro: George V). For information in English, tel: 08 36 68 31 12 daily 9am–8pm except Christmas Day, 1 January and 1 May. Other branches in the main train stations, airports and terminals.

For detailed information on Paris and surrounding areas, contact CRT 73–75 Rue Cambronne, 75015 Paris, tel: 01 45 67 89 41; Gare de l'Est, tel: 01 46 07 17 73; Gare du Nord, tel: 01 45 26 94 82; Gare de Lyon, tel: 01 43 43 33 24; Tour Eiffel, tel: 01 45 51 2215.

Getting Around

Orientation

Paris, capital of France, is one of the most densely populated urban centres in the world. Divided into 20 *arrondissements* (districts), greater Paris is home to 8 million people. Paris is traversed by the Seine River, dividing the city into two – the Right Bank and the Left Bank. A constant flow and interchange of citizenry from one bank to the other takes place over its 35 bridges. The larger Right Bank is home of Paris commerce and government, and is where most of the historic monuments, the great boulevards and museums can be found. The Left Bank, on the other hand, is the stronghold of the intellectual community. Although the city is now ringed by high-rise suburbs and satellite towns, its essential character has been preserved in a way few other cities have paralleled.

Public Transport

The Metro: Operates 5.30am–12.45pm; its comprehensive map and signs make it virtually impossible to get lost; the lines are identified by number and the names of their terminals. It operates in conjunction with the RER, suburban regional express trains which operate on four lines, identified as A–D. Flat fare tickets can be bought from metro stations and some tobacconists. For metro details, tel: 08 36 08 7714.

The *Paris-visite* card is valid for three or five consecutive days on the metro, bus and railway in the Paris/Île de France region. It also gives discounted entry to various tourist sites; available from main metro and SNCF stations and the airports. The *Formule 1* card allows an unlimited number of trips in any one day on the metro, bus and suburban trains and the night buses (it extends as far as Disneyland, Paris). Buy it from metro offices or the Central Tourist Office in the Champs Elysées (*see left*).
Buses: City buses, which operate 6.30am–8.30pm, are efficient and punctual. They are numbered and all stops have clear maps giving directions. Metro tickets are valid on the buses; one or at most two tickets are required depending on the zones travelled. You can also buy tickets from the driver.

Where to Stay

Accommodation

The Office de Tourisme de Paris on the Champs-Elysées and its branches can supply a list of hotel accommodation in every price range, or they can book you a room for a nominal fee.

Attractions

What's On

Consult *Pariscope* or *L'Officiel des Spectacles* for a guide to events in Paris. Both weekly guides are sold at newsstands. They list the current exhibitions in museums, art galleries and exhibition halls, as well as theatre events and current films. There are also sections on night entertainment and where to eat. The tourist office's monthly *Paris Selection* also gives a choice of what's on in town.

Sightseeing Tours

First-time visitors to Paris can acquaint themselves with the city by taking the all-city sightseeing coach tour organised by Cityrama, 4 Place des Pyramides 75001, tel: (01) 44 55 6000; or Paris Vision, 214 Rue de Rivoli 75001, tel: (01) 42 60 3125. The double-decker glass-topped buses travel the tourist route covering the major landmarks. The Paris Illuminations Tour, offered by the same companies, gives a breathtaking view of Paris by night. You can also discover Paris from the deck of a glass-roofed river boat as it glides down the Seine. Contact Bateaux Mouches, tel: (01) 40 76 9999.

Shopping

Elegant department stores such as Galeries Lafayette and Au Printemps are on the Right Bank, as are the expensive shops of the Champs-Elysées. For younger (and cheaper) fashions try the Left Bank, particularly around St Michel and St Germain boulevards.

The flea market (Marché aux Puces) opens on Saturday, Sunday and Monday (Metro: Porte de Clignancourt). For flowers and plants: Île de la Cité (Quai de la Corse), Monday–Saturday 8am–7.30pm (Metro: Cité). Other street markets are at Rue Mouffetard, and Rue Poncelet (Metros: Rue Poncelet and Rue Cler, respectively). Daily 9am–1pm and 4–7pm except Monday and Sunday morning.

Further Reading

General
France Today, by John Ardagh. London: Pelican.
Easy Living in France, by John P Harris. London: Arrow Books.
The French, by Theodore Zeldin. New York: Random House.
A Holiday History of France, by Ronald Hamilton. London: The Hogarth Press.
Pauper's Paris, by Miles Turner. London: Pan Books Ltd.

Other Insight Guides
Other books in the *Insight Guide* series highlight destinations in this region: *Insight Guides:* France, Burgundy, Corsica, Normandy, French Riviera, Provence, Loire Valley, Brittany, Alsace and Paris. The *Insight Pocket Guide* series, designed to help readers without a lot of time plan their trips precisely, include: *Pocket Guides*: Alsace, Brittany, Corsica, French Riviera, Loire Valley, Paris and Provence. Many of the Pocket Guides come with handy pullout maps. *Insight Compact Guides* cover Paris, Normandy, Brittany, Burgundy, French Riviera and Provence.

BELGIUM

Getting Acquainted

Area: 30,520 sq km (11,780 sq miles).
Situation: Belgium lies in north-west Europe. It has borders with France to the west and south, Luxembourg to the south-east and Germany to the east. The Netherlands and the North Sea mark its northern border.
Capital: Brussels.
Highest point: Botrange 694 metres (2,272 ft)
Population: 10 million.
Language: Flemish, French and German.
Religion: Roman Catholic.
Time Zone: Central European Standard Time.
Currency: the Euro.
Weights & Measures: Metric.
Electricity: AC 220 volts; it is recommended that you bring an adapter with you. Plugs are continental two-pin round.
International dialling code: 32
Public Holidays: In addition to those mentioned in the General Europe Introduction, the following holidays are recognised: Belgian National Day (21 July) and Armistice Day (11 November).

Getting There

By Air
Air Canada, British Airways and a number of other foreign airlines link Belgium with all parts of the world. The main gateway is the Brussels National Airport at Zaventem. Located only 10 km (6 miles) from the city centre, it is linked by railway to the Central (Centrale/Centraal), North (Nord/Noord) and South (Midi/Zuid) stations. The rapid rail

trains depart every 20 minutes from the airport and from Central Station 6am–11pm. Additionally, the Airport–City Express travels between the airport and the South Station three times an hour.

By Rail
The majority of destinations in Belgium can be reached easily from other parts of the continent by train, and many international lines run through Belgium. Rail/car/ferry services are available. International trains stop at the three main railway stations in Brussels: Brussels-North, Brussels-Central and Brussels-South. These stations are linked by rail and provide connections to further destinations in Belgium. For information contact: National Belgian Railways Association (NMBS), Shell Building, Ravenstein 60, Box 24, 1000 Brussels. Tel: 02-219 28 80 (Dutch), or tel: 02-219 26 40 (French).
By Channel Tunnel: The direct rail service from London to Brussels through the Channel Tunnel is operated by Eurostar (tel: 08457 881 811 in the UK). The journey time is 2 hours and 40 minutes.

By Road
Bordered by the Netherlands to the north, France to the south, and Germany and Luxembourg to the east, Belgium can be reached by a number of European "E" routes, namely: E5, which links London and Cologne, via Brussels; E10, which passes through Antwerp and Brussels from Amsterdam or Paris; and E10/E40, which runs from Antwerp through Brussels to Luxembourg.
The fastest means of getting from the UK to Belgium by car is with Le Shuttle (tel: 08705 353535), the Channel Tunnel service taking cars and their passengers from Folkestone to Calais. In summer there are up to four trains an hour.

By Sea
Jetfoil, passenger and car ferries link the Belgian ports of Ostend and

Zeebrugge year-round with various points in England. In connection with most crossings, there are direct train services to the main Belgian cities.

Practical Tips

Medical Services
Pharmacies close on Saturday afternoon and all day Sunday. However, in emergencies, consult the weekend editions of the local papers for the duty rotas of pharmacies, doctors, dentists and vets. Pharmacy rotas are also posted in pharmacy windows.

Emergency Numbers

Police: 101
Ambulance (Red Cross Service): 02-649 1122.
Accident and Fire Brigade: 100
SOS Youth: 02-512 9020.
Bruxelles Accueil (in all languages): 02-511 27 15 or 02-511 81 78.

Lost credit cards:
● American Express,
tel: 02-676 2111
● Diner's, tel: 02-206 9800
● Eurocard, MasterCard, Visa,
tel: 070-344 344

Tipping
Taxis, most restaurants, hairdressers, etc. very considerately include your tip in the bill, in the certainty that you couldn't fail to be impressed by the service. Ushers at some cinemas and theatres expect a small tip for taking your ticket, while toilet attendants will make your visit a misery if you pass their saucer without leaving a few coins.

Postal Services
Post offices are open Monday–Friday 9am–6pm (large transactions will not be handled after 5pm), Saturday 9am–noon. Smaller branches may close for lunch noon–2pm, close by 4 or 5pm and on Saturdays. Mail boxes are red. The South Station post office in Brussels is open 24 hours a day.

Telephones
Most public telephones are operated by phone cards, which are available from post offices, kiosks and newsagents. Apart from the old coin-operated phones, they can all be used for international calls.
  Telegrams can be sent by dialling 1225 or via your hotel reception.

Tourist Offices

In Belgium
Brussels Tourist and Information Office, Brussels Town Hall, Grand' Place, 1000 Brussels, tel: 02-513 8940, fax: 02-514 4538, theatre and concert booking service 0800 21221, e-mail: tourism.brussels @tib.be. Open: summer: daily 9am–6pm; winter: 10am–2pm; closed Sundays in January and February.
Belgian Tourist Office, 61 Rue du Marché-aux-Herbes, 1000 Brussels, tel: 02-504 0390, fax: 02-504 0270. Open: November to April Monday–Saturday 9am–6pm, Sunday 9am–1pm; May, June, September, October daily 9am–6pm; July and August daily 9am–7pm.
Belgian Tourist Reservations, 111/4 Boulevard Anspach, 1000 Brussels, tel: 02-513 7484, fax: 02-513 9277. Hotel reservations.

Tourist Offices Abroad
Japan: Tameike Tokyo Building, 9F 1–14, Akasaka–1–Chome, Minatoku Tokyo. Tel: 03 3586 7041; fax: 03 35 12 3524.
UK: 225 Marsh Wall, London E14 9FW, fax: (020) 7531 0393
US: 780 Third Avenue, Suite 1501, New York, NY 10017. Tel: (0212) 7588130; fax: (0212) 3557675.

Consulates & Embassies
Australia: Guimard Center, Rue Guimard/Guimardstraat 6–8, tel: 02-231 0500.
Canada: Avenue de Tervuren/Tervu-renlaan, tel: 02-741 0611.
Ireland: Rue Froissart/ Froissartstraat 189, tel: 02-230 5337.
UK: Rue d'Arlon/Aarlenstraat 85, tel: 02-287 6211/287 6267.

US: Boulevard du Régent/Regent-schapstraat 25–27, tel: 02-508 2111.

Getting Around

By Air
Since the longest distance across the country from southeast to northwest is only 314 km (212 miles), there is not much need for domestic air services.

By Rail
Belgium has extremely good trains that cover practically the whole country. In addition, many international express services link the country with Paris, Amsterdam and many German cities. The Belgian National Railways (Société Nationale des Chemins de Fer Belges – SNCB) offers rail travellers a wide range of flat-rate excursions, mini-trips (both inside and outside of Belgium), group excursions, charter excursions and tourist packages. One of the best deals is the *B-Tourrail* ticket which is valid throughout the entire railway network for five days within a 17-day period. The TTB ticket is similar to the B-Tourrail but is also valid for bus, tram and metro. Train information may be obtained from: Belgian Railways (SNCB), tel: 02-555 2525.

By Road
Distances are relatively short and motorways serve most of the country with the exception of the mountain regions of the Ardennes. Access to all roads is free, there are no toll roads in Belgium.
Motoring Advice: In the northern part of the country, road signs appear in Dutch – in the southern part, in French. Several towns and villages have two names, one in each of the official languages, but it is important to note that road signs only show place names in the language of that particular region. Snow tyres are permitted only in exceptional weather conditions. In case of accident, with personal injury, call the emergency number 100 to request help.

Brussels

Where to Stay

Accommodation

Visitors to Brussels will find a large selection of hotel accommodation in every price range. Many of the larger hotels offer special bargain rates for weekend stays. Hotels must post their room rates at the reception desk and are permitted to charge only these prices on your final bill.

In the city's official hotel guide you will find a complete list, including addresses and prices, of the 120 or so hotels in the city. This guide is available at the Tourist Offices on Rue du Marché aux Herbes (Grasmarkt) 61 and in the Town Hall (TIB). It is also possible to book accommodation at both these places. Belgian Tourist Reservations will also book a hotel room for you. They can be contacted at 111 Boulevard Anspach, 1000 Brussels, tel: 02-513 7484, fax: 02-513 9277.

Transport Advice

The following organisations are good sources of transport information:
● Royal Automobile Club of Belgium (RACB), Aarlenstraat 53, B-1040 Brussels, tel: 02-287 0900.
● Touring Club de Belgique (TCB), 44 Rue de la Loi, B-1040 Brussels, tel: 02-233 22 11.

What's On

There's plenty of culture and nightlife to be taken advantage of. All information concerning cultural activities in Belgium can be obtained from the various branches of the Belgian Tourist Office, tel: 02-513 89 40. Tourist Information Brussels (TIB) publishes What's On, a weekly guide to entertainment in Belgium. Information about scheduled events in Brussels is contained in the weekly English-language magazine The Bulletin.

Shopping

Belgium is noted for a number of goods, among them hand-beaten copperware from Dinant; crystal from Val-Saint-Lambert of Liège; diamonds from Antwerp; handmade lace from Bruges, Brussels, Binche and Mechelen; tapestries from Mechelen, Sint-Niklaas, Brussels and Ghent, and sporting guns from Herstal, for which Liège is world famous. Credit cards are accepted everywhere and many shops offer the tourist special terms exclusive of Value Added Tax on certain types of goods.

Language

Three official languages are spoken in Belgium: Flemish, a variation of Dutch, in the north, French in the south and German in the east. German is only spoken by a small minority of people. English is widely spoken in hotels, restaurants, shops and places of business, and is more welcome than French in Flanders (the northern, Flemish-speaking area).

Practical Tips

Business Hours

Shops are usually open Monday–Saturday 9am–6pm, although some of them close on Monday. There are a few late-night shops in the city centre, and the neighbourhood corner store may stay open until 9pm. It's best to ask around as to the best after-hours shops and chemists. Banks are open 9am–4pm or 5pm. On Friday, some larger stores and supermarkets stay open until around 9pm.

Emergency Numbers

Police and Gendarmerie: 101
Accidents: 100
Fire: 100
Doctor: 24 hours, 02-479 1818 or 02-648 8000
Dentist: Monday–Saturday 9am–7pm, 02-426 1026 or 02-428 5888
Ambulances (for non-emergencies) 24 hours: 02-649 1122
Pharmacies: Those open out-of-hours are posted in every pharmacy window.

Postal Services

Normal post office hours are Monday–Friday 9am–5pm. Some offices are open on Friday evening and Saturday morning. The office at the South Station (Gare du Midi) is open every day, 24 hours a day.

Telecommunications

Coins are accepted by some public telephones; "telecards" come in various denominations. To call other countries, first dial the international access code 00, then the country code: Australia 61; US and Canada 1; UK 44. If using a US credit phone card, call the company's access number below: AT&T, tel: 0800 10012; MCI, tel: 0800 10012; Sprint, tel: 0800 1014.

Getting Around

Orientation
Brussels can be likened to a shallow bowl. The old heart of the city is the lower city, including the Grand Place. The upper city, strictly speaking, is the area east of the Grand Place, around Avenue Louise. But as the city has expanded, it has spread over the low hills in all directions. Brussels is a metropolitan district combining 19 local government units called *communes*, one of which is Brussels city (Bruxelles in French, Brussel in Dutch).

Public Transport
The excellent metropolitan public transport network, operated by STIB, offers tickets for single journeys, a 5-journey card bought from the driver, a 10-journey card bought from an STIB or rail station, and a 24-hour card, which can be used as often as desired on bus, tram or metro lines within the city. The 5- and 10-journey tickets must be "punched" in a platform or on-board machine, each cancellation being valid for same-direction travel by one person on the bus, tram and metro network, within a 1-hour period.

The Metro: There is a fast and modern metro service consisting of two main lines which connect the eastern and western parts of the city. The underground network is supplemented by the three Pré Metro lines. Pré metro means that the completed underground tracks are also used by trams. Many metro stations contain murals and sculptures by distinguished Belgian artists.

Bus/Tram: What applies to the metro applies also to these services, although buses can be reduced to near-immobility in rush-hour. The tram is usually the fastest way to travel.

Trains: The above-ground train service is also good, but not so handy within the city limits.

By Road
Travelling by car in the city 8am–7pm, Monday–Saturday (except maybe in July and August), tends to be nasty, brutish and long. If you bring a car, you would do well not to use it for sightseeing. All the usual international car-hire companies, plus some local ones (try Rent-A-Car, 263 Avenue de la Couronne, tel: 02-649 6412), have offices in Brussels. Trams and buses always have traffic priority, as, usually, do vehicles coming from the right, unless the road is posted with orange diamond signs.

City Tours
Chatterbus (for individual – and individualistic – guides): 12 Rue des Thuyas, tel: 02-673 1835; De Boeck's (throughout Belgium): 8 Rue de la Colline, tel: 02-513 7744; and ARAU (for architecture and history): 55 Boulevard Adolphe Max, tel: 02-219 3345.

Shopping

There are numerous areas in Brussels where you can shop to your heart's content. In the Lower City you'll find plenty of shops at the Place de Brouckère, the Place de la Monnaie, along the Boulevard Anspach (predominately fashion boutiques and book stores), and on Rue Neuve, including the City 2 shopping complex. The smaller galleries off Rue Neuve, for example the Passage du Nord and the Galerie du Centre, have a wide range of unusual shops.

The Rue du Beurre is good for food and gift shops. The Rue du Midi is another well-known shopping beat, where there are quite a few art supply shops and music stores. One of the best places to go window shopping is in the glass-roofed arcades of the famous Galerie Saint Hubert, which was constructed in 1847, the first covered shopping mall to be built in Europe. Rue Antoine Dansaert is the place to find ultra-fashionable and expensive boutiques.

Fancy shops with internationally recognised designer names are concentrated in the Upper City. Streets to look out for here include Avenue Louise, Chaussée d'Ixelles, Boulevard de Waterloo and Avenue de la Toison d'Or. The most chic arcades are also located here. You'll find both the Galerie Espace Louise and the Galerie Louise at the Place Louise; while the Galeries de la Toison and the Galerie d'Ixelles are located at Porte de Namur.

The department stores are open continuously 9am–6pm. They are closed on Sunday and public holidays, but stay open until 8pm on Friday evening.

The city has many markets. Antique market: Grand Sablon (Grote Zavel), Saturday 9am–6pm, Sunday 9am–2pm.
Flower market: Grand Place (Grote Markt), daily 8am–6pm.
Bird market: Grand Place (Grote Markt), Sunday 7am–2pm.
Flea market: Place du Jeu de Balle (Vossenplein), daily 7am–2pm.
Food and Textile market: Place Bara (Gare du Midi/Zuidstation), Sunday 5am–1pm.

Further Reading

General
Guide Delta Bruxelles. Lists around 1,700 restaurants.
The Great Beers of Belgium. By Michael Jackson, the world authority.
History of the Belgians by A. de Meeiis. A colourful and wide-ranging history of the Belgians.

Other Insight Guides
Insight Guides: Belgium and Brussels are companions to this book. *Insight Pocket Guide*: Brussels is designed to help readers without a lot of time plan their trips precisely. *Insight Compact Guides* cover Belgium, Bruges and Brussels.

NETHERLANDS

Area: 33,950 sq km (13,000 sq miles)
Area Below Sea Level: one-fifth
Population: 16 million
Capital: Amsterdam
Seat of Government: The Hague
Time Zone: GMT + 1 hour in winter, + 2 hours in summer (last weekend in March to last weekend in September)
Language: Dutch
Religion: Roman Catholic (34 percent), Protestant (25 percent)
Weights and Measures: Metric
Electricity: 220 volts AC, round two-pin plugs
National Airline: KLM Royal Dutch Airlines
International Dialling Code: 31 + 20 (Amsterdam), 70 (The Hague), 10 (Rotterdam)
Public Holidays: In addition to those in the Introduction, the Netherlands celebrates Good Friday; Easter Sunday; the Queen's Birthday (15 April), Liberation day (5 May) and Whit Sunday.

Getting There

By Air

Most visitors from America or other parts of Europe fly into Schiphol Airport, 14 km (9 miles) southwest of Amsterdam. The airport is connected with 196 cities in 90 countries. Very regular flights link Schiphol with all major European airports, and there are several flights a week from North America, Canada and Australia. KLM is the national airline. KLM information in the UK, tel: (020) 8750 9000; in North America, tel: 1 800 374 7747.

By Rail

Day and night services operate from London (Liverpool Street) to the Netherlands via the Hook of Holland – journey time is around 12 hours by ferry, 10 hours by jetfoil. There are good rail connections to all parts of the country from the main ports of arrival and very regular services to the Netherlands from Brussels, Paris, Antwerp, Cologne and Hanover.
By Channel Tunnel: The Eurostar Channel Tunnel train (tel: 08457 881881) links London to Brussels in 2 hours 40 minutes, from where there are fast connections to destinations in Holland.

By Road

Holland has an excellent network of roads, and signposting is good. But, once you're in the cities, a car is often more of a hindrance than a help. From the Hook of Holland to Amsterdam, travel time is roughly 3 hours 30 minutes.
Le Shuttle: The Channel Tunnel service taking cars and their passengers from Folkstone to Calais on a drive-on-drive off system, takes 25 minutes to Calais, from where there are fast motorway connections up to Holland.

By Sea

From the UK, P&O Stena (tel: 0870-570 70 70) operates two sailings a day from Harwich to the Hook of Holland: High Speed Service: 3 hours 40 minutes. North Sea Ferries (tel: 01482-377 177) has a daily sailing from Hull to Rotterdam, taking 14 hours. Sheerness Travel Agency (tel: 01795-666 666) is one of the main east coast agents dealing with this route. The fastest sea route from the UK is from Dover to Ostend via Hoverspeed's seacat (tel: 0870-524 0241), which takes about 2 hours.

Practical Tips

Medical Services

The standard of medical and dental services in the Netherlands is very high, and most major cities have an

Emergency Numbers

● **Amsterdam (code 020)**
Police/ambulance: 112
SOS doctor/
dentist/chemist: 592 3434
Lost property
(noon–3.30pm daily): 559 3005

● **The Hague (code 070)**
Police/ambulance: 112
SOS doctor/dentist: 345 5300
(night):   346 9669
Lost property: 310 4911

● **Rotterdam (code 010)**
Police/ambulance: 112
Doctor: 420 1100
Dentist: 455 2155

emergency doctor and dental service. Enquire at your hotel, tourist information centre, or consult the introductory pages to local telephone directories.

Business Hours

Normal shopping hours are 8.30 or 9am–6 or 6.30pm. Late-night shopping is usually Thursday. Food stores close at 4pm on Saturday. All shops close for one half day a week, often Monday morning.

Tipping

Service charges and VAT are included in restaurant and bar bills. An extra tip of 10 percent can be left for extra attention or service but this is by no means compulsory. Taxi meters also include the service charge, though it is customary to give an extra tip. A lavatory attendant is usually given a small tip.

Postal Services

Main post offices are open Monday–Friday 8.30am–6pm, Saturday 9am–noon. Stamps are available from post offices, tobacconists, newstands and machines attached to the red and grey letter boxes.
    Poste restante facilities are available at the main post office. You will need a passport to collect your mail.

Telephones

Telephone boxes are mainly green, but are also recognisable in more compact and contemporary styles. Most take phonecards and/or coins. You find them in post offices, large stores, cafés and in some streets. Larger post offices have international call facilities which work out cheaper than using a hotel phone. Beware of hole-in-the-wall shops offering so-called cheap long-distance telephone services, as many of them are actually overpriced.

The code for dialling Holland from abroad is 00 31. Most telephone numbers have 10 digits (the old area code now forms part of the number, including the initial '0' which is deleted when calling from abroad). To make an international call from Holland, dial 00 + the country code: 44 for the UK and 1 for the US and Canada. AT&T, tel: 06-022 9111; Sprint, tel: 06-222 9119.

Getting Around

By Air

Schiphol, near **Amsterdam** is the Netherlands' principal airport. Amsterdam Schiphol railway station is located below the arrivals hall. Trains leave for the principal Dutch cities every 15 minutes or so

between 5.25am and 0.15am, and every 60 minutes or so during the remaining period.

Rotterdam has a small airport served by flights from Amsterdam, London and Paris, located 15 minutes from the city centre. A regular local bus service runs between the airport and the city.

Eindhoven and **Maastricht** both have airports, principally for domestic flights.

Domestic flights within the Netherlands are operated by KLM City Hopper.

For further information, tel: 020-474 7747.

By Rail

Netherlands Railways (Nederlandse Spoorwegen) has a network of express trains linking major cities. A fast direct train every 15 minutes links Schiphol airport and Amsterdam. There is an hourly night service between Utrecht, Amsterdam, Schiphol, The Hague, Rotterdam and vice versa. Frequently-stopping trains connect to smaller places. There are at least half-hourly services on most lines and 4–8 per hour on busier routes. It is not possible to reserve seats on these services.

For further information about public transport information and tickets:

Amsterdam GVB
1 Stationsplein,
Centraal Station
Tel: 0900-9292; (Monday–Friday 8am–10pm, Saturday and Sunday 9am–10pm).
Nationwide
Tel: 0900-9292.

For information on international trains, tel: 0900-9296. More information on train travel in Holland may be found in the free booklet, *Exploring Holland by Train*, published in English.

By Road

The Netherlands has a dense and modern toll-free road system. The smaller country roads are in excellent condition. There are 42 touristic routes of some 80–170 km (50–105 miles) some of which continue into neighbouring countries.

There are ferry services on secondary roads crossing rivers and canals. Most ferries are equipped to carry cars and in general the fares are not high. You may also be required to pay nominal fees for the use of tunnels, bridges and dams which appear frequently throughout the country.

Motoring Advice: To drive in the Netherlands, you must carry a current driving licence (an international licence is not

Tourist Information

Tourist information offices (Vereniging voor Vreemdelingen-verkeer – or VVV for short) are clearly marked and usually located just outside the railway station in every main town and city. Here the multilingual staff will answer all your questions, provide maps and brochures, handle your accommodation bookings and reserve tickets for the theatre. There is a charge for most of these services. It is useful to carry passport-sized photographs for various identity cards you may purchase.
The registered address of the head office is:

VVV Amsterdam Tourist Office
P.O. Box 3901
1001 AS Amsterdam
Tel: 06-3403 4066 or
0900-400 4040
Fax: 020-625 2869
To visit in person, go to: 10 Stationsplein (white building across the road to the left outside the Centraal Station). Open: daily 9am–5pm. There are also **VVV** offices inside the Centraal Station, (open 8am–8pm Mon–Sat, 8am–5pm Sun), and at 1 Leidseplein, Amsterdam, (open daily 9am–5pm). If you wish to write to a town tourist office, address the letter **VVV** and the name of the town.

Australia: Suite 302, 5 Elizabeth Street, Sydney, NSW 2000.
Canada: 25 Adelaide Street East, Suite 710, Toronto, Ontario M5C 1Y2,
 tel: 04 16 36 63 1577.
UK: PO Box 523, London SW1E 6NT, tel: 0891-200277; fax: 020-7828 7941.
US: 355 Lexington Avenue, (21st Floor), New York, NY 10017, tel: 0212 370 7367;
225 North Michigan Avenue, Suite 326, Chicago, Ill 60601, tel: 0312 8190300;
90 New Montgomery Street, Suite 305, San Francisco, CA 94105, tel: 0415 543 6772.

necessary); vehicle registration document; Green Card insurance policy and a warning triangle for use in the event of an accident or breakdown.

Waterways
There are scheduled boat services from major cities throughout the country and boat tours, excursions and trips operating on the various bodies of water in Holland.

Boat Charter: Around the IJssel-meer and in the northern provinces of Groningen and Friesland, boat rental agencies offer a range of craft, some of which have living accommodation. Another area popular with those who enjoy boating is Zeeland province.

Canal Tours: A popular way to get to know Amsterdam is by taking a canal tour; numerous companies operate from the canal basin opposite Centraal Station and tickets can be booked in advance from the nearby VVV office. Tours take an hour or more; candle-lit dinner cruises are also available. Fuller information is given in the Excursions section.

Canal Buses: While canal tours are geared essentially to visitors, you can also use Amsterdam's canal bus system. Modern glass-topped launches (equivalent to the Parisian *bâteaux mouches*) will pick you up at various points of the city and take you through some of the loveliest parts of Amsterdam.

Day tickets with unlimited use are available. Be prepared to queue in summer.

The Museum Boat Service: This stops at nine major museums at 75-minute intervals – well worth considering if you intend doing a lot of sightseeing. You can buy a day ticket from the VVV office opposite Centraal Station, where the boats leave. There is now also a canal bus offering a regular service through the canals between the Rijksmuseum and Centraal Station.

Public Transport
Tickets are sold in the form of *Nationale Strippenkaart* to be used on buses, trams, metro and the train between certain stations anywhere in Holland. The easiest place to buy the cards is at a **vvv** office (or tel: 0900-4004040; fax: 020-625 2869), though they are also sold at railway stations and many newsagents and tobacconists. You can also buy tickets from the bus or tram driver, but they cost more than tickets purchased in advance.

Transport routes are divided into zones; you must cancel one strip for your journey and one strip for each zone you travel through (i.e. cancel two strips for one zone, three strips for two zones, and so on). The stamp on your *stripenkaart* is valid for one hour. Within that time you can change from one route to another, or from one form of transport to another without cancelling more strips. An alternative is an unlimited travel ticket (called a *dagkaart*), valid for one, two or three days.

Tram 20 is a circle tram with two different routes which take you around Amsterdam and stop close to most of the city's museums and tourist attractions. The trams run daily from 9am–7pm every 10 minutes. One ticket entitles you to unlimited use of the tram for one day.

Where to Stay

It is wise to book in advance in the summer and the holiday season and, in the case of North Holland, during the bulb season (April–May). This is especially true of Amsterdam, where the central hotels are usually booked up June–August. However, it is worth telephoning hotels at short notice in case they have cancellations. You can book directly with the hotel – the reservations desk will invariably speak English. Alternatively, you can book in advance through:
The Netherlands Reservation Centre, P.O. Box 404, NL-2200 AK Leidschendam, tel: 070-419 5500, fax: 070-419 5519.

Attractions

There are more than 600 museums in Holland, with 440 of them listed in the *Attractions* booklet from vvv offices. The entry price varies; some museums are free. A Museum Year Card gives free admission to all of them.

Most museums are open from Tues–Sun 10am–5pm. On public holidays they are normally open Sunday hours.

At VVV offices bearing the *i – Nederland* sign, visitors can in addition obtain information on cultural activities and even order tickets for concerts and theatre productions. Another useful source of information is the *Time Out* section of the *Holland Tribune*, an English-language periodical available at hotels and tourist offices in the provinces of North and South Holland and on all KLM flights.

Brown café notice-boards are another good source of information on local events.

Sightseeing by Air

Flights over south Limburg, neighbouring Germany and Belgium from Maastricht airport are organised by Air Service Limburg, tel: 043-364 5030.

The flights are charged by the hour; there is a minimum of two passengers and a maximum of three.

Amsterdam

Practical Tips

Medical Services
The most central hospital is the Onze Lieve Vrouse Gasthuis, Le Oosterparkstraat 197, tel: 5999111.

The main hospital is the Academisch Medisch Centrum, Meibergdreef 9, tel: 5669111. Both hospitals have an out-patients and casualty ward.

Chemists (*Apotheek*) are normally open Monday–Friday 9am–5.30pm or 6pm. Late-night chemists operate on a rotating basis.

Emergency Numbers

Police: 6222222.
Ambulance: 5555555.
For urgent medical or dental treatment, contact the **Central Medical Service**, tel: 6642111 (SOS Doctor). Open 24 hours.

Postal Services
The main office is at Nieuwezijds Voorburgwal 182, behind the Royal Palace. Open: Monday–Friday 8.30am–6pm, 8pm on Thursday; Saturday 9am–noon. Parcels are handled at the post office at Oosterdokskade 3–5pm. Open: Monday–Friday 8.30am–9pm, Saturday 9am–noon. Stamps are available from post offices, tobacconists, news-stands and stamp machines attached to the red and grey letter boxes. *Poste restante* facilities are available at the main post office – you need a passport to collect your mail.

Telephones
For international calls, it's easier to go to Telehuis, Raadhuisstraat 48 (open 24 hours), where you can talk in a booth for as long as you like and pay when you finish.

Tourist Information
See the information under the main Netherlands section.

Consulates
Australia: Koninginnegracht 23, 2514 AB Den Haag. Tel: 070 630983.
Canada: Sophialaan 7, 2514 JP Den Haag. Tel: 070 614111.
UK: 44 Koningslaan. Tel: 673 6245.
US: 19 Museumplein, Amsterdam. Tel: 020-664-5661.

Getting Around

Orientation
Amsterdam, capital of the Netherlands and its most populous city with 750,000 inhabitants, sits on the River Amstel, supported by stilts, sometimes known as polders, driven 59 ft (18 metres) into the marshy ground below, enabling parts of the city to spring up where there were once only waterways. Built on a design of expanding horseshoe canals that fit one within the other, the city contains some 4,000 17th-century merchants' houses and warehouses and over 1,000 bridges.

Financial and economic centre of the Netherlands, Amsterdam is also part of the so-called Conurbation Holland area, which mainly comprises the provinces of North and South Holland and contains the country's major industries and its largest cities (Rotterdam and The Hague).

From the Airport
Shuttle trains leave Schiphol Airport every 15 minutes for Amsterdam Central Station during the day, and once an hour at night. Travel time is under 20 minutes. Trains also run to the RAI station and to Amsterdam Zuid for the World Trade Center, both in the south of the city. KLM operates a coach service to the city every half an hour, but it's over twice the price of the train. There is also a much cheaper public bus service linking the airport to the city.

By Road
Driving within the city centre is best avoided. If you do take a car, be prepared to contend with parking problems, mad cyclists, narrow canal streets (often blocked by delivery vans), the complexity of the one-way systems and trams which always have right of way.

If you arrive by car, the best thing to do is leave it in a car park and go the rest of the way by public transport. The multi-storey Europarking at Marnixstraat 250 usually has space and is within walking distance of the city centre.

Amsterdam makes a good base for day trips. Distances to Dutch towns of interest are short: The Hague 33 miles (52 km), Utrecht 27 miles (43 km), Delft 39 miles (62 km).

By Rail
A wide and very efficient network of rail services operates throughout the country. Fast electric trains link Amsterdam with most Dutch towns on an hourly or half-hourly basis. It is well worth finding out about excursion fares, which include entrance fees to museums and other attractions, as well as the return rail fare.

Public Transport
Unless you are travelling out of the centre you are unlikely to need the buses or metro. Within the city the prominent yellow trams are easily the best means of getting around and not expensive as long as you master the ticket system. The GVB office outside the station has information on the system in English and sells the various types of tickets. You can either buy individual tickets (which is the most expensive way of travelling), Rover tickets, which are valid for 1, 2 or more days' travel, or *strippenkaart* – strip tickets, in multiples of 6, 10 or 15; the more you buy, the cheaper they come. These are valid for one hour's travel and the amount you use depends on the zones you cover.

The GVB transport office in front of Central Station provides free public transport route maps. The best general map is published by Falkplan, called *This is Amsterdam*.

Attractions

What's On

The Amsterdam Tourist Office (vvv) publishes *Amsterdam This Week,* a weekly guide to the city's art, culture, restaurants and shopping. Also available, for a nominal fee, is a weekly programme of concerts and theatres, which includes English-speaking productions. The vvv Box Office at Stationsplein 10 provides advance bookings for theatres, operas, ballets and concerts. It is open Monday–Saturday 10am–4pm and reservations must be made in person, not over the telephone. Another useful source of cultural information is the monthly magazine *Amsterdam Times,* available at hotels and tourist offices.

After dark, entertainment focuses on three main areas: Leidseplein, popular with tourists and with locals for restaurants, lively discos and nightclubs; Rembrandtsplein for clubs, cabarets and strip shows pandering to slightly older tastes; and the Red Light District, notorious for scantily dressed women sitting in windows and for notice-boards saying "room to hire".

Strip shows, porn videos and sex shops centre on the main canals of Oude Zijds Voorburgwal and Oude Zijds Achterburgwal. The smaller, sleazier streets leading off these two canals are best avoided, and you are advised never to take photographs.

On an entirely different note, you could spend the evening on a candle-lit canal cruiser, with wine and cheese or full dinner provided.

In any case, try out one of the numerous brown cafés, a classic grand café with a reading table and more of a modern ambience, or, alternatively, one of the new-wave bars, with cool, whitewashed and mirrored walls, an abundance of greenery and a long list of cocktails. Some cafés and bars have live music, often jazz or blues. They usually post notices in the windows announcing events.

Shopping

Bargains are a rarity but browsing is fun, particularly in the markets and the small specialist shops. For general shopping the main streets are Kalverstraat and Nieuwendijk, for exclusive boutiques try P.C. Hoofstraat and for the more off-beat shops, head to the Jordaan northwest of the centre where many of the local artists live. Two unusual shopping centres are worth a visit: Magna Plaza opposite the Royal Palace and Kalvetoren on Kalverstraat.

The vvv Tourist Office provides a series of useful shopping guides, which give maps, route descriptions, places of interest and a list of addresses and shop specialities.

Coach Tours

These may be booked through any **vvv** office. All depart from Amsterdam.

City Sightseeing

Duration 2–3 hours. Summer, 10am daily. Winter, 2.30pm daily. A drive through Amsterdam which takes in an open-air market, a windmill, the Royal Palace and a visit to a diamond-cutting workshop. Plus, in winter, a ticket for a canal ride.

Marken and Volendam

Summer, 10am and 2.30pm daily. Winter, 10am daily and 2.30pm Sunday only. Duration approx 3 hours. A chance to see the traditional costumes still worn by many residents in these old fishing villages. Also included is a visit to "De Jacobs Hoeve" cheese farm at Volendam or to the cheesemaker "De Catharina Hoeve" at the Zaanse Schans, plus windmills.

Grand Holland Tour

Summer 10am daily. Winter 10am Tues, Thurs and Sun. Duration 8 hours. Lunch not included. First to the flower market at Aalsmeer (or to a clog factory on Saturday and Sunday), on to a porcelain factory in Delft, Rotterdam and then The Hague, including, in summer, the miniature village of Madurodam.

Tulip Fields and Keukenhof Flower Exhibition

10am and 2.30pm daily. 25 March–14 May. Duration 3 hours. A drive through the colourful flower-growing region with a visit to a bulbgrower and the Keukenhof flower exhibition.

Alkmaar Cheese Market and Windmills

9am departures every Friday from 21 April–15 September. Duration 4 hours. Alkmaar on Fridays shows the traditional market life of old Holland. Porters in ancient dress carry cradles heaped with yellow cheeses. Then to de Zaanse Schans to visit a windmill.

Steam Trains

● **Hoorn-Medemblik** (Noord-Holland): historic steam train ride through characteristic landscape and attractive villages. Open May to beginning of September (except Monday).
● **Goes-Oudelande** (Zeeland): steam train ride through typical South Beveland landscape with fields divided by hedges. Open: mid-May to beginning September and Christmas holiday.

Further Reading

General

Of Dutch Ways, by Helen Colijn, Dillon Press Inc, Minneapolis, Minnesota.
Dutch Art and Architecture 1600–1800, by Jakob Rosenberg et al, Penguin, London.
The Story of Amsterdam, by Anthony Vanderheiden, Rootveldt Boeken, Amsterdam.

Other Insight Guides

Insight Guides: Amsterdam and the Netherlands are companions to this book, from Apa Publications award-winning series.

GERMANY

Getting Acquainted

Area 357,000 sq km (138,000 sq miles)
Capital Berlin
Highest mountain Zugspitze (2,962 m/9,152ft)
Longest river Rhine (865 km/536 miles)
Largest island Rügen (930 sq km/358 sq miles)
Population 82 million
Population density 229 per sq km (593 per sq mile)
Language German, plus small minorities speaking Frisian and Sorbian. There is also a wide range of regional dialects.
Religion About one third Protestant, one third Roman Catholic, one third other religions or agnostic/atheist.
Time Zone Central European Time (MEZ), one hour ahead of Greenwich Mean Time. Summer Time (+ 1 hour) runs from the end of March to the end of October.
Currency The Euro.
Weights and measures Metric
Electricity 220-volts, two-pin plugs. UK visitors will need an European adapter plug.
International Dialling Code (49)
Public Holidays
In addition to those listed in the Introduction, the following public holidays are celebrated in Germany: Good Friday, National Holiday (17 June) and Unification Day (3 October). In some Catholic parts of the country, the following are also considered to be public holidays: Epiphany (6 January) and Corpus Christi Day. In the Protestant parts of West Germany, Repentance Day, which usually falls on the last Wednesday in November, is also celebrated.

Getting There

By Air

Most air-routes into Germany lead to Frankfurt airport. Germany's other international airports are: Berlin, Bremen, Düsseldorf, Hamburg, Hanover, Cologne, Munich, Nuremberg, Saabrücken, Münster/Osnabrück, Dresden and Stuttgart. Lufthansa, the national airline, serves most of the world and has a domestic service.

Terminal 1 at Frankfurt Rhein Main airport can be reached by train, so the centre of Frankfurt (Hauptwache) is only 15 minutes away. This is where you can join the main German inter-city rail network. A reliable public transport system, usually a shuttle service, links all German airports with the nearest city centre(s). Taxis are, of course, also available.

By Sea

There are ferry connections from northern Germany (Hamburg and Rotterdam) to Scandinavia and the UK (Scandinavian Seaways sailings on the Harwich–Hamburg route). The port of Warnemünde has sailings to Trelleborg in Sweden.

These shipping companies operate services to Germany from the UK:
Scandinavian Seaways: Harwich/Newcastle-Hamburg
Stena Line: Harwich-Hook of Holland
Seafrance: Dover-Calais
P&O Stena Line: Dover-Calais
Hoverspeed: Dover-Ostend/Folkestone-Boulogne/Dover-Calais (Seacat)
North Sea Ferries: Hull-Rotterdam, Hull-Zeebrugge
Ferry connections also link Germany with Norway, Denmark, Sweden, Finland, the Russian Federation, Latvia and Lithuania.

By Rail

It is now possible to travel through the Channel tunnel on Eurostar, a fast train service from London Waterloo Station to continental Europe (Paris and Brussels). Several German cities can be reached via express train from Brussels. Booking is not essential outside peak hours. For more details, contact:
German Rail
UK Booking Centre
PO Box 687A
Surbiton
Surrey KT6 6UB.
Tel: 0870 2435363 (information, general enquiries and reservations).

From northern Europe, the best train connections to the north of Germany are from the Hook of Holland in the Netherlands. Trains leave in the direction of Venlo and Emmerich. The south of Germany is better reached via Ostend, from where trains go to Aachen and Cologne, connecting with Euro-City and Inter-City trains to the southern federal states. From the UK, ferry links with the Hook of Holland are via Harwich and Ostend via Dover.

By Road

Bordered by Denmark to the north; the Netherlands, Belgium, Luxembourg and France to the west; Switzerland and Austria to the south; and the Czech and Slovak republics to the east, Germany can be reached by numerous European motorways.

Practical Tips

Pharmacies

Pharmacies (*Apotheken*), which are open 8am–6.30pm, carry a list of neighbouring pharmacies open for emergencies during the night and on weekends.

Emergency Numbers

- **Police** 110
- **Fire brigade** 112
- **Ambulance** 115
- **Operator** 03
- **National directory enquiries** 11833
- **International directory enquiries** 11834

All accidents resulting in injury must be reported to the local police station.

Business Hours

Most shops are open 9.30am–6 or 6.30pm. Small shops such as bakeries, fruit and vegetable shops and butcher's shops open as early as 7am, close for 2 hours midday, re-open around 3–6.30pm. Shops in railway stations and airports are usually open until late, some until midnight. Business hours are usually 8am–5.30pm. Government offices are open to the public 8am–noon.

Tipping

Generally, service charges and taxes are included in hotel and restaurant bills. However, satisfied customers usually leave an additional tip or at least the small change. It is also customary to tip taxi drivers and hairdressers 10 percent, and cloakroom attendants a few coins.

Postal Services

Post offices are generally open from 8am–6pm Monday–Friday and 8am–noon on Saturday. Station and airport post offices in all larger cities are open until late in the evening on weekdays and some are open 24 hours a day.

Telecommunications

Most public telephones now require telephone cards, which are sold at post offices, newspaper stands and some other shops. There are only a few kiosks left that take coins, and they are useful for making short local calls only.

The privatisation of German Telekom is bringing rapid change to the world of telecommunications. Private companies are offering phone calls at cheaper rates, but their systems are not always very convenient for the irregular user.

Two such companies are Mobilcom (01019) and Mannesmann Arcor (01070). You must prefix your call with their 5-figure number.

Every town has its own dialing code and these are listed under the local network heading in the telephone directory. If you have difficulties getting through, it's worth checking the code as many have changed recently. Most new telephone booths (grey and pink) are not supplied with telephone books, but main post offices usually have a complete up-to-date set for public use. Using directory enquiries can be quite expensive.

Numbers starting with 0130 and 0800 are free of charge.

Embassies & Consulates

Australia: Godesberger Allee 105–107, 53175 Bonn. Tel: (0228) 810330, fax: 376268.
Canada: Friedrich-Wilhelm-Strasse 18, Bonn, D-53113. Tel: (0228) 9680, fax: 9683904.
New Zealand: Bundeskanzlerplat 2–10, Bonn 1 D-53113. Tel: (0228) 228070; fax: (0228) 221687.

UK: Friedrich-Ebert-Allee 77, 5300 Bonn 1. Tel: (0228) 91670.
US: 29 Dreichmanns Avenue, Bonn D-53170. Tel: (0228) 3391; fax: (0228) 3391

Getting Around

By Air

The main domestic airports are interconnected by regular Interflug, Aero Lloyd and Lufthansa services. From within Germany, Berlin can now be reached by a number of airlines including Euro Berlin and Interflug.

Lufthansa, with its main base in Frankfurt-am-Main, is the main provider of domestic air services. Deutsche BA and Eurowings also operate regular services between the major cities and several regional airlines fly to smaller destinations. If you book in advance (14 days minimum) and aren't in possession of a rail pass, flying can be a cheaper option than travelling by rail.

From Frankfurt Airport there is a 15-minute shuttle service (S15) to the main transport junction, the Hauptwache, where the suburban railway (*S-Bahn*) and the subway (*U-Bahn*) meet. From this point you can travel to town by public transport. Alternatively, bus number 61 shuttles between the airport and the town centre (Sachsenhausen). Official taxis are ivory-coloured Mercedes or BMW models with a black TAXI sign on the roof.

Tourist Information and Tourist Offices Abroad

Anywhere in Germany where tourists are expected you should find a tourist authority or information office (marked with an "**i**"). Write to the office of your destination for information.

German National Tourist Offices are in the following cities:

● **Chicago**
401 North Michigan Avenue, Suite 2525, Chicago IL 60611-4212, USA
Tel: 312-6440723
Fax: 312-6440724
● **London**
18 Conduit Street

London W1S 2XN
Tel: 020-7317 0908 (or 09001 600100 for brochures only)
Fax: 0207495 6129
E-mail: gntolon@d-z-t.com
● **Los Angeles**
Wilshire Boulevard Suite 750
Los Angeles
CA 90025, USA
Tel: 310-5759799
Fax: 310-5751565
E-mail: gntolax@aol.com
● **New York**
East 42nd St
Chanin Bldg, 52nd Floor

New York, NY 10168-0072, USA
Tel: 212-6617200
Fax: 212-6617174
● **Toronto**
Bloor Street East
North Tower, Suite 604
Toronto, Ontario M4W3R8, Canada
Tel: 416-9681570
Fax: 416-9681986
e-mail: germanto.direct.com
● **Sydney**
P.O. Box A 980
Sidney South NSW 1235, Australia
Tel: 00612-92678148
Fax: 00612-92679035

By Rail

Every day the Deutsche Bahn AG (DB) operates some 33,000 passenger trains over a 40,000-km (25,000-mile) domestic network, as well as many international through services. The high-speed network now covers about 3500km (2000 miles) of track and is still being extended.

An hourly service runs to and from more than 50 major towns and cities in the Republic by the intercity trains (IC). The new states are now included in the IC-network. IC trains do not run at night. If you wish to travel at night you're better off boarding a D-Zug, which travels more slowly because it makes more stops on the way. Another type of train, the E-Zug, stops even more frequently, but has the advantage of reaching the smaller towns. Many overnight trains have couchette cars.

Interregio (IR) trains look very stylish indeed in their postmodern blue-white design, and these transport travellers at two-hourly intervals from city to city. Euro-City (EC) trains connect major European towns and cities but are rather expensive.

It is possible to take your own bicycle on many trains for a small extra fee, but because of limited space it is advisable to call the Fahrrad-Hotline in advance to ensure both you and bicycle get on, tel: 0180-3194194.

By Road

Germany is renowned for its 13,600 km (8,500 miles) of motorways, the autobahnen. Autobahnen are marked with an "A" on blue signs; regional roads with a "B" on yellow signs.

The ADAC (Allgemeiner Deutscher Automobil Club) provides road assistance free of charge if the damage can be repaired within half an hour. If it takes longer, you will have to pay for the repair and parts yourself. Road assistance is also free of charge and all recovery costs will be refunded if you have an insurance certificate. Make sure you carry the necessary forms.

Motoring Advice

If your car breaks down on the motorway use the orange telephones at the roadside. Black triangles on roadside posts indicate the direction of the next telephone.

Waterways

Regular, scheduled boat services operate on most rivers, lakes and coastal waters including the Danube, Main, Moselle, Rhine and the Elbe and Weser with their estuaries, lakes Ammersee, Chiemsee, Königssee and Lake Constance; also on Kiel Fjord and from the mainland to Helgoland and the East and North Frisian islands. Special excursions are conducted on practically all navigable waters.

By Bus

National Buses Buses are a primary means of transport in cities and connect the smaller villages in the countryside.

There is no national coach network in Germany. The overland buses are a substitute for the railway system: wherever there are no railways, however remote, there will be a bus. You can pick up information on regional buses at railway stations and tourist information centres.

The so-called *Europabusse* are a cheap way of travelling between cities, many departing from main railway stations. *Bahnbusse* (buses owned by the German railway) operate services that link towns with smaller villages in the country. In remote parts of the country this is usually the only form of public transport.

Among the different bus companies, Europa Bus Dienst (European Bus Service), run by the Deutsche Touring GmbH, offer some fascinating itineraries designed primarily with tourists in mind, and thus following scenic routes.

The BerLinienbus links Berlin with many cities and popular tourist areas in both Germany and the rest of Europe.

City Buses A widespread network of public transport systems is available in every large city. Those cities with a population of 100,000 and more offer an efficient bus system that runs frequently and usually very punctually. You can buy the bus tickets from the driver or at machines in the bus or at the bus stop. In large cities like Berlin, Hamburg, Cologne, Munich, Frankfurt and Stuttgart, the bus lines are integrated with the underground (U-Bahn) the tram, and the over-ground (S-Bahn) into one large public transport system. The same ticket may be used for all four means of transport.

By Tram

Trams (Strassenbahn) run on rails throughout the cities. The speed at which they travel allows for sightseeing, although there is the danger of getting into a traffic jam. Look out for yellow signs with a green "H" at bus and tram stops; they list the schedules.

By Underground

Underground (*U-Bahn*) stations are usually identified by a sign showing a white "U" on a blue background. Every station has detailed route maps displayed on the wall. The *S-Bahn* will transport you at about the same speed as the *U-Bahn*.

Where to Stay

Travellers should have no problem finding accommodation anywhere. In the peak season (June–August) it is advisable to book in advance if you are visiting a popular place. You may do so through the DIRG, reservation service TIBS, Yorck-strasse 23, D-79110 Freiburg. Tel: 0761-8858150; fax: 0761-88581.

Attractions

What's On

Most larger towns and resorts publish a "What's On" type of booklet which can be obtained from tourist office, bookstalls and hotels whenever they are available.

Shopping

Germany, being a popular tourist destination, offers lots of souvenirs. The shop to look out for is the Andenkenladen which has anything from valuable souvenirs to all sorts of knick-knacks.

In practically every town you will find a *Fussgängerzone* pedestrian zone with all kinds of shops, big department stores, and small specialised shops. Cigarettes, cigars and tobacco may be bought in newspaper shops which also stock postcards, writing supplies, magazines and newspapers.

Language

The written language of Germany is High German (*Hochdeutsch*). Spoken German, however, varies in dialect from region to region. Since English is widely taught as a first foreign language in school, and due to the long presence of allied forces and their media in West Germany, the country has one of the highest percentages of at least rudimentary English skills.

Berlin

Practical Tips

Medical Services

Most major hospitals keep ambulances specifically for accidents and emergency rooms. There are free emergency phones in front of larger post offices and elsewhere; emergency telephones posts are common in suburbs.

Emergency Numbers

- **Police** (Polizei): 110
- **Ambulance and Fire Brigade** (Notarzt und Feuerwehr): 112
- **Emergency Medical Service** (Ärztliche Notdienst): 310031
- **Emergency Chemist's Service:** 01141
- **Emergency Dental Service:** 01141

Postal Services

In Berlin, most post offices are usually open Monday–Friday 8am–6pm, and on Saturday 8am–noon.

Post offices on Friedrichstrasse railway station and at the Palast der Republik open Monday–Saturday 6pm–midnight, Sunday 8am–midnight; in Tegel Airport Monday–Friday 7am–9pm; in the International Congress Centre Monday–Friday 9am–1pm and 1.45–4pm.

Telecommunications

The dialling code for Berlin from outside the city is 030. National Telephone Information: 010. International Telephone Information: Tel: 11834. If you want to send a telegram you can do so at the post office or use the freephone service: dial 0800 33 01131 for inland, or 0800 33 01134 for telegrams to foreign countries.

Tourist Information

Information is available from the Berlin Tourist Information office, Europa Centre, tel: (030) 262 6031. The office is open Monday–Saturday 8am–10.30pm, Sunday 9am–9pm.

Tourist Offices

All kinds of information is available from the Berlin Tourismus Marketing GmbH (BTM), Am Karlsbad 11, D-10785 Berlin. Tel: 25 00 25; fax: 25 00 24 24; e-mail: reservation@btm.de internet: http://www.berlin.de

The main information office, located at the **Europa Center** (Budapester Strasse entrance), is open 8am–10pm Monday–Saturday, 9am–9pm Sunday. Another information office is situated at the **Brandenburg Gate** and is open daily 9.30am–6pm, and there are info points at Tegel Airport (main hall), open daily 5am–10.30pm, at the Dresdner Bank, Unter den Linden 17, Monday–Friday 8.30am–2pm, Tuesday and Thursday also 3.30–6pm, as well as in the KaDeWe department store, Monday–Friday 9.30am–8pm, Saturday 9am–4pm.

Potsdam Information, Am Alten Markt, Friedrich-Ebert Str. 5, 14467 Potsdam. Tel: (0331) 27 55 80; fax: 275 5899. Hotel reservation, tel: (0331) 275 58-55. Open: 9am–8pm Monday–Friday, 9am–6pm weekends.

Getting Around

Public Transport

The Berlin transportation services (BVG) operate underground trains (*U-Bahn*), fast-trains (*S-Bahn*), bus lines, tramlines in the eastern part of the city, a well-organised network of buses running throughout the night as well as boat connections crossing the Havel River between Wannsee and Kladow. The quickest way of getting around the city is on the underground system's 10 different lines.

Further information is available around the clock by calling BVG Customer Services, tel: 030 752 7020.

By Road

There are more than 1.2 million cars cruising the streets of Berlin Finding a parking place in the city is a real challenge. If you still want to drive into the city, it is best to park your vehicle at one of the Park-and-Ride areas and hop on a bus or underground.

Throughout the city no-parking and no-stopping zones are strictly patrolled as well as the time-limited parking zones. At those zones you have either to set a parking disk or – more often – to pay for a ticket at a machine (coins only, no change) for a specified time in advance.

Parking offenders can expect to pay a hefty fine to retrieve their car should it be towed away. If this should happen to you, contact either the nearest police station, for example the one at the Bahnhof Zoo, or call the main radio headquarters, tel: 110.

Useful telephone numbers:
AVD (Automobile Club of Germany) traffic information service: Tel: 240091.
ACE (Auto-Club-Europa) breakdown service: Tel: 01802-33 66 77
ADAC (German Automobile Association) urban breakdown service: Tel: 1802-22 22 22.
Weather Report: Tel: 1164.
Road Conditions: Tel: 1169.
Taxis: Tel: 194 10, 690 22, 26 10 26, 21 01 01, 21 02 02, 44 33 22 or 96 44.

Attractions

The best way to get a feel for what is going on in Berlin is to take a look in either of the city magazines, *Tip* or *Zitty*. You'll find current events and performances listed under the headings Theatre, Dance, Music, Film, Cabaret, Fine Arts, etc. The Berlin brochure *Zu Gast* in Berlin and the weekly calendar which appears in the Wednesday edition of the *Tagesspiegel* will both help you to decide where to go and what to do.

Information, tickets, books, posters and brochures for various festival events and performances are also available at Berlin Tourismus Marketing GmbH - see details above.

Sightseeing Tours

The cheapest tour is to hop on any bus, tram or S-Bahn and ride from one end to the other. You can get a good look at much of the city from the seat of a double-decker bus – the bus no. 100 takes in almost all of Berlin's great sights as it travels from Bahnhof Zoo to Alexanderplatz (*see Public Transport: By Bus*).

In summer excursion steamboats and other boats belonging to the Stern und Kreis Schiffahrt depart from various places in the city. The tours offered range from a two hour inner-city trip to whole day excursions in and around Berlin. The schedule can be obtained from

Guided City Tours

● **Art: Berlin Kunstführungen durch Galerien und Ausstellungen.** Guided tours of galleries and exhibitions and city tours on various subjects (architecture, Jewish life). Kufsteinerstr. 7, Schöneberg, 10825 Berlin, tel: 85728182.
Berliner Geschichtswerkstatt. In summer, city tours by ship. Golzstrasse 49, (Schöneberg), 10781 Berlin, tel: 2154450.
Berlin Walks. Nicholas Gay conducts walking tours in English on various subjects. Tel: 3019194.
Kultur Büro Berlin. Zeit für Kunst e.V. Guided city tours with emphasis on the history of art. Greifenhagener Str. 62, 10437 Berlin, tel: 4440936.
Schöne Künste: Kulturhistorische Stadtrundfahrten. The "Music and Theatre City Berlin" bus tour with sound clips. Tel: 7821202.
StattReisen Berlin. City walks with social history and political emphasis, also in English, French and Italian. Wide range of different subjects. Malplaquetstr. 5, 13347 Berlin, tel: 4553028.
Velotaxi. Organise sightseeing tours by bicycle. Tel: 44358990.

Stern und Kreis Schiffahrt, Puschkinallee 16/17, 12435 Berlin, tel: 536360-0.

Other boat companies offering tours on Berlin's waterways are: **Reederei Bruno Winkler,** tel: 3499595. **Reederei Riedl,** tel: 6913782. In Potsdam: **Weisse Flotte Potsdam,** tel: 0331-2759210.

Bus Tours: All of the companies below organise daily tours of Berlin. Tickets can be purchased on the bus.
Berliner Bären Stadtrundfahrt (BBS): Alexanderplatz, c/o Forum Hotel, 10178 Berlin, tel: 35195270. Departure point: corner Rankestr./Kurfürstendamm opposite memorial church and Alexanderplatz/Forum Hotel.
Berolina Stadtrundfahrten: Meinekestrasse 3, 10719 Berlin, tel: 88566030. Departure point: corner Meinekestr.1/ Kurfürstendamm.
Busverkehr Berlin (BVB): Kurfürstendamm 229, 10719 Berlin, tel: 8859880. Departure point: Kurfürstendamm 225, opposite Café Kranzler.
Severin und Kühn Berliner Stadtrundfahrten: Kurfürstendamm 216, 10719 Berlin, tel: 8804190. Departure point: corner Fasanenstr./Kurfürstendamm.

Nightlife

Because Berlin is pretty much open 24 hours a day, going from a drink at a bar or two right into the thick of city nightlife is relatively effortless.

In what was once West Berlin, the hotspots are in Charlottenburg around Savigny-Platz, Wilmersdorf (south of the Ku'damm), Schöneberg (near Winterfeldtplatz) and Goltzstrasse. Legendary Kreuzberg has two main meeting points: around Bergmannstrasse and Marheinekeplatz or in Oranienstrasse near Mariannenplatz.

Some areas of the former East Berlin are booming. The crowds, especially those wishing to show off their latest outrageous outfit, tend to meet in Mitte, mainly along Oranienburger Strasse, around the ruined Tacheles Cultural Centre (awaiting new investment) and the stylishly restored Hackesche Höfe. The social scene in Prenzlauer Berg around Kollwitzplatz is more relaxed and diverse. Here you will find students, artists, tourists and locals all having a good time.

Shopping

There's only one rule that applies to shopping in Berlin: there's nothing that you can't buy. The free guide *Shopping in Berlin* is available from the Tourist Information Centre.

Further Reading

General

Germans, by George Bailey.
The Germans, by Gordon Craig.
Toward Understanding Germany, by Robert H Lowie.
Get to Know Germany, by Ian MacDonald.
New Germany at the Crossroads, by David Marsh.

Other Insight Guides

Other books in the *Insight Guide* series highlight destinations in Germany, and include: *Insight Guides:* Germany, Berlin and Frankfurt.
The *Insight Pocket Guide* series, designed to help readers without a lot of time plan their trips precisely, include: *Pocket Guides:* Bavaria, Berlin and Munich. Many of the Pocket Guides come with handy pullout maps. *Insight Compact Guides* cover Berlin and Munich.

SWITZERLAND

Getting Acquainted

Area: 41,285 sq. km (15,935 sq. miles)
Maximum distance: North-south 220 km (135 miles), east-west 348 km (215 miles)
Length of the border: 1,882 km (1,170 miles)
Population: 7.3 million (with 19.5 percent foreigners)
Capital: Berne (pop. 126,000)
Largest cities: Zurich (pop. 342,000), Geneva (172,000), Basel (170,000), Lausanne (116,000)
Languages: Swiss-German (63.7 percent), French (19.2 percent), Italian (7.6 percent), Romansch (0.6 percent), Other languages, 8.9 percent
Religion: Catholic (46.1 percent) Protestant (40 percent)
Currency: Swiss franc (SFr)
Time Zone: Central European Time (GMT + 1 hour, + 2 hours in summer)
International dialling code: 41 then 31 (Berne), 61 (Basel), 22 (Geneva), 21 (Lausanne), 1 (Zurich)
Public Holidays: In addition to those listed in the Introduction, the following legal holidays are also observed in Switzerland: Good Friday and Switzerland National Holiday (1 August).

Getting There

By Air

The five international airports in Switzerland are: Zurich, Geneva, Basle, Lugano and Berne. Swissair and Crossair, the two Swiss airlines, connect Switzerland with 110 cities in 70 countries. The airports in Zurich and Geneva have their own train stations which are part of the national fast-train

network, several trains each hour run between the airport and the main railway station. The Basle-Mulhouse airport is actually situated in France; the journey by bus from here to the Swiss train station in Basle SBB takes about 25 minutes. There are regular connections between the Zurich, Basle and Geneva international airports. Regular and charter airlines as well as local air-taxi services fly in and out of the Berne-Belp, Lugano-Agno, Gstaad-Saanen, Sion and Samedan-St Moritz airfields.
The national carrier is **Swissair**. Its offices abroad include:
UK: Swiss Centre
3 New Coventry Street
London W1V 8EE
Reservations
Tel: 020-7434 7300
Fax: 020-7434 7219.
US: 628 Fifth Avenue
New York, NY 10020
Tel: 800-221 4750
Fax: 212-969 5747; and

Fly-Rail Services

With "Fly-Rail Baggage", train passengers don't have to lug their baggage around the airport any more. Instead, it is unloaded from the plane on to a train and forwarded directly to its destination point (in 117 train stations, mostly in cities and the larger holiday resort areas). The same service applies for the return trip: you can send your baggage – up to 24 hours in advance – directly through to your hometown airport from the town where you've been staying. Travellers may also check in at 24 train stations (including Basel, Berne, Geneva, Lausanne, Lugano, Lucerne, Neuchâtel, St Gallen and Zurich) and obtain a boarding pass up to 24 hours prior to departure.
Further information regarding Fly-Rail services, plane and railway timetables can be found in the **Fly-Rail Brochure**, available at every train station in Switzerland.

222 Sepulveda Blvd
15th Floor El Segundo
California 90245
Tel: 800-221 6644
Fax: 310-335 5935.

By Rail
Intercity trains connect Switzerland with all large cities in the surrounding countries. These trains have comfortable first and second class compartments and leave every hour. Intercity, fast and regional trains have direct connections to all cities and most holiday resort areas; certain trains travel directly to Swiss holiday areas. For further information contact the Swiss Tourist Information Centres (SVZ) or Swiss Federal Railways, tel: 051 220 1111.

By Road
Travellers can enter Switzerland by car from all neighbouring countries after passing through border customs on main thoroughfares primarily motorways. In addition, there are numerous smaller border posts, but these are not necessarily open around the clock.
Motoring Advice: Motor vehicles weighing up to 3.5 tons (including trailers and caravans) are charged SFr30 per year for what is commonly referred to as the *motorway vignette* (a sticker you place on your windshield that permits you to drive on Swiss motorways). This is valid from 1 December to 31 January (14 months). They can be purchased at borders, post offices, petrol stations and garages in Switzerland and in other countries from automobile associations and Swiss Tourist Information Centres. The sticker should be fixed to the left edge of the vehicle's front windshield. Hire cars come with a valid vignette. *The Best Roads of Switzerland for 30 Francs*, from SSVZ offices, has information on tolls on motorways and other roads.

Useful Addresses
Tourist Offices Abroad
Australia: Brian Sinclair-Thompson, c/o Swissair, 33 Pitt Street, Level

8, NSW 2000 Sydney. Tel: (0)2-9231 3744; fax: (0)2-9351 6531
Canada: 926 The East Mall, Etobicoke (Toronto) Ontario M9B 6K1. Tel: 416-695 2090; fax: 416-695 2774
UK: Swiss Centre, Swiss Court, London W1V 8EE. Tel: 020-7734 1921; fax: 020-7437 4577.
US: Swiss Center, 608 Fifth Avenue, NY 10020, tel: 212-757 5944; fax: 212-262 6116; 222 North Sepulveda Blvd, Suite 1570 El Segundo, Los Angeles CA 90245, tel: 310-335 0125; fax: 310-335 0131.

Practical Tips

Emergency Medical Services
All chemists have duty rota lists on their doors. Many doctors speak English and many hotels have house physicians. Doctor's fees and hospital costs are high. All hospitals have emergency wards with doctors on 24-hour duty, as do major rail stations.
Every city and the larger villages have a number for an emergency doctor. This can be found in local newspapers or on the general information number 111, which can also give you the addresses and phone numbers of the nearest 24-hour pharmacies.

Business Hours
Offices are open weekdays 8am–noon and 2–6pm, closed on Saturday. Shops are usually open 8am–12.30pm and 1.30–4pm. In larger cities they are also open during lunch time. Shops are often closed Monday mornings, but they stay open until 9pm on Wednesday or Thursday.

Emergency Numbers

In case of an accident, first dial the appropriate area code, then 144 to alert ambulances and other emergency vehicles.

● **Police**: 117
● **Fire brigade**: 118
● **Breakdown service**: 140

Business hours mentioned here apply to the different service industries. There are also local and regional differences.
In large cities, banks and bureaux de change are open Monday–Friday 8.30am–4.30pm and closed on Saturday. In the countryside these hours are Monday–Friday 8.30am–noon and 2–4.30 or 5.30pm. Closed: Saturday.

Tipping
Officially in Switzerland all services are included in the price, but it is wide-spread practice to honour good service by tipping. In restaurants, the bill is normally rounded up to the next franc for snacks, and two or three francs extra is usual for a dinner.

Postal Services
Post offices in large cities are open 7.30am–noon and 1.45–6.30pm throughout the week. On Saturday they are open until 11am. Stamps can be purchased at post offices, postcard kiosks and stamp machines. Mailboxes are yellow and set in the wall.

Telecommunications
The Swiss telephone system is entirely automatic. Public telephones in post offices and booths have directories in several languages. Most telephones take phonecards, on sale at post offices, newsagents and railway stations. For directory assistance dial 113; international calls 114 or 191; information (in English) 111. For calls made at hotels, substantial service charges are levied.
Telegrams can be sent from any Swiss post office or by dialling 110. Rates can be also be obtained at this number. Lucerne's Main Telegraph Office is at Bahnhofstrasse 3a.

Tourist Information

The Swiss National Tourist Office (SNTO) maintains agencies abroad (see above). Detailed tourist information in Switzerland may be obtained from the head office in Zurich (Tödistrasse 7, 8027 Zurich, tel: 01-288 11 11; fax: 01-288 1205).

If in other tourist centres, you can get information from the local tourist offices of 11 major touristic regions located throughout the country. To obtain their addresses, visitors can call tourist information, tel: 120.

Consulates & Embassies

UK: *Embassy/Consulate*, Thunstrasse 50, 3000 Berne 15, tel: 031-359 7741. *Consulate*, Rue de Vermont 37–39, 1202 Geneva, tel: 022-918 2422. *Consulate*, Via Sorengo 22, 6900 Lugano, tel: 091-950 0606.
US: *Embassy/Consulate*, Jubiläumsstrasse 93, 3001 Berne, tel: 031-357 7011. *Consulate*, Rout de Pré-Bois 29, 1216 Geneva-Cointrin, tel: 022-798 1615.
Canada: *Embassy/Consulate*, Kirchenfeldstrasse 88, 3000 Bern 6, tel: 031-357 3200. *Consulate*, Rue de l'Ariane 5, 1202 Geneva, tel. 022-919 9200.
Australia: *Embassy/Consulate*, Chemin de Fins 2, 1218 Geneva/Grand-Saconnex, tel: 022-799 9100. *Consulate*, Via Pretorio 7, 6900 Lugano, tel: 091-923 5681.

Getting Around

Public Transport

Offizielle Schweizer Kursbuch gives the schedules for and offers on all railways, mail buses, boats and mountain trains and the most important connections to foreign countries.

By Air

There are three international airports and over 40 smaller airfields in Switzerland, most of which organise flights over the Alps in good weather. Crossair connects Basel, Geneva and Zurich and Lugano and Berne.

By Rail

More than 5,780 km (3,400 miles) of dense, electrified railways open up the remotest sections of the country with trains every hour at least. More than 100 trains call at Zurich Airport each day. The swiftest connections are by fast, intercity trains. For further information contact one of the Swiss Tourist Information Centres (ST), located in many European countries and overseas.

Swiss Federal Railways is referred to by its initials, which vary between the official languages: SBB (German), CFF (French) and FFS (Italian). There are approximately 86 trains with dining cars and 325 trains with mini-bars in operation every day. If you plan to travel in a large party or during mealtimes, you'd be wise to reserve a table in advance from the **Swiss Dining Car Association**, Zurich, tel: 01-444 5111; fax: 01-271 6456.

By Road

Switzerland has a dense network of main and subsidiary roads covering over 64,600 km (40,000 miles), of which 9,350 km (5,810 miles) are highways. Twenty five major roads running over the alpine tunnels form one of the main attractions for visitors; depending on the snow, they are open from May or June to late autumn. Special rail facilities are provided for motorists wishing to transport their cars through alpine passageways.

More road information can be obtained from the Swiss National Tourist Office or any of the two Swiss Automobile clubs:
Automobile-Club der Schweiz (ACS) Wasserwerkgasse 39 CH-3000 Berne 13. Tel: 031-328 3111 Fax: 031-311 0310.
Swiss Touring Club (TCS) Chemin de Blandonnet 4 CH-1214 Genève-Vernier Tel: 022-417 2727 Fax: 022-417 2020.
Federal Traffic Police Bundesamt für Polizeiwesen Abt. Strassenverkehr Bundesrain 20, 3003 Berne Tel: 031-322 1111 Fax: 031-322 5380.

Waterways

Regularly scheduled boats cruise all the big Swiss lakes. There are steamships to put you in a nostalgic mood on Lake Geneva, Lake Zurich, Lake Brienz and Lake Lucerne. It's also possible to take a trip along the Rhine, Rhône, Aare and Doubs rivers. Details from tourist offices.

By Coach

The alpine postal motor coach (PTT) network takes travellers through the

Motoring Advice

For information on road conditions in Switzerland (for instance whether or not a road is passable, whether or not ice is present, etc.), tel: 01-163 (German), 022-163 (French), 091-163 (Italian).

You can tune into Swiss radio traffic reports issued by the police after the regular news every half hour on the hour and at half past.

During winter, information on road conditions is read out daily at 5.30am, 6.30am, 7.30am and 12.15 pm Monday–Saturday, and forecasts for the coming night are broadcast daily after the 6pm and 10pm newscasts. Foreseeable traffic obstructions registered by the police (construction sites, detours, etc.) are announced after the news report at 5.30am, 6.30am, 7.30am and 12.15 pm.

Emergency phones are found at intervals of 1.5 km on motorways; the direction of the nearest phone is indicated by arrows. Super highways are identified with green directional signs; main roads are numbered and have blue signs.

Foreign car drivers can dial 140 (the same telephone number applies throughout Switzerland) for help in the case of a breakdown.

principal mountain roads and covers regularly more than 6,800 km (4,000 miles). Some of the most spectacular stretches are included in the itinerary of the Europabus system. Conducted tours by rail, postal motor coach or private bus are regularly organised in many towns and resorts. The local tourist office can supply all necessary details.

Where to Stay

There are around 6,000 hotels, motels, pensions, mountain sanatoria and health resorts in Switzerland, amounting to more than 266,000 beds. There are 360,000 beds in chalets and holiday apartments and 7,300 youth hostel beds. Modest tourist resting-places have 226,000 couches and camp-sites have a further 238,000 places. For more information and brochures, contact the **National Tourist Office**, Tödistrasse 7, 8027 Zurich, tel: 01-288 11 11; fax: 01-288 1205 or one of the Swiss Tourism Offices abroad.

The *Swiss Hotel Guide,* published annually by the Swiss Hotel Association, is available from the Swiss National Tourist Office. Further information and prices can be found in the free regional and local hotel listings. These are available from regional tourist associations.

Attractions

What's On
The Swiss National Tourist Office (SNTO) publishes an annual calendar of events including complete details on music festivals, art exhibitions, sightseeing, trade fairs and sporting events, as well as a listing of more than 100 museums and art collections available to the public.

Nightlife

Disregard the rumour that nightlife in Switzerland is pretty provincial; in larger cities you'll find a wide variety of bars, clubs, opportunities to dance and discos. Some of the well-

known holiday resort areas also offer attractive places to spend an evening, as well as world-class entertainment programmes. For further, information enquire at a local tourist information centre or ask the hotel concierge.

Shopping

If you're searching for something typical and of good quality, try one of the Schweizerischen Heimatwerk (Swiss Handicraft) shops, located in many cities and well-populated areas. They are nearly always staffed by competent sales assistants. In smaller towns it's best to purchase articles directly from the source, i.e. the company or artist.

Language

Switzerland is one of the most multilingual countries in Europe with four national languages. German is spoken in central and eastern Switzerland; French in the west; Italian in the southern part of the country and 1 percent of the population speaks Romansch in south-eastern Switzerland. People who work with visitors usually speak several languages, including English.

Further Reading

General
The Alps, by Ronald W. Clark.
Switzerland, by Christopher S. Hughes.
The Swiss and their Mountains, by Sir A.H.M. Lunn.
Antiquities and Archaeology, by R. Sauter.
Why Switzerland, by Jonathan Steinberg.
Switzerland Exposed, by Jean Ziegler.

Other Insight Guides
Insight Guide: Switzerland and *Compact Guide*: Switzerland are companion volumes to this book, from Apa Publications' award-winning series.

AUSTRIA

Getting Acquainted

Area: 83,838 sq km (32,370 sq miles).
Capital: Vienna.
Highest Mountain: Grossglockner 3,797 metres (12,657 feet).
Population: 8.1 million.
Language: German.
Religion: 78 percent Roman Catholic.
Time zone: Central European Time (GMT plus one hour).
Currency: the Euro.
Weights & Measures: Metric.
Electricity: AC220 volts.
International dialling code: 43.
Public Holidays: In addition to those listed in the Introduction, Austria celebrates: Epiphany: 6 January; National Holiday: 26 October; Day of the Immaculate Conception: 8 December.

Getting There

By Air
Austria's national carrier, Austrian Airlines, operates daily direct services to most European capital cities from Vienna's Schwechat airport and less frequently from Salzburg, Graz, Linz, Klagenfurt and Innsbruck. Some 36 carriers, including most major European airlines, fly between Vienna and national capitals.

By Rail
There are two main stations in Vienna: the Westbahnhof serves Germany, France, Belgium and Switzerland and the Südbahnhof serves the Balkans, Greece, Hungary and Italy.

Other major international trains are the *Prinz Eugen* (Hanover–

Vienna), the *Arlberg Express* (Paris–Vienna via Switzerland) and the *Holland–Vienna Express* (Amsterdam–Vienna). Anyone wishing to arrive in style could catch the *Orient Express* on a weekly run to Budapest with stops at Innsbruck, Salzburg and Vienna.

For passenger information in Vienna, tel: 0222-1717.

By Road

There are approximately 70 international bus lines connecting Austria to other foreign countries. There are no direct bus services from Northern Europe. Would-be bus travellers are advised to travel to Munich and change to the rail network.

Travelling to Austria by car from Northern Europe is a long and arduous journey, best achieved by travelling through Germany to take advantage of the toll-free and excellent motorway network. Beware of attempting to enter the country via the less busy alpine passes, which can be closed at night and in the winter. Motorways are free in Austria.

A Green Card for insurance purposes is not mandatory although it is advised; red accident triangle, seat-belts and first aid kit are mandatory, however, for all vehicles travelling on Austrian roads.

Practical Tips

Emergency Medical Services

Chemists operate a rota system for night and Sunday duty. Information about medical emergencies is available from the local police or from the telephone directory.

Emergency Numbers

- **Fire Brigade:** 122
- **Police:** 133
- **Ambulance:** 144
- **Information:** 16
- **Crisis Intervention Hotline:** 1770
- **Vienna Radio Medical Service:** 141
- **International Aircraft Rescue Service:** 02732-70007.

Useful Telephone Numbers

Vienna flight information, tel: 7007-2233.
Railway Service Office, tel: 1700.
Railway information, tel: 1717.
ARBÖ Breakdown Service, tel: 123.
ÖAMTC Breakdown Service, tel: 120.
ÖAMTC European Emergency Service, tel: 982-8282.

Business Hours

In general, shops and businesses in Austria are open workdays from 8am–6pm and on Saturday 8am–noon. Banks are open Monday, Tuesday, Wednesday and Friday 8am–12.30pm and 1.30–3pm.

Tipping

It is usual to leave a 10–15 percent tip when the service has been good.

Postal Services

Post offices are generally open from 8am–noon and 2–6pm. A few are open on Saturday from 8–10am. Railway post offices in the large cities are open 24 hours. Stamps are available from post offices and tobacco kiosks. Letter boxes are yellow.

Telecommunications

Telephone calls may be made from the post office and telephone kiosks. Some public telephones require the use of a telephone card, obtainable from post offices. For operator-assisted long-distance calls: 1616
Telephone enquiries: 1611
Telegram service, tel: 190.
Telephone services, tel: 1621.

Getting Around

By Air

There are direct flights from Vienna to the cities of Graz, Klagenfurt, Linz, Salzburg and Innsbruck. For details consult airline schedules.

Schwechat airport is located 15 km (9 miles) to the East of the city (25 minutes' drive on the motorway). Its terminals were modernised in 1988, and it has an information booth – tel: (0222) 700 72233 – in the arrival hall which is

open from 9am–10pm daily. An express bus service which operates every 20 minutes between 6am–7pm and every 30 minutes from 8am–9pm, links the airport with Vienna's two main railway stations and the City Air Terminal next to the Hilton Hotel. For information tel: 0222-5800 2300. A train service operates between the central station and the airport every hour on the hour from 7.30am–8.30pm.

By Rail

The Austrian Federal Railway System maintains about 5,800 km (3,625 miles) of track and is connected with both the Eastern and Western European railway networks. There is a small fee for seat reservation. Passengers pay a surcharge on TEE and IC trains but the price of reserved seating is then contained within this additional charge.

Trains Vienna–Graz and Vienna–Salzburg depart at 1-hour intervals. Trains Vienna–Innsbruck and Vienna–Villach leave at 2-hour intervals.

Nearly all daytime trains have dining cars; night trains have sleeping compartments and couchettes. There are a number of fare reductions on offer. For information contact:
Vienna, tel: 0222-1717.
Graz, tel: 0316-1717.
Klagenfurt, tel: 0463-1717.
Linz, tel: 0732-1717.
Salzburg, tel: 0662-1717.
Villach, tel: 04242-1717.

By Road

Approximately 70 international bus lines connect Austria to other countries. The Austrian public bus service primarily links places not served by the railway network. Nearly all tourist areas offer bus excursions into the surrounding countryside.

Motoring Advice: There is a traffic report broadcast on Channel 3 (Ö3) every hour following the regular news edition. Programmes may be interrupted to announce especially nasty traffic conditions. In and around the city of Vienna the radio station Radio Blue Danube broadcasts regular traffic reports in English and French 7–10am, noon–2pm and 6–8pm.

The police must be called to the scene of all car accidents in which any persons are injured. Foreigners should fill out the accident form entitled *Comité Européen des Assurances*. ÖAMTC and ARBÖ maintain breakdown services along the most important thoroughfares; non-members may also take advantage of these services for a somewhat higher price than members.

Useful numbers:
ÖAMTC Breakdown Service: Tel: 120.
ARBÖ Breakdown Service: Tel: 123.
ARBÖ Emergency Service: Tel: 782528.
ÖAMTC European Emergency Service: Tel: 922245.

Tour suggestions:
A tour across the Alps; a tour around Grossglockner; from Salzburg to Salzkammergut; Carinthian Lakes tour.

Waterways

From the beginning of April until the end of October boats operate on regular schedules along the Danube. Vienna is connected to Budapest and Passau. There are also boats running on a regular basis on all larger lakes in Austria.

Along the stretch from Vienna to Budapest, the Donau-Dampf-schiffahrts-Gesellschaft Blue Danube (the Danube Steamship Company, Handelskai 265, operates the hydrofoil to Budapest.

The hydrofoil makes three trips form Vienna to Budapest and three return trips from Budapest to Vienna daily. For more detailed timetable information tel: 0222 588-800.

There is a hydrofoil service between Vienna and Bratislava. Boats depart Vienna at Reichsbrücke from Wednesday to Sunday at 9pm and 9.30pm and arrive in Bratislava at 10.30am and 11pm. The hydrofoil leaves Bratislava at 5pm and 5.40pm arriving in Vienna at 6.45pm and 7.25pm.

Where to Stay

On just about every street in tourist-oriented towns you'll find at least one *zimmer frei*, tourist information, sign. Staff can give you a listing of local, privately-run accommodation.

Attractions

Opera, theatre and classical music performances: Austrian calendar of events, the Austrian Tourist Office Centre. Tel: (0222) 587 2000. Baroque music concert dates and literature about the *Barockstrasse*: Austrian Tourist Office Centre in Vienna 5, Margaretenstrasse 1, tel: (0222) 587 2000 and at Austrian Tourist Office agencies overseas. National Theatre Ticket Reservations: 1 Goethegasse 1. Tel: (0222) 514 440. Open: Monday–Saturday 9am–5pm.

Shopping

Austria has an abundance of high quality, valuable and hand-made articles including glassware, jewellery, chinaware and winter-sports equipment.

Language

Of the 8 million population, 98 percent speak German.

Vienna

Practical Tips

Emergency Telephone Numbers

Ambulance: 40144.
Emergency Doctor: 141. Daily 7pm–7am.
Chemist (after hours): 1550.
Psychiatrist: 9, Fuchsthalergasse 18, tel: 318 419.
International Chemist: 1, Kärntner Ring 15, tel: 512 2825.
Poison Centre: 9, Lazarettgasse 14, tel: 434 3439.

Postal Services

Hauptpostamt (main post office), 1, Fleischmarkt 19, tel: 51590. Open 24 hours.

Tourist Offices

Vienna Tourist Board
Obere Augarten-Strasse 40, II, tel: 211 1401; fax: 216 8492. Detailed information about Austria can be found at local tourist offices. The nine federal provinces maintain their own tourist boards.

Austrian National Tourist Office
Österreich Werbung 1040 Vienna, Margaretenstrasse. 1, tel: 222-587 2000.

Tourist Offices Abroad
UK: Austrian National Tourist Office, 30 St George Street, London W1R 0AL. Tel: 020-7629 0461, fax: 020-7499 6038.
US: Austrian National Tourist Office, PO Box 1142, New York NY10108-1142, tel: 212-944-6880; fax: 310-477-5141 and PO Box 491938 Los Angeles CA 90049, tel: 310-477-3332; fax: 310-477-5141.

Embassies & Consulates

Australia: IV, Mattiellistrasse 2, tel: 512 8580.
Canada: I, Laurenzerberg 2, tel: 531 3830.
South Africa: XIX, Sandgasse 33, tel: 326 4930.

UK: III, Jauresgasse 12,
tel: 713-1575.
US: IX, Boltzmanngasse 16,
tel: 313 390.

Getting Around

A car is superfluous in Vienna. The town has an excellent urban and regional transport systems, including subway; fast subway; local and regional trains; trams and buses. For information about public transport in Vienna contact the Vienna Tourist Office, tel: 0222-211 1401.

Shopping

The most elegant and expensive shops, as well as art galleries and antique shops, can be found in the inner city area between Hofburg, Graben and Kärntner Strasse. Opening hours for shops are Monday–Friday usually 9am–6pm, Saturday 9am–12.30pm.

Almost every district within the city has an open-air market. There are also temporary markets which are held on Tuesday and Friday. The most famous of these markets is the Naschmarkt. There is also a flea market in the vicinity every Saturday at 4–5, Wienzeile, Kettenbrückengasse.

The Naschmarkt is held along the Wienzeile near Kettenbrückengasse. At certain times of the year, other traditional markets are held across the city. These include:
All Saints' Market
(Allerheiligenmarkt) in front of gates 1-3 of the Central Cemetary (early November).
Christmas Market
(Christkindlmarkt) in December in front of the Town Hall.
Lenten Market
(Fastenmarkt), XVII, Kalvarienberggasse (February–March)
Confirmation Market
(Firmunsgsmarkt) at Whitsun on St Stephen's Square.

Goods in Austria are subject to VAT of 20 percent or a luxury tax of 32 percent.

Further Reading

General
Austria, Empire and Republic, by Barbara Jelavich. Cambridge University Press.
Clash of Generations, by Lavender Cassels. John Murray.
Dissolution of the Austro-Hungarian Empire, by J.W. Mason. Longman.
The End of Austria-Hungary, by L. Valani. Knopf.
The Fall of the House of Habsburgs, by Edward Crankshaw. Penguin.
The Hapsburg Monarch, by Arthur J. May. University of Pennsylvania.
Mayerling: the Facts behind the Legend, by Fritz Judtman. Harrap.
A Nervous Splendour, by Frederic Morton. Little.
Nightmare in Paradise: Vienna and its Jews, by George E. Berkley. California University Press.

Insight Guides
There are *Insight Guide* titles to both Austria and Vienna. The *Insight Pocket Guide* series, designed to help readers without a lot of time plan their trips precisely, includes *Pocket Guide: Vienna*. The *Insight Compact Guide* series has titles covering Vienna and Salzburg.

BUDAPEST

Getting Acquainted

Population: 1.8 million (the population of Hungary is 11 million).
Area: 203 sq miles (525 sq km)
Language: Hungarian
Religion: Roman Catholic (67 percent); the rest are mostly Calvinist and Lutheran.
Time Zones: Hungary is in the Central European Time Zone. Summer time, as elsewhere in mainland Europe, is from the last weekend in April until the last weekend in September, when clocks are moved forward by one hour.
Currency: the Forint (Ft or HUF).
Electricity: AC 220 volts
Weights and Measures: Metric
International Dialling Code: 361
Public Holidays: In addition to those listed in the Introduction, Hungary commemorates National Day (15 March), Constitution Day (20 August) and Republic Day (23 October).

Getting There

By Air
Many airlines fly to Budapest's Ferihegy airport. Malév, Hungary's national airline, uses the Ferihegy terminal 2A, all others use Ferihegy **2B**. There are regular flights to and from all European capitals and major cities, several Balkan cities, a number of Middle Eastern cities and New York.

Malév has offices around the world and desks in the main Budapest hotels. International airlines flying to Hungary have offices in the centre of Budapest.

The most reliable way to get into town is by minibus. It stops at most big hotels, from where you can catch a taxi. The minibus will pick you up as well. ask your receptionist, or call 296 8555. Beware of taking a taxi from the airport. The incidence of over-charging is high.

General flight information. Arrivals tel: 296 8000; departures tel: 296 7000.

By Road

Travellers coming from Budapest will probably want to drive in through Vienna, from which a motorway (A4) leads almost to the crossing at Hegyeshalom. There are more crossings further to the south. If driving through Carinthia in Austria, you may want to cut through Maribor, Slovenia and drive in through Letenye.

Motorists need a valid driving licence, a sticker showing which country they're from, valid vehicle registration documents and insurance green card.

Drink Driving

Beware: there is a total drink-and-drive ban in Hungary. The legal limit is **0.0 milligrams**, and there are strict rules and harsh penalties if you have been drinking anything at all.

By Rail

Rail travellers to Budapest usually have to change trains at the West Station in Vienna (the journey continues from the South Station, Wien-Süd). Arrival is at the Keleti pályaudvar (Eastern Railway Station) in Budapest. Some long-distance international trains have coaches going directly to Budapest: the Oostende-Vienna Express (Cologne-Frankfurt-Nürnberg-Passau-Linz); the Orient Express (Paris-Kehl-Stuttgart-Munich-Salzburg); the Wiener Waltzer (Basel-Zurich-Innsbruck-Salzburg). For the trip from one station to another you should allow at least half an hour; the Metro is a lot faster than a cab. For rail service information, tel: 461 5400.

By Sea

The Hungarian Mahart company and the Austrian DDSG-Donaureisen company operate jetfoils and hovercraft between Vienna and Budapest (and elsewhere). The trip is picturesque but not necessarily cheap. Your local travel agent should be able to help you with information.

You can also write to or call: DDSG-Donaureisen, Handelskai 265, A-1021 Vienna, tel: 01 729 2161. Or try Mahart, Belgrad rakpart, Budapest V, tel: 318 1743

Practical Tips

Medical Services

Medical aid is available around the clock from the following clinics: Falck SOS Hungary: Budapest, Kapy utca 49/B, tel: 2000 100. SOS Dental Clinic: Király utca 14, tel: 267 9602/269 6010.

Accidents

Accidents have to be reported to the police (tel: 107) within 24 hours, and forms need to be filled out even for minor collisions. Report any accident – even if it wasn't your fault – to **Hungaria Insurance** Kerepesi út 15, tel: 1087
Hungarian Automobile Club Emergency Service, tel: 345 1744. 24 hour service. Foreign languages are spoken at this number.

Pharmacies (Gyogyszertar)

Almost all strong medicine is only available on prescription. Payment must be made in cash. The normal opening times are Monday–Friday 8am–6pm, Saturday 8am–2pm.

Business Hours

Times tend to vary; generally, shop trading hours are Monday–Friday 8am–6pm and Saturday 8am–1pm,

Emergency Numbers

- **Police**: 107
- **Fire Brigade**: 105
- **Ambulance/Emergency Rescue Service**: 104

with some shopping centres open on Sunday. Museums are open Tuesday–Sunday 10am–6pm, and mostly closed Monday.

Tipping

Gratuities are included in the price, but it's usual to add an extra 10–15 percent of the final sum as a tip.

Postal Services

Post offices are open Monday–Friday 8am–7pm (except in smaller towns and villages) and 8am–2pm (at the latest) on Saturday.

The post offices at the west and east train stations in Budapest are open 24 hours. At the main Post Office (8am–7pm), Budapest V. Varoshaz utca 9–11, tel: 118 5398.

Telecommunications

Digital lines ensure good quality calls. Public phone boxes use 10, 20, 50 and 100 forint coins or phone cards, available from tobacconists, post offices, shops and petrol stations.

To dial outside Budapest: 06 + prefix without the 0 + number. To dial internationally: 00. Useful country codes: Australia 61; Canada and US 1; UK 44. Foreign language directory enquiries (7am–8pm); international: 199; inland: 198; international operator 190.

Tourist Information

Tourinform offices are omnipresent in Hungary, beginning with border crossings, the airport, and train stations. They provide many services including hotel reservations, changing money, etc. If you are staying in a more expensive hotel, you will probably have a tourist office in the lobby. Tourinform offices in Budapest: **Oktogon**, VI, Liszt Ferenc tér 9–11, tel: 322 4098.
Western (Nyugati) Railway Station Main Hall, tel: 302 8580
Buda Várinfo in the Buda Castle,` I, Tárnok utca 9–11, tel: 488 0453.
Downtown, V, Vörösmarty square Tourinform Head Office and Police Info Office, tel: 438 8080; Süto

Tourist Offices Abroad

Tourist information abroad on Hungary is available from either a travel agency specialising in Eastern European travel, a branch of the IBUSZ travel agent, Malév (the Hungarian airline) or the nearest Hungarian consulate or embassy.

● **UK: Hungarian National Tourist Office,** 46 Eaton Place, London SW1 8AL, tel: 020 7823-1032, fax: 020 7823-1459.

● **US: Hungarian National Tourist Office,** 150 East 58th Street, 33rd floor, New York, NY, 10155-3398, tel: (212) 355-0240, fax: (212) 207-4103.

utca 2. (Deák tér) tel: 438 8080; or Pest side of Elizabeth Bridge, V, Március 15. tér 7. tel: 266 0479.

Embassies

British Embassy, V, Harmincad utca 6, tel: 266 2888.
US Embassy, V, Szabadsag tér 12, tel: 475 4400. After-hours emergency, tel: 475 4703.

Getting Around

By Rail

The metro operates daily 4.30am–11pm. Tickets (best bought in bulk in advance) can be obtained from vending machines, at stations, at the tobacconists, at the Metro ticket offices and in travel agencies. Budapest has three metro lines; all intersect beneath Deák tér in the centre of Pest.

Hungarian Rail (MAV) has an extensive but comparatively expensive rail network.

MAV customer service office: VI, Andrassy ut 35. Monday–Friday 9am–5pm. National information: tel: 461 5500. International information: tel: 461 5400.

Car Rental

You have to be 21 and you will need your driving licence and passport in order to hire a car. Credit cards are accepted as a means of payment. Listed below are the main car rental companies with their contact details.
Avis, V, Szervita tér 8, tel: 318 4240, 318 4158.
Budget, I, Krisztina krt. 41-43, tel/fax: 214 0420.
Europcar Interrent, VIII, Ülloi ut 60-62, tel: 477 1080, fax: 477 1099. Also at Ferihegy 2 Airport, tel. 296 6610.
Hertz Worldwide, tel: 296 0999, fax: 296 0998.

Public Transport

Buses and Trams: In the city buses and trams cost the same as the metro and run at the same times; some trams and blue buses run at night. The lines with red numbers are express bus lines, only stopping at important traffic intersections.

Yellow buses travel long-distance routes. Most of them leave from Erzsebet tér, near Deák tér. Timetables and price lists are available daily by calling: 317 1173.

Where to Stay

Contact IBUSZ or the international Tourist Information Service TOURINFO in Budapest for a list of recommended hotels and a reservation service.

Attractions

What's On

Budapest in Your Pocket provides useful listings; the *Budapest Sun* is a paper written by and for the expat community. Hotels and tourist agencies have monthlies containing advertising.

Sightseeing

There is the nostalgic funicular railway (Sikló) up to the Castle from the bank of the Danube, daily 7.30am–10pm; the rack railway from Sziagyi Erzébet fasor in the northwest of Buda and Buda Hill, daily 4.30am–midnight, journey time 25 minutes; and the Libegó chairlift to the Janós-hegy observation point in the east of the city, daily 9am–5pm, 15 minutes.

Language

Hungarian belongs to the Finno-Ugric family of languages. Its only relations in Europe are Finnish and Estonian.

Further Reading

Budapest 1900 by John Lukács.
Hungary: The Rise and Fall of Feasible Socialism by Nigel Swain.
One Minute Stories by István Örkény.
The Habsburg Monarchy 1809–1918 by AJP Taylor.
Under the Frog by Tibor Fischer.

Other Insight Guides

Other books in the *Insight Guide* series highlight destinations in this region: *Insight Guides*: Hungary and Budapest. The *Insight Pocket Guide* series, designed to help readers without a lot of time plan their trips precisely, include: *Pocket Guides*: Hungary and Budapest. Many of the Pocket Guides come with handy pullout maps. *Insight Compact Guides* cover Budapest.

WARSAW AND KRAKÓW

Getting Acquainted

Area: Poland is 690 km (430 miles) east-west and 650 km (400 miles) north-south. The total land area encompasses 312,680 sq. km (120,720 sq. miles).
Population: 38.61 million.
Language: Polish.
Capital: Warsaw.
Religion: 97 percent Roman Catholic. The remaining population is composed of about 575,000 Russian Orthodox, 267,000 Protestants, 80,000 Old Catholics, 5,200 Muslims and 5,000 Jews. Throughout the country there are more than 12,500 churches.
Time Zone: GMT plus one hour. When it is noon in Warsaw it is 6am in New York and 8pm in Tokyo. Daylight Saving is in effect May–October when one hour is added.
Currency: Polish złoty (zł or PLN), divided into 100 groszy (gr).
Weights & Measures: Metric.
International dialling code: 48.
Electricity: 220 volts. Sockets take two round pins.
Public Holidays: In addition to the holidays listed in the Introduction, Poland commemorates Constitution Day (May 3), Corpus Christi (in June) and National Independence Day (11 November).

Getting There

By Air
A new terminal was added to Warsaw's Okecie International Airport in 1992 to handle the increasing number of flights both by LOT, the Polish national airline, and international carriers. There are regular direct non-stop flights to Warsaw from New York and Chicago. Domestic flights link Warsaw to at least 11 cities and towns within the country. Virtually all the major European carriers fly to Warsaw from their home bases.

Okęcie Airport also has its own bus line, **City Line**. The bus stops at the all the larger hotels and operates every 20 minutes between 6am–11pm. (On Sunday and public holidays every 30 minutes.) Buy a ticket on board the bus. It's a little more expensive than the regular buses.

LOT also organises a luxury car service **Fly&Drive** into the centre of the city. Or you could phone for a taxi – do not take a taxi from the taxi station at Okęcie unless you must because they are far more expensive than ordering by phone.

Useful Numbers

● **Warsaw International Airport (Okęcie):** Arrivals tel: 022-650 4220; Departures tel: 022-650 3943, 846 1700/31, 846 5603.
● **Reservations and tickets:** Tel: 022-846 9645/952/953; business class tel: 0800-225757.
● **Domestic flights:** Tel: 022-650 1750.

By Sea
Regular passenger ferry services link the Polish ports of Swinoujsie and Gdansk with Denmark and Sweden.

By Rail
There are regular daily services from London's Liverpool Street Station. On Saturdays (in season) charter couchettes are available on the train from Liverpool Street. Journey time from England is about 31 hours. EuroCity trains connect Warsaw with Berlin. Passengers who use this connection have links with Cologne, Wiesbaden, Karlsruhe, Hamburg, Frankfurt and Munich. All fast and express trains run on international links. Trains have 1st and 2nd class carriages, berths, sleepers and restaurant cars. Almost all international trains arrive at Warsaw Central Station, located in the city centre.
International and domestic information: tel: 9436;
Reservations: tel: 8256033

Travelling from Germany to Poland by train is relatively cheap. It is not worth obtaining the reduced Interail Pass for people under 26 as travel within Poland is so cheap. Most trains to Poznan and Warsaw pass through Berlin and Frankfurt am Oder. During the summer a motorrail service connects Hanover and Ilawa.
Direct trains to Poland:
Paris–Cologne–Düsseldorf–Hanover –Berlin–Poznaø–Warsaw
Cologne–Hanover–Leipzig–Wroclaw–Warsaw
Frankfurt-am-Main–Bebra–Wroclaw–Warsaw
Munich–Dresden–Wroclaw–Katowice
East-West Express: London–Hoek van Holland–Berlin–Warsaw–Moscow
Chopin Express: Vienna–Warsaw
For further information:
POLRES, Al. Jerozolimskie 4400-024 Warsaw. Tel: 022/8272588.

By Road
The main European road routes across Poland are the E12 from Germany through Prague to Wroclaw, Lodz, Warsaw and Bioalystok, the E14 from Austria through the Czech Republic to Swinoujscie and on to Sweden, and the E8 from Germany through Poznan and Warsaw and on to Russia. Be warned that border formalities between Poland and Lithuania can be extremely trying and complex.
By Coach: Regular weekly services run most of the year by luxury, air-conditioned coach with bar and toilet from the English Midlands via London, across the Channel to Poland. The journey time is around 36 hours.

The Polski Express goes either from London via Amsterdam to Poznan and Warsaw; or from London or Manchester/Birmingham to Wroclaw, Katowice and Kraków.

Practical Tips

Emergency Medical Services

Western visitors can get medical attention in any city clinic. Treatments and hospital stays must be paid for in cash. Most four- and five-star hotels have a doctor on call to deal with emergencies. Make sure you take out adequate medical insurance.

Emergency Numbers

- **Ambulance**: 999
- **Fire**: 998
- **Police**: 997
  Loss or theft of credit cards can be reported at the following credit card hot lines:
American Express:
Tel: (022) 625 4030
Diners' Club, MasterCard, EuroCard and Visa:
Tel: (022) 515 3000 or 513 3150
Visa and MasterCard:
Tel: (022) 659 2713.

Business Hours

Most businesses are open weekdays from 9am–6pm. Shops open 10am–6pm Monday to Friday and 9am–2pm on Saturdays. Some food shops at 6am. In general shops are closed on Sundays, but more and more larger stores are staying open all week. There are plenty of small neighbourhood shops open 24 hours a day.

Banks open Monday to Friday 8am–6pm without lunch break. Post Offices open Monday to Saturday, 8am–8pm. The main post office in Warsaw is open 24 hours.

Postal Services

Stamps are available wherever postcards are sold. The main post offices in large cities are open around the clock; others open Monday to Saturday 8am–8pm. Telegrams can be sent from many hotels.

Telecommunications

It is advisable to purchase one of the recently introduced phone cards. These cards (remove a corner before use) are available from post offices and kiosks. If you have to use one of the old coin-operated telephones, then you will need to buy one or more of the tokens (A = 1 unit, C = 6 units) from a post office or kiosk. The service is now generally very good. Until recently, it was often necessary in smaller towns to dial out via the operator, but now almost everywhere has its own dialling code. A leaflet listing dialling codes can be obtained at post offices.

Useful Numbers: Inland directory enquiries: 913
International directory enquiries: 908
International Area Dialling Codes:
Tel: 930. To call abroad from Poland, dial 00 and then the country code, eg UK 44.

Faxes: In most large hotels and main post offices you can both send and receive a fax. In addition, the best hotels offer an office service including access to computers and printers.

Telegrams: These can be sent from any post office. The number of words and speed (normal or express) determine the cost.

Tourist Offices

Tourist Offices in Warsaw:
1/13 Plac Zamkowy,
Warsaw 00-297.
Tel: (022) 6351881.
Tourist Offices Overseas:
Germany: Polnisches Informationszentrum fr Touristik, Waidmarkt 24, 50676 Köln.
Tel: (0221) 230545. Fax: 210465.
Netherlands: Pool Informatiebureau voor Toerisme, Leidsestraat 64, Amsterdam 1017 D.
Tel: (020) 625 3570
Fax: 623 0929.
Sweden: Polska Statens Turistbyra, Kungsgatan 66,
Box 449, S-10128 Stockholm.
Tel: (08) 216075, 218145
Fax: 210465.
UK: Polish National Tourist Office, 1st floor, Remo House, 310–312 Regent Street, London W1R 5AJ.
Tel: (020) 7580 8811.
USA: Polish National Tourist Office, 333 N Michigan Avenue, Suite 224, Chicago, IL 60601.
Tel: (312) 236 9013
Fax: 236 1125.

Embassies & Consulates

Australia: ul. Estooska 3/5, 03 903 Warsaw. Tel: 6176081; fax: 617756.
Canada: ul. Matejki 1/5, 00-481 Warsaw. Tel: 6298051; fax: 6296457.
UK: Al. Rox 1, 00-556 Warsaw. Tel: 6281001/5; fax: 6217161.
US: Al. Ujazdowskie 29/31, 00-540 Warsaw. Tel: 6283041; fax: 6288298.

Getting Around

By Air

From Warsaw airport you can catch a flight at just about any time on LOT Airlines to Gdansk, Bydgoszcz, Katowice, Koszalin, Kraków, Poznan, Slupsk, Szczecin, Wroclaw and Zielona Gora. Tickets may be purchased at all LOT and Orbis branch offices, or at Warsaw International airport, tel: (022) 650 1750.

By Rail

The entire country is connected by an extensive railway network of about 16,000 miles (26,000 km). A reservation is needed on both express and regular trains. Trains are not always punctual. There are comfortable, non-stop express trains complete with dining cars running between Warsaw and Gdansk/Gydnia, Poznan and Kraków. Travelling by railway in Poland – even taking into account recent price increases – is still reasonable. Tickets are available at train stations, at Orbis or in POLRES agencies (tel: 022-365055). For information on transfers and connections, enquire at the railway station. Tel: 9436 for international and domestic rail information. Tel: 8256033 for reservations.

By Sea

Coastal boat tours offer the following trips 1 May–15 October: Gdansk–Sopot–Hel, Gydnia–Jastarnia, Gydnia–Helsowie,

Szczecin–Swinoujscie and
Miedzyzdroje. Inland boat traffic
includes journeys down the Vistula
(Warsaw–Gdansk), through the
Masurian Lakes
(Wegorzewo–Gizycko–Miko-
lajki–Nida–Ruciane), and along the
Elblag–Ostroda Canal.

By Road
Tickets for the public transport
systems can be bought at kiosks.
Remember to cancel your ticket
every time you transfer.
Combination rail and bus tickets are
available. The National Bus Network
(PKS) is about 118,000 km
(73,000 miles) long and composed
of country, city and night buses.
Trams and trolleybuses: At every
stop, and in all trams and
trolleybuses, a schedule and route
is posted.
Taxis: A vacant taxi has a lighted
sign. The best place to hail one is
at a taxi rank in front of a hotel,
station or department store. It is
also possible to phone for a radio
taxi (ask in your hotel for details).
This usually works out cheaper, as
independent drivers, who are not
linked to companies, are more likely
to overcharge their passengers. At
night, and for journeys into the
outlying countryside, fares are
usually 50 percent higher.
   To overcome the problems of
inflation, taxi meters show only a
base unit. To calculate your fare,
the driver multiplies the number of
units by a number on an authorised
list (normally this factor is shown on
a sticker on the passenger door).
Check that the taxi meter is
switched on as soon as your
journey starts.

Attractions
What's On
The dates for concerts, opera and
theatre performances are in the
calendar of events from the Tourist
Office.
Tours: Since the political
turnaround, privately-owned small
and medium-sized travel and
service agencies have sprung up
offering excursions and local

services. ORBIS, Mazurkas Travel,
PTTK, Air Tours or Trakt (tours of
Warsaw and surroundings) all
organise city tours and excursions
and provide a good service.

Further Reading
Atlas of Warsaw's Architecture, by
J.A. Cicki Chro and A. Rottermund.
**Heart of Europe: A short history of
Poland**, by Norman Davies.
History of Polish Culture, by
Bogdan Suchodolski.
The Polish August, by Neal
Ascherson.
Book of Warsaw Palaces, by T.S.
Jaroszewski.
Warsaw: The Royal Way, by Jerzy
Lileyko.
A Way of Hope, by Lech Walesa.

Other Insight Guides
Insight Guides: Poland and Eastern
Europe are companions to this
book, from Apa Publications' award-
winning series. *Insight Pocket
Guide*: Krakow is designed to help
readers without a lot of time plan
their trips precisely. *Insight
Compact Guides* cover Poland.

PRAGUE

Getting Acquainted
Area: 497 sq km (190 sq miles).
Population: 1.2 million.
Language (everyday): Czech and
some Slovak (both in the Slavonic
language family, along with Russian
and Polish).
Language: English and German
(business); Czech and Slovak.
Religion: Roman Catholic.
Time Zone: GMT plus 1 hour Oct–
Mar; GMT plus 2 hours Apr–Sept.
Currency: Czech Koruna (Kč), called
"crown" in English.
Weights & Measures: Metric.
Electricity: AC 220 volts. Two-pin
plugs or adaptors are needed for
British appliances.
International dialling code: 420
(Czech Republic) + 2 (Prague).

Planning The Trip
Entry Regulations
Czech customs controls are rigid. To
avoid misunderstandings, check on
anything you're unsure about
beforehand. Upon entering the
country, you'll be given a leaflet
explaining the customs regulations.
   Visitors should note that
antiques more than 50 years old
can only be taken out with a special
permit, which may be difficult to
obtain. Non-commercial items (i.e.
not intended for resale) of unlimited
value can be exported from the
Czech Republic without an export
permit.

Getting There
By Air
Prague's expanded, modernised
Ruzyně airport lies about 20 km
(13 miles) northwest of the city.

There are direct flights from most European capitals, New York, Montreal and Toronto. You can get detailed flight information from the Czech airline CSA, which has offices in many major cities.

By Rail
There are direct trains to Prague from Stuttgart and Munich (an 8-hour trip), Frankfurt (10 hours), Berlin (6 hours), Hamburg (14 hours), and Vienna (6 hours).

Most trains from Southern Germany and Austria come in at the main Wilsonova Station (Hlavní nádraží). Trains from the west stop at Prague-Holešovice Station and many proceed on to Wilsonova. Other destinations in the country can be reached via Prague.

Further information about rail travel can be obtained from the main station in English, French or German, tel: 2422 3887/4200.

By Road
There are many official border crossings with Germany and Austria. Expect some delays until border crossings are open to all vehicles from other nationalities.
By Bus: There are a great many different bus tours to the Czech Republic from Germany, Austria or Italy which include overnights.

By Sea
The Cologne-Düsseldorf passenger shipping line offers cruises from Berlin and Hamburg via Dresden to Prague. These last between 4 and 7 days. The *Princess of Prussia* does a one-day journey from Dresden. Ask your local travel agent for details.

Practical Tips

Emergency Medical Services
Emergencies are treated in every city clinic. Visitors now have a number of options if they require medical treatment. The **American Medical Centre** at Janovského 48, Prague 7, tel: 807756, 807757, 807758 has a 24-hour service, with house calls available. All doctors speak excellent English. Be sure

you have health insurance or the fees – which otherwise must be paid in cash – are very high.

Chemists' shops are open during normal business hours and have information and addresses for emergency services.

Emergency Numbers

● **Ambulance:** 155
● **Fire:** 150
● **Police:** 158
● **Dental emergency hotline:** 1097
● **Lost Property:** tel: 2422 6133.
Lost or stolen credit cards:
● American Express: tel: 2421 9978.
● MasterCard: tel: 2442 3135.
● Visa, Diner's Club: tel: 2412 5353.

Tourist Information
The **Prague Information Service** (**PIS**) has an office at the Old Town Hall in Old Town Square, Prague 1. Here you can obtain information about Prague, including city maps and the free monthly booklet *Prague Cultural Events*, containing helpful information and addresses.

Business Hours
Most grocery shops are open weekdays 7am–6pm; certain specialised shops 10am–6pm. Many smaller shops close for two hours at midday. On Saturday, stores close between noon and 1pm; the large department stores, however, are an exception, keeping weekday hours at weekends.

Banks are open Monday–Friday 8am–5pm with an hour for lunch. Exchange offices work 8am–7pm daily; some remain open until 10pm. For a slightly higher commission, you can exchange money at the larger hotels (24 hours).

Tipping
In general, a service charge is included in the bill. However, it is customary to round up the sum when paying. Because prices are so low, satisfied foreign customers

may be inclined to give the waiter more than the 10 percent service charge; local diners will probably not follow suit.

Postal Services
Stamps can usually be bought wherever postcards are sold. Ask about prices for letters and postcards when you get to the country, as postal rates are continually rising.

Orange and blue mailboxes are everywhere. Larger post offices are open Monday–Friday 8am–6pm, Saturday 8am–noon; smaller branches are open Monday–Friday 8am–5pm at the latest. The main post office is at Jindrisska 14 and is open 24 hours a day.

Telecommunications
There are two models of telephone in the Czech Republic – if they work. One takes 2-, 5- and 10-crown coins and can only be used for local calls. Most telephones, though, accept only phonecards, which can be purchased in post offices or from newsagents. If you want to call abroad, your best bet is to go to a post office or hotel; the latter, of course, adds a surcharge of 20–30 percent.

In most major hotels, you can receive or send a fax or telex. First-class hotels generally make office services available to their guests. Directory enquiries (Prague and the Czech Republic) Tel: 120 International enquiries Tel: 0139 and 0149.

Embassies & Consulates
UK: Thunovska 14, Prague 1, tel: 224 510/533 370.
US: Trziste 15, Prague 1, tel: 53 66 416.

Getting Around
By Air
From Prague, you can reach Brno, Bratislava, Karlovy Vary, Kosice, Ostrava, Sliac, Piestany and Tatry-Poprad by air. CSA (the national airline representatives) can give information about other connections. In the UK, tel: 020-

7255 1898/1366 for information about CSA flights; in the US, tel: 212-765 6022/6545.

In Prague itself tickets, reservations and flight information are available from: V celnici 5, Prague 1, tel: 2010 4310/2011 3743. The office is open Monday to Friday 7am–6pm, Saturday 7am–3pm. The office is located near the metro station Náměstí Republiky (exit the metro either at Náměstí Republiky or Masarykovo nádraží).

By Rail
Fare and scheduling information are available in Prague, tel: 2422 3887/4200.

You can get train tickets at Prague Railway Station or from the Cedok office at Na prikope 18, Prague 1. Unfortunately, to do so you'll have to queue up in the morning until noon and you won't be able to pick up your tickets until the following day – after queuing once again.

If you'd rather not go through this rigmarole, try one of the many local travel agencies.

By Boat
In peak season (1 May–15 October), sight-seeing tours along the Moldau depart from Prague. Information can be obtained from the quayside on the Rasin bank at the Palacky Bridge or from one of the many tour companies.

Public Transport
You can buy tickets at shops, at the kiosks of the Prague Public Transport Executive, and at hotel receptions, as well as from the automatic ticket machines at some tram stops and in all metro stations. In buses and trams, you must cancel a new ticket every time you change vehicles. In the underground, you can transfer as often as you wish within 90 minutes. Children and pensioners ride free.

Buses and the metro system link the suburbs and the city centre, or service longer routes.

The Prague underground is a quick and convenient way to get around. You can reach all of Prague's major sights with the three lines, and it's easy to transfer from one to another. Underground stations are marked with a large 'M'. Service begins at 5am and ends at midnight. For tourists, the 24-hour ticket is a bargain.

Trams in this city are slow and old-fashioned, but offer a good way to see Prague (particularly Line 22, which runs past many tourist attractions).

After midnight, taxis are the only way to get anywhere in Prague, apart from a few night bus routes. There are plenty of taxi stands in the city centre and in front of the large hotels. Make sure the meter is switched on. You can recognise official taxis by their taxi plates and the licence number in the interior. Two reputable firms with English-speaking dispatchers and reasonable rates are AAA, tel: 1080, and Profi Taxi, tel: 1035.

Where to Stay

Finding a hotel room in Prague is getting easier all the time, but if you'd like something cheap it's necessary to book far in advance. Reserving a hotel room in Prague during the peak season can be a hopeless endeavour. One alternative is to book through a travel agency, another is a private room. Many agencies rent out rooms in the centre of Prague.

Attractions

There are concerts (and leaflets) everywhere in Prague. You can book tickets for concerts and opera in the major houses through foreign travel agencies before you arrive.
To get tickets, we recommend going directly to the box office in order to get the best price, since ticket agencies may mark up prices significantly or charge a commission. You can also buy tickets through various tourist agencies, but expect to pay a hefty commission.

Further Reading

The Good Soldier Swejk, by Jaroslav Hasek. Penguin.
Prague Chronicles, by Ludvik Vaculik. Readers International.
Utz, by Bruce Chatwin. Picador.
We the People: The Revolution of 1989, by Timothy Garton-Ash. Granta.

Other Insight Guides
Other books in the *Insight Guide* series highlight destinations in this region: *Insight Guides: Eastern Europe, Czech and Slovak Republics*, and *Prague*. The *Insight Pocket Guide* series, designed to help readers without a lot of time plan their trips precisely, includes *Pocket Guide: Prague*. *Insight Compact Guides* cover the Czech Republic and Prague.

ITALY

Getting Acquainted

Area: 301,245 sq km/116,280 sq miles.
Capital: Rome.
Highest Mountain: Mont Blanc (4,760 metres/15,616 ft).
Principal rivers: Po, Tiber, Arno and Volturno.
Population: 57 million.
Language: Italian.
Religion: Roman Catholic.
Time Zone: Central European Time (GMT plus 1 hour).
Currency: the Euro.
Weights & Measures: Metric.
Electricity: 220 volts. You will need an adaptor to operate British three-pin appliances and a transformer to use 100–120 volt appliances.
International Dialling Code: 39.
Public Holidays: In addition to those holidays listed in the Introduction, the following are celebrated: Epiphany (6 January), Liberation Day: (25 April), Corpus Christi Day, Republic Day (2 June), Sts Peter and Paul Day (29 June), Victory Day (4 November), Conception Day (8 December).

Getting There

By Air
Air connections to Italy are provided by the national carrier, Alitalia, among many others. Both Rome and Milan have excellent services from many European capitals and some of the major cities including London (mainly from Heathrow but also from Gatwick).

By Rail
Frequent and fast train services link Italy with her neighbours – France, Switzerland, Austria and to a lesser

extent, the former Yugoslavia. There are also several through expresses from all other major European cities, calling en route at various Italian cities.

By Road
Bordered by France and Switzerland to the northwest and Austria and the former Yugoslavia to the northeast, Italy can be reached by a number of European routes and motorways.

When calculating the cost of travelling to Italy by car, allow for motorway tolls as well as accommodation en route and petrol. If you want to travel by toll-free roads in Italy, get hold of the Italian State Tourist Office's *Traveller's Handbook*.

The cost of travelling to Italy from the United Kingdom by scheduled coach is not much cheaper than travelling by air. National Express Eurolines run from London Victoria, via Paris and Mont Blanc, to Aosta, Turin, Genoa, Milan, Venice, Bologna, Florence and Rome.

By Sea
Sea links exist between Brindisi in the southeastern tip of Italy to Patras, Greece; between Venice and Egypt via Piraeus in Greece; and between Genoa and Malaga in Spain.

Practical Tips

Medical Services
For minor complaints, seek out a *farmacia*, identified by a sign displaying a red cross within a white circle. Trained pharmacists give advice and prescribe drugs, including antibiotics. Normal opening hours are 9am–1pm and 4–7pm, but outside these hours the address of the nearest *farmacia* on emergency duty will be posted in the window.

Business Hours
Shops are usually open 8.30 or 9am–1pm and 3.30 or 4–7.30 or 8pm, with some variations in the north where the lunch-break tends to be shorter and shops therefore close earlier. In areas serving

Emergency Numbers
● **Police:** 113, or 112 for the armed police (*Carabinieri*).
● **Ambulance:** 116
● **Public Emergency Assistance:** 113.
These numbers and their services operate on a 24-hour basis, and the number 113, in the principal cities, will answer in the main foreign languages.

tourists, hours are generally longer than these. Shops often close on Monday (or Monday morning only). Some close on Saturday. Almost everything closes on Sunday. In most resorts and large towns, there are markets once or twice a week.

Tipping
In nearly every restaurant, a service charge is included in the bill. Tipping above this is discretionary, but much appreciated, especially when service has been good. Although *pane e coperto*, an outdated cover and bread charge, has been officially eliminated in most cities, some restaurants have been slow in phasing it out.

Taxi drivers should be tipped 10 percent. In hotels it is customary to tip the chambermaids and the head waiter at the end of your stay. Custodians of sights and museums also expect a tip, particularly if they have opened something especially for you.

Postal Services
Post office hours are usually 8am–1.30pm, but every town has a main post office open throughout the day. The post office can also provide such services as *raccomandata* (registered), *espresso* (express) and *via aerea* (air mail) to speed up delivery of letters.

You can receive mail addressed to Poste Restante, held at the *fermo posta* window of the main post office in every town, picking it up personally with identification.

A very fast delivery service, CAI-post, is also provided by the post office to send important documents almost all over the world in 24–48 hours.

Stamps may also be purchased from tobacco shops, which can supply information about Italian postal codes.

Telecommunications
Public telephones are found almost everywhere in Italy, but especially in bars, which practically double as telephone offices. From some bars, but mostly from post offices, you can call a *scatti* (ring first, pay later). Most public telephones now take phonecards (*carta telefonica*) and these are available in various denominations from tobacconists, post offices or news-stands. There are only a few coin-operated phones left. In the major cities, such as Milan and Rome, it is possible to hire a mobile phone.
Directory enquiries: 12
International enquiries: 176
Reverse charge (collect) calls: 170.

If you have no small change, phone card or tokens, it is best to make international and collect calls from the public telephone offices (PTP). For numbers both within and outside your area, dialling must be preceded by "0" and then the area code, which you can obtain from

Information. The area codes of main cities are: Rome (06), Milan (02), Florence (055), Pisa (050), Venice (041), Turin (011), Naples (081), Como (031), Palermo (091). If you are dialling from outside Italy, you **keep** initial zeros.

By Air
Italian mainland cities are linked by air with each other and with Sicily and Sardinia. Services are operated by Alitalia, ATI and Aermediterraniea. Bookings for all domestic flights can be made at any travel agency. Alitalia, main office in Rome, tel: 6562 8246

By Rail
The cheapest, fastest and most convenient way to travel is by train. Train information is available from the *Uffici Informazioni* at most major stations, listed in the telephone directory under *Ferrovie dello Stato*.

The state-owned Ferrovie dello Stato (FS) extends over the entire country and into Sicily, which is linked by train ferries across the Straits of Messina. There are also railway services in Sardinia. Trains come in five basic categories:

accelerato, diretto and *locale* are all slow trains with many stops; *Expresso* trains are faster and *Rapido* is an express.

When travelling considerable distances or along major lines, the faster *InterCity* and *EuroCity* services are the best bet – the supplemental charge being well worth the time saved and the comfort. The *Pendolino* is the fastest and most comfortable train, and requires a supplemental charge and a reservation. It is a good idea to buy tickets and make reservations for the *IC/EC* and *Pendolino* in advance, and this can be done at any travel agency as well as at the station.

Public Transport
Each province in Italy has its own inter-city bus companies and each company has its own fares and lines. It is worthwhile taking buses, especially when you are going to the mountainous interior, where they are generally cheaper and faster than the train.

By Road
Autostrade (expressways) are excellent and numerous. However, these are all toll roads so your ticket must be kept and given up

Tourist Information

General tourist information is available at the Ente Nazionale per il Turismo (ENIT), Via Marghera, 2/6 Rome. Tel: 497 1222. The ENIT also has offices on the 15th Floor, 630 Fifth Avenue in New York City, tel: 212 245 4822 and in the UK at 1 Princes Street, London W1R 8A7, tel: 020-7408 1254.
In every major town you will find the Ente Provinciale per il Turismo (EPT) or the Azienda Autonoma di Soggiorno e Turismo. For their addresses and phone numbers, check the directory or the *Yellow Pages* under "Enti". Main cities have a "travel tips" named *Tuttocittà* together with the directory.

Almost every town in Italy has a **Touring Club Italiano** (TCI) office, which provides free information about points of interest. Telephone numbers are listed in the local telephone book. The club also produces some of the best maps and food – and wine – guides.

Provincial Tourist Offices (EPT)
Rome: Via Parigi, 5. Tel: 488 99253. There are also offices at Stazione Termini, tel: 06-4871270, and Fiumicino Airport, tel: 06-65956074. Open: daily Monday–Saturday 8.30am–1pm and 2–7pm.
Milan: Stazione Centrale. Tel: 669 0432/0532. Open in Summer: 9am–12.30pm and 2–6.30pm, in

winter until 6pm. Closed: Sunday. Piazza del Duomo. Tel: 809662. Open: Monday–Saturday 8am–7pm; Sunday 9am–noon and 1.30–6pm.
Florence: Via Manzoni, 16. Tel: 23320. Open: Monday–Friday 8.30am–1.30pm and 4–6.30pm, Saturday 8.30am–1pm. More central and efficient, but open to personal callers only, is the Azienda Autonoma di Turismo, Provincia-Comune di Firenze, Via Cavour, 1R. Open: Monday–Saturday 9am–2pm.
Venice: San Marco, 71F. Tel: 522 6356. Open: Monday–Saturday 9am–12.30pm and 3–7pm; also an office in the station, tel: 719078. Open: daily 8am–7pm.

when quitting the *autostrada.* Tolls are variable, as are speed limits in Italy, calculated according to the engine capacity of the car. Get a copy of the Italian Tourist Office's *Traveler's Handbook* to familiarize yourself with these differences. Fuel discount coupons are available to tourists; so are *autostrada* toll discounts. Apply at ENIT offices abroad and at frontier crossings. For information on current road conditions, dial 194.

Motoring Advice

The Automobile Club d'Italia (ACI) has offices at all main frontier posts, offering emergency breakdown services. Throughout Italy, tel: 116 for quick towing and/or repairs. Members of the automobile associations can get help from the ACI (Italian Automobile Club); Via Marsala 8, I-00185, Rome, tel: 49981.

Attractions

What's On
All cultural information can be obtained from ENIT and EPT offices, and the newspapers.

Almost every town in Italy has a Touring Club Italiano (TCI) office, which provides free information about local points of interest. Telephone numbers are listed in the local telephone book.

Shopping

The flea markets and street stalls in Florence are a bargain-hunter's paradise where particularly good buys on leather goods, scarves and clothes are available. Other major cities have similar markets, albeit not as cheap.

Popular souvenirs include blown glass from Venice, decorative and beautifully produced paper from Florence, high fashion from Milan and Italian shoes anywhere. Export licenses are required for antiques, works of art and items worth over 1 million lire.

Rome

Practical Tips

Emergency Medical Services
The Italian *farmacia* is open during shopping hours and at least one operates at night and on weekends in each district of Rome. The schedule of pharmacists on duty is posted on every pharmacy door and in the local papers.
Emergency number (fire, ambulance, police): 113

Postal Services
Rome's main post office at Piazza San Silvestro is open 8.25am–2.30pm for ordinary postal services, till 7.40pm for urgent matters, and round the clock daily (except Saturday until 1pm) for telegram services.

The Vatican runs its own postal service, reputed to be faster than the Italian service. It does not always live up to this, but when visiting St Peter's, buy Vatican-issued stamps for your postcards and post them immediately: they are only valid in the Vatican City's blue postboxes. The postmark may interest your correspondents.

Telephones
To obtain telephone directory assistance for numbers in Italy, dial 12. Dial 176 for international directory enquiries and 0176 for intercontinental enquiries.

Tourist Information
Main headquarters are located in Via Parigi 5, tel: 488 99253. There are also offices at Stazione Termini, tel: 06-4871270, and Fiumicino Airport, tel: 06-65956074. Open: daily Monday–Saturday 8.30am–1pm and 2–7pm. They provide helpful services from sightseeing to brochures and maps.

Embassies & Consulates
Canada: Via Zara 30. Tel: 445 981.
UK: Via Venti Settembre 80. Tel: 482 54 41.
US: Via Vittorio Veneto 121. Tel: 46741.

Getting Around

By Air
Rome is served by two airports: Leonardo da Vinci, commonly referred to as Fiumicino, located 30 km (18 miles) southwest of the city; and Ciampino, located 16 km (10 miles) southeast. Fiumicino mainly handles scheduled air traffic, while Ciampino is used by most charter companies.

From Fiumicino, there is a frequent train service to the city, every 20 minutes to Stazione Ostiense and every hour to Stazione Termini. It's a short taxi ride to most hotels from Termini, a little longer from Ostiense. A taxi from Fiumicino to the centre will cost around €42.

From Ciampino, the best way to reach the centre is by taxi. Expect to pay about €35.

For flight information, at Fiumicino tel: 65951; for Ciampino, tel: 794 941.

By Rail
Most international trains arrive at Termini Station, which is connected to other parts of the city by both the A and B lines of the subway.

The official taxi stand is in front of the station. Do not be tempted by the offers of "taxi" from unofficial cab drivers loitering about the station interior.

The station and the area around it are pretty seedy at night.
General Information
Train enquiries, tel: 147-888088.
Lost property, tel: 4836682, by platform 22. Open: daily 7am–11pm.
Station police, tel: 4882588.
Left luggage, near platforms 1 and 22. Charged per piece per 12-hour period. Open: 5.30am–12am.

By Road
Rome is completely encircled by a motorway, the Gran Raccordo Anulare (GRA), intersected by various roads leading from other Italian cities. A1 leads north to Florence; E1 leads to the west coast and Genoa; and A2 leads south to Naples. There are frequent

traffic jams during the rush hour. Europabus travels between London and Rome all year round.

Public Transport
Rome has two underground railway lines (*metropolitana* or metro), line A and line B, which pass most of Rome's popular tourist sights. A big red letter M marks the entrance to the underground and tickets are sold at each station. A complete network of buses and trams covers the whole city, providing frequent service until midnight and a special night service *(servizo notturno)*, details of which are given at every bus stop. Routes are well indicated on green and white signs at every bus stop (*fermata*) and the service number, starting point and destination are shown on the vehicles. Tickets (*biglietto*) must be purchased in advance at tobacconists, bars or news-stands.

Where to Stay
The Italian Tourist Office has up-to-date hotel information, available at the air terminal at Termini Railway Station. Although they cannot book rooms, they do have a comprehensive list of hotels in Rome and the surrounding area.

Alternatively, the Hotel Reservation Service, operating from a booth in Stazione Termini opposite platform 10, open daily 7am–10pm, makes commission-free reservations in Rome and other cities.

Nightlife
In a capital with remarkably little nightlife, the most popular custom is to linger well past midnight over dinner at the innumerable outdoor restaurants where roaming minstrels and guitarists play. The Trastevere area has small, reasonably priced restaurants and taverns and is the best place to meet the locals. However, Testaccio is fast taking its place as a slightly more "alternative" location. The Ludovisi district around the Via Veneto has the largest number of big hotels, famous cafés, nightclubs and restaurants but most

What's On
For the most comprehensive listings of what's on in Rome, pick up *Romac'è*, the weekly booklet that comes out on Thursdays and is available from news stands. Listings are in Italian with an abbreviated section in English. *Time Out Rome* comes out monthly in Italian with a brief English section. It carries articles and reviews as well as listings.

Look out also for *Roma Pagina Gialle* (Yellow Pages for tourists) at the Rome tourist office (EPT) or larger hotels. It's published in five languages, and lists all you could possibly wish to know about Rome.

are very expensive. Not all of the city's discotheques charge entrance fees, but they're usually very crowded and drinks are never cheap. A few larger establishments have dance floors and cabarets, and there's dancing in the lounges of some hotels.

Rome's *Daily News* advertises current English-language films at the Pasquino in Trastevere.

There's an outdoor opera almost every evening at the ruined Baths of Caracalla (Terme di Caracalla), an easy bus or taxi ride from the city centre. Equally popular sound and light performances are at the Forum and outside Rome in Tivoli. People-watching at the Trevi Fountain and the Spanish Steps also lasts well into the night during summer months.

Shopping
Via del Corso, Piazza di Spagna and Via del Babuino mark the boundaries of the classic window-shopping area. Here you can find everything from designer jeans to hand-crafted jewellery and antique furniture. Nearby Via della Croce and Via del Corso offer fashion at more accessible prices.

Streets around Piazza Navona, the Pantheon and Campo de' Fiori offer unusual hand-crafted artisanal

Carnet di Roma, available free from the EPT, also lists events on a monthly basis.

English-speaking guides and interpreters can be hired from a variety of sources: from the main EPT office, hotels and travel agencies; from the Guides Centre located at 12 Rampa Mignanelli; in the *Yellow Pages* under "Traduzione," and in many Rome newspapers which often carry advertisements offering such services. There are also guides near most of the major tourist attractions, and portable recorders with commentaries in English can often be hired.

goods and a range of smaller boutiques. The Campo de' Fiori is an interesting quarter to amble around and is still home to craftsmen, art restorers and market traders. This is a traditional working-class mix with a genuine feel that is fast dying out in trendy Trastevere.

Via del Babuino, Via Margutta, Via Giulia, Via dei Coronari and Via del Pellegrino are the main streets for antiques, *objets d'art* and paintings.

Via Nazionale is an undistinguished but relatively inexpensive shopping street, with a wide range of basic clothes.

Via Cola di Rienzo, the thoroughfare linking the Vatican with the Tiber (and Piazza del Popolo on the other bank) is lined with small boutiques and elegant shops selling a wide range of goods.

Via della Conciliazione, the street linking the Vatican with Castel Sant'Angelo, offers a wide range of religious artefacts. These include Vatican coins, statues, stamps, religious books and souvenirs. Similar objects are on sale on the streets around the Vatican itself and on Via dei Cestari, which runs between the Pantheon and Largo Argentina.

Via del Governo Vecchio is one of the best streets for stylish second-hand clothes, as are the markets at Porta Portese and Via Sannio.

Further Reading

The Italians, by Luigi Barzini. New York: Bantam Books.
Four Wonders of Italy: Rome, Florence, Venice, Naples. Allan & Unwin.
Italian Hilltowns, by Norman F Carver. Documan Press.
Art Treasures of Italy, by Bernard Denvir. Orbis Publications.
Italian Journey 1786–1788, by Johann W. von Goethe. North Point Press.
Italian Hours, by Henry James. Greenwood Press.
Twilight in Italy, Sea and Sardinia, Etruscan Places, by D.H. Lawrence. Viking Press.
The Land and People of Italy, by Frances Winwar. Harper & Row.

Other Insight Guides

Other books in the *Insight Guide* series which highlight destinations in this region are: *Insight Guides:* Italy, Rome, Bay of Naples, Tuscany, Umbria, Florence, Venice, Northern Italy, South Tyrol, Sardinia and Sicily. The *Insight Pocket Guide* series, designed to help readers without a lot of time plan their trips precisely, are: *Pocket Guides:* Florence, Milan, Rome, Sardinia, Sicily, Tuscany and Venice. Many of the Pocket Guides come with handy pullout maps. *Insight Compact Guides* cover Florence, Italian Lakes, Italian Riviera, Milan, Rome, Tuscany and Venice.

CROATIA

Getting Acquainted

Situation: Croatia (Hrvatska) lies on the eastern side of the Adriatic Sea facing Italy, between Serbia and Bosnia-Herzogovinia
Area: 56,500 sq km (21,800 sq miles)
Coastline: 1,780 km (690 miles)
Number of islands: 1185 (66 inhabited).
Population: 5 million.
Language: Serbo-Croatian.
Capital: Zagreb (population 1 million)
Religion: Roman Catholic (75 per cent), Eastern Orthodox (10 per cent)
Currency: kuna. (£1 is about 12 kuna; US$1 is about 8 kuna)
Time: Central European Time
Electricity: 220 volts; European round-pronged plugs
International dialling code: 385, plus 1 (Zagreb), 20 (Dubrovnik)
Public Holidays: In addition to the holidays listed in the Introduction, Croatia commemorates the following: Statehood Day (30 May), Antifascist Struggle Day (22 June), Day of National Thanksgiving (5 August).

Getting There

By Air

Croatia's national airline, Croatia Airlines, operates direct scheduled flights from London Heathrow airport to Zagreb, Split and Dubrovnik. Flying time from Heathrow is just over 2 hours. Croatia Airlines also connects Zagreb with other European capitals and some other major European cities, but has no direct flights to the US. Cheaper charter flights normally fly to the coastal towns of Dubrovnik, Split and Pula.

By Rail

Trains run from Austria, Germany, Hungary, Italy, Romania and Yugoslavia to Riejka, and Zagreb. The easiest and most convenient train route is from Trieste via Koper in Slovenia.

By Road

Coming from Italy, there are nearly 30 crossing points between Croatia and Slovenia, as well as numerous border points along Croatia's other international borders. Frequent buses run from Trieste into Croatia via Koper.

To enter Croatia by car you need a green insurance card. The principal road into the country from Western Europe is the E70, from Trieste, Italy, to pass through Slovenia for border crossings south for Istria and Dalmatia, or East for Zagreb.

Coach: A weekly coach service, run by Eurolines departs from London Victoria Railway Station direct for Zagreb and from Trieste, Italy, you will find frequent daily coaches to towns in Istria as well as a night bus to Dubrovnik. In addition, private companies run international services connecting Croatia with neighbouring countries, as well as Austria, Switzerland, France, Germany and Slovakia.

By Sea

There are regular boat connections between Italy and Greece and Croatia's Adriatic coast. It's possible to arrive in Dalmatia by ferry from Italy. Through summer, Jadrolinija, the Croatian national ferry company, rund regualr services from Ancona to Split, and from Bari to Dubrovnik. Another Croatian company, SEM, and the Venice-based Italian company Adriatica also covers the Ancona-Split route. Ferries run throughout the year, though less frequently in winter.

Emergency Numbers

- **Police:** 92.
- **Fire:** 93.
- **Public emergency, including medical assistance:** 94.

Practical Tips

Medical Services
Payment is necessary to see a doctor, private or public, and travel insurance is recommended.

Business Hours
Usual hours are from around 8am–7pm on weekdays, closing at 2pm on Sat. Along the Adriatic coast shops often close for an hour or two in the middle of the day.

Telecommunications
For operator assistance with a telephone call, T901. Public telephones use phonecards – 50, 100, 200 and 500 units – available from post offices and small newspaper shops.

Tourist Information
Local tourist offices (Turist Biro) are in Rijeka, Split and Dubrovnik and the larger travel agencies are also a good source of local information. Tourist information is available on the net: http://www.htz.hr

Getting Around

Croatia Airlines runs a regular bus service to and from Zagreb airport with departures every 30 minutes. In Split and Dubrovnik, airport buses leave 90 minutes prior to hte plane's take-off.

Buses: are the fastest and most convenient way to travel up and down the Adriatic coast. Seats can be purchased in advance from the larger bus stations, though for local routes any bus can be flagged down and the fare paid to the driver. A comprehensive coach network connects all parts of the country, from major cities to the smallest and most remote villages. Coaches do get busy in Summer though, and some journeys are slow and tiring.

Car hire: is available in most resorts and as well as the familiar multinational companies there are local car rental companies that often offer better rates.

Taxis: are readily available in all major towns and tourist resorts. As in any other European country, drivers are obliged to run a meter and the price is calculated on time and distance.

Where to Stay

Contact your Croatian National Tourist Office for holiday information, including accommodation.

Climate & When to Go

The Croatian coast has a Mediterranean climate: Summer is hot and dry, spring and autumn are mild, winter is cool and humid. In contrast, the Dinaric Alps, backing the Dalmatia coast, have hot summers and cold winters with large amounts of snow.

The tourist season runs from April to October. The best months to visit for hiking and biking are April through May and September through October when the countryside is at its most colourful and temperatures are not too high. The sea is warm enough to swim by mid-May and can remain so until early October. If in search of lively nightlife, with cultural events and parties on the beach, visit in August. However, remember that it does get hot and very busy. Car drivers have to queue for hours to board ferries for the island and many hotels and private rooms are booked up in advance.

GREECE

Getting Acquainted

Situation 39°N, 22°E
Area 131,950 sq km (50,950 sq miles), including around 25,050 sq km (9,670 sq miles) of islands
Capital Athens
Population 10.7 million. Greater Athens and Piraeus have a population of 4 million. Thessaloníki, the second-largest city and a university town, has nearly 1 million residents, and the most-populated island is Crete, with just over half a million inhabitants
Language Modern Greek
Literacy 95 percent
Religion Predominantly Greek Orthodox Christianity, with small minorities of Muslims, Catholics, evangelical sects and Jews
Currency the Euro
Weights and measures Metric
Electricity 220V, two-pin plugs (see also What to Pack)
International Dialling Code 30 (Athens: 1)
Time Zones Two hours ahead of Greenwich Mean Time. The clock is advanced one hour, from the last weekend in March to the last weekend in September, for extended daylight hours
Public Holidays In addition to those listed in the Introduction, Greece commemorates the following: Epiphany (6 January), Moveable Clean Monday (First Day of Lent), Evangelismós/Annunciation (25 March), Moveable Good Friday, Moveable Orthodox Easter, Moveable Pentecost Monday/Aghíou Pnévmatos (50 days after Easter), "Ohi" Day, National Holiday (28 October), Gathering of the Virgin/Sýnaxis tis Theotókou (26 December)

Getting There

By Air
The Greek National Airline, Olympic Airways, and many major international airlines link Greece with all five continents. The main gateway is Hellinikon East and West Airport, 10 km (6 miles) from the centre of Athens. Hellinikon West exclusively handles domestic and international flights of Olympic Airways (tel: 969 9111), while Hellinikon East (tel: 969 4111) handles all other international airlines. The new airport being built at Spata should begin operating in time for the 2004 Athens Olympics.

Olympic Airways operates express bus services every half hour between 3.30am–8pm from West Hellinikon to the Olympic Airways City Terminal at 96 Syngrou Avenue. Express buses also run from East Hellinikon to the City Terminal at 4 Amalias Avenue.

By Rail
There are trains connecting Thessaloniki and Athens with most major cities throughout Europe. For some destinations it may be necessary to change. Car-carrying sleeper trains connect Brussels, Düsseldorf, Cologne, Frankfurt and Stuttgart or Ljubljana in Slovenia, and from Milan on to Brindisi for the car ferry to Patras.

By Road
Bordered by the former Yugoslavia and Bulgaria to the north and Turkey to the northeast, Greece can be reached by a number of European "E" routes. The western border with Albania is closed.

By Sea
An extensive summer network of ferries links Italy with Greece. Many ferries, especially on the short routes, run all year round. Venice, Ancona, Brindisi and Bari are the Italian ports, while Corfu, Igoumenitsa and Partras serve Greece; some services go to Piraeus. The shortest routes are from Brindisi to Corfu (about 9 hours) and Patras (16–18 hours), the latter has a bus connection to Athens.

Practical Tips

Business Hours
All banks are open from 8am– 2pm Monday–Thursday, closing at 1.30pm on Friday. In heavily visited areas, however, you may find banks open additional late-afternoon hours and on Saturday mornings for currency exchange.

The schedule for business and shop hours is more complicated. Business hours vary according to the type of business and the day of the week. The main thing to remember is that businesses generally open at 8.30am and close on Monday, Wednesday and Saturday at 2.30pm. On Tuesday, Thursday and Friday most businesses close at 1.30pm and reopen in the afternoon from 5pm to 8.30pm.

Tipping
Hotels, restaurants and nightclubs add 15 percent but a little extra is expected. This figure rises to 20 percent around Christmas and Easter. Round up the charge on the taxi meter to the next 10 drachma.

Postal Services
Most local post offices are open weekdays from 7.30am until 2pm. The main post offices in central Athens (on Eólou near Omónia Square and on ´S yndagma Square at the corner of Mitropóleos Street), however, are open weekdays

Emergency Services

Chemists are open during normal shop hours but a number of them stay open day and night. Duty rotas are displayed in the local newspapers and in chemists' windows, or tel: 107 for information. Free first aid treatment is available at Red Cross clinics and English-speaking doctors and dentists advertise in *This Week in Athens*.

7.30am–8pm, Saturday 7.30am–2pm and Sunday 7.30am–1pm.

Postal rates are subject to fairly frequent change, so you'll do best to enquire at post offices. Stamps are available from the post office or from many kiosks (*perptera*) and hotels, which charge a 10–15 percent commission. Make sure you know how much it is to send a letter or postcard, though, as kiosk owners tend not to be up to date with latest international postal rates. Bear in mind that sending the attractive, large-format postcards costs letter-rate postage.

Telephones
The easiest way to make telephone calls is to purchase a telephone card from a kiosk and use a phone booth. Cards come in three sizes: 100 units, 500 units and 1,000 units, with the largest ones representing the best value. Otherwise, you may find a telephone at a kiosk, where you will pay a small charge for a local call.

You can also make long-distance calls from any one of the many kiosks which have metered phones. However, a call from a kiosk will cost considerably more than from a cardphone, or from the new-style coin-op counter phones, which are often found in hotel lobbies and restaurants. Calls from hotel rooms typically have 100 percent surcharge on top of the standard rates.

Tourist Information
The National Tourist Organization of Greece (GNTO) has offices abroad in Sydney, Montreal, Tokyo, London, New York, Los Angeles and Chicago as well as major European cities. Their head office (EOT) is in Athens at 2 Amerikas, tel: (01) 3310561/2, with information desks at the East Hellinikon Airport. Other tourist offices are located in the various tourist areas of Greece as well as at the major frontier crossings. The Greek Tourist Police are often a mine of information too.

Tourist Offices Abroad

Australia: 51–57 Pitt Street, Sydney NSW 2000. Tel: 9241 1663/4.
UK: 4 Conduit Street, London W1R ODJ. Tel: (020) 7734 5997.
US: 645 Fifth Avenue, Olypmic Tower, New York, NY 10022. Tel: (212) 421 5777.

Getting Around

By Air

Olympic Airways maintains a remarkably extensive network of internal air routes, most of which link Athens with other cities and towns plus the islands, but one or two link Thessaloniki to, for example, Crete or Rhodes. Between Athens and Thessaloniki there are about eight flights a day, more at peak holiday times. Air Greece, a smaller carrier, also offers internal flights.

By Rail

Greece does not have a very extensive railway system, and travelling by train is generally slow, but cheap. It has one main route from Athens north to Thessaloniki, where it splits. One section goes to the former Yugoslavia, another to Bulgaria and the third to Istanbul. Another rail system operates from Athens and Piraeus to the Peloponnese peninsula via Corinth. The trains are run by the Greek Railways Board (OSE) whose main offices are in Athens (1-3 Karolou Street, tel: 5240601). For train and ticket information in Athens, try 31a Venizelou St, tel: 3131 376; recorded timetables, tel: 145 (internal) and 147 (international).

By Road

A vast network of bus routes, called the KTEL, spreads across Greece; KTEL is a syndicate of bus companies whose buses are cheap, generally punctual and will take you to almost any destination that can be reached on wheels. Among Greeks it's a popular way of travelling, so you will have good company. KTEL buses on the more idiosyncratic rural routes often have a distinct personal touch. Many drivers decorate and treat the bus with great care. They are proud of it and how they drive it.

The most important thing to note about KTEL is that in larger cities there will be different bus stations for different destinations, which can be complicated if you don't know the information before setting out. Travelling from Thessaloníki to Halkidhikí, for example, you will leave from one station, and to Ioánnina, from another; Athens has two terminals, while Iráklion in Crete has three.

Waterways

The ferry network is both extensive and complicated with schedules constantly changing, although on trunk routes they are reliable.

Boats are run by a variety of companies and fares quoted in the brochures don't include taxes, which can add up to 10 percent of the fare. All the larger ferries carry cars and pre-booking is absolutely essential, except in the quieter winter weeks. Be warned: in August, the first two weeks see rough seas when the annual *meltemia* wind blows; and around the 15th (Assumption Day), boats are crowded with pilgrims travelling to and from Tinos.

Details and reservations can be made at any tourist agency or the various shipping and ferry offices in Athens and Piraeus. Always double-check departure times.

At the other end of the naval spectrum, you will find a scheduled hydrofoil service to certain islands, whose network has expanded greatly in recent years. This is the executive way to island hop; hydrofoils are more than twice as fast as the ferries and about twice as expensive.

By Car

Major frontier points are open night and day. The conflict in the former Yugoslavia means that this route into Greece is not advisable. Tolls are charged on the two main motorways: Athens–Katerini and Athens–Patras.

Attractions

What's On

Cultural information can be obtained from GNTO offices, the monthly magazine, *The Athenian*, and the glossy *This Week in Athens*, available at kiosks and hotels respectively.

Nightlife

Metropolitan "nightlife" in Greece, which is to say Athens and Thessaloniki, can be roughly divided into bars, live music clubs, discos, and the *boîtes*, *tavérnes* and clubs with live Greek music.

Shopping

The quality of Greek handicrafts is usually quite high. Cotton clothing is a well-fashioned buy; embroidered items, handcrafted jewellery, and durable-but-crude leather goods are also favoured purchases. On higher-priced items, by all means bargain.

Motoring Advice

It is suggested that visiting foreign motorists have an international driving licence (available only through the automobile club in your home country; ELPA in Greece has ceased issuing them), but in practice it is not required. Neither is an insurance Green Card. The Automobile and Touring Club of Greece (ELPA) offers information and assistance and their vans patrol the main routes. ELPA runs a rescue service (Assistance Routiere) within a 37-mile (60-km) radius of Athens, Larissa, Patras and Thessaloniki. Tel: 104.

Athens

Practical Tips

Medical Services

Pharmaceuticals are produced to international standards, and a rota system is used to ensure that a pharmacy is open somewhere in your part of the city at all times. Dial 107 for the pharmacy roster in Greek, or check the cards posted in pharmacy windows for the address nearest you.

Most downtown pharmacists speak English, and Greek pharmacists are often very helpful in assisting visitors with treating minor ailments such as diarrhoea, colds and sunburn.

Ideally, your travel insurance should cover airlifting out to northern Europe, if not home. If you do fall ill in Athens, seek out a reputable private doctor through your hotel, or embassy. The British and American embassies will supply a list of GPs and specialists, including dentists upon request. As with pharmacists, a telephone roster service is available, but only in Greek: tel: 105.

Hospitals

The best private hospital and the children's hospitals are located in Ambelokipi and Maroussi, an area just north of the Hilton, and are listed here. A complete listing of the city's public hospitals can be obtained by phoning the Tourist Police on 171.

KAT Hospital, Nikis 2, Kifissia, tel: 801 4411 for accidents.
Children's Hospitals: Agia Sofia, Thivon and Mikras Assias streets, tel: 777-1811; Aglaia Kyriakou, Thivon and Levadias streets, tel: 777-5610.

Emergency Numbers

- **Police emergency**: 100.
- **Tourist Police**: 171.
- **Ambulance**: 161
- **Coastguard patrol**: 108.

Telephones

To contact the domestic operator, tel: 151/2. For the international operator, tel: 161/2.

Tourist Office

National Tourist Organization of Greece (GNTO)
The GNTO head office (EOT) is at 2 Amerikas, tel: (01) 3310561/2, with information desks at the East Hellinikon Airport; and 1 Karageorgi Servias Street.

Other tourist offices are located in the various tourist areas of Greece as well as at the major frontier crossings.

Embassies & Consulates

All embassies are open Monday–Friday, usually from 8am–2pm.
Australia: 37 Dimitris Soutsou Street. Tel: 644 7303.
Canada: 4 Gennadiou Street. Tel: 7239511.
Ireland: 7 Vasiliou Constantinou Street. Tel: 723 2771.
New Zealand: Xenías 24, Ambelókipi (tel: 77 10 112).
UK: 1 Ploutarchou Street. Tel: 723 6211.
US: 91 Vasilissis Sophias Avenue. Tel: 721 2951.

Getting Around

By Rail

Greek trains are a delight if you enjoy travelling for travelling's sake, but a frustrating experience if getting there quickly is more important. Timetables and tickets may be purchased at OSE offices located at 6 Sina Street; or 1 Karolou Street, tel: 524 0601/5; 524 0646/8. There are two stations, one serving the Peloponnese; the other, the north.

Metro: A major expansion of the Athens metro system is underway, with new lines scheduled to be operating in time for the 2004 Olympics. The existing line between Piraeus and Kifissia is clean and reliable and connects Piraeus with Monastiraki and Omonia. City centre stops are at Thisseion, Monastiraki, and Omonia. Tickets are separate

from those used on buses and trolleys and are available only at the stations.

By Sea

In 1997 the GNTO finally had a stab at producing a comprehensive, impartial ferry timetable, *Greek Travel Routes* (from booking agents and GNTO offices). Whether they will continue with it is uncertain, but this timetable is far superior to the privately published *Greek Travel Pages* (from larger bookshops in Athens), which may not list firms that do not advertise).

Alternatively, tourist information offices supply a weekly schedule, and most offices hang a schedule in a conspicuous place so you can look up times even if the branch is closed. This should, however, not be relied on implicitly.

In general, for the most complete and up-to-date information on each port's sailings the best source is the port police (in Piraeus and most other ports), known as the *limenarhío*.

Be aware that when you enquire about ferries at a travel agent, they will sometimes inform you only of the lines with which they are affiliated.

Hydrofoil: The Flying Dolphin service is speedy, but more expensive than the ferries and liable to cancellation in anything more than a stiff breeze. However, these insect-like craft, which originally ran tours up and down the Volga River, are a pleasant way to travel to the Saronic Gulf islands, especially at the "sharp end", which is non-smoking or, on hot days, in the stern, where there is a small deck. The most reliable and durable companies are:
Ceres Flying Dolphins, 8 Aktí Themistokléous, Piraeus.
Tel: 01/42 80 001 or fax: 01/42 83 526 (preferable, as the voice line is usually engaged).
Dodecanese Hydrofoils, Platía Kýprou, Mandhráki Harbour, Rhodes. Tel: 0241/24 000.

By Road

Drive at your peril in Athens during the rush hour. The twin perils of traffic jams and pollution reached such heights in the capital that a law was introduced: on even days of the month only cars with even-numbered licence plates are allowed in the centre; on odd days only those with odd-numbered plates. This has, unfortunately, done little to improve the congestion, noise and smog in Athens

Taxis: On entry, ensure that the meter is switched on and registering 1, rather than 2 which is the rate from midnight–5am. Don't be worried if you find yourself joined, en route, by a large cross-section of Athenian society going roughly your way. It is perfectly legal for drivers to pick up as many people as is comfortably possible, and charge them all individually. The tariff regulations are posted on cards in all taxis, with very reasonable flag down and minimum fares.

There is a surcharge from airports, seaports, railway stations and bus terminals; passengers may also be charged a small fee for luggage.

In recent years various radio taxi services have started up in Athens and most other larger towns. They can pick you up within a short time of your call to a central booking number. You pay more, but this is well worth it if you want a car at a busy time of day or if you're laden with luggage and have a flight or boat to catch.

By Bus

Travelling by the regular Athens blue buses is a fairly miserable way of getting around the city. They are crowded and hot, and the routes are a mystery even to long-time residents. However, they are reasonable, at under 100 drachmas per ticket. Tickets, good for trolleys as well, are sold in books of 10 from specific news kiosks and special booths at bus and metro stations, and at various non-strategic points around the city. Most bus services run until midnight.

Separate services run to air and sea ports, and these can be useful. The Express service of distinctive blue and yellow double-decker buses runs from Syntagma Square (on Amalias Avenue) to both airports at regular intervals: buy your tickets at the kiosk by the stop. The Green bus 040 runs from Filellinon Street (near Syntagma Square) to Piraeus 24 hours a day, every 20 minutes (every hour after 1am). The Orange bus runs from 14 Mavromateon Street, Areos Park, and takes approximately 1.5 hours.

Trolley Bus: Marginally faster and more comfortable than the regular bus service, the yellow trolleys serve points of tourist interest; number 1 links the centre of the city with the railway stations, numbers 5 and 9 pass the archeological museum, and number 7 does a triangular circuit of the central districts.

Attractions

Greek News Weekly, published on Saturday night, is interesting and informative, with a regular "What's On" section. *The Athenian: Greece's English Language Monthly,* is just that, with features covering Greek politics, topics of interest and the arts. A mini-magazine, *This Week in Athens,* has been published for many years by the National Tourist Organization of Greece, and is available at GNTO offices.

Further Reading

Greek Unorthodox, by Elizabeth Boleman-Herring. Foundation Publishing.
Greece Without Columns: The Making of the Modern Greeks, by David Holden. J.B. Lippincott Co.
A Foreign Wife, by Gillian Bouras. McPhee Gribble/Penguin Books.
A Literary Companion to Travel in Greece. Richard Stoneman (ed.). Penguin Books Ltd.
Roumeli: Travels in Northern

Greece, by Patrick Leigh Fermor. Penguin Books Ltd.
Unknown Athens: Wanderings in Plaka and Elsewhere, by Liza Micheli. Dromena.

Other Insight Guides

Other books in the *Insight Guide* series highlight destinations in this region: *Insight Guides:* Greece, The Greek Islands and Crete. The *Insight Pocket Guide* series, designed to help readers without a lot of time plan their trips precisely, include: *Pocket Guides:* the Aegean Islands, Athens, Crete and Rhodes. Many of the Pocket Guides come with handy pullout maps. *Insight Compact Guides* cover Athens, Crete and Rhodes.

SPAIN

Getting Acquainted

Area 504,880 sq. km (194, 885 sq. miles).
Capital Madrid.
Population 39.2 million.
Language Spanish (Castilian), plus Catalan, Basque and Galician.
Religion Roman Catholic.
Time zone One hour ahead of Greenwich Mean Time (GMT).
Currency the Euro.
Weights and measures Metric.
Electricity 220 volts.
International dialling code 34.

Public Holidays

The overwhelmingly Roman Catholic character of Spain is reflected in its holidays which, in addition to those listed in the Introduction, include among others:
Epiphany: 6 January
St Joseph's Day: 19 March
Good Friday
Corpus Christi Day
St James's Day: 25 July
Feast of the Assumption: 15 August
Columbus Day: 12 October
Conception Day: 8 December
Various other saints' days are observed locally.

Getting There

By Air
The national carriers Iberia and Aviaco and many foreign airlines maintain regular flights to more than 30 international airports in Spain. There are many foreign charter companies which arrange periodic flights to the country.

Iberia, whose main offices in Madrid are at Calle Velázquez, 130, operates all regular Spanish carrier flights abroad and domestic connections, the latter jointly with its subsidiaries Aviaco (headquarters at Maudes, 51) and Viva Air (Zurbano, 41).
● **Iberia information and reservations:** Serviberia, tel: (91) 400 500. However, Iberia is usually more expensive than other companies, so shop around. Halcón Viajes, a chain of travel agents, is popular and offers competitive prices (tel: 91 300 600 to find your nearest office); Viajes Marsans, tel: 91 115 947, is also good, and runs special offers.

By Rail
Major destinations in Spain are linked by direct trains to points in France and Switzerland. Three overnight through trains run to Barcelona and Madrid from Paris. A similar day train runs between Geneva and Barcelona via Lyon, Avignon, Montpellier and Perpignan. Many other trains link the Franco-Spanish border, Portugal and Italy directly with Spain.

By Road
Bordered by France and the Principality of Andorra to the north and Portugal to the west, Spain is accessible via a number of European motorways and other main roads. Regular ferry services allow drivers to enter the southern tip of Spain from Morocco and Santander from Great Britain. Main motorways are: N-I (Madrid–Irun); N-II (Madrid–Barcelona); N-III (Madrid–Valencia); N-IV (Madrid–Andalusia); N-V (Madrid–Extremadura); and N-VI (Madrid–La Coruña).
By Bus: The Estación del Sur de Autobuses at Calle Canarias 17 is Madrid's main bus station and most of the major bus companies covering the long-distance routes use this terminal.

By Sea
Various foreign shipping companies, operating more than 50 scheduled lines, bring passengers to Spain. Contact a travel agent for details.

Practical Tips

Medical Services
Spain has countless chemist shops or *farmacias*, each identifiable by a big, white sign with a flashing green cross. They are open approximately 9.30am–1.30pm and 5–8pm Monday–Friday; 9am–1.30pm Saturday.

Emergency Numbers

● **National Police:** 091
● **Municipal Police:** 092
● **Emergency Medical Care:** 061
● **Fire Department:** 080.
● **Red Cross Emergency:** (91) 522 2222 in Madrid.

Business Hours
Shops are open 9.30am or 10am–1.30 or 2pm and then reopen again in the afternoon from 4.30 or 5pm–8pm, or a little later in summer. Most are closed on Saturday afternoons and all day Sunday. However, major department stores are open without interruption six days a week 10am–9pm, and frequently on Sunday.
Banking: Hours vary slightly from one bank to another. Most open 8.30 or 9am–2pm weekdays and 9am–12.30 or 1pm on Saturday. All are closed Sunday and holidays. Several banks keep major branches in the business districts open until 6pm.

Tipping
As a guideline, tipping is frequent in bars, cafeterias and restaurants (8–10 percent), taxis (5 percent), cinema and theatre ushers (15–25 ptas), and bellboys (according to services rendered).

Postal Services
The few existing district post offices are only open 9am–2pm on weekdays, 9am–1pm Saturday and closed Sunday. Principal post offices are open 9am–2pm and

4–7pm for general services. Post boxes are silver-coloured and in two parts – one marked *ciudad* (for local mail) and the other marked *provincias y extranjero* (for the rest of the country and abroad). Stamps are sold at post offices and at the *estancos*, or tobacconist shops.

Telephones

Coin and card operated telephone booths are everywhere. Wait for the tone, deposit the necessary coins and dial the number. For long-distance calls you may need to insert several coins before dialling. You can also purchase a phone card in various denominations at any tobacconist.

For overseas calls, it's probably better to go to the offices of Telefónica (the Spanish telephone company), or to privately run telephone shops where one can talk first and pay later and not have to worry about having enough coins. (If you ring from your hotel room, you will be charged a lot more than you would on a public phone.)

To make a direct overseas call, first dial 07 and then wait for another dial tone before dialling the country and city codes. It is cheaper to call before 8am and after 10pm. There are no additional discounts at weekends.

If you need information, operator assistance or wish to reverse the charges, tel: 008 (for Europe) or 005 (for the rest of the world).

Tourist Information

Tourist information is available at Plaza Mayor, 3. Tel: (91) 566 5477.

Tourist Offices Abroad
Canada: 2 Bloor Street West, 34th floor, Toronto, Ontario M4W 3E2, tel: (416) 961 3131.
UK: 22–3 Manchester Square, London W1M 5AP, tel: (020) 7486 8077.
US: 665 Fifth Avenue, New York City, NY 10103, tel: (212) 759 8822/28; 845 N. Michigan Avenue, Suite 915, Chicago,

The following numbers may be helpful – though in some cases you'll need good Spanish. Information on Spain, tel: 003.

Getting Around

By Air
Both Iberia and Aviaco operate a wide network of routes within Spain, linking all the main cities.

Iberia's main offices are at Calle Velázquez 130, 28006 Madrid. Iberia has ticket offices at Calle Velázquez 130. For flight information and reservations: Serviberia, tel: (91) 400 500. Iberia has ticket offices at Calle Velázquez 130, or you can buy an air ticket at any travel agency.

Aviaco, Iberia's subsidiary airline, only services domestic flights, while Viva Air covers international routes. The planes are generally older and smaller and fly less-frequented routes. Aviaco is at Maudes 51, in Madrid, tel: 554 3600; and Viva Air at Zurbano 41, tel: 349 0600. Iberia is usually more expensive than other companies, so we recommend you shop around.

By Rail
The Spanish National Railways (Red Nacional de los Ferrocarriles Espanoles or RENFE) provides extensive local service within the country. There are various types of trains in Spain: Talgo, Inter-city, ELT (electric

Illinois 60611, tel: (312) 944 0215/16; 8383 Wilshire Boulevard, Suite 960, 90211 Beverly Hills, California, tel: (323) 658 7188/93.

Consulates & Embassies
Australia: Plaza Descubridor Diego de Ordás, 3. Tel: (91) 441 9300.
Canada: Núñez de Balboa, 35. Tel: (91) 431 4300.
UK: Fernando el Santo, 16. Tel: (91) 319 0200.
US: Calle Serrano, 75. Tel: (91) 577 4000.

unit expresses), TER (diesel rail cars) and ordinary semi-fast and local trains. Supplementary fares are levied on all express trains. On all expresses you must either have a reserved seat or have your ticket endorsed at the station before going on board.

For information from RENFE, tel: 328 9020.

Unlike the new national services, the regional trains between cities tend to be slow. The Costa del Sol between Malaga and Fuengirola is served by an efficient commuter service, every 20 minutes. A train ride in the grand style of the Orient Express is offered by the Al-Andalus Expresso. Operating May to October, this deluxe train visits Seville, Córdoba, Granada and Málaga with option of a visit to Jerez.

Public Transport
Spain has an excellent bus network, cheaper and more frequent than trains. On major routes and at holiday times it is advisable to buy your ticket a day or two in advance.

By Road
The cities, towns and regions of Spain are linked with nearly 144,000 km (90,000 miles) of roads and highways. If you take the minor roads, expect bad surfaces and large potholes. The number of toll roads is increasing, particularly in the north and east and around Madrid.

Motoring Advice: The roadside SOS telephones are connected to the nearest police station, which sends out a breakdown van with first aid equipment. There is a small charge for work done and spare parts used. The automobile clubs of Spain are the Real Automovil Club de Espana (RACE) and the Touring Club de Espana (TCE).

International car hire chains have airport offices and offer collect and deliver services. Local companies are cheaper and will arrange to meet you on arrival if you book.

The following addresses and telephone numbers may be useful: Real Automovil Club de España,

Jose Abascal 10, Madrid.
Tel: 593 3333.
Real Automovil Club de Catalunya,
Santalo 8, Barcelona. Tel: 200
3311.
Touring Club de Espana, Modesto
Lafuente, Madrid. Tel: 233 1004.
    In the event of a breakdown in
Madrid, tel: 754 3344; in
Barcelona, tel: (93) 209 5737; in
Valencia, tel: (96) 333 2805; in
Santander, tel: (94) 223 9435.

Where to Stay

The complete hotel and *paradores*
list, *Guia oficial de hoteles*
published at Easter, is available
from national tourist offices. It is
advisable to book in advance,
especially at popular resorts during
summer or at festival times. Larger
towns have Brujula offices, the
official room-finding service, which
charges a small fee. They have
offices at stations, airports and on
main roads which lead to cities.

Attractions

Information on cultural activities
can be obtained at national, local
and city tourist offices.

Shopping

Well-known Spanish souvenirs
include damasquino jewellery,
knives and swords from Toledo;
ceramics from Toledo, Valencia and
Seville; filigree silver from Córdoba;
botas (wine-skin bottles),
castanets, Spanish dolls and
bullfight posters.

Madrid

Getting There

By Air

Most international airlines have
flights to Madrid. The airport
(Barajas) is 16 km (10 miles) from
the city centre. To get into the city
from the airport, there is a bus
service which runs regularly
(depending on the time of day) to
the underground bus terminal at the
Plaza Colón. The Aeropuerto-Colón
bus operates from 4.45am through
the day until 1.30am. From
4.45–5.45am the buses are
hourly, after that they are every 15
minutes until 7am; from
7am–10pm, they are every 10/11
minutes, and then every 15
minutes until 1.30am. For bus
information, tel: 431 6192.
    If taking a **taxi** from the airport
into Madrid, avoid unofficial cab
drivers. Official Madrid taxis are
white with red stripes painted
transversally across the doors. An
additional fee will be added to the
fare as an airport surcharge, and
each large piece of luggage will also
be charged for. On Sunday, holidays
and after 11pm, there is a further
surcharge.

By Rail

The main train stations in Madrid
are Chamartín Station; Principe Pio
(Norte) Station and Atocha Station.
RENFE train information and
reservations, tel: 563 0202.
Reservations, tel: 328 9020.
    Two trains leave Paris for Spain
every night: the Expreso Puerta del
Sol, which has old-fashioned decor,
couchettes, and carries cars; and
the Talgo Camas/couchette, more
modern and comfortable, with
beds. Both arrive at Chamartín
station, from where you can get the
metro or a taxi to the centre.
    Train information from RENFE, tel:
(91) 328 9020.

By Bus

The two main bus stations in
Madrid are Estación Sur de
Autobuses, tel: 468 4511/4200;
and Auto Res., tel: 551 7200.
For radio taxis, tel: 547 8200;
teletaxis 445 9008 and for metro
information in Madrid, tel: 522 5909.

By Car

The car journey from London and
northern Europe takes a minimum
of 24 hours (in a fast car, without
an overnight break). Allow 6 hours
from the Spanish border at Irún to
Madrid. Burgos is a good stop-off to
visit the magnificent cathedral and
eat well. You need a green card, log
book and bail bond, and it's
advisable to carry an International
Driving Licence.
    For information on road
conditions, tel: 900 123 505.

Practical Tips

Emergency Medical Services

A green or red cross identifies a
chemist (*farmacia*). Outside shop
hours go to a *farmacia de guardia*,
listed in chemist's windows and in
the newspaper.
    If you need emergency medical
treatment you will be taken to the
Urgencias (casualty) at a large
hospital or the local Ambulatorios,
which are open 24 hours a day
(addresses in the windows of
pharmacies and in the
newspapers). The Anglo-American
Medical Unit, Calle Conde de
Aranda 1, tel: 4351823, gives
bilingual attention 24 hours a day.
The Official Association of Dentists
runs a 24-hour, seven-days-a-week
clinic for emergency dental care, at
Calle Padilla 68, 5 D. Tel: 402
6421 or 402 6422.

Business Hours

Shops are open 9.30 or 10am–1.30
or 2pm and then reopen again in the
afternoon from 4.30 or 5–8pm, or a
little later in summer. Most are
closed on Saturday afternoon and
Sunday. However, the major
department stores like El Corte
Inglés and Galerías Preciados are
open without interruption six days a
week, 10am–9pm, and frequently on
Sunday, despite the protests of
small shopkeepers.

Postal Services

Most offices (*correos*) are open Monday–Friday 9am–2pm and Saturday to 1pm. Alternatively (and quicker) buy stamps in an *estanco* (tobacconist) and use either a yellow or red (*express*) postbox. Telegrams are sent from post offices or tel: 522 2000. The ornate central Palacio de Correos, in Calle Alcalá opposite Cibeles fountain (8.30am–10pm) is much faster than other post offices. Most hotels have a fax service.

Telephones

You can phone from a box (they have instructions in English, but are often out of order), from bars (more expensive, but more relaxed as you don't need the right coins) or from hotels (up to four times the normal rate). There are also public phone offices (Palacio de Correos, Gran Vía 30, Puerta de Recoletos 41); major credit cards accepted, pay after the call. If you are using a US credit phone card, dial the company's access number below, then 01, and then the country code. Sprint: tel: 900 99 0013; AT&T: tel: 900 99 0011; MCI: tel: 900 99 0014.

Tourist Information Offices

Torre de Madrid, Plaza de España. Tel: 364 1876.
Chamartín railway station. Tel: 325 9976.
Barajas airport (international arrivals). Tel: 305 8656.

Getting Around

Public Transport

The Metro: The quickest way of moving around the city, the metro runs 6am–1.30am. The 10 lines (120 stations) are labelled by number, colour and final destination. Bulk buying tickets for 10 journeys saves up to 50 percent. You can get a metro map at the ticket booth. For metro information, tel: 522 5909.

By Bus: More than 150 routes are covered by red and yellow air-conditioned buses, which run from 6am–midnight. Tickets for both are

Attractions

Perhaps the best way to get to know Madrid is to start off with a general city tour to get your bearings. Tours are available through the local tourist agencies, and the Tourist Board of the Madrid Town Council occasionally organises walking tours and excursions out of the city. For further information, contact the Madrid Tourist Office on Plaza Mayor 3, tel: 566 5477.

There are three magazines about Spain printed in English: *Lookout* and *In Spain*, both

a flat price. A reduced-price ticket for 10 journeys can be bought in an *estanco* (tobacconist's/newspaper kiosk). Night services leave on the hour from Plaza Cibeles. Buses for out-of-town trips, belonging to various private companies, go mainly from the Estación Sur de Autobuses (Calle Méndez Alvaro espquin Calle Retama. For information, tel: 468 4511/4200).

Buses run 6am–midnight. For municipal bus information, tel: 401 9900.

By Taxi: Taxis can be hailed with relative ease in main thoroughfares, found at a *Parada de Taxi* (taxi stand, indicated by a large white "T" against a dark blue background) or requested by phone. For taxi pick-up, call Radio-Teléfono Taxi, tel: 547 8200; Radio-Taxi Independiente, tel: 405 1213 or 405 5500; Teletaxi, tel: 371 2131; Radio Taxi Asociación Gremial, tel: (91) 447 5180.

Shopping

Madrid offers visitors every shopping possibility from all the regions of Spain. For craft work, leather goods, footware and furniture, try the state-run Artespaña shops (Velázquez 140; Hermosilla 14; Ramón de la Cruz 33; and at the La Vaguada shopping centre in north Madrid). Department stores and tourist shops are in the

published monthly, and the Madrid weekly, *Guidepost*, which gives performance listings. Information regarding cultural events can also be found at the Madrid Tourist Office.

Tickets for plays, concerts, films, bullfights and soccer matches can be bought at Galicia, Plaza del Carmen 7, tel: 531 2732 or 531 9131. Tickets for bullfights and soccer games only are sold at the small stores and booths set up along Calle Victoria, a small street off the Puerta del Sol.

centre between Puerta del Sol and Plaza Callao, and along the Gran Vía. Select shops and international boutiques line Calle Serrano and its adjoining streets in the Salamanca area. Designer shops are in Calle Almirante, just off the Paseo de Recoletos. The streets directly to the west of Almirante lead into one of Madrid's crime zones.

Further Reading

As I Walked Out One Midsummer Morning, by L. Lee. Penguin.
A Rose for Winter, by L. Lee. Penguin.
The Assassination of Federico García Lorca, by Ian Gibson. Penguin.
Federico García Lorca: A Life, by Ian Gibson. Faber & Faber.
Barcelona, by R. Hughes. Simon & Schuster.
South from Granada, by Gerald Brenan.
The Spaniards: A Portrait of the New Spain, by John Hooper. Penguin.
Tales of the Alhambra, by Washington Irving. Miguel Sánchez.

Other Insight Guides

Other books in the *Insight Guide* series highlight destinations in this region: *Insight Guides:* Spain, Southern Spain, Catalonia, Madrid, Barcelona, Gran Canaria, Northern Spain, Tenerife and Mallorca and Ibiza.

PORTUGAL

Area: 92,072 sq. km. (33,549 sq. miles) including Madeira and the Azores.
Capital: Lisbon
Principal rivers: Douro, Guadiana, Lima, Minho, Mondego and Tejo (Tagus).
Population: 10 million
Language: Portuguese
Religion: Roman Catholic (97 percent)
Time Zone: GMT (summer time Mar–Oct GMT + 1); the Azores are 1 hour behind continental Portugal.
Currency: the Euro
Weights and measures: metric
Electricity: 220 volts AC, continental-style round plugs.
International dialling code: outgoing 00; incoming 351

Getting There

By Air
TAP Air Portugal is Portugal's national airline and has wide international links. Many major airlines make non-stop direct flights to Lisbon from capital cities in Europe and other continents. You may also, from some countries, fly directly to Oporto in the north and Faro in the south. Links with London are particularly good. From New York and Boston there are several flights a week.

By Rail
Nowhere in Portugal is yet linked to the superfast TGV system, but there's a busy international (and national) train service. A daily train makes the Paris–Lisbon run, and the Paris–Oporto route. Madrid–Lisbon (usually twice a day) takes around 10 hours. There are routes from northern Spain (Galicia) or southern Spain (Seville) into Portugal. These tend to be slow and time-consuming.

For information about train services from any station in Lisbon (or for the rest of the country) tel: (01) 888 4025.

By Road
Good roads link Portugal with its neighbour Spain at numerous border points. Main east-west routes to Lisbon are from Seville via Beja; Badajos via Elvas; Salamanca via Viseu. Driving from England, via the Channel ferries, allow three days; or, via Plymouth–Santander or Portsmouth–Bilbao, two.

Public Holidays

In addition to the public holidays listed in the Introduction above, the following dates are holidays in Portugal: Anniversary of the Revolution (25 April), Portugal and Camões Day (10 June), St Anthony's Day/Lisbon only (13 June), Saint John's Day/especially in Oporto (24 June), Republic Day (5 October), All Saints' Day (1 November), Restoration Day (1 December), Day of the Immaculate Conception (8 December).

Practical Tips

Business Hours
Most stores open for business Monday–Friday 9am–1pm and about 3–7pm. Stores are open on Saturday 9am–1pm, and closed Sunday and holidays. Major banks are open Monday–Friday 8.30am–3pm and are closed Saturday, Sunday and holidays.

Tipping
A tip of 10 percent is sufficient in restaurants and for taxi drivers. Barbers and hairdressers receive the same or a little less. Theatre ushers also expect a small tip.

Postal Services
Most offices open Monday–Friday 9am–6pm; smaller branches close

Telephones

Phones equipped for international calls are located in all areas and accept coins, Telecom cards or credit cards, although the older phones taking coins are fast disappearing. Instructions are written in English and other major languages.

You can make calls – international and local – from post offices. Go to the window for a cabin assignment and pay when the call is finished. In Lisbon there is also a phone office in the Rossio, open everyday 9am–11pm; in Oporto, there is one in Praça da Liberdade (same hours).

Many village stores and bars have metered telephones. Phone first, pay later, but be prepared to pay more than the rate for pay phone or post office calls. Calls made from hotels are higher still.

To reach an English-speaking international operator, tel: 098 (intercontinental service) or 099 (European service). To call direct to the US or Canada, dial 097-1, plus the area code and phone number. For other countries, dial 00 plus the country code and phone number, omitting the initial zero. Dial slowly.

Telephone numbers in Portugal change with infuriating frequency. To get a current number, dial 118. But be warned – that could change, too.

Telegrams and Faxes
You may place telegrams by phone (tel: 10) or from a post office, but it is expensive. Fax machines which operate in all major post offices.

for lunch 12.30–2.30pm. In larger cities, the main branch may be open on weekends. Mail is delivered Monday–Friday; in the central business districts in the larger cities, it is delivered twice a day.

To buy stamps, stand in any line marked *selos*. To mail or receive packages, go to the line marked *encomendas*.

Getting Around

By Air
TAP has a daily service between Lisbon and Oporto, Faro and Covilhã. Flights run several times weekly between Lisbon and Bragança, and Lisbon and Portimão.

By Rail
Trains in Portugal range from the comfortable and speedy *rápidos* to the painfully slow *regionais*. Generally the most efficient routes are the *rápido* Lisbon–Coimbra–Porto and the Lisbon–Algarve lines. Some *rápidos* have first-class carriages only; others have a very comfortable second-class as well.

The *directos*, which make more stops and travel more slowly have both first- and second-class compartments; second-class here is likely to be less comfortable than in the *rápidos*. Finally, the *semi-directos* and especially the *regionais* seem to stop every few feet and take longer than one could have believed possible.

For information on train services, call (01) 888 4025.

By Road
Bus networks are private but many systems have adapted their name from the former Rodoviária Nacional so that, for example, the main bus company in the far north is now Rodoviária Entre Douro e Minho. Only the Algarve bus company dropped the word Rodoviária, calling itself Eva Transportes.

Outside the routes between major cities, the bus is often faster than the train, and the bus system is certainly more extensive. This is particularly true in the north and between the smaller towns in the Algarve and Alentejo.

There are quite a few private bus lines which tend to specialize in particular routes or areas of the country. Many travel agencies can book tickets on a private line or may even run their own.

Public Transport
Oporto's public transport is limited to buses and trams – the trams to be phased out – and Coimbra's to electric buses. Both these systems run on the same principal as Lisbon's system: you may either pay the driver a flat fee, or buy prepaid modules and validate the number required by the length of the journey. You may buy modules and get information from bus company kiosks in both Oporto and Coimbra.

Attractions

Nightlife
Nightlife in Portugal means different things to different people. For some, it's a jug of wine and a night of *fado*. For others, it's a flashy disco, or a night at the neighbourhood café.

For a list of just about everything going on in the city and larger towns consult *Agenda de Lisboa*. Even if you can't read Portuguese, the listings are comprehensible.

Shopping

Portuguese handicrafts range from hand-carved toothpicks to wicker furniture to blankets and rugs. The most famous Portuguese handicrafts include ceramic tiles (*azulejos*) and pottery, Arraiolos rugs, and embroidery and lace work.

Language

If you speak Spanish you can read Portuguese and understand most speech. There are also slight similarities with written French. At Turismo and in virtually all hotels and many restaurants you'll find the major European languages fluently spoken.

Lisbon

Getting There

By Air
Lisbon's Portela Airport is on the outskirts of the city. A taxi to the city centre will cost you around €8–10.

In all Portugal's cities, taxis are plentiful and cheap. In the city, they charge a standard meter fare, with no additions for extra passengers. (They carry up to four people.) Outside city limits, the driver may use the meter or charge a flat rate per kilometre, and is entitled to charge for the return fare (even if you don't take it). You should tip taxi drivers about 10 percent.

Buses to and from the airport are: Nos 44, 45 and 83. Express bus No. 91 travels direct between the airport and Santa Apolónia station, in the city centre just off the Praça do Comércio.

By Rail
Lisbon is not yet linked to the superfast TVG system, but there's a busy international (and national) train service. Trains from across Europe arrive at Santa Apolónia station.

Practical Tips

Medical Services
In Lisbon, there is always a pharmacy open somewhere. If you can't find one dial 118 (or get someone else to) for the *Farmácias de serviço*. Hospitals are mostly big and chronically overfull. The staff are overworked and underpaid. Some visitors head for the British Hospital, 49 Rua Saraiva de Carvalho, Tel: 395 50 67.

When you need the police, an ambulance or the fire brigade, tel: 112.

Business Hours
Most shops are open 9am–1pm and 3–7pm weekdays and mornings only on Saturday. Offices often start later and finish earlier. Major banks are open Monday–Friday

8.30am–3pm. The bank at Lisbon airport is open 24 hours, as is the airport's post office. The most central post office in Lisbon, in the Restauradores, is open 8am–10pm.

Postal Services

Most post offices are open 8.30am–6pm. The central post office at Praça dos Restauradores is open 8am–midnight, and offers the best service to tourists. The airport post office opens 24 hours. Stamps are *selos*.

Telephone

The international access code is 00. After this, dial the relevant country code: Australia 61; Canada 1; UK 44; US 1. If you are using a US phone credit card, first dial the company's access number listed below: AT&T: Tel: 05017-1288; MCI: Tel: 05017-1234; Sprint: Tel: 05017-1877. If you have problems, tel: 099 for Europe international, 098 for intercontinental and 090 for interurban. To call Portugal from overseas, get an international line then tel: 351, followed by 1 for Lisbon. Inside Portugal, Lisbon's code is 01.

Tourist Information

Tourism/Turismo at the central Palácio Foz, Praça dos Restauradores. Tel: 346 3643.

Consulates & Embassies

UK: Rua de São Bernardo, 33. Tel: 21 392 4000.
US: Avenida das Forças Armadas, 16. Tel: 727 3300.
All embassies are listed in the Lisbon phone book under the word *Embaixada*.

Getting Around

By Rail

Train/Metro: Santa Apolónia is the main train station for national and international rail travel. The Rossio station serves such places as Queluz and Sintra. From Cais do Sodré, on the waterfront, electric trains make the run to and from Cascais.

Lisbon also has a Metro system with 24 stations on lines that fan out in a rough W from the Rossio. Extended for Expo '98, the metro is principally useful for travel in the central zone of the city. The system is easy to use and very cheap. Above ground, stations are marked with a big M. Tickets for any distance can be bought at the ticket counter, or from a machine (which has instructions in English and French as well as Portuguese); you can also buy booklets of tickets. There's also a Campo Pequeno station, close to the bullring. The zoo, if you want to go there, is at Sete Rios station. For information tel: 355 8547.

By Road

Excellent service is provided cheaply by the numerous black-and-green cabs of Lisbon. A meter operates within the city, but it is switched off at Lisbon's city limits.

Bus/Tram: Lisbon can be packed with traffic, but the buses and trams go everywhere at surprising speed – except during rush hours (avoid them). Buy booklets of tickets (and maybe a route map) from the hatch at the back of the Santa Justa Elevador in the Baixa. A week's tourist pass, for all municipal transport (buses, trams, *elevadores*, the electric cable cars) is available. Daily tours are offered to Lisbon and nearby sights by coaches parked below the park in Praça Marquês de Pombal. An antique tramcar makes daily 2-hour tours in summer from the Praça do Comércio.

Motoring Advice

It's no pleasure driving in the city. For out-of-town trips there are numerous car hire companies at Lisbon airport and in the city. Avis, for example, has an office conveniently located in the garage of the Hotel Tivoli in the Avenida da Liberdade. Rental prices are cheaper than in most European countries. Petrol, however, costs more than in most countries.

Waterways

To cross the Tejo, a crucial exercise for thousands of commuters living in south bank towns, there are ferries all day from the Praça do Comércio and from the Cais do Sodré. To cross downriver, there's a ferry at Belém which goes to the small port of Porto Brandão. Some people make the trip as an outing, often to eat lunch on the other side.

Further Reading

The Portuguese: The Land and the People, by Marion Kaplan. Penguin.
They Went to Portugal, by Rose Macaulay. Penguin.

Other Insight Guides

Companion books include: *Portugal*, *Lisbon* and *Madeira*. The *Insight Pocket Guide* series, designed to help readers without a lot of time plan their trips precisely, include books on *Algarve* and *Lisbon*. Many of the Pocket Guides come with handy pullout maps. *Insight Compact Guides* cover *Portugal*, *Algarve*, *Lisbon* and *Madrid*.

Feedback

We would welcome your feedback on any details related to your experiences using the book "on the road".
Things change ever more rapidly in the world of travel, making some mistakes and omissions inevitable in a book of this kind. We are ultimately reliant on our readers to keep us in the picture. The more details you can give us (particularly with regard to addresses, e-mails and telephone numbers), the better. Please write to us at:

Insight Guides
PO Box 7910
London SE1 1WE
United Kingdom
Or send e-mail to:
insight@apaguide.demon.co.uk

ART & PHOTO CREDITS

Peter Adams 111, 170, 177, 179, 357, 358, 364, 384
AKG London 184T
Emanuel Ammon 199
Ping Amranand 26, 27, 55, 67
Archiv Gümpel 38
Archives for Art & History 31R
Apa Archive 146
Tony Arruza 61, 294T, 372/373, 374/375, 376, 380, 381, 383, 385, 386, 387, 388, 389, 390, 391
Anzenberger/Sattleberger 229
David Baltzer 46, 57
Gaetano Barone 50
David Beatty 329
Lisa Beebe 345, 349
Yann Arthus-Bertrand/Altitude 91L
Bildarchiv Preussischer Kulturbesitz 43
Bodo Bondzio 2B, 4/5, 112, 112T, 113L, 130, 135, 153, 169, 186, 256
The Bridgeman Art Library 36, 95T, 278
Marcus Brooke 304, 305, 306
Sigfried Bucher 183
Douglas Corrance 63, 115
Pierre Couteau 72/73
Jerry Dennis/Apa 17, 134, 137, 245, 246, 246T
John Decopoulos 25
Pete Didlsheim 52
Annabel Elston/Apa front flap bottom, back flap top, 90L, 91R, 91T, 92T, 94T, 132T, 136T, 228T, 232, 286T, 287, 352T
Piero Fantini 262
Lee Foster 64
Klaus D. Francke/Bilderberg 330
Ann Frank Stichting 150T
French Tourist Office 20/21
Wolfgang Fritz 126, 173
Guglielmo Galvin/Apa 149, 151, 156T, 388T

G. Galvin & G. Taylor/Apa 291T, 292T
Glyn Genin/Apa 296R, 296T, 297, 330T, 331L
Patrizia Giancotti 267
Michael Von Graffenried 209R
Frances Gransden/Apa back cover left, front flap top, 264T, 266T, 268T, 270, 274, 276T
F. Gransden/M. Read/Apa 169T, 270, 264T, 274
Albano Guatti 70/71
Manfred Hamm 95, 392
Blaine Harrington 54, 224, 359
Herb Hartmann 170T
Han Hartzuiker 138/139
Harald Hauswald 158/159
D & J Heaton 80/81
K. Heinz & S. Kraemer 167
Christoph Henning/Fotoarchiv 65
Albert Heras/Prisma 355
Michel Hetier 97, 103
Hans Höffer 220, 252/253, 292
Heidelberg Tourist Office/Loosen Foto 172
Houserstock 171, 298/299, 300, 304T
Imagen 59
A.P. Interpress 45
Michael Jenner 5B, 110L/R, 212/213, 224T, 285, 346, 348
Caroline Jones spine bottom, back cover center left, 4B, 107, 358T
Jon Jones/Sygma 47
János Kalmár 2/3, 10/11
Catherine Karnow 53, 62, 89, 90R, 101, 113R, 121
R. Kiedrowski 14
Ingeborg Knigge 133
Kodia Photo 302, 303
Bob Krist 3B
Wolfgang Kunz/Bilderberg 312
Dennis Lane 281
Robin Laurence/Apa 187, 187T

Lyle Lawson 15, 29, 33, 39, 58L, 100, 102, 294T
Lelli & Massasotti/Scala 48/49
Till Lesser/Bilderberg 160/161, 185
Magnum Picture Library 58R
Deiter Maler 214
Bildverlag Merten 8/9
Ros Miller/Apa back flap bottom, 282T, 283
Jean Mohr 200
Ingrid Morató 353
Kai Ulrich Müller 166
Museu Nacional de Arte Atiga 32
Museum of Cycladic Art 24
Ben Nakayama 291, 293, 295
Christine Osborne 152
Jurgens Ost/Europa Photo 236/237, 244
P.A. Interpress 45
Erhard Pansegrau 184
Photo Bibiotheque Nationale 37, 105T, 250T
Alexander Van Phillips/Apa 78/79, 108, 131
Eddy Posthuma de Boer 156
US Press 210/211
Mark Read/Apa back cover center right, 170, 174, 174T, 175L, 175R, 176, 221, 223, 249, 250T, 366T, 367, 368T, 369, 386T
G.P. Reichelt 162
Andrej Reiser/Bilderberg 6/7, 94
Dirk Renckhoff 176T
Paul Van Riel 92, 96, 155, 266R
Salzburg Tourist Office 232R
Othmar Seehauser 68/69
Tim Sharman 238, 247
Jeroen Snijders/Apa 104L/R, 104T, 360, 361, 362, 363
Tony Souter 240, 241, 243, 266/267

Jon Spall/Apa 227, 231, 232T, 233
Spectrum Colour Library 16
Achim Sperber/Bilderberg 222
Stone 12/13, 18/19, 74, 88, 105, 109, 188/189, 122/123, 124/125, 190/191, 194, 198, 265, 277, 284, 286, 290, 308/309, 310/311, 316, 319, 322, 323, 324, 331R, 334/335, 336/337, 356, 365
Storto 209L
Jeremy Sutton-Hibbert 307
George Taylor/Apa 120, 120T
Topham Picturepoint 31L, 42, 66, 147, 201T
Transglobe 230
Alberto Venzago 192/193
Rolf Verres 180
Karel Vlcek 234/235
Joseph F. Viesti 338, 344
Hanna Wagner 60
Bill Wassman 19, 93, 114T, 157, 181, 200T, 208, 225, 226, 228, 254/255, 263, 264, 266L, 268L/R, 269, 271, 275, 279, 282, 288, 289L/R, 296L, 347, 354, 368
Bill Wassman/Apa back cover right & bottom, 115T, 116, 116T, 117, 117T, 118, 118T, 119,

142, 150, 154, 154T, 201, 202, 202T, 203, 204, 204T, 205, 206, 207, 208T, 208, 317, 318T, 320R, 320T, 321
Stephan Weiner 136
Roger Williams 351, 352, 362T
Phil Wood/Apa 181T, 182, 182T, 242T, 294, 320L, 325, 328, 382T
Adam Woolfit 82
George Wright 140/141

Pages 98/99: *Top row left to right:* RMN/Herve Lewandowski, Lauros/Giraudon, Lauros/Giraudon, Leimdorfer/Rea/Katz. *Centre row left to right:* Lauros/Giraudon, Lauros/Giraudon. *Bottom row all by:* Lauros/Giraudon.
Pages 188/189: *Top row left to right:* Phil Wood, Wolfgang Fritz, Marton Radkai, AKG London. *Center row left to right:* Marton Radkai, Wolfgang Fritz, AKG London. *Bottom row left to right:* Marton Radkai, Verkehsverein Landshut, Wolfgang Fritz.

Pages 272/273: *Top row left to right:* Blaine Harrington, AKG London, AKG London, Blaine Harrington, Scala, Blaine Harrington, AKG/Erich Lessing, AKG/Erich Lessing, AKG London.
Pages 332/333: *Top row left to right:* Terry Harris/Just Greece, Steve Outram, Terry Harris/Just Greece, B&E Anderson. *Centre row left to right:* Steve Outram. *Bottom row left to right:* G. Sfikas/Ideal Photo SA, G. Sfikas/Ideal Photo SA, Steve Outram, Terry Harris/Just Greece.
Pages 370/371: *Top row left to right:* Imagen MAS, AISA, Andrea Pistolesi, Imagen MAS. *Centre row left to right:* JD Dallet, Imagen MAS. *Bottom row left to right:* Imagen MAS, Imagen MAS, AISA.

Map Production
Keith Brook
©2002 Apa Publications GmbH & Co.
Verlag KG Singapore Branch, Singapore

Cartographic Editor **Zoë Goodwin**
Design Consultants
Carlotta Junger, Graham Mitchener
Picture Research
Hilary Genin, Britta Jaschinski

Index

Numbers in italics refer to
photographs

a

Aachen 27, 186
Aalsmeer *156*
Adriatic 53, 289–90, 296, 301–6
Aegina (Eghina) 325
Aeolian islands 297
Agincourt 102
Aiguablava *361*, 362
Aix-en-Provence 113–14
Akrotiri 329
Albania 67, 306, 307
Alberobello 296
Albi 112
Albufeira *389*, 390
Alcobaça 386
Alentejo 388
Alexander the Great 26, 295
Algarve 388–90
Algeciras 369
Alicante 364, *370–71*
Alkmaar 155
Almería 368
Almuñécar 368
Alps 75, 115, 120, 195, 199–200,
    202, 206–9, 215
Alsace-Lorraine *52*, *74*, 121
Altamira 358
Amalfi coast *294*, 295
Amboise 107
Amiens 101–2
Amsterdam 144–51
    Anne Frank Huis 150–51, *150*
    Begijnhof 149
    cafés 150, 151
    canals 149
    Historisch Museum 149
    Jewish Quarter 150–51
    Joods Historisch Museum 150
    Koninklijk Paleis 147, *151*
    markets 151
    Museum Amstelkring 149
    Museum Het Rembrandthuis 150
    Museum Willet-Holthuysen 150
    Nieuwe Kerk 147
    nightlife 151
    Oude Kerk 147
    Rijksmuseum 149
    Stedelijk Museum 149
    Van Gogh Museum 149
    Westerkerk 151
Andalucia 366–8
Andorra 361
Angelico, Fra 275, 277, 293

Angers 108–9
Antibes 116
Antwerp 136
Apeldoorn 157
Arab influences 18, *28*, 28–9
    see also **Moors**
Aragón 360
Arcachon 110
architecture 17, 18, 28, 44, 52
Ardennes 102, 137
Arezzo 290
Argos 327
Arles 112, 113
Arlon 137
Arnhem 157
Arona 286
Arras 101
Arromanches 103
art 17, 34, 38, 40, 44
art deco 44, 151
art nouveau 17, 40, 121, 132,
    150, 187, 221, 224, 254–5
Ascona 209
Assen 157
Assisi *256*, 292
Asturias 357–8
Athens *310–11*, 313, 317–21
    Acropolis 316–9, *316*
    Daphne 321
    Monastiráki 319, 320
    Mt Lykavittós 321
    Omonia 319
    Parthenon 25, 317
    Piraeus 313
    Pláka 321
    Sounion *308–9*, 321
    Syntagma Square 319
    Tower of the Winds 319
Athos, Mt 323
Augsburg 180
Austria *10–11*, 17, 33, 35–40,
    214, 215–33
    Carinthia 215, 229, 230–31
    Graz 231
    Innsbruck 227–9
    Minimundus 231
    Salzburg 35, *210–11*, 232–3
    Salzkammergut *212–13*, 215,
    231
    Styria 231–2
    Tyrol 215, 227–30
    Vienna 35–6, 215, 221–5
    Vorarlberg 215, 227
    Wachau 233
Austro-Hungarian Empire 18, 40,
    41, 43, 239
    see also **Habsburgs**
Auvergne 111
Avignon 112–13

Avila 359
Avranches 102
Azay le Rideau 108

b

Bach, Johann Sebastian 174, 176
Baden-Baden 183
Baeza 367
Balkan coast *47*, *298–9*, 301–7
Barcelona 40, 52, 351–5
    Barri Gòtic 352–3
    Cathedral *352*
    La Rambla 351–2
    La Ribera 353–4
    Miró Foundation 52, 355
    Modernist city 354–5
    Montjuïc 355
    Museu d'Art Contemporani 351
    Museum d'Art Modern 354
    Palau de la Música Catalana *353*
    Parc de la Ciutadella 354
    Pedralbes 355
    Picasso Museum 354
    royal city 352–3
    Sagrada Família 354–5, *354*
    Tibidabo *355*
Bari 296
Baroque 17, 34–5, 131, 177, 181,
    207–8, 224, 228, 231, 241–2,
    267, 283, 301, 390
Basel *8–9*, 205
Basques 15, 339, 359–60
Bastogne 137
Batalha 386, *387*
Battle of the Bulge 137
Bauhaus School 44, 52, 169,
    173–4
Bavaria 16, *60*, *173*, 176–82
Bayeux 103
Bayreuth 176
beaches 52–3
Beaugency 105
Beaune 120
Beethoven, Ludwig van 36, 38,
    185, 224
Belfort 121
Belgium 39, 41, 46, 57–8, 127–37
    Antwerp 136
    Ardennes 137
    Bruges *122–3*, *134*, 135, *136*
    Brussels *124–5*, 128–33
    coast 135
    Ghent 136
    Liège *135*, 137
    Limburg 137
    Wallonia 137
    Waterloo 37, 136
Bellágio *54*, 286, *287*

Bellicourt 102
Bellini 282
Benidorm 53, 363
Bergamo 287
Berlage, H.P. 153
Berlin 57, 167–71
    Berlin-Mitte 167, 169
    Botanical Gardens 171
    Brandenberg Gate 158–9, 169
    Breitscheidplatz 28, 168
    Cathedrals 170, 171
    Charlottenburg Palace 171
    Dahlem 171
    Europa-Center 167, 168
    Friedrichstrasse 167
    Gendarmenmarkt 170
    Kurfürstendamm 166, 167–8,
        170
    Museum Island 167, 171
    Musikinstrumentenmuseum 169
    Neue Nationalgalerie 169
    Neue Synagoge 171
    Reichstag 52, 167, 169
    Schaubühne 168
    Scheunenviertel 167, 171
    shopping 168
    Tiergarten 169
    Unter den Linden 167, 169–70
    Wall 45, 47, 168, 169
    Zeughaus 170
    Zoologischer Garten 169
Bern 204–5
Bernese Oberland 190–91, 199, 209
Bernini, Gianlorenzo 34, 264, 267,
    268, 269, 271
Besançon 121
Beuys, Joseph 187
Biarritz 110
Bilbao 52, 360
Biot 116
Bismarck, Otto von 39, 41, 110,
    167
Black Death 30
Black Forest 182–3, 188
Blanes 361
Blois 107, 108
Bocuse, Paul 55, 120
Bodensee 207–8
body language 56–7, 56
Bologna 288
Bonn 185
Bonnard, Pierre 117
Bordeaux 64, 110
Borger 157
Borromini, Francesco 267
Bosch, Hieronymus 34, 133, 154
Bosnia-Herzegovina 40
Botticelli, Sandro 35, 271, 275,
    276

Bouillon 137
Boulogne 101, 102
Bouvines 102
Brac Island 305
Braga 385
Brahms, Johannes 250
Bramante 34
Brandenburg 173
Braque, Georges 117, 149, 157
Bratislava 225
Brea, Louis 118
Brecht, Bertholt 44
Bremen 187
Brenner Pass 285
Brescia 287
Brindisi 296
Brittany 12–13, 15, 17, 101,
    104
Bruckner, Anton 224, 233
Bruegel, Pieter 34, 135, 154
Bruges 122–3, 134, 135, 136
Brunelleschi, Filippo 275
Brussels 128–33
    Atomium 133
    Cathédral St-Michel 132
    Grand-Place 124–5, 131, 133
    Hôtel de Ville 131
    Magritte Museum 133
    Manneken Pis 131, 132
    Musées des Royeaux des Beaux-
        Arts 133
    Palais du Roi 133
    Place du Grand Sablon 133
    Royal Domain 133
Budapest 225, 239, 249–51
    Buda 249–50
    Castle Hill 249–50, 250
    Chain Bridge 249, 250
    City Park 251
    Mátyás Church 250
    museums 249, 250, 251
    Parliament 251
    Pest 250–51
    St Stephen's Basilica 251
Bulgaria 40, 57, 313
bull-running 360
bullfights 112, 336–7
Buñuel, Luis 44
Burgos 358
Burgundy 15, 28, 29, 64, 100,
    120, 120–21
Byron, Lord 199, 202, 203, 272,
    279, 307, 321
Byzantine 28, 279, 293, 323

C

Cabo São Vicente 388
Cadaqués 362

Cádiz 369
Caen 102, 103
Cagnes-sur-Mer 116
Cahors 111
Calabria 296–7
Calais 101
Caldas de Monchique 389
Calder, Alexander 117
Calella de Palafrugell 362
Calvin, John 31, 201
Camargue 113
Camões, Luis de 386, 387
Canaletto 171, 174, 278, 279
Cannes 66, 116
Cap d'Antibes 115, 116
Capri 295
Caravaggio 50, 171, 267
Carcassonne 112
Carnac 104
carnivals 14, 126, 160–61, 186,
    188–9, 224;
    see also festivals
Cascais 383
Cassis 114
Castelnaudry 112
Castile 270–71, 358–9
Catalans 15, 33, 38
Catalonia 339, 360–61, 363
Catholic Church 30–31, 34
Cavallini, Pietro 266
Cavour, Camillo 39
Cavtat 306
Cefalù 297
Cellini, Benvenuto 34, 276
Cervantes, Miguel 345, 349, 364
Cézanne, Paul 40, 91, 114
Chagall, Marc 93, 116, 117, 118,
    121, 137, 149
Chambord 106, 109
Champagne 121
Chaplin, Charlie 204
Charlemagne 27, 28, 186, 221
Chartres 28
Chaumont 107
cheeses 56, 60, 147, 155, 192–3,
    204, 207
Chelib 389–90
Chenonceaux 107–8
Cheverny 105
Chianti 292
Chillado, Eduardo 364
Chillon, Château de 203, 204
Chinon 108
Chirico, Giorgio de 44
Christianity 27–31
Christmas markets 177, 189
Chur 208
Cicero 27
Cimabue, Giovanni 292

Cimiez 118
cinema 17, 44, 96, 116, 247
civil wars 45, 67
Cluny 28, *29*
Cocteau, Jean 44
Coimbra *376*, 386
Cold War 46
Colmar 121
Cologne (Köln) *14*, 45, 185–6, *186*, 189
colonialism 18, 40
Columbus, Christopher 29, 33, 347, 352, 388
communications 18, 41, 67, 75
communism 43, 45, 46, 47
Como, Lake *54*, 286, *287*
Constance, Lake 207–8
Constantinople 279
Coppet 202
Córdoba 367
Corfu (Kerkyra) 326, *328*
Corinth 327
Corot, Jean-Baptiste 102
corruption 53–4, 257
Costa Blanca 363–4
Costa Brava 361–2
Costa Daurada 362–3
Costa del Sol 368–9
Costa de la Luz 369
Costa Verde 357–8, 377, 385–6
Côte d'Azur 114–19
Coulon 109
Courbet 102
Crécy 102
Creglingen 178
Crete (Kriti) 330, *331*, *332*
crime 53–4, 61–2
Crimean War 38
Croatia 37, 43, *47*, *298–9*, *300*, *301*, 301, 303–6
Crusaders 28–9, 31, 279
Cuenca 364
cultural heritage 17, 18, 34–6, 38
Cyclades 328–9
Czech Republic 225, 239–43
Czechoslovakia 37, 43–4, 45, 46, 47

d

D-Day landings 103
Da Gama, Vasco 33, 281, 383, 388
Dahlem 171
Dalí, Salvador 44, 154, 349, 362
Dalmatia 304–6
Damme 135
Dante Alighieri *22*, 30, 275, 289
Danube, River 180, 221, 224, 225, 233, 239, 249–51
Dark Ages 29–31
Darrës 307
Davos 208, *209*
Deauville 102
Degas, Edgar 40
Delacroix, Eugène *37*, 91
Delft 154
Delphi 323–4, *324*
democracy 25, 41, 47
Den Haag 153
Den Helder 157
Denmark 39, 46
Derain, André 40
Dessau 173–4
Dieppe 102
Dijon 120
Dinard 104
Dinkelsbühl 179, 188
Disneyland Paris *19*, 97
Dodecanese 330–31
Domenichino 270
Don Quixote 364
Donatello 34, 275, 276
Donnauwörth 179
Dordogne 111
Dortmund 186–7
Drenthe *156*, 157
Dresden 45, *174*, 175
driving 54
Dubrovnik *47*, *298–9*, *306*
Dufy, Raoul 96, 102, 116
Dunkirk 102
Dürer, Albrecht 34, 171, 177, 184, 222
Durnstein 233
Düsseldorf 186, 188
Dvorák, Antonin 38, 243

e

Edam 155
education 29–30
Eghina (Aegina) 325
Eisenerz 232
El Cid 29, 358
El Escorial 349
El Greco 34, 320, 348, 364, 365
El Maestrazgo 364
Elche 364
Emme 207
Enkhuizen 155
Enlightenment 35, 36, 38
Ensor, James Sidney 133, 137
Erasmus 30
Ernst, Max 205
Erzberg 232
Estepona 369
Estoril 383
Etna 297
European Community (EU) 46–7, 54, 55, 121, 313
Evian les Bains 202, 203
Evora 388
Evvoia (Euboea) 324–5
Expressionists 40, 133
Extremadura 365
Eze 119

f

Faro 390
fascism 44, 58
Fátima 386
Fauves 40
Ferdinand, Archduke *42*, 43, 229
Ferragudo 389
festivals 108, *188–9*, *254–5*, 306, *359*, 363, 364, 367; see also carnivals
Feuchtwangen 179
Figueres 362
Filippo Lippi, Fra 275
film 17, 44, 96, 116, 247
Flanders 102, 135
Flemings 15, 34, 57–8, 127, 131
Florence 34, *70–71*, *252–3*, 274, 275–7
  Bargello 276
  Duomo *274*, 275
  Galleria dell'Academia 277
  Neptune's Fountain *275*
  Palazzo Pitti 276
  Palazzo Vecchio 28, *34*, 276
  Piazza del Signoria 275
  Piazza Santa Maria Novella 277
  Ponte Santa Trinità 277
  Ponte Vecchio 276, *277*
  San Lorenzo 277
  Uffizi *35*, 276
Fontainebleau 34
Fontainebleau School 99
Fontaine-de-Vaucluse 113
Fontenay 120
food 18, 55–6, *80–81*, 83, 127, 301, 305, 306, 360
football 16
Foster, Sir Norman 52
Fragonard, Jean-Honoré *98*
France 17, 30, 33–9, 44, 83–121
  Alsace-Lorraine *52*, *74*, 121
  Atlantic coast 109–10
  Brittany *12–13*, 15, 17, *101*, 104
  Burgundy 15, 28, *29*, 64, *100*, *120*, 120–21
  châteaux *78–9*, 105–9
  Côte d'Azur 114–19

Disneyland *19*, 97
Dordogne 111
French Alps 115, 120
French Revolution 36–7, 202
Loire Valley *78–9*, 104–9
Normandy 102–3
northern regions 101–4
Paris *6–7*, 28, 52, 89–99
Provence 112–15
Pyrenées 111
Riviera 117–19
southwest *20–21*, 111–12
wines 64, *74*, *82*, 108, 110
Francis of Assisi *98*, *292*
Franco, Francisco 44, 47
Franco-Prussian War 39
Frankfurt 52, 184
Frederick the Great 171, 173
Freiberg 176
Fréjus 115
Friedrich, Caspar David 175
Friesian Islands 157
Fuengirola 369
Füssen 180

g

Galicia 339, 357
game fishing 389
Garda, Lake 287
Gardone Riviera 287
Garibaldi, Guiseppe *39*
Gaudí, Antonio 40, 351–2, 354–5
Gauguin, Paul 40, 137, 175, 205
Genève (Geneva) 200–202
Cathedral *200*, 201
Lake *201*, 202–4
Musée d'Horlogerie 201
Palace of Nations *202*
Reformation Wall 201
Genova (Genoa) 285
Germany 17, 39–45, 57, 163–89
Bavaria 16, *60*, *173*, 176–82
Berlin 45, 47, 52, *57*, 167–71
Black Forest 182–3, 188
Christmas markets 177, 189
coast 187
East 45, 173–7
Fairytale Road 187
festivals *188–9*
Harz 173
München (Munich) 181–2
Rhineland *14*, 45, 184–7
Romantic Road 177–8
Thuringia 176
wines 64, 184–5, *185*, 187
gestures 56–7
Ghent 136
Ghiberti, Lorenzo 275

Ghirlandaio, Domenico 271, 275, 277
Giacometti, Alberto 117
Giambologna 276
Gibraltar 339, 369
Gien 105
Giorgione 171, 282
Giotto 34, 275, 292
Girokastër 307
Girona *362*
Giverny 97
Goethe *38*, 174, 176, 272
Gothic 17, 28, 187, 205, 208, 228, 231, 241, 283, 291
Goya, Francisco de 345, 347, 348, 369
Granada 367–8
Grasse 115
Graz 231
Great Schism 30–31
Greece 24, 25–6, 38, 44, 45, 46, 47, 313–33
Athens *310–11*, 313, 317–21
flora *332–3*
islands *72–3*, 324–6, 330–33
Magna Graecia 293, 296, 297
mainland 323–4
Peloponnese 327–8
Grenoble 120
Grimm, Brothers 187
Gropius, Walter 52, 174
Grossglockner 229–30, *229*
Gruyères 204
Gstaad 209
Guadalupe 365
Guimarães 385
Guincho 52
Gutenberg, Johannes 30, 184

h

Haarlem 154–5
Habsburgs 27, 31, 33, 221–2, 223, 228
Hague (Den Haag) 153
Hals, Frans 133, 147, 149, 154
Hamburg 187
Hamelin (Hameln) 187
hand-shaking 58
Harburg 179
Haro 359
Haydn, Joseph 36, 224
health 41, 59
Heidelberg *172*, 183–4
Hemingway, Ernest 281, 286, 360
Henry the Navigator 383, 386, 388
Herculaneum 294–5
heresies 31
Hitler, Adolf 43, 44–5, *44*, 90

Hoek van Holland 154
Holbein, Hans 184, 205
Holy Roman Empire 27, 33, 35, 37, 184, 208, 221
Honfleur 102
Hooch, Pieter de 149
horses 108, *220*, *221*, 222, *291*, *303*, 369
Horta, Victor 132
Hugo, Victor 94
Huguenots 31, 109
humanism 30, 277
humour 57, 65
Hundred Years' War 30, 106
Hungary 37, 38, 43, 44, 46, 47, *236–7*
Budapest 225, 239, 249–51
hunting 60
Hussites 31
Hvar Island *302*, 305–6, *305*
Hydra (Ydhra) 325
Hyères 114–15
hygiene 59

i

IJsselmeer *155*
immigrants 57–8
Impressionists 40, 91, 169
independence 15, 37–8
Ingres, Jean-Auguste-Dominique 91
Innsbruck 227–9
Hofburg 228–9
Old Town 228–9
Schloss Ambras 229
Stiftkirke Wilten *226*, 229
Tiroler Volkunstmuseum 229
Winter Olympics 229
Interlaken 199, 209
International Brigade 44
Ionian islands 326
Ischgl 227
Isea, Lake 287
Istra 303–4
Italy 37, 38–9, 40, 41, 46, 58, 257–97
Adriatic 53, 289–90, 296
Amalfi coast *294*, 295
Apulia 296
arts 17, 28, 34, 44
Bay of Naples 293–5, *293*
Calabria 296–7
Florence 28, 34, *70–71*, *252–3*, *274*, 275–7
Lakes *54*, 286–7
northern regions *48–9*, 285–9
Po Valley 288–9
Rome 34, 263–73
Sicily 296, 297

Tuscany 28, 59, 290–92
Umbria 292–3
Venice 17, 28, 34, 37, *278*, 279–83
wines 64, 292

j

Jaca 360
Jaén 367, *371*
James, Henry 269, 283
Jerez de la Frontera *369*
Jesuits 31, 283
jet set 58–9
Jews 44, 58, 150–51, 167, 171, 243, 247, 263, 272, 283, 365, 367
Joan of Arc *30*, 102, *105*, 106
Joyce, James 285
Juan Carlos, of Spain 59–60, *59*
Jugendstil 17, 40, 187, 221, 224
Julius Caesar 26–7, *26*
Jumièges 102
Jura 121, 202, 204–5

k

Kalamata 328
Kálymnos *329*
Kandinsky, Vasily 117, 154, 205
Karlsruhe 183
Keats, John 269
Kefallonia 326
Kempen 135
Kerkyra (Corfu) 326, *328*
Keukenhof *152*, 156
kissing 58
Kitzbühel 227, 229
Klagenfurt 230
Klee, Paul 186
Klimt, Gustav 40, 223, 224
Knokke-Heist 135
Knossós 330, *331*
Koblenz 184–5
Kokoschka, Oskar 40, 224
Köln (Cologne) *14*, 45, 185–6, *186*, 189
Koper 303
Korcula *300*
Korda, Alexander 44
Korinthos 327
Kos 331
Kosovo 67
Kotor 301, 306
Krafft, Adam 177
Kraków 239, 246–7
    churches 246–7
    Cloth Hall 246
    Florian's Gate 247

Jan Matejko's House 247
    Royal Castle 247
    Szotayski Museum 247
    Town Hall Tower 246
Krems an der Donau 233
Kriti (Crete) 330, *331*, *332*
Krk Island 304

l

La Mancha *334–5*
La Rochelle 109
La Turbie 119
Lagos 388
Lang, Fritz 44
languages 17, 18, 38, 62, 65–6, 83, 200, 301, 377
Languedoc 112, *113*
Laredo 358
Lascaux *20–21*, 111
Lauda 178
Lausanne 202–3
    Cathedral 203
    Olympic Museum 203
lavatories 59
Le Caillou 136
Le Corbusier *52*, 121
Le Havre 102
Le Pen, Jean-Marie 58
Le Rozier 112
Le Touquet 102
League of Nations 43, 44, 202
Lecco 286, 287
Léger, Fernand 116
Léhar, Franz 224
Leibnitz, Gottfried Wilhelm 174
Leiden 154
Leipzig *174*
León 358, *370–71*
Leonardo da Vinci 34, 98, 275
Lichtestein, Roy 186
Liechtenstein 17, 200, 208
Liège *135*, 137
Lille 101
Limburg 137
Linz 233
Lipica 303
Lisbon 381–3, 387–8
    Alfama 381
    Avenida da Liberdade *383*
    Baixa 382
    Belém 383
    Castelo de São Jorge 381
    Chiado 382
    Fundacão Calouste Gulbenkian 383
    museums 383
    nightlife 382, 383
    Praça do Comércio 381

Rossio *381*, 383
    São Roque 382
    Sé (cathedral) 381
    Torre de Belém 383
Liszt, Franz 250
literature 41, 44
Ljubljana 303
Lloret de Mar 362
Locarno 209
Loches 105
Loire Valley *78–9*, 104–9
Lokrum Island 306
Lollards 31
Lombards 15, 28
Lorenzetti 291
Lorraine 121
Louis XIII 97
Louis XIV 23, 35, 91, 97, 98
Louis XV 36
Louis XVI 36
Louis XVIII 37, 98
Lourdes 111
Loyola, Ignatius 31
Lübeck 187
Lucerne 206–7
    Kapellbrücke *206*
    Lake 199, 206–7
    Löwenplatz 207
    Wagner Museum 207
Lugano, Lake 208–9, 286
Luther, Martin 31, 173
Lutherstadt Wittenberg 173
Luxembourg 46, 137
Lyon 120

m

Macedonia 313
Machiavelli 275
Madrid 345–9
    Morería 346
    museums 347, 348–9
    nightlife 347
    parks 349
    Plaza Dos de Mayo *347*
    Plaza de España 346–7
    Plaza Mayor 346
    Plaza Puerto del Sol 345–6
    Prado 345, *348*
    Rastro flea market *346*
    Royal Palace *344*, 346
mafia 64, 257
Mafra 387
Magdeburg 172
Maggiore, Lake 208–9, 286
Magna Graecia 293, 296, 297
Magritte, René 44, 133, 137, 154
Mahler, Gustav 224
Main, River 178, 184

Mainz 30, 184, 189
Málaga 368–9
Manet, Edouard 91
Maní *327*, 328
Mann, Thomas 281
Mannerism 34
Mantegna, Andrea 171
Marbella 369
Marconi, Guglielmo 41
Marken *153*, 155
Marne, River 102
Marseille 114
Martini, Simone 291, 292
Masaccio 276
Matejki, Jan 247
Matisse, Henri 40, 96, 116, 117, 149
Matterhorn *198*, *208*, 209
Mechelen 136
Medici family 34, 276
Mediterranean Sea 52, 53
Meier, Richard 52
Melk, Abbey of 233
Menton 119
Mérida 365
meteorite crater 179
Metternich, Prince Clemens 37, 38
Michelangelo 34, *98*, 135, 222, 270, 271, 275, 276, 277
Mies van der Rohe, Ludwig 169
Milan *48–9*, 257, 285
millennium celebrations 67
Minoans 25
Mira *374–5*
Miró, Joan 44, 117, 349
Mljet Island 306
Modena 288
Modernismo 17, 354–5
Modigliani, Amedeo 96
Monaco 17, 118–19, *118*
monarchies 59–60
monasteries 28, 29, 207, 321, *322*, 323, 355, 360, *362*, 363, 386, 387
Mondrian, Piet 149, 153, 157
Monet, Claude 40, 91, 97, 102, 154
Mons 137
Monsaraz *372–3*
Mont Blanc 199, 200
Mont Ventoux 113
Mont–St–Michel 53, 103–4, *103*
Montafon Valley 227
Monte Carlo *41*, 118
Montenegro 40, 301, 306
Montreux 203–4, 209
Montserrat 355
Moore, Henry 157
Moors 18, 28, 29, 366, *367*,

367–9, 389–90
Morella 364
Moselle, River 184–5
Mozart, Wolfgang Amadeus 35–6, 224
München (Munich) 181–2
  beer gardens 181
  Oktoberfest *160–61*, *181*, 182, *188*
  Schloss Nymphenburg 182
  Schwabing 181
mushrooms 108
music 38, 41, 151, 203, 207
Muslim influences 18, 28, *307*
Mussolini, Benito 44, 264, 272, 287
Mycenae 25, 320, 327
Mykines 327
Mykonos 328–9

n

Nafplio 327
Namur 137
Nancy 121
Nantes 104
Naples (Napoli) 293–4
  Bay of 293–5, *293*
  Castel Nuovo 294
  Herculaneum 294–5
  Pompeii 294–5
  Teatro San Carlo 294
Napoleon 37, 89, 98, 99, 136, 169, 221, 306
nationalism 37
nature 60–61, 157, *332–3*
naturism 52–3, 305, 306
Naxos 329
Nazaré 386–7
Nazis 44, 45, 177, 243, 289
Neo-classicism 17
Netherlands 33, 34–5, 37, 46, 143–57
  Amsterdam 144–51
  Arnhem 157
  coast 153–4, 157
  Delft 153
  Den Haag 153
  Drenthe *156*, 157
  flower growing 151, *152*, *156*
  Haarlem 154–5
  IJsselmeer 155
  Paleis Het Loo 157
  Rijksmuseum Kröller-Müller 157
  Rotterdam 153–4
  Veluwe 157
  windmills 143
  Zeeland 157
  Zuiderzee 155

Neuchâtel 204
Neuschwanstein *180*
Nice 117–18, *117*
Nietsche, Friedrich Wilhelm 174
Nîmes 112
Nördlingen 179
Normandy 102–3
Normans 17, 28, 102, 103
North Sea 52–3
Nürnberg (Nuremberg) 176–7, 189
Nyon 202

o

Olympia 328
Olympus, Mt 323
Oostende 135
OPEC 221
Orange 112, 113
Orléans 105
Ottoman Empire 18, 38, 40, 43
Oviedo 357

p–q

Padova (Padua) 285
Palamós 362
Palermo 297
Palladio 34
Pamplona *336–7*, *359*, 360
Paolozzi, Eduardo Luigi 157
Paris 36, 37, 46, *88*, 89–99
  Arc de Triomphe 89, 92, *93*
  cafés *95*, 96
  Champs-Élysées *91*, 92, *93*
  Commune 39
  Disneyland *19*, 97
  Eiffel Tower 90, *96*
  Forum des Halles 93–4
  La Défense 90, *90*
  La Madeleine 92
  La Villette *67*
  Latin Quarter 94–5, *94*
  Left Bank 90, 94–6
  Louvre 52, 89, *91*, 98–9
  Luxembourg Gardens 95
  Marais 93–4
  Montmartre 90, 92–3, *92*
  Montparnasse 96
  Musée de Cluny 95
  Musée d'Art Moderne de Paris 96
  Musée d'Orsay 91
  Musée de l'Armée 96
  Musée Picasso 94
  Notre-Dame 94
  Opéra de Paris 93
  Palais de Chaillot 96
  Panthéon 95

Pigalle 93
Place de la Concorde 91–2
Place Vendôme 92
Place des Vosges 94
Pompidou Centre 90, 94
Sacré-Coeur 90, 93
Sainte Chapelle 94
St-Germain-des-Prés 95
Tuileries 6–7, 89, 91
Versailles 35, 89, 97
Parnassus, Mt 323
Paros 329
Patra 328
patronage 34
Pax Romana 16, 27
Pei, I.M. 52, 90, 99
Peninsular War 37
Peñiscola 363
Périgord 111
Persian Empire 25, 26, 295
Perugia 292–3
Perugino, Pietro 271, 288
philosophers 36
Picardy 102
Picasso, Pablo 94, 96, 116, 137, 157, 186, 338, 348, 354, 369
Picos de Europa 357, 358
Piero della Francesca 290, 292
Piran 303
Pirandello, Luigi 44
Pisa 291–2, 291
Pisarro, Camille 40
Piz Buin 227
Platja d'Aro 362
Plato 25
Ploumanac'h 104
Po Valley 288–9
Poblet 362, 363
poetry 30
Poitiers 109–10
Poland 17, 37, 38, 43, 45, 47
    Kraków 239, 246–7
    Warsaw 45, 238, 239, 245–6
Pompeii 294–5
Ponti, Giovanni 52
Port Aventura 363
Port-Lligat 362
Portimão 389
Portofino 285
Portugal 29, 32, 33, 41, 44, 46, 47, 52, 377–90
    Alentejo 388
    Algarve 388–90
    Costa Verde 377, 385–6
    Lisbon 377, 380, 381–3, 387–8
    Oporto 377, 384, 385
    port wine 382, 385
Positano 295
Post-Impressionists 40

Potsdam 173
poverty 47
Prague 46, 234–5, 239, 241–3
    Castle 240, 241
    Charles Bridge 240, 241, 242, 243
    Jewish State Museum 243
    Loreto church 242
    Museum A. Dvorák 243
    National Theatre 243
    New Town 241, 243
    Old Town 243
    St Nicholas' Church 242
    St Vitus's Cathedral 241
    Strahov Monastery 242
    Waldstein Palace 242
    Wenceslas Square 243
Praia da Rocha 389
prehistoric remains 20–21, 104, 111, 111–12, 157, 358, 368
primitive art 135
Primorska 303
Provence 112–15
Prussians 15, 16, 37, 39
Puccini 267, 270
Puerto Bánus 369
Pula 304
Pyrenées 111, 360
Queluz 387
queueing 61

r

Rab Island 304
racism 57–8
railways 40
rainfall 63–4
Raphael 34, 171, 175, 264, 266–7, 268, 288, 292
Ravello 295
Ravenna 289
Realists 169
Redon 157
Reformation 31, 173, 189, 201
Regensburg 180
Reggio di Calabria 296–7
Reims 121
religion 27–31
Rembrandt 35, 133, 147, 149, 150, 153, 154, 171, 175, 184, 223
Renaissance 29–31, 34, 98, 109, 111, 120, 208, 228, 231, 246, 301, 367
    Italian 30, 34, 264, 272, 275, 276, 277
Reni, Guido 34
Renoir, Auguste 40, 91, 116
Rhine, River 154, 156, 184–6, 189

Rhodes (Rodhos) 331
Rhône, River 113, 120, 199, 200, 209
Richard the Lionheart 233
Riheka 304
Rimini 53
Rioja 359–60
Ripoll 361
Risorgimento 38–9
roads 54
robbery 61–2
Rocamadour 111
Rodin, Auguste 96, 101, 157
Roman Empire 16–17, 26–7, 156, 184, 186, 231, 319, 331
    France 112–13, 115, 118, 119
    Italy 263–5, 267, 272–3, 289, 294
    Spain and Portugal 359, 365, 390
Romanesque 17, 28, 205, 208, 246–7, 285, 301, 304, 355, 360, 361
Romania 40, 45, 57
Romaticism 38
Rome 34, 263–73
    Baths of Caracalla 265
    Baths of Diocletian 270
    Capitoline Hill 263
    Castel Sant'Angelo 270
    Colosseum 264–5, 264, 272–3
    Constantine's Arch 265
    Forum 263, 265
    Laterano 265
    Palatine Hill 263, 265
    Pantheon 267–8
    Piazza Navona 268
    Piazza Venezia 263–4
    Porta Portese 266
    St Peter's 262, 267, 270, 271
    Santa Maria della Vittoria 269–70
    Santa Maria Maggiore 270
    Sant'Andrea al Quirinale 269
    Sant'Andrea delle Valle 267
    Sistine Chapel 34, 271
    Spanish Steps 268, 269
    Trastevere 266
    Trevi Fountain 269
    Vatican City 271
    Via Vitt. Veneto 268–9
    Villa Farnesina 266–7
Ronchamp 52, 121
Ronda 369
Roses 361, 362
Rothenburg ob der Tauber 178–9, 179
Rotterdam 153–4
Rouen 102

Rousseau, Jean-Jacques 38, 105, 200, 202
Rovinj 304
royal families 59–60
Rubens 34, 98, 133, *136*, 137, 171, 174, 184, 222, 223, 276
Russia 35, 37, 38, 40, 43, 47

s

saffron 364
Sagres *388*
St Anton an Arlberg 227
St Gallen 207–8
St Johann 227, 229
St Malo 104
St Moritz 208
St Omer 101
St Paul de Vence 52, 117
St Rémy de Provence 113
St Tropez 66, 115
Saint-Emilion *110*
Salamanca 358
Salò 287
Salzburg 35, *210–11*, 232–3
    Domplatz 232
    Hohensalzburg 233
    Mozart *232*
    Old Town 233
San Gimignano *290*
San Marino 289–90
San Sebastian 360
Sanlúcar de la Barrameda 369
Sanssouci 173
Santander 358
Santiago de Compostela 357
Santoríni (Thira) *25*, 329, *330*
Sarajevo *43*
Saranda 307
Sarlat 111
Saronic Gulf islands 325
Sartre, Jean-Paul 95
Saumur 108
Savonarola, Girolamo 275
Scheveningen 153
Schiele, Egon 40, 224
Schiller, Friedrich 38, 176
Schinkel, Karl Friedrich 170–71, 173
Schoenberg, A.F.W. 224
Schubert, Franz Peter 224
Schwyz 207
seasons 75
Secession movement 40, 224
Seefeld 227
Segovia 359, *370*
Serbs 40, 43
Sert, Josep Lluis 52, 117, 355
Setúbal *386*, 388

Seurat, Georges Pierre 157
Seville 339, 366–7, *366*
Shelley, Percy 265, 269
Sicily *294*, 296, 297
Siena 28, 291
Sierra Nevada 367, 368
Silves 389–90
Sintra 387
Siracusa 297
Sitges 362
Skiathos 325
skiing 41, 46, 59, 75, 199, 200, *209*, 215, 227, 229, 360, 368
Slavs 28
Slovenia 43, 301, 303
social security 41
socialism 39, 40
Solynieve 368
Somme, River 102
Sorrento *294*, 295
Soutine 96
Spain 18, 28, 29, 33–4, 37, 44, 45, 46, 47, 339–71
    Andalucia 366–8
    Aragón 360
    Asturias 357–8
    Barcelona 40, 52, 351–5
    Basque country 15, 339, 359–60
    Castile 358–9, *370–71*
    Catalonia 339, 360–61, *363*
    Costa Blanca 363–4
    Costa Brava 361–2
    Costa Daurada 362–3
    Costa del Sol 368–9, *368*
    Costa de la Luz 369
    Costa Verde 357–8
    Extremadura 365
    Galicia 339, 357
    La Mancha *334–5*
    Madrid 345–9
    Rioja 359–60
    wines 64, 357, 359, 362–3, 369
spas and springs 183, 231, 251, 389
Split 304–5
Sporades 325
status 62
Steen, Jan 149
Stile Liberty 17
Stoss, Veit 177
Strasbourg 121
Strauss, Johann *224*
Stresa 286
Stromboli 297
student unrest 46
Stuttgart 182–3
suffrage 41
Supetar 305

surfing 52, 110
Surrealism 44, 93, 133
swearing 60
Switzerland 39, 41, 46, *194*, 195–209
    Alps 195, 199–200, 202, 206–9
    Basel *8–9*, 205
    Bern 204–5
    Bernese Oberland *190–91*, 199, 209
    Lake Geneva 200–204, *201*
    Lausanne 202–3
    Lucerne *206*, 206–7
    Lugano 208–9
    Montreux-Vevey 203–4
    Swiss National Museum (Nyon) 202
    Swiss National Museum (Zürich) 205
    Ticino 208–9
    Valais 200, 209
    Vaud Riviera 202–4
    Zürich *16*, 195, 205–6

t

Tamariu 362
Tapies, Antoní 364
Taranto 296
Tarifa 52, 369
Tarn, River 112
Tarragona 363
Tauberbischofsheim 178
Tavira 390
Taxenbach *227*
Tchaikovsky 38
television 62–3
Tell, William *199*, 206
theatre 17
Thessaloníki 323
Thira (Santoríni) *25*, 329, *330*
Thirty Years' War 31, 178, 179
Thun 209
Thuringia 176
Ticino 208–9
Tintoretto 34, 282, 283
Tirana 307
Titian 34, 171, 223, 276, 282, 283
toilets 59
Toledo 364–5, *365*
Tomar 386
Tongeren 137
Torino (Turin) 285
Torremolinos 369
Tortosa *363*
Tossa de Mar 362
Toulon 114
Toulouse 112

Toulouse-Lautrec, Henri 112
tourism 41, 46, 67, 75, 199, 279
Tournai 137
Tours 108
trade unions 41
transport *16*, 18, 41, *162*
Trás-os-Montes 385
Trebeurden 104
Tregastel 104
Trento 285
Trier 184
Trieste 285, 303
troubadours 30
Trujillo 365
Turin (Torino) 285
Turkey 43, 313, 330
Tuscany 28, 59, 290–92
Tyrol *68–9*, 215, 227–30, 285

u

Uccello, Paolo 34, 275, 277
Umbria 292–3
United Nations (UN) 202, 221
universities 29
Uri 206
Utrecht 156

v

Vaison-la-Romaine 113
Valais 200, 209
Valencia 363
Vall d'Aran *360*
Valladolid 358
Vallauris 116
van Eyck brothers 133, 135, 136, 223
Van Gogh, Vincent 40, 91, 113, 149, 154, 157
van Ruisdael, Jacob 149
Van de Velde, Willem *33*
Vasari, Giorgio *34*
Vatican City 271
Vaucluse 113
Vaud Riviera 202–4
Velázquez, Diego 34, 223, *348*
Veluwe 157
Vence 117
vendetta 64–5
Venice 37, *278*, 279–83
  Biennale 17
  Campanile 281, *282*

Castello 283
Doge's Palace 28, 281, *282*
Grand Canal 279, 281–3
Murano 283
Piazza San Marco 279–81
Rialto *282*
San Michele 283
San Polo 283
Verdon, Gorges du 115
Vermeer, Jan 35, 147, 149, 153, 223
Verona 285
Versailles 35, 89, *97*
  Treaty of 43, 44
Vesuvius 294–5
Vevey 204
Vézelay 120–21
Viana do Castelo 385
Vidal, Gore 295
Vielha 360
Vienna 35–6, 215, 221–5
  balls 222, 224
  Belvedere 223–4
  Boys' Choir 224
  Burgtheater 222
  Hofburg 221–2, *221*
  Karlskirche 224
  museums 221, 222–4
  Prater 224–5
  Ring 222
  Schloss Schönbrun *225*
  Secession movement 40, 224
  Spanish Riding School 221, *222*, 231, 303
  Stephansdom 223
  Woods 215, 225, 233
Vietnam War 46
Vigo 357
Vikings 18
Villach 231
Villandry *78–9*, *107*, 108
Vimy 102
Vitoria 360
Vivarini 296
Volendam 155, *157*
Volos 323
Voltaire 95, 105, 173, 202, 203
Vosges 121

w

Wachau 233
Wagner, Richard 176, 207, 281

Wallonia 137
Walloons 131, 137
Warsaw *45*, *238*, 239, 245–6
  Namiesthikowski Palace 246
  Old Town *238*, 245
  Royal Castle 245, *246*
  St Anna's Church 245
  St John's Cathedral 245
  Saxon Gardens 246
  University 246
  Zygmunt's Column 245
Waterloo 37, 136
Watteau, Jean-Antoine 171
weather 63–4
Weimar 176
West Friesians 157
wildlife 60–61, *332–3*
William the Conqueror 102, 103
wines *15*, 64, 233, 292, 304, 382, 385
  see also France; Germany; Spain
Wingene 135
World War I 40, 43, 102, 121, 239
World War II 45, 102, 103, 105, 137, 154, 157, 168, 175
Wörther, Lake 230–31
Würzburg 177
Wyclif, John 31

x–y

xenophobia 65–6
yachting 59, 66–7, *66*, 301
Ydhra (Hydra) 325
Yugoslavia 43, 45, 57, 67, 301, 313
Yvoire 202

z

Zadar 304
Zagreb 303
Zakynthos 326
Zaragoza 360
Zermatt *198*, 209
Zola, Émile 113
Zuiderzee 155
Zürich *16*, 195, 205–6

✸ INSIGHT GUIDES

The world's largest collection of visual travel guides

Insight Guides – the Classic Series that puts you in the picture

Alaska
Alsace
Amazon Wildlife
American Southwest
Amsterdam
Argentina
Asia, East
Asia, South
Asia, Southeast
Athens
Atlanta
Australia
Austria

Bahamas
Bali
Baltic States
Bangkok
Barbados
Barcelona
Bay of Naples
Beijing
Belgium
Belize
Berlin
Bermuda
Boston
Brazil
Brittany
Brussels
Budapest
Buenos Aires
Burgundy
Burma (Myanmar)

Cairo
Calcutta
California
California, Northern
California, Southern
Canada
Caribbean
Catalonia
Channel Islands
Chicago
Chile

China
Cologne
Continental Europe
Corsica
Costa Rica
Crete
Cuba
Cyprus
Czech & Slovak
   Republics
Delhi, Jaipur & Agra
Denmark
Dominican Republic
Dresden
Dublin
Düsseldorf

East African Wildlife
Eastern Europe
Ecuador
Edinburgh
Egypt
England

Finland
Florence
Florida
France
France, Southwest
Frankfurt
French Riviera

Gambia & Senegal
Germany
Glasgow
Gran Canaria
Great Britain
Greece
Greek Islands
Guatemala, Belize &
   Yucatán

Hamburg
Hawaii
Hong Kong

Hungary

Iceland
India
India's Western
   Himalaya
India, South
Indian Wildlife
Indonesia
Ireland
Israel
Istanbul
Italy
Italy, Northern
Italy, Southern

Jamaica
Japan
Java
Jerusalem
Jordan

Kathmandu
Kenya
Korea

Laos & Cambodia
Lisbon
Loire Valley
London
Los Angeles

Madeira
Madrid
Malaysia
Mallorca & Ibiza
Malta
Mauritius, Réunion
   & Seychelles
Melbourne
Mexico City
Mexico
Miami
Montreal
Morocco
Moscow

Munich

Namibia
Native America
Nepal
Netherlands
New England
New Orleans
New York City
New York State
New Zealand
Nile
Normandy
Norway

Old South
Oman & The UAE
Oxford

Pacific Northwest
Pakistan
Paris
Peru
Philadelphia
Philippines
Poland
Portugal
Prague
Provence
Puerto Rico

Rajasthan
Rhine
Rio de Janeiro
Rockies
Rome
Russia

St Petersburg
San Francisco
Sardinia
Scandinavia
Scotland
Seattle
Sicily
Singapore

South Africa
South America
South Tyrol
Southeast Asia
   Wildlife
Spain
Spain, Northern
Spain, Southern
Sri Lanka
Sweden
Switzerland
Sydney
Syria & Lebanon

Taiwan
Tenerife
Texas
Thailand
Tokyo
Trinidad & Tobago
Tunisia
Turkey
Turkish Coast
Tuscany

Umbria
USA: On The Road
USA: Western States
US National Parks: East
US National Parks: West

Vancouver
Venezuela
Venice
Vienna
Vietnam

Wales
Washington DC
Waterways of Europe
Wild West

Yemen

Complementing the above titles are 120 easy-to-carry Insight Compact Guides, 120 Insight Pocket Guides with full-size pull-out maps and more than 100 laminated easy-fold Insight Maps